PUBLISHERS/EDITORS:	V. Vale, Marian Wallace
ASSISTANT EDITOR:	Yimi Tong
GRAPHIC DESIGN:	Matthew Petty
COPY EDITOR:	Scott Campbell
INTERNS:	Christine Curran, Ami Tallman, Jen Lasky
PRODUCTION CONSULTANTS:	Andrea Reider, Valentine & Kay Wallace
DESIGN CONSULTANT:	Judy Sitz
COMPUTER CONSULTANTS:	Mason Jones, Ron Klatchko, Seth Robson
PUBLICITY:	Jules Sears
THANKS FOR SUPPORT:	Anne Jaso, Mira Prinz, Tara Keller, Mary Dowd, Melissa Dunn, Gentry Lane, Satu, Mateo, Mary Ricci
THANKS FOR PHOTOS:	Mark Jordan, Jim Knell, Cindy Russell, Carolyn Terry, & Everyone Else who supplied photos & posters
FINANCIAL ADVISORS:	Carol & Dennis Hamby
LAWYER:	David S. Kahn, Esq.

◆

SWING! *The New Retro Renassiance*

BOOKSTORE DISTRIBUTION: SUBCO, PO Box 160 or 265 South 5th, Monroe OR 97456.
 TEL: 800-274-7826 FAX: 541-847-6018
NON-BOOKSTORE DISTRIBUTION: LAST GASP, 777 Florida St, San Francisco CA 94110.
 TEL: 415-864-6636. FAX: 415-824-1836.
U.K. DISTRIBUTION: AIRLIFT, #8 The Arena, Mollison Ave, Enfield, Middlesex U.K. EN3 7NJ.
 TEL: 181-804-0400. FAX: 181-804-0044.
AUSTRALIA DISTRIBUTION: TOWER BOOKS PTY LTD, PO Box 213, Brookvale 2100, Australia.
 TEL: 02-9975-5566 FAX: 02-9975-5599

For a catalog send SASE or 2 IRCs to:
V/SEARCH
20 Romolo #B
San Francisco CA 94133
TEL: (415) 362-1465
FAX: (415) 362-0742
EMAIL: research@sirius.com
WEB SITE: vsearchmedia.com

Printed in Hong Kong by Colorcraft, Ltd.

20   19   18   17   16   15   14   13   12   11   10   9   8   7   6   5   4   3

Front cover: Photo of Johnny & Cari Swing by Cindy Russell. Icons: Vise Grip's 1947 Cadillac; Mark Jordan's spectators and tie; Bimbo's sign; Sam Butera's sax; and Frances Lynne's cameo. Cover Design: Marian Wallace. Back cover: Photo by V. Vale. Dance collages pages 18, 164, 191, 215 by Yimi Tong with photos by V. Vale

Table of Contents

● = dance photo-collages

PUBLISHERS

PIONEERS

BANDS & MUSICIANS

DANCERS

RECORD LABEL, CARS, BIKES, ETC.

CLUBS

INFORMATION & MORE

Introduction

"The year 2000 will bring rule by multinational corporations that will make you nostalgic for nationalism."
—Michael O'Donoghue
"Perhaps the zoot suit conceals profound political meaning; perhaps the symmetrical frenzy of the Lindy Hop conceals clues to great potential power."
—Ralph Ellison, *Negro Digest #4*, 1943

As the end of the 20th century approaches and the remnants of past cultural underground movements have become co-opted by the larger machine, the question on everyone's mind is: "What's next?" In other words, having passed through the initial howl of the Beats, the "Tune-in, Turn-on, Drop-out" resistance of the Hippies, and the complete anti-authoritarianism of Punk, what new form of social and cultural rebellion could possibly emerge? Ironically enough, it is a movement that uses the very same society it criticizes as its reference point: the retro-swing movement.

At first glance this movement seems to be more about nostalgia than social criticism, but a closer look will reveal a different form of rebellion: one that chooses optimism for building community and a sense of its own unique

> ## A closer look will reveal a different form of rebellion: one that chooses optimism for building community and a sense of its own unique identity.

identity. The swing movement is about cultural rebellion in its most subversive form: one that uses the symbols of the status quo for its own intents and purposes. This is achieved through the simple means of rejecting corporately-dictated consumption and embracing forgotten and/or ignored aspects of the American experience (e.g., music, dance, manners, clothing, etc.).

While this book is an oral history of how the retro-swing movement evolved, it is also an exploration of how individuals pioneered a way to live *with style* by recycling and pastiching a galaxy of "finds" from garage sales, thrift stores, flea markets and estate sales. In a sense, economics determined, but did not limit, their aesthetics. The most visible signifiers of this movement involve aesthetic choices in clothes and music, and these are no longer merely about originality, but quality and increased awareness. People consciously seek out second-hand Union-made American clothes that don't fall apart after the first washing. People consciously seek out older forms of music that have not been put through the corporate music industry's

sanitized and stilted face-lift. And, most importantly, people have consciously sought to revitalize partner-dancing, reclaiming a vital form of social interaction that computers and technology can never provide.

Despite surface differences involving clothing and hair styles, all undergrounds share a deep discontent with the "culture" that major media disseminates on their radio and TV stations, newspapers, magazines, billboards, etc. In the world of the eternal present, there is no need for history; the only requirement is the acquisition of the "newest and latest" products. What is at the foundation of the swing movement is its search for American history, a search for its lost roots. It is no accident that this movement is preoccupied with the years roughly between the end of World War I and the beginning of the Vietnam War. Those years mark the United States' true boom as a country where optimism and hope for the future were at their zenith. Those involved in this movement have had the intuitive understanding that what they seek is not an academic history of America, but a social history whose heart lies in the popular art forms of the people. Thus the hunger for American roots music, dance forms, old paperbacks and magazines, vintage hypermasculine and ultrafeminine clothing creations, classic cars, tattoos, etc. This movement allows people a chance to be proud of being American without the chauvinism and jingoism that has marred the past.

The new swing movement best exemplifies an understanding of American history in the musical forms that it celebrates, which include swing, jazz, blues, hard country, rockabilly, Western Swing, acappella, and doowop. This music is the hybrid offspring of America's ethnic make-up: African-American, Euro-American, Mexican-American, *et al.* This diversity is part of what makes the swing movement so unique. And oddly enough, the proliferation of new "roots" musicians and bands, which we're now seeing, was facilitated by the invention of the compact disc, which brought about the massive re-release of thousands of obscure recordings in every genre which were formerly impossible to locate, or prohibitively expensive. Basically, our American roots music heritage became restored to us.

As Jacqui Malone stated, "At the Savoy, black musicians and dancers, armed with the musical innovations of Louis Armstrong, helped develop the formula for what was eventually called 'swing music,' which swept the country during the Great Depression." (*Steppin' on the Blues*, p. 101) Judging by the number of morose models featured in the ad campaigns, the nineties have also been a kind of New Great Depression *of the spirit.* Despite alleged economic prosperity, homelessness is more pervasive than ever; lack of job security has never been so pandemic; and (thanks partly to AIDS) social relations are incredibly complex and conflicted—fraught with peril and subject to sudden termination. Society has fragmented into tens of thousands of special interest groups vying for public attention. Life has become complicated, requiring infinite levels of sensitivity, attentiveness and "negotiation" at every turn, and the net result is perpetual exhaustion—almost anomie. Not to mention the information overload inundating us all.

Depression may be caused by "mental" factors but ultimately resides in the body. So the body must provide the "cure." Enter the inexplicable neo-"swing movement" of the fin-de-siecle. Drawing upon all the wild dance music of the 20th century that *led up* to "rock'n'roll," it is aided by the return of the most spirited partner-dancing in American history. Rather than just passively watching "entertainment," the "audience" is firsthandedly experiencing joy and abandon as they visually and kinetically express the rhythms and surges of the live swing music which is still blazingly "new" to most listeners raised on rock'n'roll.

"Albert Murray calls the African American public dance a ritual of purification, affirmation and celebration. It helps drive the blues away and provides rich opportunities to symbolically chal-

---

"The sense of being perfectly well-dressed gives a feeling of inner tranquility which religion is powerless to bestow."—Ralph Waldo Emerson

---

lenge societal hierarchies by offering powers and freedoms that are impossible in ordinary life. At a dance, anyone with the right moves may become king or queen of the floor."—Jacqui Malone, *ibid*, p. 1. The corporate-business-transnational capitalist "control system" has nearly succeeded in stripping away all the rituals and rites of passage that infused meaning and significance into human relations. Institutions which formerly facilitated *sympatico* people meeting each other are now almost non-existent; Internet and want-ad romances seem pathetic, pitiful surrogates, underscoring how frightfully enormous the dimension of alienation has become—threatening to eclipse us all. With the swing movement a bit of ritual has been restored: dancing is *the* way to meet girls and guys, and with the new emphasis on manners and grace borrowed from earlier decades, radically improved social relations now seem accessible and near at hand. (Being naturally pessimistic, we will not speculate further on this.)

When cultural stagnation makes it necessary to set about *re-ordering* society, pioneers step forth to provide inspiration based on links to past creative achievements. The end of the 20th century is a period of great trepidation regarding the future. It makes profound sense to carefully review and evaluate the achievements of this past century, make our choices, and integrate our selections toward the goal of living out the remainder of our lives as creatively and meaningfully as possible, with deep responsibility toward our loved ones. Freed from the shackles of the time period in which they were created, all of our cultural choices can "come together" into a colorful mosaic that reflects more "authentic" values in which pleasure, freedom, spontaneity as well as deep ethics are united. (By the way, being into "swing" does *not* mean turning one's back on social/political awareness.)

Aesthetic elation—everything that makes living intensely in the moment exciting—is not a bad philosophical yardstick for judging experience. And now many people are deriving aesthetic

pleasure from a multitude of formerly ignored sources—Petty girls art, Heywood-Wakefield furniture, old travel/railway brochures, etc. The '90s have been described as "the decade of past decades," and with the collapse of High/Low cultural distinctions, even ordinary household objects from '40s Sears catalogs are being viewed as objects of beauty. After all, it was American design genius ("Yankee ingenuity"), widespread ideals of "democracy," plus a drive to continuously implement technological advancements, that all combined to raise the quality of life for millions on a scale hitherto unprecedented in history.

Interestingly enough, much of the backbone of the new swing movement is provided by people who are in their 50s–80s: swing jazz historian George T. Simon; Jon Lundberg, vintage clothier and social historian; bandleader Sam Butera; the Lindy Hop pioneers Frankie Manning (83) and Norma Miller; the senior musicians playing with Lavay Smith, Bill Elliott, the New Morty Show and Vise Grip's big bands, to name but a few. This underground is *de facto* combating society's vile obsession with the cult of perpetual youth, actively seeking to integrate all of the wisdom and insight which older creative pioneers can bestow, recognizing there is an enormous heritage out there which must be energetically reclaimed before it disappears forever.

It is our hope that this book plays a role in inspiring a major renaissance of creativity based upon reinvestigation and reclaiming of 20th-century American "roots" achievements—not just in music, but in all creative fields. And lest any Puritanical "wannabe revolutionary" disparage the significance of stylish clothing, we quote Ralph Waldo Emerson: "The sense of being perfectly well-dressed gives a feeling of inner tranquility which religion is powerless to bestow." Add to that an observation by clothing manufacturer William C. Browning: "If it be true that the condition of a people is indicated by its clothing, America's place in the scale of civilized lands is a high one. We have provided not only abundant clothing at a moderate cost for all classes and citizens, but we have given them the style and character in dress that is essential to the self-respect of a free, democratic people." This book attempts to trace the rise of the '90s neo-swing movement as a way of life well-suited for the next century.

—V. Vale (with thanks to Marian Wallace, Yimi Tong, and the more than 90 persons interviewed for this project)

And another thing . . .

Historical note on the origins of the "swing movement": In 1989 two key events occurred: Royal Crown Revue formed in Los Angeles, and Jay Johnson opened his art deco bar, the Deluxe, on Haight Street in San Francisco—the first 7-night-a-week place where the pioneers who started the "swing lifestyle" could meet regularly (for free), talk, sip martinis (at that time viewed as completely passé), parade their latest thrift-store finds and share information about musical discoveries, the finer points of vintage clothing, accessories and hairstyles, and last but not least, begin learning how to swing dance. At that time, nobody knew how to partner-dance; the "tough guys don't dance" attitude ruled. Today dancing has become *the* way to meet somebody, and guys (as well as girls) who don't know how to dance are clearly at a disadvantage.

Another point: the swing movement was made possible by the rockabilly scene, in which D.I.Y.-type persons accustomed to being marginalized for their pompadour hairstyles, retro Western-style clothing and obscure musical preferences, had the chutzpah to support the swing lifestyle/archetype as it emerged. In our opinion, the musical parameters of the neo-"swing" movement encompass all 20th-century American roots music you can partner-dance to, including (but not limited to) rockabilly, Hillbilly Jazz, Hot Jazz, Western Swing, etc.

The *Swing Time* staff: (clockwise from top) Mr. Lucky, Thomas Burchfield, Michael Moss, Mark Jordan, Aaron Seymour, Fritz Striker & Susan Lake (center). Sept. 1997 Photo: Mark Jordan

Michael Moss is the urbane, witty publisher of *Swing Time* magazine, a historical and cultural reference-quality publication which has championed the "swing movement" since its first issue in summer, 1995. For a 4-issue subscription send $17 ($25 overseas) to 30 Baker #B, San Francisco CA 94117. (A few back issues are available.) Michael's interview is followed by one with *Swing Time* photographer Mark Jordan.

INTERVIEW WITH MICHAEL MOSS

♦ VALE: *You've been in the swing scene from early on. Was it being in the right place at the right time?*

♦ MICHAEL MOSS: I had been reading a lot of Kerouac and really liked the way he talked about jazz—particularly bop. So I went looking for it. I lived for 12 years in the Haight-Ashbury and I met Pete Devine and Craig Ventresco when they were playing ragtime music with a washboard and acoustic guitar on a street corner. They're incredible players, so I would just kick back and listen to them. Eventually, we became friends. I would go to their house and they would play old tunes from the '20s and '30s. One day they said, "Hey, let's go for a drink at the Deluxe." They brought me there and I went, "Wow, this place is cool."

The Deluxe is a 1940s-era bar that has changed almost nil since it was originally built. It had been a gay bar for 20 years, and in 1989 was sold to Jay Johnson who wanted to do a '40s nightclub/cocktail bar. The decor is art deco with wood paneling; it's got a "blue collar" elegance. I started making that my home base, hanging out and meeting people.

I was there one night when a band came in and set up their equipment. I wasn't really paying attention, but eventually they started playing and it was this really souped-up, almost punk rock-sounding swing music! I thought, "What is this? I've never heard anything like it." It was Royal Crown Revue. At that moment I became a swing junkie.

By that time, I had already done some homework on the history of jazz. My first interest was Dixieland, and then I went through Trad Jazz, early swing, swing, bebop, modern cool jazz, and then stopped. What Royal Crown Revue did was help me realize what I liked best, which were the rhythms and melodies of swing music.

♦ V: *What year was Royal Crown playing small clubs like the Deluxe?*

♦ MM: They actually played the Deluxe until about two years ago. I first saw them back in '92. I'd been hanging out at the Deluxe for awhile, but there hadn't been much live music. Mr. Lucky was a big part of the original scene, crooning his almost-karaoke show—he'd bring in tapes and sing old Sinatra tunes.

Royal Crown had been working away at this new hybrid sound for some time, and they already had a following. That first night I saw them, the audience suddenly transformed from the usual Haight street crowd to a room full of zoot-suitin' crazies—

♦ V: *Already?*

♦ MM: Already. There was definitely a real underground clique. It was a clique because none of those people are around anymore. They were very snotty in a lot of ways, but they were the first people I saw doing this '40s thing, and they knew the band. (I'm talking about 20 or 30 people.) When Royal Crown started playing the Deluxe is when the scene really started going. They would come up every month or two from L.A. and play there—that was the *only* place. The Deluxe didn't have a cabaret license, so there was no advertising; it was all word-of-mouth. In January, 1993 I was sitting at a bar in the lower Haight and a guy in a '40s suit came up and sat down, pulled out a cigarette and a book of matches, lit the cigarette, then slid the matches over to me. There was a notice on the matches that Royal Crown was playing at Nancy Myers's speakeasy the next night. That was the advertising! Very hip.

Those were my favorite days of the scene, when it was compact and tight with high creative energy.

♦ V: *Everyone was at least an artist in the way they dressed—*

♦ MM: I thought they were more like *rebels*. At the time, piercings and tattoos were hitting it big, and with the degeneration of popular music (you could make it with a drum machine and a few rhymes), it was a way to yell back at all that. To me, this was a very rebellious, very punk thing to do. If you walked down Haight Street in '92 wearing a zoot suit, you got a helluva lot more looks than if you had 40 thousand tattoos and piercings. The "swing look" had a stronger statement to it, and I was attracted to that.

Naturally, the fantasy of '40s glamour was certainly a part of it—and I do stress the word "fantasy." In actuality, that decade was far from glamorous due to World War II, as well as lasting effects from the Great Depression. We have an over-glamourized vision of that period, thanks to Hollywood. But, again, it had a certain punk element.

And it was certainly grass roots; it was a backlash against the lack of aesthetics in modern design. It was very energetic. The thing that was so wonderful was that everybody was real close and everybody knew each other. We banded together like a small group besieged by the rest of the world. This was not something that was *packaged* for us; this was a *choice* made by a lot of young people at the same time.

♦ V: *And this was happening all over the world simultaneously. It was a zeitgeist emerging—*

♦ MM: Women wanted to be feminine again; men wanted to be more masculine. Everybody got their hair cut. My hair was short at the time, but a few years before that I had long hair. It was nice to see the sexes separate and enjoy their differences once more. The Gap is about as mainstream as you can get. Their clothes are baggy, drab, and unisex. In the early days of the scene, people dressed very individualistically—not what we now call "Retro Nazi." It wasn't like you had to be absolutely '40s, like the Art Deco Society or something. Guys and gals were mixing all kinds of styles and creating a new thing; it was very exciting. The energy level at concerts was intense because there was no dilution from outside sources. The Deluxe, for about a three or four year span was, without doubt, the CBGB's of Swing—

Guitar-driven, three-chord rock had been dominating the airwaves for 40 years, and this music sounded so incredibly fresh—it sounded *brand-new.*

♦ V: *Or San Francisco's Mabuhay of Swing—*

♦ MM: Yes. There was no other place for swing, and all like-minded bands came through there. Now that swing has grown, some bands are big before they even get here. The Deluxe has had to move on to other forms of entertainment (mainly jazz) because swing has just gotten too out-of-hand. But in the early days, it was a little sweat box.

♦ **V: How many people fit?**

♦ **MM:** Legally? [laughs] I would say that sometimes 200 people were packed in; there'd be no room to move. But we all knew each other, so nobody minded.

♦ **V: What were those early conversations like? Everyone must have been sharing discoveries of various kinds—**

♦ **MM:** Exactly. That's why that period was so exciting: everything was a discovery. Somebody would say: "Look at these cuff links I found!" Or, "Have you ever listened to this band?" And for me, the music was the greatest attraction. Guitar-driven, three-chord rock had been dominating the airwaves for 40 years, and this music sounded so incredibly fresh—it sounded *brand-new*. It was all discoveries: old movies, music, clothing . . . We'd go on treasure hunts to thrift stores and have so much fun; somebody would pull up in a vintage car and we'd all pile in. Everything we were looking for was old—but brand-new!

♦ **V: What I like about the first issue of Swing Time is how you treat it as an emerging culture, it's not just about music—**

♦ **MM:** For those who are deeply into it, it *is* a lifestyle. It's not just music you go and hear on Friday night. I consider it to be the Golden Age of American Culture. Without waxing too Mickey Spillane, you can embrace these American icons and art forms. Jazz is the *great American art form,* and right behind that is Hollywood filmmaking—

♦ **V: —and all the unknown graphic and clothing designers of the '40s and '50s, and the car designers that are being rediscovered. Plus the architects.**

♦ **MM:** Absolutely.

♦ **V: And it's also furniture and knickknacks, which you can still afford—**

♦ **MM:** Well, you could at the time. Naturally, all that stuff has become real popular; the demand has pushed prices way up. But there are so many different angles, like the design of the advertisements and artwork—that was the Golden Age of Illustration as well. In modern advertising, a lot of that is coming back—

Women wanted to be feminine again; men wanted to be more masculine. Everybody got their hair cut.

♦ **V: Yeah, like the Camel ads—**

♦ **MM:** Right, even in commercials. You see Max Jerome and the graphics they use, as well as the music . . . People finally realize that the ads and computer graphics of the '80s really stunk. There are some things that you just can't improve on. Design and manufacturing were so big before 1966, and things were made to last. When you look at new products, design isn't even a factor in most cases, and as far as "built to last" goes—forget about it! "What's hot today is passé tomorrow." That was another attraction to all this stuff: from the smallest item to the largest (like the

Chrysler Building), everything had an aesthetic beauty. I'm glad people are paying attention to this again.

♦ **V: Those great '40s gabardine shirts are being preserved—**

♦ **MM:** Yeah, people aren't wiping up oil spills on their driveways with them anymore.

♦ **V: All of the above is why I consider this a whole renaissance—**

♦ **MM:** An entire generation or two somehow skipped over all of this, and that's partly why it's so powerful. It's removed from us far enough that we can rediscover and claim it as our own. This is important. All youth is rebellious, and this is a *nice* rebellion. I've been quoted saying, "Our rebellion is conservative." And there are so many elements to it. Earlier, it was a grass roots movement, but it has definitely moved into the "product" format now.

♦ **V: It's a liberating experience to undergo being stigmatized. If you're wearing your '40s suit among grungy Haight street people, you're definitely being stigmatized; you're definitely an outsider.**

♦ **MM:** That's what was so fun about the beginning. Now we have second, third, and fourth generation bands that were inspired by Royal Crown Revue. The scene is beyond fourth generation at this point. In the beginning, the creativity was extremely intense because everybody was there for the same reason and the same attitude, which by and large is not known anymore. We try to preserve it in *Swing Time* and keep that basic spark alive, but I think it gets dissipated as more and more people with less passion move in.

♦ **V: Sure, the same thing happened in punk—**

♦ **MM:** It'll happen with anything. What's so funny about it is: nobody realizes that it *is* a social rebellion.

♦ **V: I remember posing this question to myself ages ago: when the parents have grown up with rock music, what are their kids going to use for rebellion? More rock music? The "swing thing" just had to be it.**

♦ **MM:** Right, because a lot of these kids have hippie parents and what's anti-hippie? Frank Sinatra! [laughs] "Hey, we're not going to do acid; we're going to have a martini!" Talking with a lot of kids, I know this is a definite factor. Many of them are former punks, skins, and Mods, and a lot of their parents come from a hippie, Joan Baez background. But the interesting thing about this movement is that it *includes* the parents . . . and the *grandparents!* It's really amazing. We can be radical within our age group and social world, but at the same time, what we're doing can be and *is* embraced by other generations. They might not understand a band like Cherry Poppin' Daddies, but they do like the fact that this is going on and is considered hip. "It's hip to be square," as a really lame recording artist once said. And it kind of is. I love it too because it's given all these square high school band guys jobs! [laughs]

♦ **V: That's true.**

♦ **MM:** Imagine you're in high school and it's 1985: "What do you play?" "I play guitar and get all the chicks!" "What do you play?" "I play saxophone." Forget about it! [laughs] But now, the saxophone player is the hot stud.

I don't want to sound displeased about the popularity of swing because that's actually what I'm fighting for. But I do fondly remember the first spark, which was by far the most intense. The

Pre-Swing Time :Deluxe Comix published by Joel Dylan Loya, includes contribution by Michael Moss.

bands weren't as developed and everything was more raw. I'm happy the bands have evolved, but there is something to be said about that original energy.

♦ **V: *Sure, before everything gets codified and set in stone.***

♦ **MM:** Hopefully, our magazine will create the archetype, instead of some major money guys that don't give a damn coming in and blasting the market with a bunch of crap. We're happy that the swing movement is still pretty much run by swing people.

♦ **V: *What's your overview of this as a global movement—or has it always been a global movement?***

♦ **MM:** Actually, it has. What we've done with the magazine is found a way to connect the dots by building a network. The most interesting fact about the swing movement is that these bands started spontaneously around the *world* at the same time, with basically the same age group. And nobody had any knowledge of each other. Everybody just decided to do this at once, and to me, that's absolutely fascinating. The question on everybody's mind is: *Why?* And why now? Nobody really has an answer.

♦ **V: *I was astounded that there's been a Lindy Hop/swing dance group in Sweden for ten years—***

♦ **MM:** That dance never went away. The Lindy Hop Societies have been very well-organized and in place since the '40s. Now we're seeing an infusion of younger people. The Lindy Hop people are direct *benefactors* of the swing movement. I don't want any confusion about this: the swing people brought this music into the public's eye, and *then* the Lindy Hop people discovered this was happening and, consequently, moved in. But they had nothing to do with the *creation* of this movement.

Dancing is a byproduct of the swing scene. In the original days, there weren't any dancers because nobody knew how. A few people started watching old films and figured moves out. Girls started dragging guys out on the dance floor because guys were too "cool"; we didn't want to embarrass ourselves. Eventually we all did, and it became a phenomenon. Now, dance is one of the biggest and most visible aspects, but it didn't have anything to do with the *initial* creation of the scene.

♦ **V: *Some people criticize the swing scene because it "isn't political"—***

♦ **MM:** My thought about that is: THANK GOD FOR THAT! I think that's part of its popularity. Swing is escapist entertain-

Covers above L to R: #1, #2, and #3; below L to R: #4, #5, and #6.

L to R: Timmie Hesla, Mr. Lucky, Tanya Castle, Suzi Hutsell, Thomas Burchfield, Richard Olsen, Pat Johnson, Kevin "Frenchy" Houle, Michael Moss, Rand Alexander, Mark Jordan, Susan Lake, Aaron Seymour, Morty Okin and Vise Grip. Back row: the Shufflin' Molasses Brothers at Hi-Ball Lounge in S.F., Sunday, 3-10-96. Photo: Mark Jordan

ment—it's nice to go to a concert and listen to music that isn't bombarding you with how awful the world is. Anyway, it's a bit self-righteous for 18-year-old guitar players to proclaim having all the answers. A friend of mine who was a good friend of Bob Dylan's back in the early '60s said that although he could write these incredible songs and sound like a prophet, he was an extremely naive kid.

♦ V: *There is an inadvertent political edge to this scene: most of the "products" being purchased do not benefit the major corporations.*

♦ MM: You're right. There are political statements being made, but nobody's getting on a soap box. We're not, for the most part, consumer-oriented. We don't give a damn about the hottest, newest records or fashions coming off the racks. We're interested

---

Grunge and rap were probably the biggest factors in instigating the swing movement.

---

in preserving American icons and classic designs. In fact, those in the scene who are more forward-thinking are deliberately trying to put a new spin on the music and everything.

For instance, bands that simply copycat the old guys won't go anywhere. Big Bad Voodoo Daddy does what I like best: rock with the swing sound, but drawing from 97 years of 20th century music. Probably the most well-known band in the country right now is Squirrel Nut Zippers because of their massive success on MTV, but they're really a '30s hot jazz band. They're more Louis Armstrong than Louis Jordan. If you listen to Lavay Smith, you'll hear a lot of Bessie Smith. If you listen to Bill Elliott's big band from L.A., you'll hear a Glenn Miller influence. That's part of the beauty of this movement: people are drawing from all different parts of the century. Ska and rockabilly are big factors, and so is rock'n'roll.

♦ V: *I think it was Eddie Nichols who called it the Greaser-*

Punk-Rockabilly-Swing scene—

♦ MM: [laughs] He's the visionary of the scene, so he should know. He's all of those things and much more.

♦ V: *I was happy to hear that he came out of a punk background—*

♦ MM: A lot of the major players and major bands are ex-punks: Vise Grip, Big Bad Voodoo Daddy, Royal Crown, Squirrel Nut Zippers (they come from more of an "alternative" scene, but close enough), The New Morty Show, etc. It's a common denominator throughout the scene. Personally, I came from a more Bob Dylan/Grateful Dead background—

♦ V: *Well, that was once "alternative." Bob Dylan wasn't exactly the punk rock of his time, but his first four albums were definitely trying to shake things up—*

♦ MM: And he did a good job at it. What has always attracted me more than anything is excellent songwriting. Naturally, I think the greatest songwriting took place from the turn of the century to the mid-'50s, when songwriters were just that: songwriters. The Beatles messed things up. They were good songwriters too, but all of a sudden you had to be *both* a songwriter and a performer; songwriting as an art form has suffered ever since. Just because you can play guitar and sing doesn't mean that you have a complete understanding of harmony and lyrics. A lot of the great performers never wrote songs, like Elvis and Sinatra. The sad fact now is that we don't have Tin Pan Alley at all anymore. There are no more Rodgers and Harts, Harold Arlens, or George Gershwins, etc.

♦ V: *You're talking about structures that have disappeared from our society—*

♦ MM: Right. That's another strong aspect of the swing movement: trying to put those structures back in place: The chordal make-up of the song, the lyrical content, the way the lyrics flow off the music, etc. All these little things are important and have been overlooked for the longest time.

♦ V: *Particularly witty, rhyming lyrics—*

♦ MM: Well, they've been doing that in rap, but it's not very fun to listen to. Actually, I think grunge and rap were probably the biggest factors in instigating the swing movement. All of a sudden people were screaming for melody—*screaming* for it! There's nothing more moving than a beautiful melody, and you don't hear that in rap or grunge because a lot of components that make up music are missing.

♦ **V: Most everyone today has gone through a "Save the Whales" picketing stage. But being into swing doesn't preclude you from being political—**

♦ MM: Right. Not to say that there aren't fights that need to be fought—it's just nice to be able to get away from it, even for just an evening. Swing is like baseball: a common denominator that can pull people together from all different backgrounds. Kids can work a bum job shucking videos all day and at night put on a dashing suit and go out in the world and be treated with a certain amount of respect.

> A lot of kids coming into the scene don't realize that originally this was a very "punk" thing to do. We started out trying to make a *social statement.*

♦ **V: The word "retro" somehow makes people think this scene lacks an originality of its own—**

♦ MM: Some people think nothing new is being invented in this scene, but you've got to have some *background* to be an artist. People are being inspired by a whole "new" body of culture that's been neglected.

♦ **V: If I were a writer, I would be studying the art forms of Raymond Chandler and Dashiell Hammett—**

♦ MM: That's exactly what I did: read Chandler, Hammett and a bunch of lesser-known pulp writers. I love the simple sentences and the interesting combinations of words. One of my favorite Chandler quotes is, "He was as inconspicuous as a tarantula on an Angel Food cake." What a great line! A lot of the pulp writers were really talented and have been overlooked because of the *genre* in which they wrote.

♦ **V: In this swing movement, there have been attempts to revivify vintage American slang—**

♦ MM: I'm not too fond of that because for a lot of people, it's an act. A guy like Eddie Nichols—that's just who he is; it comes from the heart. But if someone comes up and says, "Hey, Daddy-O!" it makes you feel like throwing up on your spectators! I think people need to be honest and be themselves.

One thing I want to emphasize is: it's the '90s, man, we got computers, and they're good. Let's not get lost in this idea that the past was better because it wasn't. Obviously, there were creative aspects that were phenomenal. But do you really want to live in 1940 where you can die from TB, or have to go kick the Nazis' asses again? The great thing about the '90s is that it seems like *whatever* you're into is cool; anything is possible and that's part of the fun. You can do the disco '70s, or the mod '60s; even the '80s are making a comeback, and the '50s has always been hanging around. *This is the decade of past decades.*

People really haven't dressed up since the '50s and early '60s, yet it's a fun thing to do. Even the early hippies were dressing up, but they had their own "Charlatans" ['60s vintage-dress band] kind of style. They had a costuming that was elegant in its own funky way. The punk scene was very anti-fashion and made its statement in a strong way, but that paves the way for dressing up again. After so many decades of slumming it, girls feel wonderful when they're wearing a stunning dress and guys feel great when they wear a nice suit; it brings a feeling of self-respect.

♦ **V: What caught my eye were the hardcore tattooed punk women who'd switched to swing. I think it's because of the** *extreme partner-dancing—*

♦ MM: This didn't start out as a squeaky-clean, white American, middle-class movement. Usually, the most radical changes that happen in life are unforeseen. *This* particular style is an easy one to stay with because the fashions are timeless.

♦ **V: At a recent show, you said that you hardly knew anyone there. That happened to me in punk, too: suddenly, no one I knew came anymore.**

♦ MM: In San Francisco, the core group that once was is no longer with us. They've gone on to other things. I know a big factor was that a lot of these people just wanted to do it because it was *different.* Now, they have to do something different because it's not different anymore! I feel that way at times, too. A lot of kids coming into the scene don't realize that originally this was a very "punk" thing to do. We started out trying to make a *social statement.*

♦ **V: Is that why you started publishing?**

♦ MM: Let me begin by saying we have the most talented people on the *Swing Time* staff: artists, photographers, writers, etc (and editor Susan Lake rules the world!) but rarely do they get any praise or affirmative feedback. And when you're doing a magazine without any money, that's what you need—it's the gas that keeps you going. We want people to realize why we're doing this—not to aggrandize ourselves, but to promote the movement. If we get any accolades, it's because we've worked for it. The things that I've lost for the things that I've gained sometimes bum me out, but for the most part everything's going just fine.

I had intense anger at the way mainstream press treated the emerging swing movement as a passing fad—a *novelty.* But I also had an insatiable curiosity about wanting to know what's going on out there, wanting to connect all these scenes together. I thought the best way to find out more was to start publishing: try to inform people about what's going on, and help promote the scene in an honest way. I'm proud to be a part of independent publishing because mainstream media is bullshit. **V**

L to R: Mark Jordan, Eddie Nichols, Vise Grip at El Rey, L.A., 1995.

INTERVIEW WITH MARK JORDAN

Mark Jordan is the ace photographer who has documented the "swing scene" as an insider from the very beginning of *Swing Time* magazine. Mark is also the dance partner of Mango, from Work That Skirt. He has the haircut, the clothes, the accessories, the interior furnishings, the 1942 pin-up calendar, and—last but not least—the car, a beautiful maroon 1938 Buick in mint condition.

♦ *VALE: How can you tell a vintage double-breasted suit from a recent one?*

♦ MARK JORDAN: The '40s suits have a much smaller "v" [where the tie is exposed] than more recent models, and they have *two* buttons that need to be buttoned in front, whereas the newer models have only one button. Also, the older ones often have a tag on the inside pocket that says "Union Made," or a label from an old store that's no longer in existence. Sometimes the older suits have substantial shoulder pads as well. And usually, there's no center vent in the back—that started in the '50s (and the vents got bigger with time). The pants are unmistakable, too—older pants fit a good two inches higher above the waist than modern pants. In the middle of the back they often have a small "v" opening (which helps them fit better), plus the pleats go all the way up to the top, as opposed to more recent waistbands which have a seam running horizontally through the belt loops (under the loops, of course) like a pair of Levis. They also usually have suspender buttons inside the waistband—if they don't, you can have a tailor sew them inside (or do it yourself).

I have about a dozen suits, but my favorite is a navy blue pin-striped double-breasted suit from the '40s. One of my suits has a two-button single-breasted coat; you can tell it's from the late '40s because the lapels are quite wide. I recently found a vintage gray suit for just $50, but the pockets had been used so much they bulged out. So I had them sewn up—now the suit looks fine!

By the way, I keep a pack of "Cedar Scenter" in my closet; moths love to eat vintage wool suits! You need shoe trees, too.

♦ *V: How can you recognize a vintage tie?*

♦ MJ: During World War II a lot of ties were made out of *nylon*

I have quite a few vintage silk ties and there's something about the *feel* and look of the material that's different.

---

rather than silk, because all the silk was being used for parachutes. If they were hand-painted they often say so on the inside label—I have several of those. You can still find nice vintage ties for about $20. Besides ties with vivid abstract or art deco designs, I have several with floral or foliage patterns, palm tree beach scenes and Hawaiian themes. My prize tie shows an old San Francisco cable car scene, Chinatown, etc—I splurged and paid $100, but I *had* to have it! With vintage silk ties, there's something about the *feel* and look of the material that's different from

The prized Chinatown tie. Photo: V.Vale

ties of today. There's a great book, *Fit to be Tied* (by Rod Dyer and Ron Spark; Abbeville Press) and the writer apparently owned 3,000 vintage ties—he could probably go the rest of his life without wearing the same one twice!

Another thing—besides being significantly wider (4½"), vintage ties are several inches shorter (average length 50"), because pants used to come up higher. Some of them have a two-tone effect; the top half of the tie is a solid dark contrasting color, so by the time you've tied the tie, you have a dark color knot and a lighter design beneath—pretty cool!

♦ *V: What kind of shoes do you wear just day-to-day?*

♦ MJ: Actually, I *always* wear spectators—I have about 9 pairs of black-and-white and brown-and-white ones. My oldest pair I paid $2 for; they're brown-and-white and the leather's cracking. My best pair is by Allen-Edmonds; they cost something like $260 but for the rest of your life you can send them to the factory to be refurbished, and they're extremely comfortable. Probably my least comfortable spectators were by Florsheim. I also have two pairs of plain black wingtip shoes. Dana [from Work That Skirt] just found me a pair of spectators in Las Vegas—I wear size 12, so friends are always on the lookout for me because my size is hard to find.

Another thing—accessories are pretty important. I have a collection of various tie clips, like this sword tie clip—I have about 15 of those. Underneath there's a pin that goes through your shirt, but at each end is a little "clip" that keeps your tie down on each side [see cover]. You never want to put a pin through your tie—tie tacks are not allowed!

I also have several vintage watches and some of them are curved to fit your wrist better [shows them from the side]. I'm always on the lookout for these in good condition; sometimes you can find one for $50. I have one that looks like new. I have an old pocket watch with a long chain, old pocket knives, cigarette cases, a cigar cutter, some old fountain pens, old rings, lighters and a tiny hip flask. I even have old matchbooks, skeleton keys and various political badges, like this old one saying "Dewey for President."

♦ *V: What about hats?*

♦ MJ: I finally found a beautiful old Borsalino [like San Francisco Mayor Willie Brown now wears] at an antique shop in Boston; the lady sold it to me for $40 but it's probably worth $400. It's light-grey, and you can tell it's older, not only from the inside label, but because the crown is significantly higher. I haven't worn this much because it's higher and I'm just not "used to it" yet. Here's a black Stetson Twenty (shows inside label). This hat is probably from the '30s, because "Stetson Twenty" means that it originally sold for $20. The brim turns down, and it's kind of "pointy" toward the front. The older Stetsons have a heavier, more solid-feeling felt; the new ones are made cheaper—the company was bought by someone else. Compare it to this new hat (gray); the felt feels a lot lighter. However, I wear this gray hat a lot because I look good in it; the proportions are *just right*—and if anything happens to it, I can probably replace it immediately.

I also have several beautiful antique hatboxes, some with old stickers on them, and that's what I store my hats in to keep the dust off.

♦ *V: But what do you wear just casually, every day?*

♦ MJ: Today I'm pouring concrete, so I'm wearing some classic old-looking sneakers, regular dark-blue Levis [with the cuffs turned up], a plain white T-shirt and a dark green old shirt (with two flapped pockets) that's torn, so I can wear it for doing work like that. In my closet I also have a number of "dead stock" vintage gabardine wool shirts with two flapped pockets, in various colors (gray, brown, off-white, etc). I have about eight casual coats from the late '40s, and my favorite one is in gray gabardine with two flapped chest pockets, kinda short. I have a longer one that's similar, with two diagonal slashed hand pockets, but now I don't like it as much as the shorter ones—also, it got a cigarette burn (one of the hazards of the "swing lifestyle"). They're all gabardine in different colors: brown, maroon, light gray, tan, etc. I also have a light gray flannel patch-pocket single-breasted sport coat from the early '50s.

♦ **V: What does "dead stock" mean?**

♦ **MJ:** It just means it was sitting around in a warehouse for 50 years, but was never worn. I *know* this one shirt I got recently was

---

I'd finally gotten almost everything, and then it occurred to me that the last missing element was the car.

---

dead stock, because it was still folded in the original creases—you could just *tell.*

♦ **V: You even have some vintage Dashiell Hammett books with their dust jackets, including one I've never seen before, Woman In The Dark—**

♦ **MJ:** That came out fairly recently—nice art deco dust jacket. And this Dashiell Hammett book, *The Maltese Falcon,* is an exact reproduction of the first edition which would have cost $3000! It's put out by Otto Penzler of the Mysterious Press in New York. Besides Dashiell Hammett's *The Big Knockover, The Thin Man, Red Harvest* and a few others, there's a biography of Hammett by Joe Gores. I have most of my Raymond Chandler books next to Henry Miller's *Tropic of Cancer*—a different flavor of vintage! Here's an excellent new book from England, *Forties Fashion and the New Look,* by Colin McDowell. A museum in London is having an exhibit of '40s fashions right now.

♦ **V: Your house is full of beautiful pieces—**

♦ **MJ:** Even the phones are all vintage rotary-dial . . . I was lucky; I found this dark green art deco sofa and two armchairs for $700 and they're in perfect condition; I don't think the person selling them knew what they were. Needless to say, they're made much better than anything you could find for a much higher price at a

Mark's maroon 1938 Buick. Photo: V.Vale

Mark Jordan wearing a vintage tuxedo like Humphrey Bogart wore in *Casablanca* and a traditional grosgrain (wide-ribbed or wide-grained fabric) bowtie. Art Deco replica lighter contains secret compartment for folded up $100 bill (or what have you). New Year's Eve '97 at Bimbo's (8½ Souvenirs, Jay Johnson & His Ultra Deluxe Orchestra, and Frenchy with East Bay Ray (ex-Dead Kennedys), on guitar. Photo: V. Vale

modern furniture store. Everything else I found a piece at a time, like this old clock or that art deco end-table that holds some of my '40s magazines, like *Look, Screen Guide, Photoplay,* etc. All the various lamps, radios and ashtrays are old. This huge old three-foot-tall radio was pretty cheap because it takes up so much room, but just look at the woodwork—*that's* craftsmanship! On my roll-top desk is a heavy reproduction of the Maltese Falcon statue; I got it in a mystery bookstore for $20.

In the kitchen everything's old: the refrigerator, the toaster, the clock radio, and this great antique bar I found not long ago. It looks like an old wood cabinet; when the door opens from the top, a light goes on, showing the full display of glasses, etc—beautiful! There's several old tea sets (decorative teapots and cups); this dragon set is from Japan. Nothing was super-expensive; you just have to really *look.*

I consider myself as having gotten into the "swing scene" rather late. But over the past few years I've really gotten immersed in the "lifestyle": I've found the clothes, furniture and things to put on the walls. I'd finally gotten almost everything, and then it occurred to me that the last missing element was the car. I started searching through the Internet and found this old 1938 maroon Buick in Maine for $9,000, and it was practically in perfect condition. The dashboard is a work of art, with bakelite plastic and chrome detailing everywhere, there's a floor stick shift, and the upholstery is perfect—like sitting on a long luxurious sofa. And it runs great, too. [knock on wood] As soon as I got it I drove it to a show at Bimbo's and parked it in front! There's nothing like putting on some great old clothes, taking your gal (who's dressed like a knockout in a vintage outfit) and driving to a show in your classic old automobile! ▼

Screamin' publisher Gabrielle Sutton and regular contributor Ken Mottet, Nov. 1997. Photo: Jim Sutton

Gabrielle Sutton publishes *Screamin'*, subtitled "Your Guide to American Hi-Style." For a 6-issue subscription send $18 ($27 overseas) to Hi-Style Enterprises, POB 577370, Chicago IL 60657. Sample issue, $4.

♦ *VALE:* **Screamin'**, **Swing Time** *and* **Grindstone** *all started around the summer of '95. It seems there was a zeitgeist in the air—*

♦ GABRIELLE SUTTON: We started *Screamin'* because there were a lot of fanzine publications covering the rockabilly-roots-rockin' scenes that weren't doing the job, in that they didn't take their subjects very seriously. *Swing Time* focuses on swing/jump music and dancers; they don't deal with rockabilly-psychobilly or stray too far from the mold. On the other hand, *Grindstone* is *too* liberal; in the issues I saw they were expanding the definition of the "scene" to include Social Distortion and some really punked-out things that were *way* outside our parameters.

> ### We wondered, "Why don't we have a really good publication here in America, that disseminates solid information and comes out regularly?"

The reason we do what we do is: a) we don't think it's just the music that's important; usually, if you're crazy about the music, you like all the other parts of the lifestyle that go with it: antiques-collecting, architecture, cars, etc. b) we expand the defi-

nition to include post-war American retro stylings that usually don't get any exposure: Latin Jazz, surf or cocktail— genres that aren't so far away from the mold.

We were espousing that rockabilly really has its roots in swing, jump, Latin jazz and other genres. Also, it's not just "nostalgia": bands are playing it now, and there are clothes and other products that people don't realize are firmly rooted in the design elements and virtues from America's heyday. We cover "post-war American coolness." [laughs] Anything from the mid-'40s through the early '60s that was truly American in design and virtue.

♦ *V: Tell us about your production—*

♦ GS: We're basically a two- or three-person operation. My husband does some of the art direction. Actually, what *really* instigated our magazine were three publications which we used as "standards" when we started. The first was *Kicks* magazine out of New York, done by Billy Miller and Miriam Linna who run Norton Records. It was only published every few years, whenever they felt like it. It was a very dense and wonderful publication, but it didn't come out often enough.

Then we had this English magazine, *Southern & Rockin,* which is a great publication that gives a ton of information: reviews, calendars, mail order, for mostly rockabilly music on the European scene (which in my opinion isn't as good as the American), but they were at least keeping the scene vibrant. It was dense and regularly published, although not much on looks.

The third publication we became aware of was *Continental*

Restyling, published by a French guy out of London. It had the feel, the style and the scene that we liked, but content-wise, the attitude basically was, "If it's not 'authentic,' doesn't sound exactly like it did in the '50s and isn't recorded on the same equipment, then it's not really good." We felt this did a great disservice to bands like Ray Condo, who are writing original material, recording it on digital equipment and doing a great job.

American rockabilly music is really the most "alternative" music out there—*nobody's* playing it on the radio!"

Our magazine came out as a reaction against *Continental Restyling's* attitudes. We wondered, "Why don't we have a really good publication here in America, that disseminates solid information and comes out regularly?"

♦ **V: So you're fully immersed in this lifestyle: in your clothes, house, car and all the music you own—**

♦ **GS:** Within reason! [laughs] We wear our love on our sleeves, but I don't do a beehive every morning to go to work. There's a sharing of information within this "scene." We keep our eyes peeled and scan the newspapers, and every time there's an obituary or relevant article, we rip it out and put it in a pile. The Internet keeps you posted; if you type in "rockabilly" you'll find a tremendous dialogue going on all the time that keeps you posted on things like hair grease, and what band's coming into town, etc.

There's also half a dozen rockabilly festivals happening now; Denver and Indiana have good ones. There's a vintage car show on the East Coast. You go to these, the scene gets together, and you learn stuff from other people: "Hey man, I like your jeans; where did you get them?" "Funny you should ask! Levi's is reissuing the big 'E' ones again." You get leads from other magazines and follow 'em up.

♦ **V: Do you have any collecting specialties?**

♦ **GS:** My husband has quite a collection of old hair grease from the '40s. In this scene, there's a real danger of having a pompadour and people mistaking it for some kind of *Happy Days* nostalgia. Some people don't understand that there are still people producing good music.

There's a tendency for people to categorize, so if you're labeled "swing" maybe that'll immediately exclude you from becoming Top Forty. Someone said that roots-American rockabilly music is really the most "alternative" music out there—*nobody's* playing it on the radio! If there weren't a rockabilly scene, maybe Royal Crown wouldn't have even gotten as far as they have. The people who first came to see them here were rockabilly fans who liked to dance, because nobody was swingin' in Chicago.

People here have been doing the lindy-hop and jitterbug for years but weren't sophisticated enough to call it "swing." Now there's a bunch of people out there calling it "swing" who suddenly show up in their old clothes to see a band like Royal Crown, and I think, "Where have *you* been? I've been doing rockabilly night here for six years [at Deja Vu] and I've never seen you people before." I don't respect people who ask me, "Do you lindy-hop or do you jitterbug?" I dance because I like to *dance*—I don't know what it is, but it's the steps my husband and I do and I don't know what they're called. When it gets to the point where someone says [condescendingly], "Well, you *know* . . . this is *really* a six-step," then I get a little itchy under the collar.

Just because something is rockabilly doesn't make it good—if a band sucks, you shouldn't support them no matter what they're playing! You want to like a band because of the music and not the label.

♦ **V: It seems like Chicago is a good area to find post-war American knickknacks, furniture, etc—**

♦ **GS:** Again, you're talking to someone who will buy something that isn't necessarily old, just as long as it fits the parameters of

---

Europeans do "American" much better, but they can't walk into their backyard and see crazy Americana like Graceland or Wigwam Village.

---

style that I like. Also, none of us in the circle the magazine is directed to, are antique dealers; we actually *use* it all. We buy old toasters and make our toast in them. We don't want to spend a lot of money on something that may break down two days from now. But we definitely do a lot of shopping!

♦ **V: Do you drive an old car?**

♦ **GS:** We have a "steppin' out" car: a '54 Cadillac Fleetwood that's two-tone: dark blue and light blue. It has the Continental

kit on the back, and was top-of-the-line in 1954. [laughs] It cost us $1,800—about half of what it's worth, and we've basically done nothing to it. So far it runs like a charm. But it's not our "day car." It's twenty feet long and really hard to park—it barely fits in our garage.

♦ **V: I think it's great you include articles on architecture, as well as book reviews—**

♦ GS: We approach this from a lifestyle standpoint. There's so much material out there, especially published material; in the last six months there have been three books and one TV show basically on Route 66. As far as architecture goes, we've always maintained that that's one thing we have that's a step-up on the Europeans. The Europeans do "American" much better; they're much more "authentic" and into really knowing "what it was like" in 1952 in real detail. But they can't walk into their backyard and see the original McDonald's (which was the height of '50s architecture), or some awesome bowling alley or motel or hotel, or some Frank Lloyd Wright or Mies Van Der Rohe cutting-edge buildings. Or crazy Americana like Graceland or Wigwam Village or all those wacky buildings along Route 66. We can go to drive-in movies—they've never been able to do that! If there's one thing a society does that's really a monument to its decade, it's architecture. And that includes amusement parks where

details like the signs and the miniature golf courses are just wacko America. You gotta love it!

Also, for awhile people in the "scene" thought you *had* to go to England for the Hemsby rockabilly festival which is twice a year. To be a true rockabilly person you had to pilgrimage there; Hemsby was Mecca. I think, "No way! Just take a drive down to Memphis, or go out West. Or go to your corner five-and-dime Woolsworth counter diner." We try to get people excited about what America has right here. There are so many cool and interesting things that people in the scene are into. For example, I collect bakelite bracelets. Someone else will collect bakelite box purses, or hats, or have their whole basement and rec room done in bamboo furniture, and we all share what we're into.

If you see a reference book that alludes to what you're interested in, you want to pick it up and learn more about it. We have hundreds of books like this. We've only been able to review about a dozen of them. You find out what you like and you learn how to find it! You know what you want and keep your eyes open for it, basically.

I respect anybody who knows what they like. I respect anybody who wants other people to like what they like. I don't respect people who start *telling* you what you should like. **V**

Screamin' *Mission Statement*

No denying it, old stuff is cool. Especially the music, cars, clothes, architecture and household goods created between V-J day and JFK DOA Day. Something about fender fins and hemi engines, electric guitar and doghouse bass, rayon shirts and acetate dresses, neon boomerangs and canted glass that tickles the pleasure center in many of our brains. It has nothing to do with nostalgia. It has everything to do with recognizing the best of our own culture. It has nothing to do with right-wing politics or a desire to live in the past. It has everything to do with preserving and celebrating here in America those things for which we are known throughout the world.

In postwar America, wealth and know-how came together with energy and creative cross-fertilization in what is one of the most dynamic peiods since Europe's Renaissance. Although that time has passed, plenty of us dig the styles it spawned.

We're launching *SCREAMIN'* to cover the contemporary lifestyle which doesn't really have a name. And which probably shouldn't, lest it turn into some kind of tired formula or straitjacket. The terms "rockabilly" and "rockin'" begin to describe it, but there's more than just that. Musically, there are the related forms: R&B, rock'n'roll, hillbilly, swing, surf—plus some unrelated forms like cocktail, beatnik and Latin jazz. There's vintage clothes, from a 1948 cocktail dress to a 1962 sharkskin suit, and everything between. There's antique autos, stock and custom, from fat fenders to fins. There's architecture that looks like spacecraft, furniture that looks like amoebas and kitchen appliances that look like locomotives. There's anything cool—whether pop or obscure—which might have been created last week but which is firmly rooted in postwar American culture.

The *SCREAMIN'* staff goal is to put out a magazine which is knowledgeable, useful and fun to look at. —*Screamin'* #1

Recommended Reading

American Music Flintgatan 16, S-432 35, Varberg, Sweden
Blue Suede News POB 25, Duvall WA 98109. 206-788-2776 $5
Cannot Become Obsolete (ISM) POB 1232, Lorton VA 22199-1232
Collector 436 W. 4th St #222, Pomona CA 91766. $4; $24 sub.
Continental Restyling, 9 Rue de la Libération, 88360 Ferdrupt, France. 011-33-3-2925-8864 (Send $10 cash for latest issue)
Cool & Strange Music Dana C., POB 8501, Everett WA 98201 $5
Cornfed (country), POB 220135, Brooklyn NY 11222
Dynamite c/o Andy Witter, Waldstr. 10, Dielheim 69234, Germany
Esoteric Pop Culture Robt Koenig, POB 1672, Mineola NY 11501 $3
Fashion Flashbacks (Lanajean), POB 138, San Mateo CA 94401. $4
Garage Pile POB 1061, Salt Lake City UT 84110-1061
Gearhead (Mike LaVella), POB 421219, SF CA 94142-1219. $8
Grindstone (Cameron Davis, 11288 Ventura Blvd #450, Studio City CA 91604-3149. 818-509-1257. email: grind55@aol.com $4
Hogtown News Knolis, J. Verbovenlei 79, 2100 Deurne, Belgium
Lo-Fi (cocktail/swing) POB 20357 Parkwest Sta NY NY 10025. $6
Lounge Sam W, 3010 Wilshire Blvd #92, Los Angeles CA 90010. $6
Madhouse Jump (psybil) Barnerstr. 9, 97084 Wurzburg, Germany

New Gandy Dancer (instrumental rock), Rob Bradford, 43 Humber Close, Thatham, Berkshire, England RG13 3DT
Now Dig This Trevor Cajio, 19 So. Hill Rd, Bensham, Gateshead, Tyne-Wear, England NE8 2XZ
Organ & Bongos Russell S, POB 20396, Seattle WA 98102. $5
Original Cool 4700 Colonial Av, Norfolk VA 23508. $3.
Outré Mike, 1320 Oakton Av, Evanston IL 60201. 847-866-7155.
Rhythm & Roots Review Greg, 1493 Adelle Ct, Elmont NY 11003.
Roadhouse Fever, S I Net, POB 54, Stone Harbor NJ 08247.
Rock Per-Arne Petzold. PO Box 59, Furuset 1001, Oslo 10, Norway
Rock Therapy Carlos Diaz Vallejo c/o Angel Guimera, 573° 1A Badalona, Barcelona 08915 Spain
Rockabilly Review Billy Poore. POB 100504, Nashville TN 37224.
Southern & Rocking Moved from London to Finland. At Tower?
Swivel, 6222 N. 23rd Av, Phoenix AZ 85015. 602-589-5038. $4
Texas Jamboree POB 161405, Austin TX 78716
Third Coast Music (zyd, etc) 620 Circle Ave, Round Rock TX 78664
Thrift Score (Al Hoff), POB 90282, Pittsburgh PA 15224. $2
Tiki News 2215R Market St #177, San Francisco Ca 94114

3

4

1) Dance teachers Richie Dawkins,
Olivia Hallmark [married 1-18-98!]
2) Unknown 3) Sunny Buick, Jessica
Brooks 4) Unknown 5) James Keys,
Kim Long 6) Jim Knell, Maggie
Downey winning contest 7) Mike
Galloglas, __ 8) Dens Havoc, Alicia

6

5

L.A.'s ROYAL CROWN REVUE has been credited with starting the "swing" renaissance in 1989. Members include Eddie Nichols (vocals, percussion), Mando Dorame (tenor sax), James Achor (guitar), Bill Ungerman (baritone sax), Scott Steen (trumpet), Veikko Lepisto (bass), and Daniel Glass (drums, percussion). Their recordings include *Mugzy's Move, Kings of Gangster Bop, Caught In The Act* (live CD) and *Hey Santa* (Christmas CD), all available from Hepcat, 1-800-404-4117. Check out Royal Crown's website: *rcr.com.* What follows are three interviews with Eddie Nichols, Mando Dorame, and Eddie's girlfriend, Ruth Wilson, on shopping for used clothes.

INTERVIEW WITH EDDIE NICHOLS

♦ *VALE: I always wondered what the "next big thing" after punk would be—*
♦ EDDIE NICHOLS: I couldn't have figured it out myself. I was thinking people would be putting on powdered wigs an' shit— you know what I mean? [laughs]
♦ *V: Any new social movement (beatniks, hippies, punks) has to be grass-roots, a fully-rounded "lifestyle" change, and it also has to be intense—it can't be some bourgeois, middle-*

class thing—
♦ EN: But you know what sucks: since we started doing this, a lot of that bourgeois, middle-class thing has come in. "Swing Nazis" used to really annoy me, but they don't bother me much anymore.

When I first got out here in 1984 from New York there were all these kids that I thought were *somethin'* (when I didn't know any better) parading around with fuckin' tri-mohawks and "GBH" [Grievous Bodily Harm] in studs on their leather jackets, but then they went home to—I don't know—Rancho El Segundo and daddy's mansion. It's not even about money; I would see them change their hairstyle *for the week.* There's a little bit of that going on now.

Because it's still catching on in the rest of the country, the scene's very fresh—and that's nice (despite how we rant about the old days). When we first started playing at the King King, there were just a few people who would dress up—a few *characters,* you know what I'm sayin'? And in San Francisco, I don't know if you ever met Slimm—a little cat who's a boxer? At the Deluxe in S.F. it was mostly the people who *worked* there who were into it: a handful of guys and gals, and that was about it.

The first gig we played in San Francisco was at a garage that Phil Price, this greaser from Detroit had. Big Sandy and Ronnie Dawson had played there previously, and when *we* played everybody went, "What da fuck is this?" But they loved it.

For a lot of people, this social scene's actually kinda *nice.* In some joints it's a little cornball, but San Francisco's got a pretty healthy scene and the sharpest dressers, too. Now you can go out and it's all about the *good* shit: dressin' sharp, nice car, swingin'—feeling like a *big shot* for a night, you know?

♦ **V:** *And that's new. Most people who grew up with rock music would never put on anything special to go to a rock show. The only dressing-up was for graduation or a funeral.*

♦ EN: In America we've got such a great history to pull from; there are so many things you can put together. There were some pretty hip decades going on.

From the beginning, I always put that punk energy into my music. My lyrics are usually a little *dark.*

♦ **V:** *And we're at the end of the 20th century, looking back and trying to reclaim anything great that we weren't necessarily taught in grade school—*

♦ EN: That's exactly it, man.

♦ **V:** *I recently got a 1956 Sears catalog—*

♦ EN: Ain't that nuts?! My girlfriend was showing me one of those yesterday and I was going, "Look at that—just look at those clothes!" Even in the "boot" section, they had biker boots with jewels on them! It was *happening.*

♦ **V:** *We're in a strange era where everyone's a slave to the work ethic. What we need is more leisure; a big blast of positive fun. One of the biggest attractions of this "swing movement" is the aerial dancing; after one song people are sweatin' up a storm—*

♦ EN: You know, children are the first ones to start dancing. Whenever we've played any kind of open day show, little kids respond instantly. They get out on the floor and go nuts; they love them horns and shit.

Now there are people teaching the lindy-hop everywhere. You never used to see them before and suddenly *BAM!,* they're fresh out of class and they're runnin' the show!

In one city we played, these people came up to me at a show and said, "Will you tell all the people that don't know how to dance to get off the floor?" (Like I'm going to tell people to do that at one of my gigs?!) So I announced, "Everybody who *doesn't* know how to dance, come out on the floor!" [laughs] I also said, "Ladies, please wear proper undergarments. We know you want

to show off your goodies, but . . ."

♦ **V:** *That's funny. In a way, the "flashing" of underwear is the best part—*

♦ EN: Exactly . . .

♦ **V:** *You're from Manhattan, so you must have started out with an edge—*

♦ EN: It helps. My step-grandmother sang with Bob Wills & His Texas Playboys and my dad was an entertainer. Now he's 72 but he runs around like he's much younger. He was a lounge singer in the '50s, and did Vegas, working right across from Louis Prima and all those guys. My dad was more "old school"; he was doing standards and wasn't into rock'n'roll. He stuck to his shit, then he did some Broadway tunes. My mom was a ballet dancer until my dad knocked her up and wrecked her career! [laughs]

My dad told me a funny story about the time his first wife (not my mom) busted him. He was directing a musical out of town and had "a great fling"—he tells me now about it, right? The woman sent a letter to him care of the Lands Club (it's where theater guys in New York go and drink) so it would be "safe." One of the guys at the club spotted the letter and personally delivered it to the house, where the wife intercepted it. When he came home, she had cut one leg and one arm off every suit, had his shirts in a pile all stabbed-up with ink on 'em, and chopped all his ties—there was nothing he could do. [laughs]

Self-portrait by Eddie Nichols

♦ **V:** *Now that's passion! Did your parents encourage you musically?*

♦ EN: No. They weren't even together for most of the time. I had a really shitty childhood—like most people. There were the old salad days for four or five years, then we got the evil stepfather. It was pretty horrific for fuckin' years. He was an influence on me—besides with his fist. He was a fuckin' total rebel, greaser/biker kind of guy, and was the first to introduce me to doowop and '50s *acappella.* I love that shit. My favorite thing to do is to get together with a bunch of cats and sing some doowop.

I played viola in the school orchestra for awhile and I was good. Then I got older and didn't give a shit about anything—everything started wearing out. Then I discovered punk rock. I remember the first time I saw a picture of Sid Vicious, I thought, "This is it!" I was in seventh grade and I went nuts on it.

The littlest Eddie of them all, at three or four years old.

♦ **V:** *You must have been one of the only punks in your school, and got picked on—*

♦ **EN:** I got picked on anyway. I hadn't started to dress funny, yet. I would mess up my hair but that's about it. I remember trying to decipher the Clash's lyrics for years: "What the fuck is that guy Joe Strummer saying? I can't understand a goddam word!" Now that I'm 30, I go, "Oh, *that's* what he's saying!"

From the beginning, I always put that punk energy into my music. My lyrics are usually a little *dark*. Some bands who play swing now are very "straight": happy-go-fucky. [laughs] I know that scenes come and go, but what I love about this scene is that it has reintroduced a lot of Americans and kids to old American music. It really has.

♦ **V:** *When you came to California in 1984, you probably had no money—*

♦ **EN:** Yeah, man, I ate some shit out here. I lived out on Hollywood Boulevard for a while. I thought, "Oh, shit, I gotta drag my ass out of this." So, I went on tour as a roadie for this punk band called Rigor Mortis. It was a crazy tour—actually, they broke up in San Francisco. It was their biggest show and people like Jello Biafra were there. I said, "This is your show: do your shit." Then they all got into a fight on stage and quit! [laughs] One guy kicked his fucking amp in and Big Ed was making out with this chick that looked like Phyllis Diller. It was a nightmare, man.

After the tour I had no place to live. I walked around Hollywood for three days because I didn't want to ask nobody for shit. Finally, I was fucking starving and I hooked up with one of my old buddies. I was desperate. He was an old punk I hadn't seen in years, but he was an upstanding guy who took me in. In the next two days, he bought me a pair of shoes and got me a job. I lied my ass off to get a job at this hotel as a fix-it man—I couldn't fix shit! But it was good because it really saved my ass. I wrote a bunch of Royal Crown songs on the roof of that hotel; I'd sneak up there and write.

I hate to use this tone, but the "swing lifestyle" is a "softer, gentler way to go" essentially. It's something people can feel a more comfortable with. One reason I got out of the punk scene (now don't get me wrong, I used to brawl my ass off when I was a kid, but that's 'cuz I was an angry idiot) was that it got to the point where it was literally becoming *gang wars* at the shows in L.A.

Punk was getting big in all the Los Angeles suburbs around 1983–86, and they were having huge shows at the Olympic Auditorium and the Cathay de Grande. Then it became a cop magnet; the cops wanted to close down the clubs. There was this really funny Stooges situation. The Cathay de Grande was on a corner and on the north side of the building there was a big parking

Chip off the ol' block: Eddie's dad (top) and Eddie (bottom). Photo: Jeff Higginbotham

lot where all the punks would hang out. Of course, everybody's drinking, so when the cops would pull in, everybody would run around to the other side of the block and start hanging out there. Then the cops would come to the other side, and everybody would scream and run back to the first side. The cops would only get one person out of 50 every time they did that. It would go on like that endlessly. Then they started cracking down really hard, and the Cathay closed.

♦ **V:** *Didn't you work there?*

♦ **EN:** The place was a filth hole, man. It was so scary. Everybody from Orange County up to North Hollywood would come and just abuse the shit out of that place, and my job was to clean it. I'd go downstairs in the morning and all they had on was red lights; it was like a dungeon. It was creepy and it stunk, too. Once I opened the bathroom door and there was this fuckin' roach—I've never seen one so BIG! He was as big as my hand. He checks me out and starts flying at me. But it got kind of cool towards the end.

Then the club closed, and I started doing odd jobs. Around '86 or '87, I got sick of walking around and being a bum. And that's when I got a job at the Bel Age Hotel and started playing again, mostly rockabilly. Things started going up from there.

I started getting back into the stuff that I listened to when I was a little kid: doowop and '50s music. The natural progression in Southern California was from punk to greaser. That good American look, love of old cars and doowop—it just felt right for me. I said, "Fuck it, man" and went out and bought a guitar and played in my room. I met other kids that played around town and thought it was really amazing that they could have gigs. I know that sounds stupid, but when you don't know about it . . . So, I'd just go and jam with these guys and learn as much as I could.

I was really into Robert Gordon. For awhile he went through a lot of shit. Recently he played with us and he was fuckin' great again, man—back on top. But the audience didn't know who he was when we played with him. They were Orange County kids waiting for Social Distortion to come on. Some of them were snickering, "Who's this old Elvis?" He got up and sang, "The Way I Walk." These kids didn't want their friends to know, but they were all digging it, man. He fuckin' worked them just with his presence. He could give a fuck, probably, but— [laughs]

♦ **V:** *Sometimes you can't care anymore and just do what you want. I have a lot more respect for people who have lived through hard times—*

♦ **EN:** Sure, man. That's life. I can dig that, too. You know what I've noticed lately, though? It's really hard for other people who haven't gone through that to understand where you're coming from. I see it in the way they deal with people who have drug problems; they just don't understand. I used to have the big fat drug problem, but I'm good now. Shit, it takes awhile to get over that jive, too. I fell into that, but now I'm back—back from the dead.

♦ **V: I recently saw William Burroughs in Kansas. He was 83 and still on methadone—**

♦ EN: Fuck! [imitates Burroughs' voice] "Going down to the clinic to get my dose. Godammit, that stuff tastes like shit; been drinking it for 20 years." [laughs]

♦ **V: He seemed to be healthy, though. [For the record, William S. Burroughs died of a heart attack August 2, 1997 in Lawrence, Kansas]**

Swing is attractive to old punks and rockabilly cats because it's something you *can* grow older with. And it's got a great sense of style.

♦ EN: You know what? I ran into Herbert Huncke once in New York. He just passed away. I was walking around New York and saw this guy eating ice cream on Avenue A. I said, "What's up, man?" as I was passing him. I took a harder look and it was Herbert Huncke. He said, "Hey, kid, lend me a couple bucks." And I did it just because of who he was, and then he ran off to some other little fans and probably got some more money. He looked pretty worn out, that dude.

♦ **V: It's harder to survive in Manhattan than on the West Coast.**

♦ EN: Some guys just give in to the fact that they're going to be junkies for the rest of their lives. They fucking stay down there, on the Lower East Side. If you ever want to quit, you can't do it there because it's fucking in your face every five minutes.

On Avenue A now, there's all these store fronts. You go in one and they have the ice cream bin right there. They've got vanilla, chocolate and, you open the third one, it's cocaine. It's in little bags and they just chuck 'em out to ya. Fuckin' ridiculous, man.

There was this guy in rehab with me who was a lawyer. You would never expect to see him there because he was really well-groomed; a nice, young Jewish lawyer. He was in some huge firm, popping dope behind the desk—in the office! He keeps fooling himself and sending himself to rehab, just throwing his money away. He says to me (he's just gotten out of another program and is up again), "Eddie, I'm going to move to New York to get clean." I said, "Fuck you, man." Sure enough, his habit tripled in a week.

♦ **V: New York can be pretty hardcore, but so can Los Angeles—that's why so much noir writing is set on the West Coast—**

♦ EN: That's true. Chandler, especially, is all Los Angeles. I was just driving through parts of older L.A. and it's trashed, man. It's due to poverty; there are some really cool areas that are just fuckin' turning into Third World countries. But goddamn— there's still some great stuff here, but there's just no point in hanging out. You'd have to buy some crack or get shot! And I don't want either of those, so, fuck it, I ain't goin'!

♦ **V: Did noir writing provide the philosophic underpinning of this movement for you?**

♦ EN: Yeah. This thing's already hopped-out and kids are *just* into the dancin' and shit like that. My favorite writer is David Goodis; his characters were *losers, baby!* Man, they were always losin' out—you know what I mean?

♦ **V: I hope people become encouraged to read writers like David Goodis and Dashiell Hammett—**

♦ EN: Cool; I'd love that. James M. Cain is good, too. One thing I want to touch on right now is: everybody's gettin' older all the time. I think swing is attractive to old punks and rockabilly cats because it's something you *can* grow older with. And it's got a great sense of style; there's an attraction that I attribute to *a fascination with what America used to be.* And on the *hard edge,* I attribute it to gangster movies. Almost every guy, one time or another, fancied: "Wouldn't it be fun to be a gangster for a day?" I used to read a lot of Raymond Chandler and Jim Thompson, and—it's just like, if you walk into a club, you can always tell who the new guys getting into it are, because they're really into leanin' on the bar with their fedora cocked, flippin' the same old Zippo— you dig what I'm gettin' at? And that fits a sense of fun, too.

♦ **V: What musical instruments do you play now?**

♦ EN: Guitar and a little percussion. I learned a couple of rhythms on bongos and I've been playing that in the band to add some "flavor." I don't care to be a soloist; I just want to add a little groove. It would be great to have more pieces—horns essentially. We don't need them, but I love that '30s and '40s Latin big band sound, like Xavier Cugat. He's almost Bugs Bunny-sounding; so *definitive.* Every movie you watch where they get ready to go to some nightclub, like the Copa Cabana, that's what you hear.

We're trying to keep our style and mix it up at the same time. Our sets are getting pretty diverse. We've got old school stuff from the '30s, like "The Mooch," and then we're doing our own stuff that combines those styles with something a little more faster and punk. It's working out, but it's confusing.

♦ **V: Tell us more Royal Crown history—**

♦ EN: There was a version of Royal Crown before this version. I'm talking *before* '89 when we officially started with the Stern Brothers [from Youth Brigade]. We didn't really know how to play our instruments. I was playing and learning old chord progressions, but I didn't know that's what they were. In a sense, what we did was: *we reinvented.* That's why it was so fresh, instead of somebody dressing up and saying, "We're going to do this '40s *act.*" It was a gradual process that came to fruition and developed.

♦ **V: Was this earlier incarnation your rockabilly band, the Rockomatics?**

♦ EN: No. That was right before. This is where everything gets kind of gray. It was about the same time that I went off and did that, and I was still doing the Rockomatics. I was also playing

Big Ed from Rigor Mortis and lil' Eddie share a contemplative moment ca. 1984.

with this great stand-up bass player and singer, Russell Scott. He's a band leader too, [Russell Scott and the Red Hots] so we butt heads, even though we're best friends. That's when Mando first started coming down to play. I wanted to get more into the rhythm and blues and '40s jump. Russell was very adamant as a traditionalist about what he wanted to do. We did a final gig at the Palace and then we both decided to try our own thing. And the rest is bullshit "history"—that's when Royal Crown came into being.

Rockabilly Eddie ca. 1987

♦ V: *It must have been hard keeping the band in existence, going through personnel changes, etc.*
♦ EN: The Stern brothers would leave us high and dry every time Youth Brigade could make money. I used to say it was like leaving a good-looking girlfriend, because they'd come back after a month. Mando and I used to sit there and starve our butts off because it was the only way we made a living. We were younger: "Oh, I guess we got to wait for them." Now we've got better players and that's *it.* That was a bad scene.
♦ V: *Particularly after teaming up with Mando, it seems you could weather members quitting because you've got your core.*
♦ EN: Yeah, between me and him, we can. Me and Mando could get something together anytime.
♦ V: *You said that your friend helped get you off the streets. That must have been a hard transition; Hollywood is not an easy town.*
♦ EN: It depends. I grew up not being able to ask for shit. So, it's taken me the last couple of years to learn to even speak my mind, like asking for help if I need it. The hardest time in my life was after I was playing with heroin in '87. It just got a hold of me really bad. I got strung out really hard from '93 to '96; I had a $300 a day habit for years. And I was still doing the band.

The worst year was 1995 because I was in and out. I got locked in some psych ward for two weeks and strapped down for three days. All of my old anger was coming out. I could have gotten out of the ward in about four days, but I kept trying to *break* out.

[laughs] I did get out once, through the roof. They had a Nurse Ratchet, too, who hated my ass. I was so pissed off in there, man; I felt like I was going to explode.

Then when I got out of there, I ran out and immediately got loaded because it was such a traumatic thing. They let me out and took me to a meeting (like I was going to stay?!) and I fucking bolted, man. It was like when you stick a cat in a car.

The worst thing about the psych ward was that there was no music. And there were nuts everywhere. *I* wasn't nuts; I was just a drug addict who wanted to get the fuck out of there; I never hurt anyone. I was just losing my cool. It was a heavy-ass experience.

The only thing that kept me going was a couple of brothers in there who were guards. We'd get together and sing doowop once in a while. That would lift my spirits. When I got out of there I was clean for about a month. Then I went on this run. The last day I used, man, I didn't have a place to live and was staying with friends. I was going to the methadone clinic. Then somebody sells me a bunch of Mexican Valium and I thought, "I'm doing okay; I can take a couple of these." Then I took a couple of those, a couple of that, a couple of this. And I thought, "Now I can call my dealer because I'm okay." [laughs] I had pills and drugs coming out of my ears; I got so wacked out. Then my brothers came up and got me. They sat on me for two weeks. Finally, I saw how it affected my family and how it was killing my mom. I had just given up; I spent more time in my bathroom than anywhere else. I didn't listen to music anymore and locked myself up. People would say, "Isn't life better now?" Fuck yeah, but when you're like that you don't know what life is like anymore. You don't even know what it's like *outside.* I was lucky that fate or whoever helped me to snap out of it. But if I ever want to get off the planet again, I know how to do it. I buried a lot of my old shit, finishing that addiction. It's been a really good year and a half for me so far. It's been my best years.
♦ V: *It must help to be busy—*
♦ EN: Sure. Sometimes it's just hard not to get lost along the way. After three years of the first version of Royal Crown, it got so stale. It fucking fell to pieces. It stressed the hell out of me, and looked like it was going nowhere. Then I got new guys, which was a blessing, but I was already so far into my addiction that I almost destroyed the whole thing. Fortunately, I didn't.

I'm lucky with my friends. Mando is the guy that saved my ass essentially, man. The second time I went in, before the nut ward, he came over and I was in my boxer shorts and a bloody wife-

Eddie Nichols, James Achor, Adam Stern, Jamie Stern, Mark Stern and Mando Dorame ca. 1993.

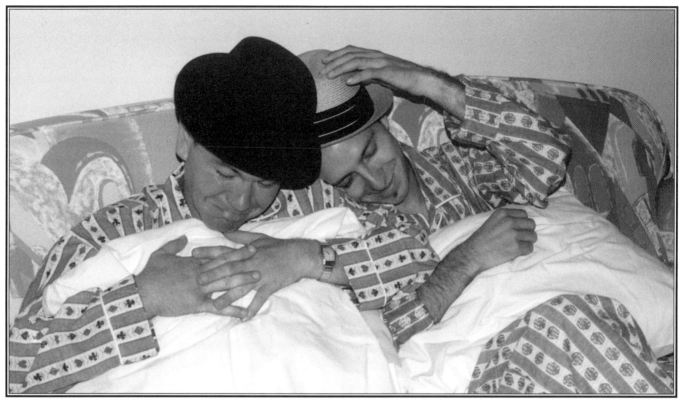

Eddie and Mando bond in Las Vegas in 1996.

beater from fuckin' banging speedballs all night. I was totally spun out of my mind. He brought me some underwear and clean T-shirts, dressed me and dragged me down to get help. He's my bro; that guy's helped me out a lot.

Mando is Mexican-American. He grew up in Watts and has a strong sense of loyalty—has a sense of family. That's just what you do and you don't even question it. It's the luckiest thing that ever happened to me.

♦ **V: You seemed to be blessed with lots of friends—**

♦ EN: Yeah, and I got two brothers. My older brother, "Ross the Boss," is a professional roadie. My younger brother, Jay-Jay is pretty multi-talented; he's a gourmet chef, a bike mechanic and a regular greaser. He had a psychobilly band called Wrecking Ball—they *were* wrecking things, too. Those guys know how to scrap—my brothers.

♦ **V: So Royal Crown's music developed out of various forms of American music (rockabilly, doowop, jump blues, etc)—**

♦ EN: Yes, it just developed. I love American music, man; I wanted to delve into something and I wanted it to be a little different.

You know what really turned me on to everything? All the Louis's, of course, but especially Louis Prima and Keely Smith. Sam Butera was Prima's bandleader in Vegas, and I recommend Sam Butera and the Witnesses on Dot Records; his shit was so bad ass, bro. He was mixing rock'n'roll with jazz; he'd do it so cool. You should hear his version of "Fever," on the *Ultra-Lounge* series.

♦ **V: Sam Butera still sells his own CDs at his shows—**

♦ EN: Hell yes. I have so many funny-ass Sam stories. [laughs] This is just the way Sam is: he and Keely Smith are doing a gig and somebody comes walking onstage. You don't do this; I don't care how famous you are. But it's Frankie Avalon; I guess he's friends with Keely. And everybody's like, "Oh look! It's Frankie!" Then you see Sam's face and you see him mouthing, "That motherfucker . . ." He's got the nastiest look on his face. He's like, [pissed-off] "Yeah, why don't you just sing something!" So, Frankie's singing with Keely and he's horrible. We go to the bar afterwards with Sam, man, and the first thing he does is order a drink and says, "That no-talent motherfuck." Goddamn! Sam's

stuff on the Dot label is such ass-kicking music. You really got to hear this shit because his voice had such soul back then.

♦ **V: His attitude about show biz is: "There's no free lunch."**

♦ EN: Sam had some hard knocks with Louis Prima. Louis kind of screwed him. There's still a lot of bad blood, even though Louis has been dead for 20 years. Sam was doing this book and Mando read it. Louis did some fucked-up shit, and Sam never got credit for any of that shit back then. It's more like a movie script, and there's stuff in that manuscript talking TRASH about Louis. But it probably is the way shit went down. Mando and I suspect that's the reason why Sam and Keely aren't playing together anymore.

♦ **V: So Keely must have seen a copy of the script—**

♦ EN: Or something. She probably didn't want some of those things said: that Louis was a hound dog. Maybe she didn't want

> ## You know what really turned me on to everything? All the Louis's, of course, but especially Louis Prima and Keely Smith.

to be embarrassed, or maybe she still has something for him, or maybe she hates him too—I just don't know.

♦ **V: Have you met any other "legends" in your travels?**

♦ EN: Besides Sam Butera, we've met James Brown. He came to one of our shows at the Hilton in Vegas. It was fuckin' righteous, man. I wouldn't go up to him, but we had this pushy Vegas manager who kept saying, "*Come on!* Get a picture with him!" We come up to him and he looks me up and down and says, [imitating James Brown] "Zoot suit! I used to have me a zoot suit when I was a kid!" The great part was that he came down to our show—they all say they're going to do it, but he did. And he *danced!* The audience was going nuts; it was so cool. He was out there scrabbling.

♦ **V: Wow—he could still dance at the age of 69!**

♦ EN: Hell yeah, man. After doin' all those drugs and gettin' all those face-lifts, and still bein' able to dance! [laughs] I'm just kidding.

I also met Jerry Lee Lewis a couple times. The last time was when we were opening for him in New York City. He walks in a half hour late with his entourage and I'm with my pal, Eddie Dixon. He wrote the theme song "Relentless" for *The Loveless,* the greaser art film with Robert Gordon. Eddie works with David Lynch and used to do bit parts in John Waters movies. He's a hillbilly who lives in New York City on Avenue A and Fourth

---

Even in school, I was always in the "out" group—but that's where you meet some of the best people.

Street—the only guy out there wrenching on his Thunderbird in the street! Sam the Sham was the preacher who married him. Anyway, me and Eddie go, "Hey, what's up, Killer?" acknowledging his presence. Jerry Lee does one of those 16th century French bows—he bends from the waist and rolls his wrists elegantly three times in a ballroom bow, and when he comes up the fourth time he flips us the bird, then smiles and waves. I thought that was way cool. It's like he was sucking it all in, and then says, "Fuck you!"

♦ **V:** *You pepper your speech with some great old street jive—*
♦ EN: I have this out-of-print book from the '30s that documents a lot of street slang, pimp slang, jail slang, hoodlum slang. Some of the stuff they came up with is fucking outrageous. For a while I used to memorize and use it, but nobody would know what the fuck I was saying. I found it pointless, except for my own entertainment value.

♦ **V:** *You draw and paint—*
♦ EN: I used to be such a people-pleaser. When I first got to San Diego I was staying at the punk rock crash house. Down there, the guys were brutal—you know, it was that Southern California muscle-bound thing in the punk scene back then. These guys

were huge tyrants and I was this skinny little 17-year-old. But I'd paint their leather jackets meticulously because I liked to draw. I would stay up all night, speed or not, and then they'd go buy me a slice of pizza after I fuckin' worked on their jacket for three days straight! I'd be like [groveling voice] "Thank you!"

♦ **V:** *In the midst of chaos, you maintained an interior life—*
♦ EN: Yeah, I really enjoyed doing those leather jackets. I'm a little too old for it now, but sometimes I feel like doing it again. Who knows—I might revert. Art takes time, man. The last time I drew I had started a picture of these boxers; it was a really great picture. I had two months of down time from the band when I first got out of rehab. I can't just sit down and draw and stop and go back to it. I'm so particular about it that I want to just spend days and days doing it all at once. And then your back hurts, goddam it!

♦ **V:** *You must have started young—*
♦ EN: Yeah. I did some good stuff when I was a kid. I run into my best friend from second grade in New York all the time; it's really weird. He gave me this booklet of stuff we used to draw. It was heinous. We'd always draw these monsters ripping the shit out of everything with bones and blood everywhere. [laughs] It was really gory stuff. We'd go at it, making whole books with little retarded sayings underneath: "This is Wolf Boy when he was 17. He killed 500 mens." [sic]

♦ **V:** *Were you influenced by* **Mad** *magazine?*
♦ EN: I was influenced by Forrest Ackerman's *Famous Monsters of Movieland.* The first thing I got when I was young was that huge *Wolfman* poster. I should have been scared; I wasn't even in first grade when I got it. I loved that monster thing . . . and *Planet of the Apes.* [laughs] My buddy in first grade and I saw this theater marquee: "Planet of the Apes Marathon." We're were like [gasp]. We saved up our money, but we didn't know that movies changed their schedules [laughs]. So, we went there on Saturday and it's the fuckin' *Legend of Boggy Creek*—a pseudo, bad "B" documentary about the Southern Sasquatch. It was so stupid, man! We were so bummed out. Oh well.

♦ **V:** *You first moved out to San Diego with your mom and then you moved up to Hollywood—*
♦ EN: Yeah, what happened was that I took an excursion up here for a gig and just stayed. That was when I started hanging out on the street. I was on pretty heavy wraps from my stepfather. I was a good kid, essentially, and was so super-disciplined that when I turned 17 I said, "Fuck living anywhere, man, I'm living out here in the streets."

It's so funny though. I go by Hollywood Boulevard today and it still looks like the same group of scrappy-assed dirty kids. There's always one kid with a mohawk, one girl with a bad mohawk, and one black kid with leopardskin spots on his head. Same with San Francisco—you still got your punks, man, but they seem to be getting dirtier and dirtier.

♦ **V:** *Or maybe you're just getting cleaner and cleaner—*
♦ EN: Maybe. [laughs] You're right, man; we were goddamn slobs.

♦ **V:** *It must have been hard to play music when you were living on the streets—*
♦ EN: I was in a real goofy mood for a couple of years; I'd crack people up and shit and make funny videos with some buddies. We were all in our early 20s and none of us knew what the hell we were going to do, so we were all fucking off. I was never stuck on

Covers for Raymond Chandler's *Finger Man and Other Stories* (1946) and David Goodis' *Nightfall* (1947).

one particular group, just a bunch of weirdos essentially. Even in school, I was always in the "out" group—but that's where you meet some of the best people. I hung out with fuckin' weirdos and rejects—the kids who would relate to you on a level other than what position you held on the soccer team.

♦ **V: In Royal Crown, I think you've attracted some real characters.**

♦ EN: Some of them *are* characters, man. Our bass player, Veikko, [pronounced VA-ko] is quite a character and very solid. He was in the Navy and he played in the circus also. He went to the music school of hard knocks. They would get a gig and fly to an island in the Pacific and there would be no landing strip. He's been through tough times and persevered, and now it's turning out the way he wanted.

Our trumpet player, Scott Steen—he's got a lip on him. We met him in San Francisco and he asked to sit in and that's how he joined the band. He's an intense player when he ain't chasin' women—just kidding!

James Achor was pretty much self-taught as a guitarist. He's a big fan of American roots music and collects tons of 78s and guitars—he'll have his own little museum someday. He's very intent on becoming a great player.

Mando's so good and original because his dad was a sax player, cholo cat, who used to take him around to the bars in Watts. Mando's played with Big Jay McNeely.

♦ **V: Ohmigod!**

♦ EN: Yeah, he's the honking sax. He was little and his dad would set him up on the bar and he'd play "Honky Tonk" and shit. He was a little guy and everyone took to him. That's why he's got the real deal going. He's my anchor. There is so much talent in the band—arrangement talent, and our drummer, Daniel Glass, is a fuckin' nut—he's great.

♦ **V: Do you have a problem with the label "swing"?**

♦ EN: I did . . . and I gave it up. What's so damn funny about it, too, bro, is that if you listened to stuff back when the scene started poppin', we had swing elements though we were playing Rhythm & Blues and Jump. Then the fedora and the whole deal with Benny Goodman came in. We've never played "In the Mood"; possibly we could, but that's a BIG, big band sound.

It's life; if you dig something, go with it.

Anyway, a bunch of kids ran with that whole "swing" label. We used to really hate it at first when all the lindy-hop kids came in, but I guess they did help build the scene.

I was just looking at news stories from '93 when things first started poppin' for us. All the headlines would be like, "Swing Is Back!" Suddenly all these kids from the suburbs started showing up, and there were "swing dance societies" coming in. Most of them were geeks who really didn't have any *edge* to them at all, but they were into the dancing. It all melded together. We lost a lot of people from the old scene when that started happening, but that's all right: "If you can't take it, then fucking get out!"

Now, I can look at things with a grain of salt. It's life; if you dig something, go with it. That faction shit was for when we were 17-year-old punks: "I don't hang out with straight-edge guys." If you want that, fine, stay in your little hole.

♦ **V: Why do you think you lost those people?**

♦ EN: We all do this in our own ways. Like the old punks looking down at the "new" punks and thinking, "I ain't hanging out here; you guys don't know shit!" kind of deal. Also, there were a lot of guys who started poppin' up and I thought they were hard. I remember a couple of cats came on the scene and they had the shit down. I figured, "They been like that for a long time, and came out of nowhere." Then I'd see them a couple of months later and they'd be into some Gucci look all of a sudden!

Eddie (far left) in his rockabilly days with Jerry Lee Lewis ca. 1988.

♦ **V: They were all surface appearance.**

♦ EN: Yeah. It blew me away. It was like, "What the fuck?"

♦ **V: Speaking of surface appearances, did your clothes evolve much in the band?**

♦ EN: Not too much, not for me. Clothes got better after the first year because I started *digging into it.* My band members are sometimes a little *casual* for me, but they do look good. Mando and myself pretty much wear cuff links, ties, etc every night.

This is going to sound cornball, but we got a style. I remember the first time I wore my collar out (like the Ricky Ricardo thing), then the rest of the band started doing it. But then some of them thought it was okay to fuckin' take off their dress jacket and not wear a tie at all. So, for the last couple of summers, I ended up sweating my nuts off because I'd be dressed head-to-toe playing Florida in 100 degree heat and 100% humidity. And the other guys wouldn't do it.

♦ **V: That's your job. It's the details. To quote Cary Grant, "It takes 260 details to add up to a good impression."**

♦ EN: Man, I'd hate to see his list.

♦ **V: He always looked so impeccable—**

♦ EN: Oh sure, he probably clipped his own butt hairs. [laughs] During a hot summer tour I might do more of a Bowery thing: the big pants and wifebeater undershirt. But I'm scared to do that because I don't want my band slobbing out on me. We want to have a look, a theme.

♦ **V: It must be tough to keep a coat on when it's 120 degrees outside. It's very punk rock to do that.**

♦ EN: [laughs] That's true. My guitar player, James Achor, used to make fun of me: "Eddie, you're the only guy walking around in black jeans, boots, and a leather jacket in the middle of the summer." And I would say, "Yeah, but I don't want to wear shorts and look like everybody else." I don't know. Whatever.

♦ **V: Do you still go to thrift stores?**

♦ EN: When you called, we were just looking at the *Recycler.* Throughout, I'm saying, "Ooh, look it this! Look it this!" My gal, Ruth, is from Phoenix and she's King Thriftshopper. Out there, there's so much good shit for a buck, but L.A.'s been picked clean. Stuff that she can get for five bucks in Arizona is $60 here and she won't buy it. Now that we need stuff, we can't get it. I'm spoiled, too, because I've been on the road. Heywood-Wakefield furniture that I can get for $300 in the Midwest is $700 or $800 in L.A. I've got all this stuff strewn out all over. I've got so much fuckin' pin-up girl art laying around my pad—that's *all* I got.

♦ **V: *What's the history of women in your life?***

♦ EN: I went through some crazy shit with women. I was 21 when I met this girl, man. She was dark and beautiful, but she had a mean dope habit. I thought I'd never do it, but when you fall in love with somebody, then you do that shit. Forget it, man. That chick died on me. She put me through hell and then died on me. It happened after we broke up, but she wrung me out. It was a nightmare. I'd come home and there'd be some guy in my fuckin' house with the door locked . . . all those things.

In my life I've known nuts, nuts, nuts, and more nuts. They were all gorgeous, man. They had some character to them. I always picked out some girl who I'd later find out was just fucked in the head. Fuckin' crazy broads. It went on like that for years, but after so many bad ones, I just started getting nice girlfriends. I've had a lot of good luck; I've got great women now—I mean, whatever. I just broke up with my girlfriend of four years, but we're still friends. And I'm living with Ruth now and she's a whopper. She's really cool, man; she wrenches on her car, always fixes things, works on projects, plays the bass. She's a greaser chick, man, simply put.

Ruth was in the punk scene when she was my age too. You know what else is cool about her? We watched a movie the other day and she said, "Who's that?" And I had to inform her it was Mel Gibson. She doesn't know any fucking thing about movies and media today; she just watches old films.

♦ **V: *You have a 1953 Hudson Bullet Car. How did you get into that?***

♦ EN: I know a few guys who are really into it. Mando has always been into it; he has a 1948 Fleetline and he's customizing a '61 convertible. It all just goes with the "swing lifestyle." [laughs] As for me, I never drove; I was always waiting to get the

car that I wanted. Five years ago, I bought a '51 Hudson, but I didn't have any money, man. I used to sit in it and pretend I was at the drive-in or something! [laughs] I'd drink beer in my car—that was my bar, essentially. And I'd stare at it and think, "Oh, boy, I wish I could fix this up . . . " But my 1953 Hudson is up and hopping; it's a beauty.

♦ *V: What color is it?*

♦ EN: It's forest green with a white top. It's cool. It's a big-ass car, man—you could put six bodies in the fuckin' trunk!

♦ *V: Do you attend car shows?*

♦ EN: As time allows. Mando goes, and my friend Ed (another one of my buddies who builds "customs") is always trying to get me to go. I love going to them, except it just makes you freak out: "Ohmigod! LOOK AT *THAT!*" That's for guys that can wrench all day on their stuff.

I recently went to a Hudson graveyard where there's about 100 cars like mine. This guy, Bill, had incredible stuff for sale, cheap. He was chewing tobacco and had this brown rim around his lips. After we left I realized that I never saw him spit—that old codger was swallowin' the shit!

♦ *V: Growing up in Manhattan, owning a car must have been a fantasy—*

♦ EN: Yeah, it was nice when I finally got one. I'm very grateful. Everything I've obtained in the last three years I really appreciate. People who just get shit handed to them don't give a damn. I'm very happy with what I got.

♦ *V: Vintage cars are these things of incredible beauty and the best of American design, all lumped into one piece of metal—*

♦ EN: There's just a *feeling* you get when you sit in one of those cars . . . My car is in good condition because I'm fixing it up, but even if the car's beat, just the aesthetics of the interior are worth it. There's all these little neat gadgets that we don't have in cars today; we've got electronics now. Everything in those cars has a purpose. All the parts complement each other; there's a niche for everything. You discover stuff all the time—and I'm not talking about rust and shit! [laughs] Those cars are the greatest—especially if you're decked out and can jump into one. It's The Bomb, man. We went out last night, actually.

♦ RUTH: [in background] Yes, we did!

♦ EN: [laughs] She hates alcohol and I said, "It sure likes you."

Cover Royal Crown Revue's first album with the Stern brothers, *Kings of Gangster Bop* (left), and their live album, *Caught In The Act* (right).

♦ **V: One thing I like about the older cars: they don't have bucket seats—**

♦ EN: Oh man, it's like a couch. You could easily put seven people in my car. It's got a lot of room. I'm starting to obsess on it. I spent *four hours* cleaning the dash yesterday. Now it looks great, but—

♦ **V: —that was thinking time, too—**

James Achor and Eddie Nichols. Photo: Mark Jordan

♦ EN: Oh yeah. It's a nice way to spend time, instead of fucking up or doing something crazy. It keeps me grounded.

Once you get hooked in, there are so many cars out there. There's the greatest car just outside of Portland right now; they want something like $4,500 for it. It's a perfect 1954 Pontiac Catalina—so beautiful. There's front trim sculpted out of chrome, and it has an Indian head made out of glass or plastic—and the face lights up! It's so cool, man! Plus the car's cherry. I was like— [gasps].

♦ **V: You're immersed in this car subculture, where you know these other car aficionados—**

♦ EN: I know a few of them. I'm still a mechanical idiot, but I'm learning. All you gotta do is get in there.

♦ **V: By changing your environment, which includes the car, you're removing yourself from the ugly, modern, trendy design of the 20th century—**

♦ EN: [Scottish accent] It's a bunch of crap! [laughs] Man, geez, driving in L.A. people are so goddamn ruthless. People are flying in front of me, and I'm in the slow lane. They're on the freeway going 70 miles an hour, and passing people on the right. It's like, "Come on, bro, you're going to fuckin' . . . " I don't know—I'm already getting into that flippin' off, swearin' thing. It's pretty bad; I gotta watch it.

♦ RUTH: [in background] People have been shot for less, Mr. Eddie.

♦ EN: My friend Ben was out here from New York, and he said, "Man, in New York if you tell someone to fuck off, it's fine or, at worst, you get into a little squabble. In L.A., you get fuckin' capped."

♦ **V: Back to the past: you said you took a break during the Stern Brothers days. I'm guessing this was when you did the "Jazz Jury" band—**

♦ EN: Yeah. Pretty much, that's what Mando put together. We've done some shows up in San Francisco. He continues to do that. He's into bebop, so it's mostly that. But because he's got a good piano player, I had the chance to get up and do some crooning. That helped—but "that don't pay the bills needa."

♦ **V: You were doing the Royal Trio and the Jazz Jury at the same time—**

♦ EN: Yeah, Royal Trio. I was doing that with J.P. He's got a band called the Big Town Seven and I would sit in with them— that's actually something I do on my time off, too. I'm kind of particular about it; when you sing all the time, people always ask you to do it on your time off. When I go out like to sit in the audience, man, I just don't want to get up—not that I'm that fuckin' good or anything, but sometimes I just want to relax. It's really hard, too, because if you turn them down, everybody's like "Mean!" and they think you're a big dick. And I'm like "Hey, I'm tryin' to rest here!"

♦ **V: You've only had four singing lessons?**

♦ EN: Yeah. I had about four vocal lessons. I took two cheapo, basic lessons and then I found this voice coach out in the Valley. I don't know why I quit going; I think I got off into being bad or something. Those lessons helped immensely. I took as many of the principles—which are the basics—and worked on those. Granted, if I had continued going I could be doing fuckin'—who's that ding dong who put *Phantom of the Opera* out? That's who this guy's students were. That kind of technical scene, but screw that. Actually, my cousin is an opera singer. He sings at places like the Met; he sings all over the world. He told me, "Eddie, don't take no more lessons. Just keep what you got and work on the basics." And sure enough, they're working out.

Basics, for me, is relaxing—they're essentially things like breathing. You know how they say, "Sing from your diaphragm." You see, people sing from their throat all the time. They scream and they lose their voice in one gig. I did 18 nights in a row and that sucked. But my voice only cracked three times the last night, and that's a pretty good run. I was only able to do that because I wasn't forcing from my throat. There's all kinds of tricks you can learn . . .

♦ **V: Do you take hot lemon juice with honey before a performance?**

♦ EN: Nah, I never do that. I drink and smoke Frankie-style

L to R: Mando Dorame, Bill Ungerman, and Scott Steen. Photo: Mark Jordan

[Sinatra]: "Who loves ya, baby?" [laughs] No, not yet, but I'll probably get to the point soon where I have to start doing it. At this point I don't have to. I think I tried it once or twice and it just made me more nervous.

The best thing that I do is croon. I haven't done any on an album, yet. But I love to croon like old Sinatra. When I get older, if I have a little money, I'm going to open my own nightclub, have a house band, cigarette girls—the whole fuckin' thing—and I'll be the singer.

My buddy Eddie Reed is really into old school big bands. Our dream is to open our own club by the year 2000. I don't know—it's getting close—but you never know what could happen in three years. That's essentially what I want to do. If I can't do it on my own, I'll go to Vegas. My father used to make a fuckin' *killing* in Vegas and that was in the '50s. What sucks, though, is that musician's wages have not gone up since the '50s. My dad was making more money back then for gigs. He used to work two months in Vegas and then go home for the rest of the year.

These kids under pseudonyms like "Valentina Violett" put on this event called the "Velvet Hammer" (at the El Rey Theater) and it was a fully retro strip show! It's girls from the scene—the greaser-punk-rock-abilly-swing scene—with a comedian, Rube Ruben. He's a little guy with a pencil moustache who looks like a cartoon pimp with his hair flattened down on his head, big rings—he winks a lot, smokes cigars—the whole 9 yards. He comes out in a plaid suit with a lobster hanging from his crotch. The girls dance to R&B and surf tunes and they all have "themes" to their costumes: the "housewife," "Venus on the Half Shell" (the "Oyster Girl" comes out of a clam). My personal favorite is a cat fight where they rip each other's clothes off—it's wild. The big clincher was the appearance of Kitten Natividad. She tells a great joke at the end, "What did one tit say to the other?" "Don't hang so low; people will think we're nuts."

♦ *V: You've written some of Royal Crown's songs?*
♦ EN: Uh-huh. And some music, but not all of it. I can't take credit for this: the reason why our band's gotten so much better is because we've got a very good horn arranger in the band now, Bill Ungerman. If it's one of my songs, I'll tell him my ideas and he has to arrange it. This is something I regret: I can hear the music in my head, but I don't have the skill to write it down. If I had fuckin' three weeks or a month to start learning how to do it, *fine,* but I don't have the time right now. Sometimes when I try to explain, musicians don't get it because they're thinking in proper terms and I'm thinking: "Boo-bop-a-doo-bop." [laughs]

You know why "standards" are great and why they still last? I realized that a lot of my early songs were very wordy with a lot of consonants. Old songs are so great because they're all

Cover for Richard Gehman's *Sinatra and His Rat Pack*

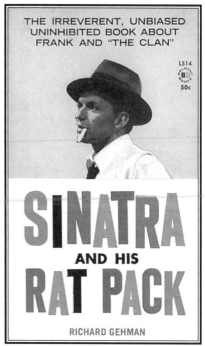

THE IRREVERENT, UNBIASED UNINHIBITED BOOK ABOUT FRANK AND "THE CLAN"

LS14
BELMONT
B
BOOKS
50c

SINATRA
AND HIS
RAT PACK

RICHARD GEHMAN

written around vowels. Like "I've got the world on a string . . ." You know what I'm saying? That's why they were great and great to sing.
♦ *V: I never knew that—*
♦ EN: Yeah, it's something to think about. They were words that were singable *and* said something. When I first started writing I would think, "God-damn, these songs are so hard to sing!" And it was because I had 50 fuckin' syllables in the words.
♦ *V: [laughs] So far you've managed to keep a private life. It's probably going to get harder and*

MYSTERY, THRILLS AND HARD-BOILED SWING!
ROYAL CROWN
REVUE
MUGZY'S MOVE

Promotional poster for Royal Crown Revue's Warner Bros. album *Mugzy's Move.*

harder—
♦ EN: I've already gotten into trouble with this. But it's also been one of the best things for building an audience. I go out to the audience and if I see someone familiar, I say Hello. I've done it ever since we started. I try to spend time with every person for just a minute. Now, I don't want to be rude, but I've found myself in some sticky situations. We'll be playing big joints and I do know a lot of the people out there, and some people want to get into long conversations.

Then there's other fans I don't even know. For instance, this woman was talking to me and I had to go onstage, so I said, "I'm sorry, but I really have to go." And she keeps on going, and then gets pissed at me. That's something I have to learn to do graciously, but I can't fuckin' please everybody. Humphrey Bogart once told Frank Sinatra, "The only thing you owe your public is a great performance." That's all you owe them, a good show, because that's what they're coming to see. You don't have to fuckin' bend over. There's a *little* more to it than that, but . . .
♦ *V: You'll just have to get better one-liners, like, "I'm sorry, but I've got to go onstage NOW."*
♦ EN: Yes. "I gotta go onstage or I'm going to kick you in the crotch! Which do you prefer?" [laughs]
♦ *V: The home (to retreat to) is really important, especially as Royal Crown gets bigger, to help you keep perspective—*
♦ EN: The pad? Yeah, it is really good. This is the most time I've had in a long time, and goddamn it I want some more of it! I don't need a lot, but there was a point where our management and booking were driving us into the ground. I was onstage one night and I almost did one of the most unprofessional things I could ever do—I was just going to drop the mike and walk off. I'd had it, man; I had been hammered into the ground. My argument with them was, "If you give me a week off, don't send me to four different places if that's my time off." I used to feel guilty about this, but if you're working two months straight with one day off a week for travel, fuck that, man, you have to recoup.

I was down in Austin, Texas and I was talking to this guy named Dale Watson. He's a country singer—a fuckin' great songwriter—and a very cool dude. He told me, "Eddie, I was doing the same thing." Then one day he started calling it his way. Sure enough, the record company didn't fire him and the managers didn't leave. He just said, "Look, if you're going to put me on this long, then this is how much time I want off." And it worked. He's kept his sanity and now he can play and enjoy it. What the fuck. If you're not enjoying it, then the audience won't enjoy it as much as they could.
♦ *V: You've got to resist those commercial pressures and*

maintain a life.

♦ EN: Definitely.

♦ V: *What's your next job?*

♦ EN: We decided to take this gig for monetary reasons: nine weeks in Vegas at the Desert Inn. That's where the Rat Pack hung out, and that's where I used to see Sam Butera. Tomorrow we're playing one of those private, pimp-your-ass gigs—where you get paid well and nobody pays attention: a corporate party or something.

We did a stint for two weeks at Disneyland in Florida because we needed bread and had just finished a tour—only the *big* bands make money on tour. Man, there were so many rules, right? I got a foul mouth. It's not that bad—I know when to control it, but geez, it's hard sometimes. We played in this "swing nightclub." It was almost too perfect; it looked like a movie set. It was called the Atlantic Dance Club on a boardwalk of the same name; it was a club and locals would come in. There's a little thriving swing scene in Orlando and there are some pretty hip people there. But then other people would come in and sit down, like we were the Country Bear Jamboree. Big fat fucking people from Minnesota: "Watch this, honey, they're freaks." And I'm going, "Hey! You moth—dirty mother freckles . . . " [laughs] I did end up swearing once. I said, "Shit!" off the mike, but everyone kind of went [Mickey Mouse voice] "What was that?" I was so afraid I was going to get the whole band canned.

♦ V: *Well, at least you're playing music . . . In the future you could probably hire someone to polish that dashboard, but I think it's better if you do it. [laughs]*

♦ EN: Oh, yeah. That's true, man. I wanna know what's going ON!

You would have loved this—it annoyed the fuck out of me! I was talking to this guy for a Houston local, left-wing rag like the *New Times* or the *L.A. Weekly.* So, I'm talking with this guy about our "Hey Pachuco!" song and I'm telling him why I wrote it and how I feel about it all. Then I get the paper and his article is nothing about music, but about our blatant disregard for the whole Pachuco movement. He interviewed sociologists and shit about if it was okay if we do this song, and told how we didn't give a fuck about it. He totally misrepresented us. It's so goddamn funny.

That song gets played on everything; it's been used for so many fuckin' things I can't even tell you. Someone told me they were playing it on the radio the other day, but bleeping out the word "Pachuco" because it was a "racist" statement. If they listened to the words of the song, it's from *this* side; it's not some establishment song. You know who used it too? Rush fuckin' Limbaugh put that song on the beginning of one of his shows! And if that moron fat fuck knew what it was about, he would have broke the fuckin' CD—or he would have deported it. Whatever. ▼

Eddie's Influences and Recommendations

PUBLICATIONS:

Goodis, David: *Of Tender Sin, The Blonde on the Street Corner, Black Friday, Of Missing Persons, Night Fall, Cassidy's Girl, The Dark Chase, The Burglar*

Jim Thompson: *The Killer Inside Me, The Nothing Man*

Chester Himes: *The Life* (about hustling, pimpin', the signifyin' monkey, etc. Lists all the codes: "Two-gun Pete," "Pimpin' Sam—shootin' gallery jive. From Holloway House: 213-653-8060.

Raymond Chandler: Everything, including any short stories. "Smart-Aleck Kill"—I love that title. "Pickup on Noon Street" is also good.

Grease Machines: From mid-'50s publications, published in 1979. Photos of George Barris, Big Daddy Roth, etc.

Old Punk Magazines: *Bomp* [U.K.], *Kicks, Zigzag*

The Pulps (cover art from pulps)

John Fante: He's depressing.

Paul Cain: *Fast One* (Black Lizard; his real name was George Sims. Wrote screenplays under the name Peter Ruric). *Seven Slayers* (short stories)—isn't that a good title for a song?

Terry Southern: *Red-Dirt Marijuana and Other Tales.*

A pile of regular "Rod" & "Custom" magazines.

MUSIC:

Sam Butera: That guy rocks, man.

Tiny Grimes: Guitar player; he rips. I don't know if he was in the Three Blazers or not.

Frank Sinatra: Almost all his records. I love Frankie, man.

Link Wray: He's almost 70 and still playing. I really wanted to see him when he played Bimbo's.

Django Reinhardt: My favorite guitar player. That's my favorite stuff to play when I play guitar, even though I can't play like him. I love those chords.

ACAPPELLA: Check Mando's list for that. Mine are all locked up.

Four Seasons: Here's someone that supposedly everyone hates; I should list it just to irk people. Frankie Valli's *Cherie & 11 Others.* They do a cool version of "Never On Sundays."

Louis Prima: *The Wildest*

Sex Pistols: *Flogging A Dead Horse.* I guess they put that out after the group was history. It had a bunch of songs they did afterwards by Steve Jones.

Clash: *Give 'Em Enough Rope*

Eddie Cochran's *Greatest Hits*

The Rejects: *Cockney Rejects*

Maximum Rock'n'Roll Album: *Not So Quiet On the Western Front Rat Music for Rat People* (San Francisco punk compilation)

Gene Vincent & The Blue Caps: It's always a battle forever between Gene Vincent & Eddie Cochran.

Sid Sings: I had the first one, with the poster, but someone snagged it. I hear he was a pretty nice fella, just a little misguided.

Slim Gaillard, Hasil Adkins, *Deaf Club LP*

FILMS:

I like warped shit and violence in movies, but not in real life.

Bad Lieutenant: The heaviest scene is when he's talkin' to Jesus!

Handgun: Fuckin' get it, bro. About 2 brothers who don't trust each other. They blow this robbery and they really fuck up. Kinda like them Goodis books, y'know.

Laws of Gravity: It's great, bro. You watch it, it looks like a documentary, but it isn't. Peter Green's in it (he was in *The Mask* & a buncha other films).

Usual Suspects: Of course. That was pretty hairy when he killed his own kids.

ROBERT MITCHUM films: He was too cool. *Night of the Hunter*—love that. He did some good *noir* films.

Metropolis: That's a great flick. Fritz Lang—sounds like a porno director or something. He probably had his little side action with the robot Maria.

Devil in a Blue Dress: It's great.

MUSIC FILMS:

Young Man With A Horn It's actually cool, got a buncha jazz cats in it. Kirk Douglas, white boy, learns the horn. Harry James does the soundtrack.

Guys & Dolls: It's my favorite cuz it's got Frank *and* Marlon.

Two Greaser Films: *The Wild One, The Loveless*

Hotrods to Hell, Cannonball Run 1 & 2, Blackboard Jungle, Rock All Night (with the Platters, etc)

SLANG:

"turn the hose on 'em" Machine-gun them.

"behind the 8-ball" If you're in trouble.

"bloodhouse worms" Men who pull in young girls for whorehouses.

Photo: Jeff Higginbotham

Mando Dorame ca. 1991. Photo: Jeff Higginbotham

INTERVIEW WITH MANDO DORAME

Tenor saxophone player Mando Dorame, Jr. is a founding member of Los Angeles-based Royal Crown Revue. He lives with Jorie Lodes, a make-up artist for independent films, video and photo sessions.

♦ *VALE: I was told that your background is Mexican-American—*

♦ MANDO DORAME: Chicano. My last name, Dorame (doe-*rah*-me) is French—somewhere along the line I had a French ancestor. My first name is pronounced "Mondo."

♦ *V: Tell us about your dad—*

♦ MD: *Pops* [Mando, Sr.] used to be a tenor sax player and has been one of my biggest influences in music and in other areas. He was born and raised in Watts, which is in South-Central Los Angeles *[ed. note: in 1994, there were 400-plus killings on the gang-inhabited streets of South-Central L.A.].* I was born and raised there as well. He was a chrome-plater and the first guy to not only chrome his whole engine but have the balls to lower a Cadillac—everybody else was trying to *buy* one first, and then just drive it around brand-new. But he actually lowered it to the ground and did all kinds of things to it. He was also in a car club with two of my uncles in the '50s, called the Night Owls, in Watts.

He was really into customizing cars. He did chrome work for Ed "Big Daddy" Roth; he chromed the "Beatnik Bandit" and a lot of Ed Roth's "inventions," if you will. He was one of the baddest chrome-platers in Watts; he chromed one of Elvis' bikes—the whole thing—in the late '50s, and did work for Jayne Mansfield, A.J. Foyt—all kinds of people.

My dad also played horn, but he never got to do it professionally. In Watts, the saxophone was a big thing during the '50s, and guys like Big Jay McNeely and Joe Houston lived in the neighborhood. He'd walk to school through an alley and hear them playing their horns from their windows. He was playing tenor for a long time, but when he had his kids he had to stop; he couldn't pursue it.

He's always been into R&B, doowop, jazz (like Gerry Mulligan and Dexter Gordon) and the more honkin' guys like Bill Doggett—that's where I get a lot of my musical background from,

because he was *always* playing these old records. When I was in junior high school I started building a collection of doowop. Later on I got into *acappella,* which is an offshoot of doowop without the instruments.

My dad played the shit out of Bill Doggett's "Honky Tonk (Part 1 and 2)" and I loved it. That was one of the first transcriptions I ever took down and learned note-for-note; I was so knocked out by it. I think I was knocked out more by the whole growlin', almost distorted sound that the sax player had—it's like he had a bad throat or something! Bill Doggett had two tenor players, Percy France and Clifford Scott, and I think it was Scott who actually played the solo on that record. I started looking for any records those guys did, trying to get that sound—which I *still* can't get! [laughs]

Then I got into the *other* side of the horn: Coltrane, Sonny Rollins and Dexter Gordon. Later I went back to listening to the earlier guys like Bill Doggett again. I'm still really into *acappella;* it's one of the only types of music that can just *lift my soul.*

Not too many people know about *acappella;* it was a late '50s, mid- to early-'60s underground sound that was going on in places like New York and Philadelphia. When the "British Invasion" came in, it knocked out doowop completely. The groups were still around, but nobody wanted to come up with the money to hire bands to back them, so eventually they started making recordings without instruments. These have an "underground" sound that didn't really surface on the West Coast. Only a few records were made, and I've been collecting 'em. Groups like Boyz II Men kinda caught on to it, but fucked it up . . . it's obvious they've listened to a lot of that. I also listen to soul music: Impressions, Sam Cook—all those guys. They're a big influence on me.

♦ *V: Did your dad take you to see live music when you were young?*

♦ MD: My dad took me everywhere—I owe every fuckin' thing to my *Pops,* man! When I was in junior high school he would take me around to all these clubs that were in the "mid" cities like Southgate, Watts, Lynwood and Compton. My dad really believed in me. He would take me to these bars, park my ass in the car (make me wait in the parking lot, go into these bars and kinda scope 'em out—usually there are live bands playing). My dad had a good way of bulldozin' people, making them do shit (including *me;* that's what dads are like).

He would go in and say to the manager, "Look, man, I got this kid in the car who can play saxophone and he's really fuckin' good. How about letting him sit in?" Usually they would go, "Uh, I don't know . . ." And then my dad would go, "Look, man, if he sucks and you don't like him, I'll help you kick his ass off the stage!" My dad is all tatted up and he's a big Mexican dude, so they would usually agree. Then he would run out and have me put my horn together in the car so I could run right in and go straight onto the stage before the owner or bartender stopped me—I was 13 or 14 years old, right? When I get on the stage everybody in the band is going, "What the fuck? This is a *kid!*"

♦ *V: [laughs] They must have thought you were "cute," though—*

♦ MD: At that time I watched every gangster movie in the world, so I always dressed in a suit. It must have been funny, now that I think about it, because I was like a midget George Raft! They would ask me what I wanted to do, and I would say "Honky Tonk" because it was a blues that *anybody* could fuckin' play. And 95% of the time I would wind up being there all night because they loved it, man. A few times, the bartenders would even bring me a drink! A lot of times the owner would even invite me back.

One time we went to the Rim Ram, which is a big steakhouse in Whittier; Big Jay McNeely was playing. It was more like a dinner place, so I could actually go up and talk to him. He let me play with him and was really cool; it's like he loved me, man. He said, "*Damn!* Would you want to play a couple gigs with me?" That never happened, but I went, "Yeah!" I remember him saying, "Man! You play like a fuckin' nigger!" I said, "Well, I'll play with you, but you just can't *pay* me like one!" He thought that was funny.

A couple of times me and my dad sat in and played with Joe Houston, too. We would open the set for him playing "All Night Long" which was his big hit. He would then come and get on the mike and say, "Well, I guess I can't play *that* tune!" My dad played tenor and I played tenor, and *two* tenors gave this big-ass sound, and Joe was on a wireless [microphone] anyway, and they always sound rinky-dink. Me and my dad had some fun times . . .

My dad hooked up with tattoo artist, Mark Mahoney—I've known him since I was as big as a potato. [laughs] He did all the

---

We had all of our influences, and listened to a lot of records, and started trying things out. Eventually it all just came together into this *thing*. It blows my mind every time I think about it.

---

tattoo work on my dad. He used to always talk to Eddie Nichols about me, and wanted to try and hook us up—at the time, Eddie was apprenticing in his shop. Finally we met, and Eddie and I have been together ever since. Mark Mahoney has always been like a godfather to me.

Mark Mahoney used to work at the Pike in Long Beach and my dad used to take me to his shop. I remember Mark being this skinny little beatnik kid with shades on, and thought he was the coolest fuckin' guy on the planet. A lot of times my dad would call up for a tattoo appointment and Mark would say, "Just come down to my house, man." So we stopped going to the Pike and just went to his house. That was the best thing in the world, because he had all these little trinkets hung up all over the place and I would look at them in awe.

As a kid, I especially liked going into Mark's bathroom, because he had stacks and stacks of "chick" magazines—every nude and porno magazine you could think of. I would come out 45 minutes later. [laughs] When you're a kid you think you're on top of everything, but I remember when I came out they'd be laughing—they knew what I was doing in there. But they never gave me shit about it; they just thought it was funny. That was the coolest thing about Mark's pad: the bathroom. I always used to bug my dad: "When you going to go over to Mark's?!"

♦ **V: You were hungry for knowledge—**

♦ MD: I got hip to a *lot* of shit early. My dad took me everywhere, and my uncle, Louie Hernandez, also—he was a guitar player, and that's who I learned my theory from. He was in the army with my dad, and in the barracks they'd play Bill Doggett tunes. My uncle was an amazing guitar player—he had his own style, but could play *anybody*. If you told him to play like B.B. King or Freddy King, you could record him and play the tape for somebody, and they would be completely fooled—that's how good he was. Back then they had the "Battle of the Bands" all the time, and he would go onstage and just *kill* everybody.

The first group I was in was the Versatiles, with all these Mexican cats including my uncle, and his wife sang—like Aretha Franklin. We played a lot of Chicano rock, Mexican music, jump blues, honky tonk, we did some Big Boy—it was a fun all-around gig, and that's why it was called the Versatiles. There was another tenor player in the band and I did the second parts—that's where I learned how to actually *play* with another horn player. This other player would beat on me all the time ("You need to go and practice more!") and I would work and work on my horn.

I would go to my uncle's house twice a week and take lessons. I worked on the horn *forever,* man. Then, my uncle cheated on his wife, and they split up, and I was bummed out because the band broke up . . . it was one of those things.

I was always into gangster clothing. First I was a little cholo kid from the *neighborhood,* so I wore khakis and Stacy Adams every day in junior high. I ironed my shirts, I put creases down the middle, had hairnets, I was in a gang—I did it *all*. I started checking out old movies and loved George Raft, so I started dressing up like that. I always tried to look sharp when I went to do a gig; I'd get dressed up in a fedora and suit. I used to think, "Wouldn't it be wild if I could have a whole band that dressed like this, playing this kind of music" (which all my friends thought was "grandpa music") "in front of my peers who would dig it? That would be fuckin' wild!"

As a kid I remember telling my dad, "Pops, there's gotta be something going on in Hollywood—why don't we go check it out?" I went to see this rockabilly band called the Mighty Hornets play the Spice Club on Hollywood Boulevard—this was about eleven years ago. That's how I got to know a lot of the guys who were around playing rockabilly and psychobilly. I got to know the bass player, Damon, and then I hooked up with Mark Mahoney and Eddie . . . I guess what I'm saying is, it's just wild how my dream came true!

I hooked up with Eddie, who's like my best friend, and he had those same dreams, too. When I met him, I thought, "This guy's like in counterpoint to me"; I thought he was really cool. We *clicked* immediately and just started taking off with this idea. We didn't *plan* this whole thing out: "We're going to dress like this and play this type of music"—we had all of our influences, and listened to a lot of records, and started trying things out (we were still learning about the music). Eventually it all just came together into this *thing*. It blows my mind every time I think about it.

You can have a dream—everybody can dream to be rich or whatever the fuck. But my dream was *to turn back time*—and

Mando at five years old.

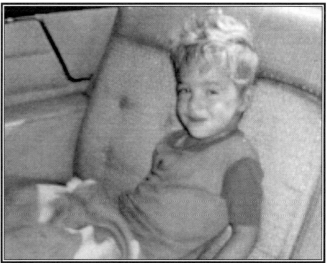

that's a hard dream to pull off! [laughs] It'd probably be easier for somebody to pursue being wealthy, than to go back and reinvent the '40s and '50s. But everywhere you go, now, there are swing bands—it's just wild. At the time, there wasn't any demand for this. Maybe Joe Jackson was doing his thing, which was kinda milquetoast, but who else? Rockabilly and psychobilly were really big, and of course punk was strong, but . . . it seemed that when we started doing our thing, within a *month* we had a good following.

♦ **V: It sounds like you started out in a rockabilly context—**

♦ MD: Yeah, we did. All our friends were really into rockabilly, and when I brought in a horn, the band *changed*. I introduced ideas that were more of a swing-vibe. I was listening to Lester Young and a lot of bebop. Eddie said that he'd always wanted to use horns in a band, and that's why it worked so well when Mark Mahoney introduced us and we tried it out. That first record we did has rockabilly in it, but it swung; it just has its own little thing. We were trying to come up with something different, but more than anything we were *learning* about all this music we loved so much.

On that first record, *Kings of Gangster Bop,* I was fuckin' learnin' how to play, and Eddie was learnin', and that's basically what that record is: a learning experience. It has its own "vibe" because we worked and played together so much that we got tight as a unit. Now, everybody's asking us for that record and wanting us to play tunes off it. There's a couple tunes I'd like to go back and re-record, now that we have three horns.

♦ **V: Can we backtrack a bit: when your dad first took you around to clubs, how did he dress?**

♦ MD: My dad always dressed sharp when he was a kid. Later on, he had to work a lot more so naturally he was mostly wearing work clothes. But when he *thought* he was getting dressed up, he would put on some brand-new khakis (Dickies), and all-black patent leather Stacy Adams (that's why *I* wore 'em as a kid; I looked up to my dad a lot). If it was hot, he just wore an undershirt (and he was all tatted up) or a plain workshirt. He wore a brim, too. He was a workin' man; he never really got *too* dressed up. He had work to do; he had to be comfortable. But I wanted my dad to be "hip," so I would starch his pants for him and crease 'em all the way up. Sometimes I'd try and get him to wear pants a couple sizes bigger. He used to go to every gig I played until

Above: Mando and Eddie in front of Bimbo's 365 Club. Photo: Mark Jordan; Below: Mando, Mark Mahoney, Eddie

maybe two years ago; he was at every damn show supporting me all the way.

I remember when I started really *noticing* the suits people wore. I used to watch a lot of old movies, including Cab Calloway films, and I had all the early *Low Rider* magazines, too. The suits I most admired were the zoot suits. I thought, "Well shit, since I'm part-Mexican, maybe I can pull it off: maybe I can wear a zoot suit onstage." So I went to this place called El Pachuco in Fullerton (which nobody knew about then) because I saw their ad in *Low Rider*. I paid $400 for a zoot suit, and starved for a week, at least. It was all black, and for a time that's all I wore.

Then I started getting them custom-made. I was hanging out with a good friend named Gary Diaz from San Diego, and we started to *really* get into the little tricks. We hooked up with old tailors, started looking at a lot of old magazines and books, and for example, began getting our belt loops lowered and cutting them in half to get "whip belts" [very thin belts] into them. Then we had *inside* belt loops made! We also got into the exact dimensions of the "fatness" of the pants at the knee, and got into raising the length above the waist. We almost went so far as putting zippers behind the cuffs (ankle chokers) so we could get our feet into the pants easier, or as my grandfather would say, "To let the gas out"—they were so tight!

Then Eddie started wearing them, and he looked good in 'em. That started so long ago; I was wearing that first suit seven years ago. I did a lot of reading up on that suit, man, and I understand there were a lot of political reasons why these Mexican kids were wearing them. They were rebelling, just the same as when cholos (or punks) get dressed up, and they got their ass beat all the time. I was trying to find information on the Sleepy Lagoon murder, and what happened during the zoot suit wars in the '40s . . . I started reading about all this, and got really "activist" in my own mind about it. So I wore that suit with *pride,* and I wore it because those were my grandparents, my ancestors.

Another thing: my grandfather was a Pachuco back in his day; he was wearing zoot suits. I used to have these long conversations with him, and he would tell me, "When you put that zoot suit on, it means a lot. It's not just a fashion thing." (It came to be *later,* in the late '40s and '50s, when Cab started putting it on, and in movies like *Stormy Weather*—the Nicholas Brothers were wearing zoots.) But when it really started, it was an East L.A. thing. These little gangs were forming to protect themselves against the sailors coming in and beating the shit out of 'em, out of racism or whatever reasons. So my grandfather used to tell me all these stories about that, and I would say, "Man, I'm going to put a zoot suit on and I'm going to stand up for *me*—for what I believe in; I'm going to stand up for all my people." And that's why I wore that suit.

My grandfather was a gigolo, man! He had a Clark Gable kind of look to him, and there was a time when he had women flying him all over the place. But you can't just sit down and talk to him about this; back then it was forbidden. Once in a while, when grandma wasn't around, he'd tell me things like, "You need this kind of shoe; you gotta get the *pointy* ones." I learned a lot from him; he was a hip guy in his day.

♦ **V: For you there's a deeper political motivation here; it's not just fashion—**

♦ MD: —for me, and Eddie, too. He also did a lot of research and got bothered by how nothing has really changed; that's why he wrote the lyrics to "Hey Pachuco!" While we were researching this we tapped into the whole Pachuco thing years ago, man.

Then I started seeing zoots pop up everywhere; the most backwards-ass white people were wearing 'em. To me, if you put a zoot on, you gotta hold your head up—you gotta have a *walk* for it! You put that thing on, it's supposed to *mean* something. I used to think, "Well, if people actually researched it and did their homework, then that's cool." But obviously it just became a fashion thing; it became so trendy—

♦ **V: As well as a mark of ostentation: "Look at me—I can afford to buy this zoot suit!"**

♦ MD: And sales at El Pachuco in Fullerton must have gone through the roof, because *everybody* was getting suits there. I've heard they've upgraded, and their suits are made better, but anyway . . . it started bothering me. I started realizing that *nobody's* doing their homework; they don't know what it means. I've always been one of them kind of cats, too, that always wanted to be different; I wanted to look different. I started seeing zoots everywhere, man, and I stopped wearing 'em! I started getting my own thing going again.

♦ **V: I fully sympathize with that—**

♦ MD: I never said all this before, but I gotta "speak my piece."

I have a pretty good collection of *Low Rider* magazines, including the first few issues. I also have a collection of another good magazine, *Q-vo*—it's all cholo writing: everybody just writing their shit up. Besides *The Zoot Suit Riots,* there aren't too many books on that subject. I look for newspaper clippings, articles in *Time* or *Life* from the early '40s . . . but mostly I learned from my family. Most histories are written by white people; if anything, they just slandered the shit out of the Mexican people.

The way I see it is: there were a lot of things that were fucked up in Mexico. Everybody wanted to come to the promised land and build something nice for their family, and they worked hard to do it. And that's what this country's supposed to be about. But it wasn't that way back then. Blacks and Asians, too, had to go through that shit. Up until the '60s when we had finally established a political movement for Latin people . . . finally we started organizing, and every person that was a good "face" figure for us pretty much got shot; assassinated. And you don't really hear about them as much as you hear about others. You have to do your homework on the history of the zoot suit riots, because there weren't too many people who wrote about it. The Mexican people still didn't have enough power to have someone to speak for us; it was too early. We didn't get anybody until the late '50s. You gotta have a family, a source who's been there and ain't gonna lie to you.

♦ **V: What's your mom like?**

♦ MD: I'm half-white; my mom was as white as they get. She's easy-going and kinda young—I think my dad met and married her when she was 17, and my mom had me when she was 18. My dad was something like 35 at the time, so he had to kinda raise *her,* too! She was from Pico Rivera. She didn't get along with her mom very well, and pretty much disowned her own family. My dad's family took her under their wing, so that became my mom's

Mando Sr., 18 years old, playing the saxophone.

Big Jay McNeely ca. 1953. Photo courtesy of Big J Records.

family. So she's kind of traditionally Mexican; that's all the food she cooks.

I remember one time my mom told me this story of when she was a little girl. *Her* mom (my grandmother) seemed to have a thing for young guys. Anyway, she came home from school with her girlfriend and found her mom, buck-naked, being chased around the house by some young guy with a hatchet in his hand! Pretty fuckin' wild.

My mom was also a writer; she's really into romance novels. She wrote a book and took it to a publisher and they were knocked out by it. But the publisher went bankrupt or folded, and my mom got rooked out of the whole deal. So from that she kinda got discouraged and doesn't write anymore. I try to encourage her. But my mom's just laid back, a really cool lovin' mom—she just loves the hell out of me. I'm just waiting to get some money so I can publish her book for her!

It was great growing up. I had a good family and that's how I thought life should be: how *I* was raised. So it's always been weird when a kid or a friend says to me, "Well, I don't have a dad." My mom and dad are still together today, and they're still so in love. I'm really proud of that, and I do everything just for them.

♦ **V: Was your mom into music, too?**

♦ MD: She's got so much soul! She listens to what's called "oldies" now, and used to go and hear groups like Thee Midniters from East L.A. She was into the same kind of music as my dad, because it's always been around the household. My mom was essentially a kid when they hooked up, so that's what she listened to. She used to always go down to Watts looking for my dad, and my dad would get upset: "You can't come down here!" He'd take her home, and she'd find her way back. My grandmother would get pissed off: "You can't have her comin' over here, man, she's white, she's gonna get jumped—you gotta *do something* with that girl!" [laughs] Then she had me, and it was just a great thing, and my bed was a dresser drawer—they didn't have money to get me a bed—but they made it nice. My dad claims that my grandmother still has that drawer somewhere—I'd love to have that. My mom's great; I really love her and she supports everything that I do.

♦ **V: Did you have any brothers or sisters?**

♦ MD: I have two younger brothers. My little brother, Brian, used to play trumpet and my middle brother, Michael, played piano but they don't play anymore. They didn't have the same interest that I did. But they're into building cars. They're chrome-platers, too; my middle brother's only 21 and he has his own plating shop. They're good kids. I have two step-sisters, too—step all over 'em. [laughs] Their names are Suzi and Lori. They're good people; I don't see them as often as I should. They probably say it's my fault.

♦ **V: What kind of car do you have?**

♦ MD: A '48 Fleetline Chevy. It's the ultimate Cholo wagon: the car that "The Bomb" got titled after. It's the second car I ever had and it's still not finished. I bought it when I was 18 for $3,200. (My first car was a '56 Ford pickup which my dad gave me, and took away from me, about ten times.) I was working at my dad's chrome shop, managing it, so that's how I was making money.

I'm almost finished with a '61 Ford Sunliner Galaxie convertible; I'm doing that like a mild custom. My dad used to always

Mando with his '61 Ford Sunliner Galaxie convertible.

customize cars back then; he lowered 'em, shaved 'em and pin-striped 'em. He knew everybody; he knew George Barris; he knew Gene Winfield; of course he was good friends with Ed Roth, and he also knew Dean Jeffries and Eric "Von" Dutch. All those guys who were customizing in Bellflower and Lynwood and all those places, my dad was around doing all the chrome on these guys' work. This was before I was born, in the '50s.

Then my dad got into building Harleys, too; he started building choppers in the '60s into the '70s. He had some really radical bikes he would show, and he won "Best Custom Bike" in a "World of Wheels" show. When Harley-Davidson used to be AMF, they flew him to Florida to some *stadium* where he gave a talk on customizing, with two Playboy bunnies beside him. Then Harley took him out to dinner. He was at a big table with all these bigwigs, and they asked him, "If you were to design a bike for Harley, what do you think would sell?" At that time Harley-Davidson was going downhill, because Honda and Yamaha bikes were selling big-time. My dad said, "Build a bike that has a hard-tail look but can give the same effect as a swing-arm" (nobody wanted the swing-arm look because it was so ugly, but if you rode a hard-tail bike, after two hours you had a hernia—but they *looked* cool). "If you can build something like that, you'd have something." Soon afterward, the Harley-Davidson soft-tail came out and just took off—that's all you see now, the soft-tail where the springs are hidden underneath; the swing-arm is history. Harley-Davidson bought themselves back from AMF, and the soft-tail was *the shit.* My dad should have been a millionaire!

♦ **V: It sounds like he turned Harley-Davidson around. There's a lesson here; corporations now routinely ask workers for suggestions in the guise of "making everybody feel they're part of the team." But it's also a way to save money on research and development. Your dad should have gotten a percentage, or a patent, or a bonus—**
♦ MD: —or *something.*
♦ **V: They picked his brain—**

♦ MD: Yeah, they did. He had no idea. The way they did it was smart. They made it seem like a big deal; they flew him out there and put him front of all these people to talk, they got him some Playboy chicks, they took him to dinner—and to my dad, it was just a "fun time" in Daytona Beach. Then they took him to the corporate dinner, where he spoke the words that should have made him rich.

Back in high school, General Motors and Fisher (or whoever) used to run contests for designing cars. And if you won, you could get your design submitted to, like, General Motors. That's how those companies got a lot of ideas; that was just a cheap way of picking people's brains.

Now Harley-Davidson is so big; they've franchised their name out to everything. Do you remember when they were trying to patent their *sound?* Honda and Yamaha were building V-twins and were getting them to sound like Harleys. I don't know if they won, but to even try and do that . . . jesus christ! I always wondered how you would go about patenting a sound?! How would you print that out? Like, "*Vroom, vroom*—that's our sound; we're suing you!"

♦ **V: Back to zoot suits: if you don't wear them so much anymore, what do you wear?**
♦ MD: I'm always trying to kinda have an *edge,* you know. Back then, just putting a suit on had an edge. I still wear a suit, but more like the early '50s patch pockets—I don't see *those* out, too much. Open collars. Sometimes I'll wear long collars, like those *Good Fellas* collars. I try to still have some style, but I'm not caught up in a certain decade—I don't give a fuck about that. It's so hard to find cool old clothes anymore. Back in high school I was probably the only kid going to vintage stores—after school, I'd sneak into them, hoping nobody saw me—it was like you're buying second-hand clothes from old folks, or somethin'. Back then, you could find double-breasted '40s or '50s suits all damn day for three or

Mando's Pop with his 1950 Chevy before it was striped by Jeffries.

five bucks. You can't do that anymore.

The same thing with records: I'd go to Salvation Army and see these old records, look at the covers and go, "This looks kinda cool. It's only a quarter or five cents. It ain't gonna hurt me to try and listen to it." I got a lot of musical knowledge this way.

You could buy all kinds of early jazz—*everything* that's popular now you could find at Goodwill. I'd take boxes of records home and play them and maybe take one to someone like Eddie and say, "Wow, listen to this!" Sometimes it was the first time I'd ever heard of a "name." You could stumble into Charlie Parker 10-inches, some of which are worth $600–$800—*if* you can find 'em.

Now you won't even see the good stuff anymore, because the Salvation Army and Goodwill stores are contracted out to rag houses. The vintage store owners come to these rag houses and pick out clothes and buy them by the pound—that's been going on for a long time. But when I was in junior high school, nobody cared. Today, everything's so picked over—you find maybe *one* record and you'll be excited: "Wow!" But back then, you could find good records all day, and they didn't cost you—you could afford to *experiment*. It's too bad that's gone—everybody kinda caught on and got hip to it.

♦ **V: I hope you kept your records—**
♦ **MD:** I keep *everything,* man. I was really into 78s, so I have crates and crates—break your back trying to lift 'em, though! Those things records keep me sane.

I also have a huge collection of old pulp books and hardbacks. I started getting into them for the cover art, and now I have a lot of early juvenile delinquency books. I just bought a collection from a friend, Che Shul, in San Francisco. They're called "J.D." books now. I have boxes of them: early '40s, '50s and even '60s. Hal Ellson (*Duke,* etc); Irving Shulman, who wrote *West Side Story*—he was one of the big writers; Orrie Hatch; Wenzell Brown (black writer); Edward De Rue; William Bernard (*Jailbait*)—there are so many great authors. I also have a collection of writings from the Beat Generation: Kerouac, Ginsberg, William Burroughs—some of them had great cover art, but those are *up the roof* now, like *Junkie* by William Burroughs or *Reform School Girl* or *Rumble.* "J.D." books are so expensive now; they're really collectible. I'm really proud of mine.

Irving Shulman wrote *The Amboy Dukes,* and Hal Ellson wrote *Duke* and *Tomboy.* Those three titles got me involved in this. I have ten copies of the first printing of *Amboy Dukes.* They're pocket books, and the cover shows this zoot-suited guy with a chain out in the air and a chick on his arm, and that pretty much started it for me; I went, "Wow—I gotta look for more of these!" I have first editions of every book by Irving Shulman and Hal Ellson. One in front of me is called *Gang Girl*; it shows this chick on the cover with the words, "The club house was her bridal suite." [laughs] When you see something like this, it just knocks you out; it's just wild. I collect all the different printings because on some books, there are six different cover paintings! Some books had the same story, but different titles— *Reform School Girl,* by Felice Swallow, was also marketed under the title *House of Fury.* Also, some writers went by different

names; *Junkie,* written by William Burroughs, was credited to William Lee. And there are so many more titles I could list . . .

The cover art has gotten really popular; now they put out books on it, plus postcards, posters—any format.

Our band has looked into a lot of history; we're into so much—not just music, but clothing and literature and films as well. If you want to do research, so much more is available now, and you can actually learn. So if we did pave the way for some other bands—

♦ **V: Or start a "swing" movement—**
♦ **MD:** I can walk into a club now and actually hear something I like on the jukebox, not just Twisted Sister—

♦ **V: I think that if just two people share a vision, they can move mountains—**
♦ **MD:** Eddie and I were probably best friends since we met. We took a liking to each other; we had so many of the same influences; we've always shared different things together . . . it's just really great to have somebody like that. He's got such incredible talent.

♦ **V: Didn't you meet Sam Butera?**
♦ **MD:** I thought Sam was really cool when he worked with Louis Prima. Not too many people knew that he sang. I tried to find everything that he sung. I found out he was still in Vegas and I was knocked out; he's one of *the guys* and he's still *around*—as opposed to, say, John Coltrane. I met Sam and he even came to see the band once.

He seems really happy but doesn't seem to enjoy talking on the phone for very long. I got to Vegas and had his home phone number and called him, and he always talks for five minutes and then he has to go . . . which is okay, because I'm talking to *Sam.* He actually acknowledges me, and if he told me to go fuck off I'd still think, "He's cool."

This one time I called him on the phone and said, "Look, Sam, I'm going to be playing," and he said, "Well, I can't make it down there 'cuz my family's sick in New Orleans and I have to wait around the phone." I had my tape player with me and I said, "Sam, I want you to listen to this tune and tell me what you think." I played this 45 that's probably lost, "Equator," and asked him, "What do you think about that?" and he went, "Where the fuck did you find that, man? That just brought back memories. Wow, that was a cool-ass tune. I'd forgotten I'd done it. Where'd you get that?"

I started playing more records I'd found, and he said, "Where'd you get all this? I don't even have these." (They were from the '50s.) So I started rapping with him, and I talked to him for like an hour—and that's unlike Sam, especially the mood that he was in. He kept asking me, about five times, "Where you playin' at? Where you playin' at?" I told him again, and said, "Look, it would be the coolest if you brought your horn down and sat in with me." And Sam goes, "Tell me about it . . . " When he said that to me, it took two seconds . . . I thought about it and hit the floor laughing so hard, because I thought it was the coolest thing I'd ever heard; five fuckin' minutes I'm laughing and poor Sam's still on

Cover of *Low Rider* Magazine and inside ad, 1978.

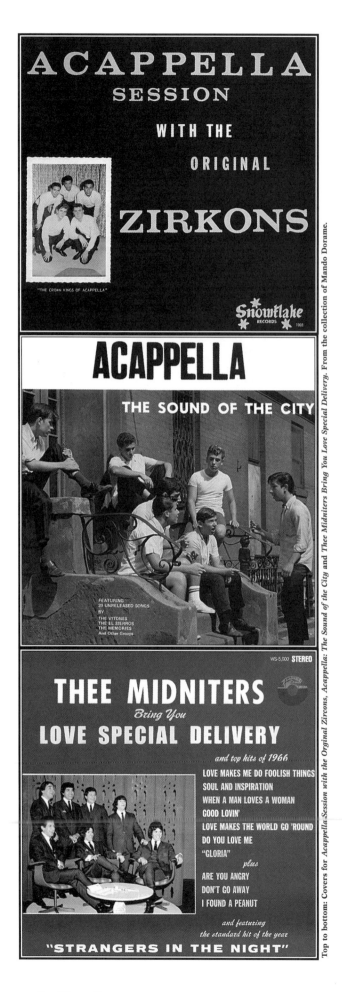

the phone. I told Eddie, and he starts laughing, and we're both laughing for ten minutes, and then I pick up the phone and Sam's fuckin' laughing—and you *never* hear him laugh. It was a cool experience. But he didn't show up for the fuckin' gig, you know . . .

Last time I talked to Sam, we started talking about mouthpieces. I said, "I've got one album where you have this mouthpiece and it sounds so cool." He said, "I've had that since I was *eighteen* years old" (and the guy's gotta be in his late '60s). He's still playing that same mouthpiece; you can't find that anymore—they don't *make* those anymore. But he said, "Next time you come to Vegas, call me up and we'll hang out. I'll take you to some music stores and we'll try out some mouthpieces." I thought, "Oh, man . . ." So I've been thinking about taking a trip to Vegas just for that—I don't fuckin' care if I'm going to play . . . just to

---

My dream was *to turn back time*—and that's a hard dream to pull off! [laughs]

---

hang out with Sam. He's a super-cool guy.

Somebody was going to make a movie about Sam, but I don't think it'll go into production. I read the script, and was told that all the words were basically from Sam. It's pretty much about him getting ripped off and treated like shit. According to him, he did a lot of arrangements and wrote a lot of originals and basically got nothing. He's a big-hearted cat, and if he is bitter, I guess he's got a right to be. I respect him in all ways, man.

Sam Butera is solely Sam Butera. There's only one reissue of him, on Bear Family, and it's *New Orleans Hot Nights*. It's early, recorded when Sam first started playing before he met Louis Prima. He put out some albums on Dot and Capitol that are impossible to find—luckily, I have 'em. He also did a lot of 45s for those labels.

Sam did the soundtrack, and had a small part in a movie called *The Rat Race* with Tony Curtis and Debbie Reynolds. Tony Curtis is a sax player, and Sam calls him up to audition him. Tony comes down to this place and starts playing horn, and Sam's making all these comments about him. Then Sam sends him to the liquor store to buy beer. By the time Tony Curtis gets back with all this beer, naive as he is (he'd just moved to New York from the Midwest; he wasn't hip to the "street" thing), his horns are gone. It's the greatest fuckin' scene, because it's Sam Butera doing it. [laughs] I actually have that soundtrack album, too, and that was on Dot. Sam's done some cool shit like that, and he's still playing, today, in Vegas.

Sam recently went into the studio and he has CDs available, from the '90s or late '80s. They're cool, but I want the *old* recordings. Everybody knows about Louis Prima, but nobody really knows how good Sam can sing—he's such a soulful singer. And the way he plays horn—he's another guy that has that growl I keep looking for; he just captured that. He knew all them guys *in the day;* Big Jay McNeely and other R&B cats were his friends. Lee Allen was his best friend who advised him to "try out" moving from New Orleans to Las Vegas. So yeah, he's one of them Italian cats that has that black sound, and it's great.

♦ **V:** *It's like you're carrying on a "tradition"—*
♦ **MD:** The funny thing about Royal Crown Revue is: in a span of nine years, we've rapidly moved through the decades. At first, we were so into bebop, then we got into early modern jazz like Miles Davis (early '50s), then I moved into Coltrane and however late he goes . . . And not just jazz, but jump blues like Louis Jordan. And before that we were listening to Cab Calloway. Now, we're listening to anything from jazz right on up to the energy of

the Ramones—it's wild.

There are so many more influences that fit into our realm. Like Cuban music, and '60s recordings from cats like Willie Bobo. I also have a big collection of Chicano recordings from the late '60s–'70s; the time of the Vietnam war when everything was so political with Chicano people. There were all these Chicano bands around, like El Chicano, Malo, and the little bands that preceded Santana, like Thee Midniters, Thee Jaguars— all these little Mexican bands. Most of their names have "Thee" in them because all the gangs were named like that: *Thee* Night Owls, *Thee* Velvet Angels. Anyway, that's a big part of my love: that type of music which is all Latin, like "Latin Rock." It's so cool, man.

That stuff is hard to get. A lot of old American recordings went to Japan; the Japanese came over and bought so much that now they have more history of old America than we do—it's amazing. But the cool thing is that they have such a love for it, they reissued practically everything. They do it by taking photos of the actual record cover and the back (and you can see that the covers are kinda fucked-up). I would rather have them take the *actual photograph* of something that's beat-up, than try and put on new artwork. They just respected the tradition so much. And the recordings are so great; they usually don't do any remastering or try and "spice it up." They just find a clean recording and put it into CD format and it sounds great. You can go to the big Tower Records in Hollywood and find a Japanese reissue of El Chicano's first recording, *Viva Tirado!* It'll cost you $25, but you can actually get it and you can listen to it. Whereas before, you had to search like hell for the record, and usually it's not in good shape.

A lot of the Blue Note records you find have been played to death. I like a lot of the "soul jazz" like Brother Jack McDuff and Richard "Groove" Holmes—that's, like, *the sound.* They used tenor players like Percy France. People bought those "biscuits 'n gravy" records and just played the shit out of 'em, partying, and spilled beers on 'em and scratched 'em, so it's impossible to find

Mando's Pop with his Harley-Davidson "Best Custom Bike" trophy and Playboy bunny.

guys buying records as soon as the boxes were pulled off the trucks. The Japanese cats were in and outta there by 6 AM. So you couldn't fuck around if you wanted to get some good shit.

Eric would come over at four in the morning and pull me out of bed and—god bless him for doing that, because I was always thankful. We'd go to the record swap meet when it was still fuckin' dark, man, and we'd be looking through records and finding little treasures. But I've kinda slacked off, because everything is so picked over now. I don't have the energy to get up that early in the morning anymore cause I'm playin' so fuckin' much . . . You can still find shit, but you gotta go to the swap meets or to the auctions. I'm a part of a lot of record auctions and a lot of book auctions for the J.D. books. But you can't find *Acappella* even at record swap meets, unless you go to New York. New York is where all the *Acappella* is *from;* I've been to Times Square Records. Strider Records in New York used to carry a lot, and I bought every fuckin' *Acappella* record he had, either through the mail or visiting there in person, and I bought a ton; I cleaned him out. About five months ago I visited him and he said, "Man, if you're comin' for *Acappella,* well you done took all that I got! We don't even have any more!" So for that kind of music . . . well, there's certain things you just can't find, no matter *what* you do.

♦ **V: You'll probably be in a position to reissue some Acappella anthologies—**

♦ MD: I've thought of that. Also, Relic Records owns the rights to a lot of *Acappella,* and you can get recordings from them. I would love to re-release some of the 45s I have; that would be really cool. There's one record called *The Sound of the City,* and it's all these teenagers singing *acappella* on the front step of a stoop in New York or wherever. I thought of putting that on a T-shirt. These are just little ideas for the future, when I'm burnt out on everything [laughs] and I can sit back and enjoy a lot of this music and help get it out there.

♦ **V: Well, I view all this rediscovering as part of a cultural renaissance that is complex; there's a lot to it . . .**

♦ MD: There is. We've been into doing what we've been doing for nine years, me and

Mando, Sr. and Dena Dorame (a.k.a. Mom and Pops) in 1997. Below: Mando with Jorie Lodes.

clean copies. If you have a clean early Blue Note Jimmy Smith or Jack MacDuff record, I'll give you whatever you want for it!

I used to go looking for doowop with a friend, Eric Maaske, who's a great tattoo artist in Orange County. We'd go to the big record swap meet in Pasadena; he would come to my house at fuckin' four in the morning—that's how nuts we were about finding records, because if you didn't get there that early, there would be all the Japanese

Mando Recommends!

ACAPPELLA RECORDS:
The Sound of the City (Times Square Records)
Acappella Session with the Original Zirkons. "The Crown Kings of Acappella." (Snowflake Records) *The Stars of Acappella.* Featuring The Five Sharks, The Valids, The Del-Capris, The Autumns, and The Zircons. (Amber Records)
OTHER RECORDS:
Thee Midniters Bring You Love Special Delivery (Whittier Records)
Malo (Warner Brothers, 1972)
Home Cookin': The Incredible Jimmy Smith (Blue Note)
BOOKS:
Brown, Wenzell: *The Wicked Streets, Run, Chico, Run, Cry Kill, Teen-Age Terror, Jailbait Jungle, The Violators* (with Israel Beckhardt)
Ellson, Hal: *Duke, Tomboy*
Shulman, Irving: *Children of the Dark, Platinum High School College Confidential, The Amboy Dukes, The Velvet Knife, Cry Tough!*
OTHER BOOKS:
Zoot Suit Murders by Thomas Sanchez
Gang Girl by Don Elliot. "She roamed in a world of wild sex!"
Jailbait by William Bernard. "Teen-age hoodlums on the loose."
H Is For Heroin by David Hulburd. "A teen-age narcotic tells her story."
OTHER PUBLICATIONS:
Low Rider Magazine, *Teen Angel*
MARK MAHONEY Tattoos 310-657-8282
J.D. BOOK SOURCE:
Ron/Kayo Books, 814 Post, SF CA 94109
    415-749-0554 open Th–Sat 11–6pm.

Eddie and the guitar player—James Achor has been with us that long, too—we've been doing it for so long. We've been involved in the music, in finding clothes, books, all types of paraphernalia—furniture, everything—for nine years. And we ain't about to stop now . . . **V**

∽ ◟ ∽ ◟ ∽ ◟ ∽ ∽ ◟ ∽

INTERVIEW WITH RUTH WILSON

For over four years RUTH WILSON was the bassist in Flathead. Among her other talents, she's a licensed manicurist and a veteran thrift-store expert. She now lives with Eddie Nichols of Royal Crown Revue in Los Angeles. In this interview she discusses thrift store shopping.

♦ *VALE: When did you start going to thrift stores?*
♦ RUTH WILSON: In high school, Arizona and Florida. I just get sick sometimes, thinking about what I've passed up. Back then I was in my punk phase and wore mostly men's clothes. In Arizona you find cool Western stuff, whereas Florida has lots of kitchen furnishings. I'm afraid my thriftin' days may be over for awhile because you can't find stuff here—there's no point thriftin' in L.A. The *beauty* of everything being so cheap is gone. I like buying things for fifty cents—but nothing's fifty cents here! At a local thrift store a full-length mirror that's $6.99 at Thrifty was marked $15!—totally out of control. I used to spend the greater part of my day thrifting, but I can't do that here. I just want to get in a band and tour so I can go places!
♦ *V: What do you read?*
♦ RW: I have a lot of magazines. I never go out and buy a new *Cosmo*—there's nothing there for me—but I have *Cosmos* from '57. People think I'm a freak when I sit on an airplane with my *Ladies Home Journal* from 1956 with a big '50s bride on the front,

but to me, *that's* what's interesting. I'll see something in an old magazine and think, "I want that!" but then realize I can't just go to a store and buy it.

I learn a lot from reading those old magazines. I was reading this article on doing laundry, and it's amazing that more housewives didn't commit suicide! They were supposed to have a box in the laundry room to keep all the clothing tags with their washing instructions on file! [laughs] The cool thing about that article—you know about orlon sweaters?
♦ *V: Sort of.*
♦ RW: Over the years I've passed up about 50 bizillion of them. You see them in the kids' section of thrift stores because they're tiny—they've shrunk. I would see them and think, "Oh, they're ruined." But from this article, I learned that before you wash them, you're supposed to place them on a piece of paper and trace the outline. They shrink when washed, so then you just stretch them back out. So now I've started buying all these tiny orlon sweaters! [laughs] The tag tells you what size they are. You learn cool stuff from reading these magazines!
♦ *V: Why did you start buying clothes at thrift stores?*
♦ RW: The older things are made better. Clothes from the '40s and '50s were meant to fit; they're tailored. They didn't have labels saying S, M, and L. And most of them are lined. They're just better quality—and the price is right! [laughs]

When I had a job where I had to wear a suit every day, I'd go to department stores and see suits that were ugly as crap and really trendy: lime green or something. And they'd be hundreds of dollars. I could go thriftin' and find some totally killer, fitted, tailored suit for four bucks.
♦ *V: I think it's great that you read old magazines instead of new ones—*
♦ RW: I have this really killer old catalog from a store called Alden's in Chicago. It had everything. Back then you could order your whole kitchen from one catalog; your steel kitchen cabinets would arrive in boxes. We have a garage full of those right now because I brought them all out from Arizona. Anyone with sense could look at those sitting out by a garbage can and realize that they are not garbage. I don't know why someone would rip those out and replace them with shitty particle board crap from Home Depot that cost $3,000. Anyway, I literally brought three kitchens' worth of '50s steel cabinets and sinks with me in the move! [laughs] But they're cool . . . as far as kitchen sinks go!
♦ *V: What else do you have?*
♦ RW: I've got a lounge chair that's tuck-and-roll, and a white naugahyde chair with bows all over it. I should mention my collection of hair dryers! [laughs] I have a '40s one and two '50s ones—they're those big chrome industrial models that look like rocket ships. Eddie doesn't think we need four, but I do . . .
♦ *V: You need your own room to do whatever you want with.*
♦ RW: If it's in a thrift store and it's from the '40s and '50s, I'll find it. For the past four years I played in a band (that just broke up in April) and made a pretty decent living. During the day I had nothing to do, so I'd drive around and thrift. I accumulated a lot of stuff, and supplemented my income by selling or trading off the things that didn't fit. Most of my clothes cost fifty cents, but they're really cool! [laughs] In Arizona you can

Cover of Irving Shulman's The Amboy Dukes (1949).

Ruth Wilson.

still find killer lady's jeans from the '50s for $2. Then you bring them to California and they're worth a lot more. It's like treasure-hunting!

♦ **V: Why don't you go to estate sales in L.A.?**

♦ RW: Because you have to be up at 7 A.M.! I could only do that if I stayed up all night.

♦ **V: Can you describe your house?**

♦ RW: Okay. I'm in the kitchen right now and I'm using our 1950s microwave—just kidding! [laughs] We have a pink and chrome '50s Dixie gas stove (some of them have a griddle in the middle; unfortunately, this isn't one of those). There's a '50s Admiral refrigerator with a big chrome delta handle. I replaced all the crappy white plastic cabinetry handles with chrome ones— much better! I'm a freak like that: I always move into rental places and put in new tile and repaint.

I just sold a '50s dinette table about three months ago and now I'm kicking myself. I have some '50s chrome dinette chairs in the garage that need to be reupholstered; fortunately, I have an upholstery machine. There's a couple '50s lamps here and there. In the bedroom, I have my grandparents' '30s vanity, dresser and nightstand. Then there's my upright bass in the corner.

♦ **V: Is that what you play?**

♦ RW: In Flathead I always played electric, but upright is my true love. And Wanda Jackson autographed it for me: "To Ruth: Keep Rockin'—Wanda Jackson."

A few months ago in Phoenix I was making a U-turn and spotted a '50s dinette table in a carport. The guy said, "We're going to have a yard sale. We just remodeled this place; the woman who lived here passed away." He said, "Take anything you want," and I swear to god she hadn't changed the decor since 1950. I cleaned the place out for $50, and he thought I was crazy. I got this really glamorous bed with a scalloped and padded ivory-

and-gold headboard—fabulous. I got a whole box of old sheets; the threads were tighter then. It was amazing.

My closet is full of vintage clothes—I don't have anything else. The only new things I buy are underwear and make-up. But you gotta have the vintage bullet bra because those old clothes were made for that. Another thing: vintage nylons are much better-made—trust me. I have really fair skin, so I've always had this problem with nylons that turn my skin a weird color. Old nylons are so sheer that it looks like you don't have anything on, except for the really cool seam in the back. You can still find them brand-new in the box, and they're usually the same price or less than new ones!

♦ **V: What's on the wall?**

♦ RW: My '50s shadow boxes contain knick-knacks: a manicure kit, a '40s clock that I need to fix. There's my Radio Flyer wagon for when I fly off the wagon like I did last night. [laughs] Eddie has original Petty girls art, which are smokey-looking because they're old. The guy who used to have them wrote all these girls' phone numbers on the back, and they're old numbers like "Elgin 5-6509," back when phone numbers still had prefixes. I don't know what he was up to! [laughs] Over the bed, we have a '40s painting of two parrots. Then we have big framed posters of Marlon Brando, Carl Perkins, the Drifters, etc over the piano.

Eddie's guitars are everywhere. Recently we bought this old Kay guitar in Florida for $25 because we were there for three weeks and were jonesin' to play. Eddie has a great-looking old guitar someone gave him that was hanging on the wall at this place they were playing in France.

Our house was built in '54—we had to ask the landlord when it was built. Last night I was going through a 1955 *House Beautiful* and found this ad for the exact same cabinets I have out in the garage. See, it helps to have old magazines!

I bought a Zero fan for $6 in Arizona and then saw a smaller version of it in L.A. for $98. I've been collecting a certain set of Samsonite luggage that's baby blue with silver sparkles in it for years and I finally have all the pieces: the hatbox (the coolest piece), wardrobe, train case, vanity case and the whole deal. I never paid more than $3 for anything. I saw some of them at an antique store and they ranged from $65–$95.

When I went to Japan, all I brought back was a pair of '50s

> I love it when people first get into swing; they get really into it and it becomes *addictive*.

"ranch girl" jeans. I had been looking in Arizona forever and could never find any, and this guy had six pairs, so I shamed him into selling me a pair for $60—way more than I would usually pay, but that was my souvenir. They were old denim (darker, the threads go vertical and horizontal and the white threads are more pronounced, whereas new denim goes at a diagonal "grain") and they zip *inside* the left pocket. Most girls' vintage pants zip with a metal zipper on the left side. I had never seen so many big "E" Levis (on Levis from the '40s and '50s, the little red tag on the rear pocket had a capital "E"; they changed to a small "e" in the late '60s).

I read an article in *Continental Restyling* that said the Levis company is getting out all their old looms to remanufacture the old fabric again. I think the old dye contained something they can't use today, so maybe they can't get the exact deep indigo blue color. I don't know what this will do for the vintage denim "collectible" market. I'm wearing a pair of cut-off Big "E" denims now and they cost me 50 cents in Colorado. I would never have paid a huge price for them; the *fun* is in paying very little.

♦ **V: Tell us about your car—**

♦ RW: I have a '59 Plymouth Belvedere with big fins; it's mint green. You know that movie *Christine?* [about a "possessed" car

> ## I swear to god she hadn't changed the decor since 1950. I cleaned the place out for $50

going on a rampage] That was a Belvedere, but it was a '58 and mine's a '59. We're the luckiest people in the world because our neighbor is a mechanical genius who fixes our cars cheap. I'm learning more about cars all the time; I can't really diagnose, but if someone else diagnoses it, then I can get the part and install it. But I don't have the foggiest idea what's wrong if the engine starts making a weird noise—our neighbor's amazing that way.

♦ **V: Eddie said you were really into old movies—**

♦ RW: In Arizona I had cable and all I would watch was AMC and the Turner Network. I don't watch the news; it just stresses me out because there's nothing I can do about it. I love everything about old movies, especially the dialogue. I don't go to modern movies. I saw *Pulp Fiction* and felt cheated. I was working as a manicurist and one of my clients came in and asked, "Have you seen the new John Travolta movie?" I had just watched *Grease* on cable for the 80th time so I was all fired up. I asked, "Is there dancing in it?" and she said, "Ummm, yeah; it's the twist." I went to see it and had to deal with this sodomy scene and watch John Travolta do the twist on heroin for ten seconds. I was so bummed

out. [laughs] I really hated it.

♦ **V: What books do you have?**

♦ RW: You gotta have *Emily Post's Book of Etiquette* and Betty Crocker's cookbook. I have this *Better Homes and Gardens* handyman book from '57. It's amazing! It has all these articles about building material, plumbing and wiring, walls and floors, windows and doors, sheet flooring in the kitchen—it's so cool! I have some *Better Homes and Gardens* decorating books from the '60s which aren't so exciting. I like the early '60s clothing and furniture, but things got a little weird after that.

I have Arthur Murray's *How To Become a Good Dancer* from 1947, and a ton of upholstery books. I collect old pattern books, like the *Bishop Method of Clothing Construction,* which is all about textiles (1959). I also have some about altering clothes from the '40s and '50s. There's a wealth of information there, especially if you *have* those clothes. Tailors today don't always know what to do, because there were specific ways to tailor some of those garments. Eddie's got a million books on pin-up girls . . .

♦ **V: Let's change the subject to dance. It was the dancing that attracted me to this whole "swing" thing—**

♦ RW: Me, too. I think our generation got ripped off in the dance department. In the '80s, it was all "alternative," so I'd go out on the dance floor and be bopping up and down and think, "What in the hell am I doing? This is idiotic!" I like swing because it's a dance with specific steps; it's a formula and no one can argue with you. I think being able to go out and dance builds up people's confidence. I had a lot of fun dancing, and there was a point where I couldn't think of anything else. I love when people first get into swing; they get really into it and it becomes *addictive.*

♦ **V: That's why swing is "sweeping the nation"!**

♦ RW: I grew up a gymnast and was in gymnastics until the ninth grade. Now I'm 30 and with swing dancing I still get to do flips, but with a "spot" [partner who supports her]—that's the way I see it. I probably can't do a standing back tuck anymore, but I can do it with a partner, so it's fun! I love the acrobatics. San Francisco has a great scene. I went there and couldn't believe some of the crazy moves I saw: totally crazy, death-defying stunts. People are becoming more and more daring . . . **V**

L to R: covers of Hal Ellson's *Duke* (1959), Harlan Ellison's The Juvies (1961), and Joe Weiss' *Gang Girl* (1957).

TIMMIE HESLA was the first ex-punk to start a "swing" band in San Francisco, anticipating the movement a decade ago.

◆ *VALE: Briefly tell us your musical history—*
◆ TIMMIE HESLA: I'm the "Moses" of the Swing movement. [laughs] From 1980 to '82 I played in the post-punk band Necropolis of Love and met a lot of people in the Bay Area music scene. In '85 I put together a group to play the Paradise Lounge called Timmie Hesla and His Orchestra (actually, it was only a quartet). At the time the Paradise was a haven where ex-punks could play fun gigs. A small lounge-type scene developed, where people wore sharkskin suits with skinny ties and sipped martinis—including Mr. Lucky, an ex-punk who had already been doing his lounge act for several years. Another act was Miss Kitty, a torch singer with a "stripper" show (the seamy side of lounge). Our band played TV mystery show songs to reggae and surf instrumental beats, etc. That same year the DNA Lounge initiated "Cocktail Cabaret Weekends" to bring people into their club before midnight. Connie Champagne & Her Tiny Bubbles played those also.

In January, 1986 I gave Brian Raffi (DNA Lounge) a proposal: if he gave me a month of weekend dates, I'd put together a big orchestra. My roommate Lou Decolator helped me set this all up. The big band was quite successful, so we were invited back to play the month of April. On June 25, 1988, Michael at Bimbo's put on his first show (to a lot of local publicity) featuring "Timmie Hesla & The Converse All-Stars" [I lived on Converse Alley, hence the name] and the Dinos, who did '50s–'60s pop songs by singers like Bobby Rydell, and Ricky Nelson—a lounge act, pure and simple. Little Roger Clark was the singer in the Dinos. (Roger and Dick Bright set the lyrics of "Gilligan's Island" to the music of "Stairway to Heaven." Recorded by Little Roger & the Goosebumps, this became a hit record until Led Zeppelin sued to have it withdrawn.)

My big band played larger venues like Bimbo's a number of times as well as warehouse parties and gigs as small as the Hotel Utah. Stephen Parr produced 2 shows at Video Free America (452 Shotwell St) and Taboo, 966 Market St. We had 13–16 members (personnel constantly shifted) and played Count Basie, Fletcher Henderson and Duke Ellington arrangements, mostly from the '30s. The band wore sharkskin suits for the Vegas Rat-Pack look (as opposed to the '30s–'40s zoot suit look). Our main problem was: we needed large places to play, and there weren't many. Also, money didn't go far, and it was easier back then to find musicians who weren't just playing for the money. Around '90 I put the big band on hold. A year or so later I ran into Paul Robinson, a guitarist who had played with Miss Kitty, and started up the big band again with him. He brought the band's musicianship up to a higher level. Some of our guest singers included Deborah Iyall and Penelope Houston. We did a New Year's Eve show at Bimbo's with Dan Hicks as guest vocalist. Paul had be working with Dan's group, and in '93 he left our big band to join him.

Probably our busiest time was the summer of '93, when we played weekly at the Club Deluxe with an 18-piece band (including Morty of the New Morty Show). We also played the Haight Street Fair that summer, with guest vocalists Pat Johnson, Vise Grip (this was his first experience singing in front of a big band), Jay Johnson (owner of the Deluxe), Sandy (from Atomic Cocktail) and Mr. Lucky. I helped Vise Grip get The Ambassadors of Swing together by finding him an arranger, Mark Allred, who has also done arrangements for me.

Our band has continued playing gigs locally at Cafe Du Nord and the Hi-Ball Lounge, and have played parties at the Glas Haus and the Liberty Ship (Pier 34, a very windy outdoor pier—we had to tie down our music stands with duct tape). My big band couldn't fit into most small clubs; several times I had to rent extra staging. My other bands include the Rat Bastards of Swing (pop-swing, lots of vocals) and Crime Scene Unit (more of a Mancini repertoire). Each one has 9–11 members.

In the '80s lounge and big band never became huge. People danced, but not the wild lindy-hopping you see now—it was more like ballroom dancing. The current version of the swing revival has its roots in the rockabilly scene, which was (and is) much more fashion-conscious; it's a "retro" lifestyle. I see a lot of bands playing places that charge as much as $25 to get in, and I wonder if they ever question this. Personally, I'm not interested in playing where my friends can't afford the cover charge, and/or have to pay $7.50 for a drink. I'm not into doing gigs just "for the money." That's the ex-punk-rocker in me. **V**

Frankie Manning is an American "living treasure," one of the few surviving innovators of Lindy Hop dancing. He still travels internationally, teaching workshops at the age of 83.

♦ **VALE: It's hard to imagine how partner-dancing can be taken much further than the Lindy Hop—**
♦ FRANKIE MANNING: But there *are* youngsters out there who are taking it a little further. They're doing things that are a little different and they're putting their own touch to it, and that's what Lindy Hop is all about. You can do the basics and still do some innovations of your own. You can add things and it still is fun.

I was born May 26, 1914 in Harlem and I'm still dancing. The Lindy Hop has certainly kept me in pretty good shape and kept me going all these years. It's good exercise and it's *enjoyable* exercise—one that you can do with somebody else; you don't have to do it by yourself!
♦ **V: Right, that's what's wrong with most exercise—**
♦ FM: [chuckles] I didn't start dancing at the Savoy, but I started out in 1927, when I was 13. I was dancing before that but that's when I started getting into Lindy Hop. Swing started in the '20s when Fletcher Henderson had his band with wonderful musicians like Louis Armstrong and Coleman Hawkins. As you know, all dancers go along with the type of music that's being played. Since the music started swinging, everyone else started going along with the music. That's how that dancing started.

I started changing the Lindy Hop from just European-style dancing to really getting down to the rhythm, down to the roots, down to the Afro-American type of *feeling*. I can say I was an innovator there. I did the first aerial! Of course, partner dancing started way back before I was born! People were doing ballroom dancing long before the Lindy Hop. The best-known American dancers were Irene and Vernon Castle then. Lindy Hop is a swing dance. With ballroom dance, there are certain rules: you have to hold your head a certain way, you've gotta hold your arm a certain way, you gotta hold your body a certain way, and Lindy Hop isn't like that. As long as you get out there and you're dancing and you're enjoying yourself and you're dancing with the music, then nobody cares if your head is held upright or not!
♦ **V: You were called "Musclehead"; what does that mean?**
♦ FM: Now you see all these athletes with shaved heads. Back in those days, that was a style also: youngsters used to go to a barber and have all their hair cut off, and I was like that, too. When I used to dance and come to a very difficult step, I'd get kinda tense, and I think the muscles in my head would stand out. [laughs] So everybody said, "That must be difficult—the muscles in Frankie's head are standing out!" That's why they called me "Musclehead."
♦ **V: In one photo from Life (June 16, 1941), Ann "Popeye" Johnson is six feet in the air, and you must have thrown her there—**
♦ FM: Yes, I'm the culprit! They called her "Popeye" because whenever she got excited, her eyes would kinda stick out of their sockets.
♦ **V: Herbert White is described as the originator of the Lindy Hop and the Suzi Q. In this Life magazine, there's photos of you and Ann doing the "Congeroo," a cross between the Conga [a Latin American dance] and the Lindy Hop. Is the "Congeroo" a name that Life made up?**

♦ FM: Actually, I coined that phrase. At the time, the Latin dance, the Conga, was very popular, and the swing world used the term "swingeroo." So we invented a dance that was a combination of "conga" and "swing." I just put the two names together; instead of saying "congeroo-swingeroo" I just said "Congeroo." So it's a swing and conga.

Herbert White was like our teacher, our mother, our father, our brother, our benefactor and everything—he actually got the group together, picked out the dancers, helped the dancers to better themselves, and I was very close to him—I was like his right-hand man. I did most of the choreography for the dancers. He would do all the booking for us. It was his group; that's why they called it "Whitey's Lindy Hoppers."

I started changing the Lindy Hop from just European-style dancing to really getting down to the rhythm, down to the roots, down to the Afro-American type of *feeling*.

♦ **V: Is this a fair description: "From the Cuban Conga, the new Congeroo retains a good deal of Latin shoulder-shaking and heel-clacking. From the old-time Lindy Hop it retains the improvised solo cadenzas and general yanking around of one partner by another"?**
♦ FM: [Chuckles] Yes . . . The Savoy did open in 1926, but I didn't start going to the Savoy Ballroom until the early '30s.
♦ **V: Well, you were young—**
♦ FM: But also I was *afraid.* There was a bunch of us, and we felt we weren't good enough to go to the Savoy, because the Savoy had a name for having the best dancers in the world there, and that was true. We were just youngsters and we didn't think we were good enough to go up there. Finally we got up enough nerve.
♦ **V: In this photo, you're wearing pants that go up very high, with suspenders—**
♦ FM: They were part of the pants. We started out wearing low-cut pants, and our shirts were coming out of our pants all the time. So we started to wear these high-belted pants with built-in suspenders, and that kept the shirts in. It was both an innovation and a costume.
♦ **V: What kind of shoes were you wearing? They almost look like tennis shoes—**
♦ FM: They were. We wore them because we would go to hotels and dance, and most of the hotel floors were very, very slippery. Before that, we just wore ordinary shoes—we didn't know anything about dancing, you see, and we'd be slippin' and slidin' all over the place! For what we were doing, throwing a girl over our shoulders, if you can't stand up on the floor, you can't be doing those kind of steps. That's when I decided to wear tennis shoes with rubber soles.

None of the girls wore big necklaces or that type of jewelry during a performance, because it would be dangerous. Your hand could accidentally catch, and that would be disastrous.
♦ **V: You're wearing a shirt with larger collar points—**
♦ FM: Well, all you have to do is get a shirt made like that, that's all! Then somebody else might see it and go, "Man, that's cool!" and they go and get themselves one, and before you know it, they're back!

◆ **V: You don't wear a coat when you Lindy Hop—**

◆ FM: Not when we're doing performances. When we just went social dancing, we always wore suit jackets, ties and shirts; back in those days that was the trend. Everything wasn't *casual* like now, when you go to a dance and the guys have their shirts out and their pants halfway down their behind . . . In those days, the girls would dress up and the fellows would also dress up. The girls would dress comfortably so they would be able to dance; the dresses would be wide at the bottom so they could move their legs. And when we went out social dancing, invariably we would be doing Lindy Hop, because that was *the thing.*

◆ **V: What are your thoughts about the coming revival of Lindy Hop?**

◆ FM: There's quite a widespread revival of it right now. I travel all over the world and in Europe it's much bigger than here in America—not so much with the bands, but the dancers. When the dance societies go out on engagements, they always travel with a band. There are a lot of jazz bands in Europe that play the music for dancing—I think, much more than here in America. San Francisco is one of the biggest places for Lindy Hop. I never thought it would be this big again. It's growing, and I'm happy to see that.

◆ **V: You've kept the spirit alive. You're an inspiration to all of us—**

◆ FM: Well, I try.

◆ **V: Can you tell us about any books on Lindy Hop?**

◆ FM: I think Norma Miller's book, *Stompin' at the Savoy,* is more accurate than any other book because she's from the same period, the '30s, and knows exactly what she's talking about.

◆ **V: I'm happy you're still alive and teaching—**

◆ FM: So am I! [laughs] **V**

More about Frankie Manning

Old *Life* magazines and videos featuring Frankie Manning and other amazing swing dancers (plus T-shirts, $20ppd) are available from Frankie's girlfriend, JUDY PRITCHETT (support her enterprise!). Introductory Frankie Manning video, "Swinging at the Savoy," $23ppd. 3 Instructional Frankie Manning videos, $23ppd *each Vol.* Norma Miller's *Swingin' at the Savoy,* an essential hardback, is available for $35ppd. Order toll-free from 1-888-50-SAVOY, Dept RS; FAX 707-964-4473 with credit card info, e-mail *savoy@mcn.org.,* or send payment to SAVOYSTLE, Dept RS, 32101 Ellison Way, Fort Bragg CA 95437. Website: *savoystyle.com.* Calif. residents add 7.5% tax. This is your one-stop for fabulous, eye-popping dance history.

Lavay Smith

Lavay Smith & Her Red Hot Skillet Lickers are pioneers of the San Francisco "swing revival"; since 1989 this world-class band has played literally thousands of shows. Their CD, *One Hour Mama* is available from V/Search, 415-362-1465. Check out the website: *lavaysmith.com*. Lavay's interview is followed by one with Chris Siebert, musical director and pianist for the Red Hot Skillet Lickers. ✆ ☎ ✆ ☎ ✆ ☎ ✆ ☎ ✆ ☎

♦ **VALE: The "swing movement" is a lifestyle—**
♦ LAVAY SMITH: It's true; it's not just about the music.
♦ *V: And it wasn't foisted on us by music industry hypesters. It seems to be very grass-roots—*
♦ LS: Yeah. As far as the style goes, people have been wearing old dresses for a long time. I've been wearing them for 10 or 15 years, since high school. But now it's in full swing. The Art Deco and Lindy-Hop Societies have existed for over a decade. Now it's all come together. A lot more "mainstream" people are learning how to dance, which is great, and more of them are wearing vintage clothing. It's not just a little scene anymore.

We're in the Information Age, and knowledge about '40s music and clothes is much more accessible. I love to read biographies of singers like Sarah Vaughan. I was out shopping and heard some techno music and it sounded so *cold*. People like to hear *real* instruments played by *real* people.
♦ *V: How did you create your "style"—*
♦ LS: Style is extremely important to evoke the period. I get my hair done by Kim Long. Finally, a few clothes companies are producing remakes, and I prefer wearing new clothes because they don't stink, hold up longer, and are sexier than a lot of "authentic" vintage. I love to wear '40s styles for day or private wear, but on stage I need to bare a little more "back." So I prefer a '50s style for stage wear.
♦ *V: Your name made me immediately think of Mamie, Clara, and—of course—Bessie Smith.*

We're in the Information Age, and knowledge about '40s music and clothes is much more accessible.

♦ LS: It's my family name. Lavay is my grandma's name—I'm Lavay Smith, Jr. [laughs] I go by two names: one for my private life and one for my professional life. I just like to keep those two worlds separate. It makes it easier to distinguish people by what they call you.
♦ *V: What's your background?*
♦ LS: My dad worked for the U.S. government and we moved to the Philippines. We loved it. I used to go sing "out in town"—that's what we called it because we lived on a naval base. Nearby was a wild city [Olongapo City] with a bunch of crazy drunken sailors and prostitutes. We used to hang out there and I would sing. This was from age 14 through 16.
♦ *V: You must have started singing before then—*
♦ LS: Yeah, I've sang my whole life. My family used to sing together a lot.
♦ *V: Did they encourage you?*
♦ LS: Oh, yeah. They knew that I was sneaking "out in town" to sing. They didn't really allow it when I was 14. But when I was 15 (hey, a whole year later!) my 18-year-old sister would take me out. It wasn't so bad because she was with me—and I was going to sneak out anyway! [laughs] I sang pop songs of the day—Blondie, etc. I used to hang out with the "Filipino Queen of Rock'n'roll," Sam Puguita. Her last name is the national flower of the Philippines. They had their own rock stars over there, and I knew 'em. [laughs] I was a big fan of the music; it was called Pinoi Rock. I lived there until I was 16; then my family moved back to L.A. and I continued singing there.
♦ *V: What kind of material did you sing in L.A.?*
♦ LS: I was writing more traditional country tunes. I was in a few groups for a couple of years, then I just sang Patsy Cline and Bessie Smith tunes with my guitar and a piano accompaniment. I mainly played in Long Beach and Huntington Beach. Then I moved to San Francisco in 1988.
♦ *V: Did moving change your musical emphasis?*
♦ LS: Yes, I was able to hook up with musicians who liked the same kind of music that I did.
♦ *V: Chris Siebert is your boyfriend, as well as the musical director of your group—*
♦ LS: I was spending time with Petey and Craig from Bo Grumpus; we were playing music on the street, hanging out and partying. I met Chris at one of their gigs. Bo Grumpus was gigging way before they knew me; they're a nationally known group now.

Photo: Mark Jordan

Craig Ventresco is one of the best ragtime guitar players in the world. Anyway, Bo Grumpus was playing at the Blue Lamp and they introduced me to Chris. Then I hired them to back me up two weeks later at a gig I got at the same bar. A lot of the songs we played were just classic blues tunes everybody knows—we didn't have time for a real rehearsal (we practiced out on the street), but it worked out fine.

There are so many good musicians in the Bay Area, you want to work with them all!

The guys had their own tunes, so they would open up the set with them and then I would come on. When you're getting a group together, it's important to find people you have a certain "chemistry" with, and we had that.

♦ **V: Was it hard playing in the street, or was it just a matter of attitude—you turned it into fun?**

♦ LS: I was learning and having a great time—I loved it. It's a good way to start because it really makes a "man" out of you! [laughs] It's a quick way to learn how to hustle—and this business is all about hustling.

♦ **V: Did you start making your musical arrangements more complicated once Chris came aboard?**

♦ LS: Well, we only had one horn for a while, so we didn't need written arrangements. But now that we have four, everything's highly arranged. Chris does that and he also writes music. Sometimes we hire copyists who use computers, but Chris usually writes out the score by hand. That's pretty Old Style. We have a lot of scores now, plus a lot of records and CDs.

♦ **V: Did you have a day job?**

♦ LS: I quit my day job about two years ago. Up 'til then I worked 10 hours a week for five years. I wanted a job where I could concentrate on the music and be able to take off whenever I wanted, so I was a bartender at Vesuvio's in North Beach; it's a great place to work. They were really flexible—I recommend it to all struggling artists! [laughs] I only worked two five-hour shifts a week.

♦ **V: Your rent must have been cheap—**

♦ LS: I lived with Chris. I was also gigging, so I had plenty of money—that was never a problem. We've been lucky right from the get-go in that we've never had to struggle for shows. I kept my day job for a long time because I wanted to only take gigs that *I* wanted to do; I never wanted to *have* to work a crappy job just to pay the rent. I'd rather serve drinks than work some shitty gig that would have been demoralizing. I turned down a lot!

♦ **V: You have a lot of weekly gigs now—**

♦ LS: Yeah, especially at Enrico's, Monday night—that's the only place I work with a small group. All the rest are with a nine-piece band. But at Enrico's, I can try out a tune and see if I like it—*then* Chris can make the arrangement. We've been at the Cafe Du Nord (Saturday) for five years and Top of the Mark (Wednesday) for about a year. We work other gigs: the Coconut Grove, the Hi-Ball Lounge, Biscuits and Blues . . .

♦ **V: Who are some influences?**

♦ LS: Like most American kids, I grew up listening to rock'n'roll, but in my late teens I discovered Bessie Smith. She led me to other blues and jazz singers. I love Louis Armstrong. My main influences are Bessie Smith, Billie Holiday, Dinah Washington, Ella Fitzgerald, Sarah Vaughan, Helen Humes and Little Esther Phillips. We played "The New Year's Jazz Festival" in Palm Springs last year and were on the same bill with Milt Jackson—I got to hang out with him. Just about a month ago, we were on the same bill as Bobby "Blue" Bland, Ruth Brown and a Roomful of

Blues at the San Francisco Blues Festival. We were able to meet Ruth Brown and that was a thrill because she's a real influence and a hero as well.

Periodically, I put together events called "Ladies Sing the Blues." I produce them and always invite two other great Bay Area singers. I've invited Denise Perrier, Sugar Pie DeSanto, Brenda Boykin, Ledisi, Patsy Smith (Carmen Getit from the Rhumba Bums), Pinkie Payne and Rhonda Benin.

♦ **V: You have a good situation in which you can try out new material and grow. Do you have regular players?**

♦ LS: Bill Stewart, one of the saxophonists we play with, is 73 years old. His father played in Cab Calloway's band, and he's played with Lionel Hampton and many others. He was there for all the changes in jazz and we really feel honored to have him. He plays his heart out every night.

We like to rotate on horns; we have about eight people for four chairs. They all know the "book" (of our arrangements) really well and we love 'em. We enjoy working with different people; there are so many good musicians in the Bay Area, you want to work with them all! **V**

INTERVIEW WITH CHRIS SIEBERT

Chris Siebert is Lavay Smith's musical director, pianist, companion and one of the most knowledgeable jazz/swing historians in the Bay Area. He's also an avid record and music book collector.

♦ *VALE: What bands have you been in?*

♦ CHRIS SIEBERT: I got my start playing in blues bands in San Francisco around '89. I played with a guy named Carlos Guitarlos, the Rhythm Sheiks, a guy named Big Bones, and I freelanced with a lot of other bands. I've done some recording with Taj Mahal and Alvin Youngblood Hart. I've also played with Snooky Pryor, who claims to have invented electric harmonica in the '40s. Those are some of my credits.

I was different from most high school teens: I really loved jazz and blues. Although I began playing blues, I've always listened to jazz. Duke Ellington was one of the first I listened to, and, a bit later, Count Basie. Like most American teens, I was also into rock as an early adolescent—just like Lavay was.

Sometimes we take big band charts and reduce them for a small band, and other times we take small band charts and expand them a little. Sometimes we make up our own arrangements.

Lavay and I met in 1989 at the the Blue Lamp bar. I was working with this band called Bo Grumpus, which plays early blues. Lavay started working with the guitar player and then ended up hiring the whole band to back her up. It became Lavay Smith and Bo Grumpus; that was the billing. Eventually, those guys went their own way. They're an excellent ragtime blues trio.

Before there was any "swing scene," Lavay and I just wanted to put together a band that played a combination of jazz and blues from the '30s and '40s. Of course, that means we're dealing with swing music: Ellington, Basie, and Ella Fitzgerald, but we're also dealing with early R&B like Esther Philips, Johnny Otis and Charles Brown (both live in the Bay Area). These people were

Lavay Smith. Photo: Kathrin Miller

pioneers of R&B and they're big heroes of ours.

♦ *V: You and Lavay have been together for a while. Just two people working as a team can overcome almost any obstacle—*

♦ CS: A great thing about working with Lavay is that we share a common vision of what "good" music is. To us, it's jazz and blues. We really think that's America's finest cultural contribution to the world. If you go to a lot of foreign countries, they'll agree with you. We're interested in the classic traditions of that music, and wanted to bring this to people who haven't had much exposure to it. And to that end we've tried to find the best musicians we can.

I think we have the best band in town, musician-wise. We're very proud of these guys and honored to be working with them. Guys like Allen Smith and Bill Ortiz on trumpet, Bill Stewart, Jules Broussard, Harvey Rob, and Hal Stein on saxophone, Larry Light on trombone, Bing Nathan on bass, Lye Randolph on

---

I thought the swing thing was going to be a quick fad. Now I think the dance factor has changed all that.

---

drums, Charlie Siebert on guitar, and Lavay and myself. It's a nine-piece little big band.

We're trying to perform music from big and small band jazz and blues from that period. Sometimes we take big band charts and reduce them for a small band, and other times we take small band charts and expand them a little. Sometimes we make up our own arrangements. Basically, we're saying: "This is America's classical music. Let's celebrate it and learn about it. Kids should study it in school and adults should be able to discuss it in an intelligent way." So, there's an element of education to this. As we educate ourselves about it, we're also exposing audiences to it.

People have said that Duke Ellington is the best composer America ever produced in *any* style of music. We agree. We have the very rare and excellent opportunity of playing this music for people in night clubs six or seven nights a week. We didn't want to be labeled a "swing" or "jazz" or "blues" band, so we do a little bit of all of them. We play some swing, some R&B, some be-bop . . .

The basic rule is that it's jazz and blues from the '30s and '40s—pre-rock'n'roll. But we don't mind breaking that rule sometimes.

In '98 you'll see Lavay Smith traveling outside of town. But mainly, we're anxious to stay in San Francisco because this is one of the best cities in the world for music. It's a good place to be based. We want to be loyal to our friends and be available regularly at places like The Top of the Mark, the Cafe Du Nord, and Enrico's—places where we've been playing for years. So, if we do any traveling, it will probably be on a short-term basis.

♦ *V: Nine people traveling is also pretty difficult—*

♦ CS: It's not cheap. Although, you'd be surprised—there are festivals all around the world that hire this type of band. We're hoping to crack into that a little bit. The first step was getting a CD out that we *liked*—and it took a long time until we were happy with it; we really wanted the first one to kick ass and sound good. The second step was promoting the CD and just getting it off the ground, which is a full-time job, especially for a little mom-and-pop operation. Being on the internet has helped.

We've gotten some good press locally; Phil Elwood, the *S.F. Examiner* jazz critic, called us "the best combo in town." It's quite a compliment because he's a historian of jazz and blues music. We also got a nice review in a national blues magazine and have been getting responses from as far away as Australia, England, and France—people wanting to find out about the band or the CD. There's a lot of possibilities and we're really excited. But the important thing is to keep the band moving musically and adding new songs to the repertoire.

♦ *V: Any comment on this wild partner-dancing revival?*

♦ CS: I think it's fantastic and I'll tell you why: jazz/blues first came about as a dance music. It was made for people who worked really hard all week, as a way for them to have some fun and joy in their lives. The combination of music and dancing is as old as humankind; they go together. As a band, it's fun for us to play for dancers because they inspire us. When you're putting out energy into an audience and it comes back to you, either in the form of applause, screaming, or dancing, then it gives you the energy to

Chris Siebert. Photo: Kathrin Miller

generate a better performance.

For a while, I thought the swing thing was going to be a quick fad. Now, I think the dance factor has changed the equation entirely, because when people invest a lot of time and money into something like dancing, they're not going to give it up overnight. These people are going out and practicing three nights a week; they're spending money, and really working at it. That doesn't just go away. In other words, it's an investment. The people who learned how to swing dance in the '40s are still doing it today as senior citizens—it's the only way they like to dance. I think these kids are going to be the same way.

We were around before there was ever any kind of "swing scene" in San Francisco or L.A. Although we go over great with the swing crowd, we're also the only band in the local scene that has played both the San Francisco Blues Festival and the San Francisco Jazz Festival, and those are for very discerning music lovers. That kind of depth, I think, is what's going to keep us going. If this fad fades, we're still going to keep doing what we do. Duke Ellington and Count Basie: their music is never going to die out! Whether there's a trend or not, there will always be people who appreciate you—if you perform the music well—and we're trying to hold ourselves up to a high standard.

♦ **V: Any comments about the vintage clothing revival?**

♦ CS: I think there are several factors. One is that fads among young people tend to go in waves, and they're usually about "reaction and counter-reaction." So, when you go through a period like the '50s when people were dressing up, then you go through a period like the '60s and '70s where they didn't. But if you look at the '80s, people did start to dress-up a little again. Look at those New Wave kids or the ska people with their little thin ties. I think a lot of this is an outgrowth of that. The truth is: I think people like to dress-up if they can do it in an affordable manner.

♦ **V: That's why "glam rock" never caught on; nobody could afford the clothes—**

♦ CS: The swing kids shop at vintage stores, where they can afford the clothes and prefer the styles.

In the '60s, we were going through an important phase in our culture and history. It was a reaction against a lot of the hypocrisy in this society. People were saying, "We're a democratic society" and we discovered we weren't so democratic. When people want to blame the protestors of the '60s for all the problems we have now, I say, "Why don't you blame the people they were protesting *against?*" There's been a lot of counter-reaction against the '60s from corporate America and the government.

Cover of *One Hour Mama.*

Duke Ellington is the best composer America ever produced in *any* style of music.

♦ **V: Not to mention revisionism. The movie "Mississippi Burning" completely rewrote history; the F.B.I. couldn't have cared less if a few civil-rights workers got murdered in the deep South—**

♦ CS: People eventually got burned-out on "revolutionary" and/or protest politics.

In the '90s, the culture is a hodge-podge of many different influences. You've got people who are into the disco '70s; other people are into punk rock (I'm talking about young people), and still others are into rockabilly from the '50s. And now there are people who are into the '40s. Maybe American culture in the future will be a smorgasboard where you just go and pick your era and style and that becomes your life. Certainly, the wave of

reissues on CDs (and with digital technology, all the different music and cultures are available on CDs and videos), people can just go out and pick their entertainment "thing." Of course, I hope people pick jazz and blues, which is still a fairly small part of the market.

Most of the new bands doing swing music aren't really in the jazz and blues category. They're more like early rock or rockabilly bands with horns added. They're very good at it, but I'm hoping more people get into jazz and blues. I hope that some of these bands, even if they may not be playing what *I* would call swing or jazz, turn on some people to jazz. They'd really be doing a big service. So this "swing movement" is definitely a good thing.

♦ **V: Tell us about the people in your band—**

♦ CS: Our alto sax player is Bill Stewart; he's a master and has been playing well over 50 years—he's 73 years old. He grew up in Chicago and went to a very famous school for jazz musicians: DuSable. His teacher was the famous Capt. Walter Dyett. His classmate and good friend was Gene Ammons, a very famous tenor saxophone player. Bill grew up during the Swing era in a musical family; his father played with Earl Hines, among others. When bebop came along he heard Charlie Parker and his style changed; he was a part of the first generation of bebop musicians. He's played with people like Lionel Hampton, Gatemouth Brown, Big Maybelle, Johnny Otis, Jay McShann, Big Joe Turner, Rex Stewart, Jesse Price, etc. He's still playing as great as ever, and we're very lucky to be working with him. He's a source of education and great music.

On trumpet, half of our jobs are played by Allen Smith, who's 72 and from the Pittsburgh area. He went on the road with Johnny Otis in 1947, and has recorded with Duke Ellington and Gil Evans. He has performed with the likes of Nat "King" Cole, Ella Fitzgerald, Frank Sinatra, Benny Goodman and Sarah Vaughan. We're very fortunate to be working with him—he's a great trumpet player and is world-renowned. He resides in the Bay Area; these are all world-class musicians who just happen to live here. Also on trumpet is Bill Ortiz, a very wonderful player who has played with Boz Scaggs, Cachao and Tito Puente. He and Allen split the trumpet chair.

On saxophone we work with (on either alto or tenor) a Bay Area legend, Jules Broussard. Jules is from Alexandria, Louisiana, and grew up playing the music of Louis Jordan and Earl Bostic. He's played with Ray Charles, Little Esther Phillips, Johnny Otis, and Big Mama Thornton. And that brings us to our drummer, Sly Randolph, who's from Harlem and has played with Sy Oliver as well as Little Esther Phillips and many other greats.

On guitar we have Charlie Siebert (my brother), on bass is Bing Nathan, on trombone Larry Leight, who splits the chair with Danny Armstrong, and finally, there are three other saxophone players we work with: Robert Stewart (he's performed with Wynton Marsalis); also on tenor sax, Harvey Robb, and finally on tenor sax, Hal Stein, who has performed with Don Byas, Erroll Garner and Charlie Parker. He's 69.

We're very happy with our CD; it's a very good representation of where we were two years ago. It came out a year ago but was recorded over two years ago. It sold over 10,000 copies, which is good for an independent jazz CD. With the players we have now, we feel our band is about five times as good. We're getting ready to put out our next CD. ◼

Rhumba Bums

Along with Lavay Smith's band, Steve Lucky & The Rhumba Bums are some of the nicest people in show biz. They include Steve Lucky (vocals/piano); Carmen Getit (vocals/Gibson 1956 ES-175 blonde hollow-body guitar); Michael "Bam-Bam" Barry (Slingerland vintage drums); Peewee McGee (1955 Cleveland tenor/'40s Martin baritone) and Scotty "Dog" Petersen (1949 Selmer alto/1965 Selmer Mark V tenor). Their website is *luckylounge.com.* and their new CD is available from V/Search (415-362-1465). What follows are interviews with Steve Lucky and Carmen Getit.

INTERVIEW WITH STEVE LUCKY

♦ STEVE LUCKY: I was born in Seattle, raised in Michigan and began my musical career in Ann Arbor playing piano. Beginning at age 8, I took classical lessons for four years and then started playing rock'n'roll organ with a band. The other members were older, and we got gigs playing weddings. At age 13 I came home after a gig and puked on my father—that ended my "professional" career for awhile.

I continued to play piano for my own enjoyment, but wasn't in a band. I listened to a lot of music and saw live music in clubs, but never thought I'd be a professional musician. At the University of Michigan, I studied ethnomusicology and got a B.A. in anthropology. When I finished college, I realized I'd never be satisfied unless I at least *tried* making a living with the music I loved, which was old rhythm & blues.

♦ *VALE: What attracted you to R&B?*

♦ SL: It was the pianistic boogie-woogie style that was most fun to play: Pete Johnson, Albert Ammons, Jay McShann, Meade Lux Lewis. I started a band, The Blue Front Persuaders, and played the Midwestern college circuit: college bars, frat parties, etc. This was a jump-swing blues band in 1980! I got to meet the piano greats Vernon "Boogie Woogie Red" Harrison (who played with John Lee Hooker) and Roosevelt Sykes. I played around there until 1987, when I moved to New York to play with Houston singer-guitarist Johnny Clyde Copeland.

I played in Greenwich Village with funky blues bands—there was no swing scene—and got to meet piano legends Pinetop Perkins and Sammy Price. I also composed for theater and dance performances and played with Joan Osborne, Blues Traveler and the Spin Doctors. I also started playing a lot in Europe with a roots-rock band, Wild Bill Durkin & the Diplomats. I got to know some promoters and spent at least a year abroad playing solo gigs. Then I brought over my own quartet, the Steve Lucky Band (piano, saxophone, bass, drums) and played various gigs.

♦ **V: When did you get together with Carmen Getit?**

♦ SL: We met in Ann Arbor in 1986—we went out a couple times but it didn't work out. She moved to NYC in the spring of

---

At age 13 I came home after a gig and puked on my father—that ended my "professional" career for awhile.

'87 and I looked her up when I moved there later that same year. This time things clicked for us in a big way, and we eventually moved in together. By '91 I had a good career going in Europe and could make my home base anywhere. Carmen wanted to move to the Bay Area, and she got an offer to manage a restaurant in Berkeley, so she moved in 1992.

♦ **V: Tell us about the Rhumba Bums—**

♦ SL: When I arrived in Berkeley in January 1993, I was hot to start a '40s-style New Orleans jump-swing band with my best friend and co-founder of the Blue Front Persuaders, drummer Marc Russell. I ran ads looking for sax players and a bassist and got a call from a guy who had played with Tom Waits and others. As we talked, I realized that we had met and played together in New York! Ralph Carney ended up playing sax with my band in the first few years; he's very original and creative.

Another response to the ad was from veteran jazzman Peter "Peewee McGee" Cornell. He can really blow, and has been our anchorman ever since. When I returned from a couple of months in Europe during the summer of '93, Marc Russell had taken a job in Chicago. Peewee recommended Michael Barry, a drummer who was getting burned out as bandleader of his own big band—it's tough to keep that many players together. Michael's solos are enormous and really musical—he's definitely got a Gene Krupa thing goin'. He's from Idaho and has this slow deliberate way of speaking.

I have a friend named Rob Sudduth. His stage name with us is Ben Whalen (been wailin'—get it?!). We both played in Rhythm Town Jive, which did a lot of Louis Jordan material. He's a great pianist and guitarist, and up until recently he did most of our gigs except in the summer when he's on the road with Huey Lewis and the News. Rob introduced us to Professsor Humphrey Bottoms (Neal Heidler), our bassist. "Hump" grew up in L.A. and has a degree in entomology from Cal. He's a very serious bassist and one of the best soloists in the band. He solos nicely with a bow.

The latest guy to join the band, Scotty Dog Petersen, moved here from Detroit. He was in the J.C. Heard Big Band in Detroit and has played with many famous musicians. A lot of people have been telling us how much better we sound lately, and some of that is due to having a pretty steady line-up; there are rarely substitute players now. But Scotty Dog's playing and stage presence is a big part of it, too.

For the first year or so, I didn't really like any one name for the band, so for every gig the band was called something different! We appeared as Steve Lucky & the Conqueror Orchestra, & the Faux PaPas, & the Alarming Charms, & the Hornswagglers, & the Talismen, & the Rampart Street Rabbit's Feet, & Horn Again, & the Rhumba Bums, & the Abstract Truth. It was like having a *nom du jour,* but nobody knew who the hell we were. Plus, some people were confusing me with Mr. Lucky, the lounge artist. Anyway, the band was a 5-piece until the fall of '94 when I convinced the band that Carmen was really a big draw for us.

🐚 🐚 🐚 🐚 🐚 🐚 🐚 🐚

INTERVIEW WITH CARMEN GETIT

♦ **VALE: Where did you grow up?**

♦ CARMEN GETIT: I grew up in a middle-class suburb of Detroit, Michigan, St. Clair Shores, where all the houses look the same. In second grade I asked my parents for piano lessons, and I played so much they had to move the piano into a separate room so they could close the door. Then my piano teacher moved away and I was so sad; I never took lessons after the fourth grade. I had some basics down, and I started playing pop tunes. My siblings would bring me music books and I would read the notes but play the timing the way I wanted to. The sheet music is usually really "stiff," with the timing straight up-and-down—it never sounded that way on the records! I think the first tune I played was "Heart and Soul"—my mama taught me that. I never knew it was a pop tune from the '40s.

My dad was Irish-American, and he and my mom were always singing, especially in the car on long trips. I have six brothers and sisters and we always sang together on trips. My aunts and uncles sang, too.

♦ **V: When did you get a guitar?**

♦ CG: In the fifth grade. My parents bought me an acoustic gui-

Steve Lucky at the Hi-Ball Lounge, 11-7-97. Photo: V.Vale

tar that was a hideous sunburst cranberry and flaming burnt orange—but it was mine! I went to this Catholic grade school (I sang in the church choir, too). We had mass once a week, and there was a group of girl guitarists who sat in the back row and accompanied the congregation. We taught each other finger-picking or rhythmic strumming—nobody took a lead. This was in the '70s, and our songbook contained folk and pop songs like the Beatles' "Let It Be"—we got to sing anything that could remotely be construed as "religious." I still have that songbook.

We taught ourselves how to sing and play pop tunes from the '70s by Cat Stevens, Harry Chapin and Carole King. Now that I think about it, that was kinda empowering—us girls just taught each other. I still played the piano for fun.

Then I went to a Catholic high school and tried to join the musicians who played for the masses, but they sort of brushed me off; I guess they had enough players. I also tried in college, but was told flat-out, "We have too many people." So in high school I didn't play much music; I wasn't growing (i.e., buying new music books and learning new songs).

In college, I started playing piano again and hardly ever played my guitar. In my dorm there was a music practice room, and late at night I would check it out and stay there for hours. I started working on pop tunes—you don't want to know what they were! [Stephen Bishop; Elton John] Then my mother bought me a subscription to *Sheet Music* magazine for a Christmas present. I started trying to learn standards like "I'm Beginning to See the Light" and "You'd Be So Nice to Come Home To."

After moving out of the dorms, it seemed like every house I rented had a piano in it. In my senior year, we had a nice piano in one house I lived in, so me and my roommates had jam ses-

Steve and Carmen in Basel, Switzerland, 1991. Photo: Daniela Thiiring.

sions. I remember an inspiring article in *Sheet Music* on an L.A. woman jazz pianist, Judy Carmichael, that highlighted her ragtime and old-style piano-playing ability, and I thought it was really cool: "A woman—right on!" I became really interested in playing music, and graduated with difficulty.

It's funny, because in 1986 I met Steve through that tune "I'm beginning to See The Light." The Steve Nardella Band (he's a harmonica player, guitarist, vocalist) in Ann Arbor at the time featured a great pianist, Mark Braun (stage name "Mr B."; he

---

I realized I'd never be satisfied unless I at least *tried* making a living with the music I loved.

---

recorded with the late jazz drummer J.C. Heard) and I really liked him. A friend of mine said, "If you like them, you'll like the Blue Front Persuaders." We went to see them and they were hysterical; their show was over-the-top with theatrics. Even my brother and his friends, who were into punk, used to go see them just for their stage show. Anyway, Steve was taking a solo and I heard the tag line from "I'm Beginning . . ." and I went, "Ohmigod, I'm trying to learn that tune!" My girlfriend said, "I can introduce you if you *want,*" and that's how we met. He came back to my house and played piano for me; he did a little dance for me in the street and got in his car and drove off. I was in awe. He was handsome, seven years older than me, and I was instantly enamored. Oddly enough, two months ago we started doing that tune! I still have that *Sheet Music* magazine, too—it's falling apart, because I worked on it so much back then.

Ann Arbor had a swing scene as early as the '70s and '80s. Steve used to teach swing dancing (with his ex-girlfriend, Vick Honeyman) at the Blind Pig in Ann Arbor. I think they started in 1983, but they called it jitterbug. They taught their lessons before the band would play. After they broke up, Vick kept on teaching with another partner. Steve and I had a couple dates taking swing dance lessons from her (that was for my benefit; he already knew how to swing dance).

There was a very influential guitar player, George Bedard, who was in a band, The Silvertones, which played blues, jump-blues, swing and rockabilly. He played a beautiful hollow-body Epiphone Emperor, and they had an upright bass in the band. Their record from 1977 is rootsy; it had a Carl Perkins tune, "Pointed Toes," "Flip Flop and Fly" (by Big Joe Turner; a lot of swing bands do this), Red Prysock's "Hand-Clapping," "Real Fine Frame" (taken from a Buddy Johnson tune called "Fine Brown Frame"), and "Tell Me What's the Reason?" (T-Bone Walker covered it). Red Prysock was a saxophonist from the '50s, but he had the wailin' jump instrumental sound.

There was a regular blues festival in Ann Arbor, with huge stars coming every year, and there was a local scene that supported blues bands. Chicago is only four hours away, so it was affordable for small clubs to bring legendary blues musicians to play Ann Arbor.

♦ *V: Why did you leave Ann Arbor for New York?*
♦ CG: I had been to New York and wanted to live there. I was afraid to pursue music, even though I loved it. My dad lost his own business and I was afraid of being poor, which as a student I had been. I'd gotten a degree in mechanical engineering. In the fall of '87 I signed a one-year engineering contract with Nissan Motor Corporation and they sent me to New York. On the day my contract expired, I quit. I hated being a woman engineer on the road, living in hotels, visiting car dealerships and meeting service managers. I had to wear business suits and heels into auto service

shops—it was so stupid.

When my contract ended I stayed in New York and worked waiting tables and teaching ballroom dance. I started living with Steve. (Steve moved to New York to be in the Johnny Clyde Copeland band, a Texas blues guitarist who had a platinum record with Albert Collins and Robert Cray.) I started losing interest in the piano the more I heard Steve play; he improvises so much, and reading songs in a music book seemed kind of mechanical by contrast. Steve started showing me basic blues guitar chords so I could play along with him. Then for my birthday in 1989 he bought me a Gibson ES-125 guitar; it had a single P-90 pickup and no cutaway, and a dot neck. The guitarist he worked with, Wild Bill Durkin, had a day job working in a guitar store, and he found it. (They call P-90's soapbox pickups; they're single coil and plastic-coated. Then later they came out with Humbuckers, which are chrome.)

♦ V: *So you started really getting into music—*
♦ CG: I was really poor when I was teaching ballroom dance and waiting tables, so after work I would go to Steve's gigs and listen to music, get inspired by people and learn from the musicians. A great guitarist, Steve Antonakas, gave me two of Mickey Baker's guitar music books which contained chord charts (Mickey had once been Louis Jordan's guitarist) and they really helped. They had all these different voicings for major sixths and minor sevenths. Before then, I only played open chords and barre chords ("Smoke on the Water")—easy ones. I took a lesson from George Bedard a couple years ago, and asked him what chords he played on certain tunes (they were *beautiful)* and he said, "They're all in those Mickey Baker books."

In New York, I became friends with Joan Osborne before she became famous, when she was singing blues. She had such a powerful stage presence, and New Yorkers are a tough audience. I met her at a time when I was struggling to do music. There weren't that many women playing, and Joan had something feminine and strong—intelligence combined with sexiness. I wanted to have that presence in my own life, not just on stage. She was vulnerable; she would really let her emotions show, and that puts *you* on the line when you do it. Nix the stage stuff and the antics, it was just her and it was so powerful.

I really was surrounded by music then, even in the dance studio—migod, did I hear some bad versions of jazz standards there! I've always liked standards, more so than Steve, so I forced them on him by copying Chris Siebert's collection of fake books as a present. Chris Siebert and Lavay Smith are so incredible, so talented and so community-minded. They're always helping to promote us, telling club owners to hire us, etc. They genuinely go out of their way to help people. I think Chris should run for political office! He was a history major at U.C. Berkeley and I think his voracious appetite for jazz and blues reflects that. He loves to give credit where it's due, and share information with people.

♦ V: *So how did you develop as a musician in NY?*
♦ CG: I had been playing on and off, but you can't really develop that way. I went with Steve on a three-month trip to Europe in 1991 (different towns in Switzerland, plus a week in Paris). I had always been intimidated in New York, because the audience was full of artists! Over the years, Steve totally turned me on to all this awesome music, and I used to sing along with it and try to get "inside" of what the singer was doing. I learned why Steve liked this person and not that one; he'd point out a musician in an ensemble and suddenly that instrument would leap out at me. So I was developing my ear, even though I wasn't necessarily applying it to an instrument—except for my voice.

Steve taught me about phrasing; anyone can play a scale, but it's *how* you place the notes that makes it swing or not. Steve has a natural feel for that in his piano playing and in his singing, too. So, he taught me a lot, just listening to music. One time I was

Steve Lucky at piano and Carmen Getit on piano, 1997. Photo: Tracy Hatch

singing a Ruth Brown tune, "Mama, He Treats Your Daughter Mean," and he said, "Hey, you do that really good!" I did it with him "live" once in Europe (I didn't know anyone in the audience, and couldn't speak Swiss/German anyway) and then I started singing it every night. That was the only song I could do.

This British swing band, The Jive Aces, was playing in the same town, and we started jamming with them. They made me sing with them. They called me up to the stage, and I didn't know how to say "No"; my heart fell into my stomach, everyone's waiting and clapping, and you're just in a dream or like hypnotized, watching yourself getting up on stage and singing. Then they asked, "Don't you know any more tunes?" and I didn't! They hired Steve to go to Paris with them and perform and I went along. On that trip I got to know Pat Reyford, a terrific musician who used to be known as Sugar Ray Ford; he's now in the Big Six.

♦ V: *Where did you play?*
♦ CG: We played two clubs in Paris that were caves, with photos of famous American blues and jazz musicians on the wall: the Caveaux de la Huchette (on the Rue de la Huchette, near the

Notre Dame). We also played The Slow Club in Paris—that's still happening. And they were teaching a swing dance lesson before the band played.

♦ **V: So in 1991, you realized you could sing—**

♦ CG: I really didn't think I could, but *other* people thought I could, so I went, "I like this, so I should really try." I also thought I wasn't good enough to just sing or just play guitar, so I'd better do both! I like guitar, but I don't get the same satisfaction that I do playing piano. There's something very rewarding about sitting down at the piano and hearing this really full sound come out; it stands alone, you don't need anything else, and it feels so good. I haven't gotten to that point in my guitar playing.

I was very fortunate to walk into a ready-made band of professional, seasoned musicians. I had to concentrate and learn the chops in a hurry to figure out how to fit in. I had to stay out of the way of the other musicians, and try to create a rhythmic feel. If someone says, "Play me a tune," I don't sound that good by myself. I used to do more finger-picking before, and now I want to play that stand-alone guitar sound, like old country blues.

In 1993, Steve went alone to Europe, but he told the club owners who booked him that next year they had to hire me, too! After I quit managing the restaurant, I started practicing seriously and was forced to learn a repertoire; we had to work up duets and other songs and Steve taught me a ton. In 1994 I went with him to play the Café des Arts in Basel, Switzerland. Steve did two 45-minute sets by himself and five sets with me *every night.* That's why we never went back!

♦ **V: Playing that much, you probably got better fast—**

♦ CG: Yeah. After I quit the restaurant in September 1993, I started teaching ballroom dance again. Steve said, "We're going into the studio to make a demo tape [recorded October, 1993] so we can get work." That was our band, The Steve & Patsy Show (me on guitar, Steve on piano, with Mark Bohn on drums and Nancy Kaspar on upright bass). My first gig with this band (which we later called The Honeymoaners, until we found out that our friend, saxophonist Ralph Carney, had a band under that name) was October 16, 1993 at Hanno's on Natoma in San Francisco.

We played as the Honeymoaners through 1994, while Steve maintained the Rhumba Bums. I gradually joined the band that year, appearing on only some gigs, mostly because the pay couldn't support a 6th player. I'm pretty sure my first paying gig with Steve Lucky & the Rhumba Bums was at the Club Deluxe in October 1994.

My parents bought me an acoustic guitar that was a hideous sunburst cranberry and flaming burnt orange—but it was mine!

In 1995 Eric Shifrin got us a Happy Hour duet gig at the House of Shields on Montgomery St—he's a terrific pianist and singer, and when Dutch at the Club Deluxe found out about it (he's the

manager), he offered us a duet every Wednesday night. We played there for over a year and called it The Steve & Patsy Show. Dutch was very supportive of us early on and still is.

♦ **V: When did you first play with the Rhumba Bums?**

♦ CG: Steve moved here in January '93 and got a gig as a solo pianist at the Lone Palm at 22nd and Guerrero and went back to play in Europe that spring. It took a while to assemble musicians for a band and get gigs. He was new in town and didn't know people. The Bums' first gig wasn't until March 1993 at the Bottom of the Hill in San Francisco. But a turning point was when the Rhumba Bums played the Cafe Du Nord Christmas party in 1993. I sat in with the band and we met Lavay Smith and Chris Siebert. Chris then got us a job at the Club Deluxe. Then the Deluxe got us into Bimbo's—Michael of Bimbo's would call Dutch and ask, "I've got this band headlining, who should we get to open for them?" People have really supported us, and when you get that kind of support, you kinda want to pass it along.

♦ **V: Why weren't you in the Rhumba Bums from the very beginning?**

♦ CG: I think it's a combination of reasons. I was teaching ballroom dance then and I was *really* into it. Also, I honestly think I wasn't ready at that point; I wasn't good enough. And Steve's initial concept was partly to prove that a swing band didn't need a guitar player, and also he had some really hot players. He couldn't afford to add a sixth person. Also, the band was playing out-there jazz pieces mixed with New Orleans R&B and swing, and I didn't have the chops to hang with the *outside* jazz stuff. And they didn't want to stop playing it; it was a thrill for the musicians—sometimes, someone would really get hot and take the whole band *way* "outside," and then everybody starts doing new things. That's a real improvisational thrill for the musicians . . . but not for swing dancers!

♦ **V: In swing dancing, you've got to be completely empathic with your partner—it's no longer you you you. You have to balance doing what you want to do, with being in synch with the other person.**

♦ CG: And that brings you to a different level of excitement. You constantly get to try some move and it's different every time you do it, depending on what your goal is. I get a thrill when I see people interpreting the different nuances in the music. I love dancing.

♦ **V: And this movement seems to be reintegrating dance with music again. I read that in the late '30s at the Savoy, when the "Lindy Hop" was being invented, the dancers were inspiring the musicians to get wilder, and the musicians in turn were inspiring the dancers. They'd have dance marathons, dance cutting contests, band cutting contests (e.g., Count Basie vs. Chick Webb)—it must have been incredible. They kept upping the ante—like, "How far can you take this wild dancing?" The bands would play a song for 20 minutes, and the dancers would almost collapse at the end. Now you see dancers sweating after just 3 minutes; what about after 20?**

♦ CG: Oh god. You knew when Steve first looked me up in New York, we went swing-dancing all the time, but we had to *find* it first, and that was really tough. We finally found a club that was doing it, and that's when I first saw FRANKIE MANNING, in 1987. It was the New York Swing Dance Society; they did Wednesday or Thursday nights at the North River Bar in Tribeca and the Swing Now Trio played. Jazz musicians that were in town would come sit in with the band. I danced with drummer Bernard Purdie; saxophonist Lew Tabackin of the Toshiko Akiyoshi Big Band sat in. It was so cool. I didn't get to dance with Frankie—I'm dyin'; I want to take one of his workshops so bad!

You have to check out the Northern California Lindy Society web site; it's called *Jump Site at ncls.com;* they let you know when

Carmen (front center) and Steve (back, with bow tie) with the Jive Aces (Pat Reyford on Carmen's right), 1991.

people come to town. Frankie Manning has a website that lists all the dance-related stuff; all the old films, books. There's a woman from Whitey's Lindy-Hoppers (the original Lindy-Hoppers that Frankie Manning was one of): Norma Miller. She still alive, still teaches, and has a book out, *Swingin' at the Savoy: The Memoir of a Jazz Dancer.* I think Frankie's website is maintained by Judy Pritchett, who I think may be his girl-friend; she lives in Fort Bragg. They have all these old film clips of dance and I want every one! If anyone wonders what I want for Christmas—well, I want all these old dance videos!

Have you seen the old Marx Brothers movie, *A Day at the Races?* There's a dance scene with Whitey's Lindy-Hoppers. It's a small scene, but so hot. Each couple comes out, and they lindy so fast—those kids can't do that now—not a lot of them.

♦ *V: You guys really are in synch with this movement*—

♦ CG: I just feel I died and went to heav-en! To be able to make a living playing music that I love?! There's a big thing I left out of this whole picture, which is: my dad was a huge music fan. He totally turned me on to all this stuff. Out of everyone in the family, I think I was the only one who loved it as much as he did. So I was the only one he could really share it with, and he was so passionate about it. If any spe-cials came on public television, it was he and I relegated to the spare room with the tiny black-and-white 6" set.

Mostly it was my dad and I who listened to the records. He had read so much about jazz, but he never made it to bebop; he could-n't "hang" with that stuff. He was into the early swing music and the Chicago ensemble jazz sound. When we listened to records, he'd go, "Listen to this such-and-such," training my ear to hear different counter-melodies that were going on. And he would dance with me. He and my mom did their version of the jitterbug.

I listened to more of a '30s sound growing up, and heard the '40s stuff on college radio stations. When I met Steve he turned me on to the stuff that I like a lot better now.

There are certain instrumentalists I want to listen to over and over again—it's like I can't get enough of them, like TINY GRIMES and His Rockin' Highlanders. There's an obscure one, BILL JENNINGS, who was also one of Louis Jordan's guitarists. But his own stuff, which is totally out-of-print (Rusty Zinn, another guitar idol of mine, turned me on to it)—that's the best music I've ever heard! There's a bunch of stuff from that era: BIG JOE TURNER (the early recordings), early T-BONE WALKER . . . I just can't stop listening to it. The late '40s, early '50s music. It's pre-rock'n'roll: guitars and band arrangements . . . all the black jump-blues bands. Big Joe Turner first recorded in 1929 and recorded through the '80s; he died around 1987.

My dad totally got me into music like Bessie Smith, who he used to call my great-Aunt, and Billie Holiday, but he didn't listen to vocalists much—mostly he was into instrumentalists: the jazz musicians of the swing era. He likes an ensemble sound; the Chicago jazz band sound. We listened to COLEMAN HAWKINS' "Body and Soul." The bands were still segregated when he was going to clubs (before he got mar-ried), so a lot of the people he was into were all these white Chicago jazz guys—but jazz then was swing.

To me, some of it sounds kinda Dixielandish. A lead instru-ment will be improvising on the melody, and another lead horn will be playing a counter-melody behind it, so you've got this polyphony going. It wouldn't necessarily make me feel: "Wow, I

L to R: Chester Whitmore, Lisa Sang, Carmen, legendary tap dancer Al Robinson, Jean Elbin, and Steve, 1997.

gotta dance!" I totally dug it, but it didn't move me as much as the stuff I was later turned on to. But it certainly helped develop my ear; the more you listen, the more you can hear.

It's a goal of mine to someday be able to read charts quicker—especially those tunes that are in a flatted key and are full of com-plicated chords with a flatted 5th and a sharp *that,* and a differ-ent chord change every quarter-bar—you know what I'm saying? And if it's a fast tune, I couldn't do it now. Sometimes Steve will help me by going, "It's kinda like *this* tune, but in a different key."

And then I'll know. Reading music faster is one of the many *next steps.*

♦ **V: *Learning to read music is difficult, and it seems boring too, compared to playing by ear and improvising—***

♦ CG: That's how I feel, exactly. I do want to learn it, but . . . Maybe I'm just greedy. You can figure out what someone's playing by ear a lot quicker, and get immediate results.

♦ **V: *Now they have videos where you can really slow down that blazing scale—***

♦ CG: —and figure out what the hell they did! Actually, what's really helped me is: I took a lesson from George Bedard, who's my idol. He's not really a great teacher. I think he could be, but he said to me, "It's all right there in that Mickey Baker book." But he put them together beautifully. He was out of the room and his wife asked (she's really cool; she deejays a radio show under the name "Lola Rebop"), "Did George tell you what his secret weapon was?" I go, "No." He had this Marantz device, a cassette player. He could plug his guitar into it, play a tape, and adjust the speed to half-time. I found an Ibanez device for $89—same thing, you put your cassette in, and you can slow down a tape to half-speed. And half-speed keeps it at the same pitch, but it also had a speed adjustment of a whole musical step, up and down, so if it were in the key of C you could play along in the key of D. And if you had a tape that was warped, you wouldn't have to retune your instrument. That thing is way cool. It's called a "Rock and Play."

There are some nights, like the last time we played the Hi-Ball, where it just feels like a "community." I don't know when this day's going to end, but I guess I'll just keep going and make new friends—be playing music in some other form and some other club. To have all these interesting people in one spot, like last night when all these really good dancers showed up—it makes me feel part of a community. I had to leave my corporate job because it was so meaningless. I never wanted to take it in the first place, but I was really broke. I remember telling my mom, "I hate this. I cannot work 9 to 5 and have the American dream of 'Don't take a vacation even if you deserve it, because you need to get ahead'!" A night like that just makes you feel happy to be alive!

♦ **V: *Everyone's craving community—***

♦ CG: I want it. That's one reason I love living on the West Coast. I live in Oakland and most of my neighbors are black and I love that. I grew up in a very segregated environment and it didn't seem natural. When I moved to New York, it was totally different and great, but it's even better here.

♦ **V: *There's a book that contains some great descriptions of the early '30s swing-dance movement,* Steppin' on the Blues *by Jacqui Malone. It says, "The Savoy's success owes as much to the famous 'battles of the bands' staged there as it does to the music and the dancers who created visualizations of the music."***

♦ CG: Ah—great! "Visualizations"—exactly. Frankie Manning's already been out here maybe twice this year. They have a night where they show old film and video clips and you can sit around and talk with Frankie. During the day he teaches the actual workshops.

There's this swing chatline *[swinglist.com]* that comes right

into your e-mail box if you contribute. It's mostly about swing dance and music. People get a little pedantic at times, but a lot of them are totally into dancing (besides the music) and they quote these statements that make you want to read all these articles and books about dance. I read this quote from Norma Miller and she says, in effect, that these moves may have looked improvisational, but everything was choreographed and calculated down to the last detail. They were having fun; it looked like it was all fun and games, but it was all choreographed.

♦ **V: *The dancers would practice alone, in solitude, working out ways to advance their art and evolve their routines, trying to do something that nobody else did so they could win the cutting contest. Imagine a hundred people doing that— dancers who were already really great to begin with. Capitalism at its best!***

Cover of *International Sweethearts of Rhythm* cassette, Oct. 14, 1946

♦ CG: CHESTER WHITMORE lives in L.A. and comes up here a lot. He teaches a lot of workshops on lindy, tap and choreography. He also leads his own jazz band; they opened the Monterey Jazz Festival last year. He has all these charts from old big bands. He's a fantastic dancer and very knowledgeable.

There was this band in the '30s and '40s called The INTERNATIONAL SWEETHEARTS OF RHYTHM, an 18-piece all-woman big band. They were called "International" because there are all these different nationalities. I've read that there's film footage, but haven't seen it. I've seen promo photos and have one of their cassettes. Chester got them back together and put them on a public television station— there's only five still alive and living all over the country, and he supplemented the rest of the 18 pieces with other woman musicians he knew in the L.A. area.

Chester teaches at the Derby and the Hollywood Athletic Club. He's constantly getting flown all over the world and is hard to get ahold of, but I was lucky enough to get him on our album. Steve wrote a piece with breaks in it, and Chester fills them in with taps!

♦ **V: *I'm glad you told me about this, because I was wondering, "Where are the women instrumentalists in this movement?"***

♦ CG: I think it's just a matter of time. A lot of the horn players came from a jazz background, and they haven't crossed over to the swing movement. There's not that many to begin with, relatively. It's not as "traditional" for women to be saxophone, trumpet and trombone players. I think of it almost like engineering— there just weren't that many women when I did it. It kinda pissed me off, y'know.

There's a great pianist, Caroline Dahl, who plays in the Rhythm Sheiks; I think she does a lot of solo work. She's also a composer, visual artist and *hot* boogie-woogie player. I think Steve met her originally in Louisville (where she's from) when he was on the road with Johnny Copeland; her band opened for them. Then there's Dizzy Burnette in Santa Cruz, who plays upright bass and sings—she's sexy, has a Brooklyn accent and calls her band the Dizzy Burnette Orchestra. Vise Grip's Ambassadors of Swing has a female drummer, Kelly Fastman—I met her when she was subbing with the Stanford Jazz Band.

Carmen and Scotty Petersen at the Hi-Ball Lounge, 11-7-97. Photo: V.Vale

There's a woman sax player who I've met; her name is Annaliese and I think the Riff Rats have hired her. And there's Suzie Laraine who plays jazz sax. She lives with Donald "Duck" Bailey who played drums with Jimmy Smith; they lived just down the street from us and we didn't know it. Suzy is the bandleader for Cynthia & the Swing Set—Cynthia's the vocalist.

There's a 15-member all-woman big band, Diva, who've been playing since 1993. They're led by Sherrie Maricle, who said, "Women in jazz is still somewhat of a novelty. We're the first band to give women the opportunity to play some serious jazz. We're top-of-the-line musicians, and not just a gimmick. A high school girl, Jessica Reiter, who publishes *Rhubarb Pie* in Santa Cruz, interviewed us and interviewed them. She's adorable and has chutzpah—she's like a kid and a woman at the same time. God, I didn't have my shit together like that when I was 16.

♦ **V:** *Do you have any other band "side projects"? A lot of people these days seem to be in at least three bands, plus work a day job—*

♦ **CG:** Steve plays Hammond B-3 organ, so we have another band that does soul jazz plus TV-lounge. It's called the "Hammond Cheese Combo"—we love puns! We played Bimbo's on a lounge bill with Herb [Herb Alpert tribute band].

♦ **V:** *B-3 organ trio music with honkin' sax is very hip now, like Brother Jack McDuff—*

♦ **CG:** I love Jack McDuff. We were supposed to see him last night at Yoshi's with Chris Siebert, but we had just flown in from Denver and were too tired. Apparently he hardly played, anyway. But I saw him the year before at the S.F. Jazz Festival at Bimbo's and it was great. Shirley Scott was also on the bill and she was stunning, beautiful, and an incredible musician who stole the show (to me, anyway) even though Jack was a total stud. She brought tears to my eyes. Our sax player Scotty Dog got hired to play the gig with Jack. Scotty got Jack to autograph a CD for me—

what a thrill.

I saw organist Jimmy McGriff last month at the SF Jazz Fest at Bimbo's. I saw Jimmy Smith at Yoshi's, and I dug it, but the guy we really like, at least on recording, is Hank Marr—Chris Siebert turned us on to him. I think he's still alive and lives in Ohio. His shit is so cool—he and Jack McDuff are my favorites. There's a deejay in San Jose who's a big B-3 lover, Pete Fallcio, and he always hosts the SF Jazz Fest organ night. I heard he brought Hank Marr out to some event in the South Bay, and man, I wish I had known! What I would do to go hear that. I e-mailed Pete to bring him out again. I've heard they haven't had him on the Jazz Fest because they don't think he has enough name recognition. They had Booker T this year, who's not a jazz player, really, but I'm sure he packed the house.

♦ **V:** *You're releasing your own CD?*

♦ **CG:** Chris Siebert turned us on to this publication, *How to Release Independent Records.* He said he wished they had read it before they produced their first CD. Chris is convinced that their CD sold well because the photo of Lavay on the cover is so good. The hardest thing is to get a photo in which all six people look good at the same time.

Steve [Lucky] usually looks great; he moves like Art Carney from *The Honeymooners*—he should have been a dancer. If you see him do improv—I just had a blast. When we were falling in love in the honeymoon phase, we used to go out dancing and he's totally improvisational—people would ask us, "Are yous two actuhs?" (we were living in New York). I was totally inspired and egged on by him. So he can do that for photos—he can mug and it doesn't look corny, it looks "fun and retro" at the same time.

♦ **V:** *Why did you get into engineering?*

♦ **CG:** I don't know; to make money. I liked all the courses I took—from math to literature—and considered being a doctor. But because my family was in that bad financial situation, I thought, "I'd better choose something so that when I graduate with my bachelor's degree, I can support myself and get out of debt." I couldn't decide. For awhile I was mad that I wasted time on that, but I'm not mad now, because I've finally found something else that I care about. V

Reference & Recommendations

Rhumba Bums, POB 8566, Emeryville CA 94662-8566.
Rhubarb Pie, POB 1165, Freedom CA 95019. $1 & two stamps.
Carmen Getit's amps: early '60s Fender Super Reverb; early '60s Ampeg Reverb-rocket.
International Sweethearts of Rhythm cassette $13ppd from Rosetta Records, 115 W. 16th St, NYC 10011. $1 for catalog.
Peter J. Silvester, *A Left Hand Like God* (on boogie-woogie)
Mezz Mezzrow: *Really The Blues*
RECORDS:
Jay McShann w/Yardbird), *The Band That Jumps the Blues*
Swinghouse [U.K. label] collection: *R&B & Boogie-Woogie*
Plas Johnson: *Bop Me Daddy* (sax instrumental)
Red Prysock, *Rock'n'Roll* (1951 hard-blowin' sax instru.)
Pete Johnson, *Pete's Blues* (House Rent Party)
Big Joe Turner, *The Boss of the Blues* ("my bible"). He's my favorite singer, especially with Pete Johnson on piano.
ARTISTS or BANDS:
Steve recommends: Andy Kirk & His Clouds of Joy (early swing band); Jimmy Lunceford; Erskine Hawkins; Bennie Moten (the first real swing band; Basie was his pianist); Hot Lips Page; T-Bone Walker (the Imperial recordings); Paul Gayten; Jimmy Liggins (brother of Joe Liggins); early Woody Herman (one of the top white bands, really burnin', not wimpy); Spike Jones (his daughter, a recording engineer, worked on our CD at Skywalker Studios); Slim Gaillard; Nat King Cole; Wynonie Harris on King Records; Lionel Hampton; Chick Webb (with Louis Jordan and Ella Fitzgerald). Carmen recommends: Dinah Washington, Helen Humes, Ruth Brown, Francis Faye

Sam Butera

Tenor saxophonist Sam Butera was born August 17, 1927. He began playing professionally at age 19, and over the years recorded 78s on the Victor, Groove and Cadence labels. In 1954 he joined Louis Prima and Keely Smith (remaining with Louis until 1975, when Louis lapsed into a coma) and achieved Hit Parade fame with recordings such as "That Old Black Magic." This interview was done on Sept 13, 1997, when Sam Butera played Bimbo's 365 Club with his band: Arnie Teich (Korg 88 keyboard & Roland synthesizer), Jimmy James (trombone), Kevin Norton (trumpet), Chris Gordon (bass), and Bob Ruggiero (drums). Sam has several CDs available, including *The Whole World Loves Italians,* available for $20 each postpaid from PO Box 42395, Las Vegas NV 89116.

♦ *VALE: What's the secret of your success?*

♦ SAM BUTERA: Here's what it's all about: *caring.* That's how I live my life. This is my 49th wedding anniversary. I've got four kids and six grandchildren, and they all live in Vegas. My oldest daughter is a vice-principal; my youngest boy is a head football coach and teacher at Bonanza High School; my youngest daughter is a secretary at the parochial school; and my oldest boy is a crap dealer at Caesar's Palace. Las Vegas has been home now for 42 years. I went there in 1954 when they had 30,000 people. Now there are 1.2 million—great city!

♦ *V: You're considered a musical godfather to this new swing movement—*

♦ SB: It's incredible how all of a sudden the kids are picking up on swing music. We just did a thing at New York, New York, the new hotel in Las Vegas. And you should see the kids that come into the lounge, dancin' and havin' a party, man! It was unbelievable. We just went to Zurich, Vienna, Paris, Italy and Frankfurt, and the kids there knew every song we had ever recorded. They called out songs I *forgot* I recorded. (In Europe, people like jazz more than they like it here.) I'm so happy, because that's good for musicians. Kids are studying, and in the years to come they'll be able to play with a big band. And that's what it's all about.

♦ *V: Making sure that culture doesn't die out—*

♦ SB: The old guy's hangin' in—that's me. [laughs] Do you know why god created the orgasm? So Italians will know when to stop!

♦ *V: You sound so young—*

♦ SB: I tell ya, I'm still *playin'* young.

Louis [Prima] and I played Bimbo's when the *grandfather* owned the 365 Club. It was the year Al and Joe Scoma opened up Scoma's on the wharf [1965]. They used to come in every night, and that's when Bimbo's had the girl in the fishbowl—

♦ *V: She's still there—*

♦ SB: Is that right? I'll be darned; I didn't realize that. Well, I'm proud of these kids. And no matter where we go, we run into them and they love this music.

When I was 19 *Look* magazine voted me "teenage instrumentalist of the year." I won that award at Carnegie Hall. There was a contest: North, East, South and West. All the Southern bands first competed in the municipal auditorium in New Orleans and we were lucky enough to win the "Big Band Contest." Then they brought us to New York City, Carnegie Hall, and from those big bands they picked an All-American Band, and from the All-American Band I was picked as outstanding instrumentalist. Among the judges were Les Brown, Spike Jones, and Nat King Cole.

♦ *V: Did you actually get to meet them?*

♦ SB: Oh, I knew them all. That's a fact, man.

In New Orleans, at the age of 20, I had my own band for many years. When I joined Louis Prima, my band was called the Nighttrainers. And when I joined Louis, I brought two guys with me to the Sahara Hotel, Las Vegas. I had forgotten to tell Louis

their names. At the end of the show, he was naming the people in the band: Louis, Keely, Sam Butera—he looked at me and I said, "The Witnesses"—that's how our band name came about.

♦ *V: So you had your own band for 7 years and then you teamed up with Louis—*

♦ SB: That's right. I couldn't pass up that opportunity. I had such respect and admiration for him, and that's why I went with Louis. But I brought my own band with me, and that made history.

♦ *V: When you had your own band, at the age of 20, you must have been the arranger. Did you go to school to learn how to write music?*

♦ SB: No, I just did it on my own: learning chord structure and things like that. However, I studied under some great clarinet teachers. Clarinet was a very important part of my life. I started with saxophone and then I went to clarinet. Jean Pacqué [sic] from Belgium, the first chair solo clarinetist with the New Orleans Symphony, was my *real* teacher.

♦ *V: What was the essence of what he taught you?*

♦ SB: Ah, you *can't* tell that. He taught me so much, and I went to lessons once a week. Boy, he sat down next to me and brother I had to play it right. Nice man; he was wonderful.

♦ *V: Did you learn discipline from him?*

♦ SB: I learned how to play *clarinet* from him. And clarinet's much more difficult than saxophone—each octave has different fingering. Whereas on saxophone they're just about the same.

I played with a lot of big bands. I had a scholarship to Notre Dame or any Southeastern college I wanted to go to, but I chose to go on the road with Ray McKinley. I was always the youngest guy in the band; now I'm the old mutha!

♦ *V: What was it like going on the road in 1946?*

♦ SB: Very hard. And there was no money. But I wanted the experience. We slept on the bus, going from one-nighter to one-nighter. It wasn't easy.

♦ *V: Did you learn a lot from Ray McKinley?*

♦ SB: Well, I learned phrasing. What taught me the most was playing with great musicians. A lot of people don't understand that.

People back east know music unbelievably. You know why? They had the Paramount Theater, the Strand, the Earl Theater in Philadelphia. And all of these theaters had big bands. So when those kids were coming up, they would skip school to hear those bands. They know music because they heard the greatest. That's where it's at, babe!

When I joined Ray McKinley, I took Peanut Hucker's place; he went with Claude Thornhill. We were working at the Hotel New Yorker. On our first night off, the older guys in the band said, "Come with us, Sam, we're going to check out 52nd Street"—there was jazz all up and down it. (And you know Louis never called it 52nd Street—you know what he called it? Fifty-*two* Street.) They took me to a place called the Three Deuces. And guess who I got to see play back-to-back? Charlie Parker and Charlie Ventura. I was never so thrilled in my life; I was crying—

Where it's at: Sam Butera in Vegas.

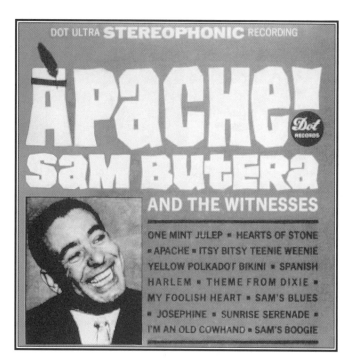
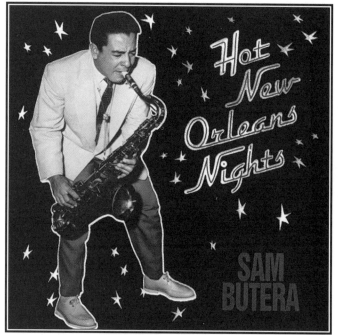

Covers of *Apache!* on Dot Records and *Hot New Orleans Nights* on Bear Family Records.

I really was. I couldn't believe it: to hear these two great musicians playing. What a thrill.

♦ **V: Leonard Feather, in his Encyclopedia of Jazz, considered you a jazz musician—**

♦ SB: You know what I am? An entertainer. I can make people laugh and make 'em smile, be happy. They enjoy what I play.

♦ **V: And while doing this, you raised a family and had a home life—**

♦ SB: I've got a wonderful wife—that's where it's at.

♦ **V: You weren't on the road as much as many musicians. Did that contribute to the longevity of your marriage?**

♦ SB: It contributed, but I love my wife dearly!

♦ **V: Weren't there a lot of places to play in New Orleans, so you didn't have to go on the road?**

♦ SB: Not no more. There's only one place you can play and that's a boat called the Treasure Chest. There's no place for me to work in New Orleans.

♦ **V: How did growing up in New Orleans influence your music?**

I was always the youngest guy in the band, now I'm the old mutha!

♦ SB: The first thing I heard was Dixieland music, but I never could get into that; it wasn't my forte. I never played any Dixieland clarinet; I played mostly concert clarinet. And when I switched to saxophone, I came up with my whole approach—at one time I was a bebopper but couldn't make no fuckin' money so that's when I went to the other style of music.

♦ **V: Did you ever have hard times, economically, like when you were figuring out you couldn't make money playing bebop?**

♦ SB: I've always managed to work. I worked behind strippers; I worked wherever I could make a dollar, 'til I got to a point in my life where I said, "Now I gotta do what *Sam* wants to do."

♦ **V: What's your take on "fame"? If you had become as famous as Frank Sinatra, then everywhere you go you'd have to have 10 bodyguards—**

♦ SB: [laughs] You know, fame isn't everything. It's doing what you enjoy doing, and making people happy. If you can't make people happy, then you're losing. And playing good music—that's *Number One*. I had a little boy walk up to me last night whose daddy is teaching him saxophone. He asked, "Mr Butera, how can I play better?" I said, "Practice." That's it.

♦ **V: Well, you probably spent 100,000 hours listening to good music and practicing—**

♦ SB: You bet! I got to hear the best players, man, and I always listened. You take a little here, you take a little there and you put it together.

♦ **V: Your father played accordion—**

♦ SB: A concertina, the little one. He played a little guitar, too, but he wasn't a schooled musician. He loved music. I started playing when I was 7 years old.

♦ **V: Did they have record players then?**

♦ SB: No, they didn't; it was shortly afterwards. The first record my father bought for me was Benny Goodman's "Please Be Kind." And he kept buying records and I kept listening. That's the only way: you listen to people play and you learn. Musicians walk up to me now and say, "I got all your CDs, Sam." I say, "Well, if it'll help you, that's fine."

♦ **V: The Bear Family CD is the only one I could find—**

♦ SB: That was done a long time ago. A lot of things have happened since then.

♦ **V: But what struck me is: I really think you have an excellent voice—**

♦ SB: [laughs] Thank you. You know, it's been a wonderful life, and I don't know—a coupla more years: *call it a day.* I'm gettin' old, man.

♦ **V: But you look so young—**

♦ SB: Preparation H every night! [laughs] My mother is 89 and has brothers and sisters in their 90s. Mama's a strong lady. My birthday just passed; it was August 17th. So I called my mother and she said, "Sam, where are you?" I said, "I'm in Atlantic City." She said, "Well, if I had known where you were, I would have called you." Then she said, "Sam, how old *are* you?" [laughs]

♦ **V: You have a brother—**

♦ SB: Just one, Joe. My mother and father are from Sicily. Mama was born in Cefalu, and my father was born in Trabia. I've never been back, but I'm going to Northern Italy in April to play.

♦ **V: How do you get inspired?**

♦ SB: Writing arrangements, it's just a *feel.* It all depends on what kind of rhythm you want to play, and you create off of that. My piano player is excellent—he does most of the writing now. I chip in my little bit, you know. In the past we played a lot of shuffle things. [demonstrates] *dinga-dinga-dinga-dinga-dinga-dinga-dinga-dinga . . .* On the new CD we just recorded, we've got a Country-Western song by Willie Nelson, "On the Road Again." But it swings; it ain't no Country & Western, you know what I mean? We got "Unforgettable"—when you hear it, you'll like it. We also got "This Little Love of Mine." They're swingers; all of 'em. "Love is in the Air/Everywhere I look around"—remember that one? "I Love You Just the Way You Are . . . *Sometimes.*" [laughs] We got a lotta great tunes.

♦ V: *It's so amazing that you're still playing—*

♦ SB: Louis was a genius. He was, in my eyes, a very special man. Did you know I did an album with Sammy Davis Jr? It's called *Sam Meets Sam: When the Feelin' Hits Ya.* It came out great; I wrote all the arrangements.

I was telling you about writing arrangements: it's the feel. You listen to the melody line of a song and it all depends on what tempo you want to do it, because that makes a great deal of difference, too. In fact, "That Old Black Magic" (that we had a big hit with) was written right here—I wrote that arrangement in San Francisco at the Fairmont.

♦ V: *Mando, from Royal Crown Revue, said you were using an original mouthpiece—*

♦ SB: I know him very well; he's a nice boy and that's a good band. I bought it when I was 18 years old and I've been playing it ever since. Guys come up to me and ask, "What kind of mouthpiece do you use?" And I say, "I use a Berg Larsen." "What kind of reed to you use?" I use a No. 5 reed—that's like a popsicle stick. See, I got very strong chops, you know. My Berg Larsen

mouthpiece was the first one to come out of England, and it was the Charlie Ventura model. People ask, "How do you get *that* sound?" and I say, "It's not Sam, it's the mouthpiece!" They ask, "Where can I find one?" and I say, "You can't, unless I die!"

♦ V: *And you used to play clarinet—*

♦ SB: With clarinet, you couldn't make any money, because people wanted to hear tenor; that was *the* big instrument with R&B. When I joined Louis I was always playing the leads on tenor.

> **Guess who I got to see play back-to-back? Charlie Parker and Charlie Ventura. I was crying—I really was.**

Now the sound we have is different from anybody else's; it's *our* sound. Next year we'll be in Las Vegas 30 weeks—thank god, we get to stay home a little bit. My wife says, "I'm gettin' lonesome, Sam!" [laughs]

♦ V: *Then you can buy a lot of presents for your grandkids—*

♦ SB: Yes, and I love 'em all.

♦ V: *Do you have any advice for musicians?*

♦ SB: To find work today is very difficult. If they want to get work, they better know how to sight-read, and it's not easy. I would say, if a young cat is coming up, if he gets an opportunity, "Be ready!" And don't say, "Oh, gee." No, say, "Put it out there and I'll read it."

♦ V: *What about with contracts?*

♦ SB: All you gotta do is read it! Don't sign nuthin' without read-

Please, ladies! Give the man some breathing room! Sam Butera (flanked by Dee Lannon on left) at Bimbo's 365 Club, 9-13-97. Photo: V.Vale

ing it—that's all I can tell you. If you don't understand it, take it to somebody who can explain it. Pay a few dollars. Then you won't get in trouble. Be ready and be prepared! Somebody gives you a job, man, just walk in there and don't be afraid.

♦ **V: When you were young, you engaged in "cutting contests" with other players—**

♦ SB: Oh yeah. I'd go *look* for jam sessions and musicians to challenge. "You got another saxophone player—I'm gonna cut him a new ass, man!" And I was prepared; I'd go look for them muthas.

You know fame isn't everything. It's doing what you enjoy doing and making people happy.

That helped me develop as a player—absolutely it gave me confidence in myself and my playing.

♦ **V: Maybe cutting contests will come back—**

♦ SB: [doubtfully] I don't know.

♦ **V: You pioneered a genre which combined Rhythm & Blues, rock'n'roll, Dixieland, and also personality-on-stage—**

♦ SB: And it all comes together and that's what people enjoy. It's a broad scope of music. People don't wanna be pushed with the same bullshit.

♦ **V: Your music appeals to all ages, from little kids to senior citizens. Whereas if you played music like Charlie Parker, only a few would understand—**

Hey, Boys! Louis, Sam and the Witnesses. Photo taken from the back cover of *Hey, Boy! Hey, Girl!*

♦ SB: Yes. An isolated group of people like Charlie Parker; mostly musicians. The average layman didn't understand what he was playing, because he never played the melody. There you go. Even today you got cats coming out with stuff that my wife or the average layman doesn't understand, even though he's playin' fantastic.

♦ **V: You emerged at a time when a number of saxophone players were coming out with a very thick, almost distorted tone—**

♦ SB: I enjoyed the playing of cats like Illinois Jacquet; he's one of the guys I learned a few things from. Coleman Hawkins—I loved the way he played. I listened to Charlie Parker a lot, I listened to Lester Young and Wardell Gray. I listened to so many guys, man, it's hard to say, "I like this guy better." Because each guy plays different; they got their own style. You can't say, "He plays better than him," because that's the way *he* plays. I play the

way *I* play. And that's it.

♦ **V: But that wonderful, thick tone—**

♦ SB: Well, you see . . . [chuckles] Let me tell ya something about that sound. When I was a kid and went to this music store for a mouthpiece, the salesman said, "This just came in from England." I said, "Let me try it." I went *"Toot!"* and said, "That's it!" I've played it ever since. That's the sound I wanted to hear. That completely changed my tone, and that's the truth.

♦ **V: What sax do you play?**

♦ SB: A Selmer Mark V or Mark VI—I can't remember. But it ain't the sax—the mouthpiece is the *thing.*

♦ **V: There are people who play a million notes in one minute like Charlie Parker, whereas your sax solos sound more like the human voice—**

♦ SB: My approach to jazz is to create something that people can understand. I can play *far out,* but I don't because I know they want to hear something they can relate to. I play a lot of melodic things. That's what I feel in my heart, so that's what I play.

I can't explain how I create these things; it just comes out. When you're playing jazz you can't go, "Well, I'm going to play this; I'm going to play that." No—it's gotta *happen.* You can't *plan.* And that's it.

♦ **V: Do you almost go into a trance state?**

♦ SB: Oh yeah. Yessir. But you gotta be playing with good musicians—that's Number One. If you don't have good players, then forget about it.

♦ **V: How do you get such a big sound with six musicians?**

♦ SB: That's the synthesizer; the voicing of the arrangements. The synthesizer is playing a harmony line to the instruments, like a string section. That's how you get the sound.

The Copa Cabana in New York was a very special place. If you played to standing room only, two shows, you were considered a star. You know what we did there? We played *three* shows a night during the week to standing room only, and *four* shows on Friday and Saturday. We were the hottest attraction in the world—but Louis wouldn't fly, so we never got to *reach out.* Then he and Keely Smith got divorced in 1961. So Louis and I went out alone together.

It's incredible what happened with this group. It was a happy thing. The people just adored Louis. And when I came into the band, I changed the whole format when I started writing all the charts. It made the band happy—*swingin'!* Nobody had that fuckin' sound.

♦ **V: You worked with Frank Sinatra—**

♦ SB: I worked with him for nine months; I was on tour with him as an opening act. We played Caesar's Palace; Camden, New Jersey; and all over doing one-nighters here and there. And he was always nice to me. I did a recording with him called *Stargazer.*

I'll tell you a story about Frank Sinatra. His pet peeve was: if he tells you to go out onstage and do 21 minutes, you better do 21 minutes. Not 22, 21. That's the way he was: "Sam, go out there and do 25 minutes." "Yessir." And I'm watching the time to make sure I don't go over. I didn't want to get him angry with me, because he was nice enough to have me with him.

I played with Sammy Davis, Jr, too; he was easy-going. He knew what he wanted, he told you, and he expected you to do just

Covers of *The Wildest Show At Tahoe* and *Hey, Boy! Hey, Girl!*, both on Capitol Records.

that. I used to hang out with him, sit down and pal around. Wonderful man, always great with me. I met Esquivel years ago when he worked at the Stardust Hotel in Vegas.

I worked with Danny Thomas; he was wonderful, too. You just can't say enough about nice people. No problems, boy. Long as you work with somebody and do what they tell you to do, and don't try to take over, then you'll get along very well.

♦ **V: *If you get the right musicians, you don't* have *discipline problems—***

♦ SB: No, you don't. I go out onstage and they know what they gotta do and they do it, man, and they have fun and the people

---

I'd go look for musicians to challenge. "You got another saxophone player—I'm going to cut him a new ass, man!"

---

laugh with them. Entertainment is making people happy—not them making *you* happy. I'm 70 years old; I can say what I want to say, and I do. But I don't make people angry; I have fun with them.

♦ **V: *You've been in feature films—***

♦ SB: I was in three movies: *Hey Boy, Hey Girl; The Rat Race;* and *Twist All Night.* There's a couple more I can't think of. We did the Dean Martin Show, Steve Allen, Mike Douglas, *A Current Affair,* Joe Piscopo, *Blast Off.* Movies: that's a waiting situation. You gotta remember your lines, and don't make people on the set angry with you. That's the whole key to it. But *be yourself*—that's what they want you for. You know the kind of part you're playing because of the lines you're learning, so you know how to act. That's about it with acting. I'm not an actor—

♦ **V: *You're a performer. What's the difference?***

♦ SB: You get before the camera, man, and a lot of times you hear, "Alright, shoot!" and forget every goddam thing. Whereas onstage, that's straight ahead; I don't worry about nuthin'. Cuz I know what I have planned, and if I want to add something I'll add it, and if I want to take it out, I will because we've got such a big "book." [repertoire] It has over 90 tunes in it.

♦ **V: *I missed you when you were playing with Keely Smith.***

Do you have anything to say about that?

♦ SB: No. I don't even want to *fuckin'* talk about it. Okay babe? Louis I loved.

♦ **V: *What do you think of Royal Crown—the zoot suits?***

♦ SB: That fits *them.* They look great 'cuz they all got the zoot suit effect and it looks fantastic. [slaps hand] It ain't one guy got fuckin' pants cut off *here* [gestures above knee] and another got pants cut off *there* [gestures below knee], y'know?

♦ **V: *How do you dress onstage?***

♦ SB: When I play, I wear a tux. The whole band wears tuxes: black. I think that looks sharp. Black bow-ties. White shirts. Black socks. Personally, I wear patent leather black loafers. And it makes a band look clean. That bullshit they got today dressin' is unbelievable. I see some of these groups and think, "Ah, man, give me a fuckin' break!" **V**

Sam Butera Discography

Albums, cassettes & CDs (solo):
The Big Horn, Big Sax & Big Voice, Wildest Clan, Atlantic City Special, Love Is In the Air, Body & Sax With A Little Soul, A Tribute to Louis Prima: Part I & II, Thinking Man's Sax, The Rat Race, He's Number One, Play It Again Sam, By Request, Live! Sheer Energy, The Whole World Loves Italians. (some are available for $20 each post-paid from PO Box 42395, Las Vegas NV 89116.)

Albums with Louis Prima:
The Wildest, Return of the Wildest, Wildest at Tahoe, Prima Show in the Casbar, Angelina, Blast Off, King of Clubs, Jungle Book, Prima '75, Prima Generation.

Other: Recorded and did arrangements for an album with Sammy Davis Jr, *Sam Meets Sam: When the Feeling Hits You.* Recorded *Stargazer* with Frank Sinatra, and did all arrangements for Louis Prima from 1954 on.

Film & TV appearances

Television: Johnny Carson Show, Merv Griffin Show, Jackie Gleason Show, Jerry Lewis Telethon, Dean Martin Show, Steve Allen Show, Mike Douglas Show, A Current Affair, Joe Piscopo Special, David Letterman Show, Paul Shaffer TV movie, Viva Shaf Vegas, plus many others
Film: *Hey Boy, Hey Girl* with Louis Prima, *The Rat Race* with Tony Curtis and Debbie Reynolds, *Twist All Night* with Louis Prima and June Wilkinson.

Sam's Book (repertoire of songs)

"Time Goes By," "Autumn Leaves," "Alexander's Ragtime Band," "Angelina," "Bill Bailey," "Bourbon Street Parade," "Body and Soul," "Buona Serra," "Can't Get Started," "Closer to the Bone," "Closing Medley" (all those songs I do toward the end of the show), "Chantilly Lace," "Clap Hands," "Cabaret," "Caldonia," "Do You Know What It Means To Miss New Orleans" (that's a medley with "Sleepy Time Down South"), "White Cliffs of Dover," "Exodus," "Exactly Like You," "For You," "For Once in My Life," "French Poodle," "Love Is A Five-Letter Word M-O-N-E-Y," "Felicia No Capecia [sic]," "I'm Just A Gigolo and I Ain't Got Nobody," "Greenback Dollar Bill," "Let the Good Times Roll," "Glowworm," "Hard-Hearted Hannah," "I'm Confessin'," "Jump Jive & Wail," "I Love You Just the Way You Are," "Josephina," "Kansas City," "The Last Dance," "Lazy River," "Love Is In The Air," "Mala Femina," "Misty," "My First, My Last, My Everything"; "Mari-youch," "I Love You More Today Than Yesterday," "My Love, Margie," "When a Man Loves a Woman," "Young Man With a Horn," "The Music Goes Round and Round," "The New Orleans Medley" ("Basin Street," "World on a String," "Night and Day," "Next Time," "Night Train," "Oh Babe," "Oh Marie," "Old Man Mose," "Old Man River," "Old Black Magic," "You Ain't No Ordinary Woman," "One Mint Julep," "The Prima Medley" (that's all those things you heard me do at the end of the show), "Pennies from Heaven," "The Pump Song," "Please No Squeeze-a Da Banana," "I'll Be Glad When You're Dead You Rascal You," "Romance Without Finance Is a Nuisance," "Rosetta," "Up Against the Wall You Redneck Mutha," "Robin Hood," "Sheik of Araby," "When You're Smiling," "Come Back to Sorrento," "St. Louis Woman," "Sunny Side of the Street," "Tiger Rag," "Turn Your Love Around," "They All Ask For You (The Monkeys Ask, the Cows Ask—Everybody)," "Them There Eyes," "I'm in the Mood for Love," "Three-Handed Woman" (She's right-handed, she's left-handed, she's underhanded, too), "The Dog" (How come my dog don't bark when *you* come around?), "I Got You Under My Skin," "Unforgettable," "Why Not," "Way Down Yonder in New Orleans," "Your Eyes Your Ass," "You're Nobody Til Somebody Loves You." Of course we have some new ones: "The Whole World Loves Italians," "On the Road Again," "Sunday Kind of Love," "This Love of Mine."
—We've got some more but I don't have them written down.

Set List (Bimbo's, Sept 13, 1997)

"When You're Smiling", "My Little Margie", "On the Road Again", "Just a Gigolo", "Tiger Rag", "Unforgettable", "Night Train", "Confessin'", "Oh Marie", "Louis Prima Medley", "Jump Jive & Wail"

INTERVIEW WITH BOB RUGGIERO

Jazz drummer Bob Ruggiero was born in New Haven, Connecticut and from the age of nine grew up in Los Angeles. He has played music professionally for two decades, and said, "I got offered more money from people like Engelbert Humperdinck and Wayne Newton. The main reason I'm doing this gig is because *I want to play with Sam.*"

♦ **VALE:** *How did you join Sam Butera?*
♦ **BOB RUGGIERO:** I saw Sam in Atlantic City in 1983 when I was playing with Freddie Bell (from Freddie Bell & the Bellboys). I was 23 and thought, "Man, I'd love to be in *this* band!" 1995 rolls around and I get a chance to audition for Sam. I was in Los Angeles at the time and I drove out to Vegas.
♦ **V:** *How did you hear about it?*
♦ **BR:** I played in Vegas a couple of months before that and heard that Sam's drummer (who had been with him for 20 years) was going to retire. I went to Vegas and auditioned and the next day Sam asked me to join. That was it; I moved. We played the Desert Inn with Keely Smith. And we're still touring constantly.
♦ **V:** *It's amazing Sam still plays, considering that he's 70. He's a role model—*
♦ **BR:** Yes, he is. He's very strong-minded. I've seen him do some incredible things. I've seen him drive ten hours on the road to a gig in L.A. and just be whipped, then come onstage and play like he'd just got up with all the energy in the world . . . and collapse after the show. When the curtain opens, Sam's got the energy. Yeah, he's incredible.
♦ **V:** *Someone said Sam mixes four genres: R&B, rock, vaudeville, and Dixieland—*
♦ **BR:** [laughs] The "vaudeville" thing is interesting. I'd have to say that's the comedy side of the show.
♦ **V:** *He really does relate personally with the audience. He makes eye contact and talks to people. I swear, he even said my name once onstage last night—*
♦ **BR:** Yeah, Sam makes everyone feel that he's performing just for *them.*
♦ **V:** *How do you learn a Sam Butera set?*
♦ **BR:** First you listen to reference tapes. You have the original Louis Prima arrangements that were done as far back as the '40s. Then you listen to a current tape or arrangement. From that you

> ### The main reason I'm doing this gig is because *I want to play with Sam.*

put in your own interpretations. So there's three approaches, and you pick out the best points.

Then you listen to how everyone in the band is responding to the way you're interpreting the arrangement, and see the boundaries of what you can play. All this is computed, thought about and processed . . . and you come out with an arrangement. And from night to night you may try different things. Or you might think, "Gee, that didn't work too well; let me do this differently." Also, a big factor is how good the other musicians are. If it's a really good band, you can play more creatively; a little more daring. If the band's mediocre, you have to hold everything together and can't test the waters that much. I think Sam's current band is probably the best he's ever had. I'm very happy to

Sam and Bob.

going on. So you have to do what drummers call "chopping wood": just keeping time, keeping it all together. There's a lot more freedom in a small band that's trying to sound like a big band than an actual big band.

♦ **V: What was it like when Keely Smith was with Sam? Is that a can of worms?**

♦ BR: Oh boy, yes it is. Let's put it this way: as a drummer, I love working with Sam as opposed to working with Keely. With Keely, I could be doing my taxes in my head while I was playing. She's a ballad singer. During the Desert Inn gigs in Vegas, she started not being able to hear herself for some reason, after doing a gig there for two years— which seems funny to me. All of a sudden she started putting plexiglass around the drums, a cover on the piano, and glass over the horns—it was sorta like, "Hmmm, she doesn't want to hear us anymore." It was strange; we had to play real quiet and laid-back; nothing like that energy you heard the other night. So after learning the material, there was not much to play.

♦ **V: Before I got into punk rock, I used to play Louis Armstrong's Hot Fives and Hot Sevens a lot. There seemed to be great freedom of improvisation, like everyone was soloing all the time—**

♦ BR: Exactly. Any song like that has a melody, then there's chord changes that they improvise over. So there is a structure, in a sense, but Dixieland is constant improvising, even underneath the melody.

♦ **V: From a musician's standpoint, this offers maximum freedom without having everything fall apart. And sometimes amazing polyphonies happen. I think that if musicians are good, even if they make a "mistake" they manage to control the problem really fast. What's your take on mistakes?**

♦ BR: If you come out of a certain solo and jump to the bridge or a different section of the song, a good musician will instantly know, "All right, I know where this is going now." And you process this: "Let's see, it was a long drive from the last gig, so we jumped ahead here and it can't be anything else." [laughs] You're thinking all of this in a split second and *everyone* just goes: "*Okay*—that's now part of the arrangement!"

Other musicians who are not as experienced would probably keep on playing, and you'd have a major conflict. Basically, it's just that they're not listening. A lot of musicians have tunnel-vision of the ears, so they keep plowing ahead. Sometimes someone like Sam just wants to go to a different section; he wants to cut short an arrangement. "Just a Gigolo" is one of our most-requested songs; we play it at every show. If we do two shows a night, sometimes Sam will start the song and just jump to the ending; maybe he's already done it a few times that night. We know exactly where he's at, within a beat, and it's different every night. You have to listen—no matter how many times you do the same material, you have to listen *all the time.* V

be a part of it.

♦ **V: There seem to be stretches where you can improvise—**

♦ BR: There's a lot of spaces where you can improvise, and there's times where you have to pull the reins back in. Some arrangements change every night. As far as the order of solos: it's often trumpet, trombone, then Sam; he's usually the last. Other times, he'll go through the whole band. So you have to keep your eyes and ears open. Last night at Bimbo's it was pretty wide open—that was a good example of Sam being in good spirits, with

---

Sam makes everyone feel that he's performing just for *them.*

---

a lot of improvising and creativity going on with the whole band.

♦ **V: Do you mean musicians surprising each other by playing some little thing no one had heard before?**

♦ BR: Exactly. That comprises about 30 to 40 percent of what you can do with Sam's arrangements. But there is also a set structure to the arrangement. That's what makes it great fun.

♦ **V: I assume everyone has the freedom to contribute suggestions, but if there's too much of that, it takes too long.**

♦ BR: Exactly. This is probably why Sam could keep musicians for 20 years: everyone is in the band because they can play well and Sam knows that and lets you play the way you want to. Everyone knows what they should be doing and *how much* they should be doing. So, there's a certain amount of freedom, and you know when to really stretch out and when to come back in. As far as how much drums I can play—it took a few months to test that. I kept stretching out further and further every night. [laughs] And Sam loved it, so I thought, "Great, this is the way I like to play, and I'm glad Sam likes it."

♦ **V: It seems like the band couldn't be better; everyone's so good—**

♦ BR: It's a fun band. If you have 15 horns like a typical big band, the drum rolls are simpler because there's so much else

Bob Ruggiero on Drums

I own several sets of drums. For miked situations in a large hall, like at Bimbo's, I use "Yamaha Recording Customs"—they have a very flat sound. At the Desert Inn in Vegas, where I'm not miked, I use my Pearl drum set; they project more naturally. However, I found a set of old 1956 Slingerland drums that are more reminiscent of the old Louis Prima/Sam Butera "sound," and I intend to start using them once we have a steady gig at the same place. When touring, I just rent Yamaha Recording Customs.

8¹/₂ Souvenirs

8½ Souvenirs L to R: Kevin Smith, Adam Berlin, Chrysta Bell, Olivier Giraud, and Glover Gill.

From Austin, Texas, 8½ Souvenirs have a unique, eclectic sound. The quintet was founded by French singer-guitarist Olivier Giraud, and includes Glover Gill (piano, accordion, kazoo), Adam Berlin (drums), Chrysta Bell (vocals) and Kevin Smith (bass). They have released three CDs to date, available from V/Search, 415-362-1465, Dept. RS). What follows are interviews with Olivier Giraud, Chrysta Bell and Kevin Smith.

INTERVIEW WITH OLIVIER GIRAUD

Olivier lives in Austin with his wife Yvette and their two cats, Bitty and Ptickette (a pun, sounds like "petite cat").

♦ *VALE: You're bringing in "The French Connection" to this swing movement, seamlessly integrating these diverse influences, and it all seems to meld together—*

♦ OLIVIER GIRAUD: That's because we don't try too hard! Individually, within ourselves, we all have different influences. I'm influenced by very different people: from David Bowie to Django Reinhardt, let's say, plus American roots music/rockabilly.

♦ *V: Did your family encourage you to be a musician?*

♦ OG: Nobody encouraged me—especially in France, where if you're a musician, you're really considered marginal. Your parents *might* encourage you to be a classical player—somebody who's "respectable." [laughs] If you're a *pluck-pluck* guitar picker, it's something you do on the side, but you have to have a real job!

I was twelve when I got my first guitar. I was on vacation on the coast and was hanging out at the swimming pool with a little girl-friend. The lifeguard had a guitar and was playing Elvis tunes and country songs. I was mesmerized—I just *had* to have a guitar. My parents said, "Okay, we'll buy you one." It was a cheap guitar, but it got me started. They didn't encourage me in any certain direction, but they wanted me to take lessons. They didn't give me a choice; they bought me the guitar and enrolled me in a classical guitar course—which I skipped, of course! I used to wrap a big bandage around my wrist and tell the teacher I couldn't play that day, and goof off for an hour until my mother picked me up.

♦ *V: How did you teach yourself?*

♦ OG: By listening.

♦ *V: So you were already collecting records?*

♦ OG: I had my parents' 45s. They listened to the EVERLY BROTHERS—for French people, they were pretty well-educated in American pop music. My parents also had BILL HALEY & the Comets, but no ELVIS. For my 12th birthday I got a 45 of "Blue Moon of Kentucky/That's All Right, Mama." In France the 45s have picture sleeves, and I looked at that cover of Elvis and said,

"Ohmigod, I want to be him!" So I started trying to play Elvis songs.

At the time I didn't even have any pocket money. But my parents saw that I had a passion there and wanted to help out, so every now and then I got a record—usually an LP. You've heard of LOS INDIOS TRABAJAROS' "Maria Elena"? That was a hit. They also had popular French music records. I started listening to all these styles mixed together, and to me it was an enchantment—I'd just gotten my own record player. I had my foot in the grown-up world, and that made the music even more striking to me. I also was fascinated by Serge Gainsbourg. Drugs and alcohol were associated with him—something really mysterious that I didn't comprehend.

♦ **V: He was "the rebel"—**

♦ OG: Yeah. His problem was: he was so darn ugly. Everybody wanted to hear his songs, but nobody wanted to *see* him! Some people joked, "We'd like to get him on TV, but you'd have to choose whether you want to see the right ear or the left." [laughs] It hurt him a lot that people were judging him so superficially. So he started writing songs for beautiful girls like Jane Birkin and Catherine Deneuve that became hits. Sometimes the girls could barely sing, but they still sounded very sexy. The songs and the lyrics were just tremendous—he was such a great writer. So I was hypnotized by Gainsbourg.

♦ **V: Did you learn his songs?**

♦ OG: Some of them, but he was a piano player writing for piano. It was not something you could easily pick up on guitar. Later, I learned more songs.

♦ **V: Did you have any friends who encouraged you?**

♦ OG: Not really. Actually, the only guitar player I encountered around school (none of my friends were musicians) was older than me, and when I would play he would just look at me like, "You worthless idiot!" Very discouraging. I never really had anybody to play with.

♦ **V: But you still kept playing—**

♦ OG: Of course! Then there was this big family catastrophe. My

Olivier's daughters, Cecile (b. Jan 31, 1989) & Juliette (b. Oct 29, 1990) in Paris, 1997.

parents were divorcing, my dad was drinking too much—it was a big mess. My little brother and sister were becoming sociopaths. So I left my parents' house. I didn't have a job. It was still the school year, so I remember . . . my parents were living right outside Paris, and I had to take the train every night to go back home from school. One night I just couldn't do it, so I slept in a train station and remained out on the street for awhile. Then I got a girlfriend.

♦ **V: What's your job history?**

♦ OG: As soon as I got out of school, I had a bunch of little jobs. I was a bellhop in a hotel—I wore a monkey suit and carried suitcases. Actually, my very first job was while I was still in school. I worked one summer just to buy a Vespa—actually, to pay for the *insurance* for one. I tricked my dad into buying it for me. He said, "If you pass your exam and switch to the next level, I'll buy you a Vespa." He was convinced that there was no way I could make it. Man, I just shifted down and took the damn exam and passed, because I wanted that Vespa so bad! It was a 50cc model—the

smaller body style. I was totally unaware of the Mods and the Who; to me it was just "the old days."

♦ **V: Well, they have beautiful design—**

♦ OG: Yes. I remember bringing a rental car with my father back to this Paris subterranean parking lot, and there was this beautiful, shiny, baby blue 125cc Vespa. It was as if a god had appeared in front of me! [laughs] From then on, I would ask my dad to bring me back Vespa catalogs and brochures. Then I passed the exam and got my Vespa. That summer my dad said, "But you know, you can't drive—you don't have insurance." I went, "I don't have any money." He said, "Well, you gotta work."

Olivier in 1965 modeling wool bathing suit.

So I began working on this farm, sprinkling plants with fertilizer and doing all kinds of jobs. But, I was traveling to work on my Vespa! I would bring a little picnic with me, and during lunch hour I would go in a neighboring field and set up this towel on the ground. I had a little Coleman stove and I would open a can and heat up some meatballs or something. It was really cool. This was all on my own, all by myself, so the memories are pretty strong—although I'm sure they're diluted!

When I got out of school, I became a bellhop for a few months. Then I got hired in a toy store. The owner was one of those rare fireworks masters. Every now and then he would get called and go with his wife and kids to do fireworks. They were this "swinging" couple, and they tried to drag my girlfriend and me into their swinging parties! This was a really weird period. I suspect my girlfriend kinda went into that, at one point! But she was beating me up, too, so I got away from her—after two years.

♦ **V: At least you found this girlfriend and had a place to stay right after leaving school—**

♦ OG: Exactly. That period was when punk was exploding, between '77 and '79. I turned 17 in 1978, and that's when punk was really accessible to everybody in France. There were tons of punk bands. I saw the DAMNED, the CLASH, SIOUXSIE, and the only concert the SEX PISTOLS did in Paris. That was pretty wild; there were fights all over the place. It was like nothing we had ever known before.

We all looked really trashy. In Paris it was the War of the Styles (or Categories). There were the Rockabilly Rebels; they had pompadours and wore leather jackets and brothel creepers. There were skinheads, and punks like myself. I remember being in the subway with my girlfriend. We were sitting on a bench waiting for a train, and on the other side, across the tracks, were these rockabilly guys and they were *big*. We started flipping them the bird and sticking out our tongues at them, and man, these guys jumped down five feet and started crossing the tracks toward us. My girlfriend and I ran for our lives! That was very scary.

I got in all kinds of trouble during those years. Somebody would come up and ask [belligerently], "What are you?" I'd reply,

"Well, what are *you?*" (You already know how it's going to end.) "You're a punk?" "Well, *whatever* . . ." "I hate punks"—*ping!* "Take that!"

♦ **V: Were you in a punk band?**

♦ OG: No. I was never really in a punk band; I was playing guitar by myself. Earlier, my family had gotten together with my grandparents and relatives and bought me an Ibanez copy of a Gibson J-200 for Christmas. (Elvis played a J-200 in his film *Loving You* [1957], but they were too expensive.)

♦ **V: You were living the punk life—**

♦ OG: Well, I didn't have any money. I didn't have much to look forward to. My family was dissolved. I had all the reasons to sink into the punk lifestyle.

♦ **V: Did you see IGGY POP in France?**

♦ OG: I was blown away; he put everybody in a trance! I knew about Iggy Pop because I was a fan of David Bowie. I think he got Iggy out of a lunatic asylum after Iggy shot Valium or something and freaked out. The punk movement for us was heavily tinted with Bowie: *Ziggy Stardust, Diamond Dogs. Aladdin Sane* was like a role model! I think Bowie was the precursor—or the curser! [laughs]

"Rock'n'Roll Suicide" had a freakin' orchestra. That's one of my favorite songs ever; that and "Five Years." I think if I had to pick a favorite songwriter, it would be Bowie. He's so diverse, smart, and takes risks—he's always on the edge. Bowie had his own sound. He always had wacky guitar players, like Carlos Alomar who is a very unusual guitar player.

Have you heard the very early Bowie ("David Jones with the Lower Third," or the "Mannish Boys")? Bowie led these bands in the '60s. I remember getting the 45s back then and I was blown away. The first album under his own name that I remember was *Images*. It was all beautiful songs you could listen to while drinking tea. Heart-ripping album. It's almost easy listening, but is written by Bowie, so it's definitely got a twist.

♦ **V: What were you doing for fun?**

♦ OG: We'd go to movies every week. For a year and a half we went to see, at least once a week, *American Graffiti, Taxi Driver, Phantom of Paradise,* and *West Side Story*. I know all the dialogue of these movies! That was part of our culture; part of how we educated ourselves. My girlfriend was always ready to go out—basically, we lived outside. We went to concerts all the time. We'd be at the front of Clash concerts making faces at Joe Strummer and going, "London's Burning! Shlaw Shlaw Shlaw!" because he had this pronunciation defect.

Olivier in Paris, "No Strings Attached," 1976

Back then I had this big acoustic guitar. I managed to save up enough money to buy a Stratocaster, but it turned out to be a fake! I loved it anyway. I got a big Fender Bassman amp that I never used because I didn't have a band. I would play things like "Rebel Rebel," but also tried to learn "Nouages" by Django Reinhardt. I gave up; it was just too difficult.

Gradually, as I was growing out of punk, I started to dig the old influences again, but from more of a guitar player's standpoint.

Olivier (third from left) with "the gang" in Paris, 1979.

That's how I became a big fan of Scotty Moore, a fascinating guitar player who had a pretty short career. He still plays occasionally, but he left Elvis to become a recording engineer very early. He played with Elvis from 1954-56, but the tours were too heavy for him—he had a family. Chet Atkins took over at one point and did a lot of sessions with Elvis in '57–'58. So Scotty Moore became one of my focal points; him and Cliff Gallup from Gene Vincent's Blue Caps.

As a guitar player, I was becoming good enough to actually *learn* the music. I still was pretty bad, but I had acquired the level of technique to "board" such pieces as "Race With the Devil" and "Be-Bop-A-Lula." I had an ear for music, and once a style or an artist entered my head, it would never really leave. So my appearance started shifting, gradually, without me suspecting it! I remember digging stuff out of the attic of my parents' house, right before my parents got separated. I dug out all these old clothes of my dad's from the '50s, and started wearing them. It was really mixed; I had baggy pants and white shirts and jackets and my hair was all greased up and dyed in various colors. It was really funky.

Then I started actively seeking out the old "stuff." I bought an old car and gradually I just got into the rockabilly thing. I have photos of me playing this big Epiphone arch-top "Emperor" guitar that I still have.

I started making money playing music in 1981.

♦ **V: What was your first gig? Or did you start out playing in the street?**

♦ OG: Oh yeah, I did a lot of that—if you consider *that* a gig! People give you a little bit of money and a lot of shit. Street musicians, especially back then, were not very popular at all. This was before artists got really aggressive about getting money from people. You'd just sit in a corner and play your music and people would give you money if they felt like it. It was illegal; you had to have a license to play in the subway. Playing in the street was tolerated, but if a cop walking by was in a bad mood, you'd get busted. I think every

guitar player and their dog has played in the street.

I played the Ibanez and sang songs like "Blue Suede Shoes" as well as songs by Bowie—pretty much everything that I'd figured out how to play. Very early on I figured out Everly Brothers' songs. I could speak a little English, but I was not even *close* to being able to figure out lyrics off a record, so I figured them out phonetically. It sounded pretty funny, actually.

Not long ago my sister got a tape from my father. My dad recorded us, every now and then, when we were talking or singing our little school songs. I heard "Love of My Life" by the Everly Brothers that my father recorded me playing a long time ago, and the "lyrics" sound ridiculous—they don't mean anything [laughs] but I am playing guitar and the chords are right. That's what's so amazing: the chords are right but the lyrics are completely wrong! I was 13 or 14 years old.

♦ **V: How did you get your first real gig?**

♦ OG: By accident I met somebody who I'm still very good friends with. In 1981 I was with a new girlfriend (thank god!) driving my first old car, a Simca Chambord (French replica of a '58 Chevy, but much shorter). On one of the rare occasions it was running, we stopped at a traffic light. Another old Simca pulled up next to us—the smaller model—and we looked over and saw these two cool-looking guys looking at us: "Hello!" So we parked on the curb and got out of the car and started talking. It felt like we were in *American Graffiti,* where people in old cars stop and talk. We introduced ourselves and it so happened I had champagne in my 'fridge, so I said, "Why don't you come back to our house and we'll have some champagne?" We went back to our house and opened up the champagne and talked, and it turned out we were all very compatible.

One of these guys was also named Olivier, and he introduced me to Thierry Le Coz of the Teen Cats. Thierry told me that Victor Leed, an awesome singer, was looking for a guitar player. I auditioned and he hired me on the spot.

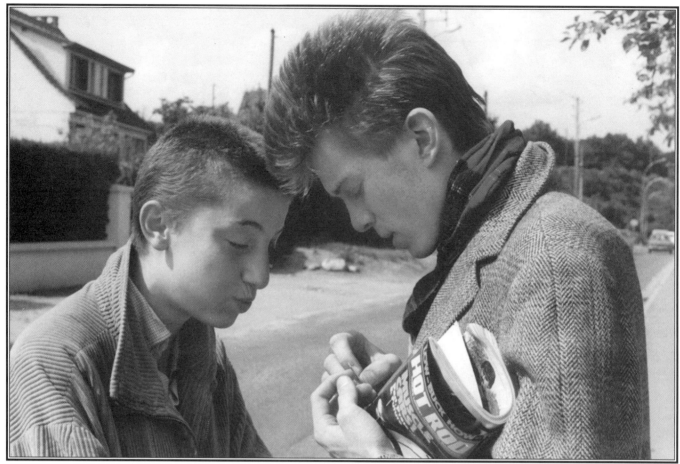

Olivier with friend in Paris, 1979. Note: *Hot Rod* magazine in hand.

♦ *V: What kind of material did you play?*

♦ OG: Elvis songs, so it just fell right in my niche—I already knew all of Scotty Moore's parts by the quarter-note! I had a guitar that was very similar to his: Epiphone's answer to Gibson's Super 400 that Scotty Moore was playing (or so I thought). He did play a Super 400, but his main axe early in the '50s was an ES-295, a goldtop with little flowers on the pickguard. So I had this big Epiphone and Victor went, "That's it—you're the guy!" The band also had an upright bass player and a drummer.

At first we played festivals and pretty big gigs—I remember

We'd play parties—not for the money but just for the sake of playing, because that's all we would do all day.

playing with Vince Taylor. Victor was a very good-looking guy, always dressed up in the coolest clothes. Then Victor, who was a non-smoker, non-drinker and very healthy, met this woman doctor who had a drug problem—she was shooting. He was totally in love with her, and sank with her. Then she died one night in his arms; by then he was already hooked. He went downhill, life became a nightmare, and that's when I left him. Victor was just impossible to be around; he was very erratic and often incoherent. He would get into these raging fits and the next second would be the most adorable guy. He made several attempts to put bands together. He died two years ago. So that was a big chunk of my youth just *pffft!*

♦ *V: But you didn't succumb to all this heroin use—*

♦ OG: No, I just kept my head straight. Maybe it's because pot always made me feel seasick, so I never went past that. I mean, I tried a couple of things, a couple of times, but it just was not my thing. I had to have my head together at all times. I'm really thankful that I had this attitude. When I was with that girlfriend who was kinda wacky—

♦ *V: The one who beat you up?*

♦ OG: Yeah, she would get on my case sometimes and she would never let go until we just got *physical*. She was strong, and I didn't want to hit her, so I'd get my ass whipped every time!

I was with Victor a solid year (but it was a *long* year). For me it was such an event. Suddenly I was playing with professional musicians on big stages and making serious money—all this thanks to Olivier and Thierry.

Around the end of '82, Thierry's second guitar player was leaving the band—he had just gotten married and was expecting a kid. These guys were young: Thierry was 17, the bass player was 18 and the drummer was 15 when I joined the band. (When I joined, they rebaptized the band "Casanova.") These guys already had a record out, were playing in festivals, touring and getting recognition from the public. I joined right when the band started doing national TV—I still have videotapes of the TV shows we appeared on. It's funny as hell when you watch them. We all looked so young and we're jumping everywhere, dressed really funky—it was cool.

♦ *V: Were you actually making a living playing music?*

♦ OG: I still had to have a job on the side. I worked for Texas Instruments when they started marketing "Speak and Spell" in France and that was a huge success. They also had "Magic Math." Another season I worked for Milton Bradley. I did this several years in a row. I would work for three months and make enough commissions to feed me for a year.

♦ *V: It's very hard to make a living as a musician—*

♦ OG: Especially in France. The other guys in the band were living with their parents—they were young.

I stayed with Thierry probably another year. One summer, at the *Fête de Musique* [music day when hundreds of musicians play at locations all over Paris], we did a big gig on Montparnasse. The band ended when Thierry moved to Austin, Texas. I was still in France, with no band.

I made a couple of attempts to form bands—that was when I started to write songs. I got a four-track cassette recorder and that took the place of playing with a band. I wrote songs and recorded them all by myself. I used my guitar to do the bass, borrowed a drum machine and a keyboard from somebody and got really fancy.

Right when I started playing with Victor, I met this really cool

---

Jackie made me sing "I'm Sorry" in the original Brenda Lee key, which is so high it's ridiculous. I pulled it off 'cuz I had to.

---

kid named Serge. He was 17 and I was about three years older. We hung out together, and like an idiot I talked him into quitting school—he was well on his way, anyway. He had a passion for the same kind of music I did, and was a record collector and guitar player. And he could *sing*. We started singing Everly Brothers songs together. By the time I left Casanova, he and I had a pretty tight thing together. We knew all of the Everly Brothers harmonies, and we both played acoustic guitar. So we'd play parties—not for money but just for the sake of playing, because that's all we would do all day. He'd come to my house in the morning and stay until five o'clock the next morning. All we'd do was play and sing.

I had met Alain, the singer for the Alligators, because the Alligators were on the same label (Big Beat Records) as Casanova, and the label took us both on tour to Algiers, along with Crazy Cavan and Freddy Fingers Lee. I met this pianist Jackie Guerard also, because he was playing with Crazy Cavan. Coming back from the tour, Jackie and his wife gave me a ride from the airport shuttle to my house. He invited me to play with him at Le Requin Chagrin, a restaurant near the Pantheon in St.-Germain on Rue Mouffetard.

I called Serge and asked him to come with me, and we started going there regularly. We were really good friends; we had the same sense of humor, and it was just a blast being together. Plus he could sing and play, so we definitely had a lot in common.

Jackie, the piano player who became a really good friend of ours, was playing with Alain in this restaurant on Rue Mouffetard. It's a very small place; the tables were literally set around the piano. Jackie started calling Serge and me up to the piano, and he accompanied us while we sang Everly Brothers songs. So we started singing in front of people, and believe it or not, we did that for over three years pretty much every night!

Jackie got another engagement in a restaurant a block down the street, Chez Felix. He would go early to Le Requin Chagrin, and at midnight switch to Chez Felix. We'd follow him and be part of his act. Serge was singing songs by himself, I was singing songs by myself, together we were doing Everly Brothers tunes, and Jackie would play old rock'n'roll standards from Jerry Lee Lewis and Elvis. The crowd would just eat it up. In between songs he would tell jokes and stories. For me this became a ritual I could not live without. I had gotten to know everybody, and both restaurants had such a warm and friendly bistro-like atmosphere. It seemed like everybody on the street knew us; it felt like I had a big family to replace the one I had lost. Every night I would dress up and go downtown and sing with Serge and Jackie.

♦ **V: How were you dressed?**

♦ **OG:** We were dressed fancy. This was the '80s, so there was a little bit of silliness, like fishnet socks and pointed shoes and bleached hair sticking straight up—that kind of stuff. I already had tattoos, and that added to the touch. My tattoo artist was Yvon, who worked right by the flea market at Clignancourt. I got tattooed in '82, '83.

So, Serge and I did this until 1987. That's when I learned how to really perform live, because we were playing for people who were eating. It was kind of a rich, blasé crowd, but we would perform well and make them laugh, and they loved it.

Jackie would put us in such situations. One night he asked me to sing "Lili Marlene." I did *not* know the lyrics, but he said, "Fake it!" I said, "Are you kidding?" He said, "Ah, just do a German accent thing." He sits me on a stool in front of everyone, takes his raincoat and wraps it around my shoulders, grabs this ice bucket shaped like a top hat and puts it on my head and starts playing the song. And then I had to do it! The only part I knew was the chorus, which I sang in a high voice while Serge and Jackie accompanied me in bass voices. I was scared to death.

♦ **V: That was a valuable apprenticeship—**

♦ **OG:** Yes. Jackie would have young people come up all the time and do some songs. He had magicians come in, too—you never knew what was going to happen. And he was an exquisite piano player; a big fan of Gainsbourg. He made me sing "I'm Sorry" in the original Brenda Lee key, which is so high it's ridiculous. I pulled it off 'cuz I had to. My voice was pretty high, so it was okay. We learned American hits; we did Fats Domino songs and all kinds of material.

I did not play much guitar during this time; I was really

Olivier (far right with cigarette) and Serge in Paris, ca. 1982.

singing. Every now and then we had to talk to the audience, because Jackie would look at us and say, "Why don't you tell these people the joke you told me before the show?" and I'd fumble to come up with a funny story. It was like being on the edge of a cliff! I would always bring my guitar, and every now and then he would have me play, but he had a theory that guitar and piano did not belong together. I think it's because I was not that great of a guitar player!

♦ **V: At that point you hadn't learned all the Django Reinhardt chords—**

♦ **OG:** But I was listening to Django, and it's the hardest thing there is. There's so much more involved than just "guitar playing," because what you're learning is not really a style. You're learning the approach to music that one guy had, so you really have to put yourself in his shoes and then let it flow out. It requires physical discipline.

♦ **V: Didn't he invent some difficult chords?**

♦ OG: Oh yeah. His music is very rich. He had an exquisite knowledge of music; he was a thorough musician although he couldn't write or read. But he just *knew*; he was an instinctive musician.

We also did a bunch of side gigs with Jackie where he would get contracts through his performances in the restaurant. People would come up to him and say, "Can you play this festival? Or this seminar?" We played a lot of big corporate parties. Jackie got his little troupe together and we'd all go play.

♦ **V: Did you have to play requests?**

♦ OG: All the time. That was difficult, especially if you didn't know the song! A lot of times it was a song you'd heard once or twice, and you'd just have to wing it. And the French public is *picky*. That was a lot of fun, and it lasted until '86 or '87.

Then there were changes. I was with somebody I had met in '84, and in '85 we separated for a year. Then in '86 we got back together and I "straightened up" and got a "real" job. I stopped going out as much, and we had two kids.

♦ **V: I can understand that pressure to get a real job—**

♦ OG: I can only say it was a real job now, because I kept it for three years. It was for a small car rental company that had several agencies spread around Paris. I kept getting raises and doing my job right, and was really enjoying it and making good friends. I'm still very good friends with a couple of the people.

Everything I did was associated with pretty wild stuff. The routine was so funny. We all were buddies and were spread out around the outskirts of Paris in different offices. We had one hour for lunch. We'd all leave at five to noon and race down to the central agency, which is south of Paris. We'd all get there at five past and go to this restaurant that we called "the Annex," because that's where we'd be if we weren't at the agency. It was a North African restaurant that served merguez (North African sausages) with green beans and french fries, and we'd kill a bottle of red wine *each*. Then we'd race back to the agency—we drove like maniacs. When we got back, we'd be real drunk and still have to perform our jobs. A bottle of wine for one person—you have to have some *training!*

We had this technique which we called EOTF, which stood for "Exploitation Optimale de Toutes Les Files," (Optimal Exploitation of All The Lanes, referring to the highway). When we were driving back we had to haul ass. It was 12 kilometers between the two agencies, and I covered it in six minutes (an average of 70–75 mph in town)! We were driving fancy company cars. Some of us were more crazy than others.

There's a big park east of Paris called le Parc de Vincennes, with a lake. One afternoon after having a good lunch, six of us went there and rented two rowboats. Then we started playing

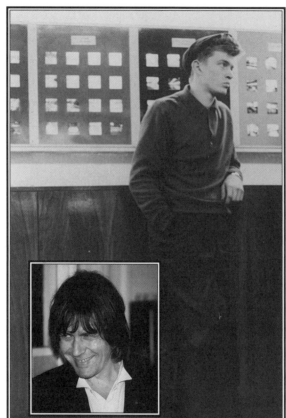

Olivier at the "Ford France" plant in Poissy, 1982. Olivier at the "Ford France" plant in Poissy, 1982. Insert: Jacky: Olivier & Serge's mentor, RIP.

"pirate." Eventually both boats flipped over, and we were all yelling and screaming, trying to get to the shore. They fined us by keeping our deposit, but I would have paid *two* deposits for the fun we had! That was the kind of atmosphere we had with our co-workers—they were all really cool guys and girls.

♦ **V: So you did this for three years and had two children. You probably didn't play much music—**

♦ OG: Not much, although I started playing a little bit of Django. But I was mainly working. We had our first kid in '89. That was after I had started coming to Austin. Let me explain: my girl-friend and I bought this 1954 Oldsmobile Rocket 88—it was beautiful. Then I got in a wreck; an 18-wheeler ran over the rear of the car! So I took two weeks off to go to the U.S. and get parts for it. November '88 I came to Austin and was blown away! I said, "Okay, I'm moving." Olivier and Thierry and all these guys I knew had moved there from France—the American Dream had beckoned. People are very friendly, the music scene is so accessible it's ridiculous. There's a university near-by that provides a very diverse cultural atmosphere. My girlfriend and I had a lit-tle bit of money put aside, so we decided to invest it. We started buying cars in America and shipping them over to France. But that took so much of our time that eventually she had to be there and I had to be here. Also, we had anoth-er kid in October, 1990: a girl. We were both going back and forth and eventual-ly she met somebody else. *Yeah . . . not good.* That was in the summer of '91.

♦ **V: Had your guitar skills gotten a bit rusty during the three years you worked for the car rental company?**

♦ OG: Kinda. But when I started going to Austin, I began playing again—in March '89 I joined a group called 47 Indians. I met Mark Rubin, who had just moved to town at the end of '89. He was the bass player for the Bad Livers—back then, he was the bass player for Killbilly. He lived on the couch of the house I was sharing for awhile. He loaned me a tape of Django Reinhardt. I was listening over and over to this and it started *working* on me. I began playing that music by ear; I don't read music. But it all made sense after awhile.

♦ **V: So, you're trying to maintain your musical career while dealing with your domestic crisis—**

♦ OG: The band was really getting tired of me going away all the time. So, I'm returning to Austin with my heart between my legs, feeling really painful and sad, and I find that the band has ousted me. I thought, "*Whatever*—I'm going to roll with the punches." If there was one point in my life that I touched the bottom, it was then. That was the toughest. Here I am, leaving everything behind, and I don't have any choice. At that point all my stuff was in Austin; I'd almost completely moved there, thinking we were all going to move, and all of a sudden this happens. I've already started a band, I have an apartment and a car. Also, being in Paris became torture, because everything reminded me of the life I did-n't have anymore.

So, I kind of talked my way back into the band, sharing a spot with this second guitar player. Then the legal immigration thing starts hanging over my head. I entered the country legally, so I'm not totally illegal, but I ended up being overstayed.

At the end of '91, I met Yvette, whom I started to hang out with, and things eventually became much more serious. She was born in Fort Worth and grew up in Dripping Springs—a *real* Texan!

♦ **V:** *What did you do in 1992?*

♦ OG: I just played with 47 Indians. At the beginning of '93 an agent got this contract to play a month in Helsinki, Finland, in a restaurant-club. When I came back from Helsinki, Yvette and I moved in together. Simultaneously, 47 Indians ceased to exist, so I had to get a job. I had gotten a one-year work permit for that engagement with 47 Indians, so I became a cab driver. During 1993, from February to September, I did nothing but drive a cab like a monster night and day, double shift. I was not playing music at all. But in my head there was this sound and this concept that I wanted to realize. So in August I called this friend and said, "Look, I want to do something that *I* want to do, not something that somebody else has asked me to do. If I'm going to do cover songs, I want to do cover songs that *I* really like." And I was really into Fellini and Nino Rota's music, Gainsbourg and Django. I wanted to combine these styles with the American music I liked, including swing from the '20s and '30s—

♦ **V:** *Oh, you somehow managed to discover that, too—*

♦ OG: That was because of my parents' records. I just loved the sound that the swing bands had in the '20s; it was so driving, *before* the whole "sweetening" period. I had some early Louis Armstrong on a jazz collection called *Storyville*. I really never was "exclusive," as far as listening to music went. Whatever my tendency of the moment was, I still always listened to everything else. When I was into rockabilly, I had to hide my David Bowie records because people wouldn't understand! [laughs]

Anyway, there was a band in Austin called the Jazz Pharoahs and I had sat in with them many times. They were a quartet doing old swing standards, with a clarinet player. I called the singer-guitarist, Tony Brussat: "Look, I want to start a band that combines all these sounds. Do you know somebody who wants to do this?" and he said, "*I'll* do it." To me, it was perfect—I loved the way he sang and he was a great guitar player, too.

We started playing together in the summer of '93. An old

Olivier when he was playing with Victor Leed, ca. 1981.

friend of Kevin's named Todd Wulfmeyer had just moved to town, and he came to my house. I told him about my project. There was this upright bass that a friend had left behind, and Todd saw it and went, "I always wanted to play one of those." And he was a very good blues and rockabilly guitar player. I said, "Well, why don't you pick it up and play with us?" So he did! We'd get together at Tony's every week and play, kind of looking for ourselves, really. We learned some Al Jolson songs, a lot of Django songs, some movie soundtracks—a lot of different mater-

ial with just two guitars and an upright bass.

Then Todd brought in a drummer from Detroit named Adam Berlin. He was staying with Todd and looking for a place to live. He liked what we were doing and we said, "Do you want to play with us?" That's how we started. We needed a name, and Tony came up with "8½ Souvenirs" after the Fellini movie and all the

L to R: Lee Rocker, Olivier, Brian Setzer, Victor Leed, Thierry Le Coz, Slim Jim, 1983.

memories that get conjured up. It's got everything in it—it's an autobiography, you know. Also, there's a Django Reinhardt song called "Souvenirs" and I think that was one of Tony's favorite French words. So that's how the band was born. It's been four years since then.

♦ **V:** *You mentioned Al Jolson—*

♦ OG: He was the king of Tin Pan Alley. Tony really wanted to do a song called "Dixie": "Is it true what they say about Dixie?" So that's one of the first songs the Souvenirs did. Jolson painted his face black and wore white gloves and pretended he was black.

♦ **V:** *Hey—are you still in touch with Jackie?*

♦ OG: Jackie died two years ago of throat cancer, all alone in his hospital room. Serge saw him just before he died. Jackie really was our spiritual father, musically.

♦ **V:** *The personnel of the Souvenirs has changed, except for Adam and yourself—*

♦ OG: The members all left for good reasons that were not necessarily related to the band itself. Tony left the band because he moved to Washington, D.C. Kathy Kiser left the band because she got married to a French guy and moved to Florida. When Juliana Sheffield left, it was because she wanted to have a solo career. Todd left because touring was wearing him out, and he wanted to spend more time with his wife—they had just bought a ranch.

♦ **V:** *Touring is very stressful—*

♦ OG: I have a hard time with it, too, but it comes with the territory, unfortunately. Since this band is really about constant evolution, switching members is just part of evolving. Each member brought their own influences and style and the band kept shifting. When Glover Gill joined, he not only brought in piano but accordion. He got the idea to play kazoo from hearing "Come Di" by Paolo Conte, an Italian singer-songwriter who plays piano and tours Europe and the U.S. occasionally.

♦ **V:** *When you played Bimbo's, your first number, "Kazango," was full of shimmering textures and sounds, almost Exotica-feeling, summoning everybody to the jungle. Did you have a synthesizer? Where did all those sounds come from?*

continued on page 76

♦ **V: I read that Django Reinhardt only had two working fingers (plus thumb) on his left hand, due to a fire. Also, that his approach to guitar was not vertical, but horizontal—**

♦ OG: That's called "linear fretting." His technique was not *strictly* linear; he played a lot of arpeggios, playing cross-neck across the fingerboard. I think that's called the "cross-board" (or "cross-neck") technique, as opposed to "linear." He also used more harmonics than any other guitar player I know of; whole chunks of solos were played in harmonics. (That's not easy.)

After Mark Rubin loaned me a tape of Django, I went back to Paris in the summer of '91 and got my first "Django" guitar, a Favino. Jacques Favino was a luthier who started his business in 1946 fixing guitars. He built the first European arch-top with f-holes. At the time, the only affordable French jazz guitars were Selmers.

We're not in an era where decisions are easy, because we have *too* many choices— back then, those guys had only one choice: take it or leave it.

Henry Selmer was a businessman. His partner was Mario Maccaferri, who collaborated to create a certain style of guitar in 1932. From 1932–33 they refined the concept: a big d-shaped soundhole with an inner wooden resonating chamber. Later on they had to give this up, because the glues were poor quality and the inner chamber would loosen and start rattling, and this was impossible to fix unless you took the whole guitar apart. Between '33 and '34, Maccaferri came up with the tiny oval soundhole design. These were archtop guitars. They made flattops, too, but the model we're interested in is an archtop with a tailpiece.

In 1934, Maccaferri left the partnership and Selmer continued making guitars with the oval soundhole, the d-hole and also a tenor model. The oval soundhole had 14 frets out of the body, the d-hole had 12 frets. The D-hole was more for rhythm guitarists, and soloists preferred the oval soundhole, because it would project better and had better tone— that's what Django played. His two rhythm guitarists played the D-holes.

Being a luthier, Jacques Favino received a lot of Selmers to fix. In 1946, when he opened his business, he started making his own models inspired by the Selmers. Joseph Reinhardt, Django's brother, would bring the family Selmers to him for repairs and restoration, so it's very possible that Favino worked on Django's guitars, but he certainly worked on Joseph's guitars. Eventually Joseph switched to Favinos because the guitars were better: they were made by one guy with better materials. They were a little more expensive.

Also, Selmer quit making guitars. In 1952, Jacques Favino was building Selmers from parts for Jean Beusher's Paris music store which had bought all the remaining stocks. Django bought his last Selmer in 1940, Model #503, and played it til the end of his life. Joseph was playing Favinos; he had a steel-string classical with a tailpiece that he liked a lot.

Favino kept on making guitars: 6-strings, 12-strings, archtops, flattops, plus a couple of upright basses. In 1983 his son Jean-Pierre took over and carried on the tradition. He actually improved models and created his own, including the "Verseau." It's one body with two opposed necks; you have to flip the guitar over to play either neck—each side is a different guitar with its own soundhole. So one side can be for classical and the other can be for jazz! It's amazing how different both sides sound—it's like playing a different guitar.

With Jean-Pierre it's just one guy doing everything, whereas most of his competition involves teams. When it comes from one brain and one set of hands, it's much more coherent. I tried other copies, and the Favinos are the best. They cost about $4000, but he's giving me a "deal" because we're good friends; I'm sort of representing his line in the U.S.

Anyway, I'm playing a Jacques Favino guitar made by the father. The way I got it was kinda weird. I came back to Paris that summer, after I started listening heavily to Django. I was still playing my big archtop Epiphone "Emperor." Serge took me to this club outside of Paris to see this French jazz guitarist who plays Django material. He was playing this Barney Kessel guitar which normally has one short, pointed cutaway, but his had *two* cutaways—it had been customized for him because he was left-handed. But he played with the strings mounted for a right-handed player. He played beautifully.

I went up to this guitarist and talked to him: "You know, I'm looking for a guitar like Django had," and he said, "This friend of mine, Marie-Ange, is a jazz guitar player. She's selling her Favino. Man, this guitar sounds like an airplane!" (which is a French expression for "it sounds great.") I visited her and it sounded awesome. She had bought it new from Beusher in the late '50s, and she sold it to me for $1,000. It was a Favino with encased metal tuning keys, thin metal tailpiece, etc.

♦ **V: Did that guitar improve your playing?**

♦ OG: Right away—sudddenly, everything was possible! The instrument you play becomes part of you. Actually, it's not an easy guitar to play, but I got used to it, and psychologically it was a complete boost.

Nowadays, a Selmer guitar lists for $25,000, and to get a good guitar of that style (but another maker), you have to spend $3,000-5,000. Finding the guitar for $1,000 was a miracle—anybody who played it just freaked. It's got such a deep sound and it's very accurate. That was a turning point for me—that and because I started playing acoustic. My Epiphone "Emperor" had three single-coil pickups built in, so I had to rely on an amp. With the acoustic, I can take my guitar anywhere and don't have to plug it in.

There's an amazing guitarist named Cal Collins who used to work with Benny Goodman, among others. He's in his fifties and has a great sense of humor. I attended a workshop he gave where he was playing an amplified archtop with f-holes. I had brought my acoustic, and he asked me to sit in with him—I felt so honored. We did a Django song together and I didn't feel disadvantaged at all—I just hit the strings harder! It worked out just fine.

It was a turning point when I started trying to get out of an acoustic guitar what I could get out of a more-easy-to-play electric. That was a big jump—I can't put enough emphasis on that. My whole body shifted.

♦ **V: How do you amplify that acoustic to play concerts?**

♦ OG: You can put a microphone in front of the guitar, but then you can't move! I tried using a De Armond violin pickup—it sounded good but didn't get loud enough. I also invented a set-up using a little lavalier microphone from Radio Shack fitted into construction foam. Since the microphone was right inside the core of the guitar, the strings were actually overdriving the mic a little bit; it had this sustain and gave me this "vintage recording" sound, very mid-rangy and cool. However, I couldn't get much volume without feedback.

When we started playing larger rooms like the Continental (300 people), I made a drastic change and switched to a purely electric sound—which is something Django did. From '43 on, he was usually recording with a French-made Stimer pickup on his guitar. I have one, actually.

♦ **V: No surprise there!**

♦ OG: From being around jazz guitarists, I knew that the De Armond "Rhythm Chief" pickups existed. Finally I found a 1952 model. I stuck it on my guitar with putty and it worked—I can play it really loud and it doesn't feed back. There's a volume knob attached to the wire of the pickup, but I'm usually full volume the whole time. One World Music, which is above the Continental Club, found it for me two years ago. In Houston I bought another one as back-up, in case something goes wrong. You can still find these because they're not very sought out—not yet, at least.

Two years ago I bought another guitar from One World Music that was the same as Django bought when he was here in the U.S. in '46. It's a small-size Epiphone Zephyr Deluxe, and it's one of my favorite guitars. It's light, it sounds incredible—it's a beautiful guitar. It's a non-cutaway f-hole archtop with one pickup next to the bridge, which gives the sound a lot of "bite." (When you move the pickup it changes the sound drastically; it's not the same guitar.) One World knew I was looking for this kind of stuff, and one day they called: "You need to come to the store." I asked, "What do you have?" and they said, "Just come in!" So I went there and freaked—I bought it on the spot. It was cheap, too: $750. This was a pre-war model, probably 1938, and older than the one Django bought.

♦ **V: Don't they get better with age?**

♦ OG: Six years over 50-some years—I don't think it makes a big difference! I played it on our first album, *Happy Feet.* I kept the Epiphone for about a year and then gave it to Serge because I knew there was no way he could find this kind of guitar in France affordably, and I knew he would appreciate it. I'm still looking for another one. It was blonde, beautiful and in immaculate shape. It had hardly been played, and it was the *same* as Django's—a big plus for me, as stupid as it may seem. These are some things you just can't help! And it had the electric Django sound; you could get that sound out of it, no problem. Part of it was because it had the pickup so close to the bridge—not your traditional jazz guitar sound.

♦ **V: What about amps?**

♦ OG: To my knowledge Django owned two different amps: Stimer amps, made by the same people who made the pickups he used. Django did not care much for equipment; he just took what was handy! His contract with Selmer said he had to use Selmers exclusively, so that's all he used. He never really tried anything else, or if he did, he didn't like it very much. It's not well-known, but on some acoustic sessions he played an acoustic Hofner. He played his Epiphone but I don't think he liked it very much.

But when he came to the U.S. he bought the Epiphone, and he also got an Epiphone Electar amp—I happen to have a 1946 Electar right here! There's a photo of Django in the U.S. playing through the exact same amp. So I play this, and I also have two small brand-new amps for the road, that I can ding around. They're all-tube Peavey Classic 30s. I use them a lot, so I always have a spare. I get a lot of volume out of these 30-watt amps because they're going through the P.A.—they put the microphone in front, and that's it.

I really like the tone of the little Epiphone amp; it has bigger tubes so the sound is warmer. Mine cost $300; however, the speaker and some of the electronics were busted. But the blonde wood case was in excellent shape. It has a wood grille in the shape of a capital "E" with a lightning bolt through it, with three horizontal and two vertical lines. It looks like an old radio. The company, Rola, who originally made the speaker, was bought by JBL. I sent it back to them and they rebuilt the speaker with the original paper filter and the same wiring material, and sent me back the speaker brand-new as if it had come from the factory 50 years ago.

I took the electronics to "Music Makers" in town. They found old capacitors that matched the original ones, and restored the electronics. The speaker board inside was busted, so I cut out a new piece of wood and got some matching fabric to stretch behind the grill, like on an old radio. Now it's restored to perfect condition—it works great. But I don't want to travel with it!

♦ **V: Do you have a preference for picks?**

♦ OG: Definitely. I use very stiff picks that are not bendable, about one sixteenth of an inch thick. Actually, I use two kinds of picks. My favorite is a French brand that is distributed by Dunlop: Dugain. They are made out of either bone, ebony, horn or coconut, and are very thick and ergonomic—they actually have a curve to them. At their thickest they're 1/8″. But these picks are $14 apiece! If I play on a stage that has wood

slats, I use Dunlop Jazz nylon picks which I buy by the hundreds. I give them away or lose them; I don't care. But I prefer the feel of the Dugain; that's what I record with. They have this really "fat" tone.

♦ **V: I may as well ask you about the strings—**

♦ OG: There's a brand you're supposed to use for these kind of guitars and this kind of sound: Argentine. They're French strings—supposedly Django used them all his life. But if you look closely at old photos, Django used banjo strings a lot! If you look at the tailpiece where the strings are attached, they have loop ends with fluffy things wrapped. In black-and-white photos you can see this very clearly—my friend Michael from Houston pointed that out. Why Django did this I don't know, but they certainly sound different.

Olivier with Casanova in Algier, 1983. Note spectators.

Argentines are very expensive; you can only find them in France where strings are very expensive. They have the most beautiful acoustic tone you can get, as far as steel strings go, and only come in two gauges: light and extra-light. We call them reds (light) and purples (x-light), because they have colored thread wrapped around the loops at the ends—that's how you can tell the gauges apart. Also: they don't last long.

However, a guy in Santa Cruz, California, started making great reproductions. He added a stiffer gauge, plus a "Gold Series" string which not only has the acoustic qualities of the Argentines, but is responsive to the magnetic pickup so they amplify better. I use these. But sometimes I just buy D'Addarios. [laughs] They're everywhere; you can close your eyes and find them anywhere you go. And they're very cheap: two sets for $8. But if I really want the good acoustic sound, I go for Argentines or the Guadalupe Manouchetones from Santa Cruz. They're $6.50 a set, and Argentines are $12 a set. This musician found enough people in the United States to justify making them—"enough" probably means 10 or 20. They're fantastic, the strings last longer, and they're only available by mail order so there's no middle-man markup.

I clean my guitar on a regular basis with lemon oil with no alcohol (very important; alcohol dissolves the varnish). It acts like a soap, but also maintains the wood. It balances the pH on the surface of the guitar and keeps it stable—plus, it makes the guitar look pretty and shiny.

♦ **V: You have to work with the material universe to get the "spiritual" tones you want—**

♦ OG: It's not being particularly "picky" wanting this or that, it's wanting what's appropriate for what you're doing. It's a long process, determining what you want. The hardest for me—and it's still ongoing—is the *tone* (especially when you play electric; it's crucial). We're not in an era where decisions are easy, because we have *too* many choices—it's confusing. Back then, those guys had only one choice: take it or leave it.

Information has to circulate so fast now, it lacks accuracy. In the process, the ability to analyze and decipher fades. Everything works as slogans; short messages that can be grasped really quick, so you get the point right away. As soon as you start trying to explain something to somebody in detail, you put them to sleep. All of the above is to say that at one point I switched to electric because it was necessary.

♦ **V: Now you have the volume you need for larger venues like Bimbo's. Without all this research, you couldn't have moved to the next level, so to speak—**

♦ OG: And it's important, because I can really do what I want. I'm much freer to play what I want to play. I have to compete with a piano, drums and upright bass. It's also great because it allows me to play my guitar of choice without having to compromise. But I learned one thing: you can't just buy pickups, stick them on a guitar, and expect the tone to come out. You really have to fiddle around for awhile. **V**

continued from page 73

♦ **V:** *How did you add your pianist?*

♦ OG: I had wanted a piano player because after playing all these gigs as a trio, I would get really tired of just hearing guitar. I needed something to expand the sound, and piano just completed everything. I actually met Glover a long time ago when I was playing with 47 Indians. Occasionally he would come to our regular gig at the 311 Club and sit in. One day he sat in with us at our Continental Club Happy Hour, and the next week played a few more songs. The week after, I spent hours at his house teaching him the other songs. Eventually he played one set, then two sets, and finally he was part of the band!

♦ OG: I don't know. We all try to get the most out of our instruments. When I play guitar, I try not to play "typical guitar." Sometimes I play octaves, which can have a horn sound. Maybe it's the voicings of our chords.

♦ **V:** *What does "Kazango" mean?*

♦ OG: It's the name of a bird. It came from a British comic strip I ran across a long time ago when I was in England. My girlfriend at the time brought me a comic strip where this little guy shoots a bow using a snake as an arrow. He stiffens it and shoots it toward a tree. "Kazango" is the sound the snake makes when it goes through the tree. When I first came to Austin, Shaun Young of High Noon let me stay at his house (I'll be eternally grateful for that) and I wrote this song while doing the dishes there. The melody was running through my head, so I dried my hands and took my guitar and recorded it.

♦ **V:** *Maybe we should leap back in time to the first Souvenirs' gigs—*

♦ OG: They were not real gigs, they were just lucky breaks we got from friends like High Noon or the Timber Wolves who let us sit in. The first real gig, when somebody actually hired the band, was at a little coffee shop called Flipnotics. The ground floor sells vintage clothing and accessories, and upstairs is a coffee shop that has live music and an outdoor patio. It's very friendly and has an "alternative" feel.

Our second big break was a weekly Wednesday "Happy Hour" (6:30 to 9:30 PM) at the Continental—that's really what launched the band. It was very stimulating; people started to believe in us. When we started, there were five people in the audience—our buddies! We were doing Federico Fellini soundtracks, Django songs, French songs and nobody knew about this music. Gradually, people who rarely went out started coming to our shows, and people unfamiliar with the music started seeking out the original records. Back then you couldn't find music like that easily, but now the local Waterloo Records has an extensive selection of Django CDs and Nino Rota's soundtracks. You can also find a lot of Gainsbourg, which you couldn't find before because there was no demand.

The Continental is a great Austin club. Steve Wertheimer, the owner, is one of the most popular club owners in Austin. He's very educated, very fair, and always treats musicians well. He's always ready to give a chance to new projects; very open to anything new—he takes risks. He had a partner, Jack Hazzard, who saw one of our first gigs and really liked it. I think he could appreciate the music because he spent a lot of time in Europe. Jack and Steve had produced an album for The Naughty Ones on their Continental Records label, and even though Jack was not really "into" the record business, they started to invest a lot of energy into us. Sometimes I wonder what the band would have become, had Jack not come along—maybe nothing at all!

Glover Gill on piano with accordian standing by. Photo: V. Vale

I've always compared this band to a mill with an open door. Anybody can walk in, and if the flour we put out is good, they stay. If the bread is good, we keep the ingredients.

♦ **V:** *So it was Glover's idea to bring in the accordion—*

♦ OG: Actually, it was my idea. Mark Rubin offered me this large Scandali accordion he had. This was in December, and I thought, "The band'll buy it for Glover as a Christmas present." He eventually discovered that the big model was limiting, and bought a smaller one.

♦ **V:** *It seems that in 8½ Souvenirs, everyone can utilize the maximum of their musical abilities—*

♦ OG: That was exactly the concept: so everybody could do what they *need* to do, what they feel like doing, without having some part laying low and unexpressed. To me, it's the ideal conditions for playing music.

♦ **V:** *And if the band's too large, individuals can't improvise as freely—*

♦ OG: Exactly. Pretty much everybody writes songs; it just takes a little bit of time for everybody to get used to how we're all working, respectively. That's gradually falling into place, and it's a good feeling.

♦ **V:** *How was "Bei Mir" brought into the mix?*

♦ OG: This was one of my favorite Andrews Sisters' songs; it's a Yiddish song. I used to do it by myself before our second girl singer, Julie, came into the band. She started singing it with me.

When we started, there were five people in the audience—our buddies!

♦ **V:** *Talk about "No lo Visto"—*

♦ OG: "No lo Visto" is just an Italian phrase I heard in a French movie; it means "I haven't seen it; I don't know what you're talking about." I just built the song around this phrase. It's about a guy in a bar in Italy who's wondering why his girlfriend left him. Then he sees this little guy at the bar who's staring at him. He's kind of drunk, so he goes up to this guy and asks him for a remedy for his sorrow. The guy indeed gives him a word of wisdom, which is, "Stay away—don't get involved."

It's funny, because I can start writing a song from many angles. It can have a story, a general idea or concept, or it can be just a hook in my head that I can't get rid of—that was the case with "Cognac." It's usually hard to write a song; I have to put a lot into it. But that's not always true, because "Souvonica" took just five minutes to write! That was another little hook I had—completely Nino Rota-ish. If you listen to "No lo Visto" and "Souvonica," the instrumental breaks are similar. For the lyrics to "Souvonica," I just made up a language using Italian, French, German, Spanish and English words. We called this language "Souvonics" (after "Ebonics")! It's the Souvenirs' language.

♦ **V:** *Americans could use a dose of multilingual ability—*

♦ **OG:** Different languages express things with such different pow-

> ## I really consider the saw as *an acoustic theremin* . . . probably the most enjoyable instrument I've ever played.

ers and notions induced. It feels good to be able to use different languages, because your range of expression broadens instantly.

About three years ago, I joined a band in Austin called the Asylum Street Spankers (and along the way picked up the musical saw). That was a big challenge for me, because I found myself being part of the rhythm section, playing mainly rhythm guitar. This allowed me to really improve my rhythm technique. It's a 10-piece band, all acoustic, no microphones. I'm playing fully acoustic with them, and the rhythm guitar definitely has to cut through.

I always thought that rhythm guitar was just as hard, if not harder than solo guitar. Playing with the Spankers really gave me the opportunity to become a rhythm guitar player who's *necessary* to the rhythm section. And since I have fewer and shorter solos, it improved those as well. The Spankers have songs that actually feature me as an acoustic guitar soloist, and for me it's heaven—it's a delight; it's wonderful.

♦ **V:** *Short solos have to say a lot in a short time—*

♦ **OG:** Exactly; it's pretty intense. And it's acoustic, so physically it's very challenging. You really have to dominate the guitar when you're playing against nine other people without amplifi-

cation, and still get the idea through to the audience. The Spankers have three CDs out, including the recent x-rated *Nasty Novelties.* So, I started splitting my time between the Spankers and the Souvenirs, but still giving priority to the Souvenirs.

I joined the Spankers about 4 months into their existence and started playing the saw with them about a year ago. I remember hearing the saw on some old French songs, and whoever was playing on them was so accurate and played such beautiful melodies—they seemed seamless. And that's what I wanted to get out of the saw. So with the Spankers, I get to play melodies and solos just like a regular instrument. That's probably the most enjoyable instrument I've ever played. It's such an instinctive instrument; there's no frets, no nothing. You just have to trust your body and your mind to find the note where it is at the right time. I really consider the saw as an *acoustic theremin.*

♦ **V:** *And it's so low-tech and simple. Except you amplify it, right?*

♦ **OG:** That's very difficult. The blade is constantly moving, so you can't attach a contact mic—if you do, what goes through the amp is the noise of the bow against the blade, and that sounds terrible. I tried a regular microphone in front, but . . . what I really want is an independent system that I can attach, like a lavalier microphone. I'm still experimenting.

♦ **V:** *The saw is so primitive, yet so microtonal—*

♦ **OG:** Plus it's so melodic and so musical—that's what's amazing about it. When I start playing the saw, people *freeze.* Because I'm not just making noises with it, I actually play melodies and that's what really startles people. I use a Stanley traditional crosscut 10-point saw. I'm trying to amplify it, because I'm looking forward to playing it with the Souvenirs.

The Spankers play swing, jazz, blues and Broadway tunes from the '20s and '30s.

♦ **V:** *So your two bands cover your various needs for self-expression—*

♦ **OG:** Actually, not quite. With some friends I occasionally like to play the old style of Django Reinhardt in the very "pure" way. And for this I have the best rhythm section I could dream of: Kevin on bass, Jimmie Dean (drummer for the Spankers), and Stanley Smith, clarinet player for the Spankers. Stan's got it down; he's *it*—he's just incredible. Every now and then we get together and do a session. At one point, this band was called the

Covers of 8½ Souvenir's *Happy Feet* and *Souvonica.*

"Rififi"—in French, that means "trouble." [laughs]

♦ **V: Your most commercial band is the Souvenirs—**

♦ OG: Definitely, and the cult band would be the Spankers. The hobby band would be the Rififi (the purist, no-money-making, fulfilling-on-the-side band). Kevin and I just jammed with Whit Smith (guitar) and Elana Fremerman (fiddle) from The Hot Club of Cowtown, who just moved to Austin, and it was amazing, so maybe there'll be yet another band! After we played the first song, we burst out laughing!

♦ **V: The Souvenirs are very romantic—**

♦ OG: Romanticism is key in that band . . . with a little dose of cynicism. "No lo Visto" is very cynical, I think. All the lyrics are sincere, but with an "ouchy" humor to them. [laughs] You always have to feel from the audience if something works, because if it doesn't, you feel like a dumb ass.

♦ **V: Obviously, Austin is a great place for you to be creative. You have three Spankers' albums out and three Souvenirs' albums—**

♦ OG: Yeah, it's a great place. The attitude is so positive, and that's something I didn't have when I first moved here. I didn't talk very much; I wasn't used to that. People are so nice here, it just blew me away. I learned expressions like "to get someone's feelings hurt." Sometimes I hear my wife say, "That's not nice," or "That's mean"—never did I hear that in France! So it changed me completely to live here.

Plus, there's something I found here that I really didn't find in France, which is the appreciation of my peers. Musicians here don't hesitate to give you a compliment if they think you deserve it. Now, it's very easy for me to communicate with people and share things with them. I owe everything to the people I have good relationships with. ▣

🐾 🐾 🐾 🐾 🐾 🐾 🐾 🐾 🐾 🐾 🐾 🐾

INTERVIEW WITH CHRYSTA BELL

Chrysta Bell joined 8½ Souvenirs in April 1997. She's been singing most of her life, but this is her first outing as a jazz singer. Nevertheless, she has the stage presence of a seasoned veteran show-biz performer—which she is. Chrysta Bell was born April 20, 1978.

♦ **VALE: Tell us some background—**

♦ CHRYSTA BELL: All my life I've been doing stuff on my own. I grew up in a recording studio! That was in San Antonio, Texas. We had an SSL 84-track digital monster console; our studio was

Chrysta Bell wearing rhinestone headdress of Brazilian drag queen, NYC, 1997.

Chrysta, age 6; recital with Pockets the Clown.

beautiful. My mom was a professional singer and she got me started in theater when I was 6 years old. In theater I was doing mostly children's musicals. I kept singing and dancing and acting through most of my childhood. It seems so like so long ago, but it really wasn't—I'm 19.

♦ **V: So your mom was a professional vocalist—**

♦ CB: She was in a rock opera called *Alice* that toured the country. When she might have done something nationally, career-wise, she had me and settled down. She did singing telegrams for a living. Her maiden name is Sunny Andrew, and her last name now is Markham. My stepfather, Mitchell Markham, owns Emerald Recording Studio with her. They co-manage, and he's a producer, engineer, composer—an amazing man.

♦ **V: This was a great environment to grow up in. Your parents must have encouraged you from Day One—**

♦ CB: They really did. I was working from age ten doing commercials, jingles, voice-over work for radio, etc. At about 15 I got very interested in singing Spanish vocals, because I lived in San Antonio and there were a lot of opportunities available to Spanish-speakers. I met a couple of producers who supposedly were going to make me the next "Selena" and all that craziness. I even did the Spanish "Star Search," but instead of singing I was a spokesmodel speaking Spanish and pretending to be a native Spaniard. I did some Spanish television shows, most of the commercials I sang and did voice-overs for were in Spanish, and I thought that Spanish TV or media was my future, but it never materialized.

I began acting while still doing musical theater. I began gaining film-acting experience, which helped me land a role in a film that aired all over Asia and was one of the top-grossing films there last year. I had the female American lead in Wong Fei Hong's *Once Upon a Time in China and America*—I was the Indian princess! I filmed a lot of footage with Jet Li, but they ended up cutting quite a bit out.

♦ **V: How did you get that opportunity?**

♦ CB: A friend, Gordon Delgado, was acting as art director and assisting on casting for this film. He put my photo in the file and they kept weeding me out: I was too white, too young, too cute for the role. Finally the director, Sammo Hung, saw my photo after Gordon had sneaked it into the file literally four or five times after it had been rejected. Sammo said, "This is the girl I want to play the part." He asked me for a private audition, and I got the role.

I was very naive about what was happening, but this director had directed many films and was world-renowned—millions of people knew him. And Jet Li is a huge Asian star. He's a charismatic man who looks really good on film, and his kung-fu moves were just amazing; he was so graceful.

They would give me my lines 30 to 40 seconds before I was supposed to say them, and then say, "Go!" I'd hesitate: "Wait a minute—am I happy, or sad, or frustrated—what's *happening* here?" They'd go, "Just act!" I'd think, "Oh, geez . . ." They would orchestrate the kung-fu scenes so ornately and everything would be just so perfect, and they'd *still* do 42 or 45 takes to make sure they had the scene! To this genre of movies, the acting was not nearly as important as the kung-fu.

♦ **V: *Nevertheless, the acting in the film seems powerful—***

♦ CB: After that movie I became interested in gaining experience with *real* acting, so I moved from San Antonio to Austin. I figured my chances would be better because a lot of directors are based there. For some reason I was drawn to the Caucus Club. It's a very classy, sophisticated joint where a lot of local politicians hang out, and it had a piano—I could see myself singing torch songs on top of it! It took me five tries to finally get a job interview, and when I mentioned to the interviewer that I was serious about singing, she said, "Well, my husband is in a band that is currently without a singer. They've been looking for one for about three months, searching L.A., New York, everywhere. They've auditioned at least 160 girls by now, but you never know—go for it." I asked, "What's the name of the band?" and she said, "8½ Souvenirs." I said, "Well, I've never heard of them, but I'll give it a try."

I got their first CD and listened to it. My audition process began at a recording studio where the band was finishing their *Souvonica* album. They said, "Hey—because you're here, why don't we just record your audition?" Luckily, I was very comfortable in the studio and their request didn't make me pee in my pants! I sang some songs, and they left me in suspense for a month—they were still in limbo with some other singers in the

Chrysta Bell recording her original songs in Emerald Studios, 1997. Photo: Jason Stewart.

audition process.

In order to get the job, I had to do an entire live show with them. This meant I had to memorize all of their repertoire of songs, which are in four different languages—*no sweat!?* This show was at the Continental Club during a Happy Hour. After the show, Olivier shook my hand and said, "Congratulations—you got the job!" A week later I went on tour to California: in San Francisco, the Hi-Ball, Deluxe, Cafe Du Nord, Bimbo's; and in L.A.: the Viper Room, the El Rey—all these beautiful clubs. I'd never been on the club circuit before, never toured before, never

sung with a swing band before, never had any experience with this type of music at all, and it was wonderful. With the Souvenirs I've met so many people and gone so many places in the eight months I've been with them.

♦ **V: *Where did you buy that rubber dress?***

Chrysta Bell as Princess Nibusia in *Once Upon A Time In China and America*, 1996.

♦ CB: If only I were as famous as that rubber dress! When I wear that, my theatrics aren't quite as apparent, because I can't move as much. If I feel I want to be "sleek," and slink around onstage, I'll wear something like that, but if I really want to move and *dance,* then I'll go with other options. Actually, the reason I really wore that is because my boyfriend told me that if I wore that dress, he'd be a legend! [laughs]

♦ **V: *I didn't realize that wearing that dress might place a certain limitation on your expressiveness—***

♦ CB: Absolutely, that's why I don't wear things like that all the time. I read one review in a San Francisco paper that said it looked as if I had melted into a Glad Bag! (Okay, whatever.) But at Bimbo's—even though it's a beautiful room, it's a very difficult room to "warm up." When people are so far away and you're high up on a stage—well, I think the Souvenirs are at their best when people are about four feet away, sweaty, probably dancing or just watching intensely. At the Continental Club in Austin, the mikes are hot, the piano is blaring in your face, the guitar is crisp, you can see Kevin sweating while he rocks his bass, and you can feel the drums. Bimbo's is fabulous in a different way: it's set up like a dream world with mermaids and red velvet, and I get to be part of the dream.

♦ **V: *Tell us about your first singing experiences—***

♦ CB: One of my first experiences was with a choir group called Peace Child, and we would sing for world peace. It was made up of children from all over Texas, and was a bit weird. I remember singing a song called "Fireball": "Fireball, burning in the sky; fireball, are we going to die?" (and we're kids, right?) Our director was like, "All right kids, imagine you're being bombed right now, and we're all going to die!" We said, [high voice] "Okay!" That was bizarre.

♦ **V: *Did you ever take any singing lessons?***

♦ CB: My first vocal coach asked me to sing some songs out of a fake book, and whichever ones I liked we would continue to work with. I was singing "Cry Me a River" one day, and my dad overheard me and said, "Chrysta Bell, you're not going to believe this, but your great-uncle wrote that song." The whole time I'd thought that it was my mom who I got all my musical ambition from, but it turned out that my father had all these musicians on his side of the family, too. We started rehearsing that tune for 8½ Souvenirs, and our piano player Glover, being a wise guy, said, "I'll give anyone a dollar who can tell me who wrote this." I went, "Arthur Hamilton," and he said, "You're right!" I went, "No shit—he's my great-uncle!" V

INTERVIEW WITH KEVIN SMITH

Kevin Smith is the bass player for 8½ Souvenirs and High Noon, a rockabilly group. For several years he toured with Ronnie Dawson. He lives with his wife, Justine, a web designer, in Austin, Texas, with their two cats.

♦ *VALE: Tell us your history—*
♦ KEVIN SMITH: I was born December 12, 1967 and grew up in Arvada, a suburb of Denver, Colorado. I graduated from high school in 1986. I was working at a Pizza Hut debating whether or not to go to college. Then I decided to put my heart into playing music.

Initially, I was into punk. The Rainbow Music Hall in Denver had all-ages shows, and I saw acts like X, the Blasters, Violent Femmes, Joe "King" Carrasco (Tex-Mex rock'n'roll from Austin, with an accordion in the band). Basically, punk led me into rockabilly—when I heard X doing a version of "Breathless," I went, "Wow, this is the *real* stuff."

I met some guys from the SHIFTERS and started going to all their rehearsals. Sometimes their bass player wouldn't show up, and I'd go, "I've got mine in the car—*I'll* do it." Gradually I worked my way into that band, playing electric bass. At the end of '87, we moved to Austin. The four of us found a duplex for $200 a month, and it became your typical teenage rock'n'roll house. We were completely broke, living on no money, but we had some legendary parties. We lived off gallon cans of refried beans, tortillas and cheese. That band was together for six months before it broke up.

I moved back to Denver to play with a band called the Jinns, but being back at your parents' house after you've moved away is a pretty traumatic experience! In mid-'88 the singer from the Shifters, Shaun Young, and I moved back to Austin to start HIGH NOON. For this band, the sound we wanted made it *necessary* for me to learn how to play upright bass.
♦ V: *Did you own an upright bass at the time?*
♦ KS: I found one in the basement of a pawnshop in Colorado for $350. It has no brand markings on it, but it's a mid-'30s, American-made playwood bass. When I bought it the neck was cracked; it needed a new bridge; I didn't know what strings to buy, etc.
♦ V: *How did you figure out what strings to buy?*
♦ KS: Through trial and error. The reason I bought an upright bass to begin with was because I'd seen Thomas Yearsley playing one with the Paladins. He really blew my mind. I didn't think you could even amplify one in a nightclub and make it sound good. He was my first upright bass hero.

Once I got back to Austin, I got my bass fixed up. We didn't have a drummer, so I had to learn the "slap style" really fast because people in Texas want to dance. Without a drummer you need a really solid rhythm guitar player and you need to create a lot of percussion in a heavy groove with the bass. I spent quite some time hurting myself and playing wrong. We were playing five or six nights a week for seven or eight years, doing four sets a night. I had no choice; I had to learn how to play and make it work, or starve.
♦ V: *How did you transition from punk to rockabilly?*
♦ KS: Early on I realized I could find cool records cheap at thrift stores. In Denver I'd met Lewis Kluge (of Rockabilly Records) who has one of the finest rockabilly collections in the world, and he got me *way* into it. He made me tapes, and told me how to look for records and what records were good—he was a big influence.

What I like about rockabilly is that there are all these threads that go back to every type of American music you can think of: hillbilly, country, jazz, rhythm & blues, conjunto (Texas border music which includes bajo sexto [like a 12-string guitar], accordion, and slap-bass). One of the things I appreciate most about Texas is the broad mix of people: from Cajuns to Czech and German polka players.

The Asylum Street Spankers. Back row: Mysterious John, Wammo, Kevin Smith, Jimmy Dean, Stan Smith. Front row: Pops Bayless, Guy Forsyth, Christina Marrs, Olivier Giraud, Josh Arnson. Photo: Todd Williams

The guitar player for the Souvenirs, Olivier, moved to Austin from Paris. I was out playing on the street one night with the singer from High Noon and Olivier came up, borrowed our guitar and played a few Scotty Moore licks. We thought, "Wow—this

47 Indians in Talin Estonia 1995 L to R: Kevin, Lisa Pankratz, Brent Gazell, Olivier

guy's amazing!" He could barely speak English, but we got to know each other. He and I and some other friends started a band called the Skyliners. I was busy with High Noon, so eventually the Skyliners got a steady bass player.

♦ **V: Where was High Noon's first gig?**

♦ KS: At the Liberty Lunch in Austin, in early '89. We wanted a real traditional rockabilly sound (like Elvis, Scotty Moore, Bill Haley, and Johnny Cash before he got a drummer—that kind of feel). I don't recall the first Skyliners gig; that may have been in '92. They probably did 40 or 50 gigs with me as bass player. The Skyliners changed their name to 47 Indians. Now the only original member is the singer.

♦ **V: With the Skyliners, the music was different—**

♦ KS: It was definitely rockabilly, but Olivier added such a unique flavor and feel—he had a different take on everything. The drummer was Lisa Pankratz, one of my best friends who now plays with Teisco del Rey. I spent two years touring with her and Ronnie Dawson. He's great; he still sounds like "Ronnie Dawson" without rehashing his old stuff. I learned so much from him. After he did his initial rock'n'roll thing, he played with the Light Crust Doughboys for years (one of the first Western Swing bands in Texas). The Light Crust's second banjo player, Smoky Montgomery, is 80 and he still gigs! One thing about the music business: you can never retire, because it's not really "work." I mean—driving 17 hours to be onstage for two hours is *kinda* like work, but it's not like digging ditches.

Kevin Smith in Finland, 1991.

♦ **V: Where did High Noon travel?**

♦ KS: Thirteen countries over about 10 years. We always did especially well in Scandinavia—in Finland there's a label called Goofin' Records (who put out records by 47 Indians), and they're a big reason why we were successful at all. The owner, Pete Hakonen, is one of the few honest people in the music industry. High Noon is still together, although we don't do as much as we used to.

♦ **V: So how did you happen to join 8½ Souvenirs?**

♦ KS: The bass player, Todd Wulfmeyer, decided he wanted to move on to other things, and I was lucky enough to get first call. I always wanted to play with Olivier. We had already been playing together in yet another band, the Asylum Street Spankers. They do gut-bucket jazz and novelty tunes—kinda like a jug band without the jug. As far as the music scene goes, Austin is very incestuous—everyone plays with everyone else. When I joined 8½ Souvenirs, I had to quickly figure out what to do with all my other projects, but it was such a great opportunity I did *not* want to miss it.

♦ **V: I like rockabilly, but why I like Western Swing, swing, jump-blues and Hot Jazz is because they go beyond three chords—**

♦ KS: Exactly. That is definitely one of the reasons I was interested in playing with the Souvenirs; I knew it would push my playing to a new level. I'm learning more about music theory, structure and everything else that is necessary to be able to play this kind of music.

Western Swing, jazz and all the swing movements are so close-knit; they're different and unique, but they're also closely related. It all adds up to a great package called "American Music." To me it's really exciting to see people listening to swing and jazz

and broadening their knowledge—everybody's getting smarter all the time!

♦ **V: People have logged a million hours listening to rock music, but have barely heard Western Swing, jump-blues, and swing—**

♦ KS: And that's where rock music came from. To me, that's what creativity is all about: hearing what happened before, and filtering it through your own unique viewpoint. And that's something the Souvenirs do very well. There are all these influences from Nino Rota and Django Reinhardt to rockabilly and 19th century classical music—all these different sources being filtered through different people to produce something new, cohesive, intelligent and fun.

♦ **V: Finally, music is allied with dance—both spur each other on again.**

♦ KS: Music is definitely based on entertainment: making people dance and have a good time. That's one reason that rock music is kinda stale right now: too much angst and negative energy. That's why a lot of people are gravitating toward the swing movement: it's enjoyable and positive.

When Bob Wills was young, he ran away to New Orleans and saw Bessie Smith sing. All of a sudden he was like, "These blues are unbelievable!" He brought that back to Texas and was playing blues on a fiddle. And that's exactly what rock'n'roll was like: hillbillies playing black R&B. This kind of cross-fertilization has been happening for 80-90 years in this country.

♦ **V: Who are your influences as a bass player?**

♦ KS: Wanna Coffman from Milton Brown & His Brownies, Milt Hinton (jazz bassist; photographer-author of *Bass Line: The Stories and Photographs of Milt Hinton.* He also recorded a CD called *Old Man Time* which contains a 45-minute interview. It's on the Chiaroscuro label). There's Bill Black (who played with Scotty Moore and Elvis). Slam Stewart is a big influence; I have a 78 of him playing with Benny Goodman on "After You're Gone," where he does an incredible bow solo. He must have done a lot of freelance work; he's on many other recordings.

Another influence is Pops Foster, who played with The Rhythm Makers and just about everybody. He was born in New Orleans in 1892 and played all the way through the history of jazz. I think Willie Dixon (house bass player who also did most of the production) was really responsible for the success of Chess Records. Chuck Berry never made a good record after he left Chess. In his autobiography, Dixon talks about how he refused to be drafted, because he didn't want to fight for a country that didn't treat him well.

♦ **V: How do you think this "retro renaissance" arose?**

♦ KS: I saw the rockabilly scene take off. I think the invention of the CD medium and the subsequent reissue craze sparked a lot of this—and that's ironic! Before, only obscure collectors could have these records. How many people have their parents' Starday 45s lying around the house? Not many. George Jones's first record (credited to "Thumper Jones" and titled "How come it?") used to be a super-rare 45, but now anybody can go to Tower Records and buy it on CD.

I hate to bring this up, but look at the success of the Stray Cats in the '80s. They sold millions of records, and they introduced me (and a lot of people) to rockabilly who might not have found it otherwise, or as quickly. They recorded all these Eddie Cochran and Gene Vincent songs, and I looked at their record going, "Who's Eddie Cochran? I better go find a record." They had a part in educating people and making it accessible. Since the time of the Stray Cats and the Blasters, people like Big Sandy and Dave and Deke have been digging more and more into all of this music and coming up with different takes on it.

♦ **V: The innovative "retro" bands all seem to wear vintage clothes—**

♦ KS: Dressing traditionally is definitely part of it. I love vintage clothes and I love looking for them, but I also love them because they're still cheap, at least in Austin. I hate to overstress the dress, because a lot of people have let that take precedence over the music. Clothes are fun, but the music is the bottom line, the supreme being.

♦ **V: I wish somebody would bring back all the great old clothes, down to the smallest detail—**

♦ KS: When I was in Japan, I bought some Levis that were an exact reproduction of jeans made in the '30s with a buckle in the

High Noon: L to R: Kevin Smith, Shaun Young, and Sean Mencher.

and to find it in a thrift store for $10—you can't complain.

In some way this fulfills the punk rock ethic I adopted when I was a teenager. Now I pick my own clothes very carefully. I have vintage things in my house but I also have a computer—I'm making my own world. I'm no longer buying what everybody's trying to sell me, I'm making my own choices.

♦ **V: Punk was a great starting point to help people develop their own, non-corporate culture. This "back-to-vintage" movement has definitely reduced profits to corporations—**

♦ KS: Look at the rise of things like vegetarianism. A lot of people are making choices that are actually going to make a difference in the future, and they're doing it logically and responsibly. Everybody's taking the best of what's come before, and making it work for them.

Another thing I enjoy about this movement and playing this kind of music: it's a never-ending educational process. For example, Cliff Gallup, who played guitar with Gene Vincent, was listening to Junior Barnard (who played with Bob Wills), and as a kid Junior was copying the jazz guitarist Charlie Christian. I want to try to absorb all these people I can and filter it all through myself, so it comes out as "me." Presently I'm learning how to play with a bow; *that* makes everything completely different!

Now all these bands are touring and spreading the word, and every day there are more and more bands. BR 549 (traditional country/rockabilly) in Nashville was signed to a major label deal (Arista) and sold 350,000 copies, and Squirrel Nut Zippers put out a record that sold over a million. How are all these things slipping through the cracks? I was used to being almost alone in this kind of thought process for so long, and now I see it filtering down to a lot of people. And personally, I agree with the way a lot of things are going . . . ▨

What I like about rockabilly is that there are all these threads that go back to every type of American music.

---

back. They have a baggy, comfortable fit and they look great . . . At first, it kinda went against my grain to wear a suit, but to find a '50s suit that fits well and is made from a nice gabardine fabric,

---

Kevin Recommends

♦ BOOKS ♦

Texas Border Music; comes with an explanatory CD
Frankie McWhorter *Cowboy Fiddler in Bob Wills' Band*
Charles R. Townsend *San Antonio Rose: The Life and Music of Bob Wills*
Cary Gincll (with Roy Lee Brown, Milton's brother): *Milton Brown and the Founding of Western Swing*, U.Illinois Press (Texas Rose Records: companion 5-CD box set)
Charles Delaunay *Django Reinhardt*
Manuel Pena *The Texas-Mexican Conjunto* (at least 24 companion LPs available on Folk Lyric)
John Edward Hasse *Beyond Category: The Life and Genius of Duke Ellington*
George T. Simon *The Big Bands*
Marshall Stearns *The Story of Jazz*
Roy Smeck's New Original Ukelele Method
Stanley Dance *The World of Swing*
Alton Delmore *The Truth Is Stranger Than Publicity* (about Delmore Brothers)
Willie Dixon *I Am The Blues*
Nat Hentoff *Listen to the Stories*
Arthur Taylor *Notes and Tones: Musician-to-Musician Interviews*

(great!)
Steve Eng *Satisfied Mind: The Country Music Life of Porter Wagoner*
Carl Perkins & David McGee *Go Cat Go: The Life and Times of Carl Perkins*
Bill Malone *Country Music U.S.A.* (pretty dry, but standard reference)
Pops Foster *The Autobiography of a New Orleans Jazzman as told to Tom Stoddard*

♦ CDs ♦

San Antonio's Conjuntos in the Fifties (Arhoolie)
The Everly Brothers *Heartaches and Harmonies* (box set; amazing bass playing & arrangements)
Slim and Slam: Complete Recordings 1938–42 (3 CDs).
Dizzy Gillespie: The Complete RCA Victor Recordings (2 CDs; includes a lot of playing by the legendary Cuban drummer Chano Pozo, who died young)
King of the Road: The Genius of Roger Miller (box set; the songs and bands are amazing. He called his music "Depressive Jazz" and does the weirdest tunes. How he slipped through the cracks in Nashville to become a power is unfathomable.)

Bob Wills: The Tiffany Transcriptions (10 CDs [?]; all great)

Slam Stewart and Major Holly *Shut Yo' Mouth* (great bass geek record; both are soloing on jazz standards. Slam sings an octave above the note, and Holly sings the same note)

Willie Dixon *The Big Three Trio* (any Big Three Trio records are great. Lot of slap-feature playing, good vocals).

Okeh Western Swing (essential compilation; an amazing record)

Duke Ellington (almost anything is great, particularly earlier recordings)

Peewee King: *Ten Gallon Boogie*

Johnny Lee Wills (Bob's brother; bassist): anything

Ronnie Dawson *Rockin' Bones* (The legendary masters. Really indicative of how unique the Dallas sound was and how unique the ideas were.)

♦ LPs ♦

The Rhythm Makers 1932 (LP, with Pops Foster)

Curtis Gordon *Rock, Roll, and Jumpin' Jive* (rockabilly-hillbilly)

The Big Three Trio *I Feel Like Steppin' Out* (Dr. Horse)

Les Paul and Trio (Tops; great small trio jazz; Les Paul without all the tricks and the sweet pop vocals. You get to hear him play jazz guitar in a straightforward context. When he switched to pop, a lot of jazz fans were very upset!)

Pioneers of the Jazz Guitar (Yazoo; a really great record)

A Collector's History of Classic Jazz (5 LPs, Murray Hill)

Ray Charles *The Genius Sings the Blues* (London-Atlantic)

Country Music's Two Guitar Greats: Merle Travis and Joe Maphis (great country guitar instrumentals; killer stuff)

Carnegie Hall Concert with Buck Owens and His Buckaroos

Charlie Christian with the Benny Goodman Sextet and Orchestra

Ellington at Newport (Columbia; one of my favorites)

Chicago Style Jazz: The Original 1927–1935 Jazz Classics

Louis Armstrong and His Hot Fives (and *Hot Sevens*)

Howlin' Wolf: His Greatest Sides

The Light Crust Doughboys: 1936 Western Swing Live (Radio Shows).

Sid King & the Five Strings *Gonna Shake This Shack Tonight* (Rockabilly-Western Swing from Dallas)

Adolph Hofner *South Texas Swing, His Early Recordings from 1935–1955*

(WWII hit him pretty hard; it didn't help having a name like "Adolph." He was playing Czech polka music and put out some early rockabilly recordings for Sarg Records, who released a whole spectrum of regional recordings. Sarg is still at a little storefront at 311 East Davis St, Luling, Texas. There are stacks of 78s that have never been played; however, you can't tell what they are because the labels were water-damaged!)

Bob Wills & His Texas Playboys 1932–41 (Texas Rose Records)

Oscar Peterson Trio *West Side Story* (great small band treatment of tunes. Bassist Ray Brown is incredible, doing everything right)

Art Tatum Trio (Brunswick 10˝ with Tiny Grimes [who's amazing] and Slam Stewart

Cats and the Fiddle (2 LPs on RCA/Bluebird. 3 tenor guitars, baritone "tipple" and upright bass. 3 and 4-part harmonies with great bass, and Tiny Grimes)

Memphis Slim *The Ambassador of the Blues* (with Willie Dixon)

Milton Brown and the Brownies (5-disc set).

Milton Brown and the Brownies *Easy Ridin' Papa* (Charly)

The Bass (ABC Impulse, 3 LP set. Charlie Hayden, Ray Brown, etc—very cool)

Speedy West & Jimmy Bryant *Two Guitars Country Style*

The Farr Brothers *South In My Soul* (instrumental back-up band for Sons of the Pioneers; they were great Western Swing/Jazz Players. Really cool stuff.)

Light Crust Doughboys: 1936–1939

Slim Gaillard *Laughin' in Rhythm, Vol One*

Quintet du Hot Club de France (Vogue, 2 LPs. This is great.)

The First Country Collection of Warren Smith (great stuff)

Write Ridge Runner Videos, 84 York Creek Dr, Driftwood TX 78619, for info on bass instruction videos involving Kevin Smith.

Instructional Videos for bass by Ray Brown are available.

Great Roy Smeck video footage; watch for it!

The Shifters L to R: Shaun Young, Manny Leon, Kevin Smith, Todd Wulfmeyer in 1988.

Ready to Rock!!!! The Big Six in 1995, L to R: Mike Sanchez, Anders Janes, Ricky Lee

Big Six

The Big Six is self-described as "England's premier Big Beat Combo." The band combines originals and numbers from the 1940s–'90s across Swing, Rockabilly, R&B, Ska, Jump-Jive and Doo-Wop to produce their own unique sound. The single "20th Century Boy" from their debut album, *Ready to Rock!*, was Number One on England's R&B charts. The Big Six's recordings are available in the U.S. from Hepcat Records, 1-800-404-4117. What follows is a conversation with drummer and band leader Ricky Lee Brawn. He's a Buddhist, a dad (daughter, Holly, 5), a theremin player, and a collector of incredibly strange music (Martin Denny, Les Baxter, etc) since 1967. In England he lives with Helen Shadow from the rockin' trio The Queen B's. Ricky Lee Brawn's contact address is: Valvemobile Location Recording Studios, PO Box 6136, London SW8 2XG, England.

♦ *VALE: How would you describe The Big Six?*
♦ RICKY LEE BRAWN: Basically, we are a group of musicians who play a hybrid sound of music. Every band says they've got a new sound, but I really think *we* have because we mix the best of several different forms: we're like James Brown's horn section meets Bill Haley's rhythm section, with some ska and a bit of glam rock.

In my opinion there are only two types of music in the world: good and bad! That means I can go to any era and pick music and turn it into our sound. Our music is based mostly on the sound from the early- to mid-'50s, but with other influences from early soul, etc.

♦ *V: You have two horn players, which is something I don't remember seeing in rock bands—*
♦ RLB: Yes. Also, I like to be in control of a situation. I've played in many bands, and I use the top players from England's swing and R&B scene, but it's quite difficult to get them together for a gig. We've got two main players: myself on drums and singer-guitarist Pat Reyford; we're there every time. The rest of the line-up is fairly fluid, but we try to keep continuity in our performance. It's all about old-fashioned entertainment, really.

There's also a bit of Spike Jones in there. We're putting some over-the-top entertainment in; we're not going onstage and tak-

ing ourselves too seriously. When it comes to music, we do take that seriously, but we like to lay back on it a bit and have some fun. This translates directly to the audience. The audience doesn't want to hear a thousand notes a minute; they want to hear things they can connect with, for their souls.

Part of the appeal of our music is the way that it's recorded. I've got my own tube studio called "Valvemobile." It's the old-fashioned way of recording: it's all mixed down into mono, using equipment that's up to 60 years old—exactly in the same way "they" would have done—so you get that big, fat, warm tube sound. This is just an add-on, really, to what we're doing. I look at the whole thing as a *package*.

♦ *V: What are some components used in your studio?*
♦ RLB: I use American RCA microphones from the '30s and '40s, plus RCA tube mixing consoles, which also come from the States. I record onto Studer tube tape recorders—they're the size of a washing machine! It's a huge set of equipment, but this type of recording is completely the opposite of the way most studios record nowadays. We don't want that ultra-clean, clinical digital sound; we want that big, fat sound. What I do is take out all the crap and go from A to B through the shortest routes. It's the path of least resistance: less is more, as they say.

♦ *V: The tube sound is definitely warmer. I've heard, on a good system, original rockabilly 78s that sound fantastic—like the band is in the room.*

♦ RLB: Yeah, they really cut them "hot." I record many rockabilly bands going for that Sun or early Capitol sound. I've spent 20-odd years researching and speaking to original engineers and performers. For example, I'm recording Bill Haley's original Comets this year, and last year I recorded Link Wray—people like that. They all want the "tube sound" and it's a *renaissance,* not just a passing phase. People want a big sound and this is how they get it.

Most of the recording I do is recorded "live" in one take using three microphones. I'll start a six-piece horn section eight feet from the microphone and signal them to walk closer in—actually fade themselves up—and that alters the sound of the microphone totally. Conversely, that's how they fade themselves out as well. You see them doing that in old films made during recording sessions: horn soloists will emerge from the orchestra and come up to the microphone.

♦ V: *How do you avoid "spillover" between all the tracks?*
♦ RLB: The secret of the sound is the spill! At my studio I've only got one track. It's a mono output from my Altec desk and I split it into stereo; it *is* stereo but it's so tight: straight-down-the-middle stereo as opposed to full-pan stereo. With multi-tracking, people always have the option to fix things, so the urgency and immediacy aren't there. To me, the performance is *everything* (including the spill), and this type of recording sorts out the men from the boys!

♦ V: *How did you get the idea to assemble this type of studio?*
♦ RLB: I started learning out of frustration—I'm actually an engineer by trade, and I learned from books and let my ears be the judge.

When I was in bands in the early '80s, we tried to recreate that sound. I would try to describe to engineers what we wanted by playing records. They would come up with what they *thought* was the sound, and I would get very frustrated because there was no bass—the sound had no balls. It's got to have a bit of *oomph* in there, and these guys couldn't get it. I thought, "Look, it must be possible to get that sound." The tube sound is here to stay; I'm sure of it.

♦ V: *Those plaid suits you wear: I first saw them on Spike Jones' band—*
♦ RLB: Exactly. Our big influence is Spike Jones and Bill Haley.

If you look at early Haley, you'll also see the plaid suits. But I've taken it a stage further, because we've also been influenced by the zoot suit. There's this *Tom and Jerry* cartoon from the '40s called "Hep Cat" (or something like that), and there's a character wearing a zoot suit and the shoulders are just ridiculous. The coat comes in really tight around the waist, like a Charles Atlas cut. Well, that's what we've done: I've exaggerated the shoulders big time; they're four inches over normal shoulders. The trousers come up above the waist; there's 32 inches at the knee coming in tight over the ankles. There's five yards of material in those suits. It's our own version of all these influences. I own all of the suits and they're all extra-large, so that no matter which musician

This isn't a fly-by-night thing, it's part of our life—it's something that we *have* to do.

plays the gig, it's likely the suit'll fit.

♦ V: *Who makes your suits?*
♦ RLB: Chris Ruocco; his family has been making suits in London for many years. He's very famous; he's the best musical tailor in London. His dad used to make suits for Cab Calloway, and cut his hair and everything else as well. Chris Ruocco has made suits for Adam Ant, Madness, Pet Shop Boys, Depeche Mode, many of the swing bands in the U.K. now—many, many bands. There was just one choice for me—he's the top tailor around.

♦ V: *Where do you get your shoes? I don't see the two-tone spectators people are wearing in the U.S.—*
♦ RLB: No, no. We don't go in for—well, we *do* go in for clichés, but they have to be our *own* clichés! We tend to want to get into the driver's seat. What we usually wear is black oxford shoes—essentially, a fairly old '30s–'40s style with a toe-cap. They're very plain English shoes, but very traditional and of very good quality. One English maker is Church's. Another two shoemakers are George Cox, and Barkers—that's a very famous maker of oxford shoes.

♦ V: *Where do your bow ties come from?*
♦ RLB: Well, we've had some for quite a few years. They were

L to R: *Ready To Rock!*, released in 1995, and *We The Boys Will Rock Ya!*, released in 1997.

original stocks made for Dean Martin—no bullshit! A lady who made suits for another band of mine went to Las Vegas, and in this old shop she found stacks of boxes of bow ties that were marked, "Especially made for Dean Martin, 1956" (or 1958). So she grabbed a few of them.

♦ *V: Describe other outfits the band wears—*

♦ RLB: The suits are always matching. We still wear the red plaid ones in our press photograph, but our other suits are green with a white plaid check; they're even brighter. They'll be featured on our new CD which we're recording right now. We prefer vinyl but we have to put it out on CD, because if we don't, it'll get bootlegged.

I've been playing this music now for 20-odd years. Most of the boys have been playing for somewhere near that. This isn't a fly-by-night thing, it's part of our life—it's something that we *have* to do. I tried giving up music in the mid-'80s to live a "conventional" life. I went back to building nuclear submarine engines and having all the trappings of what you would "normally" expect. Unfortunately—or fortunately, I should say—it didn't quite work out in the way I wanted. This music is in every pore of your body; it really is that serious. As long as you breathe life, you want to do it. I know it sounds a bit overdramatic, but that's the way it really is. I could no sooner give it up than chop off my right arm. It's as simple as that. [laughs]

♦ *V: How did you start playing music?*

♦ RLB: The first real lesson I ever had in my life was when the drum teacher at school conned me into taking music lessons, because I wanted to learn drums. This teacher finally threw me out because I wasn't practicing on the kettle drums or the triangle or some other crap he was giving me; I just wanted to play the *kit*. He said, "Get out—you'll never make a drummer as long as you live!" That was like a red rag to a bull: the best lesson he ever gave me—I was *determined* to learn then.

I started playing drums at 13, and was always into Elvis, rockabilly, Bill Haley, Glenn Miller, etc from the age of eight. My dad had an original 78 of a band called the Jodimars, and I was listening to that in 1967—I was six years old. I remember the Beatles were in the charts and the flower-power thing was going on. All that "War is over; give peace a chance" and psychedelia was going on. I remember thinking, "What the hell is this rubbish? I want rock'n'roll!" [laughs] That was the beginning of the end, I guess.

I played in Country & Western bands, middle-of-the-road type bands, playing small clubs. That was my "training." And then I started my first rock'n'roll band, the Stargazers, in 1980. It had a

Ricky Lee's parents, Rex and Wink Brawn, in 1956 dressed in Teddy Boy/Girl gear.

Ricky Lee in 1967 at the age of six.

Bill Haley-type sound and we had some records in the charts; we sold quite a few. That lasted a while. I've been in a lot of bands since then. I formed The Big Six in '94. We've played America several times and are doing really well. I'm actually in ten bands, of which many are rockabilly. There's a big rockabilly scene over in this part of the world, and has been for about 30 years.

♦ *V: It's hard to compress an entire life into one interview, but tell us a little about how you grew up—*

♦ RLB: You have to remember that in the Second World War England got bombed to hell. Some of my family got killed in it, and there were a lot of people "down," shall we say, who had the blues real bad. So when the '50s came along (and this has been told to death hundreds of times) it was a new era. People had money in their pockets, they had jobs, they had food. Previously there were people starving over here; they had food rationing until 1954. You couldn't buy chocolate or the simplest things; life felt oppressive. So when the '50s came along, there were a lot of people who wanted to let their hair down and have a good time—go out dancing—so we had a big rock'n'roll scene over here. But first it came out of America with Elvis, Bill Haley and all that.

My dad was a Teddy Boy. They wore long jackets with velvet collars, called drape suits. They also wore creepers, which are these shoes with a very thick crepe sole. The term "Teddy Boy" referred to the Edwardian look of long coats that succeeded the Victorian era. The coats are a bit like the Wyatt Earp cowboy-type of coat. The Teds wore slim jim ties, which are very thin and about an inch thick all the way down. The ladies wore big circle skirts. The Teddy Boys were quite rough and tough; there was a lot of newspaper reports about knifings and cosh boys that go around with coshes: lumps of lead that were used to take your lights out. You know, make you wish you'd never come into contact with them.

The police in England carry truncheons: a wooden club about a foot long. If you want trouble, they'll whack it over your head, no problem. They don't carry guns, just these. The Teddy Boys had quite a bad reputation. When "Rock Around The Clock" and "Blackboard Jungle" came out in 1955, they would smash up cinemas. The whole cinema would get floored; they'd go crazy. My dad wasn't really like that; he was a more sober Ted. And my mom was a Teddy Girl. It's a fantastic culture, it really is.

Along with that, you had the Ton-Up Boys, later known as the Rockers. They had the Marlon Brando "Wild One" look to a degree, but with their own style. They rode high-powered motorcycles. My dad was one of those as well.

These subcultures came out of what was, basically, happening in the States. From the research I've done, America went on to the Bobby Rydells and the more "pop" scene from about '57 or '58, and the whole rock'n'roll thing got watered down. Whereas in England, rock'n'roll stayed exactly as it was. It went to a '60s beat, but people like Carl Perkins, Gene Vincent, Eddie Cochran and Bill Haley were coming to England touring and doing TV work. They remained big over here, even through the '60s. This was a little utopia for them where they could be appreciated, and it never went away.

I was a second-generation Teddy Boy. Around 1973 I started going to rockin' clubs. There are young people still coming into that scene, but there are less now than there was then. The best time, I guess, was the early '80s when there were 14- and 15-year-old kids saying, "Hey, what's this?" At the same time, in the mid-'70s ('77 and '78), you had other kids saying, "Hey, what's this?" while looking at punk. Those were the two main cultures, but there were many others.

All that psychedelia was going on. I remember thinking, "What the hell is this rubbish? I want rock'n'roll!"

♦ **V: Is the term "rockabilly" used in England?**

♦ **RLB:** Yes, but many people prefer to use the term "rockin' scene"—that's a generic term for anything rock'n'roll—and that doesn't include Joan Jett and the Blackhearts! When I hear interviews with people from America, they use the term "rock'n'roll" to mean *anything,* but rock'n'roll for me is a specific type of music. If somebody asked me to describe rock'n'roll, I would say, "Bill Haley doing 'Rock Around the Clock'"—that to me is rock-'n'roll. So is Red Prysock, Big Al Sears, and people like Hal Singer and all those honking saxophone players—I love all that R&B sax. Bands like Bill Haley, Freddy Bell and the Bellboys, the Treniers, were essentially rock'n'roll. I think people are using "swing" the same way now, to cover what is actually a really broad subject. But I suppose it's good to have a "hook" for everyone to latch onto.

I like music wild. I like to get up on that stage, I like to sweat, work hard, get blisters on my hands, and do everything that's required to entertain the audience. For example, we played the Blue Cafe in Long Beach, California last year. The bass player laid on his back with a double bass and crawled off the stage two feet onto the floor where people were swing-dancing (we call it "jive" over here). Then he crawled on his back (still playing the bass while we're doing the song), got onto the bar and stood on the bass on the bar. Meanwhile, the bartender took this lighter fluid, spread it across the whole of the bar (where people were drinking, by the way) and lit up the entire bar—there were flames two feet high, and the guy was still playing! And that's no bullshit.

Although we're regarded as a swing band by some people, I don't regard The Big Six as one. Our new CD is going to be even more contemporary than the last, heavily relying on ska, but also doing early soul and swing as well. I'd like us to be regarded as a "contemporary dance band," along with all the hip-hop bands. The real breakthrough will happen when a band from the rock-'n'roll or swing scene crosses over and gets people from outside of that scene involved big-time. The Stray Cats did that in the early '80s; they brought in people from outside and made rockabilly and rock'n'roll world-famous, so I applaud them for that. What we're trying to do is get people into the scene, and try to get a mass market. I'm not talking about selling out or compromising in any way; we're just doing what we do, but we're trying to put it in a marketplace that can draw people in.

♦ **V: People want to get involved when they see the wild dancing; the music's almost secondary—**

♦ **RLB:** That's okay. They'll realize that without the music, they don't have the beat to dance to. You can't have one without the other. And without the audiences enjoying themselves, the bands cease to exist.

We've had a big scene in England since the early '70s. What we've had is a world-wide club, because we're not just talking about England but Japan, Scandinavia, Spain—I'm off to Munich soon to play. Our nearest equivalent to your swing dance shows are "dancings." It's modern people coming in, a lot of whom are involved with vintage clothing, but essentially it's "punters" [customers; originally, people who bet on horses] coming in to bring money into the scene—which is great.

There *is* a '40s scene where people dance '40s, but they tend to be very snobby, so I have very little time for them. I was a bit reticent when I came to America because I thought, "Oh no, it's going to be the same thing." But it was unbelievably different; I was really impressed with the American swing scene. A few years ago the people might have been into ska or another kind of music, so they're much more open-minded.

In England we have big "weekenders": imagine a holiday camp with 4,000 people staying five days. They're rockin' from midday until seven in the morning, and the bars (in two or three locations in this camp) are open all the time. People come from all corners of the world and are going crazy, listening to about 20 bands over the course of those days. In between the bands there are "record hops" where every kind of music from rockabilly to swing to rock'n'roll is played. We have three dances we do: the Jive, which is the early '50s American Jive—different from what

Song Favorites

"Fractured" 1953: Fantastic Bill Haley track!

"My Sweet" '30s: Django Reinhardt/Stephane Grapelli.

"Well Now Dig This" 1955: The Jodimars.

"Telstar" 1963: Excellent Joe Meek Production of The Tornados.

"Rock Around The Town" England 1956: Tommy Steele.

"Clarabella" 1956: The Jodimars.

"My Baby Loves Me" '50s: Charlie Gracie.

"Nab Nab" early '60s: The John Barry 7.

"Whoo I Mean Wee" '50s: Wild rockabilly of Hardrock Gunter.

"Get Off It and Go" '40s: Boogie swing of Ella Mae Morse.

"Baby Let's Play House" 1955: Elvis and a VERY BIG influence.

"Song In Blue" early '50s: Les Paul and Mary Ford.

"We Wanna Boogie" 1956: Sonny Burgess does wild/raw rockabilly.

"Caravan" 1954: Billy Jack Wills and progressive Western swing.

"Stingray!": The theme tune to cult '60s animatronic puppet show.

"Bi-I-Bickey-Bi-Bo-Go" 1956: Gene Vincent.

"Amazon Falls" '50s: Les Baxter. Enchanting!

"Rockin' Is Our Business": The Treniers.

"North Wind" '60s: Houston Wells. Another great Joe Meek production.

"Red Light" 1953: Merrill E. Moore (USA). Another big influence!

"Crazy Rythm" 1946: Bob Wills and His Texas Playboys. Great Western swing.

"French Rock" 1956/7: Johnny "Rock" Guitar (Paris, France). I don't know a thing about this guy except this is some of the wildest French rock'n'roll ever—raw, man, raw! The Stargazers cover one of his numbers and we called it "La Rock'n'roll" in 1982. It's on our CD *Rock That Boogie!*

"Jam Up" mid '50s: Tommy Ridgely.

"You Gotta Be Loose" 1958: Wailin' Bill Dell.

"Love Me": The Phantom. The wildest rockabilly track!

"The New Avengers Theme" 1996: Snowboy. This is one of my recordings. A 12-piece band all recorded onto my OLD tube gear. A big club hit over here at the moment. Released on England's Acid.

"King of the Rock": Victor Peter. This demo was sent to my U.K. agents. Victor is Portugese and sounds barking mad! It's so bad it's good, if you know what I mean!

"Barking Up The Wrong Tree" 1956: Don Woody. Fantastic sound and performance.

"Ball of Fire" '60s. I think this is the Skatelites. Excellent!

Americans do today, but just as wild (if you've ever seen *Rock Around the Clock,* that's the style they do in England). They also do something called the Stroll. You do that alone, but in a line; it's a foot-oriented thing. It's like line-dancing, and has been going on since the '40s. There's also a dance called the Bop. You do it alone to rockabilly and it's really wild—very energetic. Males and females do all of these dances. The Jive is essentially swing dancing, but it's slightly different from what you do.

♦ **V: America has Lindy Hopping—**

♦ RLB: *We* have Lindy Hopping and the swing dancing with the double pretzel— the whole thing—as well, but the main thing is the Jive. I've tried to dance with some American ladies, particularly at Bimbo's, but it was different. In England we drive on the other side of the road, so there are those sort of problems, but we get through it. [laughs]

♦ **V: Did you attend school to become an engineer?**

♦ RLB: Yes. I used to build engines for nuclear submarines, the Polaris and Trident systems, and also pumps for nuclear power stations. I did an apprenticeship which is a very regimented training schedule in college. That's what I'm really trained as, but it doesn't move me.

♦ **V: Well, I'm sure you're doing the right thing—**

♦ RLB: I know—by experience. I tried doing both; on weekends I'd fly to Switzerland or somewhere to play rock'n'roll. Then on Monday morning I'd put my other hat on and return to mediocrity. I couldn't stand it.

♦ **V: In your bands, you made a transition toward a larger band with horns. It's easier to keep four musicians together than six—**

♦ RLB: It is. But I've always played in bands with saxophones. The Stargazers had a tenor player, back in 1980. In 1982 and '83 I played in bands with multiple horns. It's nothing different. The only music we heard coming out of America at that time—and we

Ricky Lee at the Bloomsbury Theatre in London. Photo: Kitty Logan

I was impressed by the American swing scene . . . they're much more open-minded.

didn't hear a lot—was rockabilly. I thought, "Oh gawd, you have such a heritage over there; please let there be a renaissance." I was the first to applaud when bands like Royal Crown Revue and Big Bad Voodoo Daddy started getting horns. I thought it was great.

I formed the Stargazers in 1980 and left in '93, although I played in other bands throughout that time. But I had big plans to add a baritone sax player back then, to add a bit more bottom end, a bit more meatiness. I didn't know what was going on in

America at all; it's just a strange parallel. Now we stick to two horns because we can get the right phrasings, and I think it's fantastic. We're giving people good value for their money. But it's a total nightmare, of course, trying to round up six people of *quality* to actually play this music. And you earn less money. But I don't care about that; to me, the only important thing is the quality of sound. Food comes later. [laughs]

♦ **V: That's the right attitude: dedication to your vision—**

♦ RLB: Put it this way: if I was doing it for the money, I wouldn't be doing it. I mean, why give up a job where I'm earning three or four times as much? I'm not counting my studio because it's doing well, but as a musician, you struggle. You might not exactly be in poverty, but don't let anyone kid you otherwise. It doesn't matter even if you have a big record deal—

♦ **V: It's really just a handful that make the millions and get to live that "star" lifestyle.**

♦ RLB: I take all that with a pinch of salt. I keep my feet on the ground and keep my head down to a reasonable size. When I was 16 I survived a motorbike crash—I hit a lamppost at 40 miles an hour. Smoking saved me [laughs]—I used to carry a tin of rolling tobacco, and where my hip contacted the lamppost that tin absorbed most of the impact; it bent into a "V." I still have it. The funny thing is, ten years later I was diagnosed as having cancer at that exact spot on my hip. The doctors cut away a section of bone and, oddly enough, after two years the two ends of bone fused together and regrew to be as thick and strong as ever. This experience with cancer taught me, at the age of 28, what life was all about. The value of life is not about monetary things, it's about people—that's what the real value of life is to me. I feel totally *privileged* that I was able to go through that.

♦ **V: I hope you'll play continuously until you're at least 70. A lot of less-than-superstar musicians, like Cab Calloway, have played up until the day they died—**

♦ RLB: One of the best shows I've ever seen in my life was at London's huge, great Barbicon Theater. It was in 1988 and I still have the ticket stub. I joined 3,000 businessmen in suits and old granddads, and we all sat there and were enthralled by a fantastic big band that was fronted by the man himself, Cab Calloway. It was one of the best shows I've ever seen in my life. All these sober businessmen were getting up and giving it the big 'un, shouting "Hi-de-hi!" and "Hi-de-ho!" at the right times just like in the *Blues Brothers* movie. It was fantastic.

♦ **V: Back in '88, you had the foresight to attend that show—**

♦ RLB: Well, it was there, you know. The opportunities were there. Bill Haley's original Comets—now that's an amazing story. They split up in 1955 and a New York attorney made it his life's work to get them back together again. They had scattered all over America: one was a crap dealer in Vegas, one was a Halloween mask factory foreman, etc. Anyway, he got them together and they did a gig in one of these big British rock'n'roll weekenders in 1989. I was playing drums for them, and they can cut the mustard like no one else! They're going to be playing in Hollywood later this year. They're in their seventies now and, I'll tell you, people should go and see that band because that's rock'n'roll history there.

Our band brought Joey Ambrose, the original tenor saxophonist for the Jodimars, from Vegas to play with us at the Derby in Los Angeles. He tore the place apart, and he's in his 60s. Fantastic horn player.

♦ **V: Tell us some other favorite experiences—**
♦ RLB: There's a band called the Treniers who now play supper clubs in Vegas, but they were one of the hottest rock'n'roll bands around in '56 or '57—they were in a film called *The Girl Can't Help It.* They're just fantastic entertainers. Last year, they were playing for 4,000 people whose average age was in their 20s, and someone forgot to remind the singer that he was 77—he was jumping around like an 18-year-old! Rock'n'roll keeps you young (that's a cliché, of course) but it really does. It's better than anything; it's fantastic—the adrenalin is unbelievable.

Anyway, I'm pleased that kids are getting into this music now. The only thing that scares me is: I really hope it's not going to become a "novelty" and then disappear again. It went away for such a long time, and now it's back and it's building—I hope that this time it has some *staying power.* But time will tell.

♦ **V: Economics is always a factor. If you can keep a band down to six people and still have a satisfactory sound, perhaps you can keep going—**
♦ RLB: We're trying to get some big record company action, but you can't be driven by that and you can't chase rainbows. You have to deal with the realities of life, and the realities of life are doing gigs in small and large places. Luckily, when we come to America next time (this will be our third visit) we'll have built up a reputation—thankfully. And we'll be playing some fantastic clubs. We've just been taken on by one of the biggest

Ricky Lee (far right) with rock'n'roll singer Joe Brown (in white shirt) in 1979.

Nord, and the Hi-Ball Lounge. We had a great time on both tours.

I like the intimacy of a small club—jumping on the tables and going crazy. I say to the guys, "There's only one rule: there are no rules." [laughs] So, they run with it. They know they have to cut the mustard musically, but they're walking on tables amidst the audience, still playing, doing whatever—*entertaining.* Whatever they do, it must come from the heart—it mustn't be contrived in any way.

♦ **V: Tell us about your drums—**
♦ RLB: The drum kit I've got is a very well-known kit on the rock'n'roll scene. In 1980 I wanted to get some '50s drums, and very naively walked into a music shop in London and said to the salesman, "Do you have any 1950s drums?" It was around Christmas and he said, "Yeah; come back in the New Year. I've got a kit upstairs, but we have to go through the storeroom." When I returned, we went to the storeroom and were moving boxes and kits and stuff for nearly an hour—the place was completely filthy. Finally he pulled out this bass drum and my eyes nearly popped out; I couldn't believe it. He said, "How about that?" I just flipped and said, "What is it?" He said, "That's a bass drum from a 1957 Trixon kit. It's called a Starfire." The bass drum is in an elliptical shape. The usual questions I'm asked are: "Who sat on your drum?" "Where do you get skins for it?" and "Why do you play a mashed potato?" It always gets a reaction. The reason it was shaped like that was for jazz drummers, so they could have two bass drum pedals on the floor. That's why it's obviously wider at the bottom. The kit is very rare. Unfortunately, it also sounds pretty bad. [laughs] But I couldn't give a damn because I love it—I want to be chopped up and buried in that thing; it'll never leave me. It's worth thousands, but it cost me 75 pounds, the U.S. equivalent of $100—*nothing.* I've played that kit at just about every one of my 3,000 gigs.

♦ **V: Is the rest of the kit standard?**
♦ RLB: Yes. I did have another Trixon kit that had the same shape bass drum, but had a floor tom shaped like a large comma; it was four feet long! But it was too big to take on the road, so I swapped it for some recording equipment. I'm happy with my little kit. When I come to America, I've got a nice little Gretsch drumset that I brought. We've got our own little backline there now. That means a drum kit, guitar amp, double bass, double bass

Clockwise from top: Marshall Lytle, Ricky Lee Brawn, Joey Ambrose, and Dick Richards in 1989. All three men were involved with the Jodimars and/or the 1955 Comets.

"roots" agencies in America, the Tahoe Agency. They normally just take bands that have major deals, so they think we have a lot of potential. Hopefully, that will be justified.

♦ **V: At the same time, I hope you'll continue playing small clubs, too—**
♦ RLB: Yeah. Last time we came to San Francisco, we played Bimbo's. It was just about a sell-out (if I remember correctly) and it was a wild, hot, jumpin' night. The time before that was equally as wild, but on a smaller level: we played the Club Deluxe, Cafe Du

amp. That's all stored in Orange County, where we stay when we're in America. We just pick the backline up, put it in the van or whatever we're traveling in, and away we go; we're a self-contained unit. We don't have any roadies—none of that business; we do it all ourselves. We don't have any tour manager, although we do have a manager in America: Gabby from Hepcat Records. Gabby used to be roommates with Wally and Ashley from Big

Ricky Lee's 1953 Vauxhall Wyvern that he bought from the original owner.

Sandy; in fact Ashley's girlfriend, Mary, works at Hepcat along with Gabby's wife Yvonne. It's a small scene!

On our last American tour I walked into an antique store in Orange, California, where we stay with Gabby. I asked, "Do you have any vintage recording equipment?" She said, "No, but I have an old drum kit that belonged to my brother; he bought it in 1948." She brought it out and it was a white pearl Slingerland Radio King kit—that is *the* Gene Krupa kit (he's one of my drum idols—him and Billy Gussak, one of the first drummers for the Comets who played on "Rock Around the Clock" and "Crazy Man Crazy."). This drum kit is *so* rare. She said, "I want $100 for it." I said [completely deadpan], "Well, it's pretty beat up; maybe I can use it for spare parts." Meanwhile, my heart was thumping so loud I was surprised she couldn't hear it. "It's really rough; I'll give you fifty bucks for it."

She said, "Okay." I know drummers who've been looking for that for ten years!

♦ **V: You have two CDs out?**

♦ RLB: *Ready to Rock* was recorded in September '94 and released about June '95. That's two years old now. Imagine getting a band like that together, and for three days—that was so hard! We had to do a series of covers and songs that I'd written, because the guys had no idea what was in my head; I got them to do this recording just on trust. It was only then that I evolved the band, and what was in my head came down onto wax, if you like. Then they had a good idea of what I was aiming for. The second CD is being recorded now.

Now, everybody's been writing. We've replaced the piano player, Mike Sanchez,

since then. He plays in a band called the Big Town Playboys and he's just too busy to join the band permanently, because he's the singer of that group. I got this new guy named James Sumner and he's fantastic. The band we have now is very tight-knit, but I will use several musicians as long as they can cut the mustard and play with quality. I never compromise on the sound. The performance and the sound always have continuity and it always sounds the same. That's essential.

♦ **V: Do you ever play the theremin "live"?**

♦ RLB: In my new project, Johnny Bach and the Moonshine Boozers, I play a theremin that I found in London. [*ed. note:* It can be heard on the CD titled *Bach On The Bottle Again (Still Feelin' No Pain).*] I've loved that sound for a long time. I started putting it in my show instead of steel guitar. I was going through a difficult divorce when I met Helen from the Queen B's, whom I consider my soulmate; we met when they recorded at my studio. She's always wanted to have a theremin, too, and I bought her one for her last birthday. It's been amazing playing this; the rockabilly audiences have never seen anything like it—we're probably the only people in the rockin' scene who have ever used a theremin. And the kids didn't even know what it was, but it sounds almost like a steel guitar if you play it right. I've got so many projects on the go I can't tell you . . .

♦ **V: Is The Big Six on video?**

♦ RLB: My old band, the Stargazers, was in a film with David Bowie in 1985, called *Absolute Beginners.* That was from a really good book of the same title by Colin MacInnes; it chronicles the coffee bar culture scene over here in '58–'59. It was essentially rock'n'roll, but you had skiffle music, which was Big Bill Broonzy/Leadbelly type of work songs. But it was also done with a skiffle beat on washboards. It wasn't Cajun, but it had more of an acoustic sound. Anyway, in *Absolute Beginners,* I played with my band and that book was a real influence for me as well. I hope it doesn't sound like I'm name-dropping. [laughs]

♦ **V: Colin MacInnes isn't too well-known in the U.S. But America isn't the center of the world, although sometimes we like to think we are—**

The Queen B's: L to R: Mark Robertson, Helen Shadow, Angie Watts. Photo: James Jordan

♦ RLB: I go all around the world and the world is turning into one big America. I'm not saying anything about that! [laughs] I think it's important that we all keep our own identities, but there's nothing wrong with being influenced by something that's good. Rock'n'roll was born in America, but we kept the flame alive in England. Rock'n'roll now is a worldwide language. With music—of this type—you don't have to share a common language. I've played in Japan and other countries, and half the time I can't speak their language and they can't speak mine, but they understand what we're talking about with the music. Again, that sounds like a cliché, but it really is true!

Records, Bands & Books

The Stargazers:

Groove Baby Groove. EP 7″ EPCA19-24. Epic Records 1981, 4 tracks. Also EP 12″ EPCA12-1924 available.

Tales From The Crypt. LP 12″ K58406. Warner Bros. 1981. Various backing music for a "spoof" '50s detective radio play.

Hey Marie. Single 7″ EPCA2422. Epic 1982, 2 tracks. Also EP 10″ EPCA132422. Epic Records 1982, 3 tracks.

Watch This Space. LP 12″ EPC25053. Epic 1982, 13 tracks.

Tossin'N'Turnin'. Single 7″ EPC2843. Epic 1982, 2 tracks.

Ain't Nobody Here But Us Chickens. Single 7″ EPCA3013. Epic 1982, 2 tracks.

Hello! Everybody! Jump Around! LP 12″ RR22001. Rockin' Records 1988, 17 tracks.

Back In Orbit. CD/LP 12″ CH312(LP or CD). Ace Records 1991, 12 tracks.

The Speaking Clock Says . . . Rock. CD/LP 12″ JR(LP or CD)4. Vinyl Japan 1992, 12 tracks.

Rock That Boogie. CD/LP 12″ JR(LP or CD)7. Vinyl Japan 1993, 21 tracks.

Marshall and the Shooting Stars:

Airmail Special. CD/LP 12″ JR(LP or CD)9. Vinyl Japan 1994, 12 tracks.

The Space Cadets:

Lost On Earth. LP 10″ JRT8. Vinyl Japan 1995, 6 tracks.

AWAKADEEAWAKADOO. Single 7″ JON1. Vinyl Japan 1996, 2 tracks.

Astrobilly Rockin'. CD/LP 12″ JR(LP or CD)20. Vinyl Japan 1996, 14 tracks LP and 23 tracks CD.

Johnny Bach and the Moonshine Boozers:

Feelin' No Pain. LP 10″ C9RLP002. Crazy Gator Records 1996, 10 tracks.

Bach On The Bottle Again (Still Feelin' No Pain). CD/LP 12″ JR(LP or CD)30. Vinyl Japan 1997, 14 tracks LP and 16 tracks CD.

The Big 6:

Ready To Rock . . . ! CD/LP 12″ JR(LP or CD)18. Vinyl Japan 1995, 14 tracks LP and 20 tracks CD.

We The Boys Will Rock Ya! CD/LP 12″ JR(LP or CD)25. Vinyl Japan 1997, 12 tracks LP and 20 tracks CD.

Ricky Lee Brawn—Bands:

Note: I was and still am in several bands at any one time.

Doris and the Dropouts. 1974 only. Rock'n'roll.

Shillouette. 1975–6. MOR/Country.

Pebbledown. 1976 only. MOR/Country.

The Nat West Band. 1977–80. MOR/ Country.

The Stargazers. 1980–93. Rock'n'roll.

The Chevalier Brothers. 1983 only. Jump Jive.

The Tempo Toppers (later the Hatchetmen). 1983 only. R&B.

The Rock'n'Roll Prisoners. 1985 only. Rock'n'roll.

The Johnny Dumper Band. 1985–6. Elvis impersonations.

Marshall and the Shooting Stars. 1991–present. Western Swing.

The Big 6. 1994–present. Hybrid rock'n'roll.

The Space Cadets. 1995–present. Rockabilly.

Johnny Bach & the Moonshine Boozers. 1996–present. Rockabilly.

The Enforcers. 1997–present. Rocka-billy.

Killer Brew. 1997–present. Rockabilly.

The Virginians. 1997–present. Gene Vincent rockabilly.

Books:

I read mostly technical publications about recording. The BBC publications are good.

The Sound and Glory, by John W. Haley (Bill Haley's son) and John Von Hoelle (Dyne American Publishing, 1989): an excellent history of Bill Haley. The horn players position themselves a distance from their microphone and start walking toward it if they want to "fade in." I found out that's the way they used to do it.

Absolute Beginners by Colin MacInnes

Elvis Recording Sessions by Ernest Jorgensen (Denmark, Jee Prods)

Sons, Lovers, Etc by Vida Adamouli

Which (U.K. magazine by subscription only). Tests and rates every product from washing machines to cars and tells you the best performer. (But I'm not a "consumer." I don't subscribe anymore.)

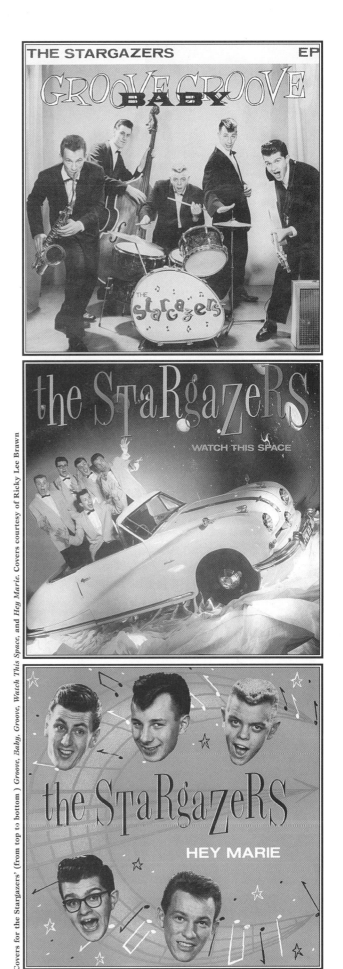

Covers for the Stargazers' (from top to bottom) *Groove, Baby, Groove, Watch This Space,* and *Hey Marie.* Covers courtesy of Ricky Lee Brawn

Beginnings...

1) March 1991, Phil Price's garage: *first* Royal Crown Revue show in S.F.—watershed event! T[?] birth of Bay Area "retro-swing lifestyle." RCR in back. 2) 1991, Marsugi's: early RCR show; n[?] Eddie playing guitar. Below: Russell Scott, L.A. 3) Fall, 1991: Royal Crown playing UC Berke[?] Sproul Plaza, back when times were tough. VINTAGE SWING PHOTOS, pp. 92-93 by JIM KNE[?]

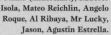

Back row L to R: Indigo Swing: Josh Workman, Little David, Bowen Brown, Baron Shul. Front L to R: Victor Estrella, Joe Pizzio (undershirt), Roberto Isola, Mateo Reichlin, Angelo Roque, Al Ribaya, Mr Lucky, Jason, Agustin Estrella.

Big Sandy at the Dollhut, Anaheim, 1995. Russell Scott on bass.

Sandy of Atomic Cocktail, singing at Natoma St, 1992.

op to R: Lauren, acques Kepler. Below: hannon Dean, Shannon icholson. Photos: Jim Knell.

Above: Javier Estrella, Fra & Jacques Kepler, "Earwig." Below: Big Sandy, Phil Price's, Feb 9, 1991.

...now

1997, Bimbo's & Hi-Ball: swing dancers include Frank Shum/Meleksah David, Rebecca/Debbie.

Johnny Dilks in Dana & Mango's living room.

At a Tony Bennett show ca. Feb 1989, at the Fairmont's Venetian Room. Top: Laurie Lee, Mr. Lucky

In San Francisco during the late '70s punk scene, lounge pioneer Mr. Lucky was (arguably) the first to dress like Frank Sinatra. In the early '80s, he began crooning Sinatra and Bacharach songs with piano accompaniment (or taped orchestral backgrounds). Over the years he's had a variety of acts. Mr. Lucky writes for *Swing Time* Magazine, where he can be contacted.

♦ MR. LUCKY: I'm doing four things at once and it's driving me a little bit nuts. I'm doing my day-job, music, painting, and writing on the side (including some poetry). I'm trying to combine Surrealist imagery, Futurism and Russian Constructivism, and my paintings (I call them "Abstract Humanism") are also based on lines from my poetry. Maybe some day I'll have a life . . . actually, life is great!

♦ *VALE: You escaped from New York—*

♦ ML: I was born in Queens. My family goes way back in N.Y.; they used to have a farm where Central Park is now. I like contrasts. One year I was living in a tepee in the woods in Nova Scotia, with animals running around. Two days later I was selling chestnuts in Times Square. [laughs] That was in my younger

---

My first band was a power-punk group called PRESSURE. I banged on anvils with little flints taped to them so that sparks would fly across the room.

---

days. I moved to San Francisco in the fall of '76 because it's easier to be creative here.

I remember saying, "In New York people do things because

they think it's going to make them some money. In San Francisco, people do things because they love to do it." I knew this gorgeous gal who moved to New York in '82, and her "take" was, "In New York, everybody talks about money. In San Francisco, everybody talks about sex." [laughs]

♦ *V: Back in the punk '70s, you dressed like Frank Sinatra—*

♦ ML: The New Wave style with early '60s 3-button suits and skinny ties suited me; I bought a lot of those suits when they were five bucks a pop. I got my pointy shoes at an outdoor used shoestand at the corner of Sixth and Mission, and have been looking for more of 'em ever since! I love all the eras; but for me, 1961 is the peak of the Golden Age—*Breakfast at Tiffany's* came out that year!

♦ *V: Tell us about your bands—*

♦ ML: My first band, in 1979-'80, was a power-punk group called PRESSURE. I banged on anvils with little flints taped to them so that sparks would fly across the room. We opened for bands like X and the Blasters, and played the Geary Temple several times. My next band was RYTH-A-RAMA, an early '60s-style novelty dance band with soulful guitar and Farfisa organ. In 1981 Dr. Demento played our 45, "Weird, Weird, Weird, Weird," to death: "He thinks she's weird/She thinks he's weird/Everybody's weird, weird, weird, weird." I said the word "weird" so many times that it lost its meaning! Live, we did "The Monster Mash" for an encore, with a tape loop of the bubbling cauldron on a tape-player I held up to the microphone. [laughs]

♦ *V: You played with Richard Kelly's Club Foot Orchestra—*

♦ ML: —and that album is N.R.M. ("Non-Rock Music," a category I invented because I thought rock music had played itself out). I played wacky percussion whenever Kelly pointed at me and gave me the hairy eyeball. His group, the Alterboys, was among the first to play TV themes like "Mission Impossible" and "Peter Gunn"; the actor Richard Edson played drums in that group and had his picture on the cover. I lived around the corner from Club Foot and helped Kelly and his girlfriend, Cindy Buff, put up some of the walls when it first got going; then I MC'd the

At Club Nine, I drove my '61 Chrysler right into the nightclub with five gorgeous gals wearing cocktail dresses. They exited the car and danced onto the stage.

album's release party (ca. April, 1981) at Gerry & Olga Gerrard's Savoy Tivoli nightclub on Grant Avenue. Club Foot was a wonderful place to do creative "experiments"—we could use a place like that in town today, no doubt about it.

By 1979 many lounges had died. As Tony Bennett said, "The '70s were not very kind." He hated that decade because he couldn't get a job and for awhile didn't have a record contract. But I love the album where he's wearing platform shoes and bell-bottoms. [laughs] At the time Sinatra was singing "Mrs Robinson" (by Simon & Garfunkel) and Mel Torme was doing hippie songs—you know, trying to update their material. All this was a big inspiration for the later Mr. Lucky Experience.

When New Wave started sputtering in 1980, I rediscovered the world of Nat King Cole and Sinatra. I went back to my dad's house, taped all his records and listened to 'em to death. I started doing this kind of music instead. Remember, we had to tape all the old records for fear the music would be lost forever. We had no idea that everything would be re-released on CD. Another thing—I started listening to KSFO; they played all this music.

In October, 1980 I played Stephen Parr's Club Generic as "Pierre Marvel and Amanda Night," and we appeared at Dog Swan's Beatnik Festival (Aug 27–28) at Richard Kelly & Cindy Buff's Club Foot. I was dressed in a sharkskin suit and fedora. The first night we did standards, originals, plus "Turn Turn Turn," "Where Have All the Flowers Gone?" and "Puff the Magic Dragon," in what came to be the Mr. Lucky style. The second night I did a performance act called "Punch and Banger," reading apocalyptic, rhyming poetry with a drummer.

Then in 1982–'83 I had the Ring-A-Ding Duo (after the Sinatra euphemism for intercourse) with pianist George Rosenberg, doing Bacharach and Sinatra material. We played parties and a couple of hotels. Then George ran off and married my girlfriend. I'm sorry the act broke up, because he was a good piano player. Then I couldn't find any musicians who wanted to play this type of music, so I went into a studio and erased the vocals off some recordings and started singing with orchestrated tape backgrounds. People say, "Oh, Lucky—he's some guy who just did a karaoke thing," but at the time, there was no karaoke. I used tapes because no musicians were interested, and I wanted a big sound. This was not a parody or a novelty; I did it because I loved the songs and nobody else was doing it.

In 1984–85 I played several times at Club Anon (run by Joegh Bullock and Marcia Crosby, the Climate Theater producers). As part of the act I made martinis onstage. On Sept 29, 1984 I sang at Steve Parr's big band show at the Swedish-American Hall, guesting with a 13-piece band, The Union Squares, above what's now the Cafe Du Nord.

In 1985-'86 I played Mrs Phillip's Bar, on the corner of 9th and Howard, every Saturday. That's an old bar where Jack Dempsey used to train in the basement. I opened for the Zasu Pitts Memorial Orchestra at the Great American Music Hall a few times.

In November, 1985 I did "Mr. Lucky Week" at Club Nine. I drove my '61 Chrysler right into the nightclub with five gorgeous gals wearing cocktail dresses. They exited the car and danced onto the stage. That was my first Mr. Lucky gig with a big dance revue. Then I also did variety shows with the Sluts-A-Go-Go (Doris Fish, Miss X, Tippi) from 1985–1990 at the 181 Club, DNA, Victoria Theater and the Oasis.

Things were pretty thin in the mid-'80s until Luther Blue, who had a punk clothing store in North Beach and then a "water bar" at Haight and Fillmore, booked me at the 530 Club on Haight Street. In '87 I did a couple of Mr. Lucky shows, with taped accompaniments, that went over quite well. Then the owner, Jay Johnson, closed the 530 Club and in 1989 opened the Deluxe. I started singing by the pool table in the back until they removed it and built a little stage. Starting in 1990, I played there every Saturday for over two years, doing Bacharach and Sinatra material, and kicked the "retro" scene off there. Slimm Buick often opened, as a stand-up comedian. Vise Grip was the doorman and he did the intro for me; Slimm also deejayed. People started dressing up, and the swing thing began gaining steam.

In the fall of '91 the Deluxe began having live music, even

I started with the Grace Slick-at-Woodstock "Good Morning, People!" bit, complete with peace signs turning into quote marks. Then I burst into "Night and Day."

though they didn't have a cabaret license. On Sundays a quiet jazz trio led by Khevan played; their last gig was Dutch's wedding party (December 8; Green Room); they backed me while I sang. I met the Psychedelic Lounge Cats (with Morty) at a Steve Parr production, Kings of S.F. Lounge, at DNA [n.d.]. With guys from that band I started Lucky & the L.S.M.F.T. Rat Pack; we did a "Lucky Goes Latin" show (doing songs from the *Sinatra Sings Jobim* LP) on 5-20-92. We played the Deluxe's third anniversary June 18, 1992.

The beloved 1961 Chrysler New Yorker in all its chrome glory. Photo: V.Vale, July 6, 1997.

DELL FIRST EDITION B165 35¢

MR. LUCKY

the handsome, hard-hitting man-about-town who plays for the highest stakes of all —life and death.

Photo: V.Vale; collage: Yimi Tong

The band mutated into the Deluxe Quartet, with Khevan Lennon, Fred Harris, Randy O'Dell and Kurt Ribak. Then I went to Europe for three weeks. When I came back, the Deluxe Quartet was playing every Sunday, and people like me started sitting in on vocals. In fall '92 Atomic Cocktail started playing every Sunday. Sept 17 I did a Las Vegas night with go-go dancers, Magic George, etc, and the next week Vise Grip debuted St. Vitus Dance (Sept 23, '92). After doing the "Mr. Lucky Experience" there in September, 1993, Dutch threw me out—it was too "far out." I came back and did a Burt Bacharach night with pianist Kevin Gerzevitz in 1995, and that was the last time I played the Deluxe.

♦ V: *Were you there when Timmie Hesla started his big band?*
♦ ML: I opened for him at a Steve Parr event in the late '80s. In 1995, Timmie played the Deluxe every Friday night for awhile. I had the pleasure of singing with his Orchestra at the Haight Street Fair; I started with the Grace Slick-at-Woodstock "Good Morning, People!" bit, complete with peace signs turning into quote marks. Then I burst into "Night and Day."

> I didn't really know what I was doing;
> I just *did* it—creativity needs a germ of
> naiveté to get the sparks flying.

♦ V: *Didn't you start going to lounge/swing shows early on?*
♦ ML: I had seen Frank Sinatra with my mother at Caesar's. In 1980 my cousins took me to the Venetian Room to see Tony Bennett, and I got bitten by the "lounge bug"—I went regularly through the '80s. I saw the Count Basie band, Jack Jones, Mel Torme with George Shearing, Joe Williams, Peggy Lee, Rosemary

Clooney, Chris Connor, and Keely Smith when she first came out of retirement. The Venetian Room was one of the last of the old supper clubs—a little window in time where the past met the present. There weren't many people on Wednesday and Sunday nights, so I got to talk to Ella Fitzgerald! I also saw Sinatra about ten times at the Circle Star Theater and Caesar's Palace.

♦ V: *When did you buy your 1961 Chrysler?*
♦ ML: In 1984. 1961 was the last year for Virgil Exner's stint as head of the design team at Chrysler. He came up with "The Forward Look" back in '57 with the low-slung, big-finned cars that Chrysler made, and in '61 made his biggest, baddest car with the Astrodome dashboard. Then Chrysler said, "Hey, everybody else is dropping the fins." Virgil refused to do that, so they fired him and shaved the fins off. They asked Virgil, "How do you like the '62?" and he said, "It looks like a plucked chicken." [laughs] I love that '61, with its dashboard, push-button transmission and everything else. So, I found one all beat-up for $600. I called it the "Fleshmobile" because it was this beige color called Sahara Sand. [laughs] I fixed it up, and since then have had a good time with that car. The car was *me.* [laughs] It still runs great and I park it in front of places I play—I hate collectors who buy old cars and just keep them in a garage.

Once it was painted, I drove it to these Rat Pack club meetings we had at Jerry and Johnny (bar at 81 3rd St; moved in 1985 to 105 3rd St) every first Friday in '86. It was an old *S.F. News* bar covered with newspaper photos, and had Louis and Keely's "Old Black Magic" and "Swing, Swing, Swing" on the jukebox. Dog Swan, Dave Microwave (of Los Microwaves), the Japanese Weekend crowd and Loretta, the first postmodern cigarette girl, would show up and we'd read from the book *Sinatra and His Rat Pack.*

♦ V: *Your car has an animal sound—*
♦ ML: That's the big engine, a 413 with the four-barrel carburetor. That engine set the record in Daytona in '61; it went 140-plus miles an hour.

♦ V: *What's the concept behind your act?*
♦ ML: The Mr. Lucky Experience evolved from a concept I wrote up in June, 1993, entitled "Mancinian, the God of Intrigue; Brubeckian, the God of Intellect; Bacharachian, the God of Heartbreak." When Sinatra came out with his new sound in the '50s, after the big band era died, he picked out songs that a guy would have sung with a megaphone in the '20s and redid them with a "swingin' style." It was a major restylization. These songs

Young Mr. Lucky

The man, the music, and the art: Mr. Lucky in his San Francisco studio. Photo: V.Vale, July 6, 1997.

were thought of as hopelessly cornball and outdated, but he realized they had great lyrics and good melodies, and he had great arrangers recast them.

My concept was to do the same thing, only draw from all eras, styles and songs. The band members all kicked in ideas. Our first show was August 28, 1993 at the Deluxe. I did songs like "Everybody Wants to Rule the World," "Luck Be A Lady Tonight," Andy William's "Can't Get Used to Losing You" and segued into "Back in Black." We played Bimbo's, Hi-Ball, the Du Nord & the Paradise. I didn't really know what I was doing; I just *did* it—creativity needs a germ of naiveté to get the sparks flying.

My latest project is the Extra-Nat'r'ls, with Kevin Gerzivitz a great pianist in his own right, Tom Byrne (samples and percussion), and Paul Ogelsby (drums). We're recording samples from Arnold Schwarzenegger movies and incorporating them into songs like "Route 66." We'll see where this takes us. We played Burning Man this year—the cocktail party just before they "lit him up." We keep building on these ideas . . . "Come Fly With Me," right?

♦ **V:** *Why do you think this swing movement needed to occur?*
♦ **ML:** The '80s–'90s were a dark period for music. With few exceptions, song lyrics were terrible. Bob Dylan, the Beatles and others ushered in the singer-songwriter and brought about the death of Tin Pan Alley. Songwriting went downhill in a big way; also, lyrics became dark, dreary and violent, reflecting the perception of the decline of the quality of life. So, how are you going to pick yourself up out of all these problems without "Accentuating the Positive," as Bing Crosby sang during World War II. Right now we're stuck in the "irony age." Sarcasm used to just be a side issue that kept everything equal and balanced, but now it's become *content.*

♦ **V:** *Creativity comes out of passion, & irony kills passion—*
♦ **ML:** A lot of young people realize this, and they see in swing music a positive force. It has taken awhile for musicians who grew up on rock riffs to learn how to play and write "swing songs," but finally people are coming up with new lyrics that are on-point for our particular era. All creativity draws on elements from the past, mixing them with what's going on right now.

♦ **V:** *These days, however, everyone needs a day job.*
♦ **ML:** You can blame the real estate racketeering conspiracy:

"Instead of spending 25% of your salary on rent, why not spend 85%?" You can no longer just work a part-time job and do creative things.

Remember that Pere Ubu song, "Life Stinks, I Need a Drink"? Now, it's like "Okay, we had a drink and now we're feeling a little better about things." [laughs]

I think it's time for "the end of trends." Trends are marketing ploys, so corporations can keep pushing new "product" for people to buy. Trends are just a way to sell stuff. Actually, trends no longer exist—they no longer have time to evolve into true trends!

♦ **V:** *What's your attitude toward clothes?*
♦ **ML:** I have a lot of gripes about contemporary shoes; people are wearing these Outer Space overpriced sneakers or heavy clodhoppers that look like club feet. You can still find black wingtips downtown—all the businessmen wear them; they're okay. I'm still looking for pointy shoes; I went to Spain thinking I could find a pair, maybe with laces on the side, but nobody had them.

> ### I think it's time for "the end of trends." Trends are marketing ploys, so corporations can keep pushing new "product" for people to buy.

Everybody now wants '40s clothes, but a lot of '40s lady's clothes look dowdy. The height of fashion for women is 1953–1965. Actually, I like all the different eras; I'm no Style Nazi. Sometimes I go out in a sharkskin suit and skinny tie and the stingy brim hat, and other nights I'll have the '40s periwinkle gabardine double-breasted suit with the wide shiny tie with a great design on it. It's hard to mix those two different styles in the same outfit—that *really* takes an artist!

A lot of guys can't afford a '40s vintage outfit, so they should just buy a decent-looking '80s suit at a thrift store. They can get a cool tie at a retro shop and look great. The point is to get a bit dressed up (or dolled up) and use a little creativity to look good, then go to a club and dance. You know, do what the original point of it all was: *have fun—with style!* Ⓥ

The New Morty Show

Ladies and gentleman . . . The New Morty Show!!! Photo: Mark Iordan

The New Morty Show does a complete '50s Vegas act updated to the '90s; it's a riotous sensory overload. Members include: Morty Okin (trumpet), Connie Champagne and Vise Grip (vocals), John Quam (keyboard), Whitney Wilson (guitar), Dave Murotake (sax), Van Hughes (trombone), Tom Beyer (upright bass), Tom Griesser (baritone sax) and Kevin Stevens (drums). Their new CD is available from V/Search, 415-362-1465. Check out the New Morty Show hotline (415-675-5673) and website: *newmortyshow.com*.

♦ **VALE: *Your show is complex! How did it evolve?***
♦ MORTY OKIN: Our greatest influence, of course, was Louis Prima and Keely Smith. We were also inspired by a '50s lounge act, Ray Anthony and His Bookend Review. I knew about Ray Anthony—he's been a trumpet player and big band leader for years—but I'd never heard of his lounge act until my friend Dutch (who works at Club Deluxe) gave me *Ray Anthony and His Bookend Review: Live at the Sahara.* I thought it was a total Louis Prima rip-off, but great because it was more cheesy. [laughs] But I wouldn't want to build anything on just the Ray Anthony material; Louis Prima was definitely our "base."
♦ *V: It makes sense they would be an inspiration to you since all of you have the trumpet in common—*
♦ MO: Yeah, definitely. They both kick my ass, but . . . [laughs] I consider myself an average trumpet player who got lucky.
♦ *V: I think vision is what creates the future.*
♦ MO: I agree with that totally. And the band has gone through a lot of changes from what was initially envisioned three years ago. Right now, I think this is where everyone in the band would like to be.
♦ *V: I think all your collective energies create something that*

surpasses what anyone could do individually. That takes a certain art and finesse, especially considering the strong personalities that make up your group.
♦ MO: Yeah, it's pretty cool. We're one of the only bands that feature a male *and* female vocalist. Vise and Connie are definitely strong points, but everyone in the band helps make it work. In a lot of bands there are "side players," but this band would not have gone where it has without everyone doing their part.
♦ *V: How has your vision been modified from what you originally conceived?*
♦ MO: The show aspect of it is the same; it's the *music* that's being modified. A lot of people in the band were part of the punk rock scene and/or into ska. Now all those influences are being brought to the fore. It's cool to do a straight-ahead swing song, then in the middle of it, inject a heavy metal lick! [laughs] It's nice to have a mix. I know a lot of our swing following in San Francisco doesn't like this too much—
♦ *V: Swing purists, let's call 'em—*
♦ MO: Swing purists . . . They don't like it too much, but when we travel, there are people who don't know how to dance and don't dress in vintage clothes who *do* love it, which is great for us

from a band standpoint. The main goal of a band is to entertain. You want to please your regular following, but at the same time, if you're traveling around to other places, you realize that the world doesn't revolve around one city. We want to have fun with

---

A lot of the swing purists resent their underground scene becoming more commercial.

---

everyone: from swing people who really know the dances and the "image" to people who just like the show and the music.

♦ **V:** *Once people get exposed to the dancing, a lot of them will go, "Gee, I want to get into this."*

♦ MO: Oh, yeah. And a lot of the swing purists resent their underground scene becoming more commercial. But from a band standpoint, again: you want everyone to be into your music. We want to get to Hong Kong so fuckin' bad. Swing and rockabilly are huge in Hong Kong and Asia. I remember seeing on *20/20*—this must have been seven years ago—they did a story on the rockabilly scene, and I was blown away at kids with pompadours two-feet high. A lot of their clothes are all remakes of vintage clothes. I'd love it if there were good remakes available now, because all the vintage stuff is mostly heavy wool or falling apart!

♦ **V:** *Wherever you travel you're going to influence people toward this style—*

♦ MO: It's a combination of us and the other bands out there. As far as this "swing" scene goes, some people take it a bit far—like any scene. There are people who think they're living in the '40s—but it's the '90s! [laughs] It's weird how there's been a complete crossover: a lot of the swing people are former punk rockers, rude boys and girls, etc. It's hilarious.

♦ **V:** *How do you want to be described?*

♦ MO: It's kind of cool to hear the different ways people categorize us. I really have no idea how to describe us: "punk/ lounge/cabaret" or "swing/punk/caba- ret"—something along those lines.

♦ **V:** *I prefer the latter, because "lounge" implies a much more passive attitude, and you guys are very energetic. Were you a "nerd" in high school, teaching yourself trumpet?*

♦ MO: [laughs] Oh, yeah. My dad is a retired band teacher. I was a big, big nerd.

♦ **V:** *Where was this?*

♦ MO: Birmingham, Michigan. Drums were my first instru- ment—for about a week. My mom said they were too loud. So, for some odd reason, I went to trumpet—

♦ **V:** *Which is even louder!*

♦ MO: Exactly. Where that rationale came from, I don't fully know. I played music from the second grade on but didn't start getting serious until my freshman year in high school—*that's* when I knew I wanted to go into music. I was mainly brought up

"classical," wanting to be in a symphony orchestra. It was only after college, where I majored in classical performance, that I real- ized it's quite impossible. [laughs] I went to Eastern Michigan University and never graduated, then moved out here in '91 to be in a funk/lounge band called the PSYCHEDELIC LOUNGE CATS—a really fun band.

♦ **V:** *How did you happen to join?*

♦ MO: They played gigs in Ann Arbor, where I was living at the time. Then one day I saw them fooling around with their trum- pets on their porch. We started talking and I ended up joining.

♦ **V:** *How could the band afford to move from Michigan to San Francisco?*

♦ MO: We never paid ourselves; all the money went into a band fund.

♦ **V:** *So, you moved out here communal-style?*

♦ MO: Oh, yeah. There were eight of us sharing a six-bedroom house.

♦ **V:** *That's big—*

♦ MO: No, not really. [laughs] Not big enough.

♦ **V:** *Did you get many gigs?*

♦ MO: The first year we did really well. I met Vise Grip the first month I was here. I went into the Club Deluxe and he was bar- tending—they had open mike nights on Sundays, so that's when

Morty Okin in the 5th Grade and now. Photo: Mark Jordan

I would go in and play with a jazz quartet. One day he said, "I'm forming a band. Do you want to be in it?" So I started doing a lot with Vise's ST. VITUS DANCE and became disillusioned with the Lounge Cats. I ended up quitting the Lounge Cats and then, a year later, got fired from St. Vitus Dance for not having an extension cord. [laughs]

♦ **V:** *What was that for?*

♦ MO: My stand light. The piano player fired me. [laughs] I played in a lot of different bands after that: UNDERCOVER SKA, VERONICA KLAUS and Her Heart and Soul Revue, SIMON'S NEW BLUE DIAMONDS, and did a lot of recording with the BROUN FELLINIS and SKANKIN' PICKLE. I played live with the REVEREND HOR- TON HEAT, but never record- ed—Vise and I would go up for a couple of songs onstage—it was awesome. He's an amazing musi- cian, lyricist, and writer.

♦ **V:** *How were you supporting yourself?*

♦ MO: For two years I was a bank teller, but for the past four-and-a-half years I've been living off music.

♦ **V:** *That's amazing.*

♦ MO: Yeah. If I died tomorrow—I mean, if I had to get a day job tomorrow—I would be thankful for the four-and-a-half years I was able to live off music. One of the lucky ones! [laughs]

♦ **V:** *It must have been stressful for you to uproot from Michigan and move to San Francisco, a strange city—*

♦ MO: It was definitely a scary move. I actually wanted to move to New York but everybody else in the Lounge Cats wanted to move to San Francisco. I'm glad I moved here. Whenever we play Vegas or L.A., when we come back it's like, "Ahhh, home . . . the ocean, mountains—yes!" We're spoiled. A lot of Vegas residents really like living there, but when we tell them what we have available here, they're like, "Oh, wow!" You know, being able to go to the symphony, having fantastic food, being able to see great music and go to night clubs seven nights a week, just walking down the street and having an incredible view, etc.

♦ **V: Did you plan to be your own bandleader?**

♦ MO: The band was formed because I was sick of being at the mercy of someone else's income. Plus, this was the music I wanted to play. Being able to go out and hustle gigs, I got the best of both worlds. Everyone in the band has played in other bands with each other, and that made it easier to form this group. Everything just worked out. I don't think any of us ever expected this kind of success at all. It's pretty weird, too, because we have no product yet.

♦ **V: That's right. There's no record—you don't even have a cassette tape?**

♦ MO: We had a crappy four-song demo of all covers—I mean, it was a good demo tape, but we had no product to sell and no product on the radio. We've been successful just based on word of mouth, which is amazing. Bands like Royal Crown Revue are really nice, and wherever they go, they put in a good word for us. Without a product I never thought this would happen. So, we're all antsy to get something out now! [laughs]

♦ **V: How did you meet Connie Champagne?**

♦ MO: I saw her and the Tiny Bubbles at the Club Deluxe; she was awesome. Then I gave her my card and said, "If you ever need a trumpet or flugelhorn player, I'd love to play." And I called her up one day and she threw me off the phone! [laughs] About a year later, she joined Veronica Klaus's Heart and Soul Revue as a back-up singer. Our drummer, Dave Rubin, and I had been playing with Veronica's group for a while.

Connie and I ended up being friends and sharing this vision. Both of us love Louis Prima and Keely Smith, and I turned her on to the Ray Anthony record. Connie sounds exactly like Keely Smith—it's really weird. So, the New Morty Show started out as just me and Connie as the band, then when St. Vitus Dance broke up, I asked Vise to join and . . . be Louis Prima! [laughs] And it worked out perfect. Connie and Vise work so well together.

♦ **V: As they say, it's a match made in heaven. What do your parents think of all this?**

♦ MO: They're so supportive. For about the past few years, we've been as tight as hell—for the first time.

♦ **V: Did they encourage you to be a musician?**

♦ MO: They encouraged me to play music, but not for a *living.* That's why we had a falling out. If I was going to get a music degree, they wanted me to get a teaching degree with it—but I didn't want to teach. Teaching is an art; I'm amazed at the patience teachers have because it's something I don't possess! So, we had a falling out for a good hunk of time. Then, about three and a half years ago, we met in Las Vegas—on neutral territory [laughs]—and it was awesome.

♦ **V: Were you playing in Vegas?**

♦ MO: No, we just decided to meet there. Then they flew out to Vegas three times in a span of three months to see the band play! They still haven't been to San Francisco to see us, but . . . My dad is retired and my mom works in the art gallery of the Jewish Community Center.

♦ **V: Tell us about working as a bank teller—**

♦ MO: I was broke when I got here; I needed to do *anything.* I started telemarketing. I had done that in college and loved it, but it was more bogus police and fire fighter organizations—total boiler room operation.

♦ **V: What's a "boiler room operation"?**

♦ MO: Basically, it means a load of crap! [laughs]

♦ **V: Would you just call up and say that you were from the Police or Fireman's Organization and try to get people to donate money?**

♦ MO: Yeah. They *were* real organizations, and some of the money was going to these institutions, but—to me, non-profit organizations are such bullshit because there *is* a profit being made and it goes to "administration." Maybe five to ten percent of all the money collected (out of, say, two million dollars—big fucking deal) goes to the actual people who need help.

♦ **V: To the kids with polio or whatever?**

♦ MO: Exactly. I don't know how it is with every non-profit group, but I'm sure for a lot of them that's how it is. But I loved it because I was good at it. So, I did that until this guy I was working with (who was also recovering from a heroin addiction) poured a boiling hot pot of coffee on my head because I had more sales than he did. [laughs] Suffice to say, I quit that job and got one as a bank teller. I actually loved that job! I learned how to budget my money and learned a lot about banking.

♦ **V: That must have served you well when you started the New Morty Show. You probably were the band's manager—**

♦ MO: Yeah. Now we're managed by Solo Music Group: Ralph Tashjian and Jay Siegan. They've made life way easier.

♦ **V: How much do you practice?**

♦ MO: When I was in college I used to practice eight hours a day—I was hardcore—but not anymore. I loved the business side and really got into hustling gigs and talking to people, so practicing became secondary. I'm just starting to get "serious" again. I've been lucky because I consider myself a good, average trumpet player, but I need to be much, much better. But the business side of this just grabbed my heart—I love it! I hope that later in life I can work for a record company or do something with the business side of music.

♦ **V: Yes, but aren't you getting a certain fulfillment from being a band leader?**

David Metzner on guitar; Tom Beyer on bass; John Quam on keyboard.

♦ MO: That's the thing: I had the best of both worlds. But then the business side became too much. Now, I can just concentrate on playing. I haven't been able to do that for a long time.

♦ V: *What responsibilities are involved in what you do? It must include making charts—*

♦ MO: When we first started out I paid a guy to do about 15 or 20 charts. Then when the band started to do well, people got committed. Now our piano player, John Quam, basically does all of the rhythm charts for the piano, bass, and guitar. As far as writing original songs, we collaborate with each other. Everybody brings something to the table.

♦ V: *It's like group arranging—*

♦ MO: To a point. Like if someone has their own song, it's how *they* want it. For some of the cover tunes that we do, I'll have something in my head and do the horn arrangements. Then we'll rehearse and I'll hone the arrangements there. But for originals, everyone has their own stuff. If something obviously doesn't sound good, we'll all give input and try to change it. It's really nice having a lot of people who are into writing. But as far as being a band leader goes—I don't advise it. [laughs] Especially not with a ten-piece band. It's a bitch. I love it, but some days you have to deal with a lot of personalities. Before we had manage-

Sing, sing, sing! L to R: Van Hughes, Dave Murotake, and Morty. Photo: Mark Jordan

---

If you're not having fun, then fuck it! What's the point of doing it?

---

ment, I was doing everything; *I* paid to get our tapes done. But for the past year, I've been able to take money out of the group's earnings to get those tapes made. Band management was a thankless job, but it was worth it.

♦ V: *Well, it is the New Morty Show and not the New Joe Schmo Show!*

♦ MO: Exactly. [laughs] I really try to keep it a democracy. But on some matters, it's impossible with ten people, and I'll make the final decision. A lot of band leaders are Nazis who make their people feel like hired guns. I guess some musicians *want* to be hired guns, but a lot of people want that commitment to be treated equal.

♦ V: *That's better for the long haul—*

♦ MO: Exactly. And some of these band leaders will take massive cuts off gigs. I don't do that. I do take a little cut to pay bills that are band-oriented.

♦ V: *That makes sense. I think most people would be happy to give you that because you're taking a load off their shoulders. You need to be fair-minded or you're going to be changing personnel all the time.*

♦ MO: Exactly! And if I was like that, this band wouldn't be what it is right now—I guarantee it.

♦ V: *Where do you rehearse with ten people?*

♦ MO: We usually go to Lennon Studios—

♦ V: *Isn't it a problem getting ten humans together?*

♦ MO: Since the band's success we don't have to deal with people's schedules. If we have a rehearsal, it's "This time, be there, or get yelled at." [laughs] And everyone's been pretty cool. Since everyone is an integral part, they all want to put something into it and see how this can grow and be successful.

♦ V: *Plus, you look like you're having fun on stage.*

♦ MO: If you're not having fun, then fuck it! What's the point of doing it? We've done a few gigs that have totally sucked.

♦ V: *You mean the audiences?*

♦ MO: Yeah; corporate parties. Most parties are a lot of fun, but of course you can't have fun all the time. So, the ones that suck, we don't give a shit about and we still have a great time anyway. People have told us they *see* that energy on stage. So if you don't know how to dance, just watching the band can be fun.

♦ V: *How do the trumpet and flugelhorn differ?*

♦ MO: The flugelhorn is a really soft, mellow version of the trumpet. It's bigger and shaped differently. There's also the pocket trumpet, which is a miniature trumpet. It's in the same key; it's the same length of tubing, just wrapped around one more time so it's half the size. I play all three of them. Some are brighter and some are a little darker-sounding. The flugelhorn is great for ballads and the trumpet is good to really cut through. The pocket trumpet is good for looks and good for *shtick.* [laughs] It's actually cool because sometimes the band gets kind of loud and the bell of the horn is closer to my face, so it's easier for me to hear.

♦ V: *Your personal monitoring system—*

♦ MO: Exactly.

♦ V: *I saw Dizzy Gillespie play a long time ago and he had his trumpet bell going 45 degrees up—*

♦ MO: Yeah, for looks. Someone sat on his trumpet one day, and he liked the look. He blew it and actually got a sound out of it. So, he had one made like that.

♦ V: *There is a total cultural sensibility to this "swing" scene—*

♦ MO: Oh, yeah, including architecture and everything else. I'll fully agree with that. A lot of designers, from clothes to furniture, are going back to those older styles. For me, I like the '50s stuff, whereas most swing people prefer the '40s stuff—

♦ **V:** *Like the double-breasted suits—*

♦ **MO:** Yeah. I don't even own one of those—

♦ **V:** *You iconoclast, you!*

♦ **MO:** [laughs] The '50s, from the cars to clothes to radios to silverware, has the coolest shit! But I would love to be able to buy a '90s ghetto blaster that looks like a '50s radio—it would be awesome! I own a record player, but not a 78 player. When I listen to music, I like it to have a clean listening quality. I know hardcore

A lot of older cats disagree with sound systems, but I'm a firm believer in technology.

record collectors disagree with me and say that some things are meant to be listened to on vinyl. I guess that's true, but having that stuff remastered on CD is awesome for me because I like hearing what every instrument is doing clearly.

♦ **V:** *Do you collect '50s paraphernalia?*

♦ **MO:** My room is pretty modern. Like I said, I love the clothes, architecture, and have some pin-up girls on the wall, but I like modern technology. I love knickknacks and gadgets—if the Sharper Image would ever sponsor me, I'd be forever grateful. [laughs] I love that shit! Everything from stereo equipment to computers.

♦ **V:** *Do you ever do horn charts on the computer?*

♦ **MO:** No, my computer's not powerful enough. Though I wish I could afford it. For the past two years I've been doing most of the horn charts, and then our trombone player, Van Hughes, does some. And Tom Griesser does a lot of charts as well. I do them on a midi keyboard with a lot of different sounds, like drums. It's a Yamaha PSR-510.

♦ **V:** *Describe your room—*

♦ **MO:** I have a bunch of awesome posters that Dutch, from the Deluxe, makes when bands play. I have two Miles Davis posters and one Dizzy Gillespie.

Below: Richard Olsen and Morty. Photo by Mark Jordan. Above: drummer, Dave Rubin.

A bunch of postcards of '50s Vegas scenes takes up a whole wall. An old Vegas felt blackjack board hangs on my door. I also have my computer and one of those cheap black modern-looking halogen lamps that everyone owns. Then there's my keyboard with a tape deck above it, so when I write music I can put it on tape. There's also my stereo system and maybe 50 records. I have about 200 CDs—I love technology, baby! [laughs] I have a ton of vintage ties and suits and crap—all the accessories. That's pretty much it.

♦ **V:** *Can you recall when people started dressing retro?*

♦ **MO:** When I moved here, a lot of people seemed to have already been into the clothes for a long time. Before I moved here, I was more into the '60s stuff—

♦ **V:** *You mean pre-psychedelic '60s?*

♦ **MO:** Yeah. Narrow lapels and three-button suits. California is more cutting-edge than anywhere else in the country. The downside is: everything's so expensive here. I remember my grandmother's house, which was mint-condition '30s, '40s, '50s every-

thing. And when she moved to a retirement home, my parents sold it all in a garage sale. They didn't get nearly as much as they could have in California because in the Midwest it's considered junk. If they had shipped that stuff to me, I would have been set for life—seriously.

♦ **V:** *Here you can go into vintage stores and learn about all this—*

♦ **MO:** Yes. And it's not so much that people look at this stuff and think, "Whoa, it's history, man—that's an antique." Here you buy it and put it in your house and *use* it! No one in the Midwest would ever think of having one of those '50s chrome dinette sets in their kitchen, except for old people. But out here, everyone's got one—it's awesome! [laughs] It was definitely culture shock when I moved here; in California I felt like I was living in Playland.

♦ **V:** *When did you get your current hairstyle? It looks so '50s—*

♦ **MO:** I started wearing it right after high school, before college. I grew up in a pretty wealthy Jewish neighborhood and my high school was Beverly Hills 90210—it was sick. I loved my childhood, but would never want to raise someone like that. It was very sheltered. I didn't start wearing vintage suits until I started college.

♦ **V:** *Did you ever go through a "grunge" period?*

♦ **MO:** Definitely not.

♦ **V:** *A horn is hardly a grunge instrument—*

♦ **MO:** I actually played with a couple of metal bands and they were a lot of fun. One out here was called MOL TRIFFID. Me and the horn section from SKANKIN' PICKLE recorded with a punk band from Japan called HIGH STANDARD. They didn't speak any English. Their record company, Fat Records, is in San Francisco, so whenever they record they fly here. High Standard are the coolest guys and they're an excellent band.

I didn't really get into METALLICA until I had a girlfriend here who was their Number One Fan. I started listening to them and thought, "Fuck, these guys are awesome." I was also always into BLACK SABBATH. In fact, when I was in the Lounge Cats we lounged up some Sabbath songs and did an Ozzy medley: "Crazy Train," "Fairies Wear Boots," and "War Pigs." It was so much fun. Anyway, I always "heard" horns in heavy metal stuff. That was another vision I had: to start a band with a six-piece horn section, two guitars, two bass players, and drums and just have it huge. It would have been a 14-piece heavy metal band with horns. But the New Morty Show is kind of turning into that! [laughs]

Horns and heavy metal mix so well together—punk, too. I think horns are starting to get more popular and moving beyond swing. It's definitely becoming more popular with harder-edge

ska bands that are doing ska punk. Like this group I played with called RUDIMENTS. NO DOUBT used to be great ska punk—now they're ska pop. But I remember fuckin' No Doubt opened up for UNDERCOVER SKA at the Paradise Lounge three years ago—they opened up for *us* in this small venue, too—then suddenly, the next thing I knew, they're huge! It was unbelievable. Then, of course, the MIGHTY MIGHTY BOSSTONES are doing ska punk and I've always loved those guys. Skankin' Pickle also did a lot of ska—more ska metal, actually.

♦ *V: Are they still around?*

♦ MO: I haven't heard their name in a long time. I'm surprised those guys never became huge. They were awesome.

♦ *V: Maybe they were too far ahead of their time—*

♦ MO: They were a couple of years too early for the ska revival, and now that ska is huge again . . . it's too bad. It's like the Psychedelic Lounge Cats—we were doing lounge five years before Combustible Edison, and now *they're* huge.

♦ *V: How did you get a consciousness of swing music?*

♦ MO: I was a classical geek for a long time. I knew Benny Goodman and Glenn Miller and liked them because my dad was into that. It wasn't until I hit college when I started getting into jazz. Swing came in my second or third year of college. So, I'm still new to a lot of this. I learned about Louis Prima in college. Before high school, I loved Thomas Dolby and the Police. I also loved Howard Jones' first album because he used horns. Any modern group that used horns I loved. I loved old Genesis—not Phil Collins—but old Genesis. Then, when I hit high school, I got serious about trumpet and went classical. In college, I expanded.

♦ *V: What kind of CDs do you own?*

♦ MO: Everything from Henry Rollins to Maynard Ferguson to Tito Puente. My collection is diverse, but not like some of my friends who have *everything.* I just can't afford everything. Vise has a lot of great shit. I have a lot of straight-ahead old jazz that wouldn't be considered swing, but still "swings." [laughs]

♦ *V: Have you started recording your CD yet?*

♦ MO: Yes, and now it's done. [laughs] It'll be on Slimstyle Records and distributed by Island Records.

♦ *V: What do you think of the whole cigar/martini drinking aspect of the scene?*

♦ MO: Clubs like the swing scene because their martini sales go through the roof. I've never really drank much. Blowing a trumpet, I'm blowing air out continuously, so I couldn't get drunk even if I wanted to. But martinis say "Good Time" to me in a different way than Miller Genuine Draft does. That's my take on drinking. As for the smoking: Yes, cigars are out of control. I don't think drinking is really a *fad,* but I think the cigar thing is a huge fad—definitely.

♦ *V: Personally, I had a total blind spot to swing and jump-blues, so I'm glad all these bands have emerged to reclaim this music—*

♦ MO: Thank you for saying what you did. There's such a major, major misconception with a lot of people. Swing is not jump-blues. Most of the "swing" bands are not swing, they're jump-blues bands. Jump-blues is what it says: high energy blues with horns. Swing is a musical term that's hard to explain if you're not a musician. If something swings, it's the combination of the backbeat of two and four on the snare drum with the ride cymbal. It's the way a lick is played in conjunction with the rhythm section. Other people would disagree: "Swing is a *lifestyle!*" No, swing is a musical fuckin' term.

♦ *V: Louis Jordan and Louis Prima have been described as more jump-blues—*

♦ MO: They are, totally.

♦ *V: I think it has something to do with the number of musicians they use—*

♦ MO: It has to do with that, but also when Louis Prima had his Dixieland orchestra, that was swingin'—I mean, that was a swing Dixieland orchestra. Glenn Miller and all the old big bands were swing, with jump-blues in there—a lot of the songs were 12-bar blues with a bunch of jazz chords and breaks (that is what I con-

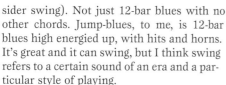

sider swing). Not just 12-bar blues with no other chords. Jump-blues, to me, is 12-bar blues high energied up, with hits and horns. It's great and it can swing, but I think swing refers to a certain sound of an era and a particular style of playing.

I guess what will happen commercially is that all of this music being revived is going to be classified under the general heading of "Swing." Even the Squirrel Nut Zippers have been labeled that, but they're '20s, '30s Hot Jazz. They're not a swing band. But at the same time, hopefully all of us bands have the same target audience who love old things. I think that's how the record industry is going to classify all of this—but it's not RIGHT! [laughs] Dammit! But whoever said the record industry was perfect!

♦ **V: Also, the true swing bands were monstrously huge—impossible to keep together today.**

♦ MO: Well, that's what happened. Smaller jazz combos started to become popular—not that jazz ever became mainstream. I think the main reason the big band era died is because clubs were not able to pay.

♦ **V: Also, amplification was introduced, so bands could have a bigger sound with fewer people.**

♦ MO: Yeah. A lot of the older cats disagree with sound systems, but I'm a firm believer in technology. This is the '90s and people's ears are trained completely different now; they're trained to listen to loud music. Take Vise's big band, for instance. We could play at Bimbo's with no sound system and the energy onstage would be just as good, but the energy in the audience would suck. As long as you've got a good sound person who knows what a big band sound should be over a sound system, it's great. I have no problem with sound systems—I love 'em.

Plus, from a band's standpoint, when you see an audience

Cover of The New Morty Show's debut album, Mortyfied!

getting into it, it gives you more energy onstage. A lot of the older cats would disagree because they grew up in a time where there were no sound systems. They played in big bands in huge halls where people would shut their mouths and listen to the music or sometimes dance, but it was a totally different time.

♦ **V: And you're going beyond swing and jump-blues in the future—**

♦ MO: Yeah, definitely. I don't necessarily get bored with a certain type of music, but we've been together for three years and bands get sick of doing the same songs. We try to add originals, new covers, and different styles as well. We like playing the punk rock and metal stuff—not all the time—but it's fun to add 'em in. We're not just playing for people; we're playing for ourselves, too.

♦ **V: You've got to please yourself to be able to please your audience—**

♦ MO: I like to do both.

♦ **V: My point is: if you please yourself, you'll shape your own public.**

♦ MO: Exactly. Those are the people you want to come see you anyway: people who appreciate what you want to do. That makes perfect sense. **V**

Morty Recommends

Travelling Shoes #1 (the Las Vegas issue), $3 from POB 206653, New Haven CT 06520-6653

As a teenager, Connie Champagne started singing in punk rock bands before singing lounge and swing during the '80s and '90s. She left the New Morty Show in Febuary 1998, and started a new version of the Tiny Bubbles with ex-Morty drummer David Rubin and vibes-master Michael Emenau. She can be contacted c/o V/Search.

♦ **VALE: Can you get packages addressed to "Connie Champagne"?**

♦ CONNIE CHAMPAGNE: Absolutely. That's my legal name now. [laughs] Through the years I've gone through several last names, and the I.R.S. doesn't like you having more than one. Every time I did a job they sent me a letter: "To whom does this social security number belong?" My accountant suggested that I just call myself Connie Champagne. Since I'd been called that for so long—even my mother slips sometimes and calls me that—I thought, "Why not?" I got a Nolo Press book on how to change your name and did it.

♦ **V: When was the first time you sang in public?**

♦ CC: The first time I ever sang in front of a crowd I was nine. All these other little girls were singing songs. The only tunes I knew all the words to were "Hello Dolly" and Nat King Cole's "Love." It spells out the word, so if you're nine, it's really easy: "L is for the way you look at me/O is for the only one I see/V is very, very extra-ordinary/E is even more than anyone that you adore." I was always a good speller!

♦ **V: Did you come from a musical family?**

♦ CC: No, they were completely unmusical. I grew up in Roseville, California. My dad's father was a career criminal—a counterfeiter by trade—but also a frustrated musician and artist. I never got to meet him because my father ran away from home when he was 14. I have an early memory of my grandmother putting on a Keely Smith wig and lip-synching in a talent show to "Old Black Magic." My mom's girlfriend had a little sister who was into the Beatles. She would come over to our house and play Beatles' albums. So, as a kid I really liked the Beatles and Keely Smith.

My grandfather, Ernie Caddel, on my mother's side, who died about five years ago, was very supportive of me. He sang and played the ukelele. He played professional football in the 1930s for the Detroit Lions. He and my grandmother told me stories of that "golden" era in the '30s and '40s. There were parts of my adolescence that were very chaotic, but his presence was really key—he always supported everything I did. And they had cool records: the Keely Smith solo record *Politely,* the Count Basie and Frank Sinatra *It Might As Well Be Swing,* Rusty Warren's *Knockers Up!*—I wasn't supposed to hear that one, but of course I played it when they were gone! In high school I discovered Dinah Washington's *Drinking Again* in a used record store. It had a wonderful cover: she has steel-gray hair and is wearing a fur coat, and you can see her profile through a glass of scotch. I love her plain, spoken delivery. She's such a great singer—not necessarily because of her technical skill, but because she's soulful and has a great way of just tossing lines off. She imbues the lyrics with a lot of meaning, irony, humor, and all that good stuff.

Connie at two years old with mom, Trudy.

♦ *V: Did your parents influence you?*
♦ CC: My mom is a big presence in my life—I love her very much. She taught me an important lesson to always keep in mind. In college, she was heavily into the Beat Scene. There was this guy who was really riding my mom's butt—metaphorically speaking—about "what a middle-class bitch she was" and how "she needed to cast off her upbringing." This guy made his own anti-freeze; it probably cost him more money, but apparently it was "cool" to do this. He was *the* hipster-dude—the one that everyone looked up to.

My mom has always been an avid reader; she read all the beat books: *Dharma Bums, On the Road,* etc. One day she happened to mention "Dean Moriarty" to this guy, and he said, "Who's *that?*" [laughs] Now that's a great lesson. My mom said, "How can you not know who that is?" This "hipster," whom everyone was in awe of, was a *bullshitter.*

♦ *V: Exactly; he was all image . . . Tell us about your musical history—*
♦ CC: I was in some really awful bands. The worst was a Steely Dan cover band—I can't remember their name. These guys were jazz musicians who thought, "We'll play high school dances and make some *money!*" But their idea of being "commercial" was to play Steely Dan songs, and they never chose ones that were popular like "My Old School" or "Deacon Blues"—they picked really obscure tunes like "Kid Charlemagne." [laughs] I *wanted* to be in a band so bad that I ignored my better judgement. I stayed with them for about a month.

Then I was in a punk band called the Queers (actually, the Napalm Queers, but "Queers" for short). We had a lot of fun, but we weren't very disciplined. I sang backup vocals for Deborah (Iyall of Romeovoid). She's wonderful to me.

♦ *V: How did you first hear about punk?*
♦ CC: When I was in high school I saw a few newspaper and magazine articles about it and thought, "These people look *interesting.*" It's so trite, now, to talk about your "painful adolescence" and all that crap, but I was living in a suburb of Sacramento and feeling isolated. Plus, I was really angry and unhappy. Everybody else was into bands like Journey and I couldn't relate to them on any level. I liked the energy of punk—that sounds like a cliché now . . .

♦ *V: It was a rebellion that was not yet set in stone.*

♦ CC: Right. You'd walk down the street and everybody would yell out the car window, "Are you Devo?"
♦ *V: So you started changing your style to be in synch with the punk scene?*
♦ CC: Yeah, I cut my hair short, dyed it black, and began wearing white make-up that gave me that "Cure" look. For Sacramento and Roseville, this was a bold fashion statement at the time. I came to San Francisco and saw shows whenever I could get a ride.

One thing that was really cool about punk and "new wave" was the fact that so many women were involved. When punk started, from the standpoint of being in a band, it went from "No Girls Allowed" to being *chic* to have a woman bass player. (I guess that's because bass is the instrument you can most quickly become somewhat competent on.) That first wave of people like Patti Smith and Deborah Harry was really appealing to me. I felt like women could be a part of this movement.

I was also in a band called Clocks of Paradise, with Brian MacLeod (drummer; recently with Sheryl Crow and Madonna)—
♦ *V: Really? [laughs] A local "success" story—*
♦ CC: Right . . . and Michael Belfer—great guitar player from the Sleepers (now he's in Black Lab). Josh, from the Black Athletes (who works at the Rainbow market now) came up with that name in a dream. It was a great band, but I was too young to appreciate it.

Those were most of the bands. Then I stopped doing that and got involved with underground theater.
♦ *V: You're a singer and a performer—*
♦ CC: I was in this underground theater group called the Dude Theater that put on plays like "Imelda: The Musical" (I wasn't in that particular one). They'd drive up to Club Nine or the DNA, do a performance on the back of a flatbed truck, and then take off. I was in "The Charlie Manson Story," which is how I became Connie Champagne. I did some research on the Manson family. The more I found out about them, the more pitiful they were—

Connie at 13 years old with her Grandfather, Ernie Caddel, in Hawaii.

♦ *V: Hardly a feminist operation—*
♦ CC: No, they're the most pathetic people and they're not "cool" in any way. A lot of theories abound as to why they did it. Personally, I don't believe it was solely about "Helter Skelter." My theory is: it had to do with the fact that Terry Melcher dropped Charlie Manson's record contract and he got really mad. In his crazed, drug-induced, hippie-fuck way, he told these really stupid people to kill everybody in Melcher's house—not realizing that it had been rented out to Sharon Tate and other people.

I was cast as "Leslie Van Houten" and, while I was researching the role, I came across a documentary on the Manson family; it included footage of this woman called "Ronnie" who had shared a cell with Susan Atkins. She'd been a gangster's moll who'd hung out in the '50s lounge scene and gotten mixed up in drugs. Susan Atkins bragged to her about being among the people who killed Sharon Tate; Ronnie freaked out (as well she should) and contacted the jailer: "This woman says she killed Sharon Tate and I want out of here!" In essence, she blew the whistle on the Manson family and was instrumental in cracking the case. Anyway, Ronnie had around 27 aliases, one of which was "Connie Champagne." When I saw that I thought, "That's the *best* name!"

I had met Scrumbly Koldwyn, of the Cockettes, and told him I wanted to play what people now call "Cocktail Nation" music. He asked, "Why don't you just do it?" and I said, "I don't know how." Then he said, "*I'll* play piano and you can sing and that's it!" We got Brad Johnson (American Music Club) and Beth Custer (Clubfoot Orchestra, Trance Mission) and formed Tabloid Mentality. We did jazz interpretations of songs like "You Can't Put Your Arms Around A Memory" by Johnny Thunders, along with the James Bond theme "You Only Live Twice." People seemed to like it.

From doing "The Charlie Manson Story" I had been thinking of calling myself Connie Champagne. Scrumbly had introduced me to Doris Fish who thought it was a great name, and immediately began calling me "Connie" all the time. She pretty much decided that's who I was. And that's how I became Connie Champagne!

Doris Fish was an incredible drag queen from Sydney, Australia. She was like a big sister or a mom in a lot of ways. She definitely had her male side—she didn't walk around the streets dressed like a girl. But she and Scrumbly helped me perceive myself as being able to do the things that I later did. They had a lot of faith in me and were both big influences. There are times when I really miss Doris . . . times when I would like to pick up the phone and ask, "What should I do?" But I can't because she's not on our plane anymore.

I was reading an article that described Doris as "a travesty of womanhood." I think she was just the opposite. She loved women. I started looking at "being a girl" as a really cool thing because of her. Her sense of humor, the things that she found interesting—she was really very underrated as an artist. Today, the RuPaul thing is great, but there wouldn't be that without a Doris. And Doris was so far beyond disco music. [laughs]

♦ **V: What did she do?**

♦ CC: She did a series of shows for the 181 Club: "Blonde Sin," "Naked Brunch," etc. And she was the producer, writer, set-designer and star of *Vegas In Space,* a feature film. We had endless benefits for that. I'm really proud that I got to be a part of that: I sang the closing-credits theme song and did a lot of voice-overs. Those were just some of the projects Doris was involved in.

After doing Tabloid Mentality for awhile, I wanted to do a

Connie during her "Queers" period, ca. 1981.

Billboard for Clocks of Paradise ca. early '80s.

drag, lounge, post-atomic cabaret act—whatever that was. I couldn't even get arrested under the name of Tabloid Mentality, but under the name of Connie Champagne and her Tiny Bubbles, we played all the time—especially at the Paradise Lounge, which at that time was a seminal place—you could do anything there. Wayne Doba was tap-dancing to "Purple Haze," Gere Fenellie would have different vocalists and she'd play her piano. Part of Tragic Mulatto, under the name of Pennsylvania Mahoney, were doing ten years ago exactly the same thing as the Squirrel Nut Zippers do today.

♦ **V: They were too far ahead of their time—**

♦ CC: Definitely. We played there Friday and Saturday nights. We didn't even have a drummer at the time. It was just piano, clarinet and stand-up bass.

♦ **V: As a creative person to survive, I think it was perfect that you found another supportive subculture, which was the gay one. I had neighbors who were drag queens; they had great clothes—**

♦ CC: Doris told me that in the '70s, they invented nostalgia because they hated '70s fashions so much. I think people like the Pointer Sisters did the "thrift thing" way before it was popular.

♦ **V: What was your first "Connie" show?**

♦ CC: The Intersection for the Arts hosted our first show in 1987, with Karen Finley also on the bill. They used to host a "Haunted House" event on Halloween with bands, and that was our first gig as Connie Champagne and her Tiny Bubbles.

♦ **V: And you got a chance to develop by playing weekly at the Paradise?**

♦ CC: Yes. And the DNA Lounge after that. They were doing cocktail/cabaret long before there was a "lounge" culture, booking Patsy Cline & the Memphis G-Spots and other groups. Then Ron Gompertz from Heyday Records (an independent San Francisco label) asked me to make a record. We made it (title: *La Strada)* in six days and—how can I put it—Roger Clark said I tried to pee on too many bushes. I think that's an accurate assessment. There are some interesting songs on it; I still like "Frenchette" quite a bit. I also like "Don't I Have the Right To Be Loved?"

♦ **V: Did you have a day job throughout all this?**

♦ CC: Yeah. I was working as a production assistant for a photographer. I also went to college [Mills College], and taught in the Young Conservatory at ACT [American Conservatory Theater] where I went to graduate school. Going to acting school will cure you of wanting to be an actor real quick! ACT was a really valuable education, but it was also like a two-year-long audition—I felt like I was walking on eggshells the whole time. Having "Connie Champagne and her Tiny Bubbles" actually saved my sanity, because I really needed something that was just *ours,* apart from school.

Stylin' Advice from Connie Champagne

♦ *V: To some people, clothing details are a big deal—*

♦ CC: —like whether or not you're wearing seamed stockings. Well, I guess it is a big deal to them in much the same way that wearing flares was during the punk days—if you wore them, you were crucified! I'm no longer concerned with the way I dress too much. I'm sensitive to it, but part of me wants to tell people to *just get over it.*

♦ *V: Didn't you get most of your wardrobe back when you could still find stuff in thrift stores?*

♦ CC: I've been collecting clothes forever. Mr David (who is also called Glamamore) made some really great reproductions for Phillip R. Ford's stage adaptation of *Valley of the Dolls* (1993). I was playing "Neely O'Hara" and when the show closed, they gave me my outfits—which was great!

I'm a big fan of Lilli Ann, a San Francisco clothing manufacturer/designer that's still around. They did the boxy Jackie Kennedy-type suits: I have a few of those. Al at Martini Mercantile found me a great '40s Lilli Ann suit which I love. Lilli Ann also did their version of the Dior "New Look" with the really cinched, wasp-waist suits and the jackets with shoulder pads. You used to be able to buy them for $20 at the Purple Heart; now you're lucky to find them for a couple hundred dollars. My favorite black sequined floor-length number came from a wonderful woman, a friend of Vise's, actually. Her name is Astrid, and I am forever in her debt for that dress. My '40s crepe dresses came from my mother-in-law, Pat. She haunts auctions in New Jersey. Those antique guys see her coming and they want to hide. She takes her vintage clothing bargain hunting *very* seriously. As corny as they are, I've always loved those Chinese silk dresses with the big slit up the side; I've got them in six or seven colors. I buy those new in Chinatown—they're pretty much like they were 50 years ago: just perfect.

♦ *V: Where do you get your shoes?*

♦ CC: I'm lucky because my feet are small. I don't have feet—I have hooves! I found a pair of 1930s shoes at Time After Time in L.A. They were marked size 3½, and were black satin with a gold cord and a Marcasite buckle.

Unfortunately, a lot of used clothing places like Buffalo Exchange and Crossroads discriminate against people with really small feet. The smallest size they carry is 6½, which I can't wear. I've gotten some great shoes at the Third Hand Store on Divisadero; it's the oldest used clothing store in its original location in San Francisco.

I also love to order shoes from Frederick's of Hollywood. You can order the shoes with the lucite heels from the catalog—everything. You can't dance in them, though—you'd break your neck. But you look real good standing there real still. Somebody once asked me how I walked in them, and I replied, "You put one foot in front of the other and cross your fingers." [laughs]

I have a pretty big collection of shoes. Friends know that I wear a size 5 or less, so when they find tiny shoes at garage sales they buy them for me. A friend just gave me a pair of green cha-cha heels he found for a dollar. I'm not very tall; I'm only five foot two—*barely.* I'm taller than Morty, but no one else. But shoes are the one item I can buy that don't have to be altered: you can buy 'em and wear 'em *that day.* Which is a luxury normal-sized people take for granted!

I love those '50s "method" movies like *The Fugitive Kind* or *Baby Doll* that feature actresses like Joanne Woodward or Carroll Baker. I love the monologue Woodward gives in *The Fugitive Kind* about "goin' jukin'." I really respect the craft involved, but that world of acting has come and gone. It's about plastic surgery now. [laughs] If you want to "make it" in show business on an acting level, I would suggest you save the $10,000 tuition and get plastic surgery.

♦ *V: I can see how in the Doris Fish context you nurtured the Connie Champagne persona and fleshed it out—*

♦ CC: —"fleshed it out" is a good way to put it. I had wanted somebody to teach me how to put on make-up and Scrumbly suggested Doris. She taught me so much more than just make-up. Doris really brought out the best in people. She liked real girls and contradicted the notion that drag queens are women-haters. Personally, I've never met a drag queen who hated women—although I've met lots of straight men that do!

After our first make-up session (which cost $40), she never charged me again. She lived in a really cool house on Oak Street that was full of "puss prints": leopardskin-print bedspreads, couches, chairs, pillows—everything. There was kitschy stuff everywhere, including a fountain with a statue of Michelangelo's David. They had a big room—they called it "The Drag Room"—where you could go in and pick whatever look you wanted.

♦ *V: It was a wardrobe room?*

♦ CC: Yeah, it had everything: wigs, scarves, boas, gowns, shoes—the full-on thing. And they weren't into looking like women, they were into looking like drag queens. So, Doris understood exactly what I was talking about, because I wanted to take it out a little further at that point.

♦ *V: It sounds like you were creating a repertoire as far from the punk scene as you could get—*

♦ CC: Hmm—it was and it wasn't. I think that punk rock, swing/lounge and drag share a common aesthetic. Among the first people to embrace punk rock were drag queens. In a way, you're embracing something that is odd, something that not everybody is into. All the drag queens I knew (like Doris Fish, Miss X and Tippi) weren't trying to look like real females (although Bambi Lake was); I'd say it was *hyper-female.*

♦ *V: How do you pick songs?*

♦ CC: For the lyrics and how I relate to what they say. I think the

An early incarnation of the New Morty Show. Photo: Rory Earnshaw

The New Morty & Connie Show

Mondays in November

audience knows real quick if you're being fake. I'm not saying everyone should get a shitty boyfriend and go to jail . . . I mean, *I* did, but I wouldn't recommend it! But it helps to experience that if you're singing a sad song and want the audience to feel the emotions involved.

Suffice to say, the stupidest thing I ever did was get hooked up with this guy who ended up dumping me on Valentine's Day for my best friend. [laughs] It sounds like a bad Country & Western song. He asked me to meet him at the Cafe Flor, and my *former*

Connie and Damian renew their vows in Vegas in 1997.

best friend showed up five minutes later. A big fight ensued and afterwards I was sitting on the street crying. The police came and I asked them to take me to the hospital—I had a black eye and bruises all over. It was really sick; it was so Billie Holiday, and stupid. Mind you, I'm not even 21 years old at this point. So, the police take one look at my dyed black hair and weird make-up and go, "We're taking you in because you don't have any identification" (I didn't have any). I got hauled away to jail by San Francisco's finest for sitting on the sidewalk crying with no identification. [laughs] Whenever I think of the lowest point in my entire life, I think that would have to be it.

♦ **V: That's the kind of experience you turn into songwriting—**
♦ CC: I was always writing songs. During the early Tiny Bubbles period, I was trying out the Tin Pan Alley approach, talking to songwriters and asking them to help me out. I've been fortunate because some really good people wrote songs for me: Mark Eitzel, John Flansburgh, J.C. Hopkins, and others. Plus, I was doing my own songs as well. One of the cool things about the Morty Show is that I've been writing a lot of songs for them. I've been co-writing with the pianist, John Quam, who is so gifted. Vise and Morty have written some cool songs together, too, and Van Hughes. I think there'll be a lot of interesting, good material on our album.

♦ **V: How did you come up with the name Tiny Bubbles?**
♦ CC: Around 1988, I used to hang out at the Pork Store Cafe on Haight Street. I'd go there for coffee every day with a friend, and there was a girl there, Marcy, who hated me. One day a bunch of us were sitting at a table and I said, "I need a name for this band I want to do." People started bandying about different names, and Marcy, very sarcastically, said, "Why don't you call it Connie Champagne and her Tiny Bubbles?" I went, "Perfect—that's it!" She was astonished, and after that she developed a liking for me and came to several shows. She was very up-front about taking credit for naming the band. She was a pal after that.

♦ **V: Do you ever play the song "Tiny Bubbles"?**
♦ CC: No. I don't do it now and I didn't do it then. It just doesn't slay me.

♦ **V: Hey, you're using slang from that era—**
♦ CC: Sometimes. But my mom told me that when *she* was a beatnik, no one actually talked like that . . . but I wish they had!

♦ **V: Yeah, that was mainly in those Beat-ploitation movies and TV shows . . . You were a pioneer of the swing/lounge/retro movement because you did it early—**
♦ CC: I just did it because I liked it. My mom being a beat, then going into the whole hippie and the '70s thing . . . The '70s was the era that I was brought up in, and it wasn't very interesting to me. To respond to your question, I didn't get up one morning and think "What's going to be the 'next big thing'?" It would still surprise me if swing became the next big thing, because it's not immediately accessible. It's romantic, it's campy and it's intelligent. But if neo-swing or hot jazz or whatever it's called ever caught on, it would be interesting to me because it takes some effort.

It's an almost totally straight-guy scene, so I'm an outcast once again. [laughs] But I've asked every guy I meet, "What's the appeal?" And it's not like they all got together on this; their immediate gut-level reaction is: "The chicks."

♦ **V: Somebody told me they were attracted by the wild dancing, because they'd never seen so many panties flashed in one night. [laughs]**
♦ CC: I think it's great. I like to dance. Partner-dancing is easy if you learn a few steps. Whoever's going to lead needs to know where they're going; they need to make that decision and not be wimpy about it. It's a lot of fun and it's always interesting because dancing is not a superficial thing—it takes a certain amount of telepathy and physical awareness. I think far too many times we've made fun of movements that incorporate dance. It's so easy to make fun of the disco era because their values and style were so incredibly superficial. But on the other hand, maybe *they* were railing against something that just got lost in history. That physical contact and communication is valuable.

You've got some people who don't want to look "uncool" while they're learning. But to me it's just one more thing to learn. How many times have you fallen off when you're learning how to skateboard, and then one day you can get up on it and you don't look stupid anymore. Like everything else worthwhile, it takes a certain amount of risk and practice. It's like going to some restaurant and eating food that you've never had before. Or listening to a particular kind of music that you didn't think you would like. It's just one more thing in life that you open yourself up to the experience of doing.

Keely Smith, Damian Monzillo, & Connie at the Desert Inn, 1995.

♦ **V: I assume that you've done some homework, listening to various female singers and have your favorites—**
♦ CC: It's interesting that you'd put it that way. When I was growing up, I used to say that I didn't like women singers at all— I liked Iggy Pop. And yet he was the first person I heard sing (and it was a brilliant cover) "One For My Baby, And One More For

the Road." I remember seeing him on some film clip, sitting in a tree and talking about how Frank Sinatra was his biggest influence. And I could see that. Everybody up until then, at least white guys, had been crooners.

So to answer your question, I didn't really like many female singers. It's that bullshit cultural misogyny most girls are spoon-fed from Day One. At the time, I liked John Lennon, Iggy Pop,

Flyer for the 1993 production of *Dolls*. Connie is third from left. Photo: Dan Nicoletta

David Bowie, Peter Murphy (Bauhaus), Ian McCulloch (Echo & the Bunnymen)—those were the singers I tried to sound like. Unfortunately for a lot of people that had to hear me back then, I was really good at it! [laughs] Then, when I started listening to different kinds of music, I really loved Dinah Washington, Julie London, Joya Sherrill—she did the original version of "I'm Beginning to See the Light" by Duke Ellington. I loved Bobby Darin and also Chet Baker.

My three favorite performers that I've seen live are James Brown, Iggy Pop, and Bernadette Peters. You'll probably think I'm really wacky now, but if you took a video of Iggy Pop and one of Judy Garland and turned the sound down and looked at their approach . . . it's real similar! There's a lot of vulnerability being displayed. Also, I think Peggy Lee's pretty happening. She's a lot more than just "Siamese Cat Song" and "Lady and the Tramp." And Keely Smith is still fantastic. You can still see her in Las Vegas and Palm Springs. She sounds exactly the same. Ella Fitzgerald sang beautifully all her life. Whereas opera singers tend to lose their voices—I dunno, we'll watch Diamanda Galas and see what happens. [laughs]

♦ **V: How did you join the New Morty Show?**

♦ CC: I was very fortunate to have met Morty. I was doing this gig with Veronica Klaus. Morty and David Rubin, a drummer, were in the band. I had actually met Morty before. He had written his name on a piece of paper in a nightclub, and at the time I was already playing with Nik Phelps, who's another horn player (Sprockets Ensemble). Anyway, Morty claims I blew him off, but I'm just going to tell you straight-up that I didn't mean to blow him off. Once we got in the Veronica Klaus band, we talked all the time. He started telling me about this band that he wanted to do, playing post-swing style material performed in lounges in the '50s and early '60s. At one point, we even did the entire sound-track to *Casino Royale*.

♦ **V: I love that album.**

♦ CC: Morty had charts made so we could play the whole thing, and I sang "The Look of Love." It's the only song I sang, but I still think it's one of the coolest things we ever did. Anyway, he said, "Would you like to join?" I said, "Sure!" and a year later (summer of '94) he called me. At first Morty sang—

♦ **V: Morty was singing? What was that like?**

♦ CC: I think he had a lot of potential. [laughs] He has a great feel for this music and a really distinctive style of playing—you can always pick Morty out. His style is very Dixieland but also modern—remember, he used to play ska. I've always liked playing music with Morty. He found some wonderful players too, like Whitney Wilson (guitarist), who is like an offspring of Robert Mitchum and Billy Zoom; John Quam (pianist), who writes wonderful songs and has a really strong background in jazz; David Murotake, a fine tenor sax player who played with Morty in Undercover Ska; and Van Hughes, an ex-mailman in his sixties, who played trombone with so many greats: Marvin Gaye, Woody Herman and Duke Ellington—he should be doing this interview!

Eventually Morty got Vise (from his own group St. Vitus Dance) into the band. I knew Vise was an entertainer, really strong, and definitely a force to be reckoned with. I think Vise and Morty met at the Deluxe. They used to have these Bloody Mary Sundays (you know: Sunday, Bloody Sunday). Vise would make his famous Bloody Marys—he's won all these awards for them. Morty asked me if I wanted to sing with Vise and I said, "Sure!" We all made a pretty good team.

The New Morty Show is an interesting band. We do have our ups and downs. It's like a big dysfunctional family; we don't always get along. [laughs] We spend a lot of time together touring and playing Vegas. Here we are, a band that started off in search of a Vegas that's long gone. And the powers that be in Las Vegas (and there are powers and they are scary) decided they were also in search of it, and wanted to bring it back. So we play Vegas a lot: the Desert Inn (Louis Prima's old stomping ground), New York, New York Hotel, Hard Rock. And we don't have to make compromises.

Connie sings . . . Photo: Rory Earnshaw

My mom had this book on Janis Joplin. One of her main credos was: "Don't compromise yourself." And that's still true. We didn't make any compromises and we actually get paid for doing what we want to do. It's a unique situation in America. Most people have to do things they hate.

♦ **V: How does the arranging get done?**

♦ CC: It depends on who comes up with the song. It could be Morty, or Van, or John Quam. The first song I wrote with John Quam was "Blue Martini." I wanted it to be a barfly song: you're a barfly, you're at the bar, and you miss your gal or your guy. And the bartender, in the middle of the song, says "Hey lady, I wrote your story. I'm here 7:30 every night on the dot." And she says to the bartender, "But listen, sister/there ain't no more sweet Mister/but this martini almost hits the spot."

Then we wrote a song called "15 Months in Jail." I don't play the piano very well, but I was playing around with chords and singing when it just *came to me.* I made a rough demo and brought it to John and he thought it was great. Then he did the horn arrangements. I really like working with him. Our producer on *Morty-fied,* Mark Eastwood, also had some cool ideas. He was inspiring, and I'm hoping to work with him again soon.

The best teacher for me, in terms of writing songs, was probably Michael Belfer. I learned the freedom to experiment over a chord progression, and let *whatever* come out . . . to just *let go* and not critique yourself because you have to allow yourself to fail. If something is good, it will survive.

♦ V: **What instruments do you play?**

♦ CC: Piano—I'm terrible! At home we had a piano, but I never had formal lessons; I taught myself. I also had a Vox Jaguar; it was like an electric organ-type instrument. I learned chording and where the notes were. It's helpful to be able to tell the musicians that you want a B-flat minor (or whatever). You can't just tell them you want it to sound "sad"—they don't get that. I ended up selling the Vox Jaguar to a band called the Amputees.

♦ V: **How do you think this wild partner dancing started?**

♦ CC: I wasn't terribly aware of it. I asked Brent at the Deluxe and he said, "Chicks." In some areas of the country, being able to dance is like a "faggy" thing. But in Los Angeles and San Francisco, it's very sexy. I guess the subtext is: if a guy knows how to dance, he might know how to do something else. I'm sure that's a big part of it.

I know that for me it started with rockabilly. When I go to Las Vegas, there's this big rockabilly, swing and ska scene. All these people hang out together in much the same that way punk, reggae, rockabilly and mod people hung out in the early '80s punk scene. Then everything splintered and became "us against them." The same thing is happening here now: swing people don't go to rockabilly shows, which is too bad.

♦ V: **Well, that's *stupid.***

♦ CC: Exactly. I pretty much like them all. If anyone comes to hear us play, I'm happy they're there. *Swing Time* magazine printed a very funny article [by editor Susan Lake] about: how do you know if you're swing, rockabilly, or lounge? They said if you're lounge you should cut your hair in a Keely Smith bob and wear a Chinese dress. The funny thing is: that's how I've always dressed. So I guess they pegged me. But I certainly didn't get up in the morning and think, "What should I be today: swing or lounge?" Whenever this splintering happens, it makes it harder to generate larger audiences.

♦ V: **You'd rather have rockabilly, ska and swing in comfortable co-existence—**

♦ CC: Sure! I like them all and it would make my life a lot easier, because I wouldn't have to exclude people when I have a party or something.

I've seen splintering among groups of people happen many times. The first group I ever belonged to was, in truth, not punk rock—I was a mod. We went to see *Quadrophenia* every midnight on Saturday and we had scooters and wore those parkas. And I still love mods. My favorite band at the moment in San Francisco is a group called the Kinetics. They're not swing at all. The piano player in that band, Marc Capelle, and the trombone player, Carroll Ashby, used to play with Veronica Klaus. I initially went to see them because of that connection. I think if the Kinetics

lived in any other city, they would be famous. I also really love Royal Crown Revue. All the players are great; Bill Ungerman does really good arrangements. Morty and Vise, I think, told them about me and I recorded with them earlier this year: a theme for a TV show. The show was cancelled, but the song may still make it on the record—I'm not sure. I loved working with Eddie Nichols. He's a wonderful singer, although I don't think *he* really knows how good he truly is.

Anyway, I'd like to see these groups stay united because there's strength in numbers. The Morty Show was playing in Southern California at the Rhino Room, and this kid told me, "We don't want this music to catch on." And I said, "Well, musicians need to be paid." If the telephone operator can be paid, why can't the musician be paid? And if people don't come to see you, you don't get paid. If it stays this cult thing that only six people attend, it's not going to last long, or we'll all have to have crappy day jobs. I'm definitely for people liking our music. I don't care whether they're "cool" or not! **V**

Influential Artists

Irma Thomas
Frances Faye: "Caught In the Act" is great!
Anita O'Day: With Benny Carter especially.
Bobby Darin: Underrated as a singer, *really.*
Chet Baker
Dusty Springfield: Yikes! She's so great!
Dinah Washington
Keely Smith and Louis Prima: Of course . . .
Current Favorites:
Frenchy (with East Bay Ray)
The Kinetics

Vise Grip

Vise Grip is a seminal figure in the Bay Area swing movement. Formerly singer for the punk rock bands Hard Attack and Eyebrows on Sticks, he went on to form St. Vitus Dance (1992) and the Ambassadors of Swing (1996)—magnificent bands that helped spread the gospel of Louis Jordan and Cab Calloway. Vise lives with his wife, artist Tanya Deason, and their boxer, Cab Calloway, in an amazing "retro" decorated apartment. Vise also sings with the New Morty Show, whose CD on Slimstyle Records is available from V/Search 415-362-1465. Tanya and Aaron Seymour (friend and *Swing Time* staff writer) were present during Vise's interview.

♦ *VALE: Unfortunately, I became aware of this swing scene relatively late—*

♦ VISE GRIP: I'm still learning every day. I've absolutely loved working with old-timers from the original swing band days, and learning the history from stories they tell. I didn't know this when I started out, but there's a real shortage of big band drummers.

In 1992 I started a 9-piece band, St. Vitus Dance, doing jump-swing inspired by Louis Jordan. This was a joint project with piano player Jerry Long. During our "career" we probably played 100 gigs, and were called the "Sex Pistols of Swing." I've always tried to project that punk energy, and still try to. Around 1994 I wanted to form a big band, the Ambassadors of Swing, and do Cab Calloway material. It took *three years* to get that band off the ground. It's been a real journey meeting all the players, but this is probably the most fun I've ever had.

This was a joint project with piano player Jerry Long. During our "career" we probably played 100 gigs, and were called the "Sex Pistols of Swing."

♦ *V: Before you started your punk band, Hard Attack, did you know you'd be a musician?*

♦ VG: Nope. I didn't even start *doing* music until I was 32 years old. I sort of fell into it and man, it happened fast. Of course, I always sang in the shower. [laughs] My father was in Vaudeville, so I was always around music. Everybody says this, but in my case it's true—it's a family thing.

♦ *V: Vaudeville in San Francisco?!*

♦ VG: Oh yeah. In fact, my dad played at the original Bimbo's during Prohibition, when it was located at 365 Market Street. It was a wild club. My dad did impersonations of Al Jolson and others who've been forgotten. It never occurred to me that I'd become an entertainer.

♦ *V: Could your dad afford to support a family working in Vaudeville?*

♦ VG: Nah, he always worked. He would do the Vaudeville at night, like every other musician.

♦ *V: Day jobs have always been with us—*

♦ VG: Yeah, we have to have the day job—that's what lets us dress up at night. [laughs] My dad had a produce truck. He worked the Richmond and Fillmore districts and sold fruits and vegetables door-to-door out of a truck; he had a scale and everything.

♦ *V: Is your family Italian?*

♦ VG: Nah, my dad was a Jewish guy. I grew up in San Francisco and I've watched it change. The Richmond used to be all Russians and the Fillmore district was really Jewish. McAllister Street—the whole block—was all kosher butchers. My grandma used to take me down there and we'd buy a chicken right out of a cage and they'd wack it over the head. Then we'd burn the feathers off and go home and eat it! [laughs] You just don't see that anymore.

♦ *V: You've probably had quite a life, even before you were 32 and started doing music. Don't you have a daughter who's now 22?*

♦ VG: Yep—did that thing. [laughs] And like everybody else, music—or the drug culture—brought it down. Before I started music, I pretty much ran the hardware store my Uncle Maury had in West Portal. I worked there for over 30 years, since junior high school. I got married and bought a house five blocks from the hardware store—my life took place basically in half a square mile. Up the hill, down the hill; up the hill, down the hill. My only involvement with music was as a listener. Probably three nights a week I was at Winterland or the old Fillmore.

♦ *V: When were you in punk bands?*

♦ VG: Around '79 I started playing my first shows at the Mabuhay Gardens, with Hard Attack. I was hanging out in that scene and used to spend a lot of time at Berkeley Square when it first opened. I was one of the original partners with the owners, Victor and Bart, but I got out just before they opened. I really got into punk because, being a little older, the energy blew me away. The controlled violence, the mosh pits, all fascinated me. Some of my favorite bands were Crime and Fang.

Change is bad sometimes, but you gotta' keep moving on. Punk, to me, is probably the most important movement that I can think of in the last 30 years. The Psychedelic movement was one thing, but punk was really, seriously *political.* The kids weren't horsing around, they were angry! Punk is there and let's hope it always will be.

♦ *V: Were you attracted to the Do-It-Yourself ethic behind punk?*

♦ VG: Exactly! [laughs] If you could bang out a couple of chords, you were ready to rumble! I was fortunate enough to catch some great English bands, including the Anti-Nowhere League. The On Broadway and the Mabuhay were like Meccas. It was an amazing time; it was insane. I hope that someday Dirk Dirksen [Mabuhay promoter] gets his documentary out. He definitely has a lot of material—he shot a video of me at the On Broadway doing a song called "Coke Nazi."

The Berkeley Square was a jumpin' place, even when it first opened. Iggy Pop, X, Adrian Belew, the Butthole Surfers and tons of great acts went through there. I was in the thick of it and watched the whole thing flourish.

♦ *V: How did you start Hard Attack?*

♦ VG: Actually Jerry Long [piano player] started it. He found *me.* We met at a wedding where he was playing in the band. They asked if I'd run up and grab the female singer, throw her over my shoulder and carry her out, so I did. That was my introduction to the world of music. [laughs] Jerry was going to teach me to play

Vise Grip. Photo: Mark Jordan

bass, but I have five thumbs, so I ended up singing. One of those "No Experience Required" type of jobs! [laughs]

As soon as I got into it, I went crazy. At that point, I probably whipped out about 25 songs. It's amazing how you go through periods when you're really productive and then you run into a wall. I'm just starting now to write again. I guess my life had become boring. [laughs]

♦ **V: You store up these things until suddenly they all come pouring out—**

♦ VG: Yeah; all of a sudden I had the opportunity to actually express something. "Coke Nazi" was one of the first songs I wrote. I was trying to think of the most extreme term I could use for someone who's addicted to that shit, because at the time, everybody had fuckin' white powder underneath every nostril they owned. "I'm a Coke Nazi/goose-stepping down my plate/Cocaine my Fuhrer/It doctrinates my mind/Cocaine rules my body and controls my life/Sieg Heil!/Coke Nazi /Can you relate?" This was a tune expressing how extreme I had gotten into it, and how it dictated my life. Most of my songs were social criticism, not much different from anybody else's, but coming from my own life.

♦ **V: Did you collaborate with Jerry to produce the tunes and arrangements?**

♦ VG: I would usually just hum out a bass line and then Jerry would write the music for it. It's really nice having someone like him, because he's an accomplished player . . . someone who could translate my ideas into music. We had a good relationship for many years and then we got into a little fight—actually, a big fight. It broke that thing up. We did do St. Vitus Dance together.

♦ **V: What year did St. Vitus Dance start?**

♦ VG: Probably around '92. Jerry was always a huge blues fan, listening to Big Joe Turner, Eddie "Cleanhead" Vinson and all those guys. We started doing Louis Jordan cover tunes together. Today everybody in the world does Louis Jordan, but back then there weren't many people doing it, except Royal Crown Revue. I still feel *they* were the ones that really kicked this "swing" thing off musically. They blew everybody's socks off. With St. Vitus Dance, I really went into jump-blues like Wynonie Harris, Louis Jordan, etc. But I kept that edge I've always had—not exactly a punk edge—but I'm intense, you know. If I'm singing Louis Jordan or Sid Vicious, it's the same energy. That's probably what's kept me going. I don't know how many times people have asked me, "Where do you get all that energy?" And I say, "Well, it ain't what it used to be!"

♦ **V: You look like you have a pretty hefty constitution—**

♦ VG: Yeah, and it's all moving down towards my belt! [laughs] It used to be on top!

Vise's dad doing his vaudeville act.

Vise, n.d.

♦ **V: The use of horns adds a different energy without losing any intensity—**

♦ VG: Horns are what really captivated me; they can really bring music out. Everybody's experimented with them, from Brian Setzer to Emerson, Lake and Palmer. Anytime you want to take something like a symphony orchestra or choir and throw it in the mix to see what it sounds like—I've always believed in that. I've used church choirs in my big band; I even had Paul from The Diamond Center introduce me one night! I'll try anything—

♦ **V: No kidding?**

♦ VG: Yeah, he introduced us at my very first show at Bimbo's! He's a weirdo, let me tell ya. It took a lot of work to talk him into coming, but when I'm on a mission "Get outta my way!" Now, I'm working on the man from the Men's Wearhouse [commercial]; I think he'll be my next victim. [laughs]

♦ **V: You once described yourself as an "old punk/gothic rocker." Where does goth come in?**

♦ VG: That's another area of music that I've always really liked: groups like Fields of the Nephilim, Sisters of Mercy, Christian Death, etc. I used to have so many black clothes I fit right into that scene. It was like, "Oh good—I don't have to buy anything this time." [laughs] I just like dark music; I always have. I think that sensibility got me into Cab Calloway—that guy was pretty dark for his time. He was singing songs about the Reefer Man and opium dens in Chinatown. He was an amazing performer and that's what got me hung up on him.

♦ **V: You saw Royal Crown for the first time around 1992?**

♦ VG: They played some warehouse parties, which were pretty big at the time. It's the old story: Royal Crown would play some club, then go down to this warehouse and start playing at two in the morning until the sun came up. And it was packed! It was really more "underground" and more of a local thing. I think San Francisco is definitely headquarters for this type of music.

Louis Jordan probably has had the biggest influence, even on the new kids' bands that are cropping up now. He's the pivotal guy that everybody copies. It makes me laugh because people say [putting us down], "All you guys do are *cover tunes*." Like these kids have heard these songs before?! [laughs] "It's not 'Stairway to Heaven,' pal. We're talking about *classics* from the '30s and '40s that you don't know anything about." And there's so much of it—a shitload of stuff; it's amazing!

I'm sure Royal Crown mentions it, but I think a big influence on them was also Louis Prima. He was the lounge king of the late '50s and '60s—that guy *owned* Vegas. Royal Crown did a lot of Prima tunes, and I know I certainly did a lot. I have some great videos; there's one of him and Keely Smith on the Ed Sullivan show.

You know who else had a big influence? I think all the kids who do swing today probably got their first taste of it from JOE JACKSON. He did a big band cover album of all Louis Jordan songs—it's pretty white toast, but the arrangements are great. He performed "Is You Is" and all the songs that people cover today. Everybody plays the exact arrangement he has and sounds like him. You can tell he's influenced a lot of people.

It makes me laugh because people say [putting us down], "All you guys do are *cover tunes.*" Like these kids have heard these songs before?!

♦ **V: One of the first times I heard horns "live" was when I saw the British ska bands (Madness, Specials, Selecter) when they first toured America in 1979-1980—**
♦ VG: There you go! Man, they put horns in another strata, that's for sure! I can't picture ska without horns; they're an integral part. Very tasty! I opened a show for Madness at the Kabuki Theater one night. Ska probably introduced horns to a lot of people of recent generations.
♦ **V: I couldn't start dressing like that and wearing those little hats—**
♦ VG: You weren't a Rude Boy, huh? [laughs] Yeah, I have a little trouble with the ska scene myself. There's this Neo-Nazi aspect to some of the kids that just turns me off. Nothing against the music. I've been to a lot of ska shows and some of those kids tend to be a little violent and rowdy, and that doesn't do much for me. The nice thing about punk was: I think I saw *one* fight the whole time I was going to shows.
♦ **V: Violence became sublimated into "art" or something—**
♦ VG: Exactly. It was an expression; it was body art! [laughs] "I'm going to swing my arms and go through that crowd if it kills me!"
♦ **V: How did you come up with "St. Vitus Dance"?**
♦ VG: There's an old Louis Jordan song called "St. Vitus Dance"—in fact, I still sing that song. It's what they used to call Parkinson's Disease: a nerve disorder or a virulent disease of the brain: "When my shoulders begin to shake/Like a boat out on the lake/When I wiggle like a snake." There's also an L.A. hard rock band called St. Vitus Dance. I met a guy from the band and he told me there was yet another band with the same name—except they were doing heavy metal. [chuckles]

There were about seven people in our band. We had three horns, at least: trumpet, trombone, and tenor saxophone. Our first show was at the Club Deluxe on Haight Street. I don't think enough credit has been given to the Deluxe as the first club to really put everything they had behind the budding swing movement. Everybody else came *after* them. Jay Johnson is the owner and he designed the place and wanted that look and scene to happen, but it was Dutch who really went to town and formed what was going to become the whole retro scene. He was influential in getting me going, because he booked us a lot. Then Nancy Myers from the Cafe Du Nord started booking swing, and then Michael Cerchiai from Bimbo's came in a little later.

In the early days, there was a crossover between rockabilly and swing, but that's almost disappeared—I don't know why. Western Swing is awesome to dance to. JOHNNY DILKS has a Western Swing band that's really wonderful.
♦ **V: When did you start dressing in suits?**

♦ VG: I started wearing suits pretty early and it was always a black double-breasted one. Even when I played with Hard Attack, I'd wear a suit—except the pants were cut off! But it was still a suit. [laughs] Every night of the week I'd watch the *Untouchables;* I couldn't get away from the double-breasted suit.
♦ **V: You must have been one of the only people to wear them back then—**
♦ VG: Let's just say I was early. I don't like to take credit for anything; I'm certainly not any "pioneer." Let's just say I was in the right place at the right time.
♦ **V: How did your look evolve?**
♦ VG: St. Vitus Dance weren't the greatest dressers of all time. Jerry and I would dress up, but it's still hard to get everybody to dress up for the big band. It's amazing: some of these guys have played with the goddamned Dorseys and every major big band, and they don't even own a tuxedo! [laughs]
♦ **V: But you're a singer/personality, and need to be more out there—**
♦ VG: Exactly. I've never considered myself much of a singer. I think I'm improving now because I'm concentrating more on it, but basically I got by on *energy*. People would come just to see what might explode.
♦ **V: Did you take singing lessons?**
♦ VG: A teacher, Kathy Ellis, was around in the '70s and '80s. I was with her for a while. She taught me breathing: where to put your air and how to use it. But I wasn't into sitting around the house going, "Aaaaahhhhh"—that wore me out! I just wanted to sing; I didn't want to do the hard work. [laughs]

The voice is an instrument. Until I met her, I never thought about having to warm it up. You can't just go out there and start screaming; you've got to learn how to use your diaphragm and open up your throat. If you're uptight, then you can't sing very well. If you're up there just to scream, then maybe it doesn't mat-

Vise in Hard Attack, ca 1982.

ter too much, but if you really want to *sing* . . . Mel Tormé didn't do that by accident; he learned how to sing.

♦ **V: *If you do anything long enough, eventually you want to improve—***

♦ VG: No question. I'm always amazed when I watch Pavarotti. He barely looks like he's breathing, he's relaxed and sweats like a

Vise and the Ambassadors of Swing on the set of *The Game.*

pig, yet all hell's coming out of his stomach—he could blow windows out. He's the Don Rickles of opera! [laughs] My wife, Tanya, is operatically trained, and she's been helping me out a lot. You know: in the pronunciation of words—everything.

♦ **V: *Do you ever go to the opera?***

♦ VG: I've been to a couple. It hasn't been that long since I've started really concentrating on other singers. I went to see Joe Williams the other night, and I watched the three tenors [Luciano Pavarotti, Placido Domingo, Jose Carreras] battle it out at Dodger Stadium. There are so many different styles. The *delivery* has become important to me. I listen to Cab Calloway probably three hours a day, just to understand the way he delivers a song—the phrasing. I really do want to learn how to sing, and it's never too late to learn!

♦ **V: *That never ends: learning how to grow creatively.***

♦ VG: If you really want to learn some history, you should phone my band director and trumpet player, John Coppola. He helped me put the big band together, and he's 68 now. When he was 15, he was already playing with a big band. He's like a prodigy, and a great storyteller. When you talk to him, you'll never call us young guys back again. He worked with Charlie Barnet, Dizzy Gillespie, Lester Young, Stan Kenton . . . He's The Man, when it comes to the *real* background. If it weren't for him, I'd still be at home trying to get a big band together! Talking to him is like sitting down with a famous philosopher. And you should have seen his face the first time the curtains went up and he saw 700 kids swing dancing!

♦ **V: *No wonder you said you were getting deep into the history—***

♦ VG: Yeah. There's a lot of great books out, and I'm still trying to catch up! I think the only one in our generation who has really done his homework is Chris Siebert, Lavay Smith's boyfriend who plays piano. Not only does he have an amazing CD and record collection, he has a closet filled to the brim with music charts. So he'll have 30 recorded versions of one song plus almost as many chart versions. It's "easy" to copy a song, but when you

know the background, and who played on which version, and all of those nuances . . . Also, Lavay Smith and the Red Hot Skillet Lickers have "stuck to their guns" doing the Ellington, Basie, Hampton, Bessie Smith stuff for *years*. In the knowledge department, they're way ahead of us.

♦ **V: *Let's backtrack to 1993. How often did you play?***

♦ VG: We were playing at least every weekend. I'd say we were very busy, considering that we weren't looking for any kind of corporate support or trying to survive off it. Whereas for a lot of groups today, "the band" is the sole source of their bread and butter.

♦ **V: *Many people are hiring swing bands to play weddings—***

♦ VG: Musicians, if they're trying to make a living, really need weddings, conventions, and corporate gigs to come into the paycheck. I know groups like Bud E. Love and Pride and Joy make a fortune doing them. They get booked by Bechtel and Rectal [laughs] and I'm afraid that's where the money is. When we were doing the clubs, we only made $40–60 a man, tops.

♦ **V: *So it was a labor of love. Did you ever get discouraged?***

♦ VG: I don't think we were expecting much—that's the answer! I know a lot of bands would like to have a record contract. That's not the farthest thing from my mind, but I could give a shit about it, really. If I can just go out and play, that means a lot more to me. It's nice if you get paid, but if somebody calls me for a benefit and it's something worthwhile—well, it's not the money that's all-important. Every big band show I do, I lose money. I could lose $1000 in a night, and I've done it.

Musicians, if they're trying to make a living, really need weddings, conventions, and corporate gigs. I'm afraid that's where the money is.

♦ **V: *Ouch! You just aren't getting paid enough?***

♦ VG: Well, I like to have stage settings. Tanya and my friend, Aaron Seymour, built all of my backdrops and themes. I'll make or buy costumes according to my themes. Like with a Jungle scene, I'll buy safari hats and hunting gear, etc, because that's what I see when I watch the old "soundies." Those old stage settings were out of this world, and I consider them a necessary part of the whole "revival" that's going on. It's not like having laser light shows and blowing smoke everywhere, it's a lot more artistic. Those old soundies look so beautiful to me, and I like to recreate that atmosphere. But it costs money. Having 19 players isn't cheap and I try to pay as high as I can because I want to keep the best players I can find. They deserve to be paid.

♦ **V: *Right. They all have to pay laundry bills after each gig.***

♦ VG: Yeah. They went to school, man. They didn't learn those instruments from sitting on their hands. They can read music faster than reading a book and that takes work. For my first big band show I hired a bunch of my friends—great players—but, man, when they got in front of those books, it was like reading Cantonese—they were lost! [laughs] But get them to solo—no fuckin' problem! And that's another thing I've learned: playing in a bigger band takes discipline.

To be good at what you're doing takes time. Even people who are born with amazing talent have to work really hard. Still, not everybody can play big band. You've got to be able to read *and* feel the music while remaining in synch with all your fellow musicians.

♦ V: *You used to work with the Barrett Brothers—*
♦ VG: Yeah, Dave and Tim from No Sisters, a new wave band with horns. We were in the middle of a show at Mick's Lounge on Van Ness and I told Dave to solo on his sax. I said, "I'll be right back" and walked out the door. I don't think he'd ever been in a situation like that. I expected him to shit in his pants, but when I came back about 20 minutes later with a bag of groceries, he was still playing! It was hilarious, especially since the guy barely knew me. [laughs]

♦ V: *Tell us about some of your shows—*
♦ VG: My favorite St. Vitus Dance show was when the Reverend Horton Heat played guitar with us. I had met him at the Deluxe and invited him to play a gig with us. So he asked for a tape and I sent it to him. He showed up and proved how versatile he really is—he played the whole show, not just one song. People think that he's just a psychobilly player, but he's absolutely amazing—he has a great feel for the music and I was just blown away by his playing. That was definitely one of my highlights.

♦ V: *One of those legendary nights that never got recorded—*
♦ VG: Right. We also did a show at the Derby in L.A. This guy, Brit Woodman, was in his 70s and had been a trombone player for Duke Ellington. He was related to one of the guys in my band, and that's how he came to sit in with us. It was such an honor to have someone of that stature on stage with us; someone who had worked the Monterey Jazz Festival and played on Ellington's *Live at Newport* album. I try to stay away from name dropping, but some things leave an *impression* on you. That was a big thrill.

The big band era was just that: an era. Harlem was loaded with monster players; it was as common as buttered toast to have amazing guys playing clubs. It was an incredible time for music.

> **Harlem was loaded with monster players; it was as common as buttered toast to have amazing guys playing clubs. It was an incredible time for music.**

They definitely set a precedent for future players. You can't pick up a saxophone and not have to deal with Lester Young eventually. Fortunately, we have recordings, even though the technology was only good enough to capture about three minutes. But in those three minutes they said a lot, fast! [laughs] They weren't doing extended dance mixes—I'll tell you that much. I still like to throw on an old 78 and hear the old scratchy sound. If these guys were recording today, they'd probably blow you out of the water!

♦ V: *Can you trace how this aerial dancing started?*
♦ VG: I think it's unbelievable. This is intense shit, man. People really get into it; people really go crazy with it. The rockabilly scene was turning toward Country & Western Swing and then the swing scene started. That's when I met Dana and Mango of Work That Skirt. They were really young when they started aerial

The Vise Squad: Vise performing with a gospel choir at Bimbo's 365 Club, with jungle backdrop.

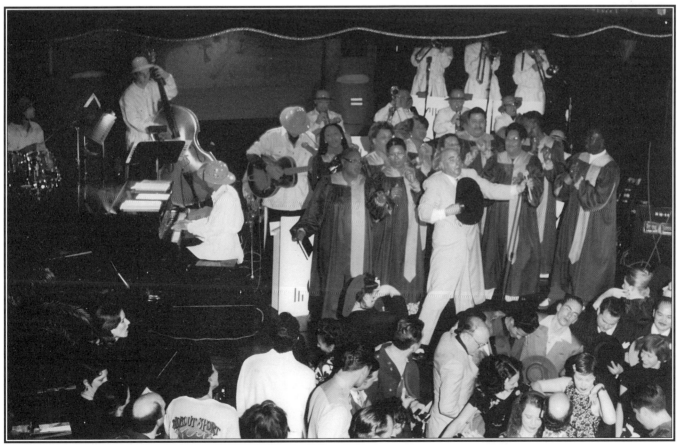

dancing at the Deluxe. I said, "Holy shit!"—everybody used to applaud and go out of their minds. Now, there's at least five studios teaching nothing but street swing or lindy-hopping. I hate to sound like an old fart, but to see couples actually holding each other again and having to *work* together . . . I turn on MTV and people are just gyrating—they don't even look at each other;

Members of the New Morty Show and Royal Crown Revue at Lake Tahoe.

they're so busy showing off their tits and ass. Whereas in the swing scene, people are actually touching each other and dancing—actually *relating*—it's pretty hip!

♦ **V: I don't think anything like this has happened in our lifetime—**

♦ VG: No. The '50s had dancing, but swing is a whole other kind of dancing. I don't remember it in the '70s, and in the '80s no one was dancing together. It's fascinating to watch, and we can't even find a room with a big enough dance floor anymore. That's a problem: the shows are starting to lose attendance because there's not enough room. The serious dancers find it way too crowded; they just can't stretch out and *dance*. These people are twirling; they need space. I think the last Royal Crown show at Bimbo's had 900 people.

♦ **V: Yeah, and it was impossible to move.**

♦ VG: That's another problem. Where are all the big dance halls they used to have? I can only imagine what might happen if we had a *real* ballroom here again.

♦ **V: It must be challenging to keep a band of seven or more people together—**

♦ VG: It's a battle, for sure. All the larger bands in the Bay Area have a hell of a time keeping players. The top-notch guys always pencil in gigs on their calendars, and if they get a better one they'll call you back: "Listen . . ." And with 17 people it's even more of a challenge getting them all together.

♦ **V: You're referring to the Ambassadors of Swing, which you formed after St. Vitus Dance ended—**

♦ VG: After St. Vitus Dance broke up I got together with Morty, who played trumpet in St. Vitus Dance. He approached me when I was trying to get this big band going. Like I said, it took some time, so meanwhile I started playing with Morty and Connie for fun.

♦ **V: I never saw Louis Prima with Keely Smith, but people say there's that same kind of chemistry onstage with you—**

♦ VG: Yeah. Connie and I are pretty matched up; it's amazing. We just kick each other in the ass all night long. And poor Morty takes a beating, too—but he deserves it! Everybody thinks he's

my son. [laughs]

♦ **V: Basically, you're continuing to research and evolve—**

♦ VG: Yeah, I want to develop myself more as an entertainer and a singer. It takes a little time, especially since you can't rehearse with a big band that often. In the old days, musicians would play all day, rehearse and then play all night. They'd have a month run somewhere and practically lived together. Today it's impossible to expect people to devote themselves to a big band.

♦ **V: I can see how after five years, you'd want to take a vacation from keeping St. Vitus Dance together—**

♦ VG: For awhile I did it all, then I handed it to Jerry. It's just so time-consuming. You can spend your life on the phone trying to get a show. I'm not much of a businessman; I'm "Mr. Let's Give It Away." [laughs] I just like to *do* the shows, you know. But now I'm in a different space: I'm older, I know what I want to do and how I want it to look, and it costs bucks. So I'll do it every four months and do it right. Then I'll go home and say, "Wow, that was pretty amazing."

I enjoy being a performer. I'm not a great singer, but the performance part of it has always been in my blood. Getting started so late in life, I've had to move pretty quickly! [laughs] What impresses me about the whole swing scene is that kids aren't so age-conscious. They can sit there and just love to death a 70-year-old saxophone player who's not wearing tight pants and piercings. It's "Gawd, this guy can play!" and not, "Gawd, what a bunch of old fuckers." These kids are there to dance, and they're into the music. They're not looking for someone to go home and masturbate to; they want to get out there and have a good time.

♦ **V: I'm still trying to figure out why this scene has such an appeal—**

Tanya, Brian Setzer, and Vise.

♦ VG: People are looking at it—not that it's water—but at how *deep* it is. There are kids who know the names of the players in all the old bands. It's not like they're reading teen magazines, they're reading books on the history of these bands—some of these kids are really learning. Let's face it, every scene has poseurs—that will always be with us—and that's fine. But I'm always impressed by meeting someone like [laughs] my wife, Tanya, who's 26. She knows more background on big band than anyone I know. Every time I have a party, I overhear her saying things like, "Wasn't he also Tommy Dorsey's second trombonist?" [laughs]

Vise and Tanya in their martini shaker-inspired kitchen, 10-25-97. Photo: V.Vale

Let's face it, kids like to come and meet other kids at swing shows, but the music overrides the "age" stigma. And this country doesn't really support old people. I have to admit, when we do a Sex Pistols' song in the Morty Show, I'm starting to get a little self-conscious: "Christ, I'm fifty-fucking years old!"

I tell you, big band music is like wine . . . it just gets better with age. I don't see this movement ending, really. I hope it *never* reaches MTV status. I guess the Squirrel Nut Zippers have opened the door as far as the "sound" goes, but I hope it never gets reduced to some fad. As to how big it will get—I'm really not sure. It all depends on how the younger kids accept this music and if they add something to it.

♦ **V:** *And come up with tunes that sound halfway decent—*

♦ **VG:** They're starting to, now that there's pressure to do your own material. Everybody realizes that you have to move on. I give Morty a lot of credit: he's thrown ska, punk, grunge, *whatever,* into the mix, trying to create *his* expression based on what he hears and sees. Things don't have to be so *religious*—we don't have to try to be Louis Jordan! You can take a chance, and if the audience doesn't like it, then you go on from there. Some of these "swing purists" are looking at the New Morty Show going, "Naw, you guys are Whitesnake now." Simply because we've tried to infuse something else into swing.

♦ **V:** *You need the freedom to try things out—*

♦ **VG:** If you watch the *Benny Goodman Story:* he wanted to play a certain style; he started jump big band music. Eventually it caught on, but at first no one wanted to hear it. So hopefully something bigger will come out of this. Maybe some real sharp kids will come along and infuse something unexpected into it and *there you go!*

♦ **V:** *I love the retro styles in this scene. I saw a girl whose theme was bing cherries: cherry earrings, necklace, cherry print dress and even a tattoo of bing cherries on her left arm—*

♦ **VG:** It's incredible how some of the women dress up! When you go to a show at Bimbo's—well, they could send the security home. All the guys leave their testosterone at the door; you don't see any tension. Everybody's there to look swanky. They don't drink beer: they want martinis and cosmopolitans. They're

stylin', man. They're going to open a door for a woman—holy shit; what a concept that is! [laughs]

♦ **V:** *We didn't grow up with this kind of dancing; it's totally new and it's not wimpy—*

♦ **VG:** Yeah. It definitely takes some work to get that down. You've got to know your partner and you've got to know what you're doing. Swing dance contests are popping up all over the place. The Morty Show played a Monsters of Swing weekend in Ventura and they had a competition in two divisions: street dancing and lindy-hopping.

♦ **V:** *There was a similar weekend here at the Great American Music Hall . . . It seems people in the scene tend to have their homes completely decked out in retro decor—*

♦ **VG:** Everybody's into the tiki bars and the ceramic figurines. It's nice.

> ### When you go to a show at Bimbo's—well, they could send the security home. All the guys leave their testosterone at the door.

♦ **V:** *It sure beats High Tech—remember that?*

♦ **VG:** Oh, yeah—I was there, babe. How about when the old avocado and mauve Rubbermaid products were big? [laughs] Christ, contact paper . . . paisley and all that shit in the '70s . . . jesus, what a fuckin' nightmare! Now, instead of that, they have faux finishes; "old art" refurbishing. People are into making everything look old.

♦ **V:** *That's okay with me; it looks better. It's definitely a whole lifestyle.*

♦ **VG:** Exactly. Tanya did an interview and said, "Should I be apologizing because there's poverty in the world? Am I supposed to stay home and not dress up?" People want to have a good time—they always have—especially during the Depression, during the war . . . Life out there can be ugly, but you have to try and get some enjoyment out of it. These kids are into dressing up, looking good and getting loaded! [laughs] The martini culture, man, that's what it is.

♦ **V: Well, as long as that respect is there—**

♦ VG: I think it's an intrinsic part of it. Where are these kids eating now? They're not going to Mel's Drive-In, they're going to

Aaron Seymour and Tanya Deason, 11-15-97. Photo: V.Vale

Alfred's on Broadway, or the Top of the Mark to have a drink. Swank not crank! [laughs]

♦ **V: I'm pretty sure swing is here to stay. I think it's being totally reclaimed.**

♦ VG: As I said in *Swing Time* magazine, I don't think it's a fad, I think it's an *awakening*. There are bands popping up every day. It seems like every city is starting to pick up steam: Austin, Chicago, New York—even smaller towns like San Jose and Petaluma, where we've played to really large crowds. It's yet another scene that had a big start right here in San Francisco.

[Tanya Deason and Aaron Seymour come in]

♦ **VALE: Tanya, tell us how you got into the "swing lifestyle"—**

♦ TANYA DEASON: I used to be a hardcore punk rocker when I was a teenager. I had a black mohawk for five years. I had a lot of fun, but I always felt there was something missing. So when I heard about swing and realized what it was really all about—reclaiming the best of American culture—I jumped in with both feet.

It made a lot of sense that after years of protesting and focus-

---

After years of protesting and focusing on what's wrong with the world, it was time for something opposite and positive: *joy;* feeling alive again.

---

ing on what's wrong with the world, it was time for something opposite and positive: *joy;* feeling alive again. Like I said in a *Bay Guardian* interview, "People are just looking not to wallow anymore. We're alive and we're here and *damned* if we're going to sit

around thinking about how awful everything is." One of the big charges by "outsiders" is that this is a politically conservative scene that wants to restore old patriarchal values. But the women in this scene are very strong, very independent and very intelligent. Yet we don't see anything wrong with having men pull out chairs for us, open doors for us, or light our cigarettes. To us that just shows respect. We believe in old-fashioned values of politeness and respect; we like to patronize small stores where we're on a first-name basis; we like to tip our mailman at Christmas—things like that.

A lot of the lifestyle is also just a real affection for an earlier time. All our friends are interested in things like old detective novels by Dashiell Hammett, so fairly regularly we'll have dinner at John's Grill, which has the Dashiell Hammett Room upstairs. We'll drive around in search of the perfect cocktail lounge, or go to Alfred's [traditional restaurant] for steaks. We love going to this old hat store, Top Hatters, in San Leandro—the owners, Ted and Marie treat Vise like their son. We're always on the alert for an old sign—whether it be on a newsstand, the side of a brick building, or inside a bar. This scene has definitely encouraged a new appreciation for architecture, furniture—*everything*. We also own the big extravagant gas-guzzling 1940s cars (we have a 1947 Cadillac; Vise used to have a beautiful 1940 Buick but it got destroyed in a fire). It's a lifestyle; it's not just the music.

There are people all over the country who are into this; it's just that in their small town they have no outlet, or community. It's still very much a subculture. But whenever we do all-ages shows, there are 16-year-old kids trying to dance and dress up. But it's like any other emerging subculture: most people are not ballsy enough to just "do it"—dare to look different and listen to a different music that's not the norm. Eventually this will get widespread enough to become "cool" or just "normal." We live with a dichotomy: we don't *want* it to grow; we just want to keep it pure and fun and personal (where we know most of the people), but at the same time, we want to make money and quit our day jobs!

One thing that may get lost as this movement gets bigger is the respect people treat each other with, the manners. It's amazing how few people on the bus will give up their seat to an older person, or how few men sitting at a bar will let a woman sit down because she's wearing 6-inch heels. It used to be that when people entered a restaurant, somebody was there to take the hats and coats. We want to hearken back to a

Vise's ties and hats. Photo: V.Vale

time when people were polite to other people. The whole "every man for himself" thing has taken over, and this swing movement is the antithesis of that. It's much more trying to thrive on a "community" standard.

Vise o' lantern.

When I first got into swing, I was really blown away by how many ex-punkers were involved. Even Dutch, who almost started the whole thing, was a hardcore L.A. punk who once had a bleached white pompadour. There's the whole subcultural aspect of staying "on the move" and always hunting for something new and different from what everybody else is doing. That's why swing has drawn people from a variety of subcultural movements.

♦ AS: Anything that's against the commercial mainstream is laudable. I went through all the phases; I did a punk rock look, a death rock look, a rockabilly look and never felt comfortable. Certainly the pale lanky death rock look didn't work for me—I'm much too large! I was a *lonely* death-rocker. Throughout all those phases it was the music that attracted me. Then when industrial and grunge and rap proliferated, melody disappeared.

♦ TD: Early Throbbing Gristle, Cabaret Voltaire and SPK were doing serious experimentation with sound, and the effect of sound on human emotional and physical states. It was so subversive that there was nothing left anymore.

♦ AS: There was a mentality: "There are no more rules anymore. You can do anything you want." The attitude was more, "I must create something different," rather than, "I must create good music." All that had its place, but now we're over the explosion of the exploration of difference and "originality."

♦ TD: There's only so many musical notes in a scale, and only so many combinations. With the industrial artists it became, "How many different noises can we incorporate?"

♦ AS: In the context of swing music history, Bill Elliott is finding a whole slew of melodies today that were missed before. Basically he asked, "What other ways in the genre can I put together notes?" Punk was supposed to be so *anarchist,* but the drumbeats are so similar and it's all three chords. I think that within swing, you can apply a rock'n'roll beat and incorporate ideas from other genres, and still have it swingin'.

♦ TD: I hope we can pull in more rockabilly and more *danceable lounge* into swing. And pull in more '50s Billy May, Frank Sinatra, Dean Martin—something to mix it up a bit more. It was a really good thing when more of the rockabilly crowd were around—they're good-time people.

♦ AS: In my case, I went from punk to rockabilly to swing. There was a time when rockabilly, country-swing and big band swing weren't that dissimilar.

♦ TD: I would rather do a show with Big Sandy or Russell Scott or Ray Condo, so there's variety. But I'm not interested in having ska there. Ska music is half skinhead and half reggae—two genres that have never appealed to me. Specials, Madness, Selecter—only a handful of bands ever pulled it off. There will *never* be a place in swing for ska!

♦ V: *Let's talk about the clothes from earlier eras—*

♦ TD: The funny thing is—nowadays, *I'm* dressed better than the millionaires! People with a lot of money don't care what they look like, because it's "hip" to wear jeans and a T-shirt. It's the cult of anonymity.

♦ AS: We're creating our own culture that's not so much mimicking. We're not just fascinated by the clothes or music, but every aspect of the culture: the politics and history, as if it were a study of the entire society. There *are* factions who are very strict about wearing a very specific decade of clothes, but they're fading away.

♦ TD: Back then, the average man only had one suit, three ties, and a couple shirts. In old Sam Spade movies, Humphrey Bogart wears the same suit the entire time.

♦ AS: You didn't have "wash-and-wear" back then; you couldn't afford to constantly be doing laundry. So clothes used to last longer. Now we're in an era of disposable clothes: a dozen pairs of jeans, 20 T-shirts; throw 'em in the wash—

♦ TD: We're in a disposable era, period. Society has become

I think that within swing, you can apply a rock'n'roll beat and incorporate ideas from other genres, and still have it swingin'.

totally disposable in just a couple decades. In this swing movement, we want things that are built to last. Everything—and that includes our relationships. We go to our neighborhood bar (the Deluxe), shop at our corner grocery store, and make an effort to establish relationships with people in the neighborhood.

♦ AS: Instead of being "every man for himself," why not put yourself out for other people? It's a better way to live.

The lonely death rocker: Tanya in 1985.

♦ **V: Tanya, how did you get into "vintage"?**

♦ TD: It was really through Vise; he'd been doing it for so long. Also, hanging out with other girls taught me: "These purses are the coveted ones. These skirts are really cool." Then you create your own style by choosing what applies to *you*. Today I gave a ton of clothes to Carla Lease from Frenchy because I realized I can't wear '50s cinch-waisted full-skirt dresses; I'm too high-waisted, so I look like an overgrown four-year-old trying to wear clothes that are too small for me! Forties' styles look better on me.

Some women like pop fashions from the earlier '60s: the Mod look or whatnot. Women who are tall and thin do the '20s flapper era perfectly. You may start out trying everything; you have to experiment a lot. You end up with a lot of things you just give away. Actually, I mix and match the eras—after all, they're all at our disposal.

♦ AS: It's not to say that

Vise, Tanya and Cab Calloway in their living room, 10-25-97. Photo: V.Vale

clothes that echo the past and are affordable.

♦ AS: DaVinci makes retro-looking shirts that look early '50s. They have a square cut at the bottom; you don't tuck them in—it's the "casual look." The sleeves go to the elbow—I was used to long sleeves, so that was a tough adjustment! You can get them from Al at Martini Mercantile on Haight St. My baggy pants all have pleats; I'm always battling that big build.

My watch is made by Fossil. It's only $30 and it shows, but it still looks "classic." I have a couple of 'em. Vise gave me my stingy brim hat—it may have been a sendover from a pal in Omaha who sends him vintage clothes. Fedoras don't really go with the casual look; a stingy-brim looks better. Vise taught me what to look for in hats as far as multiple stitching and interior lining go—there are some felt hats out there that have no lining at all, so when you sweat, you ruin them. Also, the bands rot easily. I don't use pomade; hairspray and gel work better for my thick hair. Even through my punk phase I had quasi-pompadours,

you're doing anything "wrong" if you buy an '80s double-breasted suit instead of a vintage one.

♦ TD: It's a "collecting" thing. Vise and I consider ourselves to be collectors of vintage artifacts, clothes—the whole nine yards. It takes time to learn what is actually "authentic," because a lot of stuff was remade in the '70s and usually that stuff has some horrible "twist" to it. So many men have found this unbelievable pin-stripe suit, and the pants turn out to be these elephant bell-bottoms—it's a hip-huggin total '70s disco suit! Now I can tell by

> ### You could sit in your front room 'til you drop dead, listening to great swing recordings.

the *fabric* what era it's from. There are certain fabrics that were predominant in the '40s that weren't used in other decades: nylon, gabardines, taffeta, tulle—you can pretty much tell by the fabric whether it's worth pulling off the rack.

♦ AS: I judge coats by the lapels. You can tell a '40s gabardine shirt by the way the top button closes; it's a little loop above the top. Also, note the cinched stitching around the collar and the two pocket flaps. When you wear a tie with one, the collar hangs more closely. The tie is where the statement is made!

♦ TD: Fortunately, now there are companies that are making

sometimes they were taller than at other times. I'd change colors periodically.

♦ TD: I would say the king of the stingy-brim, dark straw hat is Mr. Lucky.

♦ **V: Let's talk about music: how do you find songs to perform?**

♦ TD: We've had people watch an Ambassadors of Swing show and go, "Oh, we're going to start a band and do this song, that song, and that song." I think, "Can you not find your own material?!" I mean, it is public domain, but come on!

♦ VG: You could sit in your front room 'til you drop dead, listening to great swing recordings. There's a certain protocol that needs to be stated. If the headlining band is playing certain songs, the opening band should *NOT* play them. Before the New Morty Show opened for Sam Butera, we gave Sam our set list and he pretty much eliminated half our material! But that's the respect you give someone. We're not going to go onstage before he comes on and play all his songs. [laughs]

♦ TD: We keep finding songs nobody's revived yet: "Oh, this is awesome!" Then six months later, it's everybody's cover tune! We think, "Do your *own* research!" Vise and I spent months listening to hundreds of LPs and CDS searching for something different, energetic and that catches a mood. It took us a year until we found the *killer* arrangement of "It Ain't Necessarily So." Soon everybody will be doing it—

♦ VG: *Whatever;* just don't do it on the same show as ours! Minimal etiquette is important.

♦ AS: You could even stick with Cab Calloway, Louis Jordan and

Bill Elliott and Vise Grip (Ambassadors of Swing), Bimbo's, 11-29-97. Photo: V.Vale

Louis Prima and have enough different cover songs for ten bands to do.

♦ TD: What kills me is: there are still bands popping up who are doing the Joe Jackson *Jumpin' Jive* recording from cover to cover, no alteration—they even sing like him! That was a very important and influential CD, but to do it now—that is so tired! That

---

Nobody ever thinks of Vise's songs as covers because they're Vise. He does "Caldonia" and puts a Jewish mother into it!

---

has got to stop being the *Dick & Jane* primer of Neo-Swing.

♦ AS: Also, if you're going to do a cover, apply some personality to it, like Vise does. Vise is basically doing covers, but nobody ever thinks of Vise's songs as covers because they're Vise. He does "Caldonia" and puts a Jewish mother into it! Everybody from David Lee Roth to a million lounge singers have done "Just a Gigolo," but Vise's version is the epitome because of the *character* he brought to it. Just because a song is a cover is not the kiss of death. The pressure to be "new and exciting" is what's killing the modern music industry.

♦ TD: Nowadays, whenever an Oasis appears, 50 Oasis cover bands immediately appear. Which is not to say that won't happen in swing. When Big Bad Voodoo Daddy first appeared, they *were* Royal Crown Revue—we used to call them "Crown Lite"! Now they've changed, evolved and gone on—they laid low to make that change. Never forget, it was definitely ROYAL CROWN who blew the lid off things; they were the ones who *first* got other people into "swing." Everyone who's in a band now *owes* them.

♦ AS: There are two approaches now: 1) take the old music and ask, "How can I change it? Can I mix it with rock or ska?" 2) Or ask, "Have I learned as much as I possibly can from the Originals, and continue doing what *they* might have done?"

♦ TD: Chris and Charlie Siebert's band, The SHUFFLING MOLASSES BROTHERS (basically Lavay Smith minus Lavay), was one of the first swing bands I got into. I used to joke that going to their shows was like attending Swing 101, because before or after every song Chris would say, "This song was written in this year by this person, arranged by this person, featuring a solo on the tenor saxophone by this person—"

♦ AS: Then he'd say whether or not he was going to follow it, or what changes he had made. And on the Lavay Smith CD Chris included informative liner notes, which many bands neglect. We're all in this massive learning process, trying to understand the music.

♦ TD: Chris also explained why he chose a particular song: why it was unique. He almost forces you to train your own ear to hear the same thing; he opens your eyes.

♦ AS: I call BILL ELLIOTT the hardest-working man in the swing scene. His newest CD runs the gamut of movie soundtracks, TV shows, Latin, tango, soft swing, big band, and jump-swing. No song sounds like any other song, and he only does one cover. And that's a feat: coming up with a big-band melody that hadn't yet been conceived of. He's been true to the original sound: "I'm not going to try and change it; it was right the first time. Can I be as great as the people who originally did it?" He has a song, "I'm Beginning to Like It": "Never thought I'd see the day; Instead of slam, I swing and sway; But oh, I'm beginning to like it. I was raised on a hard-rock diet; Loved the beat that was in your face; But I've been switched to a whole new world; Filled with style and grace." My favorite line of this song is, "I switched my MTV to AMC." Ten years ago I'd ask my friends, "Did you see so-and-so on MTV last night?" Now it's, "Did you see so-and-so on AMC last night?"

♦ TD: Bill Elliott has one of the most solid, disciplined big bands I've ever heard. Vise went down to L.A. to record a song for a movie with him, and was totally blown away by the control he has over his musicians. To have an ear sufficiently trained to plot out a viable line for every single instrument—I wouldn't wish that hell on anybody!

♦ *V: I've heard that almost none of the original people in the swing movement go out anymore—*

♦ VG: They don't like being in crowded places.

♦ TD: It's nice that now we're making money, but I'll always miss going to Bimbo's and seeing 200 people I knew, literally, in one way or another. Instead of *900* people, some of whom spill beer on your nice gabardine suit that was hard to find. I say, "Don't go to Bimbo's and throw up and spill beer on people. Go to a thrash club—there you can spill all the beer you want!" 🅥

Vise's Recommendations

SOME BOOKS:
George T. Simon *Simon Says*
The Cotton Club
Songs of the '30s
Jerome Kern Collection
A Separate Cinema
The Movies Grow Up 1940-1980
Mel Tormé *My Singing Teachers*
Lionel Hampton *Hamp*
Bands, Booze & Broads
Haskins *Black Music in America*
The Great Songs of Cole Porter
Russel Wright Designs
Lucille Ball *Love, Lucy*

Jammin' at the Margins
Fabulous Fabrics of the '50s
'40s & '50s Collectibles
The Cult of Vespa
California (Union Pacific RR)
Everyday Fashions of the Forties
Sixties Sourcebook
Ted Polhemus *Street Style*
Sinatra: The Pictorial Biography
Life ("Sinatra at Eighty" issue)
Albert McCarthy *Big Band Jazz*
Ken Anger *Hollywood Babylon II*
J. Ellroy *Hollywood Nocturnes*
Alan Barbour *Bogart*

John Coppola and Frances Lynne in their San Francisco bird-watching flat. Dec. 16, 1997. Photo: V. Vale

John Coppola plays trumpet with Vise Grip's Ambassadors of Swing and other Bay Area groups, does studio work and teaches. His wife, Frances, sang with the Gene Krupa Band, Charlie Barnet and other ensembles under the name "Frances Lynne"; both occasionally lecture on swing and jazz music. The Coppolas live in San Francisco and are enthusiastic cat-lovers and bird-watchers.

INTERVIEW WITH JOHN COPPOLA

♦ *VALE: What were your feelings when you first played with Vise Grip's big band? The curtains opened and you saw several hundred kids swing dancing—*

♦ JOHN COPPOLA: I thought I was 13 years old again! It looked *exactly* like Sweet's Ballroom in Oakland, 1943. We were basically playing the same music, and the kids were dressed the same: guys in zoot suits and gals in spaghetti strap gowns. The only glaring difference was, of course, was when they turned around I saw all the tattoos! That wasn't happening with the ladies in those days. Also, these kids are better dancers. I don't mean they're *all* better than the best of the swing era dancers, but they seem studied, like they really practiced. It was really a kick for me: a time-warp.

♦ *V: I'll bet you never thought this would happen—*

♦ JC: No. Once the ballrooms folded, I couldn't see that kind of thing ever happening again. It's a surprise. A former student of mine called from Vegas and said a place just opened up there with a swing band playing the hits. He's a trumpet player who just left

Sam Butera because he didn't want to travel any longer. He said there's beginning to be a movement in Vegas; the kids come in dressed up and they dance in time—that's the main thing: you can tell a good dancer if they dance to the rhythm of the band. Those dancers used to be rare; we'd call them "rhythm dancers." That was the first thing I noticed.

♦ *V: What were the old ballrooms like? There aren't many left—*

♦ JC: No, not around here. Some of them would hold 4,000 or 5,000 people—they were huge and very popular, especially during the war years. I'm talking about the other side of the bay, because that's where I grew up and had my first musical experiences. During the war years Oakland's curfew was a few hours later than San Francisco. During curfew, everything got closed down and all the lights were turned off; they darkened the city—especially San Francisco. We had air raid warnings once in a while; there was a lot of paranoia.

The Oakland Navy Base and the Alameda Air Station formed a huge disembarkation point—all the Armed Forces came through there on their way to the Pacific to fight the Japanese. During the war, Oakland was like New Year's Eve every night; there were big parties going on nightly and they all had swing bands. That was the thing: Swing was King. Oakland was a very hip, hot town. There were *hundreds* of swing bands on the road then.

When the Swing Era was big, it was *hot.* Charlie Barnet's band would tour the South—he was known as "the White Duke" (he played a lot of Duke Ellington) and he would play the Apollo. He was one of the "white-black" bands, as they used to be called.

♦ **V: *Where were you born?***

♦ JC: I was born in Geneva, New York on May 11, 1929—I brought on the Depression! My parents grew vegetables on farmland and had a small business importing things from Italy; there was a big Sicilian colony there. We had a wind-up Victrola and a lot of records, especially opera; I heard a lot of Caruso.

In 1937 we moved to Oakland, California. By then I was listening to music; my sister Rose, who was a couple years older, had begun buying Count Basie and Benny Goodman records. We saw Goodman's band in several big movies. By the time I was 9 I was hearing a lot of good live music. The World's Fair was at Treasure Island in 1939; our grammar school went there and we heard Count Basie, the Edward Franko Goldman Band, etc. We were exposed to that music because it was the pop music of the day.

There was a radio station, KRE, in Berkeley that had a program called Open House, and I'd listen to that after school. You could phone in requests. Some of the popular music back then would be too sophisticated for people today: Coleman Hawkins' "Body and Soul" was on all the jukeboxes. In high school (around 1941) the Hit Parade Top Ten was all instrumentals! The bands brought in singers. There were a few big singers that *weren't* part of bands, like Russ Columbo and Bing Crosby (who got started in Paul Whiteman's band), but when Sinatra left Dorsey, that opened the door for solo singers, and all kinds began to appear.

The big bands were stars in their own right. Tommy Dorsey's band was an amazing assembly for awhile. He had Jo Stafford, Frank Sinatra, Connie Haines and the Pied Pipers (a vocal group); it was a huge ensemble. And he had strings—this was a package. They'd fill the stage. Glenn Miller also had singers and vocal groups; everybody had a vocal group.

♦ **V: *When did you start playing?***

♦ JC: I started seriously practicing music when I was 9—that was on trumpet in grammar school. (First I tried clarinet, but quickly switched.) By the time I got to Herbert Hoover Junior High, I had made up my mind to be a musician. I had my first serious teacher when I turned 11: Don Fraga. He was very young and also very hip. He was partial to black bands, and told me who the really great players were. He got me very interested in Basie, Ellington, Jimmie Lunceford—all the great black bands.

I had become an apprentice shoemaker to my uncle in

John playing in the Woody Herman Band at Sweets Ballroom, Oakland, 1957.

Oakland, who was a very fine mandolin player. We were right around the block from Sweet's Ballroom on Franklin St (bet. 14th–15th Sts). We'd put up posters in our window for them and they would give us passes. Inside our orthopedic shoemaking

---

Basie was playing and his band included Harry Edison, Buck Clayton, Ed Lewis and Al Killian on trumpets. That's when I realized the power of the trumpet section to carry the band.

---

shop [Service Shoe Renew Shop, 356 14th St], we had a shoeshine parlor run by a bootblack named Arthur Peoples, who was from Kansas City. In those days the guys who were shining shoes—especially the blacks—would have record players. They would put on a record and shine shoes in rhythm, almost choreographed. Arthur had all the Basie records. He had been Count Basie's valet for a short time in Kansas City, and had gotten to know Basie and Lester Young and all those cats. He'd put on these records and "pop the cloth," and catch the accents just like the drummer did.

There was a shoeshine parlor in Oakland called the Hollywood Shoeshine Parlor, with 22 shine stands. You had to wait in line because the military, especially the paratroopers, all wanted their shoes spotless. The bootblacks would get 10 or 15 guys up on chairs, put on "Rockabye Basie," and they'd all pop the cloth at the same time, catching all the accents, and the room would just be swingin'!

When I was 11, Arthur Peoples took me to Sweets Ballroom for the first time. Basie was playing and his band included Harry Edison, Buck Clayton, Ed Lewis and Al Killian on trumpets, Lester Young on tenor, and Jo Jones on drums. That's when I realized the power of the trumpet section to carry the band. Shortly after, he took me to see the Gene Krupa Orchestra with Roy Eldridge on trumpet, and that made me want to play trumpet even more. By the time I was in Tech High School, I was going to Sweets three or four nights a week!

Once the war got rolling and all these young guys were being drafted or enlisted, I began working professionally as a musician. At age 13, my first job was a one-nighter with Rudy Salvini's band, and in the summer of 1945 I played at Camp Curry in Yosemite with the Buddy Stone Band. I'd had a good teacher; he had a physical disability so he didn't go into the service. He began to hire me for jobs he would contract. I didn't have much experience, but I had the endurance; I could play loud and high and that

L to R: Woody Herman, Burt Collins, John Coppola, and Dudley Harvey at Steel Pier, Atlantic City in 1956.

There was one night when Basie was at the Paramount, Ellington at the Orpheum, Lionel Hampton at the T&D and someone else was in town, too. Another night Harry James was at the Auditorium, Dave Matthews at the Scottish Rite, Basie at the Fox Oak, Benny Carter at the old Orpheum, and Charlie Barnet at Sweets. Oakland had a lot more live music than San Francisco. Remember, there were 100,000 servicemen in town who knew they were about to go overseas, and they just wanted to party. And the ballrooms were the place to be.

♦ V: What was the situation with ladies?

♦ JC: By the late part of '42, people were flocking in from all over the country to work in the shipyards. People came from down South and the Midwest. The shipyards paid well and you could work as many hours as you wanted. America was coming out of the Depression and all of a sudden people had money, but there was nothing to spend it on! You couldn't buy a car—they didn't make them during the war.

There was rationing, although it was a bit of a joke. People couldn't buy more than four pairs of shoes a year, but who buys that many shoes, anyway? There was gas rationing, and if you did have a car, that *was* a problem. You had an A, B or C card, and if you were working in defense you could get more gas coupons. There were also meat and butter coupons, but the rationing was generous compared to England; I didn't see any skinny people.

There were a lot of young ladies coming in to work the shipyards; those were the days of "Rosie the Riveter"—remember that song? You had an influx of people who were either 4-F, or if they were really skillful, they got deferments because they were more important to the war effort in their work. The women came in and started taking over; this was really the breakthrough for hiring women in all the industries: the military, the airplane industry (when women began working on electronic parts). They actually hired dwarves or midgets to do the welding at the bottoms of ships, where it got very narrow. Everybody worked back then because there was a lot of work.

They let seniors in high school, or 16-year-old guys work in the shipyards if their parents okayed it. A lot of guys went to school only half a day and did that.

♦ V: Were a lot of young people playing in bands?

♦ JC: A band like Jack Teagarden came through and he had legal custody of Stan Getz, who was playing with him when he was 14. Zoot Sims, Al Cohen, Miles Davis—they all got to play with older musicians when they were just teenagers. Billy Eckstine's big band with Miles, Fats Navarro and Art Blakey played Sweets for a couple of weeks. When I was playing with the band that played Sweets, I was the youngest by far—the next youngest trumpet player was 45. He was too old for the service, but he had all that experience and could show me stuff. Kids got a chance to play with seasoned musicians; it was like a fast jump up. I'd see some of the big bands and there were guys 17–18 really playing great, and they'd been on the road for 4 years!

♦ V: What kind of gigs did you play?

♦ JC: I worked with a bunch of bands with 12–13 pieces. We played "stock arrangements" that had been published. A lot of them were Count Basie arrangements which I still have—I

seemed to be enough. When I started high school I began to drift away from my poor uncle and began concentrating on music, and by my senior year I was steadily working nights at Sweets Ballroom.

So, I got to hear and see all the great swing bands of that period; *everyone* came through Oakland. It was segregated. The bands would come in to work two nights, and if Monday night was "Colored Night," that's when I would go, of course. All the hip young white cats would be there, because on that night the bands wouldn't play the commercial stuff. In those days bands had to play waltzes, polkas, dances of every kind—everything. But when you caught Basie or Lunceford on colored night, they would play

---

You can tell a good dancer if they dance to the rhythm of the band. Those dancers used to be rare; we'd call them "rhythm dancers."

---

just swing and would stretch out more; the soloists got to play longer. That was the premium night. Hardly anybody danced; you'd look back and see people just deeply listening to the band. Way in the back some people might be dancing.

When a band like Basie came to town, every aspiring musician would be there early. The house band would play from 8–9, and the main band would come on at 9. So if you were really hip, you'd be there at 7:30 and listen to the house band, which was *good*. By the time Basie or Lunceford or whoever it was came on, there'd be 20 young cats grabbing their spots up front so they could study the band and try to pick up on stuff.

♦ V: What were some of the other venues?

♦ JC: Earl Hines had a big band for months at Slim Jenkins' old place on 7th St. The bands played movie theaters too. Most theaters were set up for stage shows. In Oakland they had the T&D (which ran movies and had big bands), The Orpheum, the Fox Oakland and the Paramount. Sometimes it was hard to choose.

brought them to Vise Grip and we still play them! They've held up very well. We also played pop tunes of the day. You could buy arrangements at Best Music in Oakland for 75 cents each. There were also young guys learning to arrange and writing their own stuff. A lot of good arrangers had been drafted and wrote arrangements for the Army, the Navy, and the Air Force, and those began to float down to the civilian population. Somebody knew somebody, and next thing you knew we'd have these arrangements marked "US Navy." When a tune was no longer popular, they were going to burn it, so instead of that somebody would send it to somebody else, etc. There weren't any Kinko's around back then, [laughs] so music had to be copied by hand.

In my senior year when I was working at Sweets, I played with the Gary Nottingham Band. It was an extremely good band and he had a marvelous library. He had an arranger, Marty Paich, who wrote a lot of arrangements and was brilliant. When he was 14 he could transcribe Basie or Lunceford off the records.

♦ *V: Were these bands integrated?*

♦ JC: Not Nottingham's band. In Oakland, the schools weren't necessarily segregated, although they were by neighborhoods. Most blacks went to a high school in West Oakland. There were jam sessions at DeFremery Park where we'd meet young black musicians. We used to play at the Filbert Street Boys Club; we had a 16-piece band there that was integrated. I went to Hoover and Tech High School and they were integrated. I don't remember any racial tension when I grew up in Oakland—not one incident. We'd go to West Oakland and see bands playing at Slim Jenkins' (that was a large black nightclub; Oakland's "Cotton Club") and we got in, no problem. We'd sit over in the corner and hear some great music. On summer nights when it was hot we'd leave the doors of our house open. Nobody had anything to steal!

♦ *V: Tell us about your first trumpet—*

♦ JC: My very first trumpet came from Sears Roebuck and cost $14. I blew holes in that in about eight months and took it to a repair shop and the guy said, "It'll cost you $20 to fix it!" I still have my first mouthpiece, but I don't use it. From then on, my horns were all good, professional ones.

Now I have a custom-made trumpet made by Joe Marcinkiewicz of Canby, Oregon. He's a former student. I have a lot of trumpets with different bores. I have a couple of historical horns, like an old gold-plated Conn from the '20s that I don't use;

My very first trumpet came from Sears Roebuck and cost $14. I blew holes in that in about eight months.

---

it's a piece of "trumpet jewelry"! [laughs] I have two flugelhorns; they're conical-bored and are mellower-sounding; they look like a plump trumpet. Miles brought them to the forefront in jazz, and Chuck Mangione—the guy with the hat—made them really popular. I have 10 trumpets, and four of them are out on loan to students. Some I found cheap; a couple have been given to me by former students. You gather stuff in life, y'know. Mouthpieces are like a pair of shoes; one guy may claim his is the greatest in the world and you try it and it's terrible! It's just a matter of physiognomy.

♦ *V: Who did you play with after the Gary Nottingham band?*

♦ JC: After I graduated from high school in '46 at the age of 17, I went on the road for a month and played Northern California and Oregon. Our bandleader was Bob O'Connor and his theme song was "Stratosphere." On the side of the bus it said, "From out of the stratosphere, the music of tomorrow, today." It was kind of a hip, avant-garde big band—too advanced for the times. We were booked to play a ballroom in Salt Lake City for a month, and it burned down to the ground. Also we had a bad bus; we ran into

Frances (seated on left) with the Charlie Barnet Orchestra at The Kavakos Club, Washington D.C. ca. 1948.

bad weather; everything that could go wrong, did. We found ourselves stranded in Pocatello, Idaho, without any money and everybody had to hitchhike home. When we left town, people were calling us the "suicide band."

When I came back home, I worked with Nottingham and also began working around town with some Latin bands—the big Latin bands were popular in those days. This was during the last part of the '40s. I worked with a very good big band led by Billy Shuart. Paul Desmond was lead alto player, Chuck Travis was on tenor (he works with Vise Grip now), and Allan Smith was on trumpet. The arrangements were done by a very talented arranger and composer, Keith Carr, who's still around.

Skipping along, in 1950 my main band career began to happen. Charlie Barnet was here in S.F. with a small group. He was going to expand the band and was holding auditions in Sacramento. Keith Carr had recommended me, so I went up there and got the job. I stayed with that band for a year. We toured all over the U.S.; our most notable gig was at the Apollo Theater. We played the Howard theater, too. These were black theaters, but Barnet was an unusual band who drew mixed audiences. On the posters it said "The White Duke"—he had some great arrangements and played a lot of Ellington, Basie and some bebop. That year I worked with Barnet was my biggest education; I learned more in that year than I had up to that date. We had some great musicians in the band, and that was really where I got my act together. I played first trumpet and had to take solos. I did some recordings with the band for Capitol. We did about six sides, but only two were ever released.

Around spring 1951, some guys in the Stan Kenton band heard me play with Barnet in L.A. We were playing the Oasis, and Kenton's band was at the Palladium. Kenton's first trumpet player was Ray Wetzel, a great player who had been my mentor in Barnet's band. He'd left Barnet to join Kenton, and that's when I had taken over a lot of the first chair parts. Well, Wetzel wanted to leave Kenton to join Tommy Dorsey's band, because not only had Dorsey offered him a fabulous contract, but had also offered his wife a job (she played bass), so they'd be drawing a double salary. Wetzel wanted me to take his chair with Kenton.

So the guys (who included Maynard Ferguson) came down and heard me play and the next day I got a call from Kenton inviting me to join the band. I called Barnet and it turned out he was going to take a vacation. He said I should take the job, because it would give me experience with a different kind of band. Kenton had an experimental band doing all kinds of material, whereas Barnet had a straight-ahead swing band.

I remained with Kenton for a year, then left the band because I thought I was going into the army for the Korean War. I spent some time in Oakland with my sister and father. The draft

Frances Lynne in 1958 during her tour with Charlie Barnet.

Cover of Frances' cassette, Remember, released in 1991.

board had arranged for me to play with the Ford Ord band, but it didn't happen; the war was ending. In the meantime, I had gotten married.

♦ **V:** *How did you meet your wife?*
♦ JC: When I was home for awhile, I began working "casuals" (gigs around town). Frances was a singer on some of those jobs, and we got together—you know how those things go! Our wedding date was July 28, 1952.

I went out on the road with Billy May's band and Frances went with me. I stayed with Billy for quite a while, from '52–'53. Then there were problems with money. I had been getting offers from Ray Anthony, who had a big TV show and wanted both me and my wife. In Los Angeles I left the Billy May band and came home. I worked around town playing theaters and clubs. In 1954 I went on a three-month package tour featuring Stan Kenton's orchestra, along with the Art Tatum Trio, Shorty Rogers and the Giants, and Mary Ann McCall.

In 1955 I got a call from Woody Herman. I stayed with him for three years until 1958; that was my longest road trip. Herman alternated between a big band and a small band. We had extended stays in Vegas and Tahoe with Woody's small band (an octet), and my wife would come up there.

Then I left Woody's band and came back home to stay—I was tired of traveling. I started playing theaters, clubs, the Civic Light Opera, but not much jazz. I had my own combo that played until 1962. Then Tennessee Ernie Ford came to town and I did his show for three years. He had an 8-piece band including four horns, and had great guests: Ellington, Erroll Garner, Oscar Peterson. It was kind of a "hip" show. He did his shtick, and we played gospel music, Country & Western (we had Patsy Cline on; she was a great singer). That ran its course, and I organized both a quintet and a group of ten musicians that played the Oakland's Gold Nugget and Holiday Inn, and the Premier Room in Redwood City. I also worked in the jingle business through the '60s.

In the late '60s I went on a short tour with Henry Mancini. Then I did two tours with Petula Clark. Since then, I've worked a bunch of clubs and did the theaters again—Civic Light Opera, etc. I went on tour with the "Funny Girl" show. All the arrangements were done by Ralph Burns, the same arranger for Woody Herman. I had no trouble with that music; I'd already played it for three years.

In the meantime, I worked with Gerald Wilson's band when he was here. I played with a large group working with Dizzy Gillespie at the Monterey Jazz Festival, George Shearing,

Tito Puente, Machito, J.J. Johnson (jazz trombonist). I worked the Circle Star Theater when they had a house orchestra. I did a lot of work with Nelson Riddle, with Nat Cole and Frank Sinatra. I did a couple concerts with Nat Cole at San Jose and Berkeley. He was very thin and a chain-smoker—unfiltered Camels at that. That's what killed him; he died of lung cancer. He was a great guy.

Nobody ever treated a band better than Sinatra; he acknowledged the arrangers, the soloists. We played Reagan's second inauguration ball in Sacramento, and Frank sent over the best wine to our table and picked up the tab for all the musicians. He

---

When I was with Stan Kenton, one night a guy stole a cow and put it on our bus. Yeah, there was some cute stuff.

---

came over and said how great the band was.

In recent years, I teach students. I also do summer music camps. One is sponsored by people from the Monterey Jazz Festival, and another is done by Rhythmic Concepts from Berkeley. I'm working tonight at the Pacific Union Club with a quintet, playing dinner music. Vise Grip's group played Charles Schwab's birthday party at the Palace of Legion of Honor, with the rain on the roof—great party. You know what—they canceled the first one, but we still got paid!

As far as "big band" is concerned, I work with Vise Grip and I also work with Bill Barry out of L.A. He was with Duke Ellington for years and has a lot of the Duke's arrangements. That band does a couple concerts a year.

♦ V: *It's great you're working with Vise Grip. Are you the bandleader?*
♦ JC: I've brought him some arrangements. Let's say I'm the musical advisor.
♦ V: *So which trumpet players were your main influences?*
♦ JC: Not Louis Armstrong and Dizzy Gillespie—they're so individual, they're just impossible to exactly imitate. As a teenager I transcribed a lot of Fats Navarro's solos, and I also liked Harry Sweets Edison.
♦ V: *Did anything funny happen while you were on tour?*
♦ JC: When I was with Stan Kenton, one night a guy stole a cow and put it on our bus. Yeah, there was some cute stuff. Once we showed up a night early for a gig and there was nobody there. Another time, half the band was 400 miles away from the other half at the wrong town with the same name . . .

🐾 🐾 🐾 🐾 🐾 🐾 🐾 🐾

INTERVIEW WITH FRANCES "Vocals in Velvet" LYNNE

♦ VALE: *Tell us your musical history—*
♦ FRANCES LYNNE: When I was six, I was on the Kiddies Klub [radio show] in my hometown of Austin, Texas. I started learning the lyrics of popular songs from song sheets that you could buy at drugstores, etc. They contained just the words; I learned the melodies from listening to the radio. When I became a teenager, I sang around school and town and got a reputation for this. I also sang on radio stations with the Billy Davis vocal trio; we did commercials, too. My mentors wanted me to go in the direction of Deanna Durbin; I had this "beautiful" voice that was very high and sweet. But then I fell in love with popular music and jazz.

The second part of my career began when I "joined the army," as I facetiously say. I entertained a lot at the USO and Special

Services shows, at Bergstrom Field near Austin, Texas, and Camp Swift near Bastrop, Texas. I sang with the 156th Army Band, and also did lighthearted skits "live" and for the army radio station at Camp Swift. When they broke up, they kept a small nucleus of musicians at the hospital division, and I went out and did their radio shows. These musicians became my mentors. Some of them had been in big bands, which I aspired to. As a little girl you wonder what you're going to do for your "life's work," and the general feeling was, "You can't go out to California and make it." But *these* people encouraged me.

My mother and I came out to San Francisco in 1946; someone I'd known in an army band lived there. He introduced me around, and I started to work casuals. In 1946 I got a call from a Daryl Cutler, who was forming a group with Dave Brubeck and Don Ratto. They chose me as singer, and the group was called The Three D's. Our first job was at El Borracho, a cute little neighborhood bar on Geary Blvd.

In 1947 we got hired to play the Geary Cellar, a downstairs nightclub on Geary St which is still there. When Don could no longer make it, Norman Bates joined and we changed his name to "Dorman" so we could still be The Three D's. I got some nice write-ups from Herb Caen. Stan Kenton saw me sing and was interested in having me join him, but it never worked out. I hung out with June Christy whenever she appeared with Kenton at the Edgewater, a big ballroom on the Great Highway to the right of Fulton St. We were big stuff, in a way. The place was crammed. People loved to hear Dave play the kind of music he was into, and I will say they loved me just as much. I was having so much fun doing music.

We worked jobs up and down the peninsula. When our job at the Geary Cellar ended, Paul Desmond took our group to the Band

Cover of a 1950 *Down Beat* with Frances Lynne on drums and Gene Krupa on vocals.

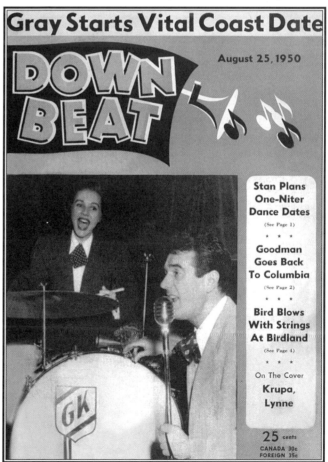

John & Frances Coppola **129**

Box in Redwood City near Stanford. The students would all come to hear Dave. I got to work with Paul and continued with Dave. We worked some jobs in Stockton—that was Dave's college town.

When all that ended, I got a call from Charlie Barnet and went on the road. First I went to Los Angeles. Charlie had asked me to talk with his arranger, Paul Villepigue. Paul was really good; he

---

When a song came out, song pluggers would come around and want you to push their song to the leader and get the leader to do it. They would wine and dine you, and that was exciting.

---

took down all my special notes and wrote arrangements just around me—I feel so fortunate.

We had to do a lot of popular songs when we got to New York. When a song came out, song pluggers would come around and want you to push their song to the leader and get the leader to do it. They would wine and dine you, and that was exciting. Then we went on the road and played theaters, clubs—a lot of one-nighters. At the time, we didn't sleep much and there were some hardships, but I look back on the experience as wonderful—you can't get that kind of experience anymore. When I was with Jerry Wald (a secondary big name band) in the summer of '49 we travelled in cars, but when I was with Charlie and Gene Krupa we always had a tour bus—that was better.

In the fall of '48 I joined Charlie Barnet. In the summer of '49 I was with Jerry Wald. In the fall of '49–'50 I went with Gene Krupa for the better part of a year. Then I came home to San

Francisco in the last part of 1950 and met John. He says he met me before, but I don't recall that. I met Johnny on a casual [one night gig] and we haven't been separated since—we dated so much and stayed out so late and early. In 1952, we decided to marry.

♦ *V: Did you sing much after that?*

♦ FL: I sang casuals; I sang with Alvino Rey's orchestra and also did a number of other gigs. I was a "single" [featured artist] at the Lido on Columbus Avenue, and sang with Nick Esposito's group at Fack's on Market St—I sang, "We'll Be Together Again," written by Frankie Laine's pianist, Carl Fisher. When casual bandleaders got a job, they would call their favorite musicians and singers first. I've worked a lot of jobs with John. I even sang an MJB coffee commercial—that paid me little residuals for five years.

♦ *V: What was it like working with Dave Brubeck?*

♦ FL: I like to tell people that I worked with him *before* he was Dave Brubeck! It was what I was meant to do. I was thrilled, and learned so much.

♦ *V: What was it like touring with Charlie Barnet's band?*

♦ FL: He was not a cuddly man to me; I did not have a fiery enough personality to suit him. The first thing he wanted me to do was dye my hair red, and I didn't do it. He tried to change my arrangement of "Body and Soul," too. The band tried to be very hip and cruel, but they didn't know I'd heard it all already. We worked the Carnival Ballroom for a month before we went on the road. So they thought they'd give me "the treatment" my first night out. They wanted to say all these bad words in front of me, but they didn't shock me in the least. Doc Severinsen was in that band, by the way.

Gene Krupa's band never did anything like that; they were all very nice. Gene liked to work crossroad puzzles and we'd play "20 Questions" on the bus. When we played ballrooms, after the first set Gene would have to change his jacket—it was totally

Frances singing with the "hospital band", Austin Texas, ca. 1944

Frances (seated on left) at the Clique Club, Philadelphia with the Gene Krupa Orchestra, 1949. Note little boy sitting in on drums!

soaked. Whenever we hit a big town, there was always some little boy coming up to him who wanted to play drums, and Gene would let him sit in. One night a young lady came up and wanted to sing "Boogie Blues," and you could tell she'd been practicing it for eons. She sang it, and then was going to sing another tune, but was so nervous she started singing "Boogie Blues" again! The band started over, and nobody made a big deal. When my tour with the Krupa Band ended, I did a two-week engagement at the Blackhawk (200 Hyde St), backed by pianist Buddy Motsinger.

You don't really get to know the leaders; they don't hang out with the musicians. I thought Gene Krupa and Jerry Wald were very nice, but again, you don't get to know them that well.

♦ V: *What songs did you do?*

♦ FL: What songs *didn't* I do?! Professionally, with the bands I sang their arrangements and what they were famous for. With Krupa, I remember singing "Cottage For Sale." With Charlie Barnet I sang "Daddy-O." Some of my influences were Billie Holiday, Anita O'Day. Growing up, I listened to the radio as much as I could and sang along. When I came to San Francisco, I loved *early* Margaret Whiting and Martha Tilton—*she's* the most underrated singer. Everybody talked about Helen Forrest (who sang with Harry James), but I thought, "The best singer is Martha Tilton." She never did get the recognition she deserved. Whenever I saw her on a TV special, she sang, "And the Angels Sing," which is not particularly great for vocalists, but that song had made her famous. She recorded it with Benny Goodman; Ziggy Elman was the trumpet player. I also liked Peggy Lee, Nat

Cole, and Fran Warren who sang with Claude Thornhill.

In those days there were a lot of great singers who sang beautifully. I guess *I'm* sort of a movie singer—it was my dream to be the one who actually sings when you see Betty Grable opening her mouth! I hope this revival of swing music encourages young women to become singers again. **V**

Frances in her high school band uniform.

Frances' Recordings

"What's Makin' Me Cry?" (backed by the Moonbeams & The Clipper Orchestra)/"Billy The Kid" (backed by the Moonbeams and the Circuit Riders). 78 on Clipper Records, 34 Hillside, NY 34, NY. Frances Lynne: *Remember.* Cassette-only release from Lark Records, 2079 Fulton St, San Francisco CA 94117. $13 postpaid.

Lee Press-On & The Nails

"Jump Swing from Hell": Lee Press-On and the Nails. Photo: Victoria Faw

Lee Press-On & The Nails is a razor-sharp swing band from Marin County led by hyperkinetic vocalist Lee Press-On. His wife, Leslie Presley, also sings; they're the "Morticia & Gomez of Swing." Current personnel include: Beau "Doc" Faw (drums), Dave "Steen" Falk (guitar), Tom "Sanction" Beyer (stand-up bass), Matt "Pouch" Cohen and Taylor "Boy Wonder" Cutcomb (trumpets), David "Babyface" Kraczek and Bob "B-flat" Thies (trombones). Saxophonists are "Amazing" Larry Sweeny (baritone), Bob "Buck" Rogers (tenor) and Mark "Marco" Donelly (alto). Their manager is Victoria Faw (Beau's wife). The Nails' live CD, recorded at Max's Hi-Ball Lounge, is available from V/Search, 415-362-1465. Their web site is *http//www.zweb.com/lpn.*

♦ *VALE: Did your friends encourage you?*
♦ LEE PRESS-ON: There's an audience for everything. George Carlin once said, "If you nail together two things that have never been nailed together before, some schmuck will buy it from you." And that's what we did. We took authentic swing music and applied it to a heavy metal aesthetic. There were at least five people in the room who thought it was cool.
♦ *V: That's funny. The marriage of Van Halen and Swing!*
♦ LPO: A *Swing Time* review of one of our shows said, "They finished with 'Hot For Teacher.' Believe me, it swings harder than it ever rocked." Which I thought was wonderful to read.
♦ *V: Tell us your background—*
♦ LPO: I'm a Marin County native. There are photos in our family album of me taking piano lessons when I was four, but I can't remember having any! Everything I play I learned by ear and by tinkering—I'm an *accomplished tinkerer.* I started on keyboards

when I was 18 and my drummer suggested I take up vibes, which is nothing but a big keyboard that you hit with sticks. So, I got a set and they're great fun.
♦ *V: What brand are they?*
♦ LPO: [low conspiratorial voice] You want to know a secret? They're not really vibes! I use a midi controller called the Mallet Kat. It's a board with three octaves' worth of foam pads on them and you hit the pads and this sends a midi message to a keyboard which in turn sends a vibe sound to an amp. The bonus is: I can also trigger tympani sounds, cartoon sound effects or *any* instrument sound with this thing. The major advantage is that it's much easier to lug around than a full set of vibes, which we *have* done on occasion. It's also very difficult to play vibes without accidentally hitting the mic with your sticks. So, I went the electronic route.
♦ *V: Well, it sounds like vibes—*

♦ LPO: Good; it's supposed to. We put fake "resonators" out in front [a triangular row of hollow pipes] to further the illusion that they actually are vibes.

♦ **V: *Here, you're more concerned with underlying principles—***

♦ LPO: Right; the *look* is everything! Actually, the vibes are the only instrument in the band that isn't completely authentic. We've also got the stand-up bass and the hollow-body guitar.

♦ **V: *That's brilliant. This is one instance where a technological advance is a good thing . . . You know, with this swing movement, the wearing of old suits seems particularly abhorrent to my male punk-rock friends—***

♦ LPO: But that's the greatest thing! When I first put the Nails together, they hated it. But that was last year. This year, it's "I've got three suits now!" "Oh, yeah? Well, I've got five!" It's so nice to see them really take pride in their appearance. Who wants to go see a band that's dressed just like you are? I like to go see a band that's dressed better than me and, me being Lee Press-On— that's hard. [laughs]

♦ **V: *It's been a long time since young people have "dressed up" on their own initiative. This has to be a reaction against years of grunge fashion—***

♦ LPO: One of my favorite cartoons is this drawing of a grunge kid looking plaintively into a camera. The caption reads, "The grunge movement is over? *Oh, no*—now I look like shit!"

It's fun to dress up, but it's not mandatory . . . You mentioned punk. The thing about the Nails is that we play traditional favorites, but our stage presence and our message isn't that much different from any really aggressive punk band. We're *in your face*, pummeling you over the head with this music. Swing was the punk rock of its day. There's a paper called *The American* (January 21, 1930) which railed against the dangers of jazz:

"Jazz ruining girls," declares reformer. "Moral disaster is coming to hundreds of American girls through the pathological, nerve-irritating, sex-exciting music of jazz orchestras," according to the Illinois Vigilance Association. "Girls in small towns, as well as big cities, in poor homes and rich homes, are victims of the weird, insidious, neurotic music that accompanies modern dancing. The degrading music is common, not only to disorderly places, but often to high school affairs, expensive hotels, and so-called society circles," declares Reverend Richard Yaro, superintendent of the Vigilance Association. Sound familiar? [laughs]

♦ **V: *I have a book about the dangers of punk rock published by some christian press—***

♦ LPO: Right. The report claims that "the Vigilance Association has no desire to abolish dancing, but seeks to awaken the public conscience to the present danger and future consequences of jazz music."

Jazz started out being frowned upon. It was played in whorehouses, not Carnegie Hall, and its major development was in the black community. There was a whole seedy element associated with jazz, much like they would have us believe punk is all about. I try to represent that onstage by putting on the heavy eye make-up and presenting a performance reminiscent of some guy hopped up on goofballs. The opium influence is at work here (Cab Calloway refers to this), because that's where jazz came from. Also, a lot of the music that *didn't* get recorded was much wilder, and that's the feel I'm trying to bring back.

♦ **V: *You've been doing research on all this—***

♦ LPO: I used to work the Renaissance Faire and I carry over a lot of their philosophy into this band venture. We try to create an accurate historical picture.

♦ **V: *So, you grew up in Marin—***

♦ LPO: My father was the chairman of the Department of Theater Arts at the College of Marin. When you live in a house with a college professor, you have no choice but to learn about what he's teaching. I've been on the stage since I was eight years old. My first performance was a walk-on part in *Inherit the Wind*—I played "Little Timmy." My mom was a registered nurse, so I could go out onstage and tear myself to pieces, and she'd put me back together! [laughs]

♦ **V: *At one Bimbo's show, you jumped into the audience and did an amazing combination of '30s jitterbugging and '80s break-dancing—***

♦ LPO: I'm also a child of the '80s—you've probably noticed

We're *in your face*, pummeling you over the head with this music. Swing was the punk rock of its day.

---

that. In my early teens I had four years of classes at Bea Blum's Dance Studio in Fairfax. The studio's still there.

♦ **V: *What was it like growing up?***

♦ LPO: I was a nerd in high school—big surprise there! I used to say that I was put on this earth so that machines would have something to talk to. [laughs] I was stamped as a genius at a very early age because of my inability to learn anything at school. And because of my father, I started hanging out in the theater, which was a source of joy for me. One reason I changed to music was because: in a band, I wasn't tied down by lines and stage directions. I could go anywhere; I could do anything. I could change the lyrics of a song if I wanted to—and no one would notice. Of course, I started the Nails to symbolically . . . RUB MY SWEAT-SOCKS IN THE GREASY PITTED FACES OF THOSE WHO DOUBTED ME! It's worked so far.

♦ **V: *[laughs] Revenge can be a powerful motive: to get back at all those creeps from your past . . . Were you ever into punk rock?***

♦ LPO: DEVO was one of my all-time favorite bands, although they're not punk in the hardcore sense of the word. But I'm actually more interested in industrial music, which is pretty much electronic punk. I remember once at a show I was hit in the nose with somebody's head. The funny thing about that was: the head came at me *sideways*. Somebody had picked up someone else by

Jumping Nails at Bimbo's 6-19-97. On bill with New Morty Show. Photo: V. Vale

the ankles and was swinging him around and he hit me. That's a fond memory! When I'm not onstage with the swing band, I'm at home generating hardcore electronic noise. That's my other great musical love. [laughs]

♦ V: Were your musical and theatrical stage backgrounds

Shopping Tips From Lee Press-On

Now you can find new retro-looking clothes. Most of the band got their suits from Siegel's (2366 Mission Street, S.F.). Another great place is H. John's in Oakland. I got a zoot suit from El Pachuco in Fullerton, run by an old Mexican-American family that has been making zoot suits since they were popular the first time in the '40s. I recently had a suit made from some snazzy material with extra wide stripes.

I found some vintage ties from the Third Hand Store on Divisadero and from Martini Mercantile next to Club Deluxe on Haight Street. But my favorite ties come from Mervyn's—you would never think that. I just picked up a Portofino hat from Martini Mercantile. The Berkeley Hat Company is a good source for hats of all shapes and sizes. I like fedoras; I've been wearing them since the blues band. Leslie recently got me a hat with a wider brim to go with the zoot suit. A friend gave me a set of vintage cuff links that say "LP" on them, so I wear those. (Obviously, they had been made for someone else with my initials.)

Queen's Shoes next to Siegel's sells two-tone shoes by Stacy Adams. I found a pair of two-tones there for just $35, made by Bernini. If you do a lot of dancing, go to Capezio and get some dancing shoes. I have a pair of wingtips and I *have* danced in them, but my favorite thing is to just get out my dancing shoes and wear spats over them. Any formal wear shop will have spats, like La Rosa's on Haight Street. The thing with wingtips is: they have to fit *very well* if you're going to do any dancing and not kill yourself. But people who don't have the budget for such things can always go to Payless. They sell shoes that look like wingtips but are made of vinyl and have rubber soles—they feel like sneakers. Right now you can't get them in two-tone at Payless, but it's only a matter of time because the swing movement is catching on like wildfire! You can also get spectators from traditional shoemakers like Churchs and Allen-Edmonds, especially around Christmastime, but they're $230–$300.

intertwined?

♦ LPO: No, it was straight theater until I was 17. Then there was an abrupt change of track: when you're in high school you want to be in a *band*. I haven't been onstage in the theater since.

My first band, which existed for about seven years in the '80s, was the John Belushi Memorial Blues Band. We played R&B and had a modicum of fame in the Bay Area. We started as just a cheap Blues Brothers impersonation, with a three- to four-piece horn section, but by the end of our career we were so much more. [laughs] Then I messed around by myself for awhile doing electronic improvisations. But I really missed horns, and for some reason wanted to be in a band that old people would enjoy.

♦ V: How did you find the musicians?

♦ LPO: My old drummer from the blues band, Beau Faw, knows more about swing than anybody I can think of; he knows who Cozy Cole played with in 1938 from June to August. [laughs] In my opinion, he's second only to Mickey Hart as far as drum knowledge is concerned. I found everyone else through my blues band, or through friends.

♦ V: What did you tell them?

♦ LPO: I just said, "We're startin' a swing band. Do you read music?" [laughs] They knew the music, but they didn't know the image that went with it. The guitar player didn't know anything about swing, so he was a little apprehensive. I knew he had what it takes because I'd heard him play, so I said, "Look, trust me, you can do this."

♦ V: How did you get into swing—

♦ LPO: My father taught me the graces of classical music, Gilbert and Sullivan, etc. He's a big classical buff, so I learned theory. As a college student in Berkeley during the '60s, my mother collected everything from Bluegrass to rock'n'roll. She was the one who turned me on to Frank Zappa—he's fabulous and remains one of my favorites to this day. She had, amongst her eclectic collection, an album called *Sorta' Dixie* by Billy May. He was one of the great arrangers.

♦ V: So you've been into swing all your life?

♦ LPO: [protests] No, no—I was *six years old* before I discovered swing music! . . . What Billy May did was take a traditional 17-piece swing orchestra and add instruments like oboes, bassoons and tympani. He came up with amazing arrangements. I suggest people check him out.

I was brought up on MGM musicals because my father also

Top: Lee & Leslie lie in their goth port-a-bed. Below: with their 1950 Mercury, 6-10-97.

Photos: V.Vale

Lee Press-On in his studio, 6-10-97. Photo: V.Vale

taught film. On Monday nights he'd show films, and once a semester he'd bring in *Singin' in the Rain*—which is the best movie musical ever made; it has incredible dancing. I learned all about Broadway, show-biz and MGM musicals.

♦ **V: Did you want to be Gene Kelly?**

♦ LPO: Who doesn't?! I'd love to be able to make a living at this kind of thing, but it's very hard to do. I appreciate the artistry behind Kelly and Astaire and the rest of them. Now thanks to the Internet, you can find stuff you could never find before. I'm beginning to track down and acquire all the movies Cab Calloway was in, whereas previously all I had were the CDs. His performance in *The Blues Brothers* is, of course, legendary. There's a great short called *Hi-De-Ho*.

   Stormy Weather is a fabulous movie musical starring Calloway, Lena Horne, Bill "Bojangles" Robinson and the Nicholas Brothers, a tap-dance duo. The Nicholas Brothers are my absolute favorite dancers of all time. I have a collection of laserdiscs, *Swing, Swing, Swing!*, which is eight hours of short subjects that Vitaphone produced. In some of these, the Nicholas Brothers were just kids—nine or eleven (in *Stormy Weather* they were teenagers). There are later films in which they're grown-up, so obviously they were dancing all their lives.

♦ **V: Being in the Renaissance Faire involved being theatrical. You were already creating an alternate persona—**

♦ LPO: What I am on onstage with Lee Press-On and the Nails is nothing like what I am in "real life." Lee Press-On is this drug-crazed monster that would just as soon kick you in the nuts than shake your hand! [laughs] Actually, I'm very shy when I'm off the stage. When I put the band together I'd had the typical experience of being dumped and was very bitter. So I said, "I'm going to have a stage character that doesn't take shit from *anybody!*" I put together an amalgam of Cab Calloway and the Joker from *Batman*. [laughs] Over the years he's mellowed a bit.

♦ **V: One reason there aren't more swing bands is because**

good horn players are hard to find—

♦ LPO: It's actually easy to get around that—*sort of.* I make up charts for everybody in the band. As long as they can follow them, they're all right. We started the band this way: "You play a horn? Great—you're in. Sit down, read this!" A lot of the boys in the horn section were *okay* when they joined, but you'd be surprised how great they can get playing every weekend for a year! [laughs]

♦ **V: If you do horn charts, you must have learned to read and write music?**

♦ LPO: Here's how the horn charts are done: I turn on my midi keyboard, arrange the song in the form of a midi sequence, save the sequence to a floppy disk, take the disk to the MacIntosh computer and call up my sheet music software program (*Finale 3.5*). *Finale* then takes my midi sequence and extrapolates a horn chart for it, which I print out and give to the band. The beauty of this

Techno and grunge were pretty much *all* you had to choose from when it came to new music.

is: the horn charts for Lee Press-On and the Nails are written by someone who not only cannot play a horn, but also cannot read music! And it's only because of my computer knowledge that I've been able to chart everything for the band. That's our other departure from authenticity.

♦ **V: Well, people starting swing bands will be doing this, too. This is another example of making the best use of technological advances. At the same time, I think part of this revival is because people are sick of synthesizer sounds, hyperfast rhythms and digital everything—**

The Fabulous Juan, dance instructor at Cafe Du Nord at Lee Press-On show, 12-8-96.

♦ LPO: Here's my reasoning for why swing is suddenly hip again. Up until the swing movement, techno and grunge were pretty much *all* you had to choose from when it came to new music (excluding World Beat, of course). You get bored with that and you're tearing through the history of music, looking for *any-thing*. You find swing music and realize there's more than three chords. Symbolically, we're taking a step forward by taking a giant step backward. Isn't that cool?

♦ V: *The main problem with swing is: the bands are larger, so it's harder to keep personnel—*

♦ LPO: Yeah, well there is that. There's actually *twelve* of us. Sometimes we pull in $600 at a club, which means each of us will come away with $50—if we're lucky. Potential bookers ask us, "Why does your band have to be so big?" The reason is: with the exception of the piano player and the guitar player, everybody in the band can only play one note at a time!

♦ V: *That's right . . . So how did you pick up your computer knowledge?*

We destroyed the Fabulous Juan and turned him into a cross-dressing lindy-hopper!

♦ LPO: Again, my dad. He was directing a version of *South Pacific* when he stepped back too far and fell into the orchestra pit. He smashed up his back big time and had to drop out of the show. He was out of work for six months, laid up and flat on his back in bed. He wanted to do something besides watch television, so he bought himself a Commodore 64—remember those?—with a whopping 64K of onboard memory. He taught himself *Basic* and then taught me. Now he's a computer programmer.

I've always loved machinery; *Star Wars* was one of my favorite

films. I'd listen to R2D2 and think, "I want to make music like that." And I do when I'm not onstage with the Nails. I've always enjoyed electronic sounds, including Walter (as he was then) and Wendy Carlos (as she is now). Her synthesized versions of the classics were a great source of listening pleasure for me as a pre-adolescent.

♦ V: *Did you ever make a living working with computers?*

♦ LPO: I'm now a freelance computer graphics engineer, with a couple of videos to my credit. Most of my jobs have been computer-related; I worked on video games and have worked at Crystal Dynamics. Again, it's all self-taught—no formal education here. The problem with a computer course is: by the time the semester has ended, everything you've learned is obsolete!

♦ V: *I didn't think the band supported you—*

♦ LPO: Oh no—$50 a night doesn't go very far. A lot of the people in the band are actually teachers. Our bass player teaches in Oakland and our drummer gives lessons regularly. The guitar player works in stocks, and the saxophone player is a financier at Autodesk Software. We also have students in the band, too. They don't have real jobs—they go to college.

♦ V: *Tell us more about how you developed the idea to do a swing band—*

♦ LPO: I wanted to do a couple of swing tunes in our blues band, but we didn't have the means—I didn't have *Finale* at that time! [laughs] I could figure out arrangements by ear, but I had no way of telling the horns, other than "You play this, and you play that." [hums horn lines] That's okay for a Motown chart, but for a swing arrangement it's difficult. We tried a couple of swing tunes with the blues band, but the audience went, "Ah, shut-up—play 'Midnight Hour' again!" You can only live with that for so long. I knew nothing about the rising scene; I just wanted to do it.

♦ V: *How many people were in the band when you started?*

♦ LPO: We started with three horns, then it was four horns, and things just ballooned. We have now what I think is the ideal arrangement: two trumpets, two trombones, three saxophones, piano, bass, guitar, drums, and vibes. And I think we're the only big band around that has vibes.

Leslie and I used to go to "swing night" at the Claremont Hotel.

♦ V: *What was the crowd like?*

♦ LPO: There were very few kids; it was mostly an older crowd, forty and up. The men were in suits and the women had big hair—big *blue* hair in some cases. They were very appreciative. They didn't dance much, but they smiled and applauded. To flash forward a few years, it was great when we played there because we pretty much had the same crowd. That was my dream: I wanted to play for old people. It's nice to play for a crowd that's so Old School they actually applaud after solos! A couple of people in the band didn't really *get it;* they asked, "Why are we playing for *these* people?" I replied, "Well, they love us—they just don't show it the same way a crazed 24-year-old would!"

We played in empty clubs for over a year: New George's in San Rafael, Club Boomerang on Haight Street, and we had a couple gigs at the Mystic Theater in Petaluma. Our second year, we broke into "real" swing clubs like the Hi-Ball Lounge. That's a great place—small, but there's a nice vibe there. We also got a gig at the Cafe Du Nord playing once a week. Finally we got to play Bimbo's, and were pretty nervous—that was our first night at that legendary club.

♦ V: *Aren't most of your shows in the Bay Area? I can't imagine paying hotels for 12 people—*

♦ LPO: Yes, but we hope to go to L.A. as soon as we figure out a way to pay for it. [laughs] If we have three shows in a row at different venues, that might do it.

♦ V: *Did your guys get discouraged?*

♦ LPO: Yeah, they did. We originally had a different bass player—he left early on because he "didn't think swing was going to be very popular." [laughs] We lost a trombone player who decided to join a rock band. But we persevered. If we weren't famous as a swing act, we were famous as a novelty act—we wanted to be the Motorhead of Swing! At Club Boomerang we started developing a following. We played to kids who didn't know how to dance then, but they do now!

♦ **V:** *Can you trace how the dancing evolved?*
♦ **LPO:** One or two couples went and learned everything and did all the hard work; then they started teaching classes. [laughs] There's Work That Skirt, Johnny Swing, and our roommate, Ritchie Dawkins. Ritchie and Johnny Swing have come to our shows and given dance lessons. We first met Johnny at the Coconut Grove. He came in wearing a bright red zoot suit and I said to myself, "Something tells me I should meet this guy." Another instructor we like is the Fabulous Juan who teaches at Cafe Du Nord every Sunday. My wife met him in belly dancing class and he ended up getting us a gig at the Du Nord, where he taught dance lessons.

♦ **V:** *He's a great Drag Queen—*
♦ **LPO:** I'm afraid we're responsible for that—at least, I'd like to think we are. Up until our Halloween show he had worn men's clothing all the time. Then we did the Halloween show where everyone dressed up goofy and he came in a dress. That was *it* for him—something clicked. He's been in a dress ever since! [laughs]

♦ **V:** *He found herself.*
♦ **LPO:** He's gay and always has been, but he wasn't a flaming cross-dresser until he was exposed to the Nails! I don't know whether that's true or not, but that's my story and I'm sticking to it. [laughs] "We destroyed the Fabulous Juan and turned him into a cross-dressing lindy-hopper!"

Lee Press-On live. Photo: Mark Jordan

♦ **V:** *What are other bands you like?*
♦ **LPO:** Lavay Smith, Big Bad Voodoo Daddy. The Cherry Poppin' Daddies—they're a ska band that does swing tunes, but the swing tunes they do are really cool. There are now bands all over the place—much too numerous to mention. Just go to the website of the Northern California Lindy Society and you'll find "everything a gate needs to know in one spot!"

♦ **V:** *What's a "gate"?*
♦ **LPO:** A gate is a guy who swings like a gate! [laughs] It's Cab Calloway slang.

♦ **V:** *Where do you rehearse in Marin?*
♦ **LPO:** There's this place that rents out storage containers for young bands to rehearse in, and the price is right. We're the only swing band there, of course. Sometimes we play at people's houses; the last rehearsal was in our living room. I give the members charts and tapes to take home. When we get together we listen to the tape, plow through the song the first time, and then fine-tune it.

♦ **V:** *Let's talk about your influences, like—*
♦ **LPO:** —the holy trinity of Louis's! That would be Prima,

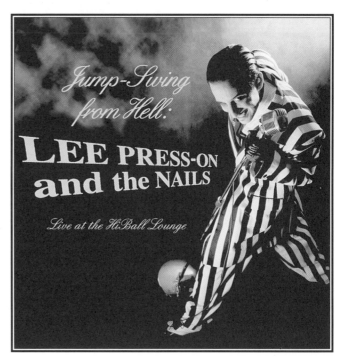

Cover of Lee Press-On and the Nails' 1997 live album.

Armstrong, and Jordan. Like I said, Lee Press-On was based on Cab Calloway, the Joker, and Dave Vanian (singer for the Damned). Also, in the film *1941* Joe Flaherty plays a character named Sal Stewart, who was sort of a cheesy bandleader-type. Oh, and there's a lot of Danny Elfman in Lee Press-On. In any Oingo Boingo photo he has this grin that made you believe he had more than 32 teeth! Other influences include Gwar, Nick Charles from the *Thin Man* films, and Groucho Marx.

♦ **V:** *With this swing movement, I hope that wit and slang are back, too—*
♦ **LPO:** If you go to our web site, I've got a complete slang page from Cab Calloway and Frank Sinatra, and a page full of slang from Dashiell Hammett and Mickey Spillane—gangster slang.

♦ **V:** *I've seen a few gay and lesbian couples swing dancing, although the scene appears mostly hetero, at this point—*
♦ **LPO:** In San Francisco there's a tolerance for pretty much everything—that's the great thing about the city. A stand-up comic named Bruce Cherry said: "In San Francisco you can play street poker: no matter how weird you are, there's always somebody weirder than you." A hand of street poker would go like this: "Okay, I see your rainbow-colored wig and raise you a Viking hat, pink spandex shorts and a fluorescent light bulb up my ass." That's the wonderful thing about San Francisco: there's a place for everyone.

♦ **V:** *Also, things have a chance to incubate here and really get going—*
♦ **LPO:** Sometimes late at night, after a show, I like to take off down the street, running and screaming and yelling. I look back at my wife and say to her, "It's all right, darling—we're in *San Francisco!"* **V**

Lee Press-On and Leslie Presley. Photo: John Carey

🐛 🐛 🐛 🐛 🐛 🐛 🐛 🐛 🐛 🐛 🐛 🐛 🐛 🐛 🐛 🐛

INTERVIEW WITH LESLIE PRESLEY

♦ **VALE: Your husband and I were talking about how swing is the first major lifestyle change since punk—**

♦ LESLIE PRESLEY: Whenever we play or go to a show, I love seeing the really heavily tattooed girls who look absolutely perfect. They have the most beautiful vintage dresses and perfectly coiled hair, and their arms (and sometimes legs and backs) are covered with tattoos. I think this swing movement marks a natural progression; people were getting sick of unpleasant clubs. This is one of the first times in my life that I haven't been accused of over-dressing when I go out.

A lot of what I know about hair and clothes I learned from watching old films—Myrna Loy is my absolute favorite. I also learn from friends; my friend Claire had the most perfect hair—it didn't look like a head of hair, it looked like a beautiful pastry or a sculpture. She said, "It's just pin curls. You get about 100 bobby pins and you can train your hair to do anything you want." She taught me how to do it, and my whole life improved! This is so completely different from ten years ago when I was trying to rat my hair. [laughs]

All I can say about vintage clothing is that it's harder to find and more expensive now. Although I prefer shopping at vintage stores, I'm for using whatever you can to your advantage. One night this girl and I were dressing up as matching candy girls and we didn't have everything we needed. I went to Nordstroms and picked out matching things, which I couldn't have done at a vintage store. And you can always return things, too, if you're not 100% satisfied. [laughs]

♦ **V: Why did you need matching outfits?**

♦ LP: At the Transmission Theater in San Francisco we were part of a show called "Jay Alexander's New Swing Circus" which played for three nights last year. At each show there were two matching candy girls—myself and a different friend each night. There were jugglers, a knife-throwing act involving a blindfolded volunteer from the audience, a trapeze girl hanging by a rope from the ceiling who did acrobatics, and Leland and I did some magic tricks. The show featured the Chaplinesque Olaf the Clown Prince, Jay Alexander's magic act, and our band. Leland did a Houdini act escaping from a box covered with chains, and I came out of a basket in which swords had been plunged. I also did a tango dance routine with Olaf in a red dress. Besides playing a full set, the band also accompanied the acts as a "pit orchestra."

I love vintage clothing, but lately I'm more interested in finding new clothing that *looks* vintage. I was repairing all my vintage clothes and was forced to learn how to do all these complicated sewing maneuvers. Then I started learning how to make dresses from the bottom up. I worked as a costumer for awhile.

♦ **V: Where do you get your shoes?**

♦ LP: Well, you definitely have to keep your eyes open. The black-and-white spectator shoes have really come back in a huge way. The Mission district has some fabulous stores, and Market Street has some shoe stores that are full of bargains. Places like Shadows that rent bridal gowns or tuxedos can also do special orders, like if you need matching outfits for the stage—that's a whole other story.

♦ LEE [in background]: I have a hole in my sock! How's *that* for vintage clothing!

♦ **V: Are there any instructional books or videos on how to do retro hairstyles, or do you just have to be shown by a person?**

♦ LP: With regard to hair, you just keep experimenting until you get something that works. By that point, I'll get bored with it and do something else.

♦ **V: Are there names for these hairstyles?**

♦ LP: A Marcel Wave is also called a Finger Wave, and that's very '20s—it's when the wave is very close to the head. Pin-curls are bigger: it's when you actually see that there's a spiral. You take your hair and wind it into a curl and bobby pin it into a shape.

♦ **V: Do you like Carmen Miranda?**

♦ LP: Oh, yeah, she's outrageous. We love old musicals and movies; it would be difficult to list them all. I love Cyd Charisse and Ann Miller—mostly brunettes—although I love Jean Harlow, too. She was very funny.

♦ **V: I love the wit in those old movies.**

♦ LP: There's not a really huge tradition of wit amongst many "scenes," I think. I really appreciate the Dorothy Parker revival that's been happening. However, she's definitely not someone to read if you're planning your wedding. She wrote about the futility of relationships and marriage; about being a sad woman left alone by men. It's not uplifting, but it's brilliant writing. And her poems that she thought were rubbish are witty and funny. You can rent *Mrs Parker and the Vicious Circle,* which is set mainly in the '20s.

I saw more panties than I've ever seen in my life—and with some of the women, I saw *more* than I ever needed to see!

♦ **V: What do you do when you're not onstage?**

♦ LP: We have a lot of people over. [laughs] Everything we do involves the band in some way. When we're not rehearsing with them, we're talking to them, making plans for them. Leland's always making new charts. We're always finding inspiration in some old musical for a song. Lee and a couple of other guys in the band—Larry and Tom—write songs. Leland writes the music and they write the words. Like Burt Bacharach and Hal David. [laughs]

♦ **V:** *Before this movement, only bourgeois people partner-danced. Now, it involves being super-gymnastic and throwing girls up in the air—*
♦ **LP:** [laughs] At the "Monsters of Swing" weekend in Ventura, I saw more panties than I've ever seen in my life—and with some of the women, I saw *more* than I ever needed to see! In fact, the emcee was yelling, "Show us your panties!" The boys in the band talk about this; I guess they regard it as an *incentive* to play better. Boys will be boys. Stockings, garter belts and tap pants (little fluttery silk shorts that a lot of the girls wear) are definitely back.

For awhile I was also calling this the "swing renaissance." It's

---

I love vintage clothing, but lately I'm more interested in finding new clothing that *looks* vintage.

---

been nice for certain people who were looking for their niche: a place to hang out and be accepted. Dressing in vintage clothing is a nice form of escape. I remember going to "rent parties" in warehouse spaces where a band would play and it wasn't exactly legal. [laughs] They'd have a little bar and charge a few dollars at the door and you'd get this fabulous entertainment for very little money. I saw St. Vitus Dance at least five years ago; Atomic Cocktail; Connie Champagne singing with her own band, Tiny Bubbles. It felt very underground, and now it's becoming the Disco of our generation.

In 1990 I saw Cab Calloway. He played the Opera House in San Francisco. Cab was amazing; he wore his signature white satin tuxedo and tails with white shoes. He sang a very jazzy, fast, jumped-up medley version of "Minnie the Moocher" and the audience lost their minds! Everyone was clapping and singing along. He sang "Minnie the Moocher's Wedding" as well. I was a little disappointed that he didn't sing my favorite song of his, "Lady With A Fan," which is the first Cab song I ever heard, back when I was 9 or 10. His voice was just as powerful as it was on the old recordings, and he danced quite a bit, which is impressive considering he must have been in his 80s by then. It was incredible to see him; I felt like I was witnessing a part of history!

My mother used to listen to old radio shows from the '30s and '40s which were broadcast after 10 PM. I loved 'em; I heard Cab Calloway, Duke Ellington, a lot of old broadcasts from the Cotton Club, as well as comedy shows: W.C. Fields, Edgar Bergen and Charlie McCarthy. I heard *The Maltese Falcon* as a radio play with the same cast that appeared in the movie, and for a while I would listen to *The Inner Sanctum* every night on my own radio. One of my favorite childhood memories is laying in the back of the family car late at night while my mother drove us home from my grandmother's house, listening to these old songs. I'd forgotten a lot of this, but seeing the Francis Ford Coppola film *The Cotton Club* brought it all back.
♦ **V:** *I haven't seen one woman musician in a swing band yet—*
♦ **LP:** Check out Steve Lucky and the Rhumba Bums; there's a woman guitar player and singer. You'd like them and she's good. Her stage name is Carmen Getit. They've been around for years . . .
♦ **V:** *Yeah. It seems that what Lee is doing now is a natural evolution out of R&B—*
♦ **LP:** I'm sitting in his studio right now, which is so jam-packed with electronic musical equipment I can't even describe it. He plays a lot of his own music, completely free of the band. I think it's good to have a lot of musical interests. There are so many people insisting that they have always been into swing and never anything else. I'm like, "*Whatever.*" [laughs] I listen to a lot of Ella Fitzgerald, but then sometimes I want to listen to Prince or Bauhaus or just anything else, like the Damned. That was my

favorite band for many years.
♦ **V:** *I was telling Lee I saw their first show here at the Mabuhay in '77—*
♦ **LP:** That's great! I was a little too young for that, but I would have gone if I could. I would have been about ten years old . . .
♦ **V:** *Are you record collectors?*
♦ **LP:** We've got a lot of old records and a huge amount of CDs. Leland also works as a swing deejay; he's doing a wedding at the end of the month. That's nice for people who want swing music but can't afford a 12-piece band—and not many people can! We love the music. That's the reason Leland started the band—that, and to impress me! [laughs]
♦ **LEE** [in the background]: —and it worked! **V**

Lee & Leslie's Albums To Take To a Desert Island

Billy May: *Sorta' Dixie*. It's my very favorite swing record of all time.
Any Cab Calloway album, especially *Are You Hep to the Jive?*
Capitol *Ultra Lounge* Series
Stan Kenton: He's good.
Raymond Scott: The guy who did "Power House."
Benny Goodman Live At Carnegie Hall.
Louis Jordan has so many albums out, it's hard to pick. He was the unsung father of rock'n'roll.
Larry Clinton: He wrote some good tunes.
Early Frank Sinatra ('40s and '50s). He was great in the MGM musicals: *On The Town, High Society.*
The Damned, Fishbone, James Brown, Frank Zappa—I seem to have wandered a bit here!
Ella Fitzgerald: *The Best of the Verve Songbooks*
The Essential Dinah Washington
Billie Holiday: *Giants of Jazz Compilation*
The Cotton Club Living Era Compilation
The Ink Spots: *The Original Decca Recordings*
Peggy Lee: *The Early Years*
Fats Waller Plays Fats Waller
8½ Souvenirs: *Happy Feet*
Harry Belafonte: *Live at Carnegie Hall*

Film & Book Choices

Any and all Buster Keaton films, any MGM musical, all the *Thin Man* films & Vitaphone shorts, *Stormy Weather, The Cotton Club, 1941, Singing' in the Rain.*
The Thin Man series, all six. Especially *The Thin Man, After the Thin Man, Shadow of The Thin Man,* and *Song of The Thin Man*
My Man Godfrey (another great William Powell film)
Swing, Swing, Swing! (A cavalcade of Vitaphone shorts)
Mrs Parker and The Vicious Circle
The Paramount period of The Marx Brothers films, especially *Monkey Business*
Five Guys Named Moe (54 minutes of Louis Jordan)
Miller's Crossing (Coen Brothers. Set during Prohibition, the best movie ever made about the Irish Mafia)
Richard the Third (with Ian MacKellan; set in the 1930s)
Pennies from Heaven (with Steve Martin, starring Christopher Walken as *Tom the Pimp!* What a hoofer!)
Zoot Suit (for the wardrobe and dancing alone.)
AND . . . The Addams Family, of course.

Of Minnie The Moocher and Me (Cab Calloway's autobiography)
Groucho and Me by Groucho Marx
Any Charles Addams compilation
Louise Brooks: a biography by Barry Paris
Lulu in Hollywood (selected writings of Louise Brooks)
The Poetry and Short Stories of Dorothy Parker
The Art of the Great Hollywood Photographers by John Kobal
Cocktail Time by P.G. Wodehouse. Very witty.
The Swing Era: The Development of Jazz by Gunther Shuller
The Complete Films of William Powell by Lawrence J. Quirk

Big Bad Voodoo Daddy

A prime mover of the "swing renaissance" is BIG BAD VOODOO DADDY from Ventura, California. Their music has been described as "psycho swing" or "big band gone wild," and their live performances are electrifying. Members include Scotty Morris (guitar, vocals), Dirk Shumaker (string bass, vocals), Andy Rowly (baritone/tenor sax, vocals), Kurt Sodergren (drums), Glen "the Kid" Marheuka (trumpet, vocals), Jeff Harris (trombone), and Karl Hunter (tenor/alto sax, clarinet, small dog voice). Their self-released CDs on their label, Big Bad Records, include *Big Bad Voodoo Daddy*, available from POB 2146, Ventura CA 93002. Check out their website at *www.bbvd.com*.

♦ **VALE:** *There's an electricity about this "swing" movement that reminds me of punk—*

♦ SCOTTY MORRIS: I feel the same way. And the kind of swing music we do is like punk rock: there's nothing mainstream about it. Cab Calloway was *not* a mainstream guy! And neither was Louis Armstrong—the press made him out to be, but Louis was *wild;* he did most of his *real* playing after-hours with a doobie in his mouth!

♦ **V:** *When did you first start playing music?*

♦ SM: When I was a little kid, there were musical instruments around the house and I started playing whatever I could. As a small boy I played trumpet; my first interest in music involved Louis Armstrong and Cab Calloway: real wild, swingin' New Orleans music with horns.

Around 1979 I discovered punk rock. I was drawn to it for the *freedom;* I felt it was absolute freedom and there were no rules. It was also Do-It-Yourself. I put the horn down because it was way cooler to be playing a distorted bass in a punk band! Hearing the Buzzcocks, the Pistols, the Clash and Elvis Costello made me really want to be involved. Here I was: this 14-year-old kid who lived on the beach and wore shorts to school, and they were something totally different with their own subculture.

At that time, Led Zeppelin, Foghat and Journey was the kind of music being played on the radio—this was pre-MTV, and kids mostly listened to the radio. Then I heard the Buzzcocks, and everything changed!

♦ **V:** *Where did you grow up?*

♦ SM: In Oxnard, between Santa Barbara and Los Angeles. Oxnard had a really great punk rock scene, with good bands like Stalag 13. It's a beach community but it wasn't Orange County. Around '81-'82 I played in a band called False Confession. We toured with bands like Ill Repute and Aggression; I wrote songs for Dr. No and helped them with their albums. I played any instrument I could to be part of the music scene—drums, bass, guitar, vocals—I pretty much did *whatever it takes* to play music during the first ten years.

Then in '89 I focused on the guitar as my main, full-time instrument. That's when I decided to make the music I really like—I guess you'd call it swing.

♦ **V:** *Also, punk changed—*

♦ SM: In the beginning the scene wasn't violent; you could go to shows and have a great time with your friends, and girls were involved. Then all of a sudden the scene changed and became violent; it turned into this circle of waving fists. I couldn't go to shows anymore, so I decided to try to create my own thing.

♦ **V:** *So you transitioned from punk to swing—*

♦ SM: I think I *always* wanted to do "swing" music, but didn't have the balls. At a certain point I became a full-time musician, touring and playing with bands and working as a studio musician. So from about '88 to '91 I was stuck in L.A., just playing *everybody else's* music. My full-time life was being a "musician." But I kept thinking, "I don't know why I don't just do my own thing. The paycheck isn't that important to me."

Finally in '91 I decided to dedicate myself to this vision of what I've wanted to do forever.

♦ **V:** *You'd seen Cab Calloway in movies—*

♦ SM: Yes. I'm a big pop art fan. I love cartoons like *Betty Boop;* Cab Calloway was behind those. For a long time I didn't even know he was an actual person; I just thought he was a character in a cartoon! Then my dad told me, "No, he's a real dude and a very heavy cat."

My dad is a real straight-ahead cool guy. He was born in Portugal, came to America, joined the service when he was 17 and saw the world for several years during World War II. He experienced life!

We've been playing this kind of music since 1992, and Royal Crown Revue has been doing it even longer, and we've never had a problem attracting crowds and making a living. You can be doing something for five years straight, and then your record comes out and suddenly you're an "overnight sensation"! Bands like us and Royal Crown were everybody's "hidden secret" until the movie *Swingers* was released—then the word was out. Some people think this music will come and go, but I think it's here to stay. If we can keep the integrity level high, *that's* what will keep us together.

I don't think swing music ever really died out, it just went underground; there were always people playing it and dancing to it. But there weren't any colorful characters coming along to reinvent it and bring it up to date—until recently, that is.

♦ **V:** *In the punk days, everyone—we were all pretty poor—did all our shopping at thrift stores, garage sales and flea markets. Now I look back and remember seeing all these splendid double-breasted suits, made of wonderful fabrics, that I passed up for $2–$5—*

♦ SM: One of the producers of the new album, Brad Benedict, is a visionary that goes beyond the word. In the '70s he had a clothing store called Heaven, selling vintage double-breasted suits and '40s

Big Bad Voodoo Daddy (with Vise Grip on bill) at Bimbo's, 11-30-96. Photo: V. Vale

ties and fedoras. He has a clothes collection that's mind-blowing; his house is like a *museum.* For him, none of this "retro" ever went away . . .

♦ **V:** *The dance and music hasn't been properly documented, because they were produced by the black community—*

♦ SM: Swing is an early form of Black American jazz. Like I said,

Louis Armstrong was an unbelievably wild American entertainer. Probably no one ever saw him do something that *he* was proud of, before 3 o'clock in the morning.

♦ **V: *People are sick of the guitar-bass-drums rock format—***

♦ SM: I think so, too. When we started out six years ago, people had no idea what we were doing, yet they liked us right away. We were wearing the suits and the hats and wing-tip shoes, yet as a band we were just a bunch of punks, really. We got up and played full-blast, really fast, wild swing music, and people just loved it.

♦ **V: *What do you think of the wild dancing being revived?***

♦ SM: A lot of times, in certain settings, the dancers are the stars, not whoever's playing. I think it's great when the audience aren't just spectators. But I didn't even know that swing dancing and our music went together until about a year-and-a-half into the band's life. We were playing, and a couple (Lee and Terri Moore from Ventura's Flyin' Lindy Hoppers) came in and just started swing-dancing as crazy as we were playing it. We started a relationship with them, and built up this giant swing movement in the Ventura area.

When we started playing the Derby in Los Angeles, that already attracted a more swing-oriented crowd. Royal Crown Revue had played there weekly and staked a claim; they were much more hip to the right dance tempos. They'd been doing it longer and had figured it all out, whereas we hadn't put the two together yet. At the Derby we learned how to work our craziness into the right tempos. That meant bigger crowds, and bigger crowds meant we could continue doing what we wanted. We really developed as a band.

♦ **V: *Compared to the old swing band recordings, the contemporary bass and drums seem a lot heavier in the mix—***

♦ SM: I think that's really my punk rock influence! On the new recording I'm going for a much more in-your-face bass and drums style. I don't try to sing like a crooner; my voice is another instrument that makes up the sound that gives you the "vibe." I try to be more of a *character* than a "nice vocalist." I torch my throat every night of the week, but I really like the way it all works together.

♦ **V: *Part of why people like swing is in reaction to "digital" sound—***

♦ SM: More than that, it may be a direct reaction to the "grunge" thing. Those people spoke very openly about sadness, depression and hard times, and people could relate to that. But then everybody got on the bandwagon. For people who have had enough of depression and angst, our music is providing the opposite: feelings that are positive and up-and-up.

♦ **V: *Why didn't the swing renaissance start in New York?***

Different style, same spirit: Scotty in the punk days. Photo: Alison Braun

♦ SM: New York has a different groove: tape-loopings and rap experiments. But, *I'm* also working on a personal project with lots of real wild loops with big-band arrangements. I have a home studio, and do soundtracks, commercials and television music—I love writing music. I get it all together at home, and if I have to take it further, I use my guys, because they're all such great players—plus being really good dudes.

♦ **V: *You compose and sketch out arrangements using loops, samples and multi-tracking—***

♦ SM: It's very quick.

♦ **V: *What are your thoughts on the difference between the big bands led by Basie and Ellington back before WWII, and today's more pared-down bands which are more economically sustainable?***

♦ SM: I think musicians were treated a lot differently. There were musicians' unions that made sure their members got paid. But the unions fell by the wayside. Big bands were replaced by smaller bands like Louis Jordan's band, with just two horns (and he played horn himself) and that cut the cost immensely. Those guys were out there jumpin', putting out the energy first and the style second.

♦ **V: *Now there's amplification, which didn't exist back then.***

♦ SM: And that's our big bonus in bringing the music into the 21st century. A band like Big Sandy isn't interested in having a big sound; they're into sounding as authentic as possible. I love Big Sandy, but I'm more interested in building onto that old sound—*adding* to it. I think Royal Crown Revue feels that way as well.

With our band, if we didn't have such crazy horn guys, well—our guys blow hard all night long; they *go for it* every single night. Most horn players won't put up with that.

♦ **V: *Does amplification help?***

♦ SM: It helps, but if you want that energy, you really gotta blow! If you blow really hard and intense, then everybody feeds off it and it becomes something entirely different—

♦ **V: *Taking the dancers to a new level of abandonment . . . Do you live the "retro" lifestyle?***

♦ SM: I was always really into thrift stores; I've worn baggy pants and wingtips and T-shirts and wifebeaters (white undershirts) and suspenders—that was always my thing, anyway. But I started to get into old vintage ties, and now I've got a large collection of vintage ties, zoot suits and pinstripe suits. I studied photos of what my heroes wore and what they looked like, and I started to emulate that.

As far as what my house looks like, it's crazy-eclectic. I collect world masks and skeletons, like Day of the Dead art. People think my house is "demonic," but the reason behind these masks is to greet good spirits. I've got devils from Mexico, skeletons from Haiti, death-masks from Bali, and most people find them horribly frightening, whereas I find them extremely comforting! I've got this 3-foot hand-carved skeleton from Haiti that's one of the scariest things I've ever seen, yet it's beautiful. It's got a big smile, and my two-and-a-half-year-old daughter looks at it and says, "Daddy, that's 'Happy'!" [laughs]

I have one mask with big horns and a tongue sticking straight out, and it has big piercing blue eyes. I bought it in New Orleans eight years ago, and it's over my fireplace mantel. It's one of the first things you see when you walk into my house.

I have a step-daughter and I went to her parents' conference with blue hair. I was part of the P.T.A., I was part of the whole everything; I just never changed my ways. I don't think what you look like or what color your hair is makes you a better parent. I'm really, really into being a parent: the education you can give to your kids and the kind of freedom of expression you can teach your kids is what's going to change the *bullshit* that's going on right now. We're just a big repercussion of all the denial that went on before us. But that's a whole different issue.

♦ **V: Did you learn how to read music?**

♦ SM: Yes, and it's very tough—it's like trying to learn how to speak Japanese! Just pick up one of those books, *Learn To Speak Japanese in One Month,* and you'll know what you're up against. Something like Japanese reminds me of music—yet once you have it, it's such a great thing to have. But it's one of the hardest things you'll ever learn.

♦ **V: Do you have a hand in charting out the arrangements?**

♦ SM: In the past, yes. But things have changed immensely since the band has taken off. With the way we're recording, who we're working with, and how we do the arrangements—it's a whole different ball game. And I really enjoy it.

In the past, I wrote the song in its entirety: all the horn lines, parts, everything. I'd show the horn players their part, either on my guitar or sing it to them, and they'd give their interpretation. As far as nuances of harmony go—*they'd* work those things out, or I'd have ideas on that.

You can do something for five years straight, and then your record comes out and suddenly you're an "overnight sensation"!

Now I sit down with our piano player, Josh, and we go over the arrangement, and I'll sing or play for him all the parts. We will then write them out and look at them and see how we can create tension and utilize the fullest degree of the horn. Previously we weren't using the horns to their fullest capacity. *Live,* it was working because there was so much energy flowing from the stage that couldn't be denied. But on record—that's another story.

So many people came up and said, "I really love the records, but compared to your live performances they're like two different things." The records seem so sterile and straight-ahead. So what we've decided to do is: really spend time "fattening up" the recordings to give you that "live" feeling. Some people might ask, "Why do you double-track the horns in the studio when you can't do that live?" Well, all that's doing is: giving you the energy that the horns *create* live, because on a recording there is no visual. What we're trying to do is create that visual in the listener's mind.

You really can evoke emotions through different sounds. A major chord can sound happy, but by changing one note (flattening the third) I can make it sad. Before, when we were doing these chords, we were really "root"-heavy on our songs. Yet when lis-

♦ **V: Who makes your zoot suits?**

♦ SM: You know, it's kind of funny because it's getting all political now. Certain people are realizing they can make *money* off these zoot suits, and they're becoming assholes. I'm looking for somebody else to make my suits who'll be cool about it. We helped bring these things back into fashion and told people where to get 'em, and now my tailor is trying to charge me double! And I don't want them for free; I think that making a zoot suit is good hard American work; it's an art form to make them. I always pay for everything; when I see bands on the road and they want to give me free stickers or shirts or CDs, I always want to pay for them because they're trying to make a living, too. What goes around comes around; it's supporting the whole system.

There's a guy on Mission Street (S.F.) who makes zoot suits and they're nice but pretty expensive. There's a guy in New York who makes 'em, but they're $1600 a suit. He makes a *real* suit, though—nothing in them is of lesser quality. My stage suits take such a beating because I sweat through them, and I wear them on the road 30–40 days at a stretch, with no time for dry-cleaning. You gotta really be careful with them. People always ask me, "How do you do it without taking your jacket off?" But I *never* take my jacket off; I always just go for it. That's the punk rock in me! . . . There's an easy way, there's a hard way and then there's *my* way!

♦ **V: What are the good shoes to buy?**

♦ SM: Stacy Adams are my favorites—I like the old ones from vintage stores, although the newer shoes aren't so bad; I use 'em on stage. They look okay. I have 3 or 4 pairs. I wear spats a lot, too—I got 'em from a place on Fillmore Street in San Francisco.

Regarding clothes, the good thing about all this is just to *be yourself.* My friend Jonathan Daniels is from New York and he still wears sharkskins and thin ties and Chelsea boots. He hangs out at all the swing shows and So What if he isn't wearing what the "elite" wears. When I say "Be yourself," well, I love to see people with mohawks, normal people, people in suits—I love a whole eclectic mix. It reminds me of the early days of punk. I don't want to be like the early Two-Tone ska guys where everybody wore dark suits with black ties and porkpie hats.

♦ **V: What kind of hats do you wear?**

♦ SM: Fedoras. Dobbs and Stetsons are what I look for.

♦ **V: How can you tell a vintage tie? Why don't they make "new" vintage ties?**

♦ SM: There's just *something* about an old tie; the knock-offs *look* like knock-offs. Salvador Dali's one of my favorite artists and he's dead now. I visited someone who had several Salvador Dali ties in perfect condition, and he told me they're worth $25,000 each!

---

tening to playbacks, we felt, "This is not the effect we're trying to get." We just hired a professional arranger, Tom Peterson, and he's phenomenally great and wonderful to work with. He's played with everybody: Glenn Miller, the Tonight Show band (with Johnny Carson) for 12 years, etc. He'll just sit down and show me better ways to do something.

♦ **V: How did you happen to meet him?**

♦ SM: Through our producers—they opened our eyes to the potential that we executed only *live.* I always wanted to just do it all myself, but these guys came in, so knowledgeable, and it all just *worked*. It's a marriage, and a real good one.

♦ **V: *The band uses a lot of syncopation and dynamics—***

♦ SM: —and that creates drama. This band had a natural chemistry from the get-go. I think if we changed one or two guys, that would ruin the whole thing. The five that started it are the five that are still there. The new producers have given us all a shot in the arm, and we're really excited.

By day, mild-mannered daddy to daughter, Sidonie . . .

♦ **V: *It's exciting when the band shouts a chorus—***

♦ SM: That's the whole Cab Calloway/Louis Jordan influence. That's the essence of what I used to love as a kid.

♦ **V: *You've also credited Gene Krupa as an influence—***

♦ SM: The thing about Gene Krupa is: he was not technically a great drummer. Bar none, there was no one better than Buddy Rich—technically, he was *the* master. I mean, Jo Jones swung harder than anybody (he was the most swingin' guy, and Buddy Rich was the most technical), but Gene is my favorite. Buddy said about him, "He wasn't the best—he was the greatest!" Gene could make you watch him.

♦ **V: *Instinct is a factor here—***

♦ SM: And I bring that to everything we do. Benny Goodman said, "Take care of the music and the music will take care of you." We started out playing music we knew nothing about, and after we had a groundwork and a sound, we decided to study the masters and develop what we have now. When we started, we just did all originals—we didn't do covers. But when we had to play *three* sets a night, that was too much—I was the only writer, and I'm a real stickler about not doing any shitty songs.

♦ **V: *Your originals sound "authentic." I hate when somebody writes an original but it just doesn't "sound right"—***

♦ SM: It "sounds like, but isn't"?! I hate those. All these bands are putting out substandard songs, whether they be swing music or . . . I'll be honest with you, swing music isn't a major force in my record listening. I listen to everything. I love all music. I love great songs and great sounds. When I hear a band with an original approach to music, I love that. But when I hear a song that sounds like somebody else, I think, "sounds like, but isn't"— that's a favorite phrase.

♦ **V: *It used to be that when a major label signed a band, the first thing they'd do was to try to break the band apart and turn the lead singer into a "star": "Oh, we can get you much better back-up musicians."***

♦ SM: And that still happens today. That's why we passed on every single deal that had ever come our way until now. It *was* pushed on us, because I'm the main songwriter and I'm the main guy and have managed the band and done all those things (and I only mean the "main guy" in that it was my vision to do this), but

100% it's the *band* that makes it sound this way. I don't know what it would have sounded like if it had been any other guys. And I credit them, as much as I credit the vision, as being the main spearhead of all this. We were dead set on signing a deal as *eight equal guys* . . . with a leader, and that's me.

We put out two records ourselves and sold 20,000 CDs without any distribution. The new record company wanted to buy both of our old records, and we said, "You're crazy! We're keeping them. That's going to be our retirement fund." I mean—I want to send my kid to college.

♦ **V: *You seemed to have anticipated (and avoided) a lot of music biz clichés. In the future I don't want to read, "So-and-so from Big Bad Voodoo Daddy died of a heroin overdose."***

♦ SM: That might be somebody else, but that's not us. We've been able to surround ourselves with really good people and have weeded out "the past."

♦ **V: *Another pitfall major labels spring on young bands: wanting the second album too soon.***

♦ SM: Right. With us, we're in complete control. Basically, I was able to produce this album. I picked all the songs, okayed all the arrangements, and was never questioned once about any song I brought to the table. I even brought in a song that had never been played live, and we just went in and recorded it. I'm really concerned about somebody coming in and changing everything we've done.

♦ **V: *Often the major record companies control the photos and artwork—***

♦ SM: I picked Todd Schorr to do the album cover, and it turned out that our producer is one of his best friends—what kind of coincidence is that?

♦ **V: *Why aren't there more women instrumentalists in swing bands?***

♦ SM: I don't know. Back then, when women vocalists were in the band, it was: "Tommy Dorsey *featuring* Anita O'Day." "Duke Ellington *featuring* Lena Horne." Women were never the mainstay. I think there will be people breaking that mold.

Photo: V. Vale

. . . and by night, BIG *BAD* VOODOO DADDY!!! Great American Music Hall, 8-30-97.

♦ **V: *What other bands do you like?***

♦ SM: I like Royal Crown Revue; I like the New Morty Show from San Francisco. I love Louis Jordan and Keely Smith, and they've got a strong element of that, especially in their new original material. I like the horn arrangements for the Cherry Poppin' Daddies; they have one of the coolest horn sections in the business. I like the Squirrel Nut Zippers; they're from that "hot" time (much earlier than swing) and I really like hot music. They have a nice New Orleans flair—they have a *lot* of different elements: a bluegrass feel, too.

♦ **V: *How did you happen to appear in* Swingers?**

♦ SM: Jon Favreau, the star and writer of the film, used to come to the Derby to see us and to dance. One night he approached us: "I know this sounds 'typical Hollywood,' but I wrote a script and would really like you guys to be in the film. It's low-budget and there's no money, but we think you'd be great." We had just done *Party of Five* and were still an "industry secret."

It was a year before *Swingers* was premiered to the executives at Miramax, Universal, etc. Next thing we knew, it was a hugely "buzzed" film. It got bought for the highest amount any independent film had ever commanded. We recorded the soundtrack in one day; it was all "live." Then we went out on the road and the crowds were much bigger—it was obvious that a lot more people had heard of us. Being in that film was a turning point in our career. To this day Jon remains a close and important friend of the band.

When we played live in the club scene in *Swingers,* I made it clear to Jon that we did not want to lip-synch, and he was really into that. So viewers saw what Wednesday night was actually like at that particular time. Sometimes it's a lot more expensive to play live, because you're using dialogue—you have to be part of another union, and it just becomes a big mess! It's ridiculous. Hollywood is a very *interesting* town. [laughs]

♦ **V: *Aren't you keeping your distance from Hollywood by remaining in Ventura?***

♦ SM: I do so much work there that I *am* part of it, but the only way to keep creative is if I stay away from it.

♦ **V: *You've played where people throw requests at you—***

♦ SM: We've played every situation you can imagine. In one week we played a party for the Grammies, a punk rock club, a jazz club, and then a full-bore concert hall. We've played private parties, society parties, corporate events, concerts, punk halls, shitholes—everything you can imagine. We've even played Country & Western bars. It keeps you working, that's for sure.

If I had a dollar for everytime somebody asked me to play "In the Mood," I would have retired by now. But I just smile and say, "You know, we don't do that one," and people are dumbfounded: "Really?" I wasn't too into guys like Glenn Miller and Tommy Dorsey. I respect their beautiful styles, but it's like music for the easy-listening, "sophisticated" white crowd.

♦ **V: *I hope you don't just play hoity-toity upper-class situations—***

♦ SM: That's the one thing we're going to try and stay away from, and keep our "class" the human race! That's kind of a pact we had with ourselves. On New Year's Eve we played Bimbo's in San Francisco, and the next day we played Club Deluxe. It was unannounced—if you knew, you knew. We just played the Fillmore; as a musician you can feel the history of the place. Henry Rollins is playing there tonight, and in the music business, I look up to him as much as I'd look up to anybody. He does lots of different things: he acts in major motion pictures, puts out

records, has a book publishing company, does spoken word and music concert tours, and never gets labeled a sell-out because he keeps it all in perspective. Just read the lyrics to his song "Starve." He would much rather starve himself and create great music and art than to become a fat, Cadillac-owning, huge-mansion, big bank account, lots of furniture, different homes in each state, kind of cigar-smoking freak.

♦ **V: *What do you think of the cigar and cocktail revival?***

♦ SM: If it's bringing somebody enjoyment and not hurting anybody else, I have no problems with it. Just as long as someone isn't burning me with a cigar or spilling it in my drink or on my clothes! If it makes you feel part of American history and culture, jump on it. Rock on!

♦ **V: *Someone from the punk days asked me, "Do I have to wear a double-breasted suit to go to a swing show?"***

♦ SM: You *don't.* You don't even have to wear anything vintage. I still have a shaved head; I have a goatee; I have body piercings and I'm 31 years old and thinking about getting my first full tattoo on my forearm. I still wear biker boots and engineer boots; I still feel just as much a punk as I ever did before. I used to slick my hair back but then I preferred a shaved head; I wore a hat a lot. I think it's really what you feel comfortable with. I'd really hate for it to

Gene Krupa on drums.

be pigeon-holed, so that people thought they'd *have* to wear just a certain style. But I also say that you should take pride in yourself when you do go out.

♦ **V: *It's a different mind-set now: going out to a "special" show.***

♦ SM: And when you feel good and you look good, you're in a good place.

♦ **V: *And some of the women look incredible—***

♦ SM: That's the best part of it.

♦ **V: *There's this spine-tingling excitement at shows that I haven't felt since early punk days—***

> **Another thing I learned from punk rock: don't take it too seriously, and try to roll with the punches when things change.**

♦ SM: That's where it's at; you've got to base what you do on that. I don't think that's something anyone can market or sell. Another thing I learned from punk rock: don't take it too seriously, and try to roll with the punches when things change. Try and see if there's still some good left in the things that happened.

I'm always looking for something new in every aspect of my life. I'm a big jazz fan and I'm also always looking for cool punk rock vinyl. Today I was at a thrift store and found Black Flag's *Black Coffee* on vinyl—I was really stoked! I went home and listened to it, made some dinner, and sung along with my daughter—she rocks out. I like to cook when I have time. The repertoire gains as you keep going; you start getting bolder and take more chances. There are hits and misses.

♦ **V: What's the food equivalent of this cultural uprising?**

♦ SM: *Good* food and good drink! I love good cabernets; I like Tanqueray and tonic. I think the finer things in life are cool—not in excess. I love martinis. Newcastle Brown Ale is my favorite; our "rider" (in our contract) states that we have to have two cases of those babies per night. Newcastle rules!

♦ **V: How do you think the trend got started to wear two-tone shoes?**

♦ SM: With us, it was a matter of looking at those old films—check out the shoes in *High Society*. Bing Crosby wears some unbelievable suits in that; some really great combinations. There's one silver-blue suit and tie combination with some two-tones . . . just check it out! Louis Armstrong is in that. There are so many more films: *Hellzapoppin'* is a big one, a standard.

I also like to read biographies, especially when they're straight from the artist's mouth so I can know what makes 'em tick.

I listen to earlier music like Big Joe Turner as well as early New Orleans jazz. I love Jimmy Rushing and Henry "Red" Allen—he's really cool. King Oliver's really happening. Louis Armstrong's *Hot Fives* and *Hot Sevens* are *the shit*—that's what originally was freaking me out as a kid. I remember looking for other kids into this kind of music and not finding anybody, especially someone who wanted to recreate it but with an edge.

♦ **V: I always thought Louis Armstrong's Hot Fives and Hot Sevens were so polyphonic, they were like Bach—**

♦ SM: They really were like that. You'd be surprised how regimented that music is. As much as that music changes every time [in live performance], it stays the same.

♦ **V: The Hot Sevens provided accessible polyphony; it seemed like your mind really could follow seven musical paths simultaneously—**

♦ SM: Never underestimate the powers of the mind! Most of the cool stuff that your mind registers is subliminal. I seem to pick out the oddest stuff that I want to hear in my music that make it sound a little bit different from other people's. I'll hear a song where the verse and chorus are terrible, but all of a sudden they'll throw in a bridge that'll turn me on because it's filling some sort of hole that I was looking for! I never try to make my bridges or choruses hokey; I always try to keep them as melodic and straightforward as possible.

♦ **V: What are your most popular songs?**

♦ SM: The first one we're going to push for the radio is "You and Me and the Bottle Makes Three"—that was in *Swingers* and people seem to really dig it. Our approach to the drums (straightahead kick drum in your face) helped beef up the song. It has a memorable hook, and you're lucky when you get one because they're few and far between. "Go Daddy-O" has been popular, plus "Mr Pinstriped Suit."

♦ **V: I've seen three different bands do "Caledonia," and each version was great—**

♦ SM: Right. You couldn't pay me enough to do that song. But I guess I'd like it if in 20 years every band and their brother did "You and Me and the Bottle Makes Three." "Minnie the Moocher" is one of the only cover tunes we do—it's a classic.

♦ **V: When I went through my "jazz" phase, which is before**

Dirk Shumaker; Great American Music Hall, 8-30-97.

punk came along, practically every record I listened to was by musicians like Charlie Parker—

♦ SM: Right. That's all I listened to *forever* until I started to get a good attitude about modern music again. All I listened to was black musicians. And that's the kind of music I play. I don't play white swing, I play wild, dark, crazy, jump Harlem music—for me *that's it*.

♦ **V: I read that when lindy hop originated, the wildest dance innovations were never seen unless you were in the black community—**

♦ SM: That's the truth. Duke Ellington has some "soundies" (short films from the '40s; the bands used to record them and then go in and do lip-synch, and do little skits as well), and he featured a really great lindy hop team that revolutionized the whole lindy hop scene. From what they're doing you can guess where it must have gone!

♦ **V: I found a 1941 Life magazine featuring wild black lindy hop dancers, Anne "Popeye" Johnson and Frankie "Musclehead" Manning dancing to the music of Erskine Hawkins—**

♦ SM: Frankie Manning is still alive! And he's still *the* guy. He's in New York. I think he's in Catalina this weekend doing the Swing Dancing Camp. Erskine Hawkins was okay; I'm not a *huge* fan of his, but I like him. I listen a lot to that music and try to get in touch with what it is and see what it's all about.

♦ **V: Well, what else is there to do but to learn more?**

♦ SM: That's what I like about the music. It's amazing what you can do with these chord structures. It's very inspirational. *It's infinite.* V

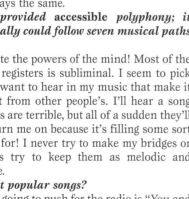

Scotty Recommends

ARTISTS:

Louis Armstrong/Jordan/Prima & Keely Smith, Henry "Red" Allen, Gene Krupa, Buddy Rich, Jimmy Rushing, Big Joe Turner

Count Basie: complete works. (Anything with Lester Young and Jo Jones on it is a keeper—that stuff swings really hard and you're not going to get any bad performances.)

Cab Calloway: the one to get that pretty much goes through the whole gamut is called *Are You Hep to the Jive?*

Duke Ellington: you can't really go wrong with the *earlier* Duke Ellington volumes of all his Harlem-influenced music.

Ultra-Lounge Series: (24 CDs) I really love *Mondo Exotica*—that's more about Martin Denny, Les Baxter, Webley Edwards, Bas Sheva—the Exotica side. *Wild, Cool and Swingin'* has Sam Butera, Peggy Lee and Bobby Darin—people may give me shit for that, but I absolutely love his voice. *Organs in Orbit* is brilliant; the weirdest thing you'll hear.

FILMS: *High Society, Hellzapoppin'*

DISCOGRAPHY:

Big Bad Voodoo Daddy (Big Bad Records, POB 2146, Ventura CA 93002)

Whatchu Want for Christmas? (Big Bad Records)

Swingers soundtrack (Hollywood Records)

Party of Five soundtrack (Reprise)

TELEVISION:

Party of Five, The Big Deal Game Show, *Access Hollywood*, E! Entertainment, Theme music for *Maggie Me & the Mambo Tree* cartoon, MTV

Crescent City Maulers

Bassist Chris Carmean founded New Jersey's Crescent City Maulers in '94 with saxophonist Tony Salimbene, drummer Lenny Zaccaro and guitarist Big Al Sagnella. Their CDs, *Screamin'* & *Harlem Hotspot* are available from Hepcat 800-404-4117, Dept RS. 👟 👟 👟

♦ *VALE: You planned "The Big Guns of Swing" weekend for October '98, in the Catskills, NY—*

♦ CHRIS CARMEAN: I'm putting it together because I love this music—it's my whole life. I grew up with swing music and now I'm in a swing band. I don't want the people who attend this festival to know what year it is for three days. Saturday night is going to be done like a '30s radio broadcast: the announcer, commercials, everything.

I really wanted to do the festival because there's nothing serious happening on the east coast. I had been to one of those rockabilly "weekenders" in England, and thought it would be great to do one here, but done *right*. It can't be too expensive and it's gotta be comfortable and classy. We've lined up Bill Elliott, Lavay Smith, 8½ Souvenirs, Blue Plate Special, Royal Crown, Squirrel Nut Zippers, Cherry Poppin' Daddies, Big Bad Voodoo Daddy, Big Six, Indigo Swing, New Morty Show and the Bellevue Cadillacs.

♦ *V: What's your background—*

♦ CC: In 1972 when I was 9 years old, my mother said, "You're taking dancing lessons!" My mom was a ballroom dancer, and my grandfather was one in New York City in the '20s and '30s. I started the lessons, and for eight years my brother, my two sisters and I did ballroom dancing and competitions. There was never any rock'n'roll in our house—all I listened to was big band, Dixieland, swing and jump-blues.

In high school I played tuba in a Dixieland band for four years. That band broke up and I did no music for awhile, then a friend introduced me to rockabilly. I learned the upright bass and met my wife—who was a singer in a rockabilly band. I thought, "Three-chord songs are a little monotonous after awhile. I prefer horns to guitars—I really want to do *swing!*" I'd been trying to get people interested in starting a swing band since '82, but couldn't find anyone. It was a long and frustrating time.

Then in March '94 I heard that a sax-playing friend left his band. He introduced me to a guitar player and a drummer. Though they never heard swing before, they managed to play it well enough. Our approach isn't "purist," but we swing *our way*.

Our first gig was at a rockabilly club. We only knew seven songs, and when we were done they said, "You gotta play the rest of the night." After that, we learned more songs,

started writing our own, and our shows got more popular.

We recorded our CD in eight hours and used it to get gigs and sell at our shows. Jack Vaughn, from Slimstyle Records, got a copy and offered us a deal.

♦ *V: How do you dress?*

♦ CC: The band wears suits. I wear one I inherited from my grandfather—a serious snappy dresser. It gets so hot here that we often have to strip down to guinea-t's [undershirts]. We also wear suspenders; I have a 32″ waist and I wear 38″ waist pants. I wear suits everywhere now—I even wear tails and tuxedo pants sometimes.

♦ *V: You play upright bass?*

♦ CC: Yeah. I broke all my wooden basses, so I switched to an aluminum one. It's light so I can throw it up in the air and toss it out in the audience. We do a New York style of swing. New York is a hard-edged town, and that's the way we feel the music.

I love it when people dance. Generally, people on the east coast are still afraid to try; they're scared of looking awkward. But one guy who *did* learn came up to me and said, "I could never get a girl until I learned how to dance."

Now we play every weekend. The New York Swing Society comes out and dances to us and, if the crowd goes crazy, we go crazy. We did one show in Montclair, closing our set with "Chicken Shack Boogie," and everybody was screaming and grabbing at us—it was hysterical. People went insane.

Oddly enough, the swing scene's bigger in New Jersey than it is in New York, and the clubs pay way better. We play at Tierney's Tavern in Montclair and the Downtown Cafe in Red Bank—the home of Count Basie (they have a Count Basie Theater there). What I like about the swing scene is: it still hasn't mutated into something horrible. ▼

The Flipped Fedoras.

One of the first New York "swing" bands is the Flipped Fedoras, led by guitarist/singer Nick Palumbo. Although he draws from a pool of musicians, his main band includes Kevin Dorn (a Gene Krupa-style drummer), Rob Susman (trombone), Tommy Russo (trumpet), Michael Hashine (alto sax), Tom Murray (tenor sax), and Tony Palumbo (bass). In Manhattan, Nick lives with his wife, Donna, an artist, and their daughter, Erin Scarlett. He can be contacted at 917-242-3428 (pager). The Flipped Fedoras CD is available from Hepcat (800) 404-4117.

♦ *VALE: It seems like the development of an east coast "swing scene" is relatively recent—*

♦ NICK PALUMBO: But I've been into this since I was a kid. My father was a swing guitar player, so I grew up listening to Django Reinhardt and all those people. Three years ago, when there was no scene at all, I said, "I'm not going to play what's on the charts; I'm going to play what comes from my heart." And that was a Mediterranean swing/jump music. The New York swing scene is new; I'd say it's a year and a half old, and we probably started it.

There were people from the West Coast swing scene moving to New York. Little by little it got bigger. A year and a half ago I started a Monday swing night at the Louisiana Community Bar & Grill (622 Broadway near Houston Street). That helped launch the scene here because it was a steady night each week where everybody could congregate. It's funny, the people who are deeply into the retro thing are the dancers—they're the hardcore people. The musicians just come in to play a gig. Except for me, of course.

[laughs] I'm on both sides of the fence.

♦ *V: What do you mean by "Mediterranean" swing?*

♦ NP: Back in the '30s and '40s, New York City was the place for jazz and swing. Then there was France, where Django Reinhardt and Stephane Grappelli started playing jazz swing with a Mediterranean flair. The group was called Le Hot Club de France. It took many different shapes and forms over the years. My father's from Italy, so that was the music he grew up. When he moved to the States in the mid-'50s, that was his style of guitar playing. You know Neapolitan music with a mandolin and an accordion?

♦ *V: Yes.*

♦ NP: Imagine these instruments swinging jazz. I'm American, but I also have that European influence. I think that's what gives my band a different twist; it has that Mediterranean flavor. It's not like 8½ Souvenirs, I caught that band a few weeks ago.

New York is funny: it's a city of everything, but at the same time it's a city of nothing. Everybody's always rushing here and there to make their payments, talking big talk about what they want to do. And nothing gets done. Meanwhile, we all sit back and read about what's going on in other places. And we ask, "What's wrong with New York City?" I think everybody's so busy running around in circles that nothing gets done.

♦ **V: The stress is high and it's hard to survive.**

♦ NP: San Francisco has a more relaxed atmosphere, which I dig. I was there about three months ago for only three days and it seemed like a week. It was great. If I had to choose another city to live in, it would be San Francisco.

I had no idea there are over 100 swing bands on the West Coast. In New York City there's *five*. The Blues Jumpers, a jump-blues band; Crescent City Maulers from Jersey—also jump-blues; the Flying Neutrinos, who are more New Orleans Dixieland; Beat Positive—more of a lounge-swing thing; and a new band called Dem Brooklyn Bums.

♦ **V: What about The Last of the International Playboys?**

♦ NP: Yeah, I *guess* so. Here's the thing, though: since there aren't many swing bands, any band that even has a shuffle in their repertoire is considered swing. It's funny. There *are* big bands in New York City, but they're the Old School type of big band that plays weddings and high society parties—sit-down Benny Goodman/Glenn Miller music. They have nothing to do with the new scene and they don't kick ass.

♦ **V: What kind of guitar do you have?**

♦ NP: A 1951 Epiphone Zephyr Regent with just one pick-up—that's it—called a New York pick-up. It's simple, there's nothing to it, but it has that fat rock/jazz sound. It's not finely detailed like the guitars Gibson was making in the '30s and '40s, with incredible wood and workmanship. Epiphones were more on the trashy side. They have a nice bite to them, but they can sing really sweet, too. I think it's a good combination for jump swing. It's a full 17" hollow-body and the color is Tobacco Sunburst. In L.A., Leo Fender (founder of Fender guitars, the first affordable electric guitar line) came up with crazy colors like Sky Blue or Fiesta

Nick Palumbo now . . . and then. Below: accompanying his father.

My father was doing lounge music back when it *was* lounge music.

Red. He'd go to auto body shops and get car paints (originally made for a Corvette or something) and spray his guitars with them.

Sometimes I play a '56 Fender Stratocaster, also in Tobacco Sunburst. I have a '64 Fender Jaguar too. The Epiphone is more my performance guitar and it's not just for the sound—people need to see something that looks like the period.

♦ **V: Do you dress "retro"?**

♦ NP: As a kid, this was the way I dressed because that's how people dressed. Remember when your folks took you to get a haircut? You just got a regular haircut; it was no big deal. This "swing revival" has been a big turnaround for me. Now I go to the barbershop and say, "Give me a regular haircut." You know, put a bit of grease in it and comb it like we did when we were kids.

♦ **V: Is your mom American?**

♦ NP: No, both my parents are from Italy. And it's a shame that the U.S. doesn't make it mandatory that kids study a second language. It's pathetic. You go to Europe and the people are so much better educated. They speak English better than some Americans, and they can even talk about American politics—we can't even do that! [laughs] I speak Italian fluently; also German, because I lived there four years.

My childhood was kind of weird: my parents were raising a family in the States with an Italian background. We'd come home with report cards and my mom would ask, "Where do I sign?" I don't remember ever bringing a pen or pencil to school. My mother never went to school and my father dropped out when he was nine. He started an apprenticeship; he's a custom suit-maker. It was a different world. If I did something wrong, it was no big deal to get a smack across the face. My father could be doing 20 years for the way he raised us! [laughs] We used to get beat up, man. It was wild. I have a child now and looking at my kid, I could never think of doing one percent of what my father used to do to discipline us. But that was what they knew.

We'd have dinner at 2 o'clock in the afternoon—who the hell does that? It was like living in Italy, only in the States.

♦ **V: Do you make your living as a musician?**

♦ NP: Yeah. I've been playing since I was a kid, and I never took lessons. When my father came to the States he made his living as a tailor and a musician in clubs. When I was eight I knew his repertoire and accompanied him on gigs. I have photos of me holding a '56 Stratocaster in my little tux, next to my father. We just did instrumentals. One day he said, "Nick, why don't you sing? There'll be more variety." And that's how I started singing.

♦ **V: What kind of clubs did you play?**

♦ NP: Classier bars and lounges. Some were in upscale restaurants where they have music in the lounge area. My father was doing lounge music back when it *was* lounge music: "Girl From Ipanema" stuff that's now retro and cool. Back then it was just pop. He used a drum machine, which I still have.

♦ **V: Did that set the foundation for what you're doing now?**

♦ NP: Yeah, it's a kick, man! I've played disco, country, blues, rock, etc. The only style of music I couldn't get into was heavy metal. I liked it, but I couldn't do the long hair and the spandex. I also did rockabilly back in the early '80s. I was doing this solo gig (just me) in Manhattan for about two years, playing upper east side Irish pubs. They'd pay a buck and a half, a free meal, drinks, and tips, and I'd walk out with 200 bucks a night. I couldn't say No to that. I was working anywhere from four to seven gigs a week. I was always playing '40s, '50s and early '60s songs in my repertoire.

One night I noticed this Aryan-looking dude sitting at the bar. After the second set, I walked over and asked where he's from. In this operatic voice, he said, "I'm from Germany." I asked what his name was: "Peter Hofmann." Then he said he needed a second guitar player for a tour, and I should come to his hotel room to audition. I knew nothing about him, but I went. I got the gig and he gave me his album to listen to. I did some research—this guy had sold 20 million units in German-speaking countries!

He does rock opera. He'll take a tune like "House of the Rising Sun" and sing it operatically with a rock band behind him. It's funny. [laughs] So, I went to Germany and ended up staying there for four years. The money was great and the work was steady. I kept on getting all these other gigs—big-scale tours playing venues with 4,000 to 12,000 people. I ended up with a small record deal.

♦ V: You had a solid musical background before you did the swing thing—

♦ NP: Yeah. I have to admit: swing is not an easy style to do. But for me, it's the easiest style to play out of all the styles I've done. I'm lucky that it's "in" now, because finally I can make a living playing music that is truly me. Come on, here I am, an east coast Italian-American, doing blues or country?! It doesn't work and it looks ridiculous. During the late '80s in New York City, country music was popular at clubs and musicians were all of a sudden "Yee-hawing." It was so un-New York that it only lasted a couple of years—thank god!

♦ V: You had a roots rockabilly band?

♦ NP: Yeah, but that wasn't me. Then there's blues—I love blues, but the musicians that do it right come from places where you eat, breathe, and live that aura and style. New York City is swing, jazz, hip-hop, etc; it's not blues or country.

♦ V: Was it hard to get started?

♦ NP: Well, three years ago lounge was the retro thing here. Luigi "Babe" Scorcia was the first retro promotor. A friend of mine, a drummer named Rocko Durubis, got a call from Luigi to put a lounge thing together, so he called me up. I said, "What the hell

---

I had no idea there are over 100 swing bands on the West Coast. In New York City there's *five*.

---

is lounge? Let's do some swing!" So we got together some tunes and started as a three-piece: me, Rocko, and Brian Lux on bass. The band was like a trashy, junk swing band that sounded horrible but looked cool. Brian is this tall Texan who's great-looking; chicks fall in love with him—he's got this Elvis vibe happening with the hair. So it started like that and Luigi was telling me, "Nick, you're doing the wrong thing; you gotta do lounge, baby, like Combustible Edison." I said, "If you want me to play your shows, how 'bout I do what *I* want to do? Otherwise get somebody else."

The first club that should get credit for supporting swing here is the Cooler, down in the Meat District—14th Street between

Ninth and Tenth Avenue. It's called the Cooler because it used to be a big refrigerator, and has this reeking odor of meat. Now there are clubs where slaughter houses used to be.

We were the first swing band that helped bring about a scene in N.Y. The Flying Neutrinos have been together for about four years, but they weren't involved in any *scene*. They and a band called Beat Positive got together with us and we started doing double or triple bands on a bill. Getting audiences to show up was difficult, and we weren't making any money. So it stopped right there. I remember we were all hanging out in bars and talking and getting drunk instead of doing gigs.

Anyway, I got a call from Mark Campbell, the manager for the Louisiana Bar & Grill: "Monday nights are dead. Let's see if we can do something with the music *you're* playing." I said, "Sure. I want to bring in a small big band with a swing sound." And that was it: it turned into a scene. I've been there a year and a half and on Monday nights you can't even *move* in the club.

♦ V: How did you find players?

♦ NP: New York City has a lot of good musicians who can read. I checked out horn players and the four guys I picked have to be the best horn section in this city. I'm not saying this because they're in my band, but because it's the truth. It was easy to get them, because "big band" is a style that horn players love and never get a chance to play. Most of them have to do laid-back "MOR" [middle-of-the-road] or play weddings just to make a living.

♦ V: You put a band together fast—

♦ NP: Yeah, in a matter of days. I had two guys make charts for about 30 tunes. We had one rehearsal and then started doing the gigs. Within eight months, the swing scene developed just from this one weekly night at the Louisiana. Everybody finally had a place. Before, it was so scattered that people had to wait for a promotor to have a "Swing Night" and pass out flyers—it wasn't consistent enough for anything to start. And the Louisiana was big enough for the scene to grow, although now it's too small—the real dancers are complaining about all the "amateurs" coming in.

♦ V: How did aerial dancing emerge in New York?

♦ NP: That kind of dancing originated in New York in the '20s and '30s in places like the Cotton Club. There's a dance school here that teaches lindy-hop, swing dancing, and ballroom dance. It's run by this French couple. They were the first to do flips in the air and wild moves. We asked them to teach dance lessons on Monday nights, and afterwards the students would come and practice at the Louisiana.

As a band we look like we're from the '40s. When we first started playing, people in the audience would just wear whatever, but now people are starting to get the garb down. I think it's just beginning—

♦ V: Right. I like the old styles better anyway.

♦ NP: They're more classic. The fabric used to be better; that's why those old suits have lasted so long. After a couple of years new suits have these permanent wrinkles or they "pill"; the fabric just wears out.

There's a clothing shop on Seventh Street in the East Village called D&L Sherny. They have never-worn clothes from the '40s (called "old new stock.") I'm not a very big guy (about 5´6½″) and a lot of clothes from that era fit me.

♦ **V:** *Right, humans were smaller then—*

♦ NP: I go into a thrift shop and I'm in heaven because everything fits, whereas the guys in my band are tall and can't find clothes easily. Back in the '80s I was in the rockabilly scene. I took all the money I had (which was $5000) out of my account, went nuts and bought all of these suits. Every time I perform on stage, I always have a good suit on, and a different one each time. I found a guy that had 500 ties from the '40s, all mint and one-of-a-kind, and bought 'em all for $1000. Some are worth $100 apiece. So, I'm set for life with clothes. I also have a 1950 Cadillac.

I had no idea that a swing scene was going to develop here; I was considering moving to the West Coast. But finally there's something happening. Now younger musicians come and ask questions about how to start a band. Timing is everything; you gotta be lucky to get into something that becomes a trend.

Fox After Breakfast invited us to appear on their TV show. A woman talked about how the swing scene is exploding here and dancers came in and started flipping each other. Everyone loved it. They called us for a second show, and now they want a third. I got a call from Verve Records because they heard about the scene. It's exciting.

♦ **V:** *Who were your major influences?*

♦ NP: Four people: Charlie Christian, early Les Paul (the Les Paul Trio), Django Reinhardt and Johnny Moore, who was a guitar player for the early Nat King Cole Trio (reissued on Laser Light). Of course, any early jump blues is good; Bear Family has released a lot. Louis Jordan was a sax player, but his guitar player was really good, whoever he was. In fact, almost anything that says "1950" or "1951" is jump. Guitar playing was coming out of jazz into "rock," and many of the guitarists were jazz players with *technique*.

During that time you hear a lot of distorted guitar, and this wasn't from effects boxes, it was because the amplifiers didn't have much power. Most of those early amps were ten or fifteen watts, compared to 100 watts now. They would distort with the volume set to "3"!

Most of the players in the new swing bands are not kids—the majority are in their 30s. It's not a style like punk where you only need to know three or four chords and can sing about death or anarchy. This is about learning; it's deep. [laughs]

♦ **V:** *And it's easier to grow old gracefully with swing—*

♦ NP: Class is definitely back in town. Trashy is still cool, but you can be trashy and classy at the same time. Just look at old photos; people used to go out in suits all the time—even to ball-games. Now you have to dance with a little finesse; it's not freak-style dancing anymore.

I am definitely appreciating music again. When I came back from Germany, I stopped doing music for two years. It sucked. To make a living I had to do anything that came my way musically. It could be a polka; if it paid $100 I was there. But after awhile, I said, "If I'm going to hate what I'm doing, I might as well hate something that makes more money." So I got a day job for two years. I lucked out and started a concession in this guy's computer store, buying and selling musical equipment. It gave me a chance to lay back and think about what I wanted to do with my life. And that's what got me to start my swing band.

As a full-time "musician" I was getting so burnt out that I did-

n't have the time to think about what I *really* wanted to do. A lot of musicians get caught up in that. Then suddenly you're 50 or 60 years old and still haven't done what you should have done.

♦ **V:** *How do you come up with new material that sounds as good as the old?*

♦ NP: As a songwriter, I find this "swing" style pretty natural to write in. If you live the lifestyle, that's what's going to come out if you're playing from the heart. I can always hear when people are *imitating*. In jazz a lot of new artists are still emerging, but people don't say, "Well, they were doing jazz in the '20s, so you can't do it anymore."

♦ **V:** *Where do you rehearse in Manhattan?*

♦ NP: We have to rent a studio. So there aren't many rehearsals!

♦ **V:** *Can you talk about the economics of keeping a band together?*

♦ NP: In New York City there are a lot of good horn players who are accomplished musicians and good readers. All my songs have horn charts, so if one of my regulars can't do it, I make a second call, third call, fourth call . . . for each player, I have four back-up guys. Depending on the gig, my band may be a whole different band—except for me. About thirty different people play in the band.

I can't offer the weekly salary that musicians need to support themselves. If one of my main guys calls and says, "I got a chance to make $300 next Tuesday," I say, "Go ahead and do it." I don't expect any commitments, because that's tough. If I had a six-month tour lined up I *would* want some commitment or contract, but that's different.

♦ **V:** *This eliminates potential for interpersonal nastiness—*

♦ NP: I don't make "loyalty" an issue at all. People kind of naturally give their loyalty, because they can do whatever they like!

♦ **V:** *How is the band's income divided?*

♦ NP: I can say this: every gig pays differently. Sometimes we do corporate parties, and those pay well. Some gigs pay lousy but are fun to do. When I can pay the guys more, they get it. When it's less, they understand and everything's cool. Right now, the iron is hot in Manhattan for this style of music. For the first time in three years it's been easier to keep the band going. Before, a player couldn't take it seriously, because I didn't have the work coming in to keep the band at a serious level. You gotta be fair, otherwise you can't keep a band! **V**

Nick with wife Donna and daughter Erin Scarlett.

Nick's Favorites

FAVORITE FILMS:
Public Enemy with James Cagney. The hairdos and the clothes are unbelievable.
The Godfather Part 1 and 2. I relate to these movies, having grown up in a traditional old world Italian family.
FAVORITE POSSESSIONS:
1950 Caddy
1956 Fender Strat
1950 and '51 Eppiphone Zephyr Regent
1964 Fender Jaguar
1940s tie collection (over 500)
Please Note: I must credit my wife and daughter with helping me pull it all together. Their constant love and support help shape all my ideas.

L to R: Bobby Trimble, Wally Hersom, Robert Williams, Ashley Kingman, and Lee Jeffries. Photo: Dave Harrison

BIG SANDY & HIS FLY-RITE BOYS have been described as "Hillbilly Boogie," "Hillbilly Bop," "Western Jive" and "Country Swing." Initially a rockabilly group, they've moved toward Western Swing, adding steel guitar and piano. Members include Robert Williams (vocals, acoustic guitar), Wally Hersom (upright bass), Bobby Trimble (drums), Ashley Kingman (guitar), Lee Jeffriess (steel guitar), and Carl Sonny Leyland (piano). They have released numerous albums and singles (including a 78), available from Hepcat (800-404-4117).

♦ *VALE: What's your background?*
♦ ROBERT WILLIAMS: I was born in Norwalk, California, a suburb of Los Angeles. My father is a welder. When I was six, our family moved to a low-income housing tract being built in Orange County. For a young married couple this seemed to be a good opportunity.

My mother is of Mexican descent, but I didn't grow up in that culture. My father is a blond-haired, blue-eyed Okie from Oklahoma. I have dark skin and dark features, and most people don't think we're related.

My dad had a lot of old country, rockabilly, Western Swing and surf records. He met my mom at a dance on the Pike in Long Beach—an amazing old amusement park. My mother had R&B, Doowop, and blues plus her older brother's records from the Pachuco/Zoot Suit Movement: Jump Blues, R&B, etc. My parents were also into old cars. To this day my dad still has a big pompadour. Some kids rebel against what their parents are into, but I really dug it.

In elementary school (early '70s), after school I'd walk to the local library and put on headphones and listen to old blues records by Big Bill Broonzy, Sonny Terry and Brownie McGhee—they had a lot of Folkways field recordings. Listening to those gave me the same feeling as watching the *Little Rascals;* I wanted

to be in a different time than where I was.
♦ *V: It's great that your parents bought records and let you play them—*
♦ RW: There was a time, though, when my father went to a Billy Graham crusade and got "saved"! He came home and tried to make us get rid of all of our records—they were "evil." I managed to hide *my* records, but unfortunately my dad got rid of a lot. Since those days my collection has grown enormously. My room is basically all records, with a little space cleared out for a bed and a path to the door!
♦ *V: Was your mother born in Mexico?*
♦ RW: No, she was second-generation. My grandparents are from Durango, Mexico. They met and got married in El Paso, Texas, and in the '30s moved to Glendale, California. My grandfather had a ranch and a grocery store in Los Angeles, and now my family (which is quite large) is spread out all over the L.A. area. My grandfather was a musician who played in bands that toured the border towns between Mexico and Texas. Then he became a preacher who had a road show featuring live music—my grandmother showed me the old photos. This was when Mexican border radio stations broadcasted jazz, blues and hillbilly music, inspiring musicians to create what became known as rock'n'roll.

♦ V: *The music you play is partially Western Swing; can you talk about that?*

♦ RW: Western Swing emerged in the '30s by boys from a country/hillbilly background who began listening to jazz musicians like Django Reinhardt. Milton Brown and Bob Wills were in a band innovating music that drew from Hot Jazz and dance music infused with ethnic European immigrant folk music: reels, fiddle dance tunes, etc. Later, Milton Brown died in a car crash and Bob Wills went on to fame and fortune.

As popular dance music changed into big band, Western Swing bands became larger, adding horn sections. Milton Brown led his through the '30s, in the '40s Bob Wills had his day, and in the '50s guys like Hank Thompson incorporated the new honky-tonk sounds. Through the years, Western Swing drew from the best music of the day. I'm trying to come up with music that draws from the best of the past, but is also very *now*—and that's a challenge.

♦ V: *There was a manic, un-bourgeois craziness in rockabilly 45s like "Love Me" by The Phantom—*

♦ RW: That song is so savage; it *is* punk. At one point in the '80s when people asked what we were into, I'd say, "Fifties punk." The Phantom's "Love Me" was our anthem!

♦ V: *When did you first start playing music?*

♦ RW: When I was in high school in '81, modern rockabilly bands began popping up. People were putting on shows at roller rinks and pizza parlors, and they were a revelation—I thought: "This is what I want to do!" A lot of the bands sounded pretty good, but the singers sounded like crap. I kept thinking, "I know I could do *at least* that good."

I was too ashamed to share these thoughts with anyone. After school I'd go home and tape myself singing along with reissue LPs of '50s songs. They had been rechanneled into fake stereo with the vocals on one side and the instruments on the other, so I'd turn down the vocal side and tape myself singing along with the instrumental side.

On my 18th birthday, my mother asked if I wanted to take guitar lessons. (She'd seen an ad where you pay for five lessons and

Bimbo's 365 Club, 9-19-97. Photo: V.Vale

get a free guitar). I said "Yes" and did that long enough to get the free guitar, but never progressed past a few basic chords—the same chords I know now! [laughs] This gave me something to sing along with at home, other than records. Also, I was able to come up with my *own* songs. I'd listen to an Elvis Presley number, change it a bit and put in my own words. It might not have been very original, but at least it was *mine*.

> I'm trying to come up
> with music that draws from the best
> of the past, but is also very *now*—
> and that's a challenge.

After a year I became a little more confident. I met other people who were into the rockabilly scene, and started going to house parties where bands were playing. I'd bring my guitar along and once in a while I'd get up the nerve to ask if I could sit in.

Just before I turned 20, in 1984, I went to a party and met some musicians from the Moondawgs. The bass player did the singing, but they wanted more of a front man. They said, "We're rehearsing next Thursday; why don't you come over and let's just mess around and see what happens." I said [casually], "Oh yeah, sure" like—no problem—but I was *so* scared! I thought, *"What am I going to do?"* I didn't think I knew enough to actually play with a band. But I went and faked my way through. I played with that band for a year before they kicked me out; the original singer got jealous and wanted his spot back. They lasted a couple more months and then broke up.

I had gotten a taste of the musician's life. We had played local shows and started getting attention from girls, and to suddenly lose that was very depressing. So I called up people I had met around town and formed another band, "Robert Williams and the Rustin' Strings" (I hated that name). We played straight rockabilly, and on a couple songs the guitarist played lap steel guitar. We played garage parties and a few clubs around town.

♦ V: *You gained experience, overcame stage fright and learned how to talk to the audience. How did you dress?*

♦ RW: I had pretty big hair. People were dressing in an exaggerated "new wave" version of the '50s. Everybody was listening to the Stray Cats, but I kept thinking, "This isn't really *rockabilly*"—from listening to my dad's records, I knew this was more like a cartoon version of it. Then I met Jason Goodman, who also had a lot of records, and we clicked. We'd be at a party hearing the Rockats or the Stray Cats or whatever cats were happening

Instruments

LEE JEFFRIESS. Guitars: 1) Chuck Wright Custom 1957 "quad-necked." 2) 1950 Bigsby triple-neck guitar originally owned by Lefty Nason, then Dusty Stewart—both from Hank Thompson's Brazos Valley Boys. AMP: custom amp, copy of Standell electronics with JBL D-130 15″ speaker.

ASHLEY KINGMAN. Guitar: Richard Allen custom, tel: 818-442-8806. Hollow-body electric/acoustic with his name inlaid in mother-of-pearl on fretboard. All handmade including pickups. Wood: birdseye maple. AMP: 1962 Vox AC-50 in Western-style custom cabinet with 2 brass cactuses on each side of JBL D-130 15″ speaker.

WALLY HERSOM. Upright Basses: Has 2 broken basses and 3 working basses. For recording uses German solid-wood carved top ('40s?). Has a 5-string Kay bass ('50s?). Tours with 1950 Epiphone plywood B-5 model. AMP: built from Fender Bassman 135, '71 modern Altec-Lansing 15″.

CARL SONNY LEYLAND. Piano: Roland FP8 88-key electric piano with a custom-made hinged wood cover (to resemble a "real" piano). AMP: Yorkville keyboard amp (with speaker and horn).

BOBBY TRIMBLE. Drums. Early-to-mid-'50s Slingerland "Radio Kings." Vintage Zildjian cymbals and Ludwig hardware, calfskin heads.

ROBERT WILLIAMS. Guitar: Richard Allen custom acoustic with his name inlaid on the fretboard.

[laughs] but we'd be in a corner discussing the Phantom or Billy Lee Riley or Johnny Burnette. I always preferred hearing the more traditional versions—

♦ V: —the roots, the originals.

♦ RW: I ended up being that way with *all* musical styles. At Tower Records I discovered rockabilly reissue albums from England and Europe, and that's where all my money went—I bought every single one! That music became a big influence on me, rather than whatever bands were "happening" at the time. Also, discovering Miriam Linna and Billy Miller's *Kicks* magazine was a big deal. They did a piece on The Phantom (Marty Lott) and printed his photo.

The photos on those albums influenced how I dressed. At the time everybody had really big pompadours overly exaggerated with hairspray, and wore bowling shirts. But Jason and I thought, "We're into this old-sounding music; let's look the part, too." So we started slicking our hair back using grease instead of hairspray—that was more authentic. While searching through thriftstores for records, we began finding old clothes, too. Back then, zipper jackets with pink-and-black diamonds on them were just sitting on the racks—things that now sell for hundreds of dollars in Hollywood vintage stores.

Little Sandy: Robert Williams in 1965 at eight months old. Below: Big Sandy!
Photo: David Harrison

At thrift stores we started picking up other things, too: knickknacks, old lamps, old furniture, and got pulled further into this retro "thing." It became a challenge to find every little piece and fixture. I was living at home, amassing all this "stuff" and putting it in the garage, and my mom ended up throwing a lot of it away. It's kind of heartbreaking recalling some of those treasures.

♦ V: You had this "other" vision of how to live, and having a co-conspirator probably helped—

♦ RW: Sure—I wasn't alone anymore; there was another "freak" into the same music. We ended up with a group of friends that shared an "authentic" approach to what started out as a '50s thing, and went farther back, as well as forward into the '60s. There was an L.A. club called The Cavern where I met these women. Their house was amazing—they had all these '50s knickknacks and furniture.

♦ V: They probably inspired you to look for the same things—

♦ RW: Oh sure! And my friend Jason was part and parcel of my development. We would walk down the street and get really angry: "developers" were tearing down these beautiful old buildings and putting up modern pieces of crap. We hated that, but there was nothing we could do about it. We thought, "Well, we'll just build our own environment to live in, and maybe it's a make-believe world, but *I'm* happy in it and I'm not hurting anybody."

♦ V: It's fun to be on the alert for beautiful buildings—

♦ RW: We almost got arrested for that once! Jason and I were walking down the street (and nobody *walks* in L.A.) because we wanted to go to a thrift store two miles away and didn't have a car. We cut through this upper-middle-class neighborhood with nice old homes. We were walking slowly, admiring the architec-

ture, and spotted an old barn behind a house. It didn't make sense being there among these '40s-style homes. On the side it said "Bible Barn."

We tried to get as close as we could, peeking over the fence, and thought it was pretty cool. Then we continued walking down the street. Suddenly two cop cars skidded to a stop right on the sidewalk in front of us, cutting us off. Apparently somebody thought we were prowlers and called the cops. They asked what we were doing and we said, "We were just looking at architecture, and saw a barn back there." One cop said, "*C'mon*—you expect me to believe that? Do you think I'm an *idiot?!*" I was wearing an old gabardine shirt and he said, "Why are you wearing a long-sleeved shirt on such a hot day? Roll up your sleeves!" like he was checking for track marks. Finally he said, "If I ever see you in this neighborhood again, I'm gonna *bust* your ass!" All because we were admiring old houses . . .

♦ V: You were persecuted for having an aesthetic different from the norm—

♦ RW: [laughs] I remember things in thrift stores I didn't buy, like great old '40s suits that none of our friends were wearing. Now we think, "Shit!" The craftsmanship and the quality used to be better. Down the street is a strip mall that's only been there about a year, and already the sign's falling down and the stucco's peeling off. That's crazy. Whereas buildings from the turn of the century are still perfectly intact. It's ridiculous!

♦ V: Tell us more about the first band you were in—

♦ RW: I was pretty lucky, because the Moondawgs were popular and played a lot. The first show I played with them was a Christmas show in Anaheim at Radio City. It had a lot of punk shows, but on certain weekends it had rockabilly night. It was an all-ages club, and was usually packed. So the very first time I ever played with a band was in front of a full house! It was pretty overwhelming. Previously I'd been kind of shy, standing in a corner by myself—I felt like I didn't quite "fit in." But I discovered I could go onstage and be somebody else, and show off! Once I got a taste for this, I loved it. By luck I fell into something that ended up being my career.

♦ V: You didn't start out playing to five people in the audience—

♦ RW: No; that happened later! At the time, rockabilly was the thing to be into in Orange County. It was a pretty big movement, with what seemed like hundreds of bands. And as quickly as it started, it faded away.

♦ V: You did classic songs in the repertoire—

♦ RW: I remember having a hard time with that first band because I wanted to do a Sleepy LaBeef song and they'd never heard of him. They wanted to do more popular songs by Eddie Cochran and Gene Vincent, like "Be-Bop-A-Lula" (and that's what audiences wanted). I felt it was more important to do some lesser known songs I was passionate about, rather than just play the "Top 40" of rockabilly.

♦ V: Then you formed "Robert Williams and the Rustin' Strings"—

♦ RW: —playing mostly original material. We were doing well, but the rockabilly scene had begun to wane. The guys I played with started getting into other things. I didn't have their full devotion—which drove me crazy, because this was *all* I wanted to do.

Then we got a shot on a local TV show called "Highway to Stardom" that was a cheapo version of "Star Search." [laughs] The guys in my band couldn't do it, so I ended up using another band called the Grave Diggers. We appeared as "Robert Williams and the Cyclones" and won that contest. In that band was a bass player, Wally Hersom, and we've been together ever since. He had a really solid slappin' style that drove the music along. Back then people would crowd around the bass player; that was the symbol of the whole "rocka-billy revival." All the girls wanted to date the bass player. Wally sings one song in our set, and whenever he does, people chant, "Wally! Wally!"

Outside of the Foothill. Photo: David Harrison

♦ **V:** *And he looks a little like Harold Lloyd or Buddy Holly—*

♦ **RW:** At the time Wally started dabbling in recording, and he ended up putting together a studio in his grandmother's tool shed with all-vintage equipment: old microphones, tape recorders, etc. Wally, Jason and I thought, "Look at all these reissues coming out. Let's put out something that *sounds* old and see if people go for it!" We made a bunch of recordings but never did anything with them.

♦ **V:** *Vintage recording equipment is now "hip"—*

♦ **RW:** It seems so obvious now; I don't know why more people didn't think of having a more traditional approach with sound equipment. All the technology they've come up with has just detracted from the "feel" they used to get—

♦ **V:** *—like in The Phantom's "Love Me"—*

♦ **RW:** My god! [laughs] After doing that show I started "bor-rowing" from the Grave Diggers. My bass player quit, so Wally joined. We lost our drummer, so Quinn, the drummer joined. At that point we became the SHAMBLES, a more driving band in a Johnny Powers' kind of way. (He did the song "Long Blonde Hair.") I shifted from a mid-'50s to a later-'50s sound.

We started doing shows in Hollywood. That was a break-through, because til then we'd only played in Orange County. We played the Anti-Club and did so well that the owners decided to host a regular rockabilly night. Other clubs followed suit, and rockabilly kinda blossomed again. Bands started to reappear and old bands got back together, once people were coming out to see rockabilly again.

♦ **V:** *This was the late '80s. How did people dress?*

♦ **RW:** The ones who dressed up wore typical '50s clothes. Women were wearing petticoats and full skirts, and then they started dressing more earlier-'50s and '40s. A few girls had Bettie Page hairdos, which are everywhere now. Some girls would wear prom dresses, others would come dressed like sexy pin-up girls, and others would go for a more "exotic" look . . . and I liked it all! Now you can see some pretty striking contrasts: a beautiful woman dressed up looking *so fine* in a vintage outfit . . . but *covered* with tattoos.

When we first started driving to Hollywood to play a show, it seemed like such a big deal—it felt like a big "road trip," even though it was only 40 minutes away! But this brought more confidence and the feeling that maybe I could *get somewhere* playing

music, beyond playing people's houses and small Orange County clubs. Besides the Anti-Club, a Hollywood club called the King King started having rockabilly nights. I remember seeing Russell Scott and his Red-Hots there, and Eddie Nichols. Eddie had been in rockabilly bands, but he always had a vision for *something else* that ended up being Royal Crown Revue.

Right when it seemed like things were beginning to happen, our guitar player quit. I was devastated. I told Wally, "Instead of looking for a new guitar player, I'd rather just start over with a new band. If you'd like to stay with me, that'd be really cool, but

> **Now, if you don't know how to dance, you're at a disadvantage. This is how you meet girls or guys.**

if you want to go ahead with the Grave Diggers thing" (which he was still doing on the side) "I understand." But he agreed to come over and play. Then T.K. Smith from the Stingrays auditioned. He could play Cliff Gallup's licks (from old Gene Vincent records) note-for-note. We jammed together and everything fell together nicely, but we still needed a drummer. I called the Grave Diggers' second drummer, Will B., and he joined. We called our new band "Big Sandy and the Fly-Rite Trio."

♦ **V:** *Where did the name "Big Sandy" come from?*

♦ **RW:** I wanted it to be "So-and-so and the ___," not just one word like the "Thunderbirds." But I felt shy about having my own name there. A lot of country artists had recorded rockabilly under other names (George Jones recorded as "Thumper Jones," and Leon Payne, who wrote so many great country classics, recorded rockabilly under the name "Rock Rogers"). At the time, I was wearing an old mechanics' jacket my uncle had given me with a name patch that said "Sandy." Wally suggested, "How about 'Big Sandy'?" He also came up with "Fly-Rite" from that Nat King Cole song, "Straighten up and fly right." So the name became "Big Sandy and the Fly-Rite Trio."

When our first album (which was recorded in Wally's studio) came out on Dionysus, I thought, "This is so cool; I never thought I'd have my own record out." Next I was amazed to see write-ups

Stylin' Tips From Robert Williams

♦ *VALE: What do you use on your hair?*
♦ ROBERT WILLIAMS: I use a blend: Murray's Pomade, which is kinda thick, along with Royal Crown, which is a lot thinner and gives me the "shine" that I like. It's just a scented petroleum jelly with some sort of wax and Lanolin. We used to spend hours teasing our hair and blow-drying it up into huge pompadours. But after awhile that seemed kinda silly. That "big hair" thing was a product of the '80s.

It's the *music* that's important. Some bands knock themselves out to get the "look" down, but if they'd only put that much effort into their music—!

♦ *V: What kind of shoes do you wear?*
♦ RW: I wear a lot of cowboy boots since our music shifted to the "country" side of the fence. I've been talking to some bootmakers about having some custom-made with my initials on them. I've also had some Western shirts made. I'll bring in an old Gene Autry photo and ask, "Can you do something like that?"

Big Sandy with BIG hair in 1985.

in little fanzines. I was working full-time at a corporate mail/xerox room where I could run off flyers and make phone calls booking shows—Big Sandy headquarters was operating out of that office!

Lee Joseph [owner of Dionysus Records] faxed me a review from an English magazine and I thought, "Wow, this is cool—somebody in England heard our record!" The review was so amazing I felt like crying. At the end it said, "If Tom Ingram doesn't bring these guys over here for one of his Hemsby [England] festivals, he's crazy." (Tom Ingram, a promoter, would bring over original artists from the States like Charlie Feathers or Sleepy LaBeef or Ronnie Dawson.) It turned out that he read the article; a couple of days later he called and invited us over.

When we arrived at Hemsby, I couldn't believe it; there were thousands of kids there. For the whole weekend it was like being in another world—everyone was completely dressed up. It was a full-on festival, with record stalls filled with amazing records, clothing stalls, old cars and hot rods—everything. This was in 1991. I was afraid the audience would be standoffish: "Let's see what *you* can do." But we got a great response that led to several more trips to England and across Europe as well. From that trip we built a whole career over there.

♦ *V: You got paid to do that—*
♦ RW: And we got treated like royalty. The money was great and people went nuts trying to pull you off the stage and waiting for your autograph. It was almost too much to take in all at once. When we came back to the "real world" in America, playing our little shows, it seemed like that had all been a dream.

Around this time our drummer, Will B., quit the band to devote more time to his family. We hooked up with Bobby Trimble, who's still with us. Bobby had been our roadie while he drummed in other bands. Just from coming to our shows, he knew all our songs. One day at a gig Will didn't show up; we had Will's drums but no Will. I thought, "What are we going to do?" But Bobby was more than eager, and he played his heart out. From that point on he was our drummer. We didn't even ask Will

what had happened; that was just *it*—Bobby was in. So it was Bobby who got to go over on our first trip to Europe.

During that trip we met Barney Koumis of "No Hit Records." He was putting out records that were pretty happening in the "rockin' scene"; in England and Europe they don't use the word "rockabilly." He asked us to record an album for his label, so when we came home we started working on one. But first we put out another record on Dionysus: a 78 single that nobody could play! We pressed 500 and they sold out right away.

Then we started working on our second album, for No Hit Records. We heard about a studio in Valdosta, Georgia with amazing vintage tube equipment that was set up exactly like an old studio—it could have been Norman Petty's studio where Buddy Holly recorded. It was owned by Mark Neill who had been in the Unknowns. He knows the old recording techniques, and in a week we recorded *On The Go*. The studio was so authentic-looking, it felt like we had arrived there in a Time Machine! But more important, we got the *sound* we wanted.

We did a couple more European tours and then got another weekly gig. Then Morrissey (of the Smiths) came to a show. It turned out that his opening act had just been forced to fly back to England, so he came to ask us to tour with him. We had a month's worth of dates set up around town, but I thought, "Shit, this is a good opportunity," so we went for it. We played 20 dates around the country in *arenas*. Once I got over the initial nervousness, I loved it. I thought, "This is cool—you can *play* with the crowd and really feed off their energy."

I got valuable experience in learning how to "work the crowd." Actually, the biggest problem was talking between songs—sometimes I start to stutter and just want to run offstage. But after playing for *that* size audiences, it was a lot easier to play club dates. I think back to when I started playing somebody's garage party and being happy with that, not thinking it would get any farther. So far it's been a cool ride!

Discographies

BIG SANDY:
"I Don't Care" (1st appearance on vinyl of Robert Williams and Wally Hersom, backing vocals; Bobbette Records, 7″ 45)
Fly Right with Big Sandy and the Fly-Rite Trio (Dionysus, 1990)
"Don't Desert Me" b/w "I'm Gonna Leave" (Dionysus, 45rpm; Jeems, 78rpm)
"On The Go" (as B.S. & the Fly-Rite Trio; No Hit, 1992)
"Jake's Barbershop" (No Hit, 1993, 4-song EP)
"Stateside Rockabilly" (3 Big Sandy tracks w/guest guitarist Malcolm Chapman, NV Records)
Jumping from 6 to 6 Big Sandy & the Fly-Rite Boys (Hightone, 1994)
Swingin' West (Hightone, 1995)
Feelin' Kinda Lucky (Hightone, 1997. Vernon McNemar, Tel: 510-763-8500; Fax: 510 763-8558. Website: *wvmc3d@earthlink.net.*
CARL SONNY LEYLAND:
"Hot Rhythm Blue Love" 45 (Rockabilly, 45)
"I Like Boogie Woogie" (Rockabilly, 10″ LP)
Blues and Stomps (No Hit, 12″ LP. U.K.)
They Call Me the Boogie Woogie Man (Dinosaur, CD)
Boogie & Blues by Carl Sonny Leyland (Jazzology, CD)
From Boogie to Rock & Roll (Honky Tonk, CD. France)
"I'm a Blues Man" (1st record w/Bob Pearce Blues Band, '81, 7″ 45)
With the KREWMEN: "I'm Gonna Get It/Ramblin" (7″ 45); "What You Are Today," "Roll Them Bones," "All Aboard," "P-Vine Blues," 4 songs on 12″ EP); "Death Letter Blues" (7″ 45).
"Town Called Blues/I'm Gonna Leave My Baby" 2 songs on Waterhole compilation LP, Germany)
Played on: *Live at the Grand Emporium* (Anson Funderburgh & Sam Myers, Blacktop) & *El Dorado Cadillac* (Billy Boy Arnold; Alligator)

♦ V: *Well, I hope you'll always play small shows—*

♦ RW: On a big stage you feel a bit removed from the audience, and you have to work harder to generate energy. Sometimes after we play a large show in San Francisco, we'll play a place like the Ivy Room in El Cerrito: a honky-tonk setting where people are drunk, crowd up around you and get sweaty. I like it when I can smell their breath and feel the heat off their bodies from dancing.

We were in Virginia when we had a blowout with T.K. Smith. We had to tell the promoter, "Well, our guitar player left," and he had to get another band to finish the rest of the tour. I was pretty depressed. By this time we had picked up a steel guitar player, Lee Jeffriess (he joined after our second album). We had met him in England and he ended up moving to New Orleans to play with a piano player, Carl Sonny Leyland (who also joined our band recently). We ran into Lee in Austin, Texas and asked him to join our band. So he was with us on the Morrissey tour. When T.K.

> ### Some girls would wear prom dresses and others would go for a more "exotic" look—and I liked them all!

left, Lee said, "I might as well fly back to England." I thought, "Oh shit, this whole thing is falling apart." I said, "Just wait, Lee; let's see what happens." We went sightseeing in Memphis and looked for records, we stopped in Austin and spent Thanksgiving with some friends, so by the time we got home I wasn't quite as depressed: "Well, we'll figure something out."

We had signed a contract to do one more tour of Europe, so we got in touch with another guitarist we'd met in England, Malcolm Chapman. When we got to England, we practiced for two days and then did the tour. We also made several recordings with him "just for fun" that were released on a compilation record.

On that trip we got reacquainted with another guitarist, Ashley Kingman, who was playing in a British band called Red, Hot and Blue. He said, "Hey, man, I'd like to come over and play with your band; let's give it a shot and try it out." I didn't know much about his playing but I knew he had become pals with Bobby. When we came home we did one show with Lee taking all the solos, and then Ashley arrived.

Almost immediately the *Los Angeles Times* called: "Are you guys playing soon?" Ashley had barely rehearsed with us, but I thought fast: "We'll call you right back." We booked a show at a club called the Doll Hut in Anaheim. The reporter came out to hear our hastily put together band, "Big Sandy and the Fly-Rite *Boys*" (we were no longer a trio). The *Times* did a photo shoot and printed a big feature. I said to Ashley, "Well, I guess you're *in* now"—remember, he had just come over to "try it out." [laughs]

Things really took off from there, because with Ashley, the band headed more in the direction of Western Swing and Country Boogie. Dave Alvin started coming to our shows. I thought, "That's cool. He doesn't say much; he watches us from the back of the room." One night he approached me on the possibility of working together. I used to see him in the Blasters, on bills with X and other L.A. roots and punk bands, and always respected everything he's done. I thought, "Even if this doesn't happen, it's great that he's into us." He got in touch with his label, Hightone Records, and they didn't know what to make of us, but Dave kept pushing for us and then went on to produce our first two Hightone records: *Jumpin' from 6 to 6* and *Swingin' West*.

Our association with Dave opened a lot of doors. We started to reach a more general audience—people who appreciate roots-oriented music (blues and folk) but not necessarily rockabilly.

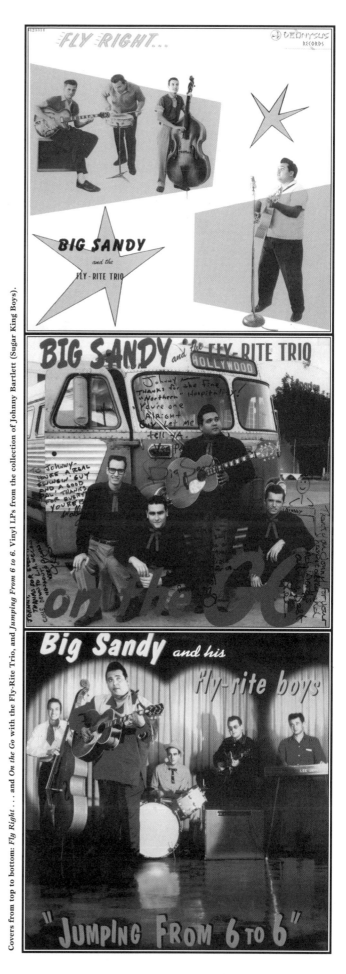

Covers from top to bottom: *Fly Right . . .* and *On the Go with the Fly-Rite Trio*, and *Jumping From 6 to 6*. Vinyl LPs from the collection of Johnny Bartlett (Sugar King Boys).

As faithful as the rockabilly audience is to us, it is a limited thing, and after awhile you start looking for a way out.

Dave took us into the Capitol Records Tower in Hollywood and that was a big deal, because so many great recordings we loved had been recorded there. You walk down the hall to the recording studio and see photos of Gene Vincent, Nat King Cole, Frank Sinatra and Buck Owens and realize they recorded in the very studio you're about to enter. You can really feel the spirit of their music in the room. We recorded for several days. On Sunday, when nobody was there, we wandered all around the building. I was looking for the vault where they kept all their master tapes, but never found it.

♦ V: How would you describe your "sound"?
♦ RW: This dance thing has really taken off, and I think that's good, because it's getting people used to rhythms other than driving, in-your-face ones. But I don't want to just be a dance band, I want to give something more for the people who *are* listening. I try to be a bit clever with the lyrics, and play around with words. With many bands, the drums are the loudest, then the guitars, and the vocals end up buried. That's not appropriate for what we're doing. I want people to be able to understand every word I sing. We have old equipment and try not to play too loud; I want to be *inviting* and pull people in.

♦ V: Maybe you're after a transparent sound rather than a "big" sound—
♦ RW: [uncertainly] Yeah. This question has been on my mind more lately. We were very pleased with the work we did with Dave Alvin, but "it was time for the little birds to leave the nest." [laughs] Had we done the newest album his way, it might have been more commercially successful, but I'm happy to be on a smaller label and have more control. Whether the record fails or succeeds, at least *we did it our way!* I hope that doesn't sound pretentious.

♦ V: What's your future direction?
♦ RW: From the '30s on, there was a healthy development in Western Swing, just as there had been in jazz, blues, country music, etc. At a certain point things got fucked-up. I don't know what happened, but I'd like to pick up the thread from that point and create something fresh. And if we can turn people on to any old, original music that's been overlooked, we'll be happy. There's enough old music *I* haven't heard yet to keep me busy; I don't think I'll ever catch up. Some people would be surprised at what I

listen to, yet I want to incorporate all of it *in a way that makes sense*—even the most oddball choices.
♦ V: *You use jazz scales, yet the music's always accessible—*
♦ RW: Our music will be headed more in that direction as we go on. We just added pianist Carl Sonny Leyland, whose main thing was boogie-woogie, but now he's attacking jazz with a vengeance. He's really hungry to learn more, and I think he's going to draw us more in that direction.
♦ V: *How did swing dance grow in popularity?*
♦ RW: People getting dressed up in '40s clothes and going to shows started as an offshoot of rockabilly. The WILD CARDS seemed to attract swing dancers. In the early *'80s* there was a group of people doing jitterbugging and swing dancing, but it faded away with the rockabilly scene in general. I always wondered what happened to those people; I guess they just "got on with their lives." But it's funny—now that it's re-emerging, I've seen some of those people out again—as if they'd never left!

I first saw signs of the oncoming explosion in San Francisco: you could just *feel* it. Every time I did a show or went to one, there would be more people dancing,

Bus Story

With the kind of music we're doing, you look at old photos and the bands all had their own bus with their name painted on the side—everyone from Bob Wills to Lefty Frizzell to Hank Thompson. We were driving outside Houston and saw a 1940s band bus for sale in a parking lot. We bought it on the spot, and the sellers left. But as we were leaving, the bus died and wouldn't start again. We hired a mechanic and stayed three or four days, and it still wouldn't work. Finally, we got in touch with the people who sold it to us and they claimed we had "done something to it" but we hadn't—we hadn't even gotten it out of the parking lot. To make a long story short, they paid us back *part* of the money, and we were out all the money we'd paid the mechanic. We just wrote it off as a lesson learned.

About six months later some friends spotted another old bus in Fayetteville, Texas, between Austin and Houston. This town was off the main highway, down a little dirt road. We went and this time gave it a good test drive before buying it for $4,500. The owner, Lee Roy Matocha, had a polka and swing band for the Czechoslovakian community—since then, I've found a couple of his old albums with the bus on the cover! We made several trips across the country and got quite attached to this bus. Unfortunately, the transmission and clutch went out recently, and I'm not sure if we're going to get it fixed. But we got so much use out of it; even if we never drive it again, it'll have been worth it. Part of our attachment came from the stories we heard, not just from Lee Roy himself, but from people who came up to us at truck stops, etc. For example, one of the band members got Lee Roy's 14-year-old daughter pregnant in that bus, and got kicked out. There are a lot of "funny" stories like that connected with the bus.

We've since bought a newer Crown '74 schoolbus for $7,500 which we're planning to customize. Now we're creating our *own* stories with this new bus. [laughs]

getting more adventurous in their moves, and getting more into the look, too. Then it started spreading. We cover the country pretty well, and now every town has their swing night or rockabilly/swing night. The dance lessons are pulling in more yuppie types. Now, if you don't know how to dance, you're at a disadvantage. This is how you meet girls or guys.

There was a time when everyone took social dancing classes as part of "growing up"—you see this in old movies, or Beaver Cleaver having to go to his dance classes. It seems like a return to that. Being a musician, I never really learned how to dance—I have the rhythm; I just don't know what to do with it! I don't know the steps, and I feel I'm at a disadvantage now. [laughs]

Dana and Mango have played a big part in this whole swing dance movement. I noticed them about three years ago when the dancing started to really take off. They did these amazing flips and aerial tosses and definitely made an impact—you couldn't help but notice them. Then they started giving lessons: Work That Skirt!

Now the dancing is filtering down to school kids. When we play all-ages shows, 14-, 15-, and 16-year-old kids are coming out, and they've got all the moves down and they're dressed up. I think, "How did it reach *them?*" Teenagers are trying to play this music and put on their own shows at pizza parlors or other places, because they can't get into clubs.

People are dressing '40s style and in other styles like rockabilly. One point I would like to make is: I think any cliquishness that divides the "swing" and "rockabilly" scenes is a shame, because personally, *I* like it all! I meet a lot of people on the road, and those who know the most about the music are generally "regular-looking," while others who are "decked out" don't know much.

A few people started out dressing in this older style to be *different.* But as more and more people do it, it becomes like the *norm.* So now, if you don't go along with it, you're kind of being a rebel against this trend. [laughs]

♦ **V: *Everything goes through cycles—***

♦ RW: And trying to be too "authentic" can make you stale. Musically, there was a period of time when I thought, "Man, I'm going to recreate this period of sound and get it down exactly—even down to the little mistakes they made—*everything.*" Then I started realizing, "This music I like—why do I like it? Because they were *innovating* at the time." So why stop that process? I'm going to take what I can from that and try and come up with something new.

I've seen a melding of punk, ska and swing all into one thing, and I wonder what's going to happen with that. There are bands that call what they play "ska music," but it's got a punk drive to it and they're dressing '40s.

♦ **V: *I like the clothing in the '40s–'50s Sears Roebuck catalogs—***

♦ RW: Certain clothes you can find all the way through them: classic styles. The way I dress is my own choice, and I'm not going to write somebody off because they're not dressed that way.

There was a time when I was never gonna buy a CD player [laughs] and I finally had to give in. I still prefer the *sound* of vinyl, but I actually almost enjoy the convenience of CDs. I do allow myself some modern conveniences, but they are just that: conveniences. In any aspect of life where there's a "new" innovation, I usually prefer what came before.

Getting back to fashion, I go to vintage shops and just can't find XL or XXL sizes. I'm thankful there are repro companies making new clothes in old styles—now I can buy them off the rack. They're making shirts that look like '40s Hawaiian shirts—to me, at least—and they're for sale at the mall. With some of the repros, the companies are even attempting to reach that earlier level of craftsmanship. You buy a *new* shirt and the buttons fall off practically the first time you wear it. Why do people put up with that? How did it get to this point? People just accept that if you

buy something new, it's going to fall apart within a couple of wearings. I think that's crazy. It makes me mad!

♦ **V: *Well, it makes them more money.***

♦ RW: In Yosemite I ran into an older acquaintance, and we started talking about the beginning of the whole vintage "thing." In the '60s, people bought clothes at thrift stores because that's all they could afford. Then they started recognizing what was what, and began collecting this and that. Other people followed suit, not to save money but because they started *trying* to dress that way. So it began out of necessity and then became fashion.

♦ **V: *In a way, I'd like the clothes corporations to start making more repro vintage clothes—***

♦ RW: It's bound to happen, but then that also kills it. And besides, you know the buttons are gonna fall off! [laughs] Ⅴ

Recommended

MAIL ORDER:
KICKS (POB 646 Cooper Station, NY NY 10003). $1 for great catalog.

Steve Hathaway 408-947-1947. 22 back issues of *Western Swing Newsletter* available; complete set $45. Latest issue $2.50, or $10 for 4 issue subscription. Website: *westernswing. com.*

FAVORITE RECORDS:
As a singer, quite a few artists have influenced me, including a number of women. I'm really into KAY STARR, especially her recordings with the Les Paul trio—those are *choice.*

We dedicated our CD, *Feelin' Kinda Lucky,* to two people who passed away this year: FARON YOUNG and RICHARD BERRY. When I was younger I looked for any music out of L.A., and Richard Berry was a big part of the '50s scene, along with Jesse Belvin and Young Jesse. They did solo work and played with vocal groups under different names, but them and a few others are responsible for a lot of '50s R&B, Doowop and vocal material that I heard growing up.

I collect home-recording discs that people used to make in recording booths in drugstores, bus stations, etc. Some people had "home" models; instead of sending a letter to a loved one, they would send a recorded message. I've found quite a few with a recurring theme of people really opening up, letting you peer inside their minds. Some stories are pretty twisted, bordering on insanity. I have a series by a woman talking in a stream-of-consciousness way, making these singularly disconnected statements. It's eerie; you wonder, "What's her story? What happened to her?" Most of these recordings are from the '40s; they're usually dated. Sometimes you find recordings of a band jamming; I've found some cool stuff along those lines.

MOVIES:
I've always been a big Robert Mitchum fan—just about anything he's in, I like. I think he's my favorite actor. He always plays himself.

Most of the movies I like fall into the "psychotronic" category and I try to check out whatever new gems get unearthed. Music has always been my main passion, but I consider myself somewhat of a movie buff. When I was a kid my father would say, "There's this cool movie on TV late tonight; you want to stay up?" [past my bedtime] I took so much from him: my musical taste; my taste for oddball, off-beat, low-budget movies. I feel lucky that I had that growing up.

MAGAZINES & BOOKS:
I try to pick up old Country& Western magazines whenever I can. In magazines, almost anything before the '60s is more interesting than what's being published now.

I found some gay paperbacks from the '50s and '60s and the cover artwork was amazing. There was one with a businessman walking down the street looking out of the corner of his eye at a gang of hoods in leather jackets. One of them is looking back; the businessman is sweating, and you can see the bulge in the leather-guy's pants—I thought it was funny. Somebody must have donated a collection to a thrift store, and I bought 'em all. My mother was cleaning my room when I was out and found them. She got really scared and had a talk with my father and he asked me [concerned], "Are you into this?" They didn't understand how I could just be into the cover art. Though my parents have been a big influence, they've never quite understood why I embraced this culture from the past. They've constantly "gotten on my case" about all the stuff I've collected.

The Hot Shots: L to R: Hiroshi Shishikura, Ken Miura, Chie Kodama, and Enocky Enomoto.

The Hot Shots are a Japanese rockabilly band featuring Enocky Enomoto (guitar, vocals), Chie Kodama (vocals, guitar), Hiroshi Shishikura (bass, vocals) and Ken Miura (drums). The Hot Shots have released two 45s, "Why Don't You Haul Off and Love Me" and "Alone With You," available from Hillsdale Records, POB 641592, SF CA 94164 ($1 for catalog); and Dionysus, Dept R/S, POB 1975, Burbank CA 91507 ($1 for catalog). Enocky's interview is followed by one with the group's female vocalist Chie Kodama.

INTERVIEW WITH ENOCKY ENOMOTO

Besides playing with the Hot Shots, Enocky Enomoto also plays with Jackie and the Cedrics, a great Japanese surf band who have toured America twice.

♦ *VALE: When did you start the Hot Shots?*
♦ ENOCKY: Three years ago. At first I played drums; I was very interested in drums. Then the guitar player left, so I said, "Okay, I'll try guitar." Then our drummer joined.
♦ *V: What kind of music did you want to play?*
♦ E: Old hillbilly, popular jazz, Western Swing—*old* music. There are many CD reissues from the 1930s, '40s. I hope they will be more popular in Japan.
♦ *V: How did you meet Chie?*
♦ E: I came to USA about four years ago and met Deke Dickerson. He said, "Do you know Chie?" She had come to Los Angeles . . . was crazy about rockabilly, and a friend of Deke, Dave, and many other rockabilly people in the USA. I said, "I don't know her," but I came back to Japan and I met her. She said to me, "I want to make an old hillbilly style band," but had no

idea how. I said, "Okay, try me."
♦ *V: How did you meet the bass player?*
♦ E: He worked in a record shop. He asked me, "Are you Enocky from Jackie and the Cedrics?" I said, "That's me!" [laughs] We talked about music, and he said, "I play upright bass." After our first bass player left, I asked him, "Shall we play together?" and he said, "Yes!" We started doing very fast rockabilly 45 songs.

Three or four years ago I came to USA and went to the Southwest and bought a 1952 Fender lap steel guitar. At first it's very easy, because open tuning is easy—*then very difficult!* I wanted to play steel guitar really well, and make a big band: trumpet, saxophone, like Bob Wills & His Texas Playboys. I love trumpet and sax in Western Swing/jazz bands; some of the trumpet is very crude ("bup-bup-bup-bup").
♦ *V: Is there a band like that in Japan now?*
♦ E: Rolling Rocks. They play rockabilly, and include fiddle, saxophone, piano—I recommend them to you. They came to USA to the 1997 Denver, Colorado rockabilly festival.
♦ *V: Jackie and the Cedrics was your first band—*
♦ E: It started July, 1990. For a long time we've played, but still not grown up. [laughs] We just keep only one style: fast! We don't

know surf music very much, but we love it. At first it was like a party or joke band, because we thought surfing music was not so cool. I didn't know about good bands like the Phantom Surfers; we only knew Joe and the Night Riders ('80s surfing) and some bands of Asian origin. But when we played, everybody said, "Great! Great!" We changed our thinking: "Surf music is cool!" That's how we started Jackie and the Cedrics.

♦♦ V: How did you meet those musicians?

♦ E: We were in the same art college. We studied design, textile design, industrial graphics. When we started Jackie and the Cedrics, I'm the most old man, already graduated. Jackie and Jelly Bean were still in school. I saw them play in a ska band, and my friend introduced us. Jelly Bean played trombone in a ska band.

♦ V: Last night, the bass player was wearing a beautiful old Western shirt, and a cowboy hat and boots, and you were wearing an old white Western shirt with two pearl-snap pockets—

♦ E: We got them in America. We came to L.A. a week ago to start our first show. We went to many stores. Now Western shirts are very expensive. I remember five years ago in America not so expensive.

On this trip I bought some 78s, LPs and 45s, but not so much. Deke Dickerson had a booth at the Pasadena Rose Bowl Record Swap. He had a Fender pedal steel guitar for sale, early '60s Model 1000: $500, good price. Very good early pedal steel guitar, hard to find; Speedy West used this. But I didn't buy it; I have no money this time. Deke has very great equipment, record collection, everything. He has an amazing house. He gave me a "Joe Maphis Newsletter" he wrote—it's great.

♦ V: Are there a lot of people in Japan who dress "vintage" or "retro"?

♦ E: Blue denim jeans, sweatshirts, and vintage sneakers are very popular. But very dressy Western style not so popular in Japan.

♦ V: In Jackie & the Cedrics, everyone wears gray matching suits—

♦ E: That's a tuxedo suit. In Japan, hotel boys wear those jackets. They cost $100–$150; not expensive in Japan brand-new. We can wash in washing machine—Jackie and Cedrics' suits good for USA tour! [laughs] Very no-good material, but good for us. Maybe polyester, I don't know.

♦ V: Where did you get your guitar?

♦ E: In Japan. It's a Fender Telecaster; the neck is Stratocaster. It's a no-good guitar: too heavy for me. I'm looking for a lightweight Telecaster, an old one. Refinished, repainted model is good for me because it's *cheap*.

♦ V: Why do you want an old one?

♦ E: I try out really old ones: 1954, '57, '58, in very expensive guitar shop in Japan. At first I thought the reissue model is okay. Then I tried original models: *amazing*—sounded really different. I think most important is if guitar body is very lightweight.

♦ V: Do you have an old amp?

♦ E: I have an old Fender, made in Japan. I'm crazy about amplifier. Amp old—guitar new. My guitar I bought for $300, but my Fender Pro Amp, 1950, I pay over $1,000 in Japan—no good! Last night I used Johnny Bartlett's very small, TV-face amp, looks so cute. Sounds very loud, but small—amazing. I think that amp doesn't need reverb effect, echo effect. I plug straight into it, and it can make good sound. Great amp!

♦ V: Do you only own one guitar?

♦ E: No, I collect bizarre guitars, very cheap Japanese guitars—I love them. I have maybe 40 guitars! Many people gave me guitars. Some people said, "My daddy has guitar, but I can't play and he don't play. If you want guitar, I give you." "Oh, please, please!" But almost always broke, no good guitars!

♦ V: How many records do you own?

♦ E: I have many '80s punk, new wave. It's hard to find 45s in Japan—America is better. Sometime people can find original 45s

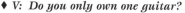

We thought surf music was just "oldies." But when we played, everybody said, "Great! Great!" We changed our thinking.

at good price at record swap meets, thrift shops, antique shops—many places. I want to look for good records in America. I came to USA with Sachiko Fujii, 5-6-7-8's older sister, drummer, she has a vintage clothes/antique shop in Japan. She came to USA and buy many antiques with me. I drove. We went to many, many antique and thrift shops: Texas, Missouri, many places in middle America, and every day we went to antique shops. At first it's very fun, but then a little bit boring because: *every day*. But I very much enjoyed finding 78 records—very cheap in antique shops.

Enocky sings his heart out at the Bottom of the Hill, 8-13-97. Photo: V.Vale

But they're almost all Frank Sinatra and pop. I look for old Hillbilly, Blues, Rhythm and Blues records. I got old records at good price—very fun. This trip I hope to go to Bakersfield.

♦ V: Do you have a lot of CDs, too?

♦ E: Yes. Bear Family is definitely a great label and it's easy to get them in Tokyo—I think there are more there than in the USA!

♦ V: What's your living situation? Are you married?

♦ E: No, I'm single. My guitars are at my papa's house. I live in a very tiny apartment—no good! My family home is very close, not in the center of Tokyo. My papa has a warehouse I use.

♦ V: What do you collect?

♦ E: Old stuff—American. It's hard to get. I got some old country music magazines in America in antique shop. I have magazines on rockabilly and blues. In Tower Records, Tokyo, it's very easy to get *Goldmine*, *Discoveries* and *Vintage Guitar* magazine, plus many other old rock magazines like *Blue Suede News*.

♦ V: Do you have other musical instruments?

♦ E: Harmonica, steel guitar, electric bass. I have an upright bass I bought from my friend for $400—bargain. That's a good price in Japan. I don't play the bass in a band, but I like to play. At first I was a bass player when I was 13. I played Beatles, Credence Clearwater Revival, Deep Purple, hard rock and punk rock: Johnny Thunders & the Heartbreakers, Ramones. I played punk rock bass long time ago. Punk rock easy to play—very good for young people. Yes: passion! *Punk rock is good.*

♦ V: Did you take guitar lessons?

♦ E: No. I learned by myself. When I started guitar, I knew tuning but I knew only two or three chords until two or three years later. Because I'm very lazy.

Cover of the Hot Shots' "Alone With You".

♦ **V: Did you watch guitar instruction videos?**
♦ E: Yeah. I watch video. I can get many good guitar instruction videos; James Burton's is very good. He used a flat-pick *and* one metal finger pick. I tried same style: great!

♦ **V: I hardly see your right hand move, yet I hear all these fast notes, and the flat-pick isn't moving that much—**
♦ E: Many people just do finger-picking or flat-picking. Metal finger-picks are good for *crispy* music. Good tone. I use one metal finger pick on my middle finger.

♦ **V: Are there other girl bands like the 5-6-7-8's in Japan?**
♦ E: Supersnazz, Pebbles. But 5-6-7-8's have a very amazing style; only one.

♦ **V: Where do you buy your boots?**
♦ E: America. They were $50 at the Pasadena Rose Bowl flea market, discounted. I hope a company will reissue boots in this style.

♦ **V: What kind of food do you like?**
♦ E: I love American food. American food is often a mixture: American-Mexican food, American-Chinese food.

♦ **V: Right, it's different than in the native countries . . . You have vintage glasses frames—**
♦ E: I bought four pairs of glasses on this tour. I also bought Ray-Ban sunglasses; they're not old.

♦ **V: Have you been in other bands?**
♦ E: Sometimes I played in different session bands, but I think no good. Like masturbation! One month ago I played with my friend from Evil Voodoo, Japanese garage band, already broken up. The drummer played drums, one guy was guitar player, Supersnazz vocalist, and I played my Flying V guitar. We played Trash R&B, but only once. Bad band!

♦ **V: Can you make a living in Tokyo playing music? Doesn't everybody have day jobs?**
♦ E: Oh, yeah. My band work is no good for my job. My job: I

Discography (all 45s)

JACKIE & THE CEDRICS: "TV Hop/Bird Dog," "Go! Honda! Go!/Velocity Stacks," "Soyokaze/Hurry Up"
THE HOT SHOTS: "Why Don't You Haul Off and Love Me" and "Alone With You."
(Also worth ordering is the rockabilly 45 by The Sugar King Boys: "Tip Top & Three Other Hits.")

make show and display, dioramas for museum, and make models—bad for health; glue very bad! Bass player works in good record store; chain store, but his store is especially country music, old hillbilly, rockabilly and '60s garage band and surfing music. I love his store; he has choice records for sale. Chie has a "normal" job; the drummer works a normal job. We don't have computers, but next month I buy computer; I want to try Internet e-mail. Jackie has computer work with an underground video company. He makes good money; is a master of computer.

♦ **V: I think it's fortunate that everyone can take time off from their jobs at the same time and come to America—**
♦ E: I don't know—maybe we *broke* our jobs! Not easy. **V**

INTERVIEW WITH CHIE KODAMA

This interview was translated by Dee Lannon, herself a gifted female rockabilly vocalist/guitarist now living in San Francisco. In Tokyo, Chie is the proud owner of a 1967 Volkswagen.

♦ **VALE: I think it's unusual that a young woman from Japan becomes a rockabilly singer and guitarist. That's something Japanese society doesn't exactly encourage—**
♦ CHIE KODAMA: I have friends in America who have influenced me, like Dee Lannon. I stayed with her in Los Angeles and got into the rockabilly scene at the Palomino. I lived with Dee for three months back in '92.

♦ **V: What brought you to America initially?**
♦ CK: I love American music, especially from the '50s, and that's why I wanted to come here. I saw Ray Campi, Mac Curtis, and Johnny Carroll play in Japan and I knew that Campi lived in L.A. I was first exposed to this music when I was 11 back in 1983 and

I want us to sound like white people singing black music.

saw the movie *American Graffiti*. I went to my first live show when I was 14 and met other people who were into rockabilly.

♦ **V: At Yoyogi Park, people play rockabilly on their radios and dance to it. Did you ever hang out there?**
♦ CK: My mother used to take me there. Yoyogi Park is a well-known site in Japan.

♦ **V: Do your parents support what you're doing with music?**
♦ CK: They're happy that I'm doing what I like.

♦ **V: What do your parents do for a living?**
♦ CK: Both my parents are hairdressers. My dad does a great job doing "retro" haircuts. They rock.

♦ **V: Where do you live in Japan?**
♦ CK: I live in central Tokyo, but my bass player is a hillbilly. [laughs] He lives in a suburb which is like a country town.

♦ **V: When did you first pick up a guitar?**
♦ CK: Two years ago. [laughs] I bought my first one for $500 through an ad in a Japanese guitar magazine. It's a mid-'50s Kay Silvertone, a cheap guitar that was sold through department stores back in the 1950s. I taught myself how to play with a book.

When the Hot Shots first got together I just sang and didn't play. Then when I started picking it up and taught myself to play chords, the band started pushing me around (they helped me along if I had any questions). [laughs]

♦ **V: How did you learn how to play scales?**
♦ CK: Enocky, my guitarist, taught me that. We started our

group when I first met him. I sent Dee a video of one of our shows before she and I ever met. Every club in Japan videotapes the show and you have the option of buying it.

♦ **V: *That's the way it should be. Last night you videotaped Dee Lannon (backed by the Hot Shots) and the Saturn V—***

♦ CK: We have six cassette tapes full of every band we've played with. I have a tripod, so I just set it up while *we* play.

♦ **V: *Who are some of your favorite singers?***

♦ CK: Clyde McPhatter, Buddy Holly . . . I want the Hot Shots to sound like late '50s/early '60s rockabilly; I want us to sound like white people singing black music. That's my goal.

♦ **V: *Which white people?***

♦ CK: [laughs] Hillbillies, except singing black music.

♦ **V: *What have you done for fun in America?***

♦ CK: I've been scouring all of the swap meets and flea markets that I can find. I've gotten the best vintage dresses here, some vintage cowboy boots, and in Los Angeles I found a 1960s Gibson acoustic guitar for $500 at the Guitar Center—that would cost $1,400 in Japan. I did good shopping!

I also found several records. I got Firehouse Five Plus Two and some '50s Dixieland Jazz from Disneyland. It's the band that used to play in the pavillion at Disneyland—I think it's called Carnation Plaza. Dee told me that Count Basie used to play there!

♦ **V: *Are you a big record collector?***

♦ CK: I have about 800 records and CDs back home in Japan. I spend $100 every week at the bass player's store, which is called Disc Union.

♦ **V: *What female singers do you like?***

♦ CK: Janis Martin, Patsy Cline, Lori Collins of the Collins Kids, Rose Maddox, and Ruth Brown (whom we cover).

♦ **V: *What do you do for a living in Japan?***

♦ CK: Right now I'm working as a receptionist for a large company. I've had many, many different kinds of jobs though. I've worked in a vintage shoe store, cashiered at an electronics store, and was a sales represenative for coffee service to offices. I was a cocktail waitress for a while at the Rocky Top Bar (just like the bluegrass song). It's in the Ginza district. You go in this tiny little door that looks like it leads to an office, then you go up this tiny little clevator, and then you open another office door and all of a sudden you're in a honky-tonk bar. That's where I met Yasu Muranaka, who played steel guitar on our recording. He didn't come to America because he's very busy playing and recording steel guitar with several bands. He's in demand.

♦ **V: *Are your parents supportive of you visiting America?***

♦ CK: Yeah, they're very happy about it. The first time I came to America, I stayed in a church (it was kind of like a hostel). My parents helped facilitate that and I stayed there for a few weeks. Then I stayed on Dee's couch for a while.

I came here in 1991 and took a road trip with the Rolling Rocks who come to L.A. every now and then. The lead singer, Wataru, comes to America a lot to buy stuff. We took a cross-country trip to Florida and back. I bought a stuffed jackalope mounted on a plaque. We visited Sun Studios, Johnny Carroll's house, the radio station that Mack Curtis worked in. When I went back to Japan, I told everyone about meeting Mack Curtis and Ray Campi and how they both still play music. No one could

believe it because they all assumed that they were dead. There was a big rockabilly band at the time, Duke and the Summits (like the Japanese Stray Cats). They contacted Ray Campi and Mack Curtis and brought them back to Japan to perform.

My second trip to America was in 1992, and that's when I met people like Deke Dickerson. I was staying with Dee and she had a weekly gig at the Blue Saloon. Anyway, this is my third trip and I'm planning to come back for this big Las Vegas rockabilly show announced for April, 1999. We don't make that much money here, so we have to save up our money again. [laughs]

♦ **V: *Is there a big retro scene in Tokyo?***

♦ CK: No, not really. In Japan, I don't really play with rockabilly bands as much as I do with punk bands. There are a couple bands, like Rolling Rocks, that people will get all '50s decked-out for. Other bands like that are Dynamite and the Rock'n'Roll Trio, the Rhythm Rockets, and the Rum and Cokes (they're one of my favorite bands). There's also a rockabilly zine in Japan called *Overheat.* They write about rockabilly in Japan and England. But most of the fanzines in Japan are about Psychobilly.

♦ **V: *Do many American rockabilly bands play Japan?***

♦ CK: A few bands like High Noon or Levi Dexter and the Rockats play in Yokahama and in Tokyo at the Gear Club. There's a club called Crocodile that is dedicated to American roots music. And there's also Club 251.

♦ **V: *Have you written any songs?***

♦ CK: Our bass player, Hiroshi, and I have written one song together. It's called "Pretend". It goes like this: "Pretend you love me/Pretend you're with me/Pretend you need me/Easing my troubled mind/Pretend you want me/Pretend you're still mine/Easing my troubled mind/I found you walking with somebody in my dreams/It means ending our love/But I can't get over you [refrain]."

♦ **V: *That sounds "authentic" . . . What's your living situation?***

♦ CK: I still live with my parents. They hate that I dress in '50s clothes; they think I look like a homeless person! [laughs] **V**

Chie Kodama at Bimbo's 8-15-97. Photo: V.Vale

Some Favorites of Chie Kodama

[Note: As previously mentioned, the Hot Shots have two 45s available for $3 each from Hillsdale Records, PO Box 641592, San Francisco CA 94164. Dee Lannon has a CD, *Town Casino,* available for $14 postpaid from Hepcat Records, PO Box 1108, Orange CA 92856 (1-800-404-4117); catalog $1.]

FAVORITE SINGERS: Don & Dewey, Clyde McPhatter, Buddy Holly, Faron Young, Ricky Nelson, Everly Bros, Big Sandy

FAVORITE RECORDS (1990s Bands): Big Sandy *Feelin' Kinda Lucky,* Russell Scott & His Red Hots *Killer Combination,* Deke Dickerson *TJ Tuck & Roll,* Sloe Gin Joes *The Sloe Gin Joes,* Dee Lannon *Town Casino,* Dalhart Imperials *There Ain't No Place,* Dave & Deke *Moonshine Melodies*

(1950s): Tennessee Ernie Ford *16 Tons of Boogie,* Jimmy & Johnny *If You Don't Somebody Else Will,* Santo & Johnny *Stereophonic,* Teen Queens *Rock Everybody*

3

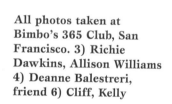

All photos taken at
Bimbo's 365 Club, San
Francisco. 3) Richie
Dawkins, Allison Williams
4) Deanne Balestreri,
friend 6) Cliff, Kelly

4

Work That Skirt! L to R: Mango, Mark, John and Dana. Photo: Mark Jordan

Dana and Mango are the dynamic dance-instruction duo behind Work That Skirt. In the Bay Area they pioneered "street swing" demonstrations at early Swing/Western Swing shows and helped develop the "retro culture dance craze" by giving hundreds of lessons in the past four years. They can be contacted at (415) 664-6946. Their instructional video is available from Slimstyle Records.

♦ *VALE: Did you dance when you were little kids?*
♦ DANA: No, definitely not. I'm amazed that we can even do what we do, because I had no dance training whatsoever—
♦ MANGO: We still have not taken a single lesson, except for ballet way back when. [laughs]
♦ D: We grew up together in Santa Rosa so we're in sync as far

as our backgrounds go.
♦ *V: Were you involved with the punk scene?*
♦ M: Yeah, but I've always been on the outskirts of everything; this is the first time I've really been *into* something. Dana, on the other hand, gets fully into everything—
♦ D: I like taking things to the limit, whether it be mod, punk

rock, new wave, raves, reggae—I even spent a summer on the Rastafarian island, man! No matter what the style or scene, really *going for it* with no namby-pambying around is much more fun.

♦ **V: How did you learn the wild aerial dancing you teach?**

♦ M: The problem with most formal dance lessons is: there's no instant gratification. You have to start with the absolute bare minimum and work your way up, and that could take *years*. We just said, "Forget it—we're going to *teach ourselves* how to do it!" So we watched movies and practiced dancing in our living room in Santa Rosa.

♦ D: A friend told us about the Club Deluxe around Christmas '93. So we drove to San Francisco to check it out. There were two couples dancing. A rockabilly band, The Barn Burners, was playing—

♦ M: It was the first time we'd ever seen live couples dancing.

♦ D: It was Brent [an early swing dancer; bartender at the Deluxe] and his partner. Looking back, they were doing very basic stuff—

♦ M: —way more basic than what goes on now. We got out on the dance floor and that's how we met Peanut (AKA Larry, another early Bay Area swing dancer); he was just totally amazed by our dancing. After we did one flip over the back, he rushed over and said, "Make sure you girls keep coming back here!"

♦ D: Then everybody told us about the New Year's Eve show featuring St. Vitus Dance—

♦ M: We went, and Vise Grip came onstage in a diaper—he was "Baby New Year." If you've ever seen Vise, he's completely bald. At that point, they were playing the Cafe Du Nord every Thursday night.

♦ D: After the show Vise asked us, "Will you come to our shows and dance? It really gets the crowd going—"

♦ M: "—and we'll put you on the guest list no matter where we play."

♦ D: The beauty of it was: all we did was flip each other—that's it. And compared to the way we dance now, it was nothing. But people were so amazed: two girls dancing and doing this thing that looked so wild. I remember thinking, "What's the big deal? We're just having a good time, joking around."

♦ M: At the time we had jobs teaching after-hours classes at the local YMCA. We'd drive to San Francisco and do the dancing, then come back to Santa Rosa and work at the YMCA. We started saving money so we could move to San Francisco.

♦ D: People always used to ask us, "Where'd you learn to dance?" Then someone said, "You guys should teach!" and that was it.

♦ **V: What's the dance philosophy of Work That Skirt?**

♦ M: With most dances (fox trot, Charleston, etc) the format is so precise that it takes forever to learn. We wanted to teach a type of dance that people could come in, take a class for half an hour, get out on the dance floor, and feel comfortable using the three or four moves that they had. It worked and people went wild for it.

♦ D: When we first moved to San Francisco I got a job managing a vintage clothing store. The owner lived in L.A. and he pretty much gave me the run of the store; I did the buying, selling—everything. At nights, that would be our studio and that's where we taught our dance lessons illegally [laughs]

♦ M: All our dance moves were written out on a piece of paper, just as informal as could possibly be.

♦ D: We started giving four-week "sessions," mostly to people who had seen us dance. Except for a one-month vacation, we have not stopped teaching our weekly dance lessons since.

♦ **V: Who thought of the name "Work That Skirt"?**

♦ D: XTC had two song titles we liked: "Work That Skirt" and "Shake Your Bag of Bones." But "Work That Skirt" was *it* for us.

♦ **V: What's your advice on clothing to wear while dancing?**

♦ M: I've ruined more 40-year-old dresses that have come to me in perfect condition; after one night they're ripped and

gone. It's so sad.

♦ D: We used to think, "Okay, we're going to a swing show, so let's dress '40s." And if we went to a rockabilly show, we wore '50s prom dresses. For hairstyle ideas, we studied old Betty Grable movies and books. We got our hair done by Dave Anthony and watched him very closely. Now, we often just do it ourselves.

It's fun; it's art. When I was in junior high and into punk rock I'd be sitting at a bus stop and people would almost get into car wrecks looking at me.

♦ M: Now people will ask me [sarcastically], "What is it—'50s night?" But I just don't care anymore about being absolutely "authentic." Even if my clothes come from the Gap, I pull it off in such a way that I still have that "look." It makes it so much easier to shop at thrift stores now because you don't have to look at the label to see if it's really old; you just buy it if you like it.

♦ D: There *are* collectors who are compelled to be very precise about everything, and I think that's silly. It doesn't matter: wear a '30s dress with '40s shoes if you want, for chrissake! Right now, I'm wearing a "modern" shirt I got in Chinatown. My shoes are from Leeds: $19! The sweater I have on is from the '50s; I got it in Santa Cruz for $2.

♦ M: After a while, looking at old movies and photo books, you start getting an "eye." Now I can pick out architecture and furniture and know what era they're from; when you get into that mindset, you just *know*.

Learn to Dance

Work That Skirt's
Dance Moves

1. Bring me in
2. Basic turn
3. Roll in
4. The Ben
5. Through the legs
6. Go for a walk
7. Go for a walk two times
8. Snapper II
9. Back stabber
10. Pretzel
11. Pretzel kick
12. Pretzel medley
13. Cinderelli
14. Midgets wrapped in leather
15. The New York
16. Work that skirt
17. Switch-a-roo
18. Rock step
19. Charleston
20. The Flip
21. Fall back
22. Grease move
23. The Jim II
24. The Fake
25. Dips: the back breaker and the pedestal
26. Going for a run
27. Swishy hips
28. Kick to the I, II

♦ D: We are very proud that our house doesn't have one modern device, except a toaster oven.

♦ M: We need another room because we need to start working on another theme—we do *theme rooms.* Our living room is tiki, our hallway is Western, our kitchen is girly '50s kitsch.

♦ *V: Do you have any hair-dressing tricks to pass along?*

♦ D & M: Moleculars!

♦ *V: What's that?*

♦ D: The Richard Caruso Curler.

♦ M: It's steam-rollers. We should be spokesmodels for this guy. [laughs]

♦ D: You put them on this weird salt-and-water machine and they get all steamy and it takes like five seconds to do your hair.

♦ M: You don't have to wear your curlers to bed like they used to. You can get major Shirley Temple curls by the time your make-up is ready. Our second tip is: go see Kim Long, our hairdresser. She's at Jaboh (1457 Haight St.). She's great. And she's been into "retro" hairstyling for a long time.

♦ *V: Do you have any other techniques?*

♦ D & M: Rats!

♦ D: They look like *S.O.S.* pads made out of nylon.

♦ M: You get them in your specific hair color: black, brown, blonde.

♦ D: If your hair's long, you take the rat and roll your hair up like a sausage and pin it. It should be very smooth and have substance underneath. We used to just *live* on rats.

♦ *V: This seems more original than the basic Bettie Page/Barbara Stanwyck "do."*

♦ M: My favorite now is the French-twist in the back with a bunch of curls on the top.

♦ D: I'm dying my bangs silver; I'm taking it to a different limit!

♦ *V: Do you ever use pomade?*

♦ D: There's a lot of hair pomades, and we've tried them all! [laughs]

♦ *V: Well, what works the best?*

♦ D: It depends on what kind of hair you have and if you're a guy or girl. For guys, Murray's rules. It's thick, like paraffin wax. There's also Royal Crown which is more petroleum-based, and then there are these oils— you could go to town! For us, all that stuff just gets rid of the frizzies. That's our big plight: get rid of frizzy hair!

♦ M: Normally, we would have afros! [laughs] Dana wears a gold tooth; she's not worried about "authenticity." It's all about having as much fun as you possibly can. You can do the glamour girl, or the sassy bad girl with the spiked heels and scarf.

♦ *V: Can you dance in heels that high?*

♦ M: Yeah, these are really good dancing shoes. They're Mary Janes with an extra high heel.

♦ D: Vintage shoes may look cool, but they're often very uncomfortable. Besides cute little lace-up granny shoes and loafers, I have a hard time with shoes.

♦ M: But they're making great shoes these days because the '40s look is back. I've found shoes at Kinney's, Macy's, etc. I look for rounded toes—nothing pointed.

♦ D: I found a pair of two-tone "spectator" shoes and wore them so much that they've been fixed about nine times. You know how saddle shoes have the black in the center? Spectators are just the opposite. You have to have good shoes on when you're dancing, or it's all over.

♦ M: For just everyday wear I love my penny loafers. And they still make those exactly like they did back in the '50s.

♦ *V: Remember when there were all these articles warning against high heels, saying they caused curvature of the spine, etc?*

♦ D: Well, worse things could happen—

♦ M: Yeah—imagine these outfits with Birkenstocks!

♦ *V: Do you still have day jobs?*

♦ M: I'm a nanny in Berkeley from 9–5:30 Monday through Friday. When that ends I'll be back in the job market.

♦ D: I work at an animation company, Wild Brain, doing office work. It's a really cool place. Their Christmas party was totally "swing" and they're all into it now. They're really supportive of me, especially when I need any time off, because I need a *lot* of time off.

♦ M: We both have jobs that are flexible. When I was hired, I walked into these people's house and they had a picture of Cab Calloway on the wall. I mentioned that I teach dance lessons and they said, "We *love* dancing; you're hired!"

♦ D: Sometimes we feel like we're always going and there's never time for rest. I work from 7:30 in the morning to 11 at night during the week. On weekends we go out and round up more business. But what would we do otherwise?

♦ *V: Talk about the press you've received—*

♦ D: We've gotten a lot of press, and our favorite interview was with a normal married Joe where we gave him a "swing makeover." [laughs] We took him shopping and he bought a tie, tie clip, a pair of spectator shoes, Murray's hair pomade, got his hair cut by Kim Long—basically we got him a whole outfit—and then took him to a party with a band and taught him how to dance.

♦ *V: You give weekly lessons at 330 Ritch Street—*

♦ M: One thing I like about that club is: the crowd is so diverse. We have a couple of really old couples—regulars—that just groove out. It's mostly people who just want to learn to dance; they're not there to show off their clothes. I also like the Deluxe, which feels like "home."

In a way we're in a catch-22 with our business. It's wonderful that there's a lot more people getting involved, but it's kind of sad, too. It's very crowded now at shows—I haven't full-on *danced* for a very long time (unless I'm performing). Like we said, the first night we went to Deluxe it was practically empty. Now if you go there on a Friday night—forget it! You can't walk from one end to the other.

♦ D: But it's been great for the bands, the bars, and great for our business.

♦ *V: The media have done their best to associate this swing phenomenon with the revival of "traditional values." And they always mention cigars and martinis—*

♦ D & M: Ugh! I hate martinis!

♦ D: Why carry that glass around—it just spills everywhere.

♦ M: But at least this group of people doesn't seem to be on speed or heroin. Admittedly, most of us drink and smoke cigarettes, but it's all legal—that much you can say for it. This scene is a lot cleaner—

♦ D: —and more respectful. A lot of people *are* trying to do things like light your cigarette.

♦ M: We know people who don't smoke who carry cigarette lighters just to do that.

♦ D: It's not like having someone light your cigarette means you're giving up yourself. I've always been a strong woman; I'm a gal and proud of it. But I do like the old values and respect.

♦ M: It's courtesy among everyone, between women *and* men. I like a man pulling out the chair for me. We've had people say, "Oh, this dancing is so sexist because the man leads." But it's tra-

Come on-a my house . . . Dana and Mango in their living room, 3-15-97. (Note Tiki bar in the background.) Photo: V. Vale

ditional for the man to lead . . . *somebody's* got to do it.

♦ D: I also think it's "growing up." When I look at punk rock kids today on Haight Street, I have a "been there, done that" attitude. After having been angry and full of angst, I think it's healthy to slow down a little and groove out on the "swing thing."

♦ M: Take time to smell the roses.

♦ V: *I don't think I'll ever get to the point where I can wear a '40s suit—*

♦ M: And you don't have to, because it's just fine to be exactly who you are.

♦ V: *At the same time, I enjoy looking at people who dress in the retro style. I saw this couple at Bimbo's and the man was wearing this bright electric blue zoot suit, but I think it was new—*

♦ D&M: That's Johnny Swing!

♦ M: My ex-boyfriend. [laughs] He gives lindy-hop lessons at the Hi-Ball Lounge.

♦ D: It was a zoot suit and it was new. You can get them made in L.A. for $500-$700. There are a few people who make them here now. The people in L.A. [El Pachuco, Fullerton] are the same people who make all of Big Bad Voodoo Daddy's and Royal Crown's. You have to get those suits made because you can't find them anymore. They're sharp. The people who actually wore them back in the '40s were few and far between, so you can't find them in thrift stores.

♦ M: If you were a real clean-cut businessman, you wouldn't be caught dead in a zoot suit back then. Nor would you wear the big-brimmed hat with the feather—that was something associated with Harlem pimps, drug dealers, hustlers, etc.

♦ D: Vise Grip has a real zoot suit he got from a preacher; what's that all about? [laughs]

♦ M: Everybody leads a double life now and then, including men of the cloth.

♦ D: Those suits are like art. Johnny was really going for it with the bright blue zoot suit up to here, the watch-chain and the

matching shoes—the whole nine yards—

♦ M: He's a plumber by day—

♦ D: Yeah, wears acid-wash jeans and a beeper. [laughs]

♦ V: *It seems that it is still possible to have a lot of style without the big bucks.*

♦ D: Men's clothes are a lot more expensive—

♦ M: But a guy can wear the same blue suit every time he goes to Bimbo's and just change his tie. Whereas if I wore the same dress all the time, people would notice.

♦ V: *What ties are preferred?*

♦ D: Wide and short. Hand-painted ones are good. Girly ties are real *in;* some people are painting them now. There are also reproductions that I think are corny.

There are people from 19 to 76, and everybody's just as fully into it as the next.

♦ M: It's because they don't use the original solid-colored ties, which are hard to come by. They use modern ties, and no matter how hard you try to make a tie look "authentic," it just doesn't.

♦ V: *Where do people get the two-tone shoes?*

♦ D: Allen-Edmonds is still making two-tones. You can get them mail order. They've been around, I think, since the '20s. They're expensive, but they're amazingly made and are warranted for life.

♦ M: Like we were saying before, you can find two-tone shoes if you just keep your eyes open; I've even found them at the mall. I just pop into every little shoe store that I see.

♦ D: There's a good store in Kensington (next to Berkeley) called Jon Lundberg's. The guy is from those days and he still dresses that way. He sells the clothes and collects them. He's old, almost 80 years old. *He* has the stories—

♦ M: He chats with all the young kids that come in.

♦ D: He's quite a character, to say the least. You can just sit down and have a history lesson for eight hours.

♦ M: There's this other friend of ours named Audrey who turned 76 this year. She still hangs out. She comes to see Lavay Smith (one of our favorite bands) every Saturday night and knows all the words to all the songs. She's always got a front-row table. Again, that's one thing I love about this swing revival: the age group is so diverse. There are people from 19 to 76, and everybody's just as fully into it as the next.

♦ V: *At swing shows, the main excitement is in watching the dancers.*

If you're having emotional problems, go out and dance. It's the cure-all!

♦ M: But it's exciting for the bands, too. When they're up there and see us dancing, they get much more excited, rather than looking out into a sitting audience.

♦ V: *That was another punk principle: trying to erase the dichotomy between the audience and the band. It was a reaction against the superstar onstage with 10,000 people sitting in an audience. I see that parallel with swing because I go as much to see the dancers as the bands. I don't have to wear ear plugs, and I can actually decipher the lyrics—*

♦ M: And usually when you go see swing bands play, the shows are in really neat places, like Bimbo's or the Great American Music Hall. The Cafe Du Nord was an old speakeasy. They're beautiful clubs, rather than going to some warehouse.

♦ D: The first time we went to Bimbo's we were late and came running in, and "Sing, Sing, Sing" was playing. It was such an overpowering experience with this huge band performing it.

♦ M: It was the first time we'd ever been there and we passed through the red curtains and went "Whoa! This is what it's all about!" That place is so beautiful.

♦ V: *In this scene, the dancing also gives people something to aspire to. In punk, anyone could do the pogo (not to mention slam dancing), but this is an art form. Nevertheless, you can take a half-hour lesson, learn four basic steps and go out on the dance floor—*

♦ D: We give them the tools and say, "Just groove out and make up your own moves." That's what we did. Then we made up names for them: the "Backstabber," etc.

♦ M: Basically, what we do is get you comfortable with dance and you take it from there and go to town.

♦ V: *At shows the dancers are drenched in sweat. It's kind of like a substitute for sex—*

♦ D: That's very true. It is romantic to dance with somebody. Even if you're not attracted to them, there is definitely something about the sweatiness and *getting down*. When I'm dancing, I'm not thinking about anything; I'm completely on this other plane. If I'm really "going for it," I'm not thinking "Okay, what's the next step?" I'm "zenned out," I'm out in left field.

♦ M: That's what we tell our students, too.

♦ D: We say, "You just have to zen out. Get zen, get down and fly."

♦ M: You can't worry about everybody watching you and all that kind of stuff.

♦ D: If you screw up or fall, you have to just run with it.

♦ V: *Many of these dance couples are so synchronized on a non-intellectual, animal-intuitive level. To me, it's a metaphor for some kind of hope that men and women can get along better in the future—*

♦ D: Yeah, we could do Swing-dancing Therapy. Ohmigod—that's a whole new world!

♦ M: Well, we have seen couples that get out there and are ready to kill each other.

♦ D: It's just like exercise. It gets your brain and your endorphins working. As a couple, you're working together, not sitting down and trying to figure something out verbally. Every time I dance I feel better. When I'm sick or have a cold, then I go out and dance and it usually clears up.

♦ M: When we were still living in Santa Rosa, we got invited to a private party at Bimbo's for one of the owners. St. Vitus Dance was playing and they asked us to come along. I was violently ill the whole day long; I must have had food poisoning or something. When Dana came to pick me up I was still sick, but I got all dressed up and ready to go. When we got to Bimbo's I thought, "Okay, I'll just have some cranberry juice and then I'll be alright." But I started getting really sick again. Dana said, "Why don't you just have one dance with me before we go home?" I danced and after that I was absolutely fine: no stomach-ache, no queasiness, no headache. I danced all night long.

♦ D: It's good for colds, stuffy noses, head colds—you'd think it wouldn't be, but it is.

♦ M: And if you're having emotional problems, go out and dance. It's the cure-all!

♦ D: That's why we're so healthy! Dance gets you going; it's *beyond* exercise. John [dance partner] and I were onstage and this older woman said to us, "Gosh, you guys are so sweaty! They've got *pills* for that now." Actually, those pills are really bad for you.

♦ M: We'd always joke about how when we walk into a club we're always so primped, not a curl out of place. But by the time we leave, we're a mess. We're sweaty, no more make-up on, the hair is down, the shoes are off . . .

♦ D: Yeah, all the jewelry is off, the pins are out. We're hobbling,

Mango and Paul at Bimbo's 365 Club. Photo: V.Vale

we've got shin bustings—

♦ **V: *Does that happen much?***

♦ D: We get kicked in the shins a lot.

♦ M: At Bimbo's especially because it's really crowded. People step on your feet . . .

♦ **V: *Those are the occupational hazards.***

♦ M: Dance at your own risk. If you're not ready to get a little bit hurt, don't even bother.

♦ D: But at crowded shows like that, there's no point for us to be dancing at all. They do this thing now called "The Cat's Corner." They did it back in the old days. It's like a break-dancing thing.

♦ M: "The Corral" is what we like to call it.

♦ D: At Bimbo's, the crowd opens up in the middle of the floor and you get to showcase your dancing. Which is as fun as anything. That's the only time you really get the room or time to get in there and *show your stuff.*

♦ M: Any other time you're dancing and bumping into people.

♦ **V: *Let's hear a bit more about swing dance injuries—***

♦ D: As of right now I'm nursing a broken foot. In the second week of July, John, Mango and I went to teach classes at the Rockin' Rhythmbilly Festival in Denver. The night before the classes were to begin, John and I were trying out this new flip move where he picks me up and throws me over him. I was wearing really high heels and landed on his shoe and fell off my shoe and broke my foot. But it took about six weeks to discover it was broken. Right now we're shooting an instructional *Work That Skirt* video, so my doctor taped up my foot. I'm waiting to get a cast on, but if it heals in a month, maybe I won't have to.

♦ **V: *Why didn't you know it was broken?***

♦ D: It hurt really bad. I started wearing really high heels and platforms because this made me feel a lot better: I could dance, walk, etc, but as soon as I put on flat shoes I couldn't walk. My doctor said that wearing platforms put a natural arch in my foot, thus facilitating healing!

♦ **V: *Can you still teach with a broken foot?***

♦ D: Oh sure, no problem. Nothing's stopping me!

My doctor said that wearing platforms put a natural arch in my foot, thus facilitating healing!

♦ **V: *Let's hear about other injuries—***

♦ D: A friend of mine, Cathy Walker, shattered her knee on the DNA floor. They had a hardwood floor that wasn't properly maintained; it was uneven, with pits in it. She was doing a flip and that was it! She had a major cast for six months.

I got injured during a video shoot at Cafe Du Nord for Cherry Poppin' Daddies and I couldn't stop because they were filming. We were doing a flip and John didn't take me over fast enough and wrenched my left arm over to the side—I landed wrong. I had to flip him, too, with the same arm, and ended up doing all this nerve damage. I couldn't move it for two weeks—it was really scary. But I had acupuncture and that really helped. I don't think Mango ever hurt herself. John never hurts himself; once in a while I step on his foot.

We were scheduled to teach swing dance to the President! It was at a party for the military base closure at Treasure Island: a swing event with Lavay Smith playing—she got me the gig. The night before, I twisted my ankle and couldn't even walk. Simultaneously, the President got called away to an emergency peace meeting in Costa Rica. The cancellation was so sudden; I had given the Secret Service my social security number and everything.

L to R: Mango, Cari Merritt, Tracy Dick, Lavay Smith, Jessica Brooks, Tammi Webster and Dana.

♦ **V: *Your near-brush with history . . . Tell us about the lindy-hop—***

♦ D: There's a lindy-hop society; they go to 435 Broadway and the Hi-Ball. They're way more specific about the music they dance to; they don't lindy-hop to rockabilly.

♦ M: There has to be a definite 8-count song, or you can't do it. You have to have a partner that knows the lindy-hop exactly the same way you do. The lindy-hop is really hard. I tried, and I think I'm a good dancer, but in two hours I didn't even get down the first basic swing-out.

♦ D: There's been a lindy-hop society since the '60s. It's mainly older people, although there is a younger crowd of people moving in. They take up too much room and they're snotty to us—[laughs]

♦ M: —because the type of dance that we do is not traditional swing. But I have a hard time with that because originally the lindy-hop was something that people *made up.* The kids listening to the music weren't counting out 8 beats as they moved their feet. Throughout the years it has become a much more contrived and precise thing. Whereas with what we do, if somebody does a dance move "wrong" and asks, "Did I do that the right way?" well, if it looked good I always say, "It wasn't exactly the way we showed you, but it looked really good and you should keep it up."

♦ D: "Street Swing" is the term we've coined.

♦ M: We started learning how to dance on the streets, with friends of ours.

♦ D: The street in front of the Deluxe was our stomping ground. It would get too crowded or too hot inside—

♦ M: —so we got out on the street and practiced doing flips and whatnot.

♦ D: With lindy-hopping it's all mapped out for you.

♦ M: On the fourth count you have to be in exactly the same spot with your partner.

♦ D: I can't get the lindy-hop. I don't *want* to get it—that's probably it. Johnny Swing teaches the lindy-hop—

♦ M: He's really good and he looks awesome when he does it. But when lindy-hoppers see what we're doing, they think we're really messing up their rhyme and reason.

♦ V: **What are some more differences between street swing and lindy-hop?**

♦ D: The lindy-hop was a made-up dance by Frankie Manning (and others) and it's different now than back then. Today's lindy-hop is a lot harder to learn. Street swing is much less formal; you're not messing up unless you drop the girl. There are more aerials and flips, whereas lindy-hop is lower to the ground and the footwork is more intricate and complicated.

In the documentary about Cab Calloway, *Minnie the Moocher,* there are amazing performances—nobody dances like that anymore. They were made of rubber bands back then, I swear! Today's lindy-hopping seems a lot more straight and narrow. But dancing's dancing; it's all fun until somebody breaks an ankle!

♦ V: **Do you object to the term "retro" at all?**

♦ M: No, I think it's kind of funny: "Retro Girls." [laughs] We're coming up with a whole new slang—

♦ D: Retrodisiacs!

♦ M: I see it as "everything being art." Now you can buy a plastic toaster, but back then you could buy this beautifully-designed chrome model. They really put care into everything they made.

♦ D: All the clothes used to be double-stitched. Clothes today aren't made like that at all. They fall apart because we're living in a disposable society.

♦ V: **In a way, the retro movement is a protest against that—**

♦ D: Yeah, it's a Recycling Movement! [laughs] One rule we have is that everything has to *work*. We can't just have a really cool clock that doesn't tell time, otherwise we'd get way out of control with stuff! I hate it when you're at a flea market and the person informs you that, "It's bakelite from the '30s," and they're charging $100 for it.

♦ M: They're telling you what era it's from and how it's worth a hundred million dollars. But it couldn't be worth that much, because it can still be found at a thrift store down the street. There's the thrill of the search, too—in a thrift store where everything else is crap, your eyes go right to something great.

♦ D: And the beauty of it is that it's probably three bucks. That's when you know it means something to you.

♦ V: **Basically, you're not supporting the consumption of new corporate products—except for shoes.**

♦ M: You've got to have some things that are modern, there's no getting past it: underwear, socks, toothbrushes . . . We had a '62 Chrysler that was cute, but it was hard to park and kept breaking down. Now we drive cars that are cheap to fill up with gas.

♦ D: Once we joked about never going into any building that was modern, and only eating in restaurants that maintained their original decor. But we never really did this. We just thought it would be so funny if we were that "anal" about this whole thing. [laughs]

♦ M: Like, we wouldn't use a product that wasn't made back then. You could buy it new today, but it would have to be a product that existed back then.

♦ D: But we broke down on something like voicemail; we needed to check our messages!

♦ V: **Do you buy old books? Or do you concentrate on old magazines, in terms of your reading research?**

♦ M: We buy lots of used coffee table books. Books on fashion. We have a book on bakelite and one on old telephones.

♦ D: I have a great book on big bands that I've learned a lot from, and a reproduction of an old 1940 Sears-Roebuck catalog including all the prices. They kill me.

♦ M: Add a zero to those old prices and that's how much everything costs now. Something that was $15 is now $150.

♦ D: We also read a lot of autobiographies, like Mezz Mezzrow's *Really the Blues.*

♦ M: He's a bit earlier than "swing," more '20s and '30s, but it's still great—especially the lingo that he uses.

♦ D: The glossary in the back is really cool. You learn what actually went on back then, whereas the movies make everything more glamorous than it really was.

♦ M: In the same respect, the way we live our lives now is a lot more glamorous than it was in the '40s. If we were girls our age then, we'd be working in the steel mill waiting for our husbands to come home from the war.

♦ D: No way would I prefer to live back then. I'd just like to go back and get the clothes and immediately return. [laughs]

♦ M: Maybe hit a few night clubs, too.

♦ D: It's not as glamorous as it was made out to be, considering what was going on: the Depression, the war, followed by the McCarthy era. I learned about all that from talking to people like Jon Lundberg—I *love* talking to old people! They tell you all these amazing stories about what actually went on; it's the greatest way to learn and to do research on music, fashion—everything. A lot of people in the swing scene are very knowledgeable about all the eras. My friend Tanya Deason (Vise's fiancee) blows me away with how much she knows about music.

♦ M: Someone like Mark Jordan [Mango's dance partner/*Swing Time* photographer] was really into the clothes and the fashion and he found the Deluxe—it's interesting how everybody converged there. More than anything, it's a group of people who share a common interest.

♦ V: **I'm trying to project four or five years down the line. Will people be sick of swing music because there wasn't enough variety of songs?**

♦ D: Swing music has always had some kind of audience, although the wild lindy-hopping went underground for a long time. But the "retro" lifestyle is here to stay. People will continue to die and their stuff will turn up in thrift stores. Sometimes I think about what will happen when we have children, because we look more like their great-grandparents—

♦ M: And the majority of the photos we take are all in black and white. If somebody came across our things just ten years from now, they'd be utterly confused: "How old were these women?"

Some dancing acrobatics at the Deluxe. Photos: Mark Jordan

♦ D: With this swing business, I think it's a passing phase for a lot of people. People will get into it and change their whole lifestyle, then they'll just mellow out and go back to "normal." Not to say it's abnormal now, it just won't be such a "hip" thing.

♦ M: But I'm always going to appreciate swing music and love old things. That'll be a part of my life forever. I think a lot of it has to do with the time in our life when "retro" hit us, too. If we were 18 and getting into this, I could see it being something we did for just a year or two. But we're at a point in our lives where we're really establishing our lifestyles. But who knows—I could become a Buddhist next week and move to New York! [laughs]

♦ *V: Can you sum up the philosophy you apply to dance?*

♦ M: Do what feels natural, what feels good and makes you happy.

♦ D: Run with it. Let go. People have so much freak-out stuff going on, insecurities and everything, that all needs to be put aside. And that's hard to do when you're trying to learn something that you've never done before, in front of a bunch of people. But if you can do it, you're really going to be quite impressed with yourself.

♦ M: When somebody is really uptight, you say, "Loosen up!" and they go, "Oh—I can just dance and have a good time?" "Yeah, that's right—that's what you're here for." All of a sudden they get the *beat* and that's what moves you. And I always say, "Don't forget to smile, everybody!"

♦ D: "I'll hold your hand!" "Have fun!"—that's all it is for me. If you're not having fun and you're not smiling, get off the dance floor godammit! [laughs] **V**

Recommendations

Books:
Big Band Almanac by Leo Walker: Good for hair-dos, fashion tips and big band info.
Really The Blues by Mezz Mezzrow: Great lingo glossary.
Continental Restyling #20: $10ppd 9 Rue de la Libération, 88360 Ferdrupt, France. 011-33-3-2925-8864
Pulp #3: $5, POB 1856, Hollywood CA 90078
Bettie Page Confidential by Bunny Yaeger, intro by Buck Henry
Woodchopper's Ball: Woody Herman's autobiography
Hot Rod by David Perry
Bands, Booze & Broads by Sheila Tracy
Once Upon A Telephone: An Illustrated Social History
Unseen Elvis: Candids of the King by Jim Curtin
Kisses ed. Lena Tabori
Art Plastic: Designed for Living by Andrea DiNoti
American Bar by Charles Schumann
Great Fashion Designs of the Forties: Paper Dolls in Full Color by Tom Tierney
50 Years of Movie Posters ed. John Kobel
Family Book of Home Entertaining by Florence Brobeck
A History of Films by John L. Fell
Good Deeds Must Be Punished by Irving Shulman
Simple Art of Murder by Raymond Chandler
Roy Rogers King of the Cowboys
Crazy Woman Blues by J.F. Burke

Movies:
Anything on AMC.
Minnie the Moocher: Cab Calloway documentary with great dancing by Frankie Manning.
Malcolm X, Swing Kids: Great dancing.
Good Clothes: *Evita, The Women* (good hair & clothes), anything with Betty Grable.

Albums
Brian Setzer Orchestra
Dave & Deke Combo: *Hollywood Barn Dance*
Bob Wills: *24 Greatest Hits*
The Life, Times & Music Series: Swing Kings
Cab Calloway: *Are You Hep to the Jive?*
Best of Big Bands: Red Norvo featuring Mildred Bailey
Viper Mad Blues: 25 Songs of Dope & Depravity
Risque Rhythm
Laughter from the Hip: 24 Jazz Comedy Classics

Swing & Western Swing Bands
Blue Plate Special (Chico), Acme Swing, Atomic Cocktail, Johnny Nocturne, Lavay Smith, Vise Grip & the Ambassadors of Swing, Johnny Dilks, Rhumba Bums.

Favorite S.F. Clubs:
330 Ritch St, Bimbo's, Cafe Du Nord, Hi-Ball, 435 Broadway, Great American Music Hall, Fillmore, Coconut Grove, Club Deluxe, The Usual (San Jose)

Hair and Make-up Tips:
"Rats": good for those big up-do's. At Beauty Supply places.
"Molecular" (Richard Carusu) Walgreens.
Make-up: MAC.

Shopping:
San Francisco: Salvation Army (better than Goodwill). Haight St: Wasteland, La Rosa, Held Over, Aardvarks, Martini Mercantile, Third-Hand Store, Old Vogue.
Berkeley: Stop the Clock, Guys & Dolls. Anywhere out of town.

Jump, jive and wail: Lee and Terri Moore.

The Flyin' Lindy Hoppers are a swing dance troupe from Ventura, California. They've done numerous performances at festivals, clubs, schools and for film/video, including Big Bad Voodoo Daddy's "King of Swing," "Machine Gun," and "You, Me and the Bottle Makes Three." Their acrobatic performances are breathtaking, and have been captured on several videos available from the Flyin' Lindy Hoppers, 343 E. Vince St, Ventura CA 93001. Their website is *FlyinLindy@AOL*. What follows are interviews with twin sisters Terri and Tammy, and Terri's husband Lee Moore.

INTERVIEW WITH LEE MOORE

♦ *VALE: You and Big Bad Voodoo Daddy are credited for starting the swing movement in Ventura—*
♦ LEE MOORE: We all started it together—us and the club, Nicholby's. My wife and I had just moved to Ventura, where I got a job working at the Chart House restaurant. We wondered if there was anything fun to do around there. Finally, someone told us to go to Nicholby's to check out this band, Big Bad Voodoo Daddy, that played "swing music." We thought it was BS, but

when we got there this killer music could be heard from outside. Nicholby's is on the second floor, so we ran upstairs as fast as we could. The place was full and there was a huge dance floor, but no one was dancing. The band was playing this psycho-swing mixture of punk, rockabilly, and swing. They were much more guitar-driven and intense in those days; their songs were almost frantic. Our dance style really matched that, so we just went out on the dance floor and started knockin' 'em dead! Back then—this was March, 1994—all we knew how to do was flips; we hadn't really learned how to *dance* yet, but it still looked pretty wild—

besides, nobody had seen that. People just went nuts watching us!

BBVD started playing once a month, and there would be a line all the way down the street. The "scene" got big fast, and the band started getting more swing-oriented. People began expecting

---

Usually when dancers perform, it's just a few couples. In our shows, you see eight to ten people going crazy. And doing crazy stuff is our "niche."

---

to see us at the shows—and we were always there, dancing. Pretty soon, BBVD started playing the Derby on Wednesday nights. I quit my job at the Chart House and we started teaching dance lessons at Nicholby's.

♦ **V: Your wife is Terri?**

♦ **LM:** Yeah. And Tammy is Terri's twin sister. There's another gal on the team that looks remarkably like her, named Alex, and another woman named Jen Salazar. Actually, there's about 10 people now in the Flyin' Lindy Hoppers.

♦ **V: Each dance seems rehearsed and so polished. You've taken partner-dancing to the next level—**

♦ **LM:** A lot of the credit goes to my wife's sister, Tammy—she's a choreographer. There's a swing-dance troupe from Sweden called the Rhythm Hot Shots. They do similar things to what we do, and they've been doing it for over ten years—they're very well-known in the swing-dance world. We decided that we wanted to do something similar to that. There are two schools of thought among dancers: the "traditional" approach, which is more of a ballroom approach, and the wild-and-crazy "club" or "street" approach.

♦ **V: As an ex-punk rocker, I go for the most wild stuff I can see—**

♦ **LM:** That's our whole approach: we want to hold on to that rawness. We don't want to look too neat and tidy. We want to be colorful and organized, but we don't want to look canned.

♦ **V: You definitely take risks. At your show, the guys were diving over each other with perfect timing—**

♦ **LM:** That's what we call "Monkey Rolls." It's funny—that's a football drill. People love the Monkey Rolls. That's our specialty. You should see when we get hired for a show at a place that's kind of sleepy and they're not ready for us. We come roaring out there, and their eyes pop out! [laughs] They don't know what hit them, man—it's so funny!

Usually when dancers perform, it's just a few couples. In our shows, you see eight to ten people going crazy. And doing crazy stuff is our "niche." It's a blast. We've probably done our "Sing, Sing, Sing" routine at least 150 times, and it's still dangerous!

INTERVIEW WITH TAMMY (CHOREOGRAPHER)

♦ **VALE: What kind of shows do you do?**

♦ **TAMMY:** Periodically, there are these "swing weekends." The first group to put one on here, on Catalina Island, was the Pasadena Ballroom Dancing Association. They started four years ago and now it's an annual event. We learned from that, and then we put on our own weekend called "Monsters of Swing." We reach a totally different market; we love the energy of a wild band playing live music in a club—that's where we feel comfortable. San Francisco recently had their first swing weekend; it was basically a knock-off of Monsters of Swing. San Diego had one, too.

Some of The Flyin' Lindy Hoppers (L to R): Jen Salazar, Chad Abbott, Terri Moore, Lee Moore, Tammy Finocchiaro, Lance Puckett, Heather Dudley, Pat Casey, and Alex Hinojosa.

It's just people doing a swing weekend in their own town.

The Rhythm Hot Shots travel around the world teaching at swing weekends; two of them will be at the San Diego event. They're a group like the Flyin' Lindy Hoppers. They consider themselves living historians and have amazing archives of dance footage, books, old magazines, etc. They watch old movies and copy the dancing almost to the tee. Basically, my goal as a choreographer and organizer is to be somewhat competitive with the Rhythm Hot Shots. It's tough, since they've been around much longer. I was very careful not to make our group an imitation of them, but we're "naturally" different because we come from a different background. Actually, both of us danced at Catalina this year, and one of their members told me, "You approach swing in a totally different manner than anyone else I've seen throughout Europe and the States." I took that as a compliment.

♦ *V: Didn't you learn from old movies yourselves?*

♦ T: Not really. But the people that taught *me* probably learned from them. Initially I learned from the Pasadena group; they taught me how to swing. They teach a variety of social dancing: ballroom, swing, country, etc, and have been around for about thirteen years. About ten years ago, they dug up some old movie footage of swing dancing and began to hunt down original members from the movies. They found a few that were still alive, got them to teach how they did it, and went on to teach other people.

So, the Rhythm Hot Shots learned from movies, Pasadena learned from the original people and movies, and everybody tries to pass that information on. *Now* I watch movies for inspiration and to see what was done, but I can't say that the bulk of my instruction came from that. Nor did the bulk of my instruction come from just being an untrained dancer "experimenting" in a club. We are fairly trained, but at the same time, we try to maintain spontaneity. We do have to be choreographed, because the stuff we do is too dangerous.

♦ *V: When I saw your act, there were three guys and four women—*

♦ T: My main guy, Lee Moore, was not there, because he had to work. Another guy hurt his knee on Friday. So, I was down two men that night, which affects my women sometimes. One of my female dancers couldn't make it either, because of work. But you got the gist of our act. Some of the big aerials were taken out because Lee wasn't there.

♦ *V: I saw plenty of aerials—*

♦ T: Yeah, but there's even more when the "real" show is put on. And if you do aerials you can't switch partners; it's too dangerous. But the same overall concept was there.

♦ *V: There was a lot of comedy, too.*

♦ T: We try to make it playful. In a club environment, we improvise a lot. We're structured in the sense that we *don't* try to hurt people on the dance floor. [laughs] We don't just memorize moves; we're versatile—we can lead and follow with different partners. Basically, you get trained to either lead or follow. You learn what to do, but you also learn how to "rough it up" enough to make it look raw. That's the hard part.

Some dancers are not trained and are very proud of the fact that they've never taken a lesson. There is this big "arrogance" thing going on now. The fact is: when you're trained, you don't hurt people.

♦ *V: Do your dance moves have names?*

♦ T: Some, but not all. Every dance has "basics" that you have to know in order to do the dance. From there, you can add creative moves.

♦ *V: Like pulling someone between your legs?*

♦ T: Those are considered aerials, lifts, and drops. But you can call them a million different names. You dip your partner, or you throw your partner (which is like an aerial), and sometimes you just lift your partner.

♦ *V: Lee was saying that you have four choreographed routines down, and you're working on a fifth—*

♦ T: We actually have about six routines: four that are really good, and two that are works-in-progress.

♦ *V: How do you improve them?*

♦ T: I don't change the routines, I just add new ones. I add variety by adding new moves. I'll improve something if I don't like a part, or if it's not coming off the way I want. But you need to be very confident about what's coming next. If a routine's constantly changing, you get insecure and that leads to mistakes. The first time you perform something new, it's never comfortable. The ones you saw on Saturday are our most comfortable; we've done them countless times. We couldn't do the newer routines because of the change in personnel.

♦ *V: Lee told me that Flattop Tom broke his ankle while dancing—*

♦ T: The worst injury I've had so far was a broken nose when I was 19—I hit a man. Other than that, we haven't had any major injuries, despite the fact that we've had to dance on precarious floor surfaces: asphalt, cement, dirt, linoleum, grass, etc.

♦ *V: Is wood the best?*

♦ T: Yes, because we do a lot of slides. If the surface isn't wood, we take out the slides from our routine. So the routine is dependent on the environment. Floor surfaces, space constraints, height requirements—ceilings can be too low or have ceiling-mounted fixtures like fans or hanging lights that are hazardous. All that affects us.

♦ *V: Isn't it better if the man is larger than the woman?*

♦ T: I have a 50-pound rule: for aerials, I prefer that the guy be 50 pounds heavier than the girl, as well as taller. But not *too* much bigger—if the girl weighs 100 pounds and the guy 250, it looks too easy and no one's impressed. Throwing around your five-year-old niece is just not as impressive as throwing around an adult female. But that's not necessarily a golden rule. There's a lot of technique involved.

♦ *V: What are other hazards?*

♦ T: Some aerials have to be learned by trial and error, which can be a very painful process. [laughs] Most injuries involve miscommunication, like when one person does a full aerial while the other person thinks it's going to be just a "prep." (The prep is the lead into the aerial; it's only half of the full move.)

♦ *V: I saw a woman come down really hard and fall forward*

Tammy Finocchiaro and Lee Moore performing New Year's 1997 at the Mirage with The New Morty Show. Photo: Terri Moore

on her hands. *Should the man be cushioning that?*

♦ T: Yes, there's escape routes out of every aerial and the guy should know them before he does a throw. When we teach, we show how to get out of a situation when it's going bad. It is the guy's responsibility to save the woman from breaking her neck. The man should be gentlemanly and take the brunt of it, because she is taking the larger risk since she has more momentum and is up in the air. The man needs extreme technique and caution; he

> **When we teach, we show how to get out of a situation when it's going bad. It is the guy's responsibility to save the woman from breaking her neck.**

should be able to control her all the way through.

Some aerials the guy has no control over. There's one where my partner throws me up in the air and there's a full release (I'm not touching anybody) and I have to come back into his arms. It takes time for the guys to accustom themselves to that.

We've learned a lot the hard way. People we teach learn quicker and faster, because they don't have to go through the trial and error we did. But there's no substitute for practice—you have to do it a million times.

♦ V: *How often do you practice?*

♦ T: The team practices once a week. Our gigs seem to come in clusters; there's seasonal highs and lows. You can work like crazy for a month and not at all the next month. Our first "professional" performance was in March '96 and by the end of that year we had performed in Vegas at the Mirage. We started out just wanting to "have fun," and had immediate popularity. Now we've done hundreds of performances.

♦ V: *Who came up with the idea to start a team?*

♦ T: That was my concept, because I'd been on teams before where I did the choreography. We started the team in January of '96 and it took two months of weekly rehearsals to get it together, with our first performance in March of that year.

♦ V: *That's all? Just eight rehearsals?*

♦ T: I came to the first rehearsal with the choreography pretty much done. I actually wrote it down on paper, and it looks like football diagrams. [laughs] It's hard because a lot of it is in my head; I have to do partner choreography by myself, and *that's* difficult. The dancers never see the diagrams; the diagrams are only for me. I don't know how other people choreograph, but I just get in a very dark room, put music on and imagine what I want to see danced to it. Then I have to think about what we're *physically* capable of doing [laughs]—sometimes that limits you.

♦ V: *Your dresses have a retro look, but I don't think they're vintage—*

♦ T: No, they're all modern. I also do fashion design, so the dresses are purchased off the rack and then altered to fit our needs. They'll be shortened and I cut them in very sharply at the waist to give them more shape. When we do our aerials, they need to be very fitted at the torso. Technically speaking, they cannot move from the torso—that's very unsafe.

♦ V: *All the material looks similar, but not identical—*

♦ T: I had to look hard for that. One of the dresses was a size 18 and I cut it down to a size eight because I wanted the extra material. I look for plunging necklines and very feminine designs, because I like contrast between the boys and the girls. The dresses can't go below the knee because they would get in our way. We can't wear vintage because of the aggressiveness of our dancing; we *shred* vintage dresses.

♦ V: *Are the dresses made of cotton?*

♦ T: No, cotton doesn't reflect well onstage. Some of them are 100% wool, but they're mostly rayon or a rayon blend. We prefer worsted wool that is very tightly woven, not winter wool. Wool is good; it absorbs a lot of sweat.

♦ **V: Where do you shop?**

♦ T: There's not one single place we shop for women's clothes, but we've found them at Macy's, Bullock's . . . A few came from second-hand stores.

♦ **V: What kind of shoes do you wear?**

♦ T: We just wear two-tones. Boys' shoes are easy to find (I just bought some tiny boys' spectators for my two-year-old daughter at Payless, and they're incredibly detailed). I've bought spectators from every conceivable place: from Payless to Macy's, and anything in between.

♦ **V: How high is the heel?**

♦ T: We prefer medium heel. It varies, but it's about an inch-and-a-half to two inches. We convert all of our shoes and have them re-soled to something soft, like rubber. When you're landing from six feet in the air, you don't want to land on solid plastic, which is what most soles are made of. We convert our shoes to tennis shoe bottoms. We have custom guys resole our shoes with two inches of foam in the heel to absorb the impact. A lot of girls like to wear more sexy shoes, but we can't because they're too dangerous. Of course, spectators that already have rubber soles make it easier.

All the girls have mandatory garters—pantyhose are not allowed!

♦ **V: In the show I saw, all the girls wore white panties. Are they custom or off-the-rack?**

♦ T: No, they're pretty much off the rack. The undergarments are supposed to match the dress. If your dress is white, your undergarments are white; and if your dress is red, so are your panties, etc. The garters are custom, but the panties (which are really dance pants) are bought off the rack. They look like regular underwear but are much thicker and are reinforced. You can buy them anywhere, like at Macy's. We flash, but we don't want to feel ridiculous.

We do very modern swing, I'd say. Most people prefer to wear authentic vintage clothing, and we're one of the most adamant about *not* wearing it! We have a vintage influence, but we put a '90s look to it. We're renegades in that regard.

♦ **V: It looks vintage but it also looks brand-new. I think that's what people really want. It's getting too expensive to find vintage, and it's way too fragile—**

♦ T: It is way too fragile. You know what? In the '40s they didn't wear 40-year-old clothes—that's the way I look at it. The clothes looked fresh and new then, but now they don't look fresh anymore—the material just shreds and cannot handle what we do. So we knock off from the past. The dresses are similar, to give us

You and me and the baby makes three: Lee, Terri, and Jessica Moore.

a "consistent" look.

♦ **V: It's nice that you wear dresses that aren't all the same.**

♦ T: There's a lot of technical details that we require. I have to open up the sleeves on all the dresses. If you raise your arm in a dress, the whole dress comes up—similar to a man's sport coat. So, I have to alter all the sleeves so that our arms can make a full revolution without the dress moving. I rip out all the seams and add fabric to the sleeve. The dresses are bought off the rack, with major alterations added later.

♦ **V: For safety reasons, you probably don't wear heavy jewelry—**

♦ T: All jewelry is banned in our routine, except for my sister's wedding ring, because her husband won't let her take it off—for reasons that are obvious! [laughs] Actually we sometimes wear certain kinds of jewelry, like earrings or necklaces. But the guys can't wear watches or anything.

You might have noticed that our dresses don't have any attachments in the middle, like a belt or belt loops. We can't have any of that. No buttons. It's primarily so that we don't get stuck on anything. If they get stuck on anything, your entire dress might get pulled off.

♦ **V: Are your hairstyles retro?**

♦ T: Our hairstyles are retro-influenced, and we do it all ourselves. I try to do them a little bit more modern, but we mostly just like them off our faces. We put them up so they look finished. I learned my lesson on how to do my hair, the hard way. A newspaper printed a photo of me doing a jump. My hair was not plastered to my head, so it made this huge fan over my head like an oversized afro. I've been embarrassed by this ever since. Now my hair is styled in a constricted way, so that it looks the same upside down as it does when I'm standing straight up.

♦ **V: What do you use on your hair?**

♦ T: I use one bobby pin in my whole hair set and then I just hairspray the rest of it.

And, of course, we use push-up bras—people laugh because I

Tammy Finocchiaro & Lance Puckett at Great American Music Hall (S.F. Swing Jam) with Big Bad Voodoo Daddy and Flattop Tom.

approve the uniforms all the way down to the underpants. It all has to match, but it's not necessarily just one brand. I'd love the men to wear matching boxers in case their pants rip, but it's harder to find them for men.

♦ **V: What are some safety requirements for men?**
♦ T: The baggy pants are a safe thing because they allow for movement, besides looking kinda cool. I've switched all my guys to short-sleeved shirts, which is really odd with a tie, but it's more casual, cooler, and functional for aerials. When men wear suits, they look like they just got off work. The ties are short because the pants are high-waisted, so they don't have to worry too much about them flying in their faces.

INTERVIEW WITH TERRI MOORE

♦ TERRI MOORE: We did a show once at the Orange County Fair. I remember a little girl in the audience turning to her mother and saying [loudly], "Oh, mama, I saw her panties!" [laughs] She was embarrassed for me, but there's nothing you can do . . .
♦ **VALE: I asked Tammy about that and she said that you buy reinforced panties that cover "things" up very well.**
♦ TM: We had one girl on our team who didn't really wear enough panty. I guess guys from quite a distance got a lot of detail. They were stoked, of course! [laughs]
♦ **V: Well, it never bothered me!**
♦ TM: I would be a little embarrassed, though. This particular girl would have died if she knew.
♦ **V: Actually, in the show I saw, all four of you were completely "together" in that department—**
♦ TM: Mine are the kind that hold your stomach in; they were the only ones that went high enough for me. I'm surprised that some girls go out wearing bikini briefs—don't they *know?* We do family shows where there's lots of kids, so we don't want to be too risqué.

They're reinforced all the way around. Somebody actually got a picture of my crotch while I was doing a cartwheel with my legs spread open, from about two feet away—it was taken in a crowded bar. Later, the photographer showed me the photo and I real-

ized that my panties were great—even that close up you couldn't see a *thing!* [laughs] He didn't know it was me, and he asked, "Have I met you before?" I said, "You have—just not from this end!" I was stunned that he was going around showing this photo to everyone.

Actually, I didn't realize panties were such an "issue" until we signed up a new girl on our team who brought it up. If you're dancing and some hair pops out—that's just not very pretty. If people think they're going to see that, trust me, they're going to be looking, and they'll get distracted. We like to take the show away from that level; it's the *dancing* that matters.

Some people wear bike tights or aerobic tights, but I think they're terrible. They look frumpy. I did this for awhile after my pregnancy because I felt self-conscious. Then I saw some footage of myself and realized I looked better revealing my chubby thighs than being covered with those awful bike tights. You can't put a

> I remember a little girl in the audience turning to her mother and saying [loudly], "Oh, mama, I saw her panties!" [laughs] She was embarrassed for me.

pretty dress on and have aerobic wear underneath—it just doesn't look right. Maybe if it were one of those lacy things—*maybe.* People should just go with the thick white briefs. You can get them at Mervyn's and they're great. Some are expensive and some aren't. Mine have held up—thank heavens—because they've really taken a beating. [laughs] They've definitely been abused.
♦ **V: Who are the women in your group?**
♦ TM: Heather's the sexy one, Tammy and I are the sporty ones, Alex is the spunky one, and Jen's the fire-plug!

The Flyin' Lindy Hoppers include: Chad Abbott, Pat Casey, Heather Dudley, Jackson Dutra, Tammy Finocchiaro, Alex Hinojosa, Lee & Terri Moore, and Lance Puckett. **V**

Johnny & Cari Swing

Johnny Swing and Cari Elizabeth teach swing dance lessons Sunday and Tuesday nights at Max's Hi-Ball Lounge in San Francisco. They organized the first San Francisco Swing Jam Weekend (Aug. 29–30, 1997) which featured Lavay Smith, Big Bad Voodoo Daddy, and Flattop Tom & His Jump Cats. Both evenings were highlighted by several levels of spectacular dance contests. They can be contacted at 415-548-8193.

♦ **VALE: How did you first find out about swing?**

♦ JOHNNY SWING: I was born in 1972 and grew up in Belmont, near San Francisco. I learned how to swing dance in high school; the school offered a ballroom dance course. That's when I started doing performances with a partner, although at the time, there was nowhere to dance.

In 1990 I moved to San Francisco. It wasn't till 1993 that a dozen of my friends and I went to an Irish bar, Pat O'Shea's on Geary Street and saw a band, the Bachelors, who were playing danceable music. That night I managed to dance with almost every girl in the room! Then I began searching out places where I could dance.

I started dating a girl who lived close to the Club Deluxe, and we began meeting there for drinks. It has a very small dance floor; only one couple could dance at a time! That was *the* place; that's where I really got into swing music, the clothes, the whole culture back when it definitely was a subculture. People dressed the part, everybody knew each other, we all went to the same shows together. In 1994 there was something to do every night: Sunday was swing night at the Cafe Du Nord, Tuesday was rockabilly night at the Ace Cafe, and all the other nights we went to the Deluxe.

I met Dana and Mango (from Work That Skirt) and starting teaching swing dance lessons with them on Sunday nights at Kimball's West on Franklin Street. After we gave our lesson, a "swing" band would play, like Indigo Swing, the Rhumba Bums, Lavay Smith. The first night only about seven people showed up, but the last night we taught (before the club closed) there were 150 people there. It was a great space, and it's a shame it closed.

For me, dancing became everything; the clothing was secondary. But part of hanging out involved dressing up and looking nice. In 1994 you could get perfect vintage suits for $30–$40 that are now going for $200–$300. It was easy to find '40s ties; you could go out on Saturday and come home with bags of clothes. Now everything's much more expensive and too hard to find.

I started having clothes made for several reasons. One, I don't like dancing in vintage suits—I don't think it looks right. I like high-waisted pants that are baggy in the leg (they add to the whole dancer look) whereas some of my suit pants are pleated but don't have enough room. I split the crotch in several of my suits, and *that's* what led me to have my clothes custom-made. Secondly, a '40s double-breasted suit coat fits really tight—it's hard to dance wild in one.

My dance partner Cari found Mary Johnson in Hollywood, and for the past two years she's been making most of our clothes. She color-coordinates our outfits to match, etc. I've had four suits and two pairs of zoot suit pants made for a grand total of just under $3000! But when you're a performer, image is everything. I also started looking for vintage reproduction clothing, like this black '50s-looking shirt jacket made by DaVinci (the Hi-Ball sells them, with their logo on the sleeve). I paired that up with a pair of black and white zoot pants made by Mary Johnson which have large white diamonds down the sides.

♦ **V: You dance so acrobatically; tell us about your shoes—**

♦ JS: I have all sorts of different shoes, depending on the outfit and surface I'm going to be dancing on. With Work That Skirt we got hired to perform in Livermore. We had to dance in 103 degree heat on concrete. Like an idiot, I wore just regular leather-soled walking shoes (spectators) but now I know better! All I can say

Cari and Johnny. Photo: Cindy Russell, Dec. 1997

is, the balls of my feet were *burning* . . .

Al from Martini Mercantile does all my shoes now. He dyes them to match my suits; he's taken a regular pair of spectators, removed the sole and shank and replaced these with a bowling sole (thick suede leather, on top of which is a thin piece of dance rubber glued on). That adds some gripping ability. Regular shoes bought off the rack are not made for dancing; they're walking shoes. The work that Al does on my shoes helps out tremendously. I also wear skateboarding shoes—they look like classic black-and-white sneakers and are made by Simple. They have a really thick sole, a nice arch support—they're like dancing on air. The only thing is, they lack the slipperiness you need sometimes. I tend to do the splits with my partner, and it's hard to do that with a sticky shoe. I was doing the splits recently at our Great American Music Hall dance contest, and at one point my shoe came off—I hadn't tied the laces tightly enough.

♦ *V: How did you meet your dance partner, Cari?*

♦ JS: While still teaching with Dana and Mango, I had met Cari while out dancing at a swing show. When I met her, she had been a gymnast for 10 years (now she coaches gymnastics), and I thought, "Wouldn't she be great as a dance partner?" But she had a boyfriend at the time, so it wasn't an option. About a month after Dana and Mango and I stopped working together (professional differences), I ran into Cari at the DNA lounge (I had started teaching my own dance lessons by then). She said she was single and I said, "How would you like to teach with me?" [laughs] That was March 8, 1996. We've been together ever since—and not just as dance partners!

When Cari and I started teaching together, she didn't know a whole lot, but at that point neither did I. [laughs] There was a particular dance I wanted to learn (the Lindy Hop) so we both started taking dance lessons. Since then we've really grown; we've been together two years. We've spent a lot of time learning how to dance, learning music structure, dance history (we've gotten a chance to learn from some of the masters who were doing it back in the '30s in Harlem, like Frankie Manning, who's 83 years old). There are other older dancers who occasionally give dance workshops; we've taken a few of those. Steven Mitchell, in my mind, is the best teacher out there.

She said she was single and I said, "How would you like to teach with me?" We've been together ever since!

♦ *V: Cari, can you tell us about any dance problems specific to women?*

♦ CE: I think the biggest issue is: the women in the dance scene don't get as much credit as the men do. It's been that way all along: the men dancers seem to be more famous than the women. There are, however, a few women out there that have made a name for themselves, and who are not in any man's shadow. Some of these have been my teachers: Erin and Tammi Stevens, Jan Olsen, Jenny Thomas.

This type of dancing is very physical, and while it's mostly women who do the aerials, guys occasionally do them, too. I fre-

Cari and Johnny, Hi-Ball, 11-14-97. Photo: V. Vale

quently do aerials with John, and right now I have a pretty messed-up right knee from a lot of landings. Since it is a very physically demanding activity, there's always the chance of injury. The difficulty of all the dancing in general is fairly balanced between "leaders" and "followers." Men have to be mentally prepared for what they're going to lead next—they can't be indecisive—and women have to be prepared to react instantly. As far as aerials go, the guys have to be strong enough and the girls have to be agile enough. A good leader will give his follower "play time" to do her thing, especially in Lindy Hop.

♦*V: Cari, how did you get into swing?*

♦CE: In 1994, when I was 19, I started going to the Ace Cafe on Tuesdays, which was rockabilly nights. At that point I hadn't done any swing dancing; I just thought it looked fun. My ex-boyfriend and I started taking swing dance lessons from the Fred Astaire dance studio in Sunnyvale. We went to the Ace until it shut down, after which we danced at random shows in different clubs. Then we broke up, and shortly thereafter I got together with John, my dance partner.

♦*V: You two organized that Great American Music Hall Swing Jam Weekend—*

♦JS: The first swing dance contest I heard about in the Bay Area took place at the Claremont Hotel a couple years ago (which Cari and I won). We got the idea to organize our own Swing Dance Weekend—that took Cari and I five months. We had ads all over, and people from NY, L.A., Seattle, Arizona, and Texas came to it. There was one semi-finalist couple: the man was from France and his partner was from London! He wore pants up to his armpits and tiny suspenders. During this weekend, we used the Hi-Ball lounge and the Broadway Studios (435 Broadway) and gave swing lessons all day Saturday and Sunday. People bought a "package" that got them into the show Saturday and Sunday nights, and got dance classes all day.

We gave classes in St. Louis Shag, the Balboa, Lindy Hop, East Coast Swing, aerials (basic to intermediate levels)—there was something for everybody. We gave out over $1,000 in cash prizes. There were two contests: the first was a Jack-and-Jill. Sixteen couples entered, and everyone had to rotate partners! From that we picked the best leaders and the best followers. The second contest was the couples contest. Friday night was the first level of elimination down to five couples for the couples contest, and eight couples for the Jack and Jill. Saturday night was the finals. Bernard and Josie from Hollywood were the winners of the couples contest.

Now it seems like the swing dance movement is growing by leaps and bounds on an international scale. The cool thing about this whole movement and everything involved is: I feel it's not something that's going to die out very easily. People have spent a lot of time and money involving themselves, learning how to dance, learning the history, the music, the fashions, etc, and for a lot of people this isn't going to go away overnight, like some fad. People just love it! Dancing is a great thing to know how to do, and once you learn it, you'll know how to do it for the rest of your life. It brings such a thrill—you can just see it on people's faces.

In this context, it's normal for a guy to come up to a girl and ask her to dance (or for a girl to ask a guy to dance). Basically this creates a much easier atmosphere for people to maybe *meet* someone, or just have fun dancing and that's it. It's all about fun: going out there and having a good time. And the music is so great, too—there's so much to discover and it hasn't been heard to death. I really can't see this ending anytime soon. **V**

Slim Style Records staff, L to R: Christina Palacio, Rusty Jones, Jack Vaughan, Bill Workman

Started by Jack Vaughn, Slimstyle Records aims to release as much music as possible by innovative swing (and related musical genre) bands. Their address is 3400 E. Speedway Ste. 118-272, Tucson, AZ 85716. Their e-mail address is: *slimstyle@earthlink.net.*

♦ *VALE: Tell us the history of your independent record company—*

♦ JACK VAUGHN: I grew up in Washington, D.C. and as a young kid was heavily into and inspired by the scene centered around Dischord Records and their D-I-Y. ethic. In 1989 my parents moved to Guatemala, where in high school I started a punk rock record label called Third World Underground to release 45s by Guatemalan garage bands such as Reagan's Colon Surgery. We kinda started the punk rock scene there, and by the time I left for Tucson in 1992 we had released about 10 records. Then I signed Jonathan Fire*Eater (New York), the Lonely Trojans, etc. plus we released four well-known compilations, *Echoes of the Nation's Capital,* which included a lot of D.C. bands. By the time I graduated from the University of Arizona in 1996, Third World Underground had produced 25 releases.

When I graduated, I had become a bit disenchanted with the music scene, and got funding to start a ska label—something I'd wanted to do for awhile. I was sitting at the kitchen table when my girlfriend, Christina Palacio, suddenly said, "You know, you should sign some swing bands!" She had become enamored of the original swing music era and had gotten into the music, and had noticed there seemed to be quite a few swing bands popping up. She'd been on the Internet and had come across the names of some of the bigger unsigned bands: The New Morty Show, Blue Plate Special, and Big Time Operator. It turned out that Royal Crown had already played Tucson at least half a dozen times, and actually I'd seen them once but hadn't realized they represented a coherent emerging movement. I had already enjoyed their CD, *Mugzy's Move,* and now everything started to fall into place.

> **As a label we're committed to releasing music from the jumpin'est swing bands out there who are doing their own thing—writing new songs, adding new twists to the music, and in general ensuring that the swing movement is here to stay and not something that can be reduced to a passing fad.**

I decided to divert the funding for the ska label into swing music instead. I'd already signed two ska bands which blended ska and swing together, Dave's Big Deluxe (Arizona) and Jimmy Skaffa (Nebraska). Christina got the phone numbers of the afore-mentioned unsigned swing bands from the Internet, and I contacted them about the possibility of putting out their records. Blue Plate Special sent me a tape and within a week we had a ten-tative deal. Nothing hap-pened with B.T.O., and the New Morty Show had already planned to sign with a major label. However, they broke with that label (I don't know why) and I immediate-ly got on the phone with their manager, Jay Siegan, and we signed a deal.

BLUE PLATE SPECIAL

In the interim I had found out about *Swing Time* magazine and contacted Michael Moss, again with Christina's Internet research help. He suggested we sign the Crescent City Maulers (New Jersey), which we did. I found and signed a local swing/rock band, Hipster Daddy-O & the Handgrenades, and Scotty Morris recommended Red & the Red Hots (Los Angeles) whom we also signed. Michael Moss and I collaborated to produce a Swing Time/Slimstyle compilation CD. Around the same time Jay Siegan told me that Dana and Mango (Work That Skirt) had opened a lot of the major swing shows in San Francisco teaching dance lessons. I thought, "Why not produce a dance instruction video with them?" I hired a San Francisco filmmaker, Rand Alexander, who had worked on the New Morty Show promo-tional video, and he put together a film crew, did the shoot, and is completing the post-production.

As things got busier, I enlisted a couple college friends who

New Morty poses with Joe Escovedo.

were into the swing scene by that time: William Slab Bacon, who had studied graphic design, and Rusty Jones, who like me does whatever it takes to get the records out. In Arizona our overhead is very low, and our financing is such that I'm able to eke out a modest existence. Bill gets paid on a per-project basis, and Rusty works part-time; he'll go full time as soon as our cash flow improves.

As a label we're committed to releasing music from the jump-in'est swing bands out there who are doing their own thing—writing new songs, adding new twists to the music, and in gener-al ensuring that the swing movement is here to stay and not something that can be reduced to a passing fad. ▼

Slimm & Sunny Buick

Slimm and Sunny Buick with vintage bikes customized by Slimm. Photo: Henry Goldfield, 12.97

One of San Francisco's prototypical "retro" couples is Slimm and Sunny Buick. Slimm has created some amazing assemblage-art bicycles, and Sunny is a tattooist specializing in "retro" designs (Goldfields, 404 Broadway, 415-433-0558; Sunny's studio 415-771-8210). They were present as the retro-rockabilly-greaser-punk scene gave birth to the "swing movement."

♦ *VALE: Tell us some background—*
♦ SLIMM BUICK: I grew up in San Francisco and started collecting records when I was about nine. When I was a kid I was going around to garage sales asking, "Do you have any records?" and picking out ones I wanted. But as I started getting into the antique business, it was like, "How much for all of them?" You save the ones you like and trade or sell the rest—that's how I ended up with so many records. I was one of those kids who didn't talk to too many other kids in school; I just hung out with old people and listened to records.

♦ *V: How did you get hired to be a DJ at the Deluxe?*
♦ SLIMM: I went there when it first opened. I had thousands of great old records, and I started giving away tapes of my favorite songs to people. After about six months, Jay Johnson offered me a job. I would ride to work on my bicycle, pulling a little red wagon absolutely loaded with LPs and 78s. I deejayed playing a variety of music: Joe Turner, Bob Wills, Sinatra, Louis Jordan and Louis Prima. I did a poster for "Las Vegas Night" March 28, 1991 and that became an annual event. It wasn't until Jay got a lounge singer named Mr. Lucky that he started giving me playlists of songs that I *had* to play. I got frustrated and left.

The first jump band I'd heard live was in Los Angeles around 1985: The Chevalier Brothers. They played really fast but stood real stationary, like watching Ricky Nelson sing. They just disappeared. Then Royal Crown showed up in 1992 at the Deluxe, and

blew people away.
♦ *V: What motivated you to make your amazing art-bicycles?*
♦ SLIMM: I think it came out of an interest in old cars and motorcycles, but I could never afford one. I looked at a lot of old hotrod magazines and kind of worked that styling into bicycles. Around 1987 I made my first low-rider BMX-type bike. It had hood ornaments from old Dodges and DeSotos on the rear fender, and had raked front forks and lots of chrome. Gradually I started

---

I would ride to work on my bicycle, pulling a little red wagon absolutely loaded with LPs and 78s.

---

making skirts and paneling. Not long ago I covered a bike in cowhide and added handlebars that looked like cowhorns. I actually put cowhorns on an earlier Western-style bike, but they proved to not be very strong.

I did one bike that was all Elvis motifs and another with a devil theme. I did one with clowns: it has a boxing glove in front attached to a shaving mirror—you push it and it springs back punching! A lot of the parts I picked up at estate sales—years later you find a use for them. I found an old smashed Buick grill for $5. Three years later I bought this cycle truck with a huge basket in front, and now it's on the front of the basket.

I did two bicycle art shows at the Du Nord; Oct 22, 1992 (Big Sandy played) and on March 17, 1996. San Francisco has a "Bike to Work" week every May: "You should be riding a bike, not driving," and I kinda go along with that. I've never really driven. I like looking at the design of vintage cars, but I wouldn't want one.

I grew up hanging around my grandfather and his neighbors, hearing all their World War II stories and listening to old records. For years I used to get beat up at school because I was listening to music like Ellington, and wearing old clothes. As a kid I wanted older stuff; I never got too excited about going to Macy's. At one point I told my parents, "Hey, give me my own money to buy my clothes with." They gave me $200 and I came back with five suits, plus shopping bags full of other clothes. They said, "You look like your grandfather!" and I said, "Yeah, it's great!" Now probably half of those kids who beat me up think it's a cool fad and are trying to buy all that stuff. You used to go to Thrift Town and find three '40s double-breasted suits a week, easy, that fit you—up until the early '90s. Basically, I have this recycling theory about trying not to waste what we have left on this planet.

♦ V: Sunny, you're associated with the rise of "retro" tattooing—

♦ SUNNY BUICK: The old tattoos make a lot of sense to me because they age well; they have a hard black outline. They're small and stand on their own, and you can collect them over the years. These days, a lot of tattooing involves ornate details, and I wonder how they'll look 30 years from now.

There's a lot of styles available now, and some people mix them up and get 'em all. That's one thing that's modern about the current swing movement—you see a *lot* of girls that are heavily tattooed. At a recent Sam Butera show there were some long-time fans: older women all dressed up, and I saw them looking somewhat scornfully at young women with tattoos. It must be weird to see something so familiar combined with something so shocking.

I work at Henry Goldfield's, an old-time tattoo shop in San Francisco. Henry has always apprenticed people in the old-style way in which you work your ass off, and *someday* he'll let you tattoo! He's got a lot of classic flash, and is one of the best at doing classic style tattoos.

♦ V: Describe some retro tattoos—

♦ SUNNY: The boys tend to get a lot of pin-up girls, anchors, stars, hearts, card suits and "Man's Ruin" (a woman with liquor, cigarettes, dice and cards). Girls, unless they're *out there* (like a punked-out swing person) mostly get tattoos on their legs and backs—not a lot of full arm tattoos (although a few have). I have these arrows on the back of my calves that suggest I have "seams," and I have anchors on the upper half of my thighs—it's my superstition that they help hold the stockings up!

Tattoo enthusiasts today take traditional designs, like two bluebirds on the chest or the Virgin of Guadalupe, and *twist* them—make the Virgin ghostly or something. We're into the good things from the past that have been forgotten, but we also have computers—it's not like we really want to *live* in the past. I wouldn't want to go back to the days of heavy-duty racism and sexism. But there is definitely a "retro" lifestyle being lived now. People may have a modern telephone, computer, and a few appliances including a stereo and television, but everything else is old, including the dishes and car.

In this movement, you're kind of "living the past in the present" with your outward appearance, including the music you listen to, the films you see, and your clothes. And being a girl into it, it's so much fun doing things like plucking your eyebrows, wearing false eyelashes on occasion, seamed stockings with garters and girdle (which are a pain in the ass sometimes), and a pointy push-up bra. Some people aren't into wearing old underwear, but I'm into it. The thrift stores and vintage clothing stores have stock that's never been used, or hardly used. The fashions of the '40s look so nice on women's figures. They play up the feminine, with accessories (gloves, purses, hats), and modern fashion has lost that. There's a lot of fashion potential now; many people enjoy going to rockabilly, Western Swing and swing shows, and they dress accordingly.

My mom was a hippie. I grew up with '60s psychedelic music, but at 15 I became interested in early '60s "garage" bands and also the '20s: no waist, short skirts and short hair. Then I got into rockabilly, then Western Swing and swing. It seems like I keep going backward in time!

♦ V: You got married—

♦ SUNNY: Slimm and I knew each other for eight years before we got married three years ago. If you're gonna get married, you may as well marry your best friend! Marriage is like riding a tandem bicycle—sometimes one person pedals more than the other, but to make it up a steep hill both people have to work hard! ▉

At a Timmie Hesla party: Smelly Kelly from Red Meat sporting a tattoo by Sunny, 11-14-97. Insert: Sunny, the girl in Bimbo's fishbowl! Photo: V.Vale

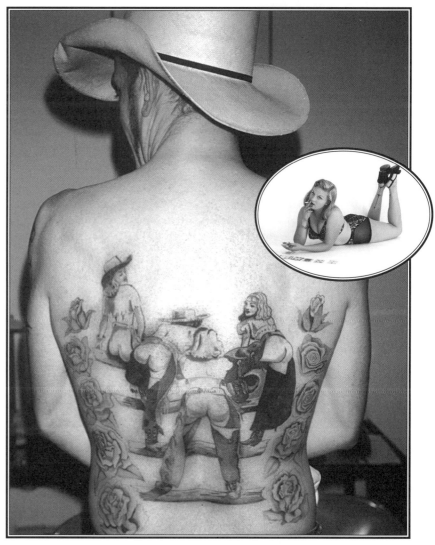

Jose & Cindy Mejia

José and Cindy Mejia were present as the Bay Area rockabilly scene incubated the "swing" movement. Raised in the Cholo subculture, José, his brother Javier and their friend, Ché Shul are credited with introducing modified vintage cars to the rockabilly-retro scene. José is an ace mechanic and pinstripe artist (leather jackets, cars, etc). Cindy is a computer technician who rebuilt and rides a vintage 1928 Indian motorcycle.

INTERVIEW WITH JOSÉ MEJIA

♦ JOSÉ MEJIA: I was born on Feb 28, 1965; my brother Javier was born Sept 16, 1968, and we grew up in San Francisco at 20th and Treat Streets. I started hanging out at 20th and Valencia. Me and my Cholo friends were in their own little world. We would occasionally see a guy on a skateboard with a mohawk in the late '70s and then started seeing more and more people like that. I wondered, "What's going on here?" It's funny to me to see old punk rockers who dress blue-collar now, because I thought they hated that—I thought that's why they became punk rockers! And it looks like they're trying to "go back," and you really can't ever go back. When I first started going to rockabilly shows, sometimes I'd see old Cholo friends drive by and they'd stop and ask me, "Hey, what are *you* doing here? These people are *weird!*" [laughs]

♦ VALE: When did you and Javier start working on cars?
♦ JM: In 1979 my brother and I bought an old 1955 Buick. For the most part we just sat in it and talked about what we wanted to do; the most we *did* to it was hang fuzzy dice! We had started buying magazines when we were about nine years old: *Hot Rod, Street Rodder*—that was the best, because it had a "custom" section. We built custom hot rod model kits and talked about what we would do. We also started going to custom car shows. I went to Catholic school, and they told us to do a project over Easter vacation, so I built a '55 Corvette model kit. We had an older cousin who had a purple '57 Chevy—he was kinda wild, and we thought, "He's so cool."

♦ V: When did you start going to rockabilly or punk shows?
♦ JM: 1987. I joined the Marines in 1983 when I was 18. While I was in the service my brother bought a '51 Mercury. In 1985 he bought a second Merc and came to visit me at Camp Pendleton. We drove to Tijuana and had it tuck-and-rolled—that was awesome. He had that car for nine years.

We grew up in the Mission district and we just *stayed* in the Mission—everything we needed was there: supermarkets, movie theaters. But when I got out of the service—my four year enlistment was up in 1987—I said to Javier, "Hey, let's go to Haight Street—I heard it's really crazy out there!" You should have seen

us the first time we left the neighborhood and started discovering San Francisco; we were pretty amazed. You start to see other subcultures and then you think, "But that's all they've got, while *we* can move on, and see more." But it's also neat when a subculture just keeps its thing going, on and on.

We saw a flyer for a rockabilly band, the Alley Boys, and we went. April, 1987 was the first time we pulled up in the '51 Merc with Tijuana tuck-and-roll to a rockabilly show—that's when we first saw that whole world. We thought, "Ohmigod, I can't believe this actually exists. These people are real greasers!" Back in '87, you'd never see custom cars parked outside rockabilly shows—just us. Now it's snowballed.

♦ **V: *So you got more and more into the rockabilly scene?***
♦ **JM:** Slowly we kept going to more shows. I became roommates with J.J. Nichols, Eddie Nichols' brother, and he told us he want-

---

The car was pink with purple flames. There was no windshield, so I wore swimming goggles to drive.

---

ed to find Royal Crown Revue a gig. Phil Price was there and he said, "Then *we'll* put on a gig!" He had a big garage near Third and Army, and everyone helped get it ready. I put up my own money to buy the beer—I remember worrying if I'd ever make my money back. (It turned out that the booze only lasted a couple of hours.) At that first Royal Crown show, almost nobody was dressed '40s—only the band. There was a group of Mods there (including members of The Loved Ones), because my girlfriend at the time was a Mod and she invited them.

That was early 1991, and for the next year it seemed like Royal Crown would drive up to San Francisco at least every couple weeks in their old RV which broke down several times. One time it hit a school crossing sign in front of our flat—it's *still* bent! Their early gigs were kinda lame; they played Marsugi's in San Jose (a pizza place), the Chatterbox in the daytime (!). Our house became Royal Crown's unofficial S.F. headquarters—other band members might stay elsewhere, but everyone would check in. (Sometimes Eddie would stay with Phil, who lived at 18th between Guerrero & Valencia, just two blocks away.) They would rehearse and set up the snare drum in our kitchen—they'd play for whoever was in the house. One time Russell Scott was in town and he and Eddie came over and stayed up all night in the kitchen singing doowop. Then Russell passed out on the kitchen floor—he was so big we couldn't move him, so we left him there!

In general, after rockabilly shows, we started having all-night parties at our house in the Mission. There'd be 80 people crammed in there.

♦ **V: *When did you actually start chopping vintage cars?***
♦ **JM:** In '87 we bought another '51 Merc that was already chopped, but not running, and we pulled the engine out, put in another one and got it running. The worst was going to shops

when we didn't know much and asking for advice. We taught ourselves by asking people, bothering people, meeting people—at a car show we'd ask, "How'd you wire that alternator?" We never chopped a car ourselves; there are some famous customizers out there, some of whom charge $5,000 for chopping a car.

Once I picked up my brother at the place where he'd had his car painted, and it was pink with purple flames. There was no windshield, so I wore swimming goggles to drive. The police pulled us over: "What the hell is this: a pink car, with purple flames?!" They made us walk off the freeway and they pushed the car off. I have a photo of the Cramps by it.

We had a lot of adventures back then—mainly involving things breaking down. We were cruising down the freeway and the 40-year-old windshield caved in—I had to prop my feet up against it while my brother drove. Then the brakes went out, and all we had was the emergency brake. We were young and foolish, so we continued to cruise; every time we had to stop, we just downshifted and pulled the emergency brake. But we shoulda gone home!

♦ **V: *How many cars have you customized?***
♦ **JM:** Besides the two '51 Mercs, I have a '31 Ford—that's the car I got married in. We're currently working on a 1960 Chevrolet Impala with a metal flake top, custom tail-lights.

Ten years ago you never used to see custom cars parked at a rockabilly or an "alternative" show, and the swing scene didn't exist. You could see plenty of chopped and channeled cars at car shows, but not at a Cramps concert. Now there are rockabilly kids getting into the cars, and kids who were formerly just into the cars are getting into rockabilly. The car shows used to be nothing but serious *truly* blue-collar, non-"alternative" people in baseball caps and Letterman jackets–fifty-year-old men with cool cars, and we'd say, "I wish there were more kids into this." Now that there are, we go, "I wish there weren't so many people into this." [laughs]

About five years ago the book *Kustom Kulture* came out. That

Trashwomen Elka, Tina & Danielle with José at the Colma Jewish Cemetery, 1993

cross-pollinated the custom car culture with "alternative" culture. I think it was the tattoo artists who introduced Big Daddy Roth to "alternative" people. Recently another book came out, *Hot Rod*, which has many photos of rockabilly and heavily-tattooed punk people with hot rods. *Gearhead* magazine appeals to the punk audience, but with a custom car influence, whereas if you pick up *Street*

Rodder, all you see is 50-year-old men with cool cars. *International Tattoo Art* (Nov '97) had a big color piece on custom cars.

Another cross-pollination has involved Mexican wrestling shows. The *real* Mexican wrestlers have their names in English; it's only the more "punk" or Americanized wrestlers who use names like "El Chicone." [laughs]

♦ *V: Outside the Greaseball, the entire block was filled with old custom cars—an awesome sight. At night one guy did a demonstration, where flames shot out of his tailpipes—*

♦ JM: Flamethrowers. They have a sparkplug tapped into the tailpipe, with separate coils, and I think they run the carburetor extra-rich. You can buy a kit now; it came out about five years ago. But before they had them, we read a magazine article about how to do this yourself.

♦ *V: Where do you live?*

♦ JM: In the Excelsior neighborhood; I bought a house. Around my neighborhood we have what we call "urban rednecks"—what I call "Level One." The 49ers rule here; so do the Giants. KMEL rules; if you listen to punk rock, you're a weirdo. It's another culture compared to Haight Street, where everything has to be alternative/underground. I can understand why a lot of punk rockers hate jocks, but now I realize that for people like my neighbors, "That's all they know." It's like they never took advantage of all the diversity in the city. It's kinda sad in a way, but also kinda "trippy."

I didn't go to the Greaseball this year; my wife and I were in Germany for the Oktoberfest. I thought it was awesome: "These Germans are crazy!" We saw a daredevil motorcycle exhibit. Coming from the Cholo world, not all the Cholos were open-minded—even now. It was when I was in the Marines that suddenly I was thrown in with people from all over and I went, "You're from Tennessee? What the hell is that?" I thought, "I gotta see more of the world." That's why as soon as I came back I said, "Jav, we're going to this rockabilly show." I like to trip off all these little subcultures. You have to stay open; you *see* a lot more. **V**

INTERVIEW WITH CINDY MEJIA

♦ *VALE: Tell us about your family background—*

♦ CINDY MEJIA: My dad was born May 13, 1920 in Calgary, Canada and my mom was born in Mexico. I was born Feb. 20, 1967 in Pacifica [near San Francisco] and I have a brother who's 6 years older. My dad was always in his basement "shop" rebuilding antique motorcycle parts—people send him orders from all over, even Australia. He raced motorcycles in the '40s, served in World War II, and then raced after the war. He still rides at the age of 77! My brother's got a bike, and his wife, too. None of us use the term "biker," we call ourselves "motorcycle enthusiasts."

My mother died of leukemia when I was nine, so then it was just the three of us. Later we got a stepmother—she was very into motorcycles and that's how my dad and her met. When I lived at home, I used to help my dad. If anything broke, you fixed it. My dad made a lot of things, like a dollhouse for me. My brother wanted a bicycle, and my dad was too cheap to go out and buy one. He took a girl's bike and welded a bar across. We learned early on that if something had to be done, you just did it. So when I got my first car, it didn't make any sense to have anybody else work on it. In our family, we never liked to be helpless.

Growing up, my parents took me all over the state to motorcycle swap meets. We went to a few motorcycle races, although those mostly had stopped in the '60s. When I was about nine, my father stuck me on a bike, and I did well until he mentioned shifting gears—that freaked me out! Growing up, motorcycles weren't that cool—low-riders were cool. Now I like 'em both.

In high school I was a Chola and started saving up money for a low-rider car. This girl I knew had a creepy boyfriend who'd found a '65 Impala that an old person was selling cheap ($1,100), but he didn't have the money yet. I went and bought it out from under him! I painted it black.

♦ *V: What jobs did you have?*

♦ CM: I've been working since I was 15! I first worked a summer job as a receptionist for a typewriter-repair shop; then I worked at A&W as a waitress. When I bought the car I was printing photographs at a one-hour photo lab.

♦ *V: Why did you want a low-rider car?*

♦ CM: Those cars were "in" in our crowd. To make a low-rider car there are certain requirements. For me, the car has to be long and "aerodynamic," and the '65 is the only Impala like that. There were '70s low-rider cars, but to me they belonged in the circus. Then there are the "bombs"—cars from the '40s, but I thought parking would be a problem. Besides, to me that was a car you got when you were older. It's funny; I just told my husband, "We're old enough that we need a bomb now!"

♦ *V: What happened to that '65 Impala?*

♦ CM: I sold it when I was 21. For the next three years I took electronics classes at a junior college and worked full-time fixing Canon copiers—I started that job when I was 19, while going to school at night. Then I went to work for a medical-electronics company, fixing non-invasive blood pressure monitors. When I was 24, I went to Munich to work for Siemens Medical as part of an "exchange program"—I saw a flyer for it at school. I worked a year and stayed another year because I had a rich boyfriend. I came back broke and lived at my dad's for awhile, and got back into the electronics industry.

I had started learning how to ride bikes before moving to Germany. When I came back, my dad offered me one of his Harleys and I didn't like it. I tried his 1930 Indian 101 Scout and thought, "This is it!" It's lower, lighter, and when you shift you can *feel* you're in gear—it's not mushy like a Harley. I felt like I was one with the bike. With the Harley, I always felt like I was sitting on top of the bike, but with the 101 you can steer it just with your legs.

My dad found a 1928 Indian 101 frame and gave it to me as a birthday present (it was crooked, so he had to straighten it). Then it took months for both of us to find the parts and put it together. I did all the wiring. The color is Indian Red; somebody who owed my dad money painted it.

♦ *V: Why do you like your motorcycle?*

♦ CM: It's responsive; different from a car. It's not the smoothest ride—that's for sure, but it's loud and it's fun. They do break down a lot. I'm real happy that José is riding now, too.

♦ *V: You haven't been in any wrecks?*

♦ CM: No. My bike has a "suicide clutch," so I have to really

> We have a saying, "Four doors—say no more." Now we go, "Oh, it's a *punk rocker!*" Somebody with purple hair can have a car with four doors.

concentrate when I ride. I don't take chances. Maybe if you have a newer bike you can, but . . . My dad's always been real careful, and he's always taught us to be real careful.

♦ *V: What's your "day" transportation?*

♦ CM: I have a company car.

♦ *V: How did you meet José?*

♦ CM: I saw him at a bunch of parties before we were finally introduced. I should have met him years earlier. But as soon as we started going out, we decided to get married—it just took a year to plan the wedding.

♦ *V: What was your wedding like?*

Cindy Mejia with her vintage 1928 Indian motorcycle, 11-30-97. Photo: V. Vale

♦ CM: It was a traditional Mexican wedding in a Catholic church, with certain rituals. We had the mariachi in the church—we got more compliments for that than anything else. Leaving, we had all the cars and some motorcycles lined up outside—that was pretty cool. And we were in José's 1931 Model A Ford—I rewired that, by the way. It's painted a primer rust color.

José's in a car club, the Royal Jokers. At the wedding most of the car people were friends of José's, and most of the bike people were friends of mine. I met the bike people mostly through my dad, and have known many of them since I was ten or younger. My dad gave us a Lincoln welding outfit as a wedding present, and now we're both getting better at welding.

♦ V: *You're just naturally very practical, I guess*—

♦ CM: Probably because my mother died and my brother and I had to *do what had to be done.* It was never, "You do this because you're the girl, and *you* do that because you're the boy." If someone had to cook, or clean, or hold something while my dad welded it, whoever was there had to do it. There was never a distinction. I have to credit my father for that; he never instilled in us what we could or couldn't do because of our gender. It's funny, because most people would think he's probably a chauvinist, 'cuz he's kinda rough around the edges, but *nope!*

Now I'm taking a computer repair course, because for the job I have now I need to know more. I'll never be done; there's always something I want to learn. José and I are planning to take a welding class. I took a machining class—that was fun.

♦ V: *Are you into rockabilly and "retro"?*

♦ CM: Yeah, that's how José and I met. If you're a Chola, then by definition you are into vintage stuff. You already like the music: the R&B oldies, *not* the Dick Clark oldies—we make a big distinction! A lot of the styles that the Cholas wear are reminiscent of the pachucas from the '40s. So we like the '40s and the '50s where the guys had the baggy pants and the girls wore beaded sweaters. In high school you had to know where all the second-

hand stores were as part of "Chola culture." Cholas were always into secondhand stuff: old clothes, old cars, old music. In high school I think I would have died if I'd heard rockabilly—that was just not "in" with us—no way. But later on, it was an easy transition. It's funny: José's got the exact same background. We went from being hardcore Cholo to running with rockabilly people.

♦ V: *The rockabilly people obviously borrowed from you; look at all the old cars outside the shows now*—

♦ CM: Yeah, but they get four-doors. I still can't figure that one out. A four-door is not cool unless it's suicide doors [where the door handles meet in the middle]. Any time an old car, especially a bomb, has four doors, it's just not cool. So it's weird when we see a nice car that has four doors; we have a saying, "Four doors—say no more." Now we go, "Oh, it's a punk rocker!" Somebody with purple hair can have a car with four doors; they don't mind. It's funny; to us you wouldn't go out of the house if you had four doors. Even if a car was super-clean, you wouldn't buy it: "Yeah, it's a cool *year,* and there's no dents, *but* it'll always be a four-door."

♦ V: *You still haven't abandoned your "retro" roots*—

♦ CM: My cousin first took me to the Deluxe in 1989, about six months after it opened. I saw the old clothes on people, and I hadn't worn that stuff in years. (You grow out of being a Chola; you just couldn't get a job looking that way. It was a natural progression to just wear jeans, or whatever.) I went, "Ohmigod, this is too cool!" and the next weekend we returned all dressed up. We went every weekend, at least once a week. The clothes were easy to find and cheap then, because nobody was doing it.

♦ V: *You have an extended family, with cousins and other relatives being an important part, whereas most "white" people don't have that*—

♦ CM: You guys move too much! My cousins are maybe five minutes away. I would never leave San Francisco because I would never leave my family. I'm mad that my brother moved an hour away!

I mean, nobody else has done that; that's really bizarre for us.

My cousin taught me about rockabilly. I remember going, "What's that?" She took me to a show where Royal Crown Revue was playing a garage party at Hunter's Point. As I walked in, there was an old motorcycle and I went, [admiringly] "Hey—what's this?!" José was there—I remember, because his brother Javier spilled beer on me. But José was just too cool. Then I went to Germany, and didn't see him again until I got back. When I got back there was a lot more going on; the Ace Cafe had events, the Paradise . . .

♦ V: So you and José were at that first Royal Crown show in San Francisco—

Javier Mejia's 1951 custom Mercury, purple with green flames.

♦ CM: Yeah, and I thought, "These guys are great! What are they doing *here?*" [laughs]

♦ V: Do you remember seeing any live music at the Deluxe besides Mr. Lucky?

♦ CM: No, there was nothing. He was the first one. And he has a nice car. The Deluxe was great; I thought, "Oh, a place to wear fur again!" My dad's ex-girlfriend was a Pachuca from the '40s and she had this stole that had padded shoulders, really cool, and she gave it to me when I was 15. I always looked up to her; she was a neat lady.

♦ V: So you were in the Chola culture—

♦ CM: We were in it *hardcore*. In high school you couldn't get away from it—the school was mostly Hispanics. Most of my girlfriends are still my friends, so we've known each other 15-plus years.

As a kid I've always liked old cars and old motorcycles. I don't look at a new car and think it looks "good," I think they've really screwed up as far as style goes. I think there's no comparison. With lots of cars you can't tell what's what; about the only new car I can recognize is a Cadillac.

♦ V: And the new Cadillacs don't look that great—

♦ CM: But at least you can tell it's a Cadillac!

♦ V: I don't want to look at this "retro movement" as some fad—

♦ CM: I'm sure it is for some people, but for the rest of us, we just

kinda giggle. When this "thing" started to be more popular and "swing" was in everyone's vocabulary again, a lot of people said, "Humph—all these new people!" I go, "Wait a minute—*you* were new a year ago!" When I first got back from Germany I went, "Wow—things have changed!" I didn't see any of the old people, and all the new people look at you like, "Where are *you* from?"

We love old stuff. I have a lot of dresses that I don't get to wear, because we're so busy. I perform in a samba group. Now, when you go out on the dance floor, people bang against you; they have no concept of space. I go out there and get stepped on and abused and I don't like to go out there. I'll go salsa dancing because they're not going to step on me. We still go to anything at Bimbo's because it's the best place in the city. We're probably going to see Brian Setzer play the Warfield on New Year's—it's big, so there's room to dance. But these days we go to more car or bike shows if we have spare time.

There's been times when vintage bikes were in, and people would buy them, and when they were bored with them, they'd sell them. Just like right now you see a lot of people on Harleys. Well later on, that just means more Harley parts for the people who are *really* into them. The mood swings back and forth. I can't wait for the time when secondhand clothes aren't "in" anymore, so I can buy them for less! **V**

Some Books and Magazines

The American Hot Rod
Hot Rods & Customs of the 1960s
Hot Rods of the 1950s
Hot Rods by Ed "Big Daddy" Roth
Barris: Kustoms of the 1950s
Custom Cars of the 1950s
Hot Rods by Pete and Jake
Confessions of a Rat Fink (Roth)
The Lowbrow Art of Robert Williams
Visual Addiction (Robert Williams)
Monster (Sanyika Shakur)
Hell's Angels (Hunter S. Thompson)
Going Down to the Barrio (Moore)
Growing Up Latino (ed. Augenbaum & Stavans)
Don't Spit on My Corner (Miguel Duran)
Always Running (Luis J. Rodriguez)
Macho! (Victor Villasenor)
Material World (Menzel)
Vargas (Taschen Publications)

The Art of the Cocktail (Philip Collins)
Vintage Aircraft Nose Art (Gary M. Valant)
The Immortal Elvis Presley
Three Seconds from Eternity (Doisneau)
The Pearl & Burning Bright (John Steinbeck)`
The Sting Man (Robert W. Greene)
Angels in the Gutter (Joseph Hilton)
Drawn and Quartered (Charles Addams)
Saints Preserve Us! (Kelly & Rogers)
A Brief History of Time (Stephen W. Hawking)
David Niven: Go Slowly, Come Back Quickly
You and Your Superstitions (Brewton Berry)
The Cycle Jumpers (Marshall Spiegel)
Hot Rod Fury (Robert Sidney Bowen)
Building and Racing the Hot Rod
Hot Rod It and Run for Fun!
Hot Rod, Crash Club, Street Rod, Rag Top, Fever Heat, Road Rocket, Here Is Your Hobby: Car Customizing: by Henry Gregory Felsen

1) Jason Pierotti's car outside 1997 Greaseball
2) Bimbo's after Vise Grip show, 1996, L to R: Susan Galvin, John Dickerman, Roberto Isola, DeAnne Balestreri, Mateo Reichlin, Anna Silva, Mike Carballo, Mario Gomez, unknown.
3) dancing at Bimbo's: Meleksah David and Paul
4) Pearl Harbor's living room, San Francisco, 10-96
5) retro tattoo on Johnny Swing by Tony Mills, 1996
6) Bimbo's, 1996: Peachy's Puff retro-cigarette girl.
All photos except #2 by V. Vale, #2 photographer unk.

Bimbo's • Hi-Ball

In San Francisco, Bimbo's and the Hi-Ball Lounge are primary supporters of the "swing" movement.

Left: Bimbo's Italian statuary in lobby. Below: Johnny & Cari's swing dance troupe show off a few steps.

Emberley & Buddy

BIMBO'S 365 CLUB

1025 Columbus Ave, San Francisco CA 94133 (415-474-0365)

is the most beautiful nightclub in America. This is because one family has owned and operated it since its beginning.

Sept 21, 1903, Agostino Giuntoli (nicknamed "Bimbo" by his mother), left the family farm in Chriesina Uzzanese, Tuscany, Italy in 1922 and worked his way to San Francisco. In 1931 he became partners with "Monk" Young, who owned the 365 Club on the 2nd floor of 365 Market Street (Bimbo bought out his partner in 1936). The gorgeous art deco club was square with a dining room and two large bars, one of which was located behind the orchestra pit and featured a stand-alone serpentine bar accommodating seven bartenders.

In 1932, with the aid of a magician friend, Bimbo implemented "The Girl in the Fishbowl": Dolfina, a nude girl who appears to be swimming amidst live goldfish. *Life* magazine (Dec 20, 1948) did a photo-feature exposing how this illusion was accomplished. Besides building up a reputation as a chef, Bimbo occasionally entertained on clarinet and mandolin. His philosophy was "There's no substitute for class," and "The club should be as comfortable as a home." With his derby, cashmere overcoats, spats and diamond-encrusted "365" stickpin, he cut a dashing figure.

During Prohibition, Bimbo's was a speakeasy with a one-way mirror in the front door, boasting the largest collection of Prohibition liquor in San Francisco. The policy was "No tie, no

entree," and they turned away Howard Hughes once. The seven-night-a-week club with shows at 8, 10:30 and 1 AM, featured big acts, nightly revues and leggy chorus lines which once included Rita Hayworth, who was paid $35 a week. In 1939, Bimbo's Sunday dinners were $1 ("and what a dinner, yeah man!").

In 1951 the club was renamed *Bimbo's* 365 Club and moved to a larger, flashier location (capacity: 685) at the former Bel Tabarin, designed by S.F. architect Timothy Pflueger ca.1937. Besides the grand ballroom (4000 sq. ft.) with a 23´x31´ main stage and an adjacent side-stage, there were the Twist Room with individual juke-boxes (r.i.p.), the dimly-lit lounge and the main bar—all decorated in rich reds and vibrant brasses. The women's room features individual vanity stations (and there are attendants in both bathrooms), the lobby showcases a marble sculpture commissioned from Italy, and there are exuberant paintings of naked women and satyrs throughout the club. Not glimpsed by the public is an enormous stainless-steel kitchen and an upstairs honeycombed with various rooms.

Among the hundreds of artists who appeared were Louis Prima, Duke Ellington, Esquivel, Buddy Rich and Frank Sinatra, Jr. By the late '60s, topless and bottomless routines, psychedelia, pressure from unions and the six-figure salaries paid to entertainers by Reno and Vegas clubs, all combined to extinguish the larger supper clubs across the U.S. Bimbo closed down on

New Year's Eve, 1969, with his favorite vocalist, Al Martino. However, the club continued to book conventions, parties and private events such as Iggy Pop's legendary appearances in 1974, the Tubes' shows in 1975 and the Crime/Weirdos punk show in 1977.

By 1979 the management of Bimbo's had passed to Graziano Cerchiai (Bimbo's son-in-law, who married daughter Diana). Among others, Bette Midler and Buster Poindexter (David Johansen of the New York Dolls) appeared at the concerts that were occasionally staged. Then in 1988 Graziano passed on the keys to his son Michael Cerchiai, then 28, who implemented a shrewd booking policy to ensure the club's survivability (just to open the doors costs an estimated $2,000). Michael's first show was on June 25, 1988, with Timmie Hesla and the Converse All-Stars, plus the Dinos in the lounge.

Bimbo's has been instrumental in developing the swing scene in San Francisco (and supporting rockabilly/American roots music), booking acts such as Royal Crown Revue, Vise Grip, The New Morty Show, Steve Lucky & The Rhumba Bums, and Big Sandy. Our thanks to Michael Cerchiai, Graziano and Diana, Gino, Anne Jaso, Mira Prinz and Tara Keller for all their assistance. **V**

SOME SHOWS AT BIMBO'S:

Atomic Cocktail • Ray Condo • 8½ Souvenirs • Johnny Dilks & His Visitacion Valley Boys • Big Sandy • Sloe Gin Joes • Sam Butera • Big Bad Voodoo Daddy • Lavay Smith & The Red Hot Skillet Lickers • Blue Plate Special • Lee Press-On & the Nails • The Collins Kids • Rockin' Lloyd Tripp and His Three Tons of Fun • The Big Six • Phantom Surfers • The Sugar King Boys • Wally's Swing World • Useless Playboys • Mr. Lucky • Johnny Nocturne • Jay Johnson • Frenchy • Jumpin' Jimes • Molasses Brothers • Saturn V (garage) • Wanda Jackson • Rosie Flores • Blue Bell Wranglers • Mingo 2000 • The Inciters and Miss Mergatroid (eccentric accordion activist) •

Outside Bimbo's 365 Club. Line includes Squeaky, Frenchy, Suzi Hutsell, Paul Russell, Monique Jennings, Fritz Striker (?). Work That Skirt video shoot in progress. Photo: V. Vale, 10-4-97.

1) Hi-Ball Dec 97: L to R: Jason Stewart, Suzi Krieger, Tobias Hampton, Johnny & Cari Swing, Singrid Fortney, Rainy Culbertson, Christian Mikkelson. 2) GB Japanese dancers

HI-BALL LOUNGE

473 Broadway, SF CA 94133
TEL 415-39SWING; *hiball.com.*

Located in San Francisco's legendary North Beach neighborhood, The Hi-Ball Lounge is presently San Francisco's only 7-night-a-week club for beginning/intermediate swing/roots music bands. Capacity is about 100 (main room 20´x100´, plus a basement for restrooms, storage and offices); perfect for seeing bands before they become huge. Bands who got a leg up still play unadvertised/"underground" shows there, like the Big Bad Voodoo Daddy event in 1997 (with a line around the block).

The sons of '50s jazz saxophonist Bob Young, Max and Sam Young grew up in a jazz milieu. The brothers opened up a blues club titled Blues (2125 Lombard; 415-771-2583) before opening up the Hi-Ball Lounge in November, 1995. Just a blue vertical neon "Hi-Ball" sign marks the club's location on the site of the former Jazz Workshop. Max and Sam implemented a retro-style decor, utilizing an existing bar near the front entrance. Retro graphics and photos of icons embellish the walls upstairs and downstairs. The stage is wrapped in red velvet with two fake palm trees; the east wall has exposed brick with booths while the opposite wall has a leopard sound-absorbent panel. Every seat in the house offers unobstructed visibility, thanks to the elevated stage, and there is a good dance floor. Sound and lights are excellent.

Sam Young also offers a line of retro clothing (at present, three bowling shirts and a shirt-jacket) which is sold at the club. On Sunday and Monday nights Spencer deejays "swing" music, and on Sunday and Tuesday nights at 7 PM Johnny & Cari Swing offer Lindy-Hop lessons (call 415-548-8193 for info). Lee Press-On & The Nails recorded their first CD at the Hi-Ball, and a Hi-Ball compilation CD is scheduled for release. Colorful "retro" postcards listing the club's schedule are available monthly; the schedule is also posted on their website. On weekends, patrons are advised to show up early; the club regularly sells out. And there is a dress code: no athletic shoes or "grunge" clothing (ripped jeans/T-shirt) are acceptable.

The Hi-Ball features acts from horn "swing" bands to the Sloe Gin Joes led by roots guitar personality Frank Novicki. The first act when the club opened was "Johnny and Ricky": Ricky Quisol (drums) accompanying dynamo boogie-woogie pianist Johnny Goetchius. The Hi-Ball offers a beautiful environment to learn or practice dancing, listen to music, or just hang out and meet people. As a friend of Max

Young's put it, "The nicest thing about going to the Hi-Ball is that no one hit on me. The guys were totally cool; they helped me learn how to dance; people were very friendly. It's a great scene for a single woman." **V**

SOME BANDS WHO HAVE PLAYED THE HI-BALL

The Mr. Lucky Experience • Sloe Gin Joes • The Chazz Cats • Atomic Cocktail • Jellyroll, Frenchy • The Hammond Cheese Combo • The Tim Hesla Big Band • Indigo Swing • The New Morty Show • Wally's Swing World • Blue Plate Special • Steve Lucky and the Rhumba Bums • The Dizzy Burnett Combo • Ben Mercato's Mondo Combo • The Chrome Addicts • The Esotericons • Acme Swing • Jumpin Jimes • Red and the Red Hots • The Mood Swing Orchestra • The Mitch Woods & his Rocket 88's • The Colorifics • Jack Duvall Combo • The Josh Jones Quartet featuring Shaharazade • Tiny James & the Swing Kings • the band formerly known as the Swinging Johnsons • The Swingin' Matt Cassell Trio • Lavay Smith & the Red Hot Skillet Lickers • Mingo 2000 • The Riff Rats • The Savoy Swingers • the Swamis • Clint Baker's New Orleans Jazz Band • Timmie Hesla's The Rat Bastards of Swing • The Richard Olsen Quintet • Campbell's Soup • Jeff Bright and the Sunshine Boys • Marcie Jean and the Swing Set • The Martini Brothers • Mood Swing Orchestra • The Dutch Falconi Orchestra • Johnny Dilks & the Rhythm Rustlers • Pee-Wee Thomas & the Safecrackers • Spo-Dee-O-Dee (from Germany) • Herb • El Camino Cha Cha Orchestra • The Colorifics • The Smoke Jumpers • The Hi-Jinx Trio • The Leopard Lounge • Bob Dalpe & Out of Nowhere •

3) Bimbo's 1-17-97 (New Morty/Lee Press-On): Richie Dawkins, Allison Williams 4) GAMH 8-30-97 (Swing Jam Weekend) 5) Bimbo's 9-19-97 (Big Sandy): Renee, Kurt 6) Bimbo's 12-31-97 Fred Stuart, vocalist extraordinaire for Blue Plate Special, a very special band from Chico, now relocated to Los Angeles.

CAFE DU NORD

2170 Market St, San Francisco CA 94114
415-861-5016. www.cafedunord.com

Was a former speakeasy, now a downstairs club with a Victorian/bordello ambiance—lurid red walls and carpeting. It boasts a long, hand-carved mahogany bar. Capacity is 250, and food is served Wed-Sat. The cover originally was $2 and was just recently raised to $5 (weekends).

The Du Nord was started by two bartenders from the Deluxe, Cindy Johnson and Jon Varnadoe, who by good fortune found a former Basque restaurant for rent. They were helped initially by an experienced restaurateur-consultant, Peter Garin. At the time Jon had $200 in his bank account and Cindy had a negative $400 balance, but the Swedish-American landlords trusted them and didn't ask for a credit check! After raising money, and with the help of carpenter-plumber friends, they opened the Du Nord on Feb 14, 1991 as a jazz club with the Unknown Giants (quartet) playing. It took awhile for "swing" to bring in a crowd on a regular basis, so initially the Du Nord was booking a wide spectrum of acts: cabaret (including drag performers), straight jazz and '50s retro Tito Puente-style salsa acts.

Early on, Tracy Dick started rockabilly-deejaying and booking "American roots music" shows; the first being the Boogie Men. Big Sandy played a number of

times
(including, Tracy's wedding, 10-8-94), and so did Royal Crown Revue. In 1992 the Du Nord started "Atomic Swing Thursdays" booking Atomic Cocktail (1st gig April 8, 1992), Lavay Smith, Vise Grip's St. Vitus Dance, Bo Grumpus (ragtime), and Russell Scott & His Red Hots. By December Lavay Smith & The Red Hot Skillet

Lickers were regularly playing Saturdays, and that has continued to date.

Virtually all the bands spearheading the "retro-swing movement" have played there: Timmie Hesla, Royal Crown Revue (at least 3-4 times), Big Bad Voodoo Daddy, New Morty Show, Atomic Cocktail, Mr. Lucky, Ray Condo, Dave & Deke Combo, 8½ Souvenirs, Lee Press-On & The Nails, Squirrel Nut Zippers (9-3-95; 1996), and many more "roots" bands. Lavay Smith has organized two "Swing for Choice" benefits, and one "Swing for Single Payer Houseplan" benefit. The Upstairs Ballroom has hosted several events featuring the David Hardiman Big Band, Rudy Salvini Big Band, and Timmie Hesla on 12-12-92. Besides numerous other colorful events such as the two exhibits of Slimm Buick's "art bicycles," the Du Nord has also hosted outlandish New Year's Extravaganzas, a Surrealist Costume Ball, and a recreation of the last dinner served on the Titanic, including the actual music played.

In 1995 Jon Varnadoe left to work at Bruno's, and Cindy remained as sole owner, with Nancy Myers booking shows. Currently, Nancy and Cindy are launching the Du Nord record label (*Market Street: A Live Compilation* released).

THE DELUXE

1511 Haight St, San Francisco CA 94117
415-552-6949

This was where the "retro-swing lifestyle" incubated in San Francisco. A former gay bar purchased by Jay Johnson and reopened June 7, 1989, the art deco setting offered a 7-night-a-week locale where people could meet, talk, listen to music and dance. Initially the music included all types of "American roots" music, thanks to early deejay-record collectors Slimm Buick and Peter Becker. Tracy Dick played rockabilly music once a week; the other nights emphasized jazz and swing. The club drew the rockabilly crowd (who like to "dress up"), including Ricky Quisol (in the '80s, he made his own zoot suit) and the four Estrellas Brothers.

Members of the Art Deco Society (whom Jay invited), early vintage-clothing aficionados like Jack "The Hat" Perkins (the first bartender hired) and Roberto Isola, and what became the "swing crowd" (about 30 people!) started congregating there. Poverty was the main reason people dressed in vintage clothes; they were the cheapest way to "look sharp." Flea-market aficionados like David Dean and college students like Dutch Penfield started dressing up and hanging out there almost nightly. The Deluxe remains a primary hangout for people early (or "deep") into the scene. Bands like The New Morty Show, Royal Crown Revue and 8½ Souvenirs still do unpublicized shows there in the spirit of the once-underground movement.

The Deluxe began in context of high-decibel "alternative" rock concerts, post-New Wave discos, enormous raves, smart drinks—in *reaction* to these, Jay Johnson wanted to have a place where people could socialize, talk and not have

to scream in each other's ears. The "Deco/Atomic" Deluxe had been remodeled in 1949, the beginning of the cocktail era, and all Jay had to do was to restore it. It was partly the design of the club that dictated a different musical emphasis (on Sinatra, Count Basie, etc) to go with the martinis served. The club was never about putting on live music shows; with two adjoining rooms (capacity 49 each), it's suited for a small torch-singer act, at best. The Deluxe didn't have a cabaret license until a couple years ago. Nevertheless, when Royal Crown Revue played several unadvertised shows there ca. '91–92 (and also at Phil Price's warehouse in 1991), they inspired the formation of local swing bands. Atomic Cocktail started early '92. Vise Grip premiered St. Vitus Dance

in Sept '92; he got a friend on the local newspaper to write about him and the Deluxe "scene." Then *CNN* came to the Deluxe to film a feature on the "swing movement," and the resulting attention brought by mainstream media (according to Jay) ruined everything! Ⅴ

Jay Johnson History

Jay Johnson's "history": Ground Zero cafe, 783 Haight St./Scott, '85–'95. 530 Club (530 Haight St), 6 months. Deluxe: opened '89. Orbit Room, 1900 Market, 415-252-9525: opened July '91.

L to R: Catrine Ljunggren (Rhythm Hotshots, SwedenL), Rob van Haaren, Diane Thomas. Photo: V. Vale, 11-97

Early Swingers

People in the Early Scene (most not mentioned or pictured elsewhere)
DELUXE: *Bartenders:* Jack Perkins, Jon Varnadoe, Cindy Johnson, Jack Stevens, John Richardson, Peter, Marinell, Dutch Penfield, Kevin Fosdick; Jeff Koch. *Doormen:* Yo-Yo, Scotty, Vise Grip; Mike Haber, Mike Daley, Fritz, Jimmy. *Waitresses:* Laurie Lee, Katarina, Paula Negri, Anna-Lisa, Holly Fagerbau. Chris "Coatcheck" Blum. Gentry Lane, Pam, Penny, Libby, Karen, Cookie, Jane. *Deejays:* Peter Becker, Slimm Buick, Tracy Dick; Phil Slash, Alexi. Klaus Haus, Annie Greiner. Oyster Bar: Big Nate, Jason Macanu. Sunday Brunch: Heather, Bob.
DELUXE CROWD [partial listing]: Vanessa Silva-D'Amelio, Diana Alden, Laura Borsh, Lisa Butterhead, Daniela, Jessica Davis, Shauna Goodkin, Laurie Gordon, Tracy/Sean Hickey (lawyer), Gerry/Steve Irwin, Janet (mar. Tim Hesla), Pat Johnson, Mark & Chris Kapka, Sara Klotz (sang at Deluxe), Kimberly Manning, Maya/Kristy, Joe Oliver, Petey (Jay's bulldog); Dave Sampson, Shannon/Ray, Alberta Sterub, Tracy, Christy Ward, Mark Whienhold. Plus people cited elsewhere by Mr. Lucky, etc.
SATU'S LIST: Mark Alvarez, Addrynn Clegg, Craig "The Pup", Karla Fixx, Peter Kirsch, Joey Myers, Paul "Ponyboy" Nelson, Robin Rocha, Che Shul (plus son & daughter), Jen Smith, Rick Tanner, Justin, Nicole Vigil.
SUNNY BUICK'S LIST: Joey Ahearn, Valerie Barnd (San Jose), Bethany, Bita & Joanne, Cammy Blackstone, Becky Cavin, Rudy Chalard, David & Donald Dean, Dens Havoc, George Huit, Jane, Jenna, Joanne, Richard Krinker, Larry (Peanut), Amy Muirhead, Liza Mae, Melissa, Chris Monda, Sam, Tammy, Carolyn Terry, Joe Ward. Corrections? Call 415 *362-1465*. V

Dance instruction by Rob & Diane

Rob van Haaren was born in Amsterdam 36 years ago and trained with Sweden's Rhythm Hot Shots by attending their yearly international swing-dance camp at Herrang, Sweden, held in July. The Rhythm Hot Shots are largely responsible for reviving the most acrobatic partner-dance of the 20th century, the Lindy Hop (the dance that American—and Nazi—white society tried to keep away from their sons and daughters). TRHS began aggressively archiving all possible documentation (surviving films, soundies, recordings, photos, magazines, books, etc) and helped locate and bring out of retirement surviving Lindy Hop dance pioneers, including Frankie Manning (who worked 30 years as a postman), Norma Miller, etc.

There are Lindy Hop societies in most countries, and dance workshops are held throughout the year: in Oslo, Norway, Finland, Switzerland, Germany, London, Singapore, Australia, Yugoslavia, Austria, Belgium, Barcelona, Holland, Belgium, France, and in America: Washington, D.C., NY, Texas, Florida, Seattle, Chicago, Ventura, Catalina Island, Boston, etc.

During World War II, American soldiers brought the Lindy Hop to Sweden (and other European countries) and the dance remained active, particularly in Sweden. In 1982 the Rhythm Hot Shots were formed; current members include founder Lennart Westerlund, plus Catrine Ljunggren, Evas Lagerqvist, Ulrika Eriksson and Eddie Jansson. They are linked to other Lindy Hop Societies. Their website is linked to the Northern California Lindy Hop Society's website & their telephone number is 011-46-8643-4058. In the Bay Area, Rob van Haaren & partner Diane Thomas ("Rob & Diane") are energetically teaching, preserving and promoting the Lindy Hop, and arguably offer the most scholarly historical and international perspective on this American-invented art form. They may be contacted at 650-579-1122.

1) pre-stage Du Nord '92: Russell Scott. Photo: Jim Knell 2) 1991 Deluxe poster 3) 1994 Deluxe calendar 4) Jay Johnson (with 17-piece Orchestra), Bimbo's, 12-31-97. 5) Deluxe pictured on cover of Deluxe Comix published by Joel Dylan 6) Deluxe July '92: Eddie Nichols, Patty Lagana 7) 1991: YoYo (sic), 1st Deluxe doorman w/Carolyn Terry 8) Deluxe '92, L to R: David Dean, Katarina Fabic, Donald Dean 9) L to R, Phil Price's garage (Phaze, 1814 Illinois St), 1991: Sunny Buick, Becky Cavin, Tracy Dick (top), Jen Smith, Valerie, Bethany 10) Atomic Cocktail at Deluxe, L to R: Ricky Quisol, Sandy Clifford, Vance Ehlers, Dan Eisenberg. (Thanks for photos, Carolyn Terry!)

Deluxe/Du Nord/Rob & Diane **195**

Speakeasies

S.F. SPEAKEASIES

In the close-knit rockabilly-greaser-punk community that incubated the swing movement, parties as well as illegal speakeasies (DIY shows charging low admission fees and selling alcohol, organized by music enthusiastics) played a major supportive role in expanding the aesthetic of the "roots" music scene to embrace swing, Western Swing, etc. The rockabilly underground had long been its own subculture, with its signature music, retro clothing, hairstyles, dances, zines, etc. It was (and continues to be) *genuinely* alternative, because its music is virtually never played on the radio—not even college stations.

A handful of energetic individuals stuck their necks out, worked hard and put on illicit events so "the community" could meet and enjoy music by innovative roots bands struggling to gain an audience. Almost everyone knew each other. Also of note: a few pioneers began dressing "vintage" and partner-dancing (as well as teaching others to partner-dance) as early as the mid-'80s.

A kind of cross-fertilization produced the current swing movement. From Northern California, the four Estrella Brothers (Agustin, Victor, Alex, and Javier who grew up in Petaluma with the 3 Kepler Brothers: Fra, Jacq, Jé) moved to San Francisco and began hosting numerous after-hours parties, first at Agustin's apartment at 3824 Sacramento St, then at an apartment at 1288 17th Avenue/Irving. Their "clan" included Allison (Victor's future wife), Tom and Jeff Orgain, Frank Tena (from Spain), Shannon and Robert Dean, Alex Haslam, Tracy, Susanna, etc. Musicians and friends would gather to jam, sing, flirt and fraternize till dawn. These parties usually followed larger concerts by better-known groups such as the Blasters, Cramps, Stray Cats, X and Paladins, or shows by smaller bands at venues such as the Chi-Chi Club (440 Broadway) run by Miss Keiko and Masa, noteworthy for numerous hanging garter belts from the walls, and the black-and-white tiled floor.

It's difficult to trace exactly how the vintage suit-fedora-wide tie style began, but persons unknown to each other began buying the clothes, partially "because they were the cheapest clothes you could find in thrift stores. And they had such great style!" (Jack Perkins). Agustin cited the Stray Cats (and even Elvis) as an influence: they wore suits, little "Ike" jackets, or baggy pink slacks with a white belt. There used to be cheaper vintage clothes stores: Fellino's at 24th/Mission and Mr Toad's on Polk St; the Third Hand Store was also an early vintage shop. These were hangouts as well as sources of knowledge, and offered flyers for upcoming shows.

By the mid-'80s the Estrella Brothers had begun dressing up (for evening adventures) in

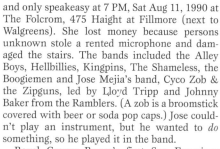

vintage clothes when, thanks to a job connection, Agustin became educated as to the fine points of quality clothing construction. When he realized a $1500 suit could be had for $25 at a vintage store (if you knew what details to look for), all the Estrellas began buying them. A second advantage was: dressed-up, it was "a piece of cake" for the underage brothers to get into over-21 clubs. Having grown up partner-dancing under the tutelage of their Mexican parents, the brothers discovered that: since so few men danced, the ones who did had a "leg up" with the ladies; additionally, it was easy and fun to teach inexperienced women how to dance. Their *modus operandi* involving rounds of cocktails and swing-dances (ultimately ending with a slow dance, and then an exit with the lady of choice) made them the envy of early scenesters at the Deluxe. Dancing began to catch on!

The Estrellas began teaching more and more people how to dance,

At Nancy's: Karla Fixx & Addrynn Clegg dancing in foreground, two rockabilly people in rear, and a mohawked punk in leather wearing a "bitch" pin! Photo: Warren Spicer

such as Jim Knell (photographer from San Jose), and welcomed others into their dancing clan, such as Tracy Dick. They also initiated partner-dancing at the Deluxe, probably as early as 1989.

In the early '90s, after three of the Estrellas moved away (Agustin to NYC; Alex and Javier to L.A.), Jose and Javier Mejia continued the "tradition" of after-hours parties at their house at 711 Treat St, again hosting numerous jam sessions by musicians. Jose and Javier, with their friend Che Shul, were custom-car aficionados associated more with musicians from the South Bay rockabilly scene, including greaser Phil Price, who as a teenager had played with '70s punk band Motor City Bad Boys in Detroit.

To return to the topic of "speakeasies," SF "Rockabilly Queen" Tracy Dick put on her first

and only speakeasy at 7 PM, Sat Aug 11, 1990 at The Folcrom, 475 Haight at Fillmore (next to Walgreens). She lost money because persons unknown stole a rented microphone and damaged the stairs. The bands included the Alley Boys, Hellbillies, Kingpins, The Shameless, the Boogiemen and Jose Mejia's band, Cyco Zob & the Zipguns, led by Lloyd Tripp and Johnny Baker from the Ramblers. (A zob is a broomstick covered with beer or soda pop caps.) Jose couldn't play an instrument, but he wanted to *do* something, so he played it in the band.

Royal Crown Revue's first San Francisco show was at a speakeasy or "barn dance" organized by Phil Price and friends at his garage, "Phaze Industries" (1814 Illinois St). Phil was mildly outraged when he heard that Royal Crown Revue couldn't get a show in San Francisco: "Fuck it man, *we'll* put one on!" He recalls having half a dozen events at Illinois St: "The parties would end when we ran out of booze; usually it would be daylight outside." What follows is a partial listing, according to available documentation:

(Some of) Phil Price's Speakeasies:

Sat Jan 5, 1991 Alley Boys ("Tracy Dick's Birthday"). BRAWL

Sat Feb 9, 1991 Ronnie Dawson, Big Sandy. 1814 Illinois. ($2 admission)

[March__, 1991] Royal Crown Revue. Primal event: birth of the retro-swing movement in S.F.

Phil recalls one speakeasy where The Loved Ones were supposed to show up and they didn't, so an improv band christening themselves "The Loveless" played: Ricky Quisol (dr), Dez Mabunga (bs), and Phil Price (gtr). Also on the bill were the Zip Guns (including Rockin' Lloyd Tripp on bass and Johnny Baker [Ramblers], plus a drummer). According to Phil, RCR played two more times. On one occasion, they played the previous night at Marsugi's, San Jose, & Eddie & Jay Nichols got their arms broken in a fracas. Big Sandy played once more (either Sat, April or Sat, July 27, 1991 with the Hellbillies and Susanna & Her Golden West Playboys). Phil recalls all these events being approximately six weeks apart. The Loveless were the opening act at *all* the shows, and once "Molly Can't Tap" [sic] played. The group had horns, and two tap dancers in lieu of a drummer! (For those interested in how the suit-fedora-wide tie fashion reignited, Loveless drummer Ricky Quisol recalls that in late '86, he opened a show for Chris Isaacs wearing a brown double-breasted suit ($10 in San Jose), fedora, and pumpkin-colored wingtips.)

Phil Price also hosted two speakeasies at The

Photo: Warren Spicer

Phil Price with Gina.

Reanimator (garage), 1100 Revere St in Hunter's Point (no dates). One featured "The Shameless" with Robert Dean (singer), Fra Kepler (gtr), Lloyd Tripp (bass), Jamie Lease (drums); and Phil Price (gtr). The Stardusters and the Barnburners also played that show.

The other speakeasy was a benefit for the Royal Jokers Car Club on Jan 21, 1994. The posters advertised three bands, but here's who actually played: Wreckin' Ball (San Jose), the Shameless, and singer-bassist Eddie McGarry's band; either the Cuban Cigars or the Boilermakers. (Eddie wrote a "hit" song titled "Emulsified"). Tamales were sold, and there was a raffle; prizes included a car coat and a car club plaque for the now-defunct Road Lords. There was supposed to be a drag race between Jose Mejia and Red Fred, but Fred blew his differential. Big Sandy wasn't scheduled to play, but he came after his show and sang a couple numbers—it was the happenin' after-hours place to go that night! Pearl Harbor also sang a number backed by Big Sandy's band.

In 1992 Slow Club bartender Fra Kepler (working with Tracy Dick) leased the location for the "American Club" at 440 Potrero/17th St so Russell Scott & His Red Hots could play (Sun, April 19 at noon). That event featured dancin'

lessons by Two Steppin' C.C. Steve, and Tracy's Easter egg hunt. On Sat, Oct 24, Fra put on another "American Club" event with Russell Scott opening for Big Sandy. The same night around the corner, the Slow Club was celebrating its anniversary, and Big Sandy played there 10-midnight as well.

Fra Kepler also hosted numerous barbecue-rockabilly-motorcycle-rock'n'roll events Sundays at the Slow Club (2501 Mariposa at Hampshire), with all-free barbecue and all-free bands. Jose and Javier Mejia would drag-race people like Danielle Pimm (from the Trashwomen). After the *Bay Guardian* complained, these Slow Club Sundays ceased. Fra also did events at the Atlas Cafe (20th/Alabama) as recently as 1997. He also did several events at a warehouse at 130 Dore Alley with bands like the Phantom Surfers, Big Sandy and the Loved Ones, and at least one event at Shotwell 59 (3349 20th St/Shotwell) with Big Sandy.

Atomic Cocktail also hosted 9 "rent parties" at their warehouse at 498 Natoma Alley near 6th Street in 1992-'94. Guitarist Whitney Wilson and pianist Johnny Goetchius were in the early Atomic Cocktail. Also, on July 31, 1993, Tracy Dick presented a big warehouse speakeasy at Army and Evans next to Secret Studios, featuring Big Sandy, Go Cat Go and the Statesiders (with Johnny Bartlett)—you had to call 861-4776 to find out the secret location.

Nancy Myers, who now books shows at the Cafe Du Nord, put on a number of speakeasies at a warehouse on at 2451 Harrison/20th St where she lived with roommate Luke Ogden. They set up a bar in the elevator, so when the police came, the "bar" could disappear into the basement. For the first event, Nancy and her friends rolled tiny invitations into little gelatin capsules and gave them out. A password was necessary to

get in. Besides the bands listed below, Nancy recalls shows with the Useless Playboys (rockabilly from Texas) and Rev. Horton Heat. The Rev never showed, but his bassist Jimbo Wallace did, and jammed with Russell Scott. Admission for events was $5, and Nancy never got arrested—she only had a couple close calls. The doormen were August Ragone, who handled the police, and Addrynn Clegg. Bartender was Marinell Stratton (who bartended at the Du Nord, and also at Tracy Dick's 1990 event).

Nancy recalls, "Back then everything seemed to be tied together: swing, rockabilly, Western Swing, punk. Nobody cared what your clothes were like, if you wore a torn dress, or if your steps were off—everyone just wanted to have fun. Now people are so concerned about `learning how to *swing dance*.' [laughs] Swing music should be enjoyed by everybody, not just people who dress up in perfect retro outfits." **V**

(SOME OF) NANCY'S SPEAKEASIES:

12.5.92 1 AM. Broun Fellinis.
Password: "Utopia."

1.9.93 Royal Crown Revue.
"Joe Sent Me."
(see opposite page illustration: matchcover invitation with password)

2.14.93 3 PM St. Vitus Massacre (Vise Grip)

2.27.93 11 PM Psychedelic Lounge Cats

3.5.93 Midnight Royal Crown Revue
(Invitation Only)

3.13.93 Midnight Russell Scott & The Red Hots
(Invitation Only)

8.14.93 Rattled Roosters
"What Else Do You Want"

10.23.93 11 PM Mando Dorame & Jazz Jury
(Invitation Only)

Early Phil Price warehouse party at Phaze, 1814 Illinois St: 2nd Big Sandy show, 1991. Note increased audience attendance (compared to Feb 9 event, photo on p.93). PHOTO: JIM KNELL.

Bay Area Rockabilly

AUGUST RAGONE "Greaseball King"

In 1984 I began working with Mike Belardes who played sax for a rockabilly band called The Kingpins (1981–1991). The band was founded by drummer Craig Ramsey and guitarist Frank Novicki (Sloe Gin Joes). Then in 1985 I moved to Japan. In 1988 I moved back to San Francisco. Guys from the Kingpins and I put together a show at the Cactus Club in San Jose called "The Monsters of Pomp" (short for "pompadour"), a precursor of the later Greaseball series. This was an all-day event featuring the first-known Bay Area appearance of Big Sandy and His Fly-Rite Trio. We did another "Monsters of Pomp" event in 1989 featuring the Kingpins, The Alley Boys (then a 3-piece rockabilly band), The Ruffnecks and The Shakin' Dominoes (both from Las Vegas).

In the fall of 1988 I was hired at the DNA Lounge (375 11th St). Mark Alvarez (former Mabuhay doorman) was already working there, and in 1989 we began booking monthly "Rockabilly Sunday" events. On November 1, 1990 we brought in Ronnie Dawson for his first Bay Area appearance; Roy Loney & the Phantom Movers were the opening act. In 1991 I hooked up with Johnny Legend, and with drummer/cool-culture encyclopediast Joey Myers (The Diablos, Sugar King Boys, etc) put together the world's first "Sleazefest" featuring B-movies, trailers and The Kingpins, Mummies, Phantom Surfers, Johnny Legend & His Rockabilly Bastards, plus the first Rock'n'Roll Mexican Wrestling Show. Johnny, myself and Barrie Evans from The Hellbillies shared a love for Mexican wrestling movies, and our event became the Incredibly Strange Wrestling shows.

The late Ace Cafe owned by Adam Fisher (former DNA deejay, with co-proprietors Bill Stone and Courtney Persinger) expanded to include live music (ca. 1992). Alvarez and I suggested "Rockabilly Tuesdays" to them, and that became the most successful night at the club. When Adam got into an auto accident during the Dirtball 500, March 1993, I stepped in to help Bill Stone, and began booking his entire schedule (jazz, blues, swing, country and rockabilly) for about 6 months, until Bill sold the Ace.

During the last year at the Ace, Alvarez and I began promoting The Stardusters, a Western Swing band formed by "Iron Mike" Braten, a drummer for The Ramblers. After the Stardusters faded, Mike founded Memphis 54 and Lost Highway, both country-rockabilly influenced bands. The Stardusters featured bassist Dave Antony (Jeff Bright & the Sunshine Boys) and Whitney Wilson (New Morty Show) on guitar. Lost Highway guitarist George Cole (Jellyfish) has since joined The Big Blue Hearts.

In late 1994 the new regime at DNA Lounge hired me as a deejay. I couldn't persuade the DNA to book a swing night, but my rockabilly nights were very successful. In 1995 I suggested a "Monsters of Pomp" festival. That took place in September under the name "Greaseball," with 10 bands. Next year we hosted 12 bands in October. In 1997 we moved it to Slim's and hosted 22 bands over Oct 11–12.

In 1995 ex-Floridian James Shelton moved to SF from LA, where he had hosted a rockabilly night at the Burgundy Room. We

August with Martha Novils at Bimbo's, to see Big Sandy, 9-19-97. Photo: V.Vale

started co-deejaying Rockabilly Thursdays at the DNA and then formed Hepcat Productions. Now we book shows at the Covered Wagon Saloon, Cafe Du Nord, Max's Hi-Ball Lounge and Blues.

Some Bay Area acts that were favorites include The Boogiemen, Silver Threads, Scott Bros, Stringbusters, Gary Claxton, Barnburners, Van Riff, Bachelors, Human Torches, Goodbye Liverpool, Wild Joe Ward, the Ramblers, Coronados, Senders, Statesiders, Shameless, Pattersons, Greasemonkeys, Diablos, Cyco Zob & the Zip Guns, Hipdrivers, Smokin' Cat Daddies, Honky-Tonk Angels, Panther Slim, the Tombstones. Other '80s "roots" bands include Rank'n'File (formerly the Dils), Silvertone (with John Silver from the Dils, Jimmy Wilsey from the Avengers, and Chris Isaac), Swingin' Possums (fronted by Johnny Genocide from KGB, etc) and the Watchmen.

San Jose-area bands included Big Hair, founded by drummer Ricky Quisol who has hosted a series of Hank Williams Birthday Parties (at DeMarco's in Brisbane, the Paradise, the Hi-Ball Lounge, etc). Big Hair had 8 members, 3 of which sang, and did C&W versions of songs like "Disco Inferno." When the band broke up, 3 bands resulted: Whistlin' Bullets (country), Kettles (rockin' country-rockabilly; both featured female singers) and Frontier Wives (country-punk; all guys).

Late '80s "roots" bands included Alley Boys (now a Social Distortion-style band), King Rocker, El Kabong, and PeeWee and His Safecrackers. PeeWee Thomas deserves a chapter all his own. There's Rockin' Lloyd Tripp & His Three Tons of Fun (Lloyd was in the Blubbery Hellbellies in the U.K.), Jeff Bright & The Sunshine Boys (who play weekly at the Deluxe) and Dee Lannon, formerly of the Coronados. Jeff Bright features the drummer for Impatient Youth! **V**

TRACY DICK "The Queen of the Rockabilly Scene"

The two camps of rockabilly and jump-swing do cross, but in some communities there is a classist attitude that one is "better" (or "cleaner") than the other. Personally, the more I learn about either, the more exciting it is. With swing, I like best the black swing bands of the '40s, because they tend to be juicier, rawer, and captured more the essence of what was really going on—which was *rebellion.*

In terms of marketability, swing/Western Swing is where it's at now. But all of the above movements came from the same place and time frame. The Western Swing movement was huge in the Bay Area in the '40s; there were all these Western Swing ballrooms. People migrated to California in the '30s and '40s from Oklahoma and surrounding states, and they brought their music with them. When WWII happened, black people who came to work in the shipyards brought their jump-swing with them. This was the first time people had had money in years, so a huge swing movement started here, and as it got popular it got more and more raw: hence, rockabilly and rock'n'roll. Then the powers that be said, "Instead of Little Richard, let's have Pat Boone." When the Beatles came, they ruined things even more.

In the later '80s I worked at Forma on Haight Street. I always saw the Blasters, the Paladins and the Stray Cats when they came to town. One night Jen Smith came up to me and said, "Here's a flyer for some other upcoming shows." Cammy Blackstone was

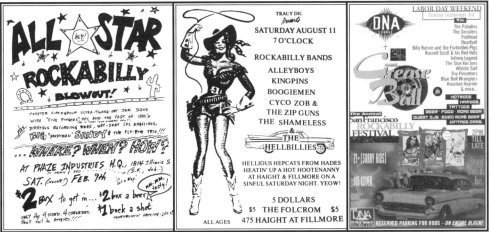

putting on country-rockabilly acts like the Diablos and Dee Lannon at the "Iron Cowboy Club" (the old Nitebreak). I went to a show in San Jose, and Tony from Terror Train (L.A.) said, "You guys are all a bunch of fuckin' pussies. You bitch and complain that there are no shows, but why don't you make it happen?" I thought, "He's talking to *me!*" So I [and my best friend, Carolyn Terry] talked Jay Johnson into letting me deejay a rockabilly show at the Deluxe. I started the day after the October 1989 earthquake, and it was a huge success, so Jay said, "I want to have a *rockabilly club!*" We did this once a month for four months, then once a week. It would have continued, except Carolyn broke up with Jay and started going out with Phil Price and the two had a big fight. Jay said, "I don't ever want to have another rockabilly in this club again!"

I continued deejaying at the Armadillo, DNA, Limbo, Zeitgeist, etc and over the years I also had private parties wherever I lived. People started contacting me at Forma to find out what was "happening." I also put out about four issues of my fanzine, *Rockabilly Deluxe,* when I was doing shows at the Deluxe. August 11, 1990, I rented a space next to Walgreen's on Haight and Fillmore, The Folcrom. I had six bands play and learned a lot about musician's egos.

I was a big blonde with a big mouth who would talk to anybody: "Come to my show!" Fra Kepler and I did a number of shows together, and Fra would put up a big chunk of change and lose it all. I booked the first [rockabilly] show the Cafe Du Nord had: the Boogiemen.

Phil Price [from Detroit] owned this garage. His girlfriend, Carolyn Terry, was my best friend, and I wanted to have a big birthday party. After we did that first party, we figured, "Why not have more?" We'd charge a few dollars if an out-of-town band needed some travel money. We had dollar shots and dollar beers! We put sawdust on the floor and bales of hay to sit on, and had big buckets of water everywhere because we were afraid someone would burn the place down. Back then, there was an incredible sense of family—just like punk was in the early days: really small, people watching out for each other, trying to help each other. Then it got more popular and things grew from that. When Royal Crown came up, it seemed so wild that a swing band would happen. (But "my" band is Big Sandy.)

At those early events, it wasn't just rockabilly kids. There were the scooter kids, the Mod kids, Johnny Bartlett and his whole "garage" crowd (including the Phantom Surfers), these scary greasers, these old North Beach blues guys, a few punks, a few hippies, and a bunch of rockabilly kids.

When the parties at Phil Price's garage (and other locations I found) started, I put up almost every band that came to town. 99% of the people never knew that I did it. I did the Honeybunch (telephone) Hotline free for years; it was a way for people to find out about rockabilly shows.

Now the Internet is fantastic, because it provides information on where things are in the world. You can't support and be a part of something if you don't know where to go! There's the rockabilly mailing list, there's swing sites, vintage record collecting sites, etc. And it's impersonal, so you don't have to worry whether you've got the hip-and-cool haircut or shoes. You just have to worry about whether you have the heart and soul and desire to enjoy it and want to find out more. One of the best things about people being into "retro" stuff, is that they help keep those things available and important, whether it's 78s or hats and shoes.

I did the booking, promoting and deejaying because I wanted to, just like so many others in the Bay Area who made this all happen. I was a small part of a much bigger picture.

Now what bothers me most is how *acceptable* swing music has become. The music that "floats my boat" is never going to be put in a radio jingle. And that music is rockabilly, hillbilly, rural blues, real country music—"our" oral history. Because it was always working class and "poor folk," it's never going to get the respect it so richly deserves.

Slow Club: Carolyn Terry's birthday party, July 1992, L to R: Tracy Dick, Bethany, Valerie Barnd, Rhea (back), Jen Smith, Carolyn Terry, Loretta DePorceri, Laurie Lee. Photo supplied by Carolyn Terry.

Swing got big because the Glenn Millers of the world adopted it, and white kids had the money to go to the big swing clubs. But jump-blues started in black clubs, honkytonks and juke joints in Harlem and other American cities. All of a sudden it's "acceptable"; it's the retro that is "okay." It didn't start out that way, and that's why there's a split now. V

Steve Hathaway

STEVE HATHAWAY has done a "classic country music" radio show for 25 years, titled "The Cupertino Barn Dance" on KKUP, Cupertino, 91.5 FM (Sunday nights, 9–midnight). He publishes the *Western Swing Newsletter* ($3 from 1733 Cheney Dr, San Jose, CA 95128. Complete set #1–22 $45; sub $15). His website is *westernswing.com*. Steve also has an archive of 16mm short music films (mostly country and jazz). His partner, VIDA LEE hosts two radio shows on KKUP, one playing swing/jump and the blues and early R&B. Here Steve discusses contemporary western swing and honky tonk bands and labels in the S.F. Bay area. ✍ ✍ ✍ ✍ ✍ ✍ ✍ ✍ ✍ ✍ ✍ ✍ ✍ ✍ ✍ ✍ ✍ ✍ ✍

On Western Swing

HIGHTONE RECORDS in Alameda is probably the best label as far as *real* country music goes. They've released three CDs by Big Sandy and the Fly-Rite Boys, one of the most danceable acts around. Big Sandy began as a rockabilly act but since adding steel guitar and piano has moved to include hillbilly boogie and Western Swing. Another Hightone artist with three CDs is DALE WATSON. Out of the rich Austin, Texas music scene, he sounds and looks like a young Merle Haggard, but all his songs are original, and like his stage presence, compelling. Another W.S. label is JOAQUIN RECORDS, who released CDs by RAY CONDO, plus LPs by earlier W.S. pioneers.

Johnny Dilks started out with a super-band of super-pickers. With as many as 16 members, it was a giant Western Swing band. He was trying for the pre-war W.S. style, and had players like guitarist Paul Mehling from The Hot Club of San Francisco, multi-instrumentalist Tony Marcus from Cats and Jammers, and steel guitarist Bobby Black, who played with Commander Cody—but it was too difficult to get all these people together. He pared the band down and as JOHNNY DILKS & The VISITACION VALLEY BOYS play regularly their brand of Western Swing and honky tonk, with a spice of cajun.

Dilks' current steel guitarist, Billy Wilson, has an occasional band called BILLY JACK & HIS WESTERN SWING BAND (which is a "play" on Billy Jack Wills). It includes Vance Terry, the living-legend steel guitarist who played with Billy Jack Wills and Jimmy Rivers. Vance played on and recorded the *Brisbane Bop* record. The band also features vibraphone. Other bands on the local scene include JEFF BRIGHT & The SUNSHINE BOYS, who play more uptown country, '60s style, but they have great original songs. Drummer Ricky Quisol leads a band called RICK & The ROUNDERS; it plays mostly '50s and '60s covers. Frank Novicki's SLOE GIN JOES (with bassist Dez Mabunga) play his unique original rockabilly songs. New on the scene is the Oakland band RED MEAT, whose debut CD features twisted originals in old style country sometimes with modern themes, like "Telephone Tag." Of course, there are zillions of rockabilly bands. (Look for the SUGAR KING BOYS and PEE WEE THOMAS & HIS SAFE CRACKERS).

LOST WEEKEND is a Western Swing band led by Don Burnham. Since 1984, when it first played Paul's Saloon as a quartet, Lost Weekend has kept a western swing presence in the Bay Area. Its most memorable performance was in 1991 at Bimbo's for the S.F. Jazz Festival, when it became a 13-piece big W.S. band complete with horn section. Among the greats playing in this band are steel guitarists Vance Terry and Bobby Black.

♦ **V:** *What is Western Swing?*

♦ **SH:** In the context of country/hillbilly music, Western Swing bands were the first to incorporate drums and electric guitar. Also introduced was the smoother (read: no twang) popular vocal style. They were doing black jazz and blues songs as part of their repertoire. And most importantly, they played to dance crowds. When rockabilly came on the scene 30 years later, it too was blending country and blues, playing to dance crowds with its driving drums, but by now the band unit was smaller, often with only the electric guitar as lead instrument. And the tempos, guitar, and vocals became harder-edged. Rockabilly was the psychobilly of Western Swing, in its day. One of the earliest rock'n'roll bands was Bill Haley and the Comets, but the previous name was Bill Haley and the Saddlemen, and before that BILL HALEY & HIS FOUR ACES OF WESTERN SWING. He, like all rockers, owes a debt to Western Swing.

Western Swing Recommendations: Recordings, Books & Periodicals

RECORDINGS AVAILABLE ON CD:

ANTHOLOGY: *Okeh Western Swing* **(CBS Special Products): 28 tracks of '30s and '40s WS—excellent starter for learning early western swing.**

ANTHOLOGY: *Hillbilly Boogie!* **(Legacy/Columbia): 20 tracks of '40s and '50s WS & hillbilly boogie—a style in itself, hillbilly boogie came out of western swing and some think it led up to rockabilly. There was a huge hit in the late '40s: "Beat Me Daddy Eight To The Bar," by Will Bradley. Then everybody started doing boogie woogie; the Andrew Sisters, and the country (hillbilly) cats; etc.**

ANTHOLOGY: WESTERN SWING ON THE RADIO (Country Routes) English Import. 20 tracks, mostly '40s WS radio transcriptions

BOB WILLS AND HIS TEXAS PLAYBOYS **1935–1973** (Rhino) 2 CD set. 36 tracks taken throughout his career from multiple labels–best Bob Wills starter collection.

BOB WILLS AND HIS TEXAS PLAYBOYS: THE TIFFANY TRANSCRIPTIONS. **9 vol. series originally issued on Kaleidoscope of El Cerrito–features arguably the best recordings Wills made. Recorded in the late '40s in San Francisco, the transcription sessions yielded the most "live" sound of their recorded output.** *Vol. 3* recommended starter.

BILLY JACK WILLS & HIS WESTERN SWING BAND (Joaquin). **2 separate CDs taken from radio transcription shows. Bob Wills' youngest brother led band in Sacramento: these groundbreaking western swing "Young Turks" incorporated late '40s R&B sounds of Wynonie Harris and Louis Jordan. Some of Billy Jack's vocals are borderline rockabilly. With electric mandolin/fiddle player Tiny Moore arranging, this was a hot little band.**

MILTON BROWN & HIS MUSICAL BROWNIES/BILL BOYD & HIS COWBOY RAMBLERS: UNDER THE DOUBLE EAGLE, **Great Western Swing Bands of the 1930's, Vol. 1 (BMG). 9 tracks by each. Seminal western swing bands. Some feel that had Brown (great singer) not died early, he and not Bob Wills would be the biggest name in western swing.**

SPADE COOLEY: SPADELLA! THE ESSENTIAL SPADE COOLEY **(Legacy/Columbia). 20 tracks from his Columbia recordings. The self proclaimed "King Of Western Swing" also recorded for RCA Victor and Decca. His unique west coast band had a fiddle section and even a harp! Check out the great steel and guitar solos in "Oklahoma Stomp."**

TEX WILLIAMS & HIS WESTERN CARAVAN: VINTAGE COLLECTIONS **(Capitol). 20 tracks—great west coast stuff. Tex left Spade Cooley and took the whole band with him, including the harp player! Best known for "Smoke! Smoke! Smoke! (That Cigarette)."**

TOM MORRELL & THE TIME WARP TOP HANDS: HOW THE WEST WAS SWUNG **(WR) series. 9 vol. series of the best western swing being made today. On these recordings, guitar/steel guitarist Tom Morrell surrounds himself with outstanding personnel and repertoire. And he writes the zany liner notes, illustrated with anthropomorphic dinosaurs, and gives everyone pet names like Pack-Rat, O'Possum, etc.**

ASLEEP AT THE WHEEL: STILL SWINGIN' **(Liberty). 3-CD box set. This collection contains a great sampling of a band that has released over 30 records over 25 years. Ray Benson has been on a "mission from God" to keep western swing alive. The once Bay Area, now Austin-based band has had some fabulous players. This is probably a good starter since it has the best of the early band, a live set, and their recent tribute to Bob Wills with superstar guests.**

RAY CONDO & THE RICOCHETS (Joaquin) **3 CDs** BIG SANDY & HIS FLY-RITE BOYS (Hightone) **5 CDs The RICOCHETS are a Vancouver based rockabilly/western jump combo. This band combined members of Ray Condo & The Hardrock Goners and Jimmy Roy's Five Star Hillbillies (both recorded on the English label**

Steve Hathaway and Vida Lee with Louis Jordan poster, 1997.

Fury). **They, along with Big Sandy & The Fly-Rite Boys, are forging new ground and gaining new admirers to western swing.**

DAN HICKS & THE HOT LICKS: RETURN TO HICKSVILLE **(Hip-O/MCA)** DAN HICKS & THE ACOUSTIC WARRIORS: SHOOTIN' STRAIGHT **(On The Spot). Not western swing, but for me, an early push in that direction. The Hot Licks collection and the newer Acoustic Warriors are full of Dan's twisted fun lyrics and toe tappin' tunes.**

COMMANDER CODY & THE LOST PLANET AIRMEN: TOO MUCH FUN **(Best Of) (UNI/MCA) and** WE'VE GOT A LIVE ONE HERE! **(Warner Bros./WEA). When I first saw them I was awestruck by this hippie-lookin' band doing rockabilly, country, and Bob Wills songs. I had to have more. Their "Best Of" and "live" records are good starters.**

BOOKS & PERIODICALS:

SAN ANTONIO ROSE: THE LIFE AND MUSIC OF BOB WILLS, **Charles R. Townsend (University of Illinois Press)**

MILTON BROWN AND THE FOUNDING OF WESTERN SWING, **Cary Ginell (University of Illinois Press)**

ENCYCLOPEDIA OF COUNTRY MUSIC, **Country Music Foundation (Oxford University Press) fall 1998 release**

THE HILLBILLY RESEARCHER, **Occasional periodical (20 Silkstream Rd., Burnt Oak, Edgware, Middlesex HA8 0DA, England)**

THE JOURNAL OF COUNTRY MUSIC, **3 issues/yr, periodical (4 Music Sq. East, Nashville TN 37203)**

SWING IN THE MOVIES
by Satu

Artists and Models (1937) Comedy with music set in the advertising world starring Jack Benny. Musical interlude with Louis Armstrong and an appearance by Connie Boswell.

Atlantic City/Atlantic City Honeymoon (1944) Musical comedy with Paul Whiteman and His Orchestra (very popular with white audiences, he called himself the King of Jazz), Louis Armstrong with a big band and Buck and Bubbles, a tremendous dance duo with a big influence on black teenagers on the East Coast.

Ball of Fire (1941) Comedy with Barbara Stanwyck featuring scenes with Gene Krupa and His Orchestra and Barbara singing! Howard Hawks' remake of *A Song Is Born,* with Krupa replacing B. Goodman.

Beat the Band (1947) Schlock with Gene Krupa in both a speaking part and featuring his orchestra in two big production numbers.

The Benny Goodman Story (1955) Benny's bio with music produced by Himself and all his notable musicians. Appearances by many fine musicians including Mary Lou Williams and Louis Prima.

Beware (1946) 45-minute musical second feature starring Louis Jordan.

The Big Beat (1957) Lots of musical numbers, no plot. Charlie Barnet, Harry James, Fats Domino, the Mills Brothers.

Boarding House Blues (1948) All black film strung together from popular vaudeville acts. Features Lucky Millinder's Orchestra with Bull Moose Jackson on vocals.

Boy! What a Girl! (1947) All black production featuring Slam Stewart (of Slim and Slam), Big Sid Catlett, dancing by the Harlem Maniacs and a Gene Krupa appearance.

Broadway Rhythm (1944) A string of song and dance numbers with Tommy Dorsey, Hazel Scott playing a boogie-woogie, and Lena Horne.

Cabin in the Sky (1942) Vincente Minelli's first film, based on a broadway play. Musical numbers with Louis Armstrong, Duke Ellington and his Orchestra Buck Washington, Ethel Waters and Lena Horne. The plot is a cringe but the music sublime and the dancing worth emulating.

Chatterbox (1943) A Joe E. Brown feature with numbers by the Mills Brothers and Spade Cooley and His Boys. Spade was a huge star in California with Oakie and Arkie immigrants from the Dust Bowl.

Crazy House/Funzapoppin' (1943) Plotless excuse for musical numbers (is this beginning to sound familiar?) Features Count Basie with Jimmy Rushing, the Glenn Miller Singers and the Delta Rhythm Boys.

Dancing Co-Ed (1939) College comedy starring Lana Turner chock full of jitterbugging and Artie Shaw, the future Mr Lana Turner.

Dixie Jamboree (1944) Comedy with music set on a showboat. Features Cab Calloway.

Drum Crazy—the Gene Krupa Story (1959) Sal Mineo plays Gene Krupa, with GK doing his own drumming.

Ebony Parade (1947) Soundie compilation with Cab Calloway, Count Basie, The Mills Brothers, and Vanita Smythe.

The Fabulous Dorseys (1947) a bio of the feudin' Dorsey brothers with both their big bands.

Follow the Boys (1944) Wartime USO tribute film featuring Ted Lewis, The Delta Rhythm Boys and Louis Jordan and his Tympany Five.

The Gang's All Here (1943) Busby Berkeley musical in Technicolor with numbers by Benny Goodman.

The Glenn Miller Story (1953) not very realistic but the scene featuring Louis Armstrong and his All-Stars with Gene Krupa is memorable.

Going Places (1938) Comedy with music and a horse, featuring Louis Armstrong and Maxine Sullivan (one of the best hairdos in swing).

Hellzapoppin' (1941) silly comedy with a famous musical number combining Slim and Slam with Whitey's Lindy Hoppers.

Here Comes Elmer (1943) Comedy with an early appearance by Nat King Cole when he still had his swinging trio, performing " Straighten Up and Fly Right" among other numbers.

Hey Boy! Hey Girl! (1959) Louis Prima/Keely Smith musical vehicle. Plot? What's that?

Hit Parade of 1937 (1936) Musical revue film featuring Duke Ellington with Ivie Anderson on vocals.

Hit Parade of 1943 (1943) Musical revue film with Count Basie and his band.

Hit Parade of 1947 (1947) Yet another musical revue film, this time with Woody Herman and his Orchestra.

Hollywood Canteen (1944) Warner Brothers acts doing a tribute to the servicemen's club of the title. Jimmy Dorsey's band accompanies most singers and does a swinging instrumental as well.

I Dood It/By Hook and By Crook (1943) Comedy of errors featuring musical numbers by Lena Horne, Hazel Scott, Lee Young and Jimmy Dorsey with his Orchestra. The dancing is great in this film; Vincente Minelli really knew how to direct a hoof number.

Jam Session (1944) Dreck with splendid performers. Louis Armstrong and His Orchestra, Charlie Barnet and His Orchestra, Jo Stafford and others. Some black musicians in white-led bands don't appear on camera as they were played by white actors. Sigh.

Jivin' in Be-bop (1947) one-hour second feature of nothing but music and dancing made for the Negro circuit. Includes Dizzy Gillespie, Charlie Parker, and all the luminaries who played with them at the time.

Killer Diller (1948) All-black production of vaudeville numbers strung together with musical numbers by Andy Kirk and his Clouds of Joy and the Nat King Cole Trio featuring Oscar Moore on guitar.

King of Jazz (1930) Early technicolor feature with the very white Paul Whiteman and his superb band, which includes Eddie Lang and Joe Venuti.

Make Believe Ballroom (1949) Musical with appearances by Jimmy Dorsey, Pee Wee Hunt, Charlie Barnet, Gene Krupa and Nat King Cole.

Manhattan Merry-Go-Round (1937) Gangster comedy with appearances by Jack Jenney, Cab Calloway, Ted Lewis and Louis Prima.

Orchestra Wives (1942) Starring the Glenn Miller Orchestra with Tex Beneke. I'm crazy about this movie and you should go see it right now. Splendid dance and song sequence by the Nicholas Brothers of "I've Got a Gal From Kalamazoo."

St Louis Blues (1958) Dopey bio of W.C. Handy with Nat King Cole as The Man. Features Pearl Bailey, Cab Calloway, Mahalia Jackson, Ella Fitzgerald, and Curtis Counce.

Second Chorus (1940) Romantic comedy starring Fred Astaire and Burgess Meredith as musicians trying to get a job with Artie Shaw's orchestra. Artie has a featured role and his band has several swinging numbers with Nick Fatool on drums.

Senior Prom (1958) Low budget musical with appearances by Bob Crosby and Louis Prima.

Seven Days' Leave (1942) Musical comedy with Lucille Ball and Victor Mature with appearances by Les Brown and his Orchestra.

Something to Shout About (1943) Backstage musical featuring Hazel Scott, queen of boogie woogie, and Teddy Wilson. My dad was in charge of entertainment for his all-black unit in Korea in 1954 and this was a popular favorite even then.

A Song Is Born (1948) A remake of Ball of Fire by the same director, Howard Hawks. Appearances by Benny Goodman, Louis Armstrong, Tommy Dorsey, Lionel Hampton, Charlie Barnet et al.

Stage Door Canteen (1943) All-star vaudeville comedy with 60 different popular entertainers including Count Basie, Benny Goodman, Xavier Cugat (hipper than you think) and Kay Kyser (squarer than you can imagine).

Start Cheering (1937) Film tailored for Jimmy Durante with a typically snappy appearance by Louis Prima.

Stormy Weather (1943) A classic all-black film with the coolest chorus girls in leopard spot. Loaded with stars and talent, including Cab Calloway, the omnipresent but in my opinion charmless Lena Horne, Slim and Slam, the Spirits of Rhythm, Cab Calloway, Fats Waller, the dancing of Bill Robinson. Also a lovely dreamlike dance sequence with the Katherine Dunham Dancers.

The Strip (1951) Murder mystery set on Sunset Strip with the orchestras of Louis Armstrong and Jack Teagarden.

Sun Valley Serenade (1941) Musical romance with Sonja Henie and the continuous presence of Glenn Miller and his Orchestra and Tex Beneke and the Modernaires.

Sweet and Low-Down (1944) Formula comedy with the continuous presence of Benny Goodman (when did this guy have a chance to make records?) and a version of his Orchestra.

Swing in the Saddle (1944) yes, it's a low-budget western with Nat King Cole. Who thought of this combo?

Swing Parade of 1946 (1946) A variety film

including the Three Stooges and Louis Jordan and the Tympany Five, always entertaining.

Syncopation (1942) A musical history of jazz from 1906 to the present (the 1942 present, that is, and strangely Negro-free). Benny Goodman, Charlie Barnet, Joe Venuti, Gene Krupa, Harry James and other luminaries doing their syncopated thing.

Thousands Cheer (1943) wartime morale booster film with Benny Carter, Ethel Waters, Bob Crosby (regrettably not with the Bobcats) and Kay Kyser and some killer costumes and dance sequences.

Top Man (1943) Donald O'Connor comedy musical featuring Count Basie and his Orchestra.

Two Girls and a Sailor (1944) Regrettably nowhere near as spicy as the title suggests, but a good excuse for Harry James, Lena Horne, Ella Fitzgerald and Xavier Cugat.

Wabash Avenue (1950) A jolly musical with Red Nichols and the Five Pennies backing Betty Grable in a version of "I wish I could shimmy like my sister Kate" Hokey but entertaining.

You Can't Have Everything (1937) A movie about a small-town girl in New York, with three appearances by Louis Prima.

❧ ❧ ❧ ❧ ❧ ❧ ❧ ❧ ❧ ❧

MOVIES WITH SPECTACULAR OUTFITS
by Satu

American Me The opening sequence is a cavalcade of high-style Pachuco outfits and even includes an authentic tattoo shop. And no one has ever beaten the American penal system for denim styling. Also a killer overview of every major So Cal pachuco look thru the '80s (Pendletons with a beehive! groomsmen in white stingy brims!)

Orchestra Wives Musicians at rest in lcisurc suits, the killer 30's gab versions, tropical shirts etc. Stylish musician's wives in polka-dotted leisure pajamas playing lethal bridge. The Nicholas brothers with the prototype patent-leather conks. Plus Caesar Romero, a style king in thc Latin mold and playboy par cxccllcncc.

Stormy Weather The zoot suit dance sequences are one of the few that show a woman's zoot suit, and while it is a costume designer's version of one, my dad who was there says it's pretty close.

Harlem on the Prairie Those colored folk bring their natural sense of rhythm and styling' flair to the wild west.

Carmen Jones Dorothy Dandridge was a style model for every hep black woman in America. The hoop earrings, the peasant top, the skirt too tight to walk in . . .

The Two Jakes Chinatown is a '70s version of the '30s, but the *Two Jakes* is costumed achingly authentically. You can tell that Jack Nicholson is in trouble from the get-go because he's wearing brown shoes with a blue suit. There is a beauty shop sequence that is mind-blowing for hair and makeup perfectionists.

The Women the original cut of this film includes a 10-minute color sequence, a complete Adrian of Hollywood fashion show. The scenes set in a department store and on a dude ranch are also priceless for detail.

Henry and June I did not want the people in this movie to have sex because then they would take off their perfect outfits. Pretty sad, huh?

The Funeral '30s mobster hi-style, including all-white suits and lots of lingerie. Will also show you how to furnish your home if you want to make a Genovese caporegime feel right at home without lifting an antipasto plate.

Goodfellas, Casino, Raging Bull Martin Scorcese is a stickler for detail and it shows. If you see a tie clip on one of his guys, rest assured that his mama would really have bought him the tie clip for Confirmation.

What's Love Got to Do with It Gentlemen, do like Ike looks, not like Ike does. Ladies, look like Tina no matter what you do.

In the Mood Forties wartime revelry done much better than *1941* which placed a kid in a zoot suit in a racially integrated servicemen's dance. Oh sure, tell me another one.

Swing Shift What Rosie the Riveter really wore, on and off duty. Also includes a trailer of doom and a cab that I would gladly ride to hell for the pleasure of watching the meter tick. Men's hair is not always right, though.

A Walk in the Clouds So there's no plot whatsoever and Keanu Reeves has the curse of period films, Bad Hair. All else is spot on, including luggage.

A League of their Own More Rosie the riveter fashions and some authentically sloppy dancing.

Swing Kids Yes, Europeans really did dress different from the Yanks. Quoting Augie Ragone: we just want to dance, we don't want to be Nazis!

Tucker Cars, cars, cars . . .

Tin Men Barry Levinson's tribute to siding salesmen in the early '60s, with cha-cha-chaing.

Pennies from Heaven The BBC original is even odder and more damaged than the American remake. Dennis Potter is a genius but you will want to kill yourself.

Paper Moon Poor and crafty, Tatum O'Neill is the reason I smoke. Includes black people which is somcwhat of a novclty.

Rambling Rose how to look like a tramp in 1935.

The Color Purple 3 decades and a variety of socioeconomic levels of colored folk. Endless source of home decor ideas.

Malcolm X Why did he look so much better whcn hc was so much badder? Some of my friends have doubted costume authenticity but to them I say—they were shopping in HARLEM.

Thunder Road Robert Mitchum is a god. He acts, he drives, he sings the title tune. Why did southern white boys go bad, listen to Negro music, and join motorcycle gangs? The war, thas why. Plus the moonshine and the incredible cars in this movie. I may start wearing my overalls out again.

❧ ❧ ❧ ❧ ❧ ❧ ❧ ❧ ❧ ❧

MORE MOVIES THAT SWING
by Yimi

Big Broadcast, The (1932): Features the top radio acts of the day: the Mills Brothers, the Boswell Sisters, Bing Crosby and the Cab Calloway Orchestra. Light-skinned Calloway is "blacked-up" because the studio feared that his racial identity would be mistaken. Calloway performs *Minnie the Moocher* and *Hot Toddy*, one of the band's few instrumentals.

Big Broadcast of 1937, The: Benny Goodman's first movie, filmed in 1936 during his second engagement at the Palomar Ballroom.

Birth of the Blues (1941): Jack Teagarden and Bing Crosby.

Black and Tan Fantasy (1929): 19-minute short. Duke Ellington's first appearance on film.

Cabin in the Sky (1943) Minnelli musical with Louis Armstrong, Duke Ellington, etc.

Dancing Coed (1938): Routine college comedy with Artie Shaw and drummer Buddy Rich. Features Shaw's third wife, Lana Turner.

Easy Come, Easy Go and **One I Love:** Jimmy and Tommy Dorsey.

Harlem After Midnight (1934): This all-black, low-budget gangster feature was shot entirely in Harlem and features Leon Gross' jumping swing band. Directed and produced by premiere black director Oscar Michaux.

Hollywood Hotel (1937): Goodman's big band roars through the classic *Sing, Sing, Sing*. The band's all there, too: Hampton, Wilson, Davis, Krupa, and the recently added Harry James. Not only considered Goodman's best film, but also the best band film in movie history. Directed by Busby Berkeley, the storyline is based on Hollywood gossip columnnist Louella Parsons.

King of Burlesque (1935): Fats Waller steals the scene by raising an eyebrow.

Kobenhvn, Kalundborg (1933): Louis Armstrong is in this feature film shot in Copenhagen for European studios. Josephine Baker was to be featured, but she canceled out at the last minute.

Mr. Chump (1937): Forgettable film that includes such lines as "Swing music makes you want to live!"

Murder at the Vanities (1934): Watch Duke Ellington improv to the rewriting of Liszt's Hungarian Rhapsody by songwriting team Sam Coslow and Arthur Johnston.

Never Too Old to Swing 1945 soundie featuring Tiny Grimes and a dance team. 3 mins.

New Orleans (1947) Musical featuring Louis Armstrong, Billie Holiday, Woody Herman, etc.

Pennies From Heaven (1936): Louis Armstrong and Lionel Hampton appear in a Haunted House nightclub sequence.

Rhapsody in Black and Blue (1932): Short featuring Louis Armstrong as a janitor who falls asleep and dreams of being in "Jazzmania" (jazz heaven) and wakes to find himself in leopard skin and soap bubbles.

Sing, Sinner, Sing (1933): Rarely seen film made for second-run houses. Features Les Hite's band and Lionel Hampton on drums. Daisy Mae Diggs is the "truckin" vocalist.

Singing Kid, The (1936): Cab Calloway makes an appearance in this Al Jolson vehicle and performs *Keep That Hi-De-Ho in Your Soul*.

You Can't Have Everything (1937): Louis Prima's swing band, then one of the few made up entirely of New Orleans players, swung *Rhythm on the Radio* and *It's a Southern Holiday*. **V**

Skip Heller & Art Fein

Skip Heller is a writer, a producer (Frenchy, Ray Campi, etc) and a guitarist/arranger who has been the bandleader behind Yma Sumac, Joey Sehee and Campi (among others). Skip lives with his wife, Sheryl Farber, in Los Angeles, and can be contacted at *lonlytown@aol.com*. His own recordings are available from Dionysus (catalog $1), Dept R/S, POB 1975, Burbank CA 91507, tel 818-848-2698.

Cameron from *Grindstone* magazine, Skip Heller, Sammy Masters, Lee Joseph of Dionysus Records, and rockabilly legend Ray Campi. Photo: Aime Joseph, Nov 1997

♦ *VALE: What are some problems with contemporary musicians playing swing?*

♦ SKIP HELLER: Drummers in particular have grown up playing through a sound system, whereas Gene Krupa, Buddy Rich, Zutty Singleton and all the other great swing drummers didn't. Today everybody gets miked. So the way the musician physically plays the instrument is different; technology has changed how musicians' hands work in relationship to their instruments. Benny Goodman played on radio shows for years, sitting in a horn section, before he became famous. There was usually just one microphone and the sound mix depended on people's proximity, so all the dynamics were supplied by the band. Now things are different; everyone plays louder than they used to.

Another thing—with the advent of electronic tuners, musicians today are more in tune. On old Duke Ellington records, Harry Carney, the baritone sax player, is slightly out of tune, and that makes the notes ring a different way, like waves bouncing against each other and fighting for control. That makes the music more interesting and "human."

♦ *V: I like mistakes in music; that's why Brian Eno's Portsmouth Sinfonia record was so much fun to listen to.*

♦ SH: Mistakes have almost been legislated out of the recording process. When you hear old Western Swing, swing, or rockabilly records, there are finger slips all over the place or trumpet players breaking the high note. Wow! You can actually hear them playing! You feel there's a human being sitting behind the instrument. I miss that. Technology is wonderful, but on the other hand, everything sounds too antiseptic.

♦ *V: I'm waiting for the return of all-night marathons. I read about one with 22 dance bands playing all night long.*

♦ SH: They would have these band "cutting contests" as well as dance contests that people would rigorously practice and rehearse for. It was considered very uncool to steal someone's unique steps. **V**

Skip's favorite Dance Floor Records

ROY BROWN "Mighty Mighty Man." Where the mid-tempo swing of the big bands stops, there starts the too-fast too-loud jump-blues of guys like Roy Milton, Wynonie Harris and Amos Milburn. This is the stuff that kept swing-based dancing alive into the '50s. Roy Brown is my favorite jump singer. "Mighty Mighty Man" is truly unbridled. Art Fein compiled a Roy disc for Rhino, and it's all meat, no fat.

ARTIE SHAW "Little Jazz." Of the white big band leaders, Artie Shaw was the coolest. He spoke four languages, married unspeakably beautiful women, wrote novels, and was arguably the most interesting clarinet player of the Swing Era. He had people like Babs Gonzales and The Mel-Tones (featuring Les Baxter) in his groups. The great trumpeter Roy Eldridge was in the band for awhile, and "Little Jazz" (the title was his nickname) was a feature for him. With this gentle foxtrot, you won't throw your girlfriend up in the air, but dance floors fill up when this comes on.

BOB WILLS & His Texas Playboys "Miss Molly." If you're looking to make the connection between rockabilly and swing, look no further. "Molly" jumps like Roy Brown, but with a kind of sagebrush veneer. All of Bob's Columbia sides are essential for a better life.

BENNY GOODMAN "Sing Sing Sing" (Carnegie Hall, 1938 Version). Jitterbuggers have forever held this one close to heart. Drummer Gene Krupa holds down that perfect jungle beat for something like ten minutes—the first extended dance mix?—and those tom-toms have the perfect "get on the floor" allure. Probably the most imitated swing band arrangement ever. I saw a film of Louis Prima playing "Sing, Sing, Sing" with Buddy Rich on drums. As the camera pans over the band, it's obvious that the war had quite an effect on music, because you see a lot of women, some really old guys and some really young guys.

CHUCK HIGGINS "Motorhead Baby." A jump boogie is a clarion call to lindy-hoppers, and this is a fine example. Higgins' one-note honking saxophone is the real deal. The frantic jumpy piano and sharp vocal are courtesy of Johnny "Guitar" Watson, my personal hero, later responsible for "Three Hours Past Midnight," "Hot Little Mama," "Gangster of Love." On this recording, the 19-year-old swingin' piano-player was a real threat to the kings of piano jump. No doubt when he switched to guitar, Cecil Gant and Amos Milburn slept better.

TINY BRADSHAW "Soft." After Illinois Jacquet introduced the squealing-honking one-note tenor saxophone solo via *Jazz at the Philharmonic*, a rash of jazz-tinged R&B instrumentals populated the post-war jump landscape. A more pure R&B honkin' sound was to be found in the records of Big Jay McNeely and Joe Houston. Bandleaders like Bradshaw and Earl Bostic were a little more genteel (at least part of the time). "Soft" is a mid-tempo jumper with the tenor sax at the fore. The piano solo predates Sun Ra's modern weirdness—and I've been told it's likely that Ra was the pianist on this date. Space-age lindy-hop music? Stranger categories have emerged.

The TRENIERS "This Is It." Nobody but nobody dethrones the Treniers for over-the-top, too-fast swing-dance jump music. For sheer mayhem, these guys are the Grail, with every sax solo sounding like the result of an on-the-bandstand strangulation. For high-speed lindy-hop like it must have been in the glory days (see Malcolm X's autobiography), "This Is It" is indeed *it*.

SAMMY MASTERS "Pink Cadillac." California rockabilly comes out of Bob Wills, Hank Thompson and other Texas/Oklahoma swing outfits. Sammy Masters' singles for 4-Star Records (of Pasadena) include the John Coltrane of hillbilly guitar, Jimmy Bryant. Big Sandy has checked these out heavily. With its jet-propelled swing rhythm, "Pink Cadillac" is a standard at every jump and rockabilly party.

ROSEMARY CLOONEY "Come On-A My House." Taking a page from the Louis Prima manual of Grease-Ball Cool, Rosie unleashes an unclassifiable slice of Italo-American Jump Pop. The near-rockabilly bass and edgy harpsichord make for one rambunctious whirl around the floor. If only everything about the Eisenhower era had been this rockin', we'd have never needed Elvis.

RED SAUNDERS "Boot 'Em Up." The B-side of "Hambone." You know those '50s teen-rock flicks where the kids are jitterbugging like mad to riff-crazy horn-section jump? This is the one non-soundtrack example I've found, and it's nearly perfect. Can be easily segued into Ruth Brown's "Mama, He Treats Your Daughter Mean."

When Harry Met Sally (1989). This soundtrack may have been most responsible for the reawakening of interest in swing. It featured Harry Connick, Jr. singing standards originally recorded by Frank Sinatra and Tony Bennett. If you want to sell music to this generation, you have to attach it to visual imagery.

CECIL GANT "I Wonder," a ballad. In 1945, a resurgence in black record labels began after WWII. Roy Brown, Wynonie Harris and Lionel Hampton ("Hey-Bop-a-Ree-Bop") made jump-blues records which are optimum for Lindy Hopping.

WYNONIE HARRIS "Good Rocking Tonight." That's what people were lindy-hopping to in 1948. It just so happened it was in an area of town that many white people were afraid to visit.

Obviously, this is a mere glimpse at a bottomless genre. But every one of these has survived a zillion plays on my home Victrola. Whenever possible, I recommend these sides as 78s. Since the disc turns faster, the bass positively roars out of the speakers. If you like these records, keep an eye out for 78s on the King/Federal, Aladdin, Apollo, Deluxe, Okeh, Excello, Chess, Checker, Aristocrat, Flip, Flair, Modern, Atlantic, Sittin' In With, Specialty, Black & White, and Fortune labels. If they're in good shape, they're not cheap. But you get what you pay for.

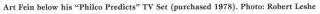

Art Fein below his "Philco Predicts" TV Set (purchased 1978). Photo: Robert Leshe

Art Fein, L.A. music critic, record collector and historian has interviewed scores of American "roots" music legends on his public access TV show, *Art Fein's Poker Party* (since 1984). Art lives with his wife Jennifer and daughter Jessica (presently 6 years old), and can be contacted at 1838 El Cerrito Pl #2, Hollywood CA 90068-3765.

Books by Art Fein

The L.A. Musical History Tour: a guide to rock'n'roll landmarks. *The Greatest Rock'n'Roll Stories* (General Publishing, Santa Monica). Basically, it's 60 stories that everybody knows, with amplification and clarification, and a bunch of others I thought were interesting, like the "Paul is dead" flap. I do get to say that MTV is the worst thing that ever happened to music and that Woodstock was a crock of shit: just a bunch of people wallowing in the mud. There were 19 other concerts just like it that summer, but this is the one where everybody got stuck in a traffic jam—*so what!*

Art Recommends Films & Books

FILM:
The Twist (documentary). It shows everything that lead up to the Twist, including some wild lindy-hopping or jitterbugging.
BOOKS:
Steve Propes' *The First Rock'n'Roll Record.* The premise is that there are 50 records that could have been the first rock'n'roll record, and he describes each one. The hilarious thing is that it *ends* with "Heartbreak Hotel." Unfortunately, there's no records to accompany it, so it'll drive you nuts. I have about 20 out of the 50. He recommends "Jazz at the Philharmonic" which is a 1942 concert at the Philharmonic Auditorium in Los Angeles. It's a jam session with Nat "King" Cole on piano, Les Paul on guitar, and Illinois Jacquet on sax. Propes contends this is the moment of the birth of rock'n'roll, and you can *hear* it—no one's ever heard that before and people are screaming. When you realize this is happening in 1942, it's a revelation.

Jim Dawson *Nervous, Man, Nervous* (by Big Jay McNeely's manager). Who'd want to do a book on a guy who plays honkin' sax, which is mostly one note over and over? Well, as Big Jay says, "It's *how* you play that note! [laughs] The honkin' sax players are like the Cramps; they're reducing musical statement to an absurd minimum.

♦ *VALE: How did you get into jump-blues and swing?*
♦ ART FEIN: In the '70s, a big deal for me was Route 66 records out of Sweden. They released records by late-'40s black combos with some big band feeling, but transitioning into the birth of R&B: jump-blues like Wynonie Harris, Roy Brown and Louis Jordan. Roy Brown, who wrote "Good Rockin' Tonight," shouted like people did in church—and to many people that was a no-no. The king of jump music was Louis Jordan, who was very popular, appearing on Ed Sullivan, etc. His big hits were tunes like "Ain't Nobody Here But Us Chickens," with funny lyrics about cops raiding after-hour joints, or people getting arrested for dancing all night. Almost all his songs were "novelty," and *that's* why they were dismissed. Jump has not really been acknowledged in music history. Even jazz scholars barely know anything about jump musicians like Wynonie Harris.

Bullmoose Jackson's "Big Ten-Inch" (about a 10″ record, of course) and Tiny Bradshaw's "Train Kept A-Rollin'" are also jump. Everything from the jump era sounds like you're riding on a train. *Any* Louis Jordan album is worth getting. He was one of the rare people who redid his hits and they're different, but just as good. He can even make you appreciate songs like "I Believe in Music"! Jump music straddles R&B or early rock'n'roll. Chuck Berry will say that Louis Jordan was his main influence. Every '50s black musician listened to him.

♦ *V: What's your take on all these new swing bands?*
♦ AF: The so-called "swing" bands like Royal Crown are great, but they're all doing jump, really. **V**

Art Recommends Recordings

Roy Eldridge *Ain't That A Shame*
Lil Green *Romance In The Dark, Why Don't You Do Right*
Wynonie Harris *Stormy Night*
Ivory Joe Hunter *Stop Rockin' The Boat, I Quit My Pretty Mama, I Need You So*
Bullmoose Jackson *I Knew Who Threw The Whisky In The Well, Why Don't You Haul Off And Love Me*
Louis Prima *Oh Babe*
Sister Rosetta Tharpe w/Lucky Millender Orch *Shout Sister Shout*
Amos Milburn *Tell Me How Long Has The Train Been Gone, After Midnight*
Roy Brown *Roy Brown's Boogie*
Ella Johnson *I Don't Care Who Knows*
Buddy Johnson Orch *Did You See Jackie Robinson Hit That Ball?*
Tampa Red *Witching Hour Blues*
Ella Fitzgerald *Flying Home*
Louis Jordan *No Sale*
Dinah Washington *Million Dollar Smile*
Ruth Brown *So Long*

A to Z of Bands

Note: Bands covered in interviews are NOT listed below. Almost all the CDs mentioned are available from Hepcat 800-404-4117, Dept RS. This directory is *incomplete*; probably a new "swing" band forms every day. Also, if your band was not listed, it's because you didn't send us your promo package, so send it for our next directory! (VG = VISE GRIP, AS = AARON SEYMOUR, TD = TANYA DEASON)

Ricky Quisol at Hi-Ball, 12-1-96.

Atomic Cocktail Ricky Quisol (dr), Sandy Clifford (voc), Dan Eisenberg (piano), Yanos Lustig (tenor sax), Troy Green (bass) are instigators of the original San Francisco "swing" uprising, playing Sundays at the Deluxe in fall '92, and hosting 9 infamous all-night rent parties at their Natoma St. warehouse in '92–'94. On 8-27-93 AC went to L.A. and were the first neo-swing band to play the Derby and the Viper Room, just before Royal Crown Revue did regular Wed. nights at the Derby. Original song "Get Swank" on Pushing the Norton CD. The name "Atomic Cocktail" came from a '40s Slim Gaillard protest song about nuclear energy.

Altruda, Joey LA, Jump with Joey
Atomic Fireballs Detroit band. 818-546-0415.
Beat Me Daddy L.A. band featuring vocalist Patty Lagana, a punk roommate of Eddie Nichols from the San Diego days who also sang occasionally with the Rock-o-matics and Mando Dorame's Jazz Jury. Band together from Oct '91-Feb '93, different lineup went to Vegas, played with Royal Crown Revue at the Shark Club, then broke up. Patty's previous bands: Urban Assault, with Sidewinder, Three Bad Jacks (Elvis, guitarist from Terror Train & Tony Portillo, drummer of THROW RAG, a Cramps-like country band with an amazing singer, Apollo).
Beat Positive John Ceparano started a NYC-based trio in late 1988. Fusing swing and lounge, the band now includes vibes and horns. In 1994 released CD *Come Out Swingin'.* Released cassette preview in 1997 of new CD *Livin' It Up.*

Have 3 songs on Lo-Fi Lee's *NYC Swing* CD, $15 from POB 20087 Greeley Square Station, NYC 10001. 718-706-0655.
Bellevue Cadillac Boston's swing band. CD titled *Black and White* $16ppd from 329 E. Main St, Norton MA 02766. *webmkt.com/cadillac/*
Big Joe & the Dynaflows. Baltimore.
Big Rhythm Combo LA band
Big Town Operator First gig Feb 2, '96 at Casbah, San Diego. Ex-rockabilly singer Warren Lovell started 10-piece jump-swing band, played Derby, Viper Room, Vegas, etc. Hot CD, *High Altitude Swing.* 619-273-7368. (web site)
The Big Town Seven. Had a chick singer & were really hot.—VG
Billard, Dave Hot Austin, Texas guitarist in the vein of Jimmy Bryant (country-jazz). Has recorded and toured with

Dale Watson and Wayne Hancock; plays with the Hot Club of Cowtown, etc.
Billie Sheets & The Blue Diamonds Veteran L.A. vocalist often favorably compared to legendary blues shouter Roy Brown. The Blue Diamonds mix West Coast Swing with

KC jazz and Memphis blues sounds. CD *Please Tell Me Why* available through Big Clock Records. 213-669-7382 or *big-clock@earthlink.net.*
Black Tie Orchestra Bay Area 19-piece private party big band featuring former "Situations"/Ms. Jello Biafra punkette Teresa Soder.
Blasters LA roots music band featuring brothers Dave & Phil Alvin. 1st LP 1980, *American Music* (now re-released). 2nd LP, *The Blasters.* Recorded other LPs and toured a lot. Dave Alvin left in 1986, replaced by James Intveld. John Bazz still in band; current drummer: Jerry Angel. Both Alvin brothers have released solo recordings & worked with other bands.
Blue Bell Wranglers Joann has amazing voice.
Blue Plate Special "A lot of bands are trying to do the rock'n'roll and swing mix, but BPS deserve praise for keeping their sets 'traditional.'"–AS After starting rockabilly band Incredible Diamonds in 1992 in Chico, CA, Todd Clark met Kevin Wright (Kingpins' vocalist) in '93 & started Blue Plate Special. Original songs include "Night Out," "A Tango of Sorrow," "Work That Skirt," "Double-Talkin' Fool" and "A Night in Havana." Many arrangements by early trombonist Jamie Vlahos. First gig early 1994: Todd rented theater & built art deco & tiki sets—did 4 D-I-Y shows. 45 out. BPS c/o 8306 Wilshire Blvd #56, Bev Hills, CA 90211. 888-908-4063.
Blue Room Boys do everything: a crazy bop song, serious blues-swing, and then "The Days of Wine & Roses." Eclectic. Anything Ralph Carney touches is stunning. He's worked with Tom Waits & others.—AS
Blues Jumpers 6-piece band's debut CD *Wheels Start Turning* has a Louis Jordan, Cab Calloway, Stax/Volt feel. 201-531-9528 or *TraMiller@aol.com.*
Brown, Junior Guit-steel guitarist fuses diff. styles of music beautifully.
Camaros Up-n-coming NYC performance art band. Jen Jones writes & sings original songs with vocalist Lee Ann Westover and Amanda Monoca on guitar. On Lo-Fi NYC Swing CD.
Candye Kane & The Swingin' Armadillos Ex-stripper doing blues-a-billy . . . but really, a lot deeper than that.
Cats & Jammers 510-534-4683.
Chazz Cats Their background has a lot of Grateful Dead/folkmusic/blues as well as a passion for roadhouse swing.

They've been expanding their style and coming up with their own music. They're from Berkeley and have a female singer (D'lilah Monroe) that's nice to look at. They do "Roadhouse Swing" & their CD sounds good. (CD $15ppd from 1410 Josephine Av, Berkeley CA 94703 or *chazzcats@aol.com*)—TD

Cherry-Poppin' Daddies Ska band from Eugene, Oregon turned swing. CD, *Zoot Suit Riot,* available.

Condo, Ray Western Swing, Rockabilly and Hillbilly Bop meld into an original sound that's authentically vintage. 2 CDs available from the Canadian original who's also a sax player. Peerless band; great live show—Ray's the "real thing." Ray Condo & the Ricochets' first gig was at the Railway Club in Vancouver, B.C. in Sept 1994. CDs $15ppd each from Joaquin Records, Dept RS, 254 Scott St, SF CA 94117. 415-621-4131.

Crazy Hot Rhythm Society Orchestra Also the MIKE HENEBRY ORCHESTRA. Private party band. Mike Henebry is very enthusiastic about keeping swing music alive. 562-431-1699 or *mhenebry@aol.com*

Crazy Rhythm Daddies Canadian swing band featuring the brotherly duo of

Blue Plate Special L to R: Adam Bankhead, Todd Clark, Nathan Dreyfuss, Fred Stuart, Phil Topping, Ken Charlson. 1997.

Trevor Baker Photography (818) 455-4016

Peter & Eric Sandmark. For self-titled CD contact Iglu Records at PO BOX 122, Station P, Toronto ON M5S 2S7, Canada; 416-944-9624.

Dem Brooklyn Bums Broccoli Bob leads this NYC group; CD available.

Johnny Dilks & His Visitacion Valley Boys Visitacion Valley (southern district of San Francisco), was a hotbed of country music in the '40s. Local punk rocker-turned roots musician plays Western Swing and hillbilly with a first-class band. Dilks has become an ace yodeler and rhythm guitarist, and has compelling stage presence. He picks great songs, like "Roly-Poly." Highly recommended.

Cynthia & The Swing Set Scat & swing from the East Bay. 510-548-5839

Dalhart Imperials Denver rockabilly. Also a more swing band version called PAPA GRANDE. 303-455-8408.

L: Flattop Tom at Great American Music Hall, 8.3.97. Photo: V. Vale. Above: Dutch Falconi & His Twisted Orchestra from Sacramento: a bountiful bevy of 20 ecstatic entertainers.

Dave & Deke (Dave Stuckey and Deke Dickerson). Defunct combo, very influential. Had duet-harmony sound like country duo Jimmy and Johnny. Dave has new band, Pappy & The Hired Hands. See "Eccophonic" entry.

Derailers '40s Bakersfield country sound from band now signed to Sire.

The Dino Martinis 6-piece Calgary band that "mixes the ultimate drink of Swing and Jump Blues." First CD: *The Bottle Collector's Lounge,* $20 from Dept RS, 28 Franklin Drive SE, Calgary, AB, Canada T2H 0T9. 403-253-7878, fax 225-2749 or (web page) *hazlettj@cadvision.com.* 2nd CD just out, (early '98). They have several TV, movie and radio show credits. Original songs.

Dizzy Burnett Hot female stand-up bass player from Santa Cruz. 408-423-2511.

Don Miller Orchestra L.A. private party 14-piece band since 1986, on "The Nanny" and "Seinfeld." CD, *This Swingin' Life,* due in Jan 1998. 818-432-8410.

Dutch (Penfield) manager and booker of the Club Deluxe, the original San Francisco swing mecca.

Dutch Falconi & His Twisted Orchestra Sacramento big band, 20-plus members. CDs *The Shoes of Despair, Crime Boss Hootenanny,* $15 ea. from 916-456-1276.

(web page) Hot! Originals!

Eccophonic. Deke Dickerson's label.

Eddie Reed Swing Band Long Beach-based vocalist-clarinetist quit his rockabilly band, The Bluehearts, in 1990 and joined a big band as an apprenticeship. In 1993 he formed a "swing" band which played its first gig April 27, 1993. His bands (usually a sextet) have played The Derby, Coconut Grove, Rhino Room, Viper Room, etc. Singer Meghan Ivey (born 12.11.78; joined Reed at age 14) and 14 other musicians appear on new CD, *Hollywood Jump.* As Ivey said, "Ella and other original big band singers were 14 or 15 when they joined bands." A dedicated musician and bandleader, Eddie Reed deserves your support. (web page)

TEL 562-434-7189

Eight To The Bar Boston band with female vocalist Cynthia Lyon. CD *Beat Me Rocking.* (web page) 203-272-0597

Elliott, Bill He has an awesome big band in L.A. and has done a lot of movie scores. Those guys kick butt. Get their 2 CDs. 310-459-1717; *swingorch@aol.com.*

Eric Ekstrand Ensemble LA band

Flattop Tom & His Jump Cats LA-based *hot* 8-piece dedicated to keeping tradional swing alive performing classic big band, jump-blues/jive and more. Tom Hall, frontman and harmonica player, is a great pro dancer, with an extensive collection of vintage swing-dance videos that often play in the background, and is a genuine character. (His day job was a gym teacher). Featured pianist-vocalist is the hot Linda "Lucky" Giandominico. First gig opening for the late, great William Clarke (Alligator Records) on Sept. 19, 1992. 2 releases out, *Jumpin' Blues for Your Dancin' Shoes* and *Rockin' and Jumpin' the Blues,* with 13 originals out of 21 cuts. Hotline: 1-888-GO FLATTOP.

Flores, Rosie In the tradition of Janis Martin and Wanda Jackson (both of whom appeared on her CD, *Rockabilly Filly),* Rosie sings classic American roots music. T.K. Smith and Russell Scott also appeared on this. Ex-Screamin' Sirens.

Above: Core members of Jellyroll: Paul Mehling, Steve Dekrone, Belinda Blair, 1997. Below Right: Kim Nalley, vocalist for Johnny Nocturne band. Below: Hot Club of Cowtown: T.C. Cyran, Elana Fremerman, Whit Smith.

Flying Neutrinos NY Universal/Grp/Fiction recording artists popular with NYC retro scene from beginning. Orig. from New Orleans. 212-802-9752; 212-924-1009.
Four Piece Suit Boston band doing film soundtrack, more lounge-swing.
Frenchy includes clarinet/sax, vibes, drums, bass, plus East Bay Ray (former Dead Kennedys guitarist). They have a good beat and a sensual female singer with a strong punk rock voice, like Nina Hagen. CD available.—TD
Friends of Dean Martinez SF lounge.
Ray Gelato A sax player amidst the Sugar Ray and King Pleasure crowd who does jump-blues. Recently he hooked up with the Good Fellas from Italy and did a tribute CD to Louis Prima that's excellent, *Ray Gelato Meets the Good Fellas.* With 3 other CDs out, he's doing well in England, and seguing into soundtracks. He just did *Inventing the Abbotts,* a love story set in the '50s.—TD
George Gee's Jump, Jive and Wailers Also has his 15-piece MAKE BELIEVE ORCHESTRA and his hand in Swing 46, NYC's 1st 7-day/week swing club. Works w/Nick Palumbo, too. 212-779-7865.
Hancock, Wayne Austin, TX pure Honky-Tonk singer-guitarist.
Heyday Records Bay Area label, CDs by Dave & Deke and Connie Champagne. 2325 3rd St, SF CA. Tel 415-252-5590.
Hipster Daddy-O & The Handgrenades Tuscon boogie-woogie, jump blues. Slimstyle CD out. 520-320-3742
Honkin' Hep Cats UK band.
Horton Brothers. Austin, Texas rockabilly-hillbilly-boogie quartet includes Shaun Young. LP on Crazy Love Records (Germany) and 45 on Echophonic. The brothers used to play horns in The Big Town Swingtet. Members also play in successor, The Jive Bombers. POB 143534, Austin TX 78714.
Hot Club Of Cowtown Dazzling performances by Western Swing heirs Whit Smith (guitar-vocals), Elana Fremerman (violin-vocals) and T.C. Cyran (upright bass) won over the last Greaseball audi-

ence. Their influences include (guitar: George Barnes and Hank Garland, Django), fiddle: Joe Venuti and Stephane Grappelli, Joe Holly and Louie Tierney [early jazzy fiddle stylists in the Bob Wills Band. Tiny Moore on mandolin. Bob Wills, Tex Williams (hot jazz and western swing). Whit and Elana were in an NYC 11-piece Western Swing band (with 3 fiddles) in '94-'96, Whit Smith & His Western Caravan (vocals: Thirsty Dave). Cassette $8ppd or CD $12ppd from POB 685335, Austin TX 78701-9998. 512-479-9219. *(web page)*
Hot Club Of San Francisco They are incredible, doing acoustic Django Reinhardt stuff—amazing. Gypsy jazz. Now Paul Maylin has this new band with a chick singer, JELLY-ROLL.—VG. 2 releases, *The Quintet of the Hot Club of San Francisco & Swing This.* 415-931-0909
Hot Rod Lincoln San Diego rockabilly trio. 3rd CD Blue Cafe. Booking: Jim 619-299-5929.
Hot Rod Trio from L.A. have a brand-new CD and a cool car club. Buddy, President. These kids are keeping up the heritage of hot rod car clubs from the '40s and '50s and they haven't "sold out" to technology updating. Their music matches their cars—it's all part of "the culture."—Vida Lee
The Hucklebucks Hard working jump blues 4-piece band from Sacramento with just released CD, *Coastin'.* Frontman Doug James also plays a mean harp and

tenor sax. First gig at Harlows in Sacramento Sept. 7, 1995. 916-448-0741
Hunter Sullivan Dallas crooner
Indigo Swing San Francisco sextet of *good* musicians led by vocalist Johnny Boyd; around since 1993. They have a loyal following. 14-track 1995 CD, *Indigo Swing.*
Intveld, James "Roots" guitarist-singer playing rockabilly since early '80s; played in later version of The Blasters. Cuts on *L.A. Rockabilly* anthology. Standout.
Jackson, Wanda. Child prodigy b. Oct 20, 1937, toured with Elvis, did "Let's Have a Party" and "Fujiyama Mama." Still tours and gets the roots crowd goin'. A living legend; see her while you can.
Jazz Passengers Former Blondie frontwoman Deborah Harry often tours as "Special Guest Vocalist" with this offshoot of the Lounge Lizards. CD out.
Jellyroll 3-part vocal jump jive from the '40s with jazzy vocalist Belinda Blair and Hot Club's Paul Mehling and Steve Dekrone, who she met busking in Paris. CD on Checker Records. 415-921-8065 or *JellySJD@aol.com*
Jimmy & Gigolos LA 213-481-1894
Jive Aces Upbeat UK band playing hot Jump R&B. CDs *The Golden Age of Science Fiction* and *Bolt from the Blue* have some great tracks. Fun dance music.

Jive Bombers New Austin, TX jump/jive combo featuring Miss Danna Dattlo from The Jubilettes and Big Town Swingtet. Shaun Young (see separate entry) plays drums. 512-912-8580
Joaquin Records, run by Jeff Richardson (who also ran Rambler and Western Records in the late '70s-early '80s) has only produced Western Swing recordings. Current releases include 2 Ray Condo CDs, Jimmy Rivers & The Cherokees: *Brisbane Bop* (Rivers was the '50s-'60s guitar king of Brisbane Western Swing, ruling the 23 Club). Past releases include recordings by Smoky Wood, Moon Mullican, Jimmie Revard & His Oklahoma Playboys, Milton Brown & His Musical Brownies, and some W.S. anthologies: Hartman's Heartbreakers: *Give It To Me, Daddy* (x-rated '30s hillbilly music featuring Betty Lou), *Swing Guitar Legend* by Argentinian Django Reinhardt-rival Oscar Aleman, and some W.S. anthologies: *Texas Sand, Devil with the Devil, Hot As I Am.* Ray Condo and Big Sandy were influenced by the above recordings. CDs $15 each from Dept R/S,

254 Scott St, SF CA 94117. 415-621-4131.

Joe Vento Big Band All-Stars LA band

John Henderson Orchestra Veteran LA band. 714-637-7655

The Johnny Nocturne Swing Band Bay area veterans now featuring Kim Nally on vocals. CDs on Rounder Records. 415-459-4215. see Nocturne

Johnny Crawford 1928 Dance Orchestra LA band. 213-962-0804 or *DanceOrch@aol.com*

Johnson, Jay Besides owning Club Deluxe which incubated the early SF swing scene, this Frank Sinatra-understudy fronts his own 17-piece Ultra Deluxe Orchestra. Black belt karate!

Jumpin' Jimes 9-piece WWII-era jump blues/swing from L.A.—they were interesting. They play the Derby all the time - AS. CD out in early '98. 805-339-9148

Jump With Joey LA band, more eclectic than swing. 2 CDs.

JW (Jeremy) plays double-neck Bigsby steel guitar with Lucky Stars, tours with Wayne Hancock.

King Pleasure & The Biscuit Boys do jump-swing. This British band dresses in bright red double-breasted suits and spectators and do a totally energetic show, with the horns choreographed. At one point the stand-up bass player jumped off the stage, his bass between his legs, playing it while walking. The drummer has his back to him banging out the drum beat on the back of the bass. They were walking through the crowd like this—it was amazing! 4 CDs available.—TD

Kings Of Pleasure new Tucson, Arizona "swing" band with CD out on Trope Records.

Kreuzer, Josie *Hot Rod Girl* CD out by the former singer of LA rockabilly band Whistle Bait.

Lannon, Dee A San Francisco native, in the '80s Dee sang for The Coronados before starting Dee Lannon and the Rhythm Rustlers. In 1991, she moved to L.A. Her first 45 was "Lasso Your Heart." In 1994 she recorded a 10″ EP, *Honky Tonk Nighttime Gal.* She toured Japan in 1993 and 1996, recording a CD, *Town Casino.* She recently recorded another CD in L.A. Dee has one of the best voices in modern rockabilly, plus great stage presence. Contact Dee c/o Blue Puffer Records, 100 First St #100-228, SF CA 94105.

L'Atome "Pre-apocalyptic sounds inspired by underwater cities" from Phoenix, OR. CD *The Flash of Light.* Note: not swing music; uncategorizable. (Web page) 541-535-4195

Last Of The International Playboys NYC 9-piece band of Vegas jazz and Latin lounge, from Rat Pack covers to orginal catchy tunes. Accordian, bassoon, horns and Latin percussive instruments mix to form a strange, refreshing punch. S/t CD $16 from Main Squeeze, 19 Essex St, NY NY 10012. (212-614-3109).

Little Big Band LA band

Little Charlie & His Nightcats Sacramento jump-blues quartet. They tour the world 300 days a year. Charlie Baty (gtr), Rick Estrin (vo, har), Ronnie James Weber (bass), June Core (drums; Louis Jordan's 2nd cousin!). Recordings on Alligator Records. 704-399-2210

Lost Continentals Atlanta rockabilly-swing. *Moonshine & Martinis.* 404-355-5580

Love Dogs 7-piece Boston band mixes Big Band jazz with New Orleans R&B to form swinging orginals since 1994. *I'm Yo Dog* on Tone-Cool Records available from Rounder. 617-491-1970.

Lucky Seven Swing Ensemble Eugene, OR jump-blues, swing. 541-683-529

Lucky Stars LA based. 213-464-LUCK. Their steel player, JW, plays double-neck Bigsby steel guitar, has toured with Wayne Hancock, and is hot.

Lucky Strikes very lounge, late-night Frank Sinatra crooning style, but traditionalist-sounding in the same way Bill Elliott is. When you listen to their CD, *12 Past Midnight,* a song may sound familiar, but it's *all* original music! They captured the style really well. The songs are all crooner love-songs.—AS 512-447-9299

Martini Brothers - now OUT OF NOWHERE

Merchants Of Venus Austin, Texas swing-based 7-piece band played first gig Sept 28, 1994 at the Carousel Lounge. Vocalist George Brainard and bassist Merrideth Jiles (MOV Prods) have a CD out, *Who Knew?,* available from POB 650037, Austin TX 78765. 512-323-9125.

Mez, DJ Dan 3 CDs out. 617-783-9333

Mighty Blue Kings Confused bandwagon-jumpers from Chicago. Mealy.

Money Plays Eight The (only?) swing band in Denver.

Mora's Modern Rhythmists Dean Mora is a LA music veteran. 818-980-8397 or *deanmora@pacificnet.net*

The Movers Boston swing/jump blues band. 603-228-4489 or *blues@tiac.net*

Nicola Miller Quintet Minneapolis chanteuse turns bars into martini lounges and often unites her basic players; since '96 with guest horns for a more swingin' time.

Nocturne, Johnny Band docs really good, hot jump-swing. Founded by tenor saxophonist John Firmin, the band has been playing swing music way before there was any viable "scene." Kim Nalley, who sings with him, is a great lady whose voice is amazing! 3 CDs on Rounder Records: *Wailin' Daddy, Shake 'em Up* and *Wild & Cool.*—AS

Olsen, Richard leads a good and enjoyable big band. He's a former member of the Charlatans, an early San Francisco's '60s band. CD available.—TD

Out Of Nowhere 6-piece band founded by the Sinatra-esque Bob Dalpe, who started singing big band standards in 1993 at The House of Shields in S.F.

L to R: Milan Moorman, Freddy Mendoza, Craig Marshall, Dave Miller, Elias Haslanger, David Levy. Pix: David Levy.

bd@ix.netcom.com.

Paladins Early '80s L.A. rockabilly band, still rockin'. Many CDs available.

Parr, Stephen Archivist of swing/lounge films and '70s-era punk rocker. In the post-punk San Francisco scene, Parr tried to promote swing consciousness with live events and film screenings, beginning in 1980 with Mr. Lucky as "Punch and Banger" (Oct 23) and "Mr. Lucky and Amanda Night" (Oct 3) at Club Generic, 236 Leavenworth St. On Sept 29, 1984 he produced "All Dressed Up and No Place to Go" at the Swedish-American Hall, 2174 Market St with The Union Squares (13-piece big band) and Mr. Lucky. Later he produced events with Mr. Lucky, the Tim Hesla Orchestra and other "cabaret" acts. Film rentals available from his company Oddball Film & Video, FAX 415-863-9771; TEL 415-558-8112.

Peachy's Puffs Retro cigarette & candy girls have returned! In S.F. 415-777-4436.

Poindexter, Buster aka David Johansen Former NY Dolls vocalist in his swingin' alter ego with a horn-section band led by Joe Delia. Several CDs of hit-or-miss repertoire on RCA.

Pritchett, Judy 32101 Ellison Way, Fort Bragg, CA 95437.

Energetically promotes Lindy Hop, Frankie Manning, Norma Miller and swing dance in general. Has videos, books, etc. for sale. (web site)

Quisol, Ricky Bay Area drummer in Big Hair, Kettles, T-Bone (with Rick Tanner & Fra Kepler), Chicken Shackers (w/Derek Felton), Susanna & the Golden West Playboys, Bachelors, Swingin' Johnsons, Johnny & Ricky, Rounders & Atomic Cocktail. Also filled in with Vise Grip's St. Vitus Dance, Lucky Stars, etc & toured w/Phantom Surfers Johnny Bartlett & Mike Lucas, plus Elka on guitar. Roots Archivist.

Radio Ranch Straight Shooters features girl country fiddle player. LA Western Swing band.

Red & The Red Hots Play Derby every Thurs. in LA. Red Young formed the band in 1984 after years of touring and recording with the likes of the Supremes, Dolly Parton and Eric Burdon. 213-876-7333. *redhot@earthlink.net*

Red Meat a comical, sarcastic country/Western Swing band. They have a good, solid collection of instrumentalists including good fiddle players. Very

entertaining! Genuine characters.—TD

The Rounders SF Honky-Tonk band led by charismatic "roots" scholar/drummer Ricky Quisol. J.B. Allison gtr, Brian Mello voc/gtr, David Phillips ped steel gtr, Tony Laborle bs. Driving! 415-468-4454.

The Riff Rats is an excellent band playing mostly covers that are well-arranged. Mike Madager is a guitarist who has been around the swing scene since the early days. He was a part of Bo Grumpus.—AS

Road Zombies. The premiere Northern California "rods and customs" car club; their cars are breathtaking and other-worldly. Range from little hotrods to ultra-cool customs. Craig Hahn, president, has a 1940 Ford that's rolling art deco. beeper: 408-322-9056. Annual party in April.—Vida Lee

Rob & Diane Bay Area Lindy Hop instructors. Rob is originally from Amsterdam and has danced all over the world; he has an international perspective on American "swing" creativity. 560-864-8127. Teach Wed at 435 Broadway.

Rob Rio & The Revolvers LA based. 818-994-2437

Rollin' Rocks great Japanese Western Swing band. Their instrumental "West Coast Excursion" sounds like a vintage pre-war W.S. song. They played the '97 Denver Rock 'N Rhythm-billy Weekend and with Bill Haley's Comets were one of the big hits of the show. On The Hill Records has released several 45s.

Ron Sunshine & Full Swing NYC Ron has jump & R&B bands. 718-768-1040.

Roomful Of Blues Playing host to a

L : Russell Scott. Below: Sloe Gin Joes: Dez Mabunga, Mike Burns & Frank Novicki.

variety of Boston musicians for the past 28 years, the most recent incarnation is a 9-piece with horns emitting a jump-blues vibe. *Under One Roof* available on Rounder Records follows up their Grammy-nominated *Turn It On! Turn It Up!*

Royal Crowns, Amazing. Boston band.

Royal Jokers S.F. car club started by Jose Mejia, Carlitos Wright (punker from Hayward) and Che Shul in late '80s. They used to drive their cars to shows like at the Chi-Chi Club or the occasional Stray Cats shows. Once Brian Setzer autographed Jose's pink chopped Merc.

Royal Cruisers Bay Area "Old fart" true '50s car club (no high-tech garbage allowed; original motors only) joined by Che Shul, now a family man. Goes to annual Pasa Robles custom car show, Memorial Day—the *only* show where you can see customs. You're not a real "rockabilly" unless you go to Pasa Robles!

Rugcutters L.A. dance troupe featuring Peter Loggins and Alicia Milo. 310-519-7926. e-mail *rugcutrs@gte.net*.

Russ Button's Swing Orchestra Trumpeter who counts Bay Area great John Coppola (now playing with the Ambassadors of Swing) as his greatest single influence, formed an authentic 30's/40's-styled big band (4 trumpets, 4 trombones, 5 saxs, piano, bass, drums, vocalist and sometimes guitar). With his motto, "Big band swing has always been about dance music and it is dance music that has driven American Popular Culture," he's one of the veterans. Newcomers to swing should rediscover him.

Russell Scott & His Red Hots b. March 6, 1967. The rockabilly scene incubated the swing movement. Inspired by the Stray Cats (and by his dad's doowop and rockabilly 45 collection), Russell Scott started a band, the Rockin' Renegades in the 9th grade (1981) which lasted past high school. They released a 45, "Gonna Rock'n'Roll/If You Love Me." Russell was intrinsically involved in the hectic '80s L.A. roots music scene. He was in a band, the Rock-a-matics, with Eddie Nichols and James Achor before Royal Crown Revue formed in 1989.

A burly 6´2˝ singer and bassist, he plays music for the love of it and is the kind of musician who finishes a gig and then goes to an after-hours party and sings till dawn. Along with the SUN DEMONS, HOT ROD LINCOLN and other L.A. groups, he performs rockabilly, but *his* way—expanded to include songs by Sinatra, Neil Diamond, Harry Belafonte and more. As he put it, "The word rockabilly includes rock'n'roll and hillbilly. And that music came from blues, swing, hillbilly and jazz. So if people get into rockabilly, they'll also get into the music that spawned it. Swing is getting big now, but it's rockabilly that opened the door." Cuts on *Pushing the Norton: The Ace Cafe Compilation,* and *Turning the World Blue: A Tribute to Gene Vincent & His Blue Caps,* plus their own CD and 10″ LP on Bear Family. 213-666-5363.

Sehee, Joey LA lounge-rock pioneer.

Set 'em Up Joe NYC 212-714-7043

Setzer, Brian Ex-Stray Cats frontman has "big" band fusing rockabilly, swing and rock showmanship.

Shagtime dance instruction by humanitarian Michael Marangio. (510) 528-7858

Sloe Gin Joes (orig. "Revelators") Bay Area long-time rockabilly stalwarts Frank Novicki (voc, gtr), Dez Mabunga aka Dez Mab (bs),Mike Burns (dr). CD recorded at Ivy Room, Albany, CA. FRANK NOVICKI: early '80s punk bands; Soul Senders; seeing The Blasters changed his life. Diablos, orig. Kingpins. 1987: *Shockwaves,* an all-instrumental surf-garage band that recorded *Primal Twang* in 1991. Toured with Rosie Flores, wrote songs for Pearl Harbour, toured with Legendary Stardust Cowboy (produced 2 albums); backed up Bo Diddley and Richard Berry. DEZ MABUNGA: First punk band Cathouse, '85. Kettles (w/Ricky Quisol, brother Fred Mabunga, singer Margo Wister). Coronados w/Dee Lannon. Shakedancer (blues). With brother Fred & drummer Joey Myers formed Freddy King & The Kings doing Freddy King instrumentals. '91 Boogiemen w/Haroun Serang (gtr), Tobin (dr). '92 8-Ball Scratch with Elka (gtr, Trashwomen), Chris Harvey (Count Backwards), singer named Slim. Von Zipper (w/Chris Harvey & Peepin' John from Count Backwards). Saints We Ain't, Juggernaut. Still in Demonics (punk). Joined SGJoes mid '96. The Sloe Gin Joes have played on shows with Ronnie Dawson, the Paladins, Big Sandy, Wayne Hancock, Royal Crown Revue, Ray Condo, The Derailers, Elvis Herselvis, and the original Comets (of Bill Haley fame). Send $12ppd (cash) for great CD from 2966 Diamond St, Box 169RS, SF CA 94131. E-mail: *sloginjoes@aol.com.* Homepage: *http://members.aol.com/sloginjoes/sgj.html.*

Smokejumpers Looking like rockabilly cats in a sci-fi movie, this band played a Christmas '97 special on cable access in San Francisco. With the guitarist's green-dyed mohawk shaped like a pine tree, the bass player's holiday nail polish and the green flattop accenting the red zoot suit on the lead singer, they *must* be from SF.

The Sophisticats

Speakeasy Spies Also play as the PAUL TURNER BIG BAND. Turner is a drummer prodigy and his Veronica Lake-ish frontwoman Karista Cook have been making the rounds of So Cal swing joints. 310-659-1748.

Spider Smith & The Sinister Seven They were an earlier swing band from Sacramento with a "standard" swing sound like Blue Plate Special. Two main guys were at an ATM and they got shot! And they were *really* good. We never heard of them again.—TD

Stardust Orchestra play very soft swing every Thursday at Coconut Grove. But when it's played right, it can take you to the '40s fast.—TD

Stillmen Superior Bay Area Rockabilly band. EP $7ppd from Star Tone, Dept RS, POB 191533, SF CA 94119.*dimlights.com.*

Sugar King Boys SF rockabilly band with Jose Espinosa (bs, ex-Blue Bell Wranglers), Joey Myers, (dr), Pete Gowdy (voc-acoustic gtr), Johnny Bartlett (hot guitarist, also in Saturn V; formerly in Phantom Surfers [8 yrs], Statesiders, Wig Torture). EP $5: Hillsdale Records, POB 641592, SF CA 94164. Send $1 for catalog; Dept RS.

Sugar Ray's Flying Fortress is led by Pat Reyford, lead singer of The Big Six. Their CD, *Bim Bam Baby,* is great.—TD

Swing Fever 18-year Bay Area veterans featuring Louie Armstrong-esque trumpet/fluegelhorn player (often at the same time) Clark Terry, and led by Bryan Gould on trombone. Bay Area chanteuse Kim Nalley often sings. 415-459-2428.

Top: Wally's Swing World. Above: Rockin' Lloyd Tripp at Bimbo's, 8-15-97.

The Swing Solution 17-piece full-blown big band from San Jose with jump as its "specialty." (Web page) 408-264-4201 or *swing@inferno.com*

Tracy Wells Big Band LA based

Tripp, Lloyd Former U.K. bassist with Blubbery Hellbillies (3 LPs, 2 45s); singer & drummer were in The Lurkers. The singer for the Pogues named the B.H. Lloyd relocated to Bay Area where he joined The Ramblers in 1987, which spun off into the Zipguns in 1990. In 1994 he started Rockin' Lloyd Tripp & His 3 Tons of Fun.

Twisters Canadian jump-blues/blues-a-billy band features hot harmonica and guitar against a slappin' rhythm section. CD, *Fulla Hot Air,* available for $20ppd from 1-800-633-8282. email *junior@smartt.com.*

Van Tassel, Susanna Austin singer-gtr

Velvet Hammer In L.A., Elvia & Michelle have revived Variety Burlesque Shows. Sizzling! $3 next catalog, 3157 Silverlake Blvd, Los Angeles CA 90039

Vibro-Champs Minneapolis rockabilly stalwarts since 1992 led by the charismatic Dave Wolfe, now incorporating swing with the addition of guest horns. (webpage) 612-874-2457 or *vibro@tt.net*

Vic Volare & His Lounge Orchestra Minneapolis crooner with swingin' elements. 612-872-9786

Wally's Swing World Santa Cruz music professor & Sinatra sound-alike Wally Trinidad (with big pompadour) fronts a 7-piece swing band. Very early in the movement; 1st gig was summer '92. Excel. cassette available for $12 postpaid. 408-423-9021 or *dodger@ihot.com*

Wild Cards were L.A. Latin guys who did a Latin version of Louis Jordan. Lead singer did the splits; very animated. Miller beer sponsored them as "next big thing." They disappeared.—Ricky Quisol

Young, Shaun Frontman of High Noon has his own solo CD out. A scholar and historian. Plays in other groups as well.

Zinn, Rusty Ace blues/roots guitarist.

THANKS FOR HELP!
Jules Sears • Eric Mittler
No. & So. Calif. Lindy Societies
MargieCormier • Lo Fi Lee • Nancy Myers
Tumbleweed Productions • Dave Wolfe
Jim Calderone • Mike Henebry
Charles Mohnike

A to Z of Swing Pioneers

Arlen, Harold *composer.* With lyricist Ted Koehler, he wrote "Stormy Weather," Cotton Club revue songs for Cab Calloway, etc

Armstrong, Louis (8-4-00–7-6-71) *trumpet, singer, cornet, leader.* Born Daniel Louis Armstrong in New Orleans, Louisiana. His wide mouth won him the nickname "Satchelmouth" (Satchmo or Satch for short). No other jazz soloist can compare in influence with Armstrong as a trumpeter, singer, entertainer, and personality. Though his style could be considered simple by today's standards, few artists have achieved his warmth and beauty. LPs include: *Fireworks, Muggles, West End Blue, Knee Drops, Weatherbird, Satchmo Sings, Louis and the Angels, New Orlean Nights, At the Crescendo w. Eddie Condon, Satch Plays Fats, Louis Under the Stars, Town Hall Concert Plus, Pennies From Heaven,* and *Porgy & Bess* with Ella Fitzgerald. Films include: *Pennies From Heaven* (1936) with Bing Crosby, *New Orleans* (1947), *The Glenn Miller Story, The Five Pennies, High Society,* and *Jazz on a Summer's Day.*

Basie, Count (8-21-04–4-26-84) *leader, piano, organ, composer.* Born William Basie in Red Bank, New Jersey. Through the 1940s, Basie maintained a band whose contagious rhythms and superlative team spirit remain unique in jazz. In 1957, Basie's became the first U.S. band ever to play for the Queen of England. That same year, his group became the first black jazz band to ever play New York's Waldorf-Astoria Hotel. LPs include: *April In Paris, Basie One More Time, Count* with Tony Bennett, *Jumpin' at the Woodside, King of Swing* and *Swingin' Count.*

Beiderbecke, Bix (1903–1931) *cornet, piano, composer.* Born Leon Bismarck Beiderbecke in Davenport, Iowa. Only after his early death from pneumonia did Beiderbecke win any acclaim for his contributions to music. Known chiefly as a cornetist, his exquisite tone and legato style of improvisation helped mark him as one of the first white jazz musicians to gain the respect of black jazzmen. LPs include: *Bix and His Gang, Bix and Tram,* and *Whiteman Days.* Books: *Young Man With A Horn* by Dorothy Baker was inspired by his life.

Berlin, Irving (5-11-1888–1989) USA's most-performed songwriter: "You write in the morning, you write at night. You write in a taxi, in the bathtub, or in an elevator. It may turn out to be very bad, but you sharpen your pencil and try again. A professional songwriter has his mind on his job all the time."

Calloway, Cab (12-25-07–11-18-94) *singer, leader.* Born Cabell Calloway in Rochester, New York. In 1931 Calloway recorded *Minnie the Moocher,* which made him a national name as a novelty "scat" singer, nicknamed "the hi-de-ho man." Calloway was the highest paid and most successful black entertainer of the prewar years. Though not considered "serious" by the musicians and critics of his time, Calloway was important as a leader of a big band that lasted until 1948. Its alumni included people like Dizzy Gillespie and Cozy Cole. Films include: *The Singing Kid* with Al Jolson, *Big Broadcast of 1933, Stormy Weather,* and *Sensations of 1945.* Book: *Of Minnie the Moocher and Me,* Calloway's autobiography.

Christian, Charlie (7-29-16–3-2-42) the first important amplified jazz guitarist; hugely influential. A must-listen.

Cole, Nat "King" (3-17-19–2-15-65) *singer, piano.* Born Nathaniel Coles in Montgomery, Alabama. Initially a solo pianist, throughout the '50s Cole became the first jazz-grounded male voice since Louis Armstrong to gain worldwide popular acceptance. Cole's was the first black jazz combo to have its own sponsored radio series (Wildroot Cream Oil '48–49) and was the first black artist to have his own series on network TV. LPs include: *After Midnight, The Piano Style of Nat "King" Cole,* and *St. Louis Blues.* Films include: *Small Town Girl, The Blue Gardenia, Hajji Baba,* and *The Nat King Cole Story.*

Cotton Club (1923-40, Lenox/142nd St) The first nightclub in America to feature all-black entertainers, premiering Cab Calloway, Duke Ellington, etc. Conceived by the first heavyweight black boxing champion, Jack Johnson. The bandstand was a replica of a Southern mansion, waiters were dressed in red tuxedos, and the tables were covered in red-and-white tablecloths. Everyone was dressed "to the max." Performers did 3

shows at night: 8:30, 11:30, and 2 AM. The Cotton Club incubated both jazz and dance in America, making many artists famous.

Crosby, Bing singer-actor. See his films!

Dorsey, Jimmy (1904–1957) *clarinet, alto sax.* Born James Dorsey in Shenandoah, Pennsylvania. (brother of Dorsey, Tommy)

Dorsey, Tommy (1905–1956) *trombone, leader.* Born Thomas Dorsey in Shenandoah, Pennsylvania. See his films!

Ellington, Duke (4-29-99–5-24-74) *composer, leader, piano.* Born Edward Kennedy Ellington in Washington, D.C. Throughout his career, Ellington searched for new forms and developments without ever losing the "essence" of jazz. His many innovations include using the voice as a jazz instrument; employing a miniature concerto form to build compositions around a soloist; and the creation of new works for special jazz concert premieres. His songs alone have made him a major 20th century musical figure. LPs include: *The Music of Duke Ellington, In A Mellotone, The Duke and His Men, At the Cotton Club, Black, Brown & Beige, A Drum Is A Woman, etc.* Books include: *Duke Ellington* by Barry Ulanov (1946) and an anthology of British writing on Duke, *Duke Ellington: His Life and Music* (1959).

Fields, Dorothy (1904–1974) *lyricist.* One of the few well-known female songwriters of the '20s and '30s. She began her career writing for Harlem nightclub productions; her first was a Cotton Club Revue, *Hot Chocolates,* which introduced Duke Ellington. Some of her songs include: *I Can't Give You Anything But Love, On the Sunny Side of the Street,* & *I'm In the Mood For Love.*

Gillespie, "Dizzy" (1917–1993) *trumpet.* Born John Birks Gillespie in South Carolina. Co-founder of the '40s bebop movement. He fused jazz with Latin music and was known for his surreal humor and bohemian dress of hipster style beret, shades and goatee that became the uniform for "modern jazz." Recordings include: *Cubana-Be, Cubana-Bop* and *Manteca.*

Goodman, Benjamin "Benny" (5-30-09–6-13-86) *clarinet, leader.* Called "The King of Swing." Historic January 16, 1938 Carnegie Hall Concert. 1940, Charlie Christian played in his sextet. Goodman is a famous swing pioneer with countless recordings available. Film: *The Benny Goodman Story* (1956).

Hampton, Lionel (4-12-09–) *vibraharp, drums, piano, leader.* Born in Louisville, Kentucky. Hampton was the first jazz musician to feature the vibraharp or vibraphone (popularly known as vibes). Also originated the "trigger-finger" style of piano playing where he used his two forefingers as if they were vibraphone mallets and played extremely fast, single note passages. Played with Benny Goodman's band before fronting his own orchestra. LPs include: *King of the Vibes, Flying Home, Swinging With Hampton.* Film: *The Benny Goodman Story* (1955).

Harris, Wynonie: Very important!

Hawkins, Coleman "Bean" (1901–1969): *tenor saxophone.* Born Coleman Randolph Hawkins in Missouri. Hawkins virtually invented the mature sound and style of the tenor sax in jazz. He was a swing player whose sound revealed his sympathies to bebop. Recordings include: *Body and Soul.*

Herman, Woody (5-16-13–10-29-87) *clarinet, saxes, vocals, leader.* First became known as "The Band That Plays the Blues." 1939 hit "Woodchoppers' Ball." "Caldonia" hit. Incubated many soloists and writers.

James, Harry *bandleader, trumpet player,* married Betty Grable. Film: *Benny Goodman Story,* 1955. Swing pioneer.

Jordan, Louis (7-8-08–2-4-75) *singer, alto sax, leader.* Born in Brinkley, Arkansas.

Jordan's combo, the Tympany Five, enjoyed a steady rise to national fame as Jordan featured himself more and more in vocal blues and novelties. Originally limited to R&B circles, he became hugely popular combining showmanship, good musicianship, a strong accent on humor and an original rhythmic vocal style. Hits include: *Knock Me a Kiss, Gonna Move to the Outskirts of Town, Five Guys Named Moe,* and *Choo Choo Ch'Boogie.*

Kenton, Stan (12-15-11–8-25-79) A progressive bandleader, he featured many solos, advanced harmonies. Worked with arranger Pete Rugolo, singer June Christy. Cult figure.

Krupa, Gene (1-15-09–10-16-73) *drums, leader.* Born in Chicago, Illinois. A main attraction with Benny Goodman's band, he became one of the important figures of the swing era and was able to start a successful band of his own in 1938. He was the first drummer in jazz history to become world-famous. LPs include: *Hey! Here's Gene Krupa, Drum Boogie, Sing, Sing, Sing, Swingin' With Krupa.* Film: *The Gene Krupa Story* (1959) with Sal Mineo as Krupa.

Lunceford, Jimmie (6-6-02–7-12-47, Seaside, OR). Innovative bandleader at poorer black clubs, became known as having most showmanlike and disciplined black jazz orchestra. A swing pioneer, he had the first orchestra to feature high-note trumpeters.

May, Billy (11-10-16–) composer, leader, trumpet. Arranger for Charlie Barnet, Alvino Rey, etc. LPs: *Jimmie Lunceford in Hi Fi, Sorta Dixie, His Big Fat Brass.*

Mezzrow, Mezz (11-9-99–8-5-72, Paris) clarinet, saxes. Dismissed in Eddie Condon's biography, *We Called It Music,* he wrote the classic, *Really the Blues,* with Bernard Wolfe.

Miller, Glenn (3-1-04–12-16-44) composer, leader, trombone. Very popular swing pioneer; died in plane crash. Film: *The Glenn Miller Story* (1954, dir. Anthony Mann).

Millinder, Lucky (8-8-00–) Innovative bandleader, mostly played poorer black clubs, *swing pioneer.* Played Savoy Ballroom, toured Europe; great sidemen. Underrated.

Morton, Jelly Roll (10-20-90–7-10-41): *composer, piano, leader, singer.* Born Ferdinand Joseph La Menthe in Gulfport, Louisiana. Had his start playing piano in New Orleans' Storyville quarter brothels. Recorded a long series of sessions under the name of Morton's Red Hot Peppers. Due to his claims of "inventing jazz in 1902" and that many famous compositions had been stolen from him, Morton was a controversial figure. LPs include: *King of New Orleans Jazz, New Orleans Memories.* Book: *Mister Jelly Roll* by Alan Lomax (1950).

Moten, Bennie (11-13-94–4-2-35) *pianist, leader.* Highly influential bandleader with brother Buster on accordion, Jimmy Rushing, Hot Lips Page, Ben Webster, etc—a hot band! After his death, his pianist Count Basie took over most of the band. CD: *Basie Beginnings* (1929-32) on Bluebird.

Norvo, Red (3-31-08–) *vibraharp, xylophone.* Born Kenneth Norville in Beardstown, Illinois. Norvo was the first to prove jazz could be played on the xylophone. LPs include: *Red Norvo and His All Stars, Windjammer City Style,* and *Vibe-Rations.*

Oliver, Joe "King" (5-11-85–4-8-38) cor-net, leader. Louis Armstrong's major influence and mentor; however, Armstrong sounds completely different.

Parker, Charlie "Bird" or "Yardbird" (8-29-20–3-12-55) *alto sax, composer.* Born Charles Christopher Parker, Jr. in Kansas City, Kansas. Parker was the leading founder of bebop, a post-swing school of jazz. His style is characterized by an expanded harmonic base to free melodic ideas, plus spontaneous inventiveness. As influential as Louis Armstrong, he was considered a prophet, a genius, and a quintessential Bohemian personality. Also, he was a junkie. Recordings include: *Now's the Time, Ko-Ko, Billie's Bounce, Ornithology, Yardbird Suite,* and *A Night in Tunisia.* Film: *Bird* (1988) starring Forest Whitaker. French book out.

Prima, Louis (12-7-11–8-24-78) *leader, singer, trumpet.* Born in New Orleans, Louisiana. With the arrival of the swing era he became a national name. He crossed over entirely into pop music, leading a dance band. In 1954, he and his wife, singer Keely Smith, formed a team which became a huge nightclub attraction in New York, Chicago, Hollywood and especially Las Vegas. Film: *Hey Boy, Hey Girl.* Also recorded with second wife, Gia Maione. Many LPs.

Porter, Cole (1893–1964) *lyricist.* A prolific songwriter known for songs that expressed the attractiveness and wealth of his social set, Porter is best known for such songs as: *I Get a Kick Out of You, I've Got You Under My Skin, Ev'ry Time We Say Goodbye, Night and Day,* and *Begin the Beguine.*

Rainey, Ma (1886–1939) *singer.* Born Gertrude Malissa Nix Pridgett in Columbus, Georgia. After many years on the road playing the black vaudeville circuits, her simple, direct blues style brought her belated fame during her peak years (1923-9). Bessie Smith was the most famous protege and emulator of Ma Rainey, who took her on tour in her show when Smith was an unknown.

Rich, Buddy (6-30-17–4-2-87) drums, singer. Big band drummer, soloist, described in Mel Torme's *Traps the Drum Wonder.*

Savoy Ballroom (3-12-26–late '50s; 140th-141st Sts/Lenox Ave) ballroom where Lindy Hop and swing jazz were incubated. Dazzling setting took up an entire city block: spacious lobby, marble staircase, orange-and-blue dancehall, mamoth mahogany floor. Dances popularized at the Savoy included the Flying Charleston, the Big Apple, the Stomp, the Jitterbug Jive, the Snakehips, the Rhumbaboogie, the Bunny Hug, the Turkey Trot, the Shimmy, the Peabody, and of course, the Lindy Hop. Only the best bands and dancers were allowed to compete in the "Battle of the Bands" and the dance "cutting contests" featuring Whitey's Lindy Hoppers, legendary tap-dancer Eddie Rector, etc. For most of the '30s, Chick Webb's band ruled. Other important clubs: Roseland Ballroom, Small's Paradise, Connie's Inn, Apollo Theater. Of note to Lindy Hoppers: the Harvest Moon Ball finals held at Central Park Mall and Madison Square Garden.

Shaw, Artie (5-23-10–) *clarinetist, leader.* Born Arthur Arshawsky. Innovative bandleader who led five bands during the swing era, one with string quartet! Autobiography *The Trouble with Cinderella* barely mentions music biz or his wives, which included Lana Turner, Ava Gardner and Evelyn Keyes.

Sinatra, Frank (12-12-15–): *singer, crooner, chairman of the board.* Born Francis Albert Sinatra in Hoboken, New Jersey. Anti-racist activist in his youth.

Singleton, Zutty (5-14-98–) drums. Along with Baby Dodds, considered foremost "trad jazz" drummer. Appeared in *Stormy Weather* '43 and *New Orleans* '46.

Smith, Bessie (4-15-94–9-26-37): The first major blues and jazz singer on records; called "Empress of the Blues." Killed in car crash.

Smith, Keely (3-9-32–) *singer,* full name Dorothy Jacqueline Keely Smith Prima. Sang on Joe Brown's children's shows, bands from Norfolk, VA. Joined Louis Prima in 1948 (age 16) and married him 7-13-53. Jazz-influenced comedienne-vocalist. Films: *Hey Boy, Hey Girl, Thunder Road.* Has own LPs out, plus many with Louis Prima. See her videos!

Teagarden, Jack (8-20-05–1-15-64) *trombonist, vocals, leader.* Charismatic trombonist who should have become a "swing" star, but signed a 5-year contract w/Paul Whiteman and got "buried" in the band. Film: *The Birth of the Blues* (1940, Bing Crosby).

Webb, Chick (William Webb, 2-10-02–6-16-39): *drums, leader* of the hottest band to play the Savoy Ballroom, won most "Battle of the Bands" contests, was broadcast nationally, produced many great records for Decca. Driving drummer, featured Ella Fitzgerald. Physically deformed but surmounted this. Died of tuberculosis. Underrated.

Waller, Fats (5-21-04–12-15-43) *piano, organ, composer, vocals.* Played stride, classic jazz, swing piano. The first jazz organist, wrote many classic songs, influenced everybody. Had his own radio program, made many recordings. Became ill while soloist at Hollywood's Zanzibar Room, and died of pneumonia. Films: *Hooray for Love, King of Burlesque* (1935), *Stormy Weather* ('43).

West 52nd St. (N.Y.) Known in the '30s and '40s as the Street of Swing because of the nightclubs that lined the street, like the Famous Door, the Onyx, and Kelly's Stables. *[Note: this directory has no claim to completeness!]*

SPENCER'S 100 Reasons to Swing

Spencer is the Sunday night swing deejay at the Hi-Ball Lounge, San Francisco. He also hosts "Spencer's" Saturday nights at the DNA Lounge, where he's worked for the past 12 years. In the late '70s he played bass and sang in Neon (first titled Punk; later, the Noise). When the lounge/swing renaissance began, Spencer was the vocalist for Timmie Hesla's Converse All-Stars, when they did shows at the DNA Lounge. In 1995 he heard about the opening of the Hi-Ball. He checked it out and thought, "This reminds me of the early punk or Goth scene: similar energy, people were dressed differently, they had a certain edge, and there was so much enthusiasm—especially in the dancers. Previously, I'd given up hope for Western civilization and had wanted to retire to an emu ranch. Now I think I'll stick around for awhile."

1 "Sing, Sing, Sing" Benny Goodman
2 "In The Mood" Glenn Miller
3 "Just A Gigiolo" Louis Prima
4 "Bei Mer Bist Du Schoen" Andrews Sisters
5 "Take The 'A' Train" Duke Ellington
6 "Fly Me To The Moon" Frank Sinatra
7 "Is You, Or Is You Ain't (Ma' Baby)" Louis Jordan
8 "The Walkin' Blues" Anyone
9 "Leap Frog" Les Brown
10 "String Of Pearls" Glenn Miller
11 "Flying Home" Benny Goodman
12 "Ain't That A Kick in the Head" Dean Martin
13 "Mack The Knife" Bobby Darin
14 "Shiny Stockings" Count Basie
15 "It Don't Mean A Thing (If It Ain't Got That Swing)" Benny Goodman
16 "Knock Me Kiss" Louis Jordan
17 "I've Got a Gal In Kalamazoo" Glenn Miller
18 "Christopher Colombus" Dinah Washington
19 "Beyond The Sea" Bobby Darin
20 "Tour De Force" Dizzy Gillespie
21 "You're Nobody 'Til Somebody Loves You" Dean Martin
22 "Fever" Peggy Lee
23 "Jump, Jive, An' Wail" Louis Prima
24 "Danke Schöen" Wayne Newton
25 "Tuxedo Junction" Glenn Miller
26 "Night And Day" Frank Sinatra
27 "5 Months, 2 Weeks, 2 Days" Louis Prima
28 "Ain't Nobody Here But Us Chickens" Louis Jordan
29 "American Patrol" Glenn Miller
30 "I've Got My Love To Keep Me Warm" Les Brown
31 "Every Day I Have The Blues" Count Basie
32 "Eager Beaver" Stan Kenton
33 "The Hornet" Artie Shaw
34 "Chattanooga Choo Choo" Glenn Miller
35 "Caravan" Duke Ellington
36 "Pennsylvania 6-5000" Glenn Miller
37 "Until I Met You" Duke Ellington
38 "Segue In C" Count Basie
39 "Sweet Lorraine" Louis Jordan
40 "Boy From Ipanema" Peggy Lee
41 "Strangers In The Night" Wayne Newton
42 "Call Me Irresponsible" Bobby Darin
43 "Just In Time" Dean Martin
44 "Midnight Swinger" Mel Torme
45 "Destination Moon" Dinah Washington
46 "It Had Better Be Tonight" Lena Horne
47 "More" Frank Sinatra
48 "Little Brown Jug" Stan Kenton
49 "Painted Rhythm" Stan Kenton
50 "Swinging The Blues" Count Basie

51 "Everybody Loves My Baby" Dinah Washington
52 "Choo Choo Ch'Boogie" Louis Jordan
53 "Sent For You Yesterday" Count Basie
54 "One O' Clock Jump" Count Basie
55 "Don't Get Around Much Anymore" Duke Ellington
56 "That Old Black Magic" Louis Prima
57 "The Lady Is A Tramp" Frank Sinatra
58 "Lazy River" Bobby Darin
59 "And Write Myself A Letter" Nat Cole
60 "Bizet Has His Day" Les Brown
61 "Stompin' At The Savoy" Benny Goodman
62 "Don't Be That Way" Benny Goodman
63 "Wild Women Don't Get The Blues" Dennis Rowland
64 "Dig That Crazy Chick" Sam Butera
65 "Sunday In New York" Bobby Darin
66 "Blue Moon" Frank Sinatra
68 "Closer To The Bone" Louis Prima
69 "Nobody But Me" Lou Rawls
70 "Killer Joe" Lionel Hampton
71 "L.O.V.E." Nat Cole
72 "Forty-Second Street" Mel Torme
73 "A Fine Romance" Ella Fitzgerald & Louis Armstrong
74 "Are You Havin' Any Fun" Tony Bennett
75 "Volga Boatmen" Glenn Miller
76 "Same Old Saturday Night" Frank Sinatra
77 "Don't Sit Under The Apple Tree" Glenn Miller
78 "On The Sunny Side Of The Street" Tommy Dorsey
79 "At The Woodchopper's Ball" Woody Herman
80 "Saturday Night Fish Fry" Louis Jordan
81 "Baby Won't You Please Come Home" Louis Prima
82 "April In Paris" Sammy Davis
83 "It All Depends On You" Frank Sinatra
84 "There Will Never Be Another You" Keely Smith
85 "I'm Beginning To See The Light" Bobby Darin
86 "Caldonia" Louis Jordan
87 "Salt Pork, West Virginia" Louis Jordan
88 "A Good Man Is Hard To Find" Les Brown
89 "Pretty Woman" Count Basie
90 "Jack The Bear" Duke Ellington
91 "Comin' Home Baby" Mel Torme
92 "Shout And Feel It" Count Basie
93 "Flat Foot Floogie" Slim Gaillard
94 "Lover's Leap" Les Brown
95 "From This Moment On" Frank Sinatra
96 "Please Don't Talk About Me" Dean Martin
97 "Can't Get Started" Keely Smith
98 "B.D.E." Count Basie
99 "Mainstem" Duke Ellington
100 "Ol' MacDonald" Frank Sinatra

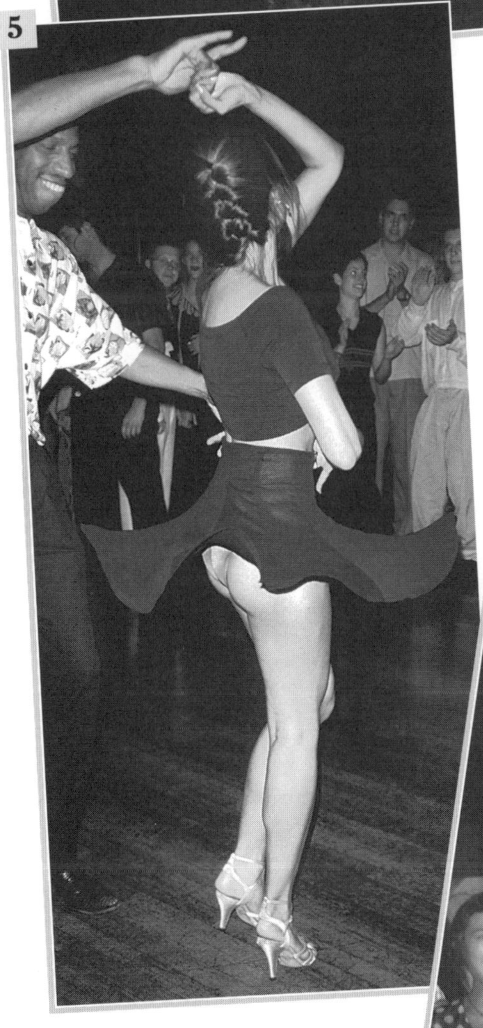

1) Du Nord 2) Bimbo's
3) Barbe and Link
4) Bimbo's: Mark Jordan,
   Suzi Hutsell
5) Great American Music Hall

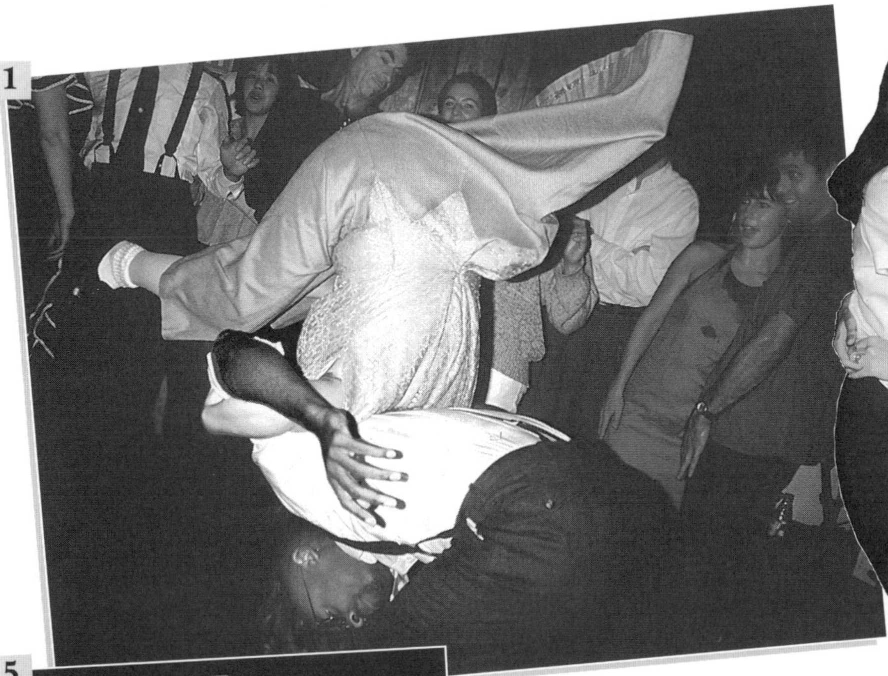

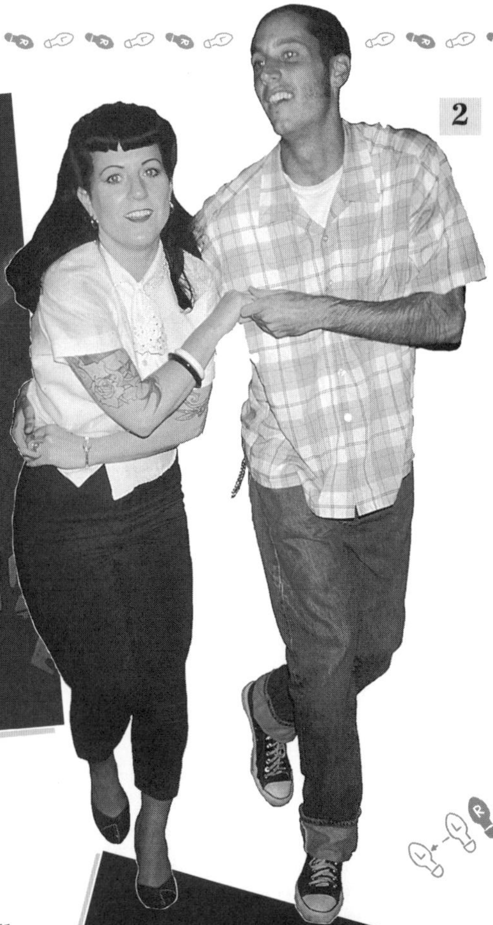

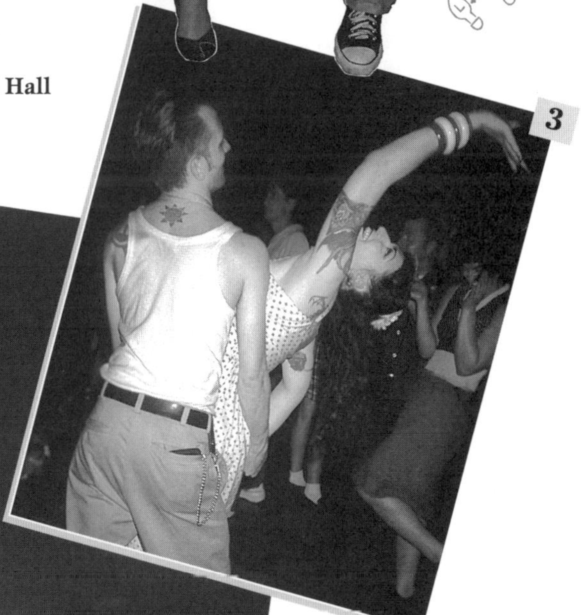

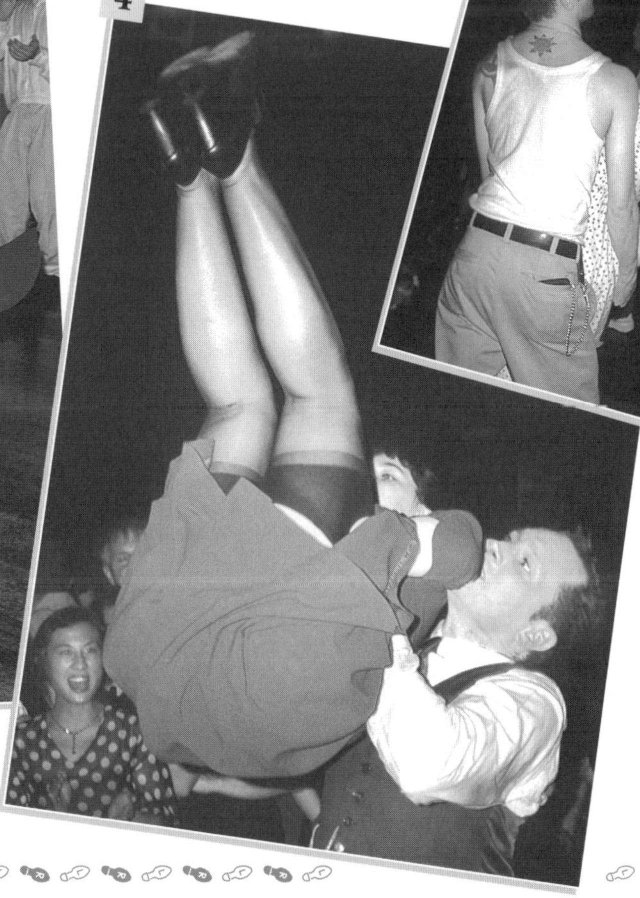

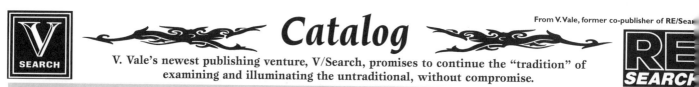

Catalog

From V. Vale, former co-publisher of RE/Sear

V/SEARCH

V. Vale's newest publishing venture, V/Search, promises to continue the "tradition" of examining and illuminating the untraditional, without compromise.

RE/SEARCH

SWING! *The New Retro Renassaince*

Q: Why are so many hardcore tattooed punks going to swing & rockabilly shows?
A: It's the dancing, man—the wildest jitterbugging and lindy-hopping since the late '30s!

With SWING! The New Retro Renaissance, V/Search documents the first major lifestyle change since punk. After a 50-year absence, partner-dancing is back with a vengeance, propelled by a new generation of bands with roots in Hot Jazz, Jump Swing, Western Swing and Rockabilly. Also documented are the exciting retro clothes, hairstyles, furnishings, vintage cars, etc saved from extinction by cutting-edge visionaries of this movement. Lavishly illustrated, with informative directories, lists of recommended recordings, books, films, etc, this is the first comprehensive guide to a new state of mind being pioneered on the West Coast. 8½x11″, 224 pp, over 350 photos & illustrations. **$17.99.**

SWING! Vol. 2 coming Spring 1999!
Call or write for details.

Music from the *Swing Renaissance:*

Each CD is $16, All six for $77. *Please read about the bands listed here in the text of the book*

8½ Souvenirs	Lee Press-On and the Nails	Lavay Smith	New Morty Show	Steve Lucky & the Rhumba Bums

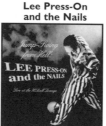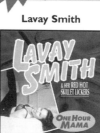

Search & Destroy, Vol. 1 & 2

By the mid-'70s the Punk aesthetic had spread out from England to America. The American Punk scene soon developed an energy and talent of its own, which was documented in its own homegrown, heavily illustrated magazine, *Search & Destroy*, edited by V. Vale between 1976 and 1979. This complete facsimile reprint of all 11 issues captures the rage, riot and revelations of an extraordinary period. Innovators such as Devo, Iggy Pop, Dead Kennedys and Ramones are featured alongside William Burroughs, J.G. Ballard, John Waters, Russ Meyer and David Lynch. This is the *real thing*, written when punk was first inventing itself. JUMBO SIZE 10x15″, 150 pp, over 150 articles and 400 photos & illustrations per volume. **Vol.1: $19.95; Vol.2: $19.95.**

SPECIAL: both volumes $30!

"Unsurpassed! The best punk rock documentation there will ever be. A library resource."–LAST GASP NEWSLETTER

Memoirs of a Sword Swallower *by Daniel P. Mannix*

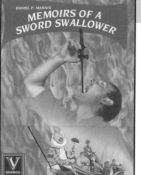

"I probably never would have become America's leading fire-eater if Flamo the Great hadn't happened to explode that night . . ." So begins this true story of life with a traveling carnival, peopled by amazing characters (the Human Ostrich, the Human Salamander, Jolly Daisy, etc.) who commit outrageous feats of wizardry. This is one of the only authentic narratives revealing the "tricks" (or more often, the lack thereof) and skills involved in a sideshow, and is invaluable to those aspiring to this profession. Having cultivated the desire to create real magic since early childhood, Mannix rose to become a top act within a season, and here is his inspiring tale. *NEW: RARE PHOTOS!* This is the first edition to include photos of the actual characters in the book, most of them taken by Mannix himself in the '30s. 8½x11″, 128 pp, 55 photos & illustrations. **$15.99.**
A few signed copies available at $30; author died 1/29/97.
"The beautiful world of outcasts and freaks banding together to form an alternate society is accurately and compassionately portrayed by an insider."–CIRCUS ARTS

ZINES! Vol. 1 & 2 *Incendiary Interviews with Independent Publishers*

In the past two decades a quiet revolution has gained force: over 50,000 "zines" (independent, not-for-profit self publications) have emerged and spread—mostly through the mail, with little publicity. Flaunting off-beat interests, extreme personal revelations and social activism, zines directly counter the *pseudo-communication* and glossy lies of the mainstream media monopoly. Vol. 1 includes in-depth interviews with publishers of: *Beer Frame, Crap Hound, Thrift SCORE, Bunny Hop,* OUTPUNK, *Fat Girl, Housewife Turned Assassin, Mystery Date* & MORE! Vol. 2 continues the investigation with *Dishwasher Pete, Temp Slave,* and *Murder Can Be Fun* & MORE. **Vol.1: 184 pp, $18.99; Vol.2: 148 pp, $14.99. Each has** over 200 illustrations & photos, quotations, zine directory, index, 8½x11″. **"These fanzines represent an almost unprecedented breakthrough . . ."–ALTERNATIVE PRESS; "An excellent look at the history of the zine movement."–AM. BOOKSELLER; ". . . a fascinating survey . . ."–PUB. WKLY.**

#16: RE/Search Guide to Bodily Fluids by Paul Spinrad

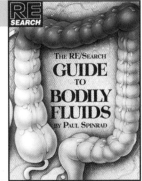

Table of Contents: Mucus, Menstruation, Saliva, Sweat, Vomit, Urine, Flatus, Feces, Earwax & more
This guide sparks a radical rethinking of our relationship with our bodies and Nature, humorously (and seriously) spanning the gamut of everything you ever wanted to know about bodily functions and excreta. Each bodily function is discussed from a variety of viewpoints: scientific, anthropological, historical, mythological, sociological, and artistic. **Topics include:** constipation (such as its relationship to cornflakes and graham crackers!); the history and evolution of toilet paper; farting; urine (including little known facts about urinalysis); earwax; smegma as well as many other engrossing topics! 8½x11″, 148pp. **$15.99**

"A stunning new release . . . *The RE/Search Guide to Bodily Fluids* is a must buy."–BIKINI
"This is an important work that shouldn't be ignored, packed with fascinating facts on excreta."
–LOADED MAGAZINE

#15 & 14: Incredibly Strange Music, Vol. 1 & 2

Incredibly Strange Music surveys the territory of neglected "garage sale" records (mostly from the '50s–'70s), spotlighting genres, artists and one-of a-kind gems that will delight and surprise. **Genres examined include:** "easy listening," "exotica," and "celebrity" (massive categories in themselves) as well as more recordings by (singing) cops and (polka-playing) priests, undertakers, religious ventriloquists, astronauts, opera-singing parrots, beatnik and hippie records, and gospel by blind teenage girls with bouffant hairdos. Virtually every musical/lyrical boundary in the history of recorded sound has been breached; every sacred cow upturned. EACH 8½x11″, 208 pp, over 200 photos.
Vol. 1: $17.99, Vol. 2: $17.99, SPECIAL: both for $32.00.

"Fans of ambient music, acid jazz, ethno-techno, even industrial rock, will find the leap back to these genres an easy one to make."–ROLLING STONE

#13: Angry Women

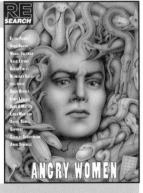

16 cutting-edge performance artists discuss critical questions such as: How can revolutionary feminism encompass wild sex, humor, beauty, spirituality *plus* radical politics? How can a powerful movement for social change be *inclusionary*? A wide range of topics is discussed *passionately*. Armed with contempt for dogma, stereotype & cliche, these creative visionaries probe deeply into our social foundation of taboos, beliefs and totalitarian linguistic contradictions from whence spring (as well as thwart) our theories, imaginings, behavior and dreams. 8½x11″, 240 pp, 135 illustrations. **$18.99**

◆ Karen Finley ◆ Annie Sprinkle ◆ Diamanda Galás ◆ bell hooks ◆ Kathy Acker ◆ Avital Ronnell ◆ Lydia Lunch ◆ Sapphire ◆ Susie Bright ◆ Valie Export ◆ and many more . . .

"The view here is largely pro-sex, pro-porn, and pro-choice . . . Art and activism are inseparable from life and being. This is the 13th step, beyond AA's 12: a healing rage."–THE VILLAGE VOICE
"This book is a Bible. . . it hails the dawn of a new era–the era of an inclusive, fun, sexy feminism. . . Every interview contains brilliant moments of wisdom."–AMERICAN BOOK REVIEW

#12: Modern Primitives

An eye-opening, startling investigation of the undercover world of body modifications: tattooing, piercing and scarification. **Articles & interviews:** *Fakir Musafar* (Silicon Valley ad executive who has practiced every known body modification); *Genesis & Paula P-Orridge* describing numerous ritual scarifications and symbolic tattoos; *Ed Hardy* (editor of *Tattootime*); *Capt. Don Leslie*; *Jim Ward*; *Anton LaVey* (founder of the Church of Satan); *Lyle Tuttle*; *Raelyn Gallina* (women's piercer) & others talking about body practices that develop identity and philosophic awareness and explore sexual sensation. 22 interviews, 2 essays, quotations, sources/bibliography & index. 8½x11″, 212 pp, 279 photos and illustrations. **$17.99**

"Through 'primitive' modifications, they are taking possession of the only thing that any of us will ever really own: our bodies."–WHOLE EARTH REVIEW
"The photographs and illustrations are both explicit and astounding . . . This is the ideal biker coffee table book, a conversation piece that provides fascinating food for thought."–IRON HORSE

#11: Pranks!

A prank is a "trick, a mischievous act, a ludicrous act." Although not regarded as poetic or artistic acts, pranks constitute an art form and genre in themselves. Here pranksters such as Timothy Leary, Abbie Hoffman, Monte Cazazza, Jello Biafra, Earth First!, Joe Coleman, Karen Finley, John Waters and Henry Rollins (and more) challenge the sovereign authority of words, images & behavioral convention. This iconoclastic compendium will dazzle and delight all lovers of humor, satire and irony. 8½x11″, 240 pp, 164 photos & illustrations. **$19.99**

"The definitive treatment of the subject, offering extensive interviews with 36 contemporary tricksters . . . from the Underground's answer to Studs Terkel."–WASHINGTON POST

"Men never do evil so completely and cheerfully as when they do it from religious conviction."–Pascal

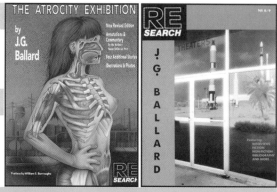

RE/SEARCH BACKLIST

The Confessions of Wanda von Sacher-Masoch

Finally available in English: the racy and riveting *Confessions of Wanda von Sacher-Masoch*—married for ten years to Leopold von Sacher-Masoch (author of *Venus in Furs* and many other novels) whose whip-and-fur bedroom games spawned the term "masochism." In this feminist classic from 100 years ago, Wanda was forced to play "sadistic" roles in Leopold's fantasies to ensure the survival of herself and her 3 children—games which called into question who was the Master and who the Slave. Besides being a compelling story of a woman's search for her own identity, strength and ultimately, complete independence, this is a true-life adventure story—an odyssey through many lands peopled by amazing characters. Underneath its unforgettable poetic imagery and almost unbearable emotional cataclysms reigns a woman's consistent unblinking investigation of the limits of morality and the deepest meanings of love. Translated by Marian Phillips, Caroline Hébert & V. Vale. 8½x11″, 136 pp, photo-illustrated. **$13.99**

"Extravagantly designed in an illustrated, oversized edition that is a pleasure to hold. It is also exquisitely written, engaging and literary and turns our preconceptions upside down."–LA READER

The Torture Garden *by Octave Mirbeau*

This book was once described as the "most sickening work of art of the nineteenth century!" Long out of print, Octave Mirbeau's macabre classic (1899) features a corrupt Frenchman and an insatiably cruel Englishwoman who meet and then frequent a fantastic 19th century Chinese garden where torture is practiced as an art form. The fascinating, horrific narrative slithers deep into the human spirit, uncovering murderous proclivities and demented desires. Lavish, loving detail of description. Introduction, biography & bibliography. 8½x11″, 120 pp, 21 photos. **$15.95**

". . . sadistic spectacle as apocalyptic celebration of human potential. . . A work as chilling as it is seductive."–THE DAILY CALIFORNIAN

"Here is a novel that is hot with the fever of ecstatic, prohibited joys, as cruel as a thumbscrew and as luxuriant as an Oriental tapestry. This exotic story of Clara and her insatiable desire for the perverse and the forbidden has been hailed by the critics."—Charles Hanson Towne

". . . daydreams in which sexual images are mixed nightmarishly with images of horror."—Ed. Wilson

Freaks: We Who Are Not As Others *by Daniel P. Mannix*

Another long out-of-print classic book based on Mannix's personal acquaintance with sideshow stars such as the Alligator Man and the Monkey Woman. Read all about the notorious love affairs of midgets; the amazing story of the elephant boy; the unusual amours of Jolly Daisy, the fat woman; the famous pinhead who inspired Verdi's *Rigoletto*; the tragedy of Betty Lou Williams and her parasitic twin; the black midget, only 34 inches tall, who was happily married to a 264-pound wife; the human torso who could sew, crochet and type; and bizarre accounts of normal humans turned into freaks—either voluntarily or by evil design! 88 astounding photographs and additional material from the author's personal collection. 8½x11″, 124 pp. **$15.95**

"RE/Search has provided us with a moving glimpse at the rarified world of physical deformity; a glimpse that ultimately succeeds in its goal of humanizing the inhuman, revealing the beauty that often lies behind the grotesque and in dramatically illustrating the triumph of the human spirit in the face of overwhelming debility."–SPECTRUM WEEKLY

Bob Flanagan, Super-Masochist

Bob Flanagan, 1952-1996, was born in New York City, grew up with Cystic Fibrosis (a genetically inherited, nearly-always fatal disease) and lived longer than any other person with CF. The physical pain of his childhood suffering was principally alleviated by masturbation, wherein pain and pleasure became linked, resulting in his lifelong practice of extreme masochism. In deeply confessional interviews, Bob details his sexual practices and his relationship with long-term partner and Mistress, Sheree Rose. He tells how frequent near-death encounters modified his concepts of gratification and abstinence, reward and punishment, and intensified his masochistic drive. Through his insider's perspective on the Sado-Masochistic community, we learn about branding, piercing, whipping, bondage and endurance trials. Includes photos by L.A. artist Sheree Rose. 8½x11″, 128 pp, 125 photos & illustrations. **$14.99**

". . . an eloquent tour through the psychic terrain of SM, discussing the most severe sexual diversions with the humorous detachment of a shy, clean living nerd. I came away from the book wanting to know this man."–DETAILS MAGAZINE

TWO by Charles Willeford: High Priest of California *and* Wild Wives

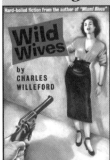

A classic of hard-boiled fiction, Charles Willeford's *Wild Wives* is amoral, sexy, and brutal. Written in a sleazy San Francisco hotel in the early 1950's while on leave from the Army, Willeford creates a tale of deception featuring the crooked detective Jacob C. Blake and his nemesis—a beautiful, insane young woman who is the wife of a socially prominent San Francisco architect. Blake becomes entangled in a web of deceit, intrigue and multiple murders in this exciting period tale. 5x7″, 108pp. **$10.99**

Russell Haxby is a ruthless used car salesman obsessed with manipulating and cavorting with a married woman. In this classic of Hard-boiled fiction, Charles Willeford crafts a wry, sardonic tale of hypocrisy, intrigue and lust. Set in San Francisco in the early fifties—every sentence masks innuendo, every detail hides a clue, and every used car sale is an outrageous con job. 5x7″, 148 pp. **$10.99**

"A tempo so relentless, words practically fly off the page."–VILLAGE VOICE

SPECIAL DISCOUNTS ☎ ☎

Just The RE/Search Library: (Save $36!) All RE/Search serials

Offer includes the *RE/Search #1, 2 & 3* tabloids, *#4/5: Burroughs/Gysin/Throbbing Gristle*, *#6/7: Industrial Culture Handbook*, *#8/9: J.G. Ballard*, *#10: Incredibly Strange Films*, *#11: Pranks!*, *#12: Modern Primitives*, *#13: Angry Women*, *#14: Incredibly Strange Music, Vol. 1*, *#15: Incredibly Strange Music, Vol. 2*, and *#16: RE/Search Guide to Bodily Fluids* by Paul Spinrad.
Special Discount Offer Only: $175 ppd. Seamail/Canada: $190.

The Classic RE/Search Library: (Save $19!) All RE/Search classic reprints

Offer includes *Freaks: We Who Are Not As Others*, *The Torture Garden*, *The Atrocity Exhibition*, *The Confessions of Wanda von Sacher-Masoch*, *High Priest of California* and *Wild Wives*. **Special Discount Offer: $68 ppd.** Seamail/Canada: $74.

The Complete Library: (Save $100!)

Includes all issues of RE/Search (both offers above), PLUS the first 5 issues of V/Search
Special Discount Offer Only: $332 ppd. Seamail/Canada: $365.

Incredibly Strange Library: (Save $13!)

Includes *Incredibly Strange Music Vol. One*, *Incredibly Strange Music Vol. Two* and *Incredibly Strange Films*.
Special Discount Offer Only: $49 ppd. Seamail/Canada: $55.

The Music Library: (Save $19!)

Offer includes *Incredibly Strange Music* CDs Vol. One & Two; *The Essential Perrey & Kingsley*; Ken Nordine's *Colors*; and Eden Ahbez's *Eden's Island*. Normally $84 with shipping and handling; NOW: all CDs only $65 postpaid! ($75 postpaid Air Mail Overseas)

S&M Library: (Save $16!)

Offer includes *RE/Search #12: Modern Primitives* , *Bob Flanagan: Super-Masochist*, *The Confessions of Wanda von Sacher-Masoch*, and *The Torture Garden*. Special Discount Offer: $52 ppd. **Seamail/Canada: $58.**

Subscriptions to V/Search

Receive the next three books published by V/Search, either our numbered interview format serials or *WHATEVER!* **$40.** Overseas/Canada: **$50.** *Please state which issue you would like your subscription to begin with (i.e., next, most recent, etc). Sorry no library or university subscriptions. Libraries and universities please place individual orders from this catalog. NEW: Retro subscription: any 3 backlist paperbacks $40.* *NOTE: Subscriptions sent surface mail only! No airmail.

ORDERING INFORMATION ☎ ☎

MAIL: V/SEARCH Publications
20 ROMOLO #B
SAN FRANCISCO, CA 94133

OR

PHONE: Orders may be placed Monday through Friday: 10 AM to 6 PM PST, fax any time TEL (415) 362-1465, FAX (415) 362-0742

Cash, Check or Money Order Payable to V/Search Publications OR Charge to Credit Card: VISA or MASTERCARD Only

SHIPPING & HANDLING CHARGES

DOMESTIC CUSTOMERS: first item $4; add $1 per additional item; for priority mail add $1 per order.
INTERNATIONAL CUSTOMERS: SEAMAIL: first item $6; add $2 per each additional item;
AIRMAIL: first item $15; add $12 per additional item.

PAYMENT IN U.S. DOLLARS ONLY
ATTENTION CANADIAN CUSTOMERS: We *do not* accept personal checks even from a U.S. dollar account! Send Cash or International Money Orders Only! (available from the post office)

SAVE YOUR INDEX! (SEE BACK OF THIS PAGE) XEROX THIS FORM OR JUST WRITE INFO ON A SEPARATE SHEET!!!

TITLE	#	TOTAL	
			NAME
			ADDRESS
			CITY, STATE, ZIP
			VISA/MASTERCARD #
SUBTOTAL			**EXPIRATION DATE and SIGNATURE**
CA residents add 8½% sales tax			
Shipping and handling (see above)			**PHONE NUMBER**
May 1998 **TOTAL**			**SEND SASE FOR CATALOG (or 4 IRCs for OVERSEAS)**

INDEX